Fundamentals of Human Resource Management

Content, Competencies, and Applications

Gary Dessler Florida International University

Pearson Education International

Acquisitions Editor: Jennifer M. Collins
Editorial Director: Sally Yagan
Product Development Manager: Ashley Santora
Editorial Assistant: Elizabeth Davis
Editorial Project Manager: Claudia Fernandes
Director of Marketing: Patrice Jones
Marketing Manager: Nikki Jones
Marketing Assistant: Ian Gold
Permissions Project Manager: Charles Morris
Associate Managing Editor: Suzanne DeWorken
Production Project Manager: Kelly Warsak
Senior Operations Specialist: Arnold Vila
Operations Specialist: Carol O'Rourke
Creative Director: Christy Mahon
Senior Art Director: Janet Slowik
Interior Designer: Karen Quigley
Cover Designer: Karen Quigley

Manager, Rights and Permissions:
 Zina Arabia
Manager, Visual Research: Beth Brenzel
Image Permission Coordinator:
 Angelique Sharps
Photo Research: Sheila Norman
Manager, Cover Visual Research &
 Permissions: Karen Sanatar
Composition: BookMasters, Inc.
Full-Service Project Management:
 Jennifer Welsch/BookMasters, Inc.
Printer/Binder: Phoenix Color Corp.
Cover Printer: Courier/Kendallville
Typeface: 10/12 Times

Credits and acknowledgments borrowed from other sources and reproduced, with permission, in this textbook appear on pages 489–490.

If you purchased this book within the United States or Canada you should be aware that it has been wrongfully imported without the approval of the Publisher or the Author.

Pearson Prentice Hall™ is a trademark of Pearson Education, Inc.
Pearson® is a registered trademark of Pearson plc
Prentice Hall® is a registered trademark of Pearson Education, Inc.

Pearson Education Ltd., London
Pearson Education Singapore, Pte. Ltd
Pearson Education, Canada, Inc.
Pearson Education–Japan
Pearson Education Australia PTY, Limited

Pearson Education North Asia, Ltd., Hong Kong
Pearson Educación de Mexico, S.A. de C.V.
Pearson Education Malaysia, Pte. Ltd.
Pearson Education Upper Saddle River,
 New Jersey

Prentice Hall
is an imprint of

www.pearsonhighered.com

10 9 8 7 6 5 4 3 2 1
ISBN-13: 978-0-13-714281-1
ISBN-10: 0-13-714281-1

To Taylor

Brief Contents

Contents

Preface

Fundamentals of Human Resource Management provides students in undergraduate and graduate human resource management courses with a comprehensive review of the human resource management body of knowledge in a relatively brief 14-chapter format.

Human resource management is the process of acquiring, training, appraising, and compensating employees and of attending to their labor relations, health and safety, and fairness concerns. The topics we'll discuss should therefore provide you with the concepts and techniques you'll need to perform the "people" or personnel aspects of management, such as s*electing* job candidates, *orienting and training* new employees, *providing* incentives and benefits, and *appraising* performance. Prior coursework in principles of management is helpful but not required for benefiting from this book.

Human resource management is an important topic, even if you never spend one day as an HR manager. Every day of your business career, you'll have to interview and hire people, and train and appraise them, for instance. Studying this book should therefore enable you to do three things. It should help *all* business students—not just human resource management majors—learn how to use essential human resource management skills like interviewing, appraising, and providing safe practices at work. It should enable you to satisfy the relevant "assessment of learning" objectives that your school's accrediting agencies may require. And it should give you a practical perspective on how managers apply non-HR personal competencies (such as ethical decision-making) and business knowledge (such as business law) when carrying out personnel tasks like screening and appraising employees.

It is my hope that studying this book will provide you with skills you will use all through your management career. Many other students around the world have found that to be the case. Publishers have translated my other human resource management textbooks into more than ten languages, so, as you read this preface, there are students in China, Russia, France, Malaysia, India, South America and the Middle East and other places who are also learning HR skills from one of my books.

Look for several specific features in this book. A boxed *Global Issues* feature highlights global aspects of human resource management, and a laptop icon points the way to human resource information system applications. HR in Practice features present guidelines and checklists supervisors can use to do a better job managing their personnel. Two boxed features show how managers use personal and business skills as part of their jobs. For example, in Chapter 5, "Selecting Employees," the *Personal Competencies* feature addresses "Building Your *Cross-Cultural Sensitivity:* Skills to Reduce Employee Selection Errors" and the *Business in Action* feature addresses *"Building Your Business Law Knowledge in Testing."*

Student Supplements

eHRM: An Internet Guide to Human Resource Management   Provides an introduction to many of the tools and resources available on the Internet for managing human resources, regardless of the type or size of the company.

Self Assessment Library 3.4 (SAL)   SAL is a unique learning tool that allows students to assess their knowledge, beliefs, feelings, and actions in regard to a wide range of personal skills, abilities, and interests. Provided scoring keys allow for immediate, individual analysis. This single volume of 69 research-based instruments is organized into four parts and offers students one source from which to learn more about themselves.

HRSim Selection Simulation   HRSim Selection reinforces the core human resource concept of recruitment and selection. This browser-based simulation is flexible enough to run in a short timeframe or in a more traditional format, which allows more time for detailed analysis and discussion. HRSim Selection immerses students in a challenging environment where they can experience a real life human resource situation.

Packages

Pearson Prentice Hall offers special pricing when you choose to package your text with other student resources. Recommended package for this text are:

Fundamentals of Human Resource Management and eHRM: An Internet Guide to Human Resource Management – ISBN # 013507388X

Fundamentals of Human Resource Management and Self Assessment Library 3.4 – ISBN # 0137158416

Fundamentals of Human Resource Management and HRSim Selection – ISBN # 0135073898

Acknowledgments

I am indebted to many people for their assistance in creating this book. I appreciate the hard work and suggestions from the reviewers of *Fundamentals*, including Wesley A. Scroggins, Missouri State University; Deborah M. Wharff, University of North Carolina Pembroke and University of Massachusetts, Lowell; and David C. Jacobs, Morgan State University. James Scheiner, Dean of the School of Business Administration at Stetson University, had a significant influence on the concept and themes of *Fundamentals*, and I am grateful for his friendship and advice. At Pearson Prentice Hall, I want to thank the team I worked with on this book, including Acquisitions Editor Jennifer Collins, Production Project Manager Kelly Warsack, Project Manager Jennifer Welsch, and Marketing Manager Nikki Jones, as well as the world-wide members of Pearson's sales team. At home, I want to thank my wife Claudia for her support, my son Derek for his advice, and of course, our newest family member, Taylor, for keeping things lively.

About the Author

Gary Dessler is a widely read author of textbooks in human resource management, and management. His best-selling *Human Resource Management, 11th edition* (Prentice Hall, 2008), is also available in 10 languages including Traditional and Simplified Chinese. Dessler's other books include *Managing Now* (Houghton Mifflin, 2008), *Framework for Human Resource Management, 5th edition* (Prentice Hall), and *Winning Commitment: How to Build and Keep a Competitive Workforce* (McGraw-Hill). His published articles and presentations include "Expanding into China? What Foreign Employers Entering China Should Know About Human Resource Management in China Today," SAM *Advanced Management Journal*, September 2006; "How to Fine-Tune Your Employees' Ethical Compasses," *Supervision*, April 2006; and "Business Models of China's Online Recruiting Sites: A Taxonomy and Implications," (co-author), paper presented at Rollins China Center Conference, December 2006. Dessler is a Founding Professor at Florida International University where he teaches courses in human resource management, strategic management, and management. He has degrees from New York University (B.S.), Rensselaer Polytechnic Institute (M.S.), and the Baruch School of Business of the City University of New York (Ph.D.). Dr. Dessler served for 3 years on the Institute of International Education's national selection committee for the Fulbright student awards; is a member of the Society for Human Resource Management, the Academy of Management, and the Authors Guild; and, as a board member for a chemical engineering and pollution control firm, serves as that firm's consulting human resource manager.

Managing Human Resources Today

1

When you finish studying this chapter, you should be able to:

1. Answer the question "What is human resource management?"

2. Explain with at least five examples why "knowing HR management concepts and techniques is important to any supervisor or manager."

3. Explain with examples what we mean by "the changing environment of human resource management."

4. Give examples of how the HR manager's duties today are different from 30 years ago.

5. List, with examples, four important issues influencing HR management today.

Introduction

When it comes to keeping good employees, the restaurant business is usually a tough sell. Hourly employee turnover typically ranges from about 110% to 135%, meaning that the average restaurant replaces just about all its employees every year or so.[1] That's particularly dangerous in a service business, where an unkind word from a hapless employee can prompt a customer to leave. Yet some restaurant managers seem to know the secret not just of keeping good employees but of keeping them happy. Bob Gamboa, general manager of a Stanford's Restaurant in Lake Oswego, Oregon, is one of them. He estimates his yearly turnover is only about 28%, several times better than the industry average. His secret? Simple yet effective human resource management practices. For example, "You have to be really picky . . . I'm selective on who I hire. I'm looking for people who want to stay."[2] He looks for people who smile easily and are friendly, and he tells them during the interview, that "if you're not the friendliest employee in the restaurant, you're not going to make it."[3] His success shows how even simple improvements in human resource management can generate disproportionately large returns for employers. ■

❶ Answer the question "What is human resource management?"

organization
A group consisting of people with formally assigned roles who work together to achieve the organization's goals.

manager
Someone who is responsible for accomplishing the organization's goals, and who does so by managing the efforts of the organization's people.

managing
To perform five basic functions: planning, organizing, staffing, leading, and controlling.

management process
The five basic functions of planning, organizing, staffing, leading, and controlling.

human resource management (HRM)
The process of acquiring, training, appraising, and compensating employees, and of attending to their labor relations, health and safety, and fairness concerns.

WHAT IS HUMAN RESOURCE MANAGEMENT?

Stanford's Restaurant is an *organization*. An **organization** consists of people (in this case, people like chefs, managers, and wait-staff) with formally assigned roles who work together to achieve the organization's goals. A **manager** is someone who is responsible for accomplishing the organization's goals, and who does so by managing the efforts of the organization's people. Most writers agree that **managing** involves performing five basic functions: planning, organizing, staffing, leading, and controlling. In total, these functions represent the **management process.** Some of the specific activities involved in each function include:

- *Planning.* Establishing goals and standards; developing rules and procedures; developing plans and forecasts.
- *Organizing.* Giving each subordinate a specific task; establishing departments; delegating authority to subordinates; establishing channels of authority and communication; coordinating the work of subordinates.
- *Staffing.* Determining what type of people should be hired; recruiting prospective employees; selecting employees; setting performance standards; compensating employees; evaluating performance; counseling employees; training and developing employees.
- *Leading.* Getting others to get the job done; maintaining morale; motivating subordinates.
- *Controlling.* Setting standards such as sales quotas, quality standards, or production levels; checking to see how actual performance compares with these standards; taking corrective action as needed.

In this book, we are going to focus on one of these functions—the staffing, personnel management, or *human resource management (HRM)* function. **Human resource management** is the process of acquiring, training, appraising, and compensating employees, and of attending to their labor relations, health and safety, and fairness concerns. The topics we'll discuss should therefore provide you with the concepts and techniques you'll need to perform the "people" or personnel aspects of management. These include:

- *Conducting job analyses* (determining the nature of each employee's job)
- *Planning labor needs* and *recruiting* job candidates
- *Selecting* job candidates
- *Orienting and training* new employees
- *Managing wages and salaries* (compensating employees)
- *Providing incentives and benefits*
- *Appraising performance*
- *Communicating* (interviewing, counseling, disciplining)

- Training employees, *and developing managers*
- *Building employee commitment*

And what a manager should know about:

- Equal opportunity and affirmative action
- Employee health and safety
- Handling grievances and labor relations

Why Is Human Resource Management Important to All Managers?

Why are these concepts and techniques important to all managers? Perhaps it's easier to answer this by listing some of the personnel mistakes you don't want to make while managing. For example, you don't want

To have your employees not performing at peak capacity

To hire the wrong person for the job

To experience high turnover

To find employees not doing their best

To have your company taken to court because of your discriminatory actions

To have your company cited under governmental occupational safety laws for unsafe practices

To allow a lack of training to undermine your department's effectiveness

To commit any unfair labor practices

Explain with at least five examples why "knowing HR management concepts and techniques is important to any supervisor or manager."

WHY STUDY THIS BOOK? Carefully studying this book can help you avoid mistakes like these. More important, it can help ensure that you get results—through people. Remember that you could do everything else right as a manager—lay brilliant plans, draw clear organization charts, set up modern assembly lines, and use sophisticated accounting controls—but still fail, for instance, by hiring the wrong people or by not motivating subordinates.

On the other hand, many managers—from presidents to generals to supervisors—have been successful even without adequate plans, organizations, or controls. They were successful because they had the knack for hiring the right people for the right jobs and motivating, appraising, and developing them. Remember as you read this book that getting results is the bottom line of managing and that, as a manager, you will have to get these results through people. This fact hasn't changed from the dawn of management. As one company president summed it up:

> For many years it has been said that capital is the bottleneck for a developing industry. I don't think this any longer holds true. I think it's the workforce and the company's inability to recruit and maintain a good workforce that does constitute the bottleneck for production. I don't know of any major project backed by good ideas, vigor, and enthusiasm that has been stopped by a shortage of cash. I do know of industries whose growth has been partly stopped or hampered because they can't maintain an efficient and enthusiastic labor force, and I think this will hold true even more in the future.[4]

Line and Staff Aspects of HRM

All managers are, in a sense, human resource managers, because they all get involved in activities such as recruiting, interviewing, selecting, and training. Yet most firms also have a separate human resource department with its own human resource manager. How do the duties of this departmental HR manager and his or her staff relate to line managers' human resource duties? Let's answer this by starting with short definitions of line versus staff authority.

Line Versus Staff Authority

authority
The right to make decisions, direct others' work, and give orders.

Authority is the right to make decisions, to direct the work of others, and to give orders. In management, we usually distinguish between line authority and staff authority. Line

line manager
A manager who is authorized to direct the work of subordinates and is responsible for accomplishing the organization's tasks.

staff manager
A manager who assists and advises line managers.

authority gives managers the right (or authority) to issue orders to other managers or employees. It creates a superior-subordinate relationship. Staff authority gives a manager the right (authority) to advise other managers or employees. It creates an advisory relationship. **Line managers** have line authority. They are authorized to give orders. **Staff managers** have staff authority. They are authorized to assist and advise line managers.

In popular usage, managers associate line managers with managing functions (like sales or production) that the company must have to operate. Staff managers generally run departments that are advisory or supportive, like purchasing, human resource management, and quality control. This "must-have" vs. "supportive" distinction makes sense as long as the "staff" department is, in fact, advisory. However, strictly speaking, it is not the type of department the person is in charge of or its name that determines if the manager in charge is line or staff. It is the nature of the manager's authority. The line manager can issue orders. The staff manager can advise.

Human resource managers are staff managers. They assist and advise line managers in areas like recruiting, hiring, and compensation. (However, we'll see that line managers also have human resource duties.)

FROM LINE TO STAFF Managers may move from line to staff positions (and back) over the course of their careers. For example, line managers in areas like production and sales may well make career stopovers as staff human resource managers (one good reason for all managers to know something about human resources). A survey by the Center for Effective Organizations at the University of Southern California found that about one fourth of large U.S. businesses appointed managers with no human resources experience as their top human resource executives. Employers assumed that these people may find it easier to link the firm's human resource management efforts to the firm's strategic goals, and might sometimes be better equipped to integrate the firm's human resources efforts with other functions like sales and finance.[5]

LINE–STAFF HR COOPERATION HR and line managers share responsibility for most human resource activities. For example, human resource and line managers in about two thirds of the firms in one survey shared responsibility for skills training.[6] (Thus, the supervisor might describe what training she thinks the new employee needs, HR might design the training, and the supervisor might then ensure that the training is having the desired effect.)

Line Managers' Human Resource Management Responsibilities

In any case, all supervisors spend much of their time on HR/personnel-type tasks. Indeed, the direct handling of people always has been an integral part of every line manager's responsibility, from president down to the first-line supervisor.

For example, one company outlines its line supervisors' responsibilities for effective human resource management under the following general headings:

1. Placing the right person in the right job
2. Starting new employees in the organization (orientation)
3. Training employees for jobs that are new to them
4. Improving the job performance of each person
5. Gaining creative cooperation and developing smooth working relationships
6. Interpreting the company's policies and procedures
7. Controlling labor costs
8. Developing the abilities of each person
9. Creating and maintaining departmental morale
10. Protecting employees' health and physical conditions

In small organizations, line managers may carry out all these personnel duties unassisted. But as the organization grows, line managers need the assistance, specialized knowledge, and advice of a separate human resource staff.

Organizing the Human Resource Department's Responsibilities

The *human resource department* provides this specialized assistance. Figure 1.1 shows the human resource management jobs you might find in a large company. Typical positions

FIGURE 1.1 HR Organization Chart for a Large Organization

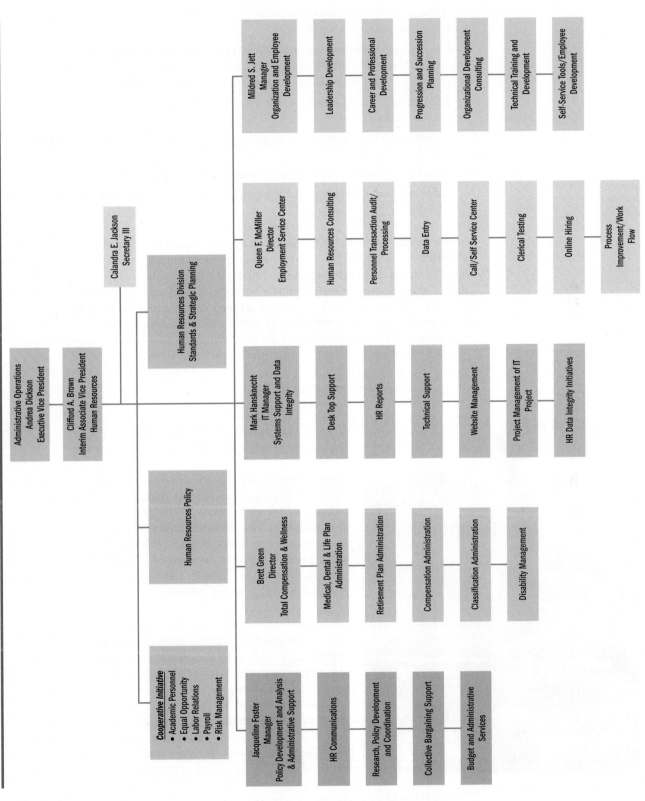

Source: www.hr.wayne.edu/orgcharts.php/hrdorgchart.pdf, accessed May 6, 2007.

include compensation and benefits manager, employment and recruiting supervisor, training specialist, and employee relations executive. Examples of job duties include:

Recruiters: Maintain contact within the community and perhaps travel extensively to search for qualified job applicants.

Equal employment opportunity (EEO) representatives or affirmative action coordinators: Investigate and resolve EEO grievances, examine organizational practices for potential violations, and compile and submit EEO reports.

Job analysts: Collect and examine detailed information about job duties to prepare job descriptions.

Compensation managers: Develop compensation plans and handle the employee benefits program.

Training specialists: Plan, organize, and direct training activities.

Labor relations specialists: Advise management on all aspects of union–management relations.

HR IN SMALL BUSINESSES Human resource management in small firms is not just a shrunken version of big-company human resource management. Employers usually have about one HR professional per 100 employees. Small firms (say, those with less than 100 employees) generally don't have the critical mass required for a full-time human resource manager. Their human resource management therefore tends to be "ad hoc and informal." For example, one survey concludes that small firms tend to use "unimaginative" recruiting practices like relying on newspaper ads, walk-ins, and word-of-mouth, and to do little or no formal training.[7] However, that certainly does not need to be the case. Techniques like those throughout this book (and in chapter 12) can boost the small business owner's "HR IQ."

Randy MacDonald and IBM reorganized its human resource management group to focus on the needs of specific groups of IBM employees.

THE CHANGING ENVIRONMENT OF HUMAN RESOURCE MANAGEMENT

In most respects, the individual supervisor's human resource management–related duties haven't changed much in many years. Managers have always been "on the front line" when it comes to responsibilities like placing the right person in the right job, and training new employees. What *has* changed rather dramatically are the human resource department's duties and how it does its job. Let's look at an example, and then more closely at why and how HR management has changed.

IBM EXAMPLE For example, Randy MacDonald, IBM's senior vice president of human resources, felt that IBM's traditionally organized human resource management department did not adequately serve the different needs of IBM's various groups of employees. The organization was not employee-focused. Instead, as is typical, it isolated HR functions into "silos" such as recruitment, training, and employee relations. This silo approach meant there was no one team of human resource specialists (recruiters, trainers, and so on) focusing on the needs of specific groups of employees (engineers, managers, and so on).

MacDonald therefore reorganized IBM's human resources function. He segmented its 330,000 employees into three sets of "customers," executive and technical employees, managers, and rank and file. Separate human resource management teams (consisting of recruitment, training, and compensation specialists, for instance) now focus on serving the needs of each employee segment. These cross-functional HR teams, working together, ensure that the employees in each segment get the skills, learning, and compensation they require to support IBM's strategy.[8]

The bottom line is that extraordinary changes have taken place in what employers expect from their human resource management departments, and in how these departments do their jobs. Let's look first at some of the trends that prompted these changes, and then more closely at the changes themselves.

Competitive Trends

Managing today is not what it was just a few years ago. Competitive, demographic, and workforce trends are driving businesses to change how they do things.

GLOBALIZATION & COMPETITION Globalization is a prime example. *Globalization* refers to the tendency of firms to extend their sales, ownership, and/or manufacturing to new markets abroad. Examples are all around us. Toyota produces the Corolla in the United Kingdom, while Dell produces and sells PCs in China. Free trade areas—agreements that reduce tariffs and barriers among trading partners—further encourage international trade. NAFTA (the North American Free Trade Agreement) and the EU (European Union) are examples.

More globalization means more competition, and more competition means more pressure to be "world class"—to lower costs, to make employees more productive, and to do things better and less expensively. As when the Spanish retailer Zara opens a new store in Manhattan, globalization pressures local employers and their HR teams to institute practices that get the best from their employees.

OUTSOURCING The search for greater efficiencies is prompting employers to outsource (export) more jobs to lower-cost locations abroad. For example, Merrill Lynch says it is having some of its security analysis work done in India. Figure 1.2 summarizes the situation. It shows that between 2005 and 2015, about 3 million U.S. jobs, ranging from office support and computer jobs to management, sales, and even legal jobs, will likely move offshore.[9]

Employers are even outsourcing human resource work. For example, several years ago BP Oil outsourced to Hewitt Associates (although in this case not abroad) its payroll, relocation, severance, and benefits administration functions.[10]

TECHNOLOGICAL ADVANCES Technology is changing almost everything businesses do. For example, technology (in the form of Internet-based communications) made it feasible for Merrill Lynch to outsource its security analysis jobs to India. Zara doesn't need the expensive inventories that burden competitors like The Gap. Zara operates its own Internet-based worldwide distribution network, linked to the checkout registers at its stores around the world. Suppose its headquarters in Spain sees a garment "flying" out of a store? Zara's computerized manufacturing system dyes the required fabric, cuts and manufactures the item, and speeds new garments to that store within days.

THE NATURE OF WORK Technology is also changing the nature of work, even factory work. In plants throughout the world, knowledge-intensive high-tech manufacturing jobs are

FIGURE 1.2

Employment Exodus: Projected Loss of U.S. Jobs and Wages

Source: Michael Shroeder, "States Fight Exodus of Jobs," *Wall Street Journal* (June 3, 2003): 84. Copyright © 2003 Dow Jones & Co., Inc. Reproduced with permission of Dow Jones & Co., Inc. in the format Textbook via Copyright Clearance Center.

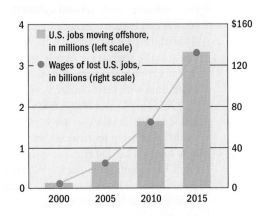

3 Explain with examples what we mean by "the changing environment of human resource management."

replacing traditional factory jobs. Skilled machinist Chad Toulouse illustrates the modern blue-collar worker. After an 18-week training course, this former college student now works as a team leader in a plant where about 40% of the machines are automated. In older plants, machinists would manually control machines that cut chunks of metal into things like engine parts. Today, Chad and his team spend much of their time typing commands into computerized machines that create precision parts for products, including water pumps.[11] Technology-based employees like these need new skills and training to excel at these more complex jobs.

SERVICE JOBS   Technology is not the only trend driving this change from "brawn to brains." Today over two thirds of the U.S. workforce is employed in producing and delivering services, not products. Between 2004 and 2014, almost all the 19 million new jobs added in the United States will be in services, not in goods-producing industries.[12]

HUMAN CAPITAL   For employers, this all means a growing need for "knowledge workers" and human capital. *Human capital* refers to the knowledge, education, training, skills, and expertise of a firm's workers.[13] Today, "the center of gravity in employment is moving fast from manual and clerical workers to knowledge workers, who resist the command-and-control model that business took from the military 100 years ago."[14] Managers need new world-class human resource management systems and skills to select, train, and motivate these employees and to get them to work more like committed partners.

Demographic and Workforce Trends

DEMOGRAPHIC TRENDS   At the same time, workforce demographic trends are making finding and hiring good employees more challenging. Labor force growth is not expected to keep pace with job growth, with an estimated shortfall of about 14 million college educated workers by 2020.[15] One study of 35 large global companies' senior human resource managers said "talent management"—in particular, the acquisition, development, and retention of talent—ranked as their top concern.[16]

Overall, the U.S. workforce's demographics are becoming older and more multiethnic.[17] At current rates, the white labor force will grow by 7%, as compared with blacks (17%), Asians (32%), and other (30%) by 2014. The labor force participation rate of women, having increased from about 40% 50 years ago to about 60% today, will remain at about 60% through 2014. As the baby-boom generation ages, the number of people in the labor force age 55 to 64 will increase by about 7 million through 2014. The Hispanic and Latino labor force will increase by about 33%.[18]

There has also been a shift to nontraditional workers. Nontraditional workers include those who hold multiple jobs, or who are "contingent" or part-time workers, or people working in alternative work arrangements (such as a mother–daughter team sharing one flight attendant job at JetBlue airlines). Today, almost 10% of American workers—about 13 million people—fit this nontraditional workforce category. Of these, about 8 million are independent contractors who work on specific projects and move on once the projects are done.

"GENERATION Y"   Some experts note that the incoming crop of younger workers may have different work-related values than did their predecessors. Based on one study, current (older) employees are more likely to be work-centric (to focus more on work than on family with respect to career decisions). Younger workers tend to be more family-centric or dual-centric (balancing family and work life). Younger workers also generally don't agree that it's "better for women to stay home" than to work, and younger fathers tend to spend more time with their children on workdays.[19]

Fortune Magazine says that today's new "Generation Y" employees will bring challenges and strengths. It says they may be "the most high maintenance workforce in the history of the world." Referring to them as "the most praised generation," the *Wall Street Journal* explains how Lands' End and Bank of America are teaching their managers to compliment these new employees with prize packages and public appreciation.[20] On the other hand, as the first generation raised on pagers and e-mail, their information technology skills will also make them the most high performing.

RETIREES One survey of human resource professionals calls "the aging workforce" the biggest demographic trend impacting employers. For example, how will employers replace these retiring employees in the face of a diminishing supply of younger workers?

Employers are dealing with this in various ways. One survey found that 41% of surveyed employers are bringing retirees back into the workforce, 34% are conducting studies to determine their own projected retirement rates, and 31% are offering employment options designed to attract and retain semi-retired workers.[21] This retiree issue helps explain why "talent management"—getting and keeping good employees—ranks as HR managers' top concern.[22]

HUMAN RESOURCE MANAGEMENT'S CHANGING ROLE

Competitive, demographic, and workforce trends like these force businesses to change how they do things. For example, more competition means more pressure to lower costs, and to make employees more productive. Most employers are therefore cutting staff, outsourcing tasks, and installing new productivity-boosting technologies. And as part of these efforts, they also expect their HR managers to "add value", in other words, to improve organizational performance in measurable ways.

Example of HR Management's Changing Role

Human resource management's role has therefore shifted to improving organizational performance by tapping the potential of the firms' human capital. Here's an example. A bank installed a new software system that made it easier for customer service representatives to handle customers' inquiries. Seeking to capitalize on the new software, the bank upgraded the customer service representatives' jobs. The bank's human resource management team gave the reps new training, taught them how to sell more of the bank's services, gave them more authority to make decisions, and raised their wages. Here, the new computer system dramatically improved revenues and profitability.

A second bank installed a similar system, but did not upgrade the workers' jobs. The employees received only enough training to use the new software. Here, the new system helped the service reps handle a few more calls. But this bank saw none of the big performance gains the first bank had gotten by expanding its reps into highly trained salespeople.[23]

There are two points to this example.

- *First,* today's employers expect their human resource managers to measurably improve organizational performance, by instituting new and improved human resource practices.[24]
- *Second*, human resource management therefore has new duties and priorities. Human resource management used to focus mostly on day-to-day administrative duties, like signing up employees for benefits. Today, it focuses less on administration, and more on strategic activities like helping the bank's employees better capitalize on their new customer service software. In other words, human resource management has evolved. Let's look at how.

④ Give examples of how the HR manager's duties today are different from 30 years ago.

The Evolution to the New Human Resource Management

Figure 1.3 helps illustrate how human resource management evolved in response to evolving trends and issues. As companies expanded in the early 1900s, employers needed more assistance with "personnel." The earliest personnel departments took over hiring and firing from supervisors, ran the payroll department, and administered benefits. As know-how in things like testing and interviewing emerged, the personnel department began playing a bigger role in employee selection, training, and promotion.[25] The appearance of union legislation in the 1930s added "protecting the firm in its interaction with unions" to the personnel department's responsibilities. Then, as new equal employment legislation created the potential for discrimination-related lawsuits, employers turned to personnel managers to provide the requisite advice.[26]

Today, competitive, technological, and workforce trends mean business is much more competitive than in the past. Human resource managers face new issues. As in the bank example, highly trained and committed employees, not machines, are often a firm's main

FIGURE 1.3 Issues Driving the Evolution of Human Resource Management

Decade	Major Business Issues	Common Titles for "HR"
Pre-1900s	Small businesses, and workers' guilds	No "HR" people
1900s	Growth of larger-scale enterprises due to effects of earlier industrial revolution, World War I	Labor Relations, Personnel
1920s	World-wide economic depression, Hawthorne "human relations" studies, first labor legislation	Industrial Relations, Personnel
1940s	World War II, growth of large diversified enterprises	Personnel Administration
1960s	Civil rights and compliance	Personnel
1980s	Growing impact of globalization and technology, and emergence of the knowledge/service economy, human capital	Personnel/Human Resources
2000s	Modern organizations, organization effectiveness, strategic HR planning	Human Resource Management

Source: Based on Richard Vosburgh, "The Evolution of HR: Developing HR as an Internal Consulting Organization," *Human Resource Planning,* September 2007, volume 30, issue 3.

competitive advantage. That means employers like Tesco have had to rethink how their human resource management departments do things. We'll see in this book that the trend today is for the human resource team to spend less time on administrative, transactional services such as benefits administration, and more time doing two main things—

1. Supporting top management's *strategic planning* efforts, and
2. Acting as the firm's *"internal consultant"* for identifying and institutionalizing changes that will help the company's employees better contribute to the company's success.

Two writers put it this way: human resource management needs to shift its emphasis from providing services to providing people-related decisions that "inform and support."[27]

IMPORTANT HUMAN RESOURCE MANAGEMENT ISSUES TODAY

⑤ List, with examples, four important issues influencing HR management today.

This shift in emphasis means that successful human resource managers find themselves dealing with at least four issues today. We'll discuss these issues in more detail later in this book, but it's useful to get a birds eye view of them in this first, introductory chapter. The issues are the need for HR managers: *to cultivate new skills; to understand strategic planning; to understand how to utilize technology;* and *to institute policies and practices that ensure fair and ethical behavior at work.*

New Human Resource Management Skills[28]

First, the evolution of HR's duties *from* supplying mostly administrative services *to* supplying more strategic and people-related consulting support means human resource managers need to develop new kinds of skills. Here are three examples.

1. First, employers and their HR teams need to find *new ways to supply traditional transactional HR services* (such as benefits administration), so as to free up the human resource manager's time for strategic, internal consulting activities.
2. Second, human resource managers have to improve their *internal consulting skills.* (For example, the bank's human resource manager devised new screening, training, and pay practices that helped the bank better capitalize on its new customer service rep software.) And,

3. Third, moving from supplying administrative services to supplying consulting and strategic ones often means outsourcing administrative services like benefits administration to outside vendors. Human resource managers therefore need to be adept at dealing with outside vendors—they must *improve their HR outsourcing skills.*

Throughout this book we'll see how human resource managers develop these and other skills.

Strategic Human Resource Management

strategy
The company's long-term plan for how it will balance its internal strengths and weaknesses with its external opportunities and threats to maintain a competitive advantage.

Every company needs a *strategy*. A **strategy** is the company's plan for how it will match its internal strengths and weaknesses with external opportunities and threats in order to maintain a competitive advantage. Thus Microsoft's strategy was to boost its Internet search capacity by trying to buy Yahoo. B&Q's strategy is to sell do-it-yourself and home improvement tools and supplies.

Whether it's the first-line supervisor or the company's HR manager, the person's main human resource-related responsibility is to use human resource management methods to produce the employee competencies and behaviors the company needs to achieve its strategic goals. This makes *strategic planning* another important HR issue. At the bank, this meant making sure the customer service reps had the pay and sales training they needed to capitalize on the new technology. At IBM it meant reorganizing human resource management around teams, each of which then focused on supporting one of three groups of employees.

strategic human resource management
Formulating and executing human resource policies and practices that produce the employee competencies and behaviors the company needs to achieve its strategic aims.

Helping top management formulate and execute its strategy is one way human resource managers add value to the company. **Strategic human resource management** means formulating and executing human resource policies and practices that produce the employee competencies and behaviors the company needs to achieve its strategic aims.

ALBERTSON'S EXAMPLE U.S. grocery retailer Albertson's Markets faced competitive pressures from firms like Wal-Mart. Albertson's top management therefore needed their human resource managers to be partners in helping the firm achieve its strategic goals. These goals included reducing costs and offering excellent service.

Albertson's HR team did this in several ways. For example, reducing personnel-related costs and improving performance meant hiring employees who had a customer-focused approach, as well as reducing turnover, improving retention, and eliminating time-consuming manual processes and procedures for store managers.

Working with its information technology department, Albertson's human resource management team also got a computer system from Unicru of Portland, Oregon (www.unicru.com). The system collects and analyzes the information entered by applicants

Albertson's HR team took steps to support the company's strategy.

online and at kiosks. It ranks applicants based on the extent to which they exhibit the customer-focused traits that predict success in retail jobs, helps track candidates throughout the screening process, and does other things, such as track reasons for departure once applicants are hired. HR managers were able to present a compelling business case to illustrate the new system's return on investment. Working as a partner with top management, its HR team thus contributed to achieving Albertson's strategic goals.[29] We'll address HR strategy in more detail in chapter 3.

HR and Technology

Technology is another important HR issue, because (see Figure 1.4) technology plays such a central role in human resource management today. Employers want to reduce the time they put into providing administrative HR services like benefits sign-ups. Technology helps them do this. It improves HR functioning in four main ways: *self-service, call centers, productivity improvement,* and *outsourcing.*[30]

Dell provides good examples of several of these applications. For example, Dell employees use the firm's intranet-based HR applications to *self-service* many of their HR transactions, such as updating personal information and changing benefits allocations. Technology also enabled Dell to create a *centralized call center.* HR specialists answer questions from all Dell's far-flung employees, reducing the need for multiple HR centers at each Dell location.

More firms are installing Internet- and computer-based systems for improving human resource function *productivity.* For example, Dell installed a Web-based applicant tracking system. This system automated the process of recruiting employees and of managing their applications and progress through the hiring process. The vendor then worked with Dell to develop customized recruiting metrics. These included, for instance, hiring managers' evaluations of the candidates. Dell can now correlate candidate performance with sources of applicants. They can therefore focus their recruiting on the more productive recruitment sources.[31]

FIGURE 1.4 Some Ways HR Managers Use Technology

Technology	How Used by HR
Application Service Providers (ASPs)	ASPs host and manage services (such as for processing employment applications) for the employer from their own remote computers
Web portals	Employers use these, for instance, to enable employees to manage their own benefits and update their personal information
Streaming PC video	Used, for instance, to facilitate distance training
The mobile Web and wireless net access	Used to facilitate employees' access to the company's Web-based HR activities
Personal digital assistants	For example, some firms provide incoming managers with preloaded personal digital assistants. These contain information the new managers need to better adjust to their new jobs, such as key contact information and digital images of the manager's new employees
Monitoring software	Used to track employees' Internet and e-mail activities or performance
Integrated human resource information systems (HRIS)	Used to integrate the employer's separate HR systems, for instance by automatically updating employee's qualifications list when he or she completes a training program
Electronic signatures	Employers can use these legally valid e-signatures to expeditiously obtain applicant and employee signatures
The Web	Managers make extensive use of the Web, as for doing salary surveys

Sources: Adapted from Samuel Greengard, "10 HR Technology Trends for 2001," *HR Trends and Tools for Business Results* 80, no. 1 (January 2001): 20–22; Jim Meade, "Analytical Tools Give Meaning to Data," *HR Magazine* 46, no. 11 (November 2001): 97 ff. Connie Winkler, "Quality Check," *HR Magazine* (May 2007): 93–98.

Dell put much of its HR services online.

Finally, technology also makes it easier to *outsource* human resource activities to specialist service providers by enabling service providers to have real-time Internet-based access to the employer's HR database. For instance, several years ago, BP outsourced its benefits management activities to Hewitt Associates. We'll address HR technology in more detail throughout the book, and in chapter 12.

Managing Ethics

ethics

The principles of conduct governing an individual or a group; specifically, the standards you use to decide what your conduct should be.

Because ethical misdeeds will torpedo even otherwise competent managers, *managing ethics* is an important human resource management issue. **Ethics** refers to the standards someone uses to decide what his or her conduct should be. Ethical decisions always involve *morality,* matters of serious consequence to society's well-being, such as murder, lying, and stealing. Newspaper headlines regarding ethical lapses (like questionably timed stock option grants at various firms) never seem to end. Given that some firms, such as the accounting firm Arthur Andersen, were literally put out of business by ethical lapses, one has to wonder what the managers were thinking.

The United States Congress passed the Sarbanes-Oxley Act in 2003. To help ensure that managers take their ethics responsibilities seriously, Sarbanes-Oxley (SOX) is intended to curb erroneous corporate financial reporting. Among other things, Sarbanes-Oxley requires CEOs and CFOs to certify their companies' periodic financial reports. It also prohibits personal loans to executive officers and directors, and requires CEOs and CFOs to reimburse their firms for bonuses and stock option profits if corporate financial statements subsequently require restating.[32] SOX does not just involve the firm's CEO and CFO. For example, every publicly listed company now needs a code of ethics, more often than not promulgated by human resources.

The human resource manager's responsibilities for ethics don't end with Sarbanes-Oxley. One survey found that six of the ten most serious ethical issues—workplace safety, security of employee records, employee theft, affirmative action, "comparable work", and employee privacy rights—were human resource management related.[33] We'll address ethics in more detail in chapter 9.

HR Certification

As the human resource manager's tasks grow more complex, human resource management is becoming more professionalized. More than 60,000 HR professionals have already passed one or both of the Society for Human Resource Management's (SHRM™) HR professional certification exams. SHRM's Human Resource Certification Institute offers these exams. Two levels of exams test the professional's knowledge of all aspects of human resource management, including management practices, staffing, development, compensation, labor relations, and health and safety. Those who successfully complete all requirements earn the SPHR (senior professional in HR) or PHR (professional in HR) certificate. The Human Resource Certification Institute recently began implementing state certifications in the U.S. Managers can take an online HRCI assessment exam at www.HRCI.org.

THE PLAN OF THIS BOOK

The basic aim of this book is to provide all current and future managers (including but not just limited to current and future *human resource managers*) with the concepts and skills they need to carry out the people or personnel aspects of their jobs.

The Chapters

We've organized the topics in the following chapters:

Part 1: Introduction
1. *Managing Human Resources Today*
2. *Managing Equal Opportunity and Diversity* What you'll need to know about equal opportunity laws as they relate to human resource management activities, such as interviewing, selecting employees, and evaluating performance appraisals.
3. *Mergers, Acquisitions, and Strategic Human Resource Management* What is strategic planning, and how human resource management contributes to mergers, acquisitions, and strategy formulation and execution.

Part 2: Staffing the Organization
4. *Personal Planning and Recruiting* How to analyze a job and how to determine the job's requirements, specific duties, and responsibilities, as well as what sorts of people need to be hired and how to recruit them.
5. *Selecting Employees* Techniques such as testing that you can use to ensure that you're hiring the right people.
6. *Training and Developing Employees* Providing the training and development necessary to ensure that your employees have the knowledge and skills required to accomplish their tasks.

Part 3: Appraising and Compensating Employees
7. *Performance Management and Appraisal* Techniques for managing and appraising performance.
8. *Compensating Employees* How to develop equitable pay plans, including incentives and benefits, for your employees.

Part 4: Employee and Labor Relations
9. *Ethics, Employee Rights, and Fair Treatment at Work* Ensuring ethical and fair treatment through discipline, grievance, and career management processes.
10. *Working with Unions and Resolving Disputes* Concepts and techniques concerning the relations between unions and management, including the union-organizing campaign, negotiating and agreeing on a collective bargaining agreement between unions and management, and managing the agreement.
11. *Improving Occupational Safety, Health, and Security* The causes of accidents, how to make the workplace safe, and laws governing your responsibilities in regard to employee safety and health.

Part 5: Special Issues in Human Resource Management
12. *Managing Human Resources in Entrepreneurial Firms* Special HRM methods small business managers can use to compete more successfully.
13. *Managing HR Globally* Applying human resource management policies and practices in a global environment.
14. *Measuring and Improving HR Management's Results* How managers can measure, assess, and improve the effectiveness of their human resource practices.

Two Special Chapter Features

SHRM, the Society for Human Resource Management, distributed its new *SHRM Human Resource Curriculum Guidebook* a few years ago. One point the *Guidebook* makes is that human resource managers need certain business and personal skills in order to best utilize their human resource management knowledge. Among other things, the *Guidebook* therefore suggests teaching human resource management in a way that blends the *HR content* with these business and personal skills. For example, in discussing equal employment law (an HR content area), tie in discussions of relevant *personal competencies* (such as "ethical decision making") and *business knowledge applications* (such as "corporate social responsibility").

Because doing so makes sense even for managers who have no intention of ever being human resource managers, we'll follow SHRM's suggestion in this book. We do this by including in each subsequent chapter from this point on two special features:

1. ***Personal Competencies features*** The boxed *Personal Competencies* features highlight relevant managerial personal competencies (skills). So, for the Managing Equal Opportunity and Diversity chapter we discuss *ethical decision-making* as a personal competency.
2. ***Business in Action features*** The boxed *Business in Action* features highlight relevant business/policy knowledge applications. Thus, for the Managing Equal Opportunity and Diversity chapter's *Business in Action* feature, you'll find a business law and public policy feature showing how California's Longo Toyota auto dealership supports its business policy goals by building a diverse workforce.

Review

SUMMARY

1. Staffing, personnel management, or human resource management includes activities such as recruiting, selecting, training, compensating, appraising, and developing.
2. HR management is a part of every line manager's responsibilities. These HR responsibilities include placing the right person in the right job and then orienting, training, and compensating the person to improve his or her job performance.
3. The HR manager and his or her department provide various staff services to line management; for example, the HR manager or department assists in the hiring, training, evaluating, rewarding, promoting, and disciplining of employees at all levels.

4. Changes in the environment of HR management are requiring HR to play a more strategic role in organizations. These changes include growing workforce diversity, rapid technological change, globalization, and changes in the nature of work, such as the movement toward a service society and a growing emphasis on education and human capital.
5. The consequence of changes in the work environment is that HR managers' jobs are increasingly strategic in nature, and these managers must also focus more on providing internal consulting expertise with respect to improving employee morale and performance.

KEY TERMS

organization   28
manager   28
managing   28
management process   28
human resource management   28
authority   29

line managers   30
staff managers   30
services   34
strategy   37
strategic human resource management   37
ethics   39

DISCUSSION QUESTIONS AND EXERCISES

1. Explain what HR management is and how it relates to line management.
2. Give several examples of how HR management concepts and techniques can be of use to all managers.
3. Compare the authority of line and staff managers. Give examples of each.
4. Working individually or in groups, develop a list showing how trends such as workforce diversity, technological trends, globalization, and changes in the nature of work have affected the college or university you are now attending or the organization for which you work.
5. Working individually or in groups, develop several examples showing how the new HR management practices mentioned in this chapter have or have not been implemented to some extent in the college or university you are now attending or in the organization for which you work.
6. Working individually or in groups, interview an HR manager. Based on that interview, write a short presentation regarding HR's role today in improving employee and organizational productivity.
7. Why is it important for a company to make its human resources into a "competitive advantage"? How can HR contribute to doing so?
8. What is meant by strategic human resource management? Give an example of how HR managers can help support their firms' strategic goals.

Application Exercises

HR in Action Case Incident 1 — Jack Nelson's Problem

As a new member of the board of directors for a local bank, Jack Nelson was being introduced to all the employees in the home office. When he was introduced to Ruth Johnson, he was curious about her work and asked her what her machine did. Johnson replied that she really did not know what the machine was called or what it did. She explained that she had been working there for only two months. She did, however, know precisely how to operate the machine. According to her supervisor, she was an excellent employee.

At one of the branch offices, the supervisor in charge spoke to Nelson confidentially, telling him that "something was wrong," but she didn't know what. For one thing, she explained, employee turnover was too high, and no sooner had one employee been put on the job than another one resigned. With customers to see and loans to be made, she explained, she had little time to work with the new employees as they came and went.

All branch supervisors hired their own employees without communication with the home office or other branches. When an opening developed, the supervisor tried to find a suitable employee to replace the worker who had quit.

After touring the 22 branches and finding similar problems in many of them, Nelson wondered what the home office should do or what action he should take. The banking firm was generally regarded as a well-run institution that had grown from 27 to 191 employees during the past eight years. The more he thought about the matter, the more puzzled Nelson became. He couldn't quite put his finger on the problem, and he didn't know whether to report his findings to the president.

Questions

1. What do you think is causing some of the problems in the bank's home office and branches?
2. Do you think setting up an HR unit in the main office would help?
3. What specific functions should an HR unit carry out? What HR functions would then be carried out by the bank's supervisors and other line managers?

Source: George, Claude S., *Supervision In Action: Art Managing Others,* 4th, © 1985. Electronically reproduced by permission of Pearson Education, Inc., Upper Saddle River, New Jersey.

HR in Action Case Incident 2 — Carter Cleaning Company

Introduction

A main theme of this book is that HR management—activities like recruiting, selecting, training, and rewarding employees—is not just the job of a central HR group but rather a job in which every manager must engage. Perhaps nowhere is this more apparent than in the typical small service business. Here the owner/manager usually has no HR staff to rely on. However, the success of his or her enterprise (not to mention his or her family's peace of mind) often depends largely on the effectiveness through which workers are recruited, hired, trained, evaluated, and rewarded. Therefore, to help illustrate and emphasize the front-line manager's HR role, throughout this book we will use a continuing case based on an actual small business. Each chapter's segment of the case will illustrate how the case's main player—owner/manager Jennifer Carter—confronts and solves personnel problems each day at work by applying the concepts and techniques of that particular chapter. Here is background information you will need to answer questions that arise in subsequent chapters. (We also present a second, unrelated case incident in each chapter.)

Carter Cleaning Centers

Jennifer Carter graduated from University in June 2005, and, after considering several job offers, decided to do what she really always planned to do—go into business with her father, Jack Carter.

Jack Carter opened his first laundrette in 1995 and his second in 1998. The main attraction of these coin laundry businesses for him was that they were capital-intensive rather than labor-intensive. Thus, once the investment in machinery was made, the stores could be run with just one unskilled attendant and have none of the labor problems one normally expects from being in the retail service business.

The attractiveness of operating with virtually no skilled labor notwithstanding, Jack had decided by 1999 to expand the services in each of his stores to include the dry cleaning and pressing of clothes. He embarked, in other words, on a strategy of "related diversification" by adding new services that were related to and consistent with his existing coin laundry activities. He added these in part because he wanted to better utilize the unused space in the rather large stores he currently had under lease, and partly because he was, as he put it, "tired of sending out the dry cleaning and pressing work that came in from our coin laundry clients to a dry cleaner eight kilometers away, who then took most of what should have been our profits." To reflect the new, expanded line of services he renamed each of his two stores Carter Cleaning Centers and was sufficiently satisfied with their performance to open four more of the same type of stores over the next five years. Each store had its own on-site manager and, on average, about seven employees and annual revenues of about $600,000. It was this six-store chain of cleaning centers that Jennifer joined upon graduating from University.

Her understanding with her father was that she would serve as a troubleshooter/consultant to the elder Carter with the aim of both learning the business and bringing to it modern management concepts and techniques for solving the business's problems and facilitating its growth.

Questions

1. Make a list of five specific HR problems you think Carter Cleaning will have to grapple with.
2. What would you do first if you were Jennifer?

EXPERIENTIAL EXERCISE

Helping "Sir Alan"

Purpose

The purpose of this exercise is to provide practice in identifying and applying the basic concepts of human resource management by illustrating how managers use these techniques in their day-to-day jobs.

Required Understanding

Be familiar with the material in this chapter, and with several episodes of *The Apprentice*, the BBC program in which business magnate Sir Alan Sugar starred.

How to Set Up the Exercise/Instructions

1. Divide the class into teams of three to four students.
2. Read this: As you know by having watched "Sir Alan" as he organized his business teams for *The Apprentice*, human resource management plays an important role in what Alan Sugar and the participants on his separate teams need to do to be successful. For example, Alan Sugar needs to be able to appraise each of the participants. And, for their part, the leaders of each of his teams need to be able to staff his or her teams with the right participants and then provide the sorts of training, incentives, and evaluations that help their companies succeed and that therefore make the participants themselves (and especially the team leaders) look like "winners" to Mr. Sugar.
3. Watch several of these shows (or reruns of the shows), and then meet with your team and answer the following questions:
   a. What specific HR functions (recruiting, interviewing, and so on) can you identify Alan Sugar using on this show? Make sure to give specific examples.
   b. What specific HR functions (recruiting, selecting, training, and so on) can you identify one or more of the team leaders using to help manage their teams on the show? Again, please give specific examples.
   c. Provide a specific example of how HR functions (such as recruiting, selection, interviewing, compensating, appraising, and so on) contributed to one of the participants coming across as particularly successful to Mr. Trump. Can you provide examples of how one or more of these functions contributed to Mr. Trump telling a participant "You're fired"?
   d. Present your team's conclusions to the class.

ENDNOTES

1. Dina Berta, "Paying Attention to Retention," *Nation's Restaurant News* 42, no. 4 (January 28, 2008).
2. Dina Berta, "Motivation Keeps Top Talent Sticking Around," *Nation's Restaurant News* 41, no. 20 (May 14, 2007): 1, 43–44.
3. Ibid.
4. Quoted in Fred K. Foulkes, "The Expanding Role of the Personnel Function," *Harvard Business Review* (March/April 1975): 71–84. See also Dave Ulrich and Wayne Brockbank, *The HR value proposition* (Boston, Mass.: Harvard Business School Press, 2005).
5. Steve Bates, "No Experience Necessary? Many Companies Are Putting non-HR Executives in Charge of HR with Mixed Results," *HR Magazine* 46, no. 11 (November 2001): 34–41. Similarly, HR managers often have non-HR duties. See "HR's Evolving Role in Organizations and Its Impact on Business Strategy: A Survey Report by the Society for Human Resource Management," May 2008, Society for Human Resource Management, 1800 Duke Street, Alexandria, VA 22314, USA.
6. "Human Resource Activities, Budgets & Staffs, 1999–2000," *BNA Bulletin to Management* 51, no. 25 (June 29, 2000): S1–S6.
7. Susan Mayson and Rowena Barrett, "The 'Science' and 'Practice' of HR in Small Firms," *Human Resource Management Review* 16 (2006): 447–455.
8. Robert Grossman, "IBM's HR Takes a Risk," *HR Management* (April 2007): 54–59.
9. Michael Schroeder, "States Fight Exodus of Jobs," *Wall Street Journal* (June 3, 2003): 84. See also Monica Belcourt, "Outsourcing—the Benefits and the Risks," *Human Resource Management Review* 16 (2006): 69–279.
10. Jessica Marquez, "Hewitt—HP Split May Signal End of 'Lift and Shift' Deals," *Workforce Management* (December 11, 2006): 3–4.
11. Timothy Appel, "Better Off a Blue-Collar," *Wall Street Journal* (July 1, 2003): B-1.
12. See "Charting the projections: 2004–2014," *Occupational Outlook Quarterly* (Winter 2005–2006). (Most recent as of 7/08. See http://www.bls.gov/emp/optd/optd003.pdf, accessed July 13, 2008).
13. Richard Crawford, *In the Era of Human Capital* (New York: Harper Business, 1991): 26.
14. Peter Drucker, "The Coming of the New Organization," *Harvard Business Review* (January–February 1988): 45. See also James Guthime et al., "Correlates and Consequences of High Involvement Work Practices: The Role of Competitive Strategy," *International Journal of Human Resource Management* (February 2002): 183–97, and James Combs et al., "How Much Do High-Performance Work Practices Matter? A Meta-Analysis of Their Effects on Organizational Performance," *Personal Psychology* 59 (2006): 501–528.
15. Tony Carneval, "The Coming Labor and Skills Shortage," Training and Development (January 2005): 39.
16. "Talent Management Leads in Top HR Concerns," *Compensation & Benefits Review* (May/June 2007): 12.
17. "Charting the Projections: 2004–2014", *Occupational Outlook Quarterly* (Winter 2005–2006): 48–50.
18. Ibid.
19. Eva Kaplan-Leiserson, "The Changing Workforce," *Training and Development* (February 2005): 10–11.
20. Nadira Hira, "You Raised Them, Now Manage Them," *Fortune* (May 28, 2007): 38–46. See also Kathryn Tyler, "The Tethered Generation," *HR Magazine* (May 2007): 41–46 and Jeffrey Zaslow, "The Most Praised Generation Goes to Work," *The Wall Street Journal* (April 20, 2007): W1, W7.
21. Jennifer Schramm, "Exploring the Future of Work: Workplace Visions," *Society for Human Resource Management* 2 (2005): 6.
22. "Talent Management Leads in Top HR Concerns," *Compensation & Benefits Review* (May/June 2007): 12.
23. www.knowledge.wharton.upe.edu, "Human Resources Wharton," downloaded January 8, 2006.
24. See for example, Anthea Zacharatos et al., "High-Performance Work Systems and Occupational Safety," *Journal of Applied Psychology* 90, no. 1 (2005): 77–93.
25. "Immigrants in the Workplace," *BNA Bulletin to Management Datagraph* (March 15, 1996): 260–261. See also Tanuja Agarwala, "Human Resource Management: The Emerging Trends," *Indian Journal of Industrial Relations* (January 2002): 315–331 and Shari Caudron et al., "80 People, Events and Trends that Shaped HR," *Workforce* (January 2002): 26–56.
26. "Human Capital Critical to Success," *Management Review* (November 1998): 9.
27. John Boudreau and Peter Ramstad, 2007, *Beyond HR: The New Science of Human Capital* (Boston College Harvard Business University: Harvard Business School Publishing Corporation): 9.
28. Except as noted, most of this section based on Richard Vosburgh, "The Evolution of HR: Developing HR as an Internal Consulting Organization," *Human Resource Planning* 30, issue 3 (September 2007): 11–24.
29. "Automation Improves Retailer's Hiring Efficiency and Quality," *HR Focus* 82, no. 2 (February 2005): 3.
30. "The Future of HR," *Workplace Visions* 6 (Society for Human Resource Management, 2001): 3–4.
31. Connie Winkler, "Quality Check," *HR Magazine* (May 2007): 93–98.
32. Jonathon Segal, "The joy of uncooking: The new corporate accountability law puts new burdens on HR in an effort to prevent companies from cooking the books", *HR Magazine* (November 2002): 52–58.
33. Kevin Wooten, "Ethical Dilemmas in Human Resource Management," *Human Resource Management Review* 11 (2001): 161.
34. "The Human Resource Certification Institute (HRCI) Announces the California Certification," http://www.hrci.org/HRCI_Files/_Items/HRCI-MR-TAB2-951/Docs/At_A_Glance.pdf, accessed 12/28/07.

Managing Equal Opportunity and Diversity

2

When you finish studying this chapter, you should be able to:

1. *Summarize the basic equal employment opportunity laws regarding age, race, sex, national origin, religion, and handicap discrimination.*

2. *Explain the basic defenses against discrimination allegations.*

3. *Present a summary of what employers can and cannot legally do with respect to recruitment, selection, and promotion and layoff practices.*

4. *Explain the Equal Employment Opportunity Commission enforcement process.*

5. *List five strategies for successfully increasing diversity of the work force.*

Introduction

Financial services giant Morgan Stanley & Co. recently settled a proposed class-action lawsuit. A number of its African American, Latino, and female financial advisors charged that the company let allegedly biased "virtually all white" branch managers decide who got the best leads, to these employees' detriment.[1] ■

SELECTED EQUAL EMPLOYMENT OPPORTUNITY LAWS

Hardly a day goes by without reports of equal opportunity–related lawsuits at work. One survey of 300 corporate general counsels found that employment lawsuits like these were their biggest litigation fears.[2] Performing day-to-day supervisory tasks like hiring or transferring employees without understanding equal employment laws is fraught with peril. Let us start at the beginning.

Background

① Summarize the basic equal employment opportunity laws regarding age, race, sex, national origin, religion, and handicap discrimination.

Legislation barring discrimination against minorities in the United States is nothing new. For example, the Fifth Amendment to the U.S. Constitution (ratified in 1791) states that "no person shall . . . be deprived of life, liberty, or property, without due process of the law."[3] Other laws as well as various court decisions made discrimination against minorities illegal by the early 1900s, at least in theory.[4] But as a practical matter, the U.S. Congress and various presidents were reluctant to take dramatic action on equal employment issues until the early 1960s. At that point, "they were finally prompted to act primarily as a result of civil unrest among the minorities and women" who eventually became protected by the new equal rights legislation and the agencies created to implement and enforce it.[5] The accompanying *Business in Action* feature provides a perspective on how laws like these come about.

public policy
Public policy consists of political decisions for implementing programs to achieve societal goals.

Business in Action   Building Your *Public Policy* Knowledge

Laws govern much of what we do and how we live. For example, traffic laws govern how fast we should drive, tax laws largely govern who pays what taxes, and equal employment laws state, with some precision, what managers can and cannot do when selecting, training, paying, and promoting and firing members of minority groups.

What may not be so obvious is that all laws invariably stem from public policy considerations. In other words, governments enact laws so as to further the government's public policy aims. Thus, if Bristol decides that it's in the best interests of its citizens to lower fuel consumption by getting everyone to ride bicycles more frequently its city government may build more bicycle lanes or designate "bicycle commuter" zones. If the people elect a new prime minister whose administration believes that lowering tax rates is a way to encourage entrepreneurs to start new businesses, it may encourage Parliament to lower the taxes that business people pay.

According to a review of the term *public policy* at *www.answers.com/topic/public-policy*, there's no one definition of "public policy." But, to paraphrase one good definition on that site, **public policy** is a course of action or inaction that public authorities choose to pursue, in order to address a problem. Put

another way, "public policy consists of political decisions for implementing programs to achieve societal goals." As with traffic and tax laws, governments express their chosen public policies by way of the laws and regulations they set, and the other decisions they make (such as how they spend their tax revenues).

The evolution of equal employment law helps illustrate how public policy considerations drive legislation. We saw that even by the early 1900s, federal public policy in the United States generally favored supporting equality at work and discouraging discrimination. Early laws supported these public policy goals. But as a practical matter, the U.S. government took little or no dramatic action on equal employment until the early 1960s. At that point, public policy changed. As we noted, "they were finally prompted to act primarily as a result of civil unrest among the minorities and women" who eventually became protected by the new equal rights legislation and the agencies created to implement and enforce it.[6]

Public policy is thus important for several reasons. First, laws almost never spring up at random; instead they flow out of the government's public policy agenda. Second, much of the political debate you see occurring around election time reflects the fact that one political party's public policy agenda is considerably different from the other's—one may believe in redistributing wealth, while the other believes in lowering the tax on wealthy people to encourage them to invest more, for instance. Third, "public policy" is not just some abstract concept. A government's public policy viewpoint drives its legislative agenda. The laws and the other decisions it makes then govern what its citizens can and cannot do. We can therefore best understand the notions of equitableness and nondiscrimination underlying equal employment laws as reflecting what our government over time saw as vital societal—and therefore public policy—goals.

A SUMMARY OF U.S. LABOR LAWS

Equal Pay Act of 1963

Equal Pay Act of 1963
The act requiring equal pay for equal work, regardless of sex.

The U.S. **Equal Pay Act of 1963** (amended in 1972) was one of the first new laws passed. It made it unlawful to discriminate in pay on the basis of sex when jobs involve equal work—equivalent skills, effort, and responsibility—and are performed under similar working conditions. However, differences in pay do not violate the act if the difference is based on a seniority system, a merit system, a system that measures earnings by quantity or quality of production, or a differential based on any factor other than sex.

Title VII of the 1964 Civil Rights Act

Title VII of the 1964 Civil Rights Act
The section of the act that says an employer cannot discriminate on the basis of race, color, religion, sex, or national origin with respect to employment.

What the Law Says Title VII of the 1964 Civil Rights Act was another of these new laws. **Title VII** (amended by the 1972 Equal Employment Opportunity Act) says an employer cannot discriminate based on race, color, religion, sex, or national origin. Specifically, it states that it shall be an unlawful employment practice for an employer[7]:

1. *To fail or refuse to hire or to discharge an individual or otherwise to discriminate against any individual* with respect to his or her compensation, terms, conditions, or privileges of employment, because of such individual's race, color, religion, sex, or national origin.
2. *To limit, segregate, or classify his or her employees or applicants for employment* in any way that would deprive or tend to deprive any individual of employment opportunities or otherwise adversely affect his or her status as an employee, because of such individual's race, color, religion, sex, or national origin.

Equal Employment Opportunity Commission (EEOC)
The commission, created by Title VII, is empowered to investigate job discrimination complaints and sue on behalf of complainants.

Title VII established the **Equal Employment Opportunity Commission (EEOC)**. It consists of five members, appointed by the president with the advice and consent of the Senate. Each member of the EEOC serves a term of 5 years. The EEOC has a staff of thousands to assist it in administering the Civil Rights law in employment settings.

Establishing the EEOC greatly enhanced the federal government's ability to enforce equal employment opportunity laws. The EEOC receives and investigates job discrimination complaints from aggrieved individuals. When it finds reasonable cause that the charges are justified, it attempts (through conciliation) to reach an agreement eliminating all aspects of the discrimination. If this conciliation fails, the EEOC has the power to go directly to court to enforce the law. Under the Equal Employment Opportunity Act of 1972, discrimination charges may be filed by the EEOC on behalf of an aggrieved individual, as well as by the individuals themselves. We explain this procedure in more detail later in this chapter.

affirmative action
Making an extra effort to hire and promote those in protected groups, particularly when those groups are under-represented.

Office of Federal Contract Compliance Programs (OFCCP)
This office is responsible for implementing the executive orders and ensuring compliance of federal contractors.

Executive Orders

Under executive orders that U.S. presidents issued years ago, most employers who do business with the U.S. government have an obligation beyond that imposed by Title VII to refrain from employment discrimination. Executive Orders 11246 and 11375 don't just ban discrimination; they require that contractors take **affirmative action** to ensure equal employment opportunity (we explain affirmative action later in this chapter). These orders also established the **Office of Federal Contract Compliance Programs (OFCCP)**, which is responsible for ensuring the compliance of federal contracts.

Age Discrimination in Employment Act (ADEA) of 1967
The act prohibiting arbitrary age discrimination and specifically protecting individuals over 40 years old.

Vocational Rehabilitation Act of 1973
The act requiring certain federal contractors to take affirmative action for disabled persons.

Pregnancy Discrimination Act (PDA)
An amendment to Title VII of the Civil Rights Act that prohibits sex discrimination based on "pregnancy, childbirth, or related medical conditions."

federal agency guidelines
Guidelines issued by federal agencies explaining recommended employer equal employment federal legislation procedures in detail.

sexual harassment
Harassment on the basis of sex that has the purpose or effect of substantially interfering with a person's work performance or creating an intimidating, hostile, or offensive work environment.

Age Discrimination in Employment Act of 1967

The **Age Discrimination in Employment Act (ADEA) of 1967**, as amended, makes it unlawful to discriminate against employees or applicants for employment who are 40 years of age or older, effectively ending most mandatory retirement.[8]

Vocational Rehabilitation Act of 1973

The **Vocational Rehabilitation Act of 1973** requires employers with federal contracts over $2,500 to take affirmative action for the employment of disabled persons. The act does not require that an unqualified person be hired. It does require that an employer take steps to accommodate a disabled worker unless doing so imposes an undue hardship on the employer.

Pregnancy Discrimination Act of 1978

Congress passed the **Pregnancy Discrimination Act (PDA)** in 1978 as an amendment to Title VII. The act broadened the definition of sex discrimination to encompass pregnancy, childbirth, or related medical conditions. It prohibits using these for discrimination in hiring, promotion, suspension, or discharge, or any other term or condition of employment. Basically, the act says that if an employer offers its employees disability coverage, then pregnancy and childbirth must be treated like any other disability and must be included in the plan as a covered condition. Court decisions, more working mothers in the workforce, and other changes are prompting more—and more successful—PDA claims. Pregnancy claim plaintiff victories rose about 66% in one recent 10-year period, while pregnancy claims filed with the EEOC rose about 39%.[9]

Progressive human resource thinking notwithstanding, one firm, an auto dealership, recently fired an employee after she told them she was pregnant. The reason? Allegedly "in case I ended up throwing up or cramping in one of their vehicles. They said pregnant women do that sometimes, and I could cause an accident."[10]

Federal Agency Uniform Guidelines on Employee Selection Procedures

Initially, the federal agencies charged with ensuring compliance with the aforementioned laws and executive orders issued their own implementing guidelines. Subsequently, the EEOC, Civil Service Commission, Department of Labor, and Department of Justice adopted detailed, uniform guidelines for employers.[11] These guidelines

> "incorporate a single set of principles which are designed to assist employers, labor organizations, employment agencies, and licensing and certification boards to comply with requirements of federal law prohibiting employment practices which discriminate on grounds of race, color, religion, sex, and national origin."[12]

They explain, for instance, what test validation procedures are acceptable, as well as how and under what conditions to validate a selection procedure. The OFCCP has its own *Manual of Guidelines*. The American Psychological Association has published its own (non-legally binding) *Standards for Educational and Psychological Testing*.

Historically, these guidelines have fleshed out the procedures to use in complying with equal employment laws. For example, recall that the ADEA prohibited employers from discriminating against persons over 40 years old because of age. Subsequent guidelines stated that it was unlawful to discriminate in hiring (or in any way) by giving preference because of age even to individuals within the 40-plus age bracket. Thus, you can't reject a 58-year-old candidate based on age, and defend yourself by showing you hired a 46-year-old.[13] (Hiring, say, a 54-year-old may provide a defense, though.)

Sexual Harassment

The EEOC guidelines define **sexual harassment** as unwelcome sexual advances, requests for sexual favors, and other verbal or physical conduct of a sexual nature that takes place under any of the following conditions:

1. Submission is either explicitly or implicitly a term or condition of an individual's employment.

Sexual harassment is unwelcome sexual advances, requests for sexual favors, and other verbal or physical conduct of a sexual nature.

Federal Violence Against Women Act of 1994
Provides that a person who commits a crime of violence motivated by gender shall be liable to the party injured.

2. Submission to or rejection of such conduct is the basis for employment decisions affecting such individual.
3. Such conduct has the purpose or effect of unreasonably interfering with an individual's work performance or creating an intimidating, hostile, or offensive work environment.

Sexual harassment is a violation of Title VII when such conduct has the purpose or effect of substantially interfering with a person's work performance or creating an intimidating, hostile, or offensive work environment. The EEOC's guidelines further assert that employers have a duty to maintain workplaces free of sexual harassment and intimidation. The Civil Rights Act of 1991 added teeth to this by permitting victims of intentional discrimination, including sexual harassment, to have jury trials and to collect compensatory damages for pain and suffering and punitive damages in cases in which the employer acted with "malice or reckless indifference" to the individual's rights.[14]

Sexual harassment laws do not just cover harassment of women by men. They also cover those occasions when women harass men, as well as same-sex harassment. The U.S. Supreme Court held (in *ONCALE*. v. *Sundowner Offshore Services Inc.*) that "same-sex discrimination consisting of same-sex sexual harassment is actionable under Title VII." It said that same-sex subordinates, coworkers, or superiors are liable under the theory that they create a hostile work environment for the employee.[15]

The **Federal Violence Against Women Act of 1994** provides another avenue that women can use to seek relief for violent sexual harassment. It provides that someone who commits a crime of violence motivated by gender and thus deprives another of her rights shall be liable to the party injured. [16]

Proving Sexual Harassment

There are three main ways an employee can prove sexual harassment.

QUID PRO QUO The most direct way is to prove that rejecting a supervisor's advances adversely affected what the EEOC calls a "tangible employment action" such as hiring, firing, promotion, demotion, undesirable assignment, benefits, compensation, and/or work assignment. Thus in one case the employee showed that continued job success and advancement were dependent on her agreeing to her supervisor's sexual demands.

HOSTILE ENVIRONMENT CREATED BY SUPERVISORS It is not always necessary to show that the harassment had tangible consequences such as a demotion or termination. For example, in one case the court found that a male supervisor's sexual harassment had substantially affected a female employee's emotional and psychological ability, to the point that she felt she had to quit her job. Even though no direct threats or promises were made in exchange for sexual advances, the fact that the advances interfered with the woman's performance and created an offensive work environment were enough to prove that sexual harassment had occurred.

Distinguishing between harassment and flirting can be tricky. The courts do not interpret as sexual harassment any sexual relationships that arise during the course of employment but that do not have a substantial effect on that employment. In one decision, for instance, the U.S. Supreme Court held that sexual harassment law doesn't cover ordinary "intersexual flirtation." In his ruling, Justice Scalia said courts must carefully distinguish between "simple teasing" and truly abusive behavior.[17]

HOSTILE ENVIRONMENT CREATED BY COWORKERS OR NONEMPLOYEES Advances do not have to be made by the person's supervisor to qualify as sexual harassment: An employee's coworkers or customers can cause the employer to be held responsible for sexual harassment. In one case, the court held that a sexually provocative uniform that the employer required led to lewd comments by customers toward the employee. When she complained that she would no longer wear the uniform, she was fired. Because the employer could not show that there was a job-related necessity for requiring such a uniform and because the uniform was required only for female employees, the court ruled that the employer, in effect, was responsible for the sexually harassing behavior. Such abhorrent client behavior is more likely when the clients are in positions of power, and when they have less reason to think they'll be penalized.[18]

Court Decisions

The U.S. Supreme Court used the *Meritor Savings Bank, FSB* v. *Vinson* case to broadly endorse the EEOC's guidelines on sexual harassment. Two more recent U.S. Supreme Court decisions further clarified the law on sexual harassment.

In the first, *Burlington Industries* v. *Ellerth*, the employee accused her supervisor of *quid pro quo* harassment. She said her boss propositioned and threatened her with demotion if she did not respond. The threats were not carried out, and she was in fact promoted. In the second case, *Faragher* v. *City of Boca Raton*, the employee accused the employer of condoning a hostile work environment: She said she quit her lifeguard job after repeated taunts from other lifeguards. The Court ruled in favor of the employees in both cases.

The Court's decisions in these cases have several important implications for employers.

First, the decisions make it clear that in a *quid pro quo* case it is *not* necessary for the employee to have suffered tangible job action (such as being demoted) to win the case.

Second, the decisions spell out an important defense against harassment suits. The Court said that an employer could defend itself against sexual harassment liability by showing two things. First, it had to show "that the employer exercised care to prevent and correct promptly any sexually harassing behavior." Second, the employer had to demonstrate that the plaintiff "unreasonably failed to take advantage of any preventive or corrective opportunities provided by the employer." The Supreme Court specifically said that the employee's failing to use formal organizational reporting systems would satisfy the second component.

Sensible employers promptly took steps to show that they did take "reasonable care." For example, they promulgated strong harassment policies, trained managers and employees regarding their responsibilities for complying with these policies, instituted reporting processes, investigated charges promptly, and then took corrective actions promptly, as required.[19]

Causes

Sexual harassment is more likely to occur under certain circumstances. The most important factor is a permissive social climate, one where employees conclude there's a risk to victims for complaining, that complaints won't be taken seriously, and/or that there's a lack of sanctions against offenders.[20] Minority women are particularly at risk. One study found "women experienced more sexual harassment than men, minorities experienced more ethnic harassment than whites, and minority women experienced more harassment overall than majority men, minority men, and majority women."[21]

Most people probably assume that sexual motives drive sexual harassment, but that's not always so. Studies suggest that *gender harassment* is the most common form of sexual harassment. **Gender harassment** is "a form of hostile environment harassment that appears to be motivated by hostility toward individuals who violate gender ideals." In one case, for instance, bosses told a high-performing female accountant to "walk more femininely [and] dress more femininely."[22]

gender harassment
A form of hostile environment harassment that appears to be motivated by hostility toward individuals who violate gender ideals.

Adding to the causes is the unfortunate fact that most sexual harassment victims don't sue or complain. Instead, either due to fear of losing one's job or a sense that complaining is futile, they quit or try to avoid their harassers. "The few women who do formally complain do so only after encountering frequent, severe sexual harassment; at that point, considerable damage may have already occurred."[23] The harassers themselves sometimes don't even realize that their abominable behavior is harassing or offending others. Sexual harassment training and policies can reduce these problems.

Several psychological and practical considerations complicate the problem. For example, women and men don't view harassment-related facts in the same way. "Women perceive a broader range of socio-sexual behaviors as harassing," particularly when those behaviors involve "hostile work environment harassment, derogatory attitudes toward women, dating pressure, or physical sexual contact."[24] Thus what is harassment to a woman may be misperceived as innocent behavior by a man.

WHAT THE MANAGER/EMPLOYER SHOULD DO Given this, employers should do two things: They should take steps (as we list in the *HR in Practice*, page 52) to ensure harassment does not take place. Second, once being apprised of such a situation, they should take immediate corrective action, even if the offending party is a nonemployee, once they know (or should know) of the harassing conduct.[25] The aims are to reduce or eliminate instances of sexual harassment and to minimize the employer's liability should such claims arise.

Note, however, that taking what courts call "reasonable" steps may not be enough to prevent harassment. This is because a sexual harassment compliance procedure may be reasonable in the legal sense, but not so reasonable to the employees who must use it. In one study, researchers surveyed about 6,000 employees in the U.S. military. Their findings made it clear that reporting incidents of harassment often triggered retaliation and could harm the victim "in terms of lower job satisfaction and greater psychological distress." Under such conditions, it's no wonder that for many of these employees, the most "reasonable" thing to do was nothing, and to avoid reporting. Managers who take preventing sexual harassment seriously therefore must ensure that the organization's climate (including management's real willingness to eradicate harassment), and not just its written rules, supports employees who feel harassed.[26] The *Personal Competencies* explains EEO's ethical aspects.

Personal Competencies

Building Your *Ethical Decision-Making* Skills

As the accompanying text explains, there is more to equal employment than just its legal aspects. Managers should understand that equal employment is also an ethical issue.

Ethics are "the principles of conduct governing an individual or a group"—they're the principles people use to decide what their conduct should be.[29] However, ethical decisions don't include just any type of behavior. For instance, deciding what flavour ice cream to buy would not, in itself, involve ethics. Instead, ethical decisions are also always rooted in morality. *Morality* means society's accepted standards of behavior. Like the Ten Commandments, morality always involves basic questions of right and wrong, such as stealing, murder, and how to treat other people. As such, how to treat employees who may be disabled, or of a different age, race, gender, or national origin than you, is almost always as much of an ethical question as a purely legal one.

Consider one recent example. A jury in Central Islip, New York, ordered Wal-Mart to pay Patrick Brady $7.5 million for violating the Americans with Disabilities Act. Wal-Mart hired Patrick, who has cerebral palsy, to work as a pharmacist's assistant in one of its stores. According to the complaint, he worked as an assistant for just one day, before the store reassigned him to collect carts and pick up trash. The complaint claims that the pharmacist didn't think the disabled man was "fit for the pharmacy job."[30]

What (if anything) is the ethical issue here? In terms of any moral or ethical code that you'd like to apply, do you think the pharmacist did the ethically right thing? Can you think of anything the pharmacist could have done here that would change your opinion? Do you think the pharmacist's actions were legal? Could they possibly have been legal but still unethical? How?

WHAT THE EMPLOYEE CAN DO An employee who believes he or she was sexually harassed can also take several steps to address the problem. However, prior to taking action, the employee should understand how courts define sexual harassment. For example, "hostile environment" sexual harassment generally means that the discriminatory intimidation, insults, and ridicule that permeated the workplace were sufficiently severe or pervasive to alter the conditions of employment. Courts in these cases look at several things. These include whether the discriminatory conduct is frequent or severe; whether it is physically threatening or humiliating, or a mere offensive utterance; and whether it unreasonably interferes with an employee's work performance. They also look at whether an employee welcomed the conduct, or instead immediately made it clear that the conduct was unwelcome, undesirable, or offensive.

The steps an employee can take include:

1. File a verbal contemporaneous complaint or protest with the harasser and the harasser's boss stating that the unwanted overtures should cease because the conduct is unwelcome. Use the employer's complaint procedure, if any.
2. If there's no complaint procedure, write a polite letter to the accused, one that provides a detailed statement of the facts as the writer sees them, describes his or her feelings and what damage the writer thinks has been done, and states that he or she would like to request that the future relationship be on a purely professional basis. Deliver this letter in person, with a witness if necessary.
3. If the unwelcome conduct does not cease, file verbal and written reports with the harasser's manager and/or the human resource director regarding the unwelcome conduct and unsuccessful efforts to get it to stop.
4. If the letters and appeals to the employer do not suffice, the accuser should turn to the local office of the EEOC to file the necessary claim.
5. If the harassment is of a serious nature, the employee can also consult an attorney about suing the harasser for assault and battery, intentional infliction of emotional distress, and injunctive relief and to recover compensatory and punitive damages.

HR in Practice

How to Minimize Liability in Sexual Harassment Claims

The EEOC says, "Prevention is the best tool to eliminate sexual harassment in the workplace. Employers are encouraged to take steps necessary to prevent sexual harassment from occurring. They should clearly communicate to employees that sexual harassment will not be tolerated. They can do so by providing sexual harassment training to their employees and by establishing an effective complaint or grievance process and taking immediate and appropriate action when an employee complains".[27]

Therefore, to minimize liability in sexual harassment claims:

1. *Issue a strong policy statement* condemning harassment. Clearly explain what's prohibited; assure protection against retaliation for employees who make complaints; and lay out a complaint process that provides confidentiality as well as prompt, thorough, and impartial investigations and corrective actions. Republish the policy periodically (see Figure 2.1 below).

2. *Inform all employees* about the policy prohibiting sexual harassment and of their rights under the policy.
3. *Develop and implement a complaint procedure.*
4. *Take all harassment complaints seriously.* Establish a management response system that includes an immediate reaction and investigation by senior management. Based on various U.S. Supreme Court decisions, employers reduce their liability when they respond to an incident in a way that's deemed adequate and convincingly calculated to prevent future incidents.
5. *Commence management training sessions* with supervisors and managers. Don't just focus on legal issues but on harassment's ethical dimension as well. In one study, trainees were actually *less* (not more) likely than were other groups to perceive an action as sexual harassment, less willing to report sexual harassment, and more likely to blame the victim. The program had focused too heavily on harassment's legal aspects, and

FIGURE 2.1

What to Cover in a Sexual Harassment Policy

The EEOC says the antiharassment policy should contain a clear explanation of the prohibited conduct; assurance of protection against retaliation for employees who make complaints or provide information related to such complaints; a clearly described complaint process that provides confidentiality and accessible avenues of complaint as well as prompt, thorough, and impartial investigations; and clear assurance that the employer will take immediate and appropriate corrective action where harassment has occurred.

Source: www.eeoc.gov/types/sexual_harrasment.html, accessed May 6, 2007.

not enough on its ethical and moral implications.[28] (See the accompanying *Personal Competencies* feature for ethical and moral implications.)

6. *Discipline managers and employees* involved in sexual harassment.

7. *Keep thorough records* of complaints, investigations, and actions taken.

8. *Monitor the harassment climate.* For example, use periodic written attitude surveys and hotlines, as well as exit interviews that uncover complaints.

Selected Court Decisions Regarding Equal Employment Opportunity (EEO)

Several early court decisions helped to form the interpretive foundation for EEO laws such as those involving sexual harassment. We summarize some important decisions in this section.

Griggs **v.** *Duke Power Company*

Supreme Court case in which the plaintiff argued that his employer's requirement that coal handlers be high-school graduates was unfairly discriminatory. In finding for the plaintiff, the Court ruled that discrimination need not be overt to be illegal, that employment practices must be related to job performance, and that the burden of proof is on the employer to show that hiring standards are job related.

protected class

Persons such as minorities and women protected by equal opportunity laws, including Title VII.

GRIGGS V. DUKE POWER COMPANY *Griggs* **v.** *Duke Power Company* (1971) was a landmark case because the Supreme Court used it to define unfair discrimination. In this case, a suit was brought against the Duke Power Company on behalf of Willie Griggs, an applicant for a job as a coal handler. The company required its coal handlers to be high school graduates. Griggs claimed that this requirement was illegally discriminatory because it wasn't related to success on the job and because it resulted in more blacks than whites being rejected for these jobs.

Griggs won the case. The decision of the Court was unanimous, and in his written opinion, Chief Justice Burger laid out three crucial guidelines affecting equal employment legislation. First, the court ruled that discrimination on the part of the employer need not be overt; in other words, the employer does not have to be shown to have intentionally discriminated against the employee or applicant—it need only be shown that discrimination took place. Second, the court held that an employment practice (in this case requiring the high school diploma) must be shown to be *job related* if it has an unequal impact on members of a **protected class**.

In the words of Justice Burger:

> The act proscribes not only overt discrimination but also practices that are fair in form, but discriminatory in operation. The touchstone is business necessity. If an employment practice which operates to exclude Negroes cannot be shown to be related to job performance the practice is prohibited.[31]

Third, Burger's opinion clearly placed the burden of proof on the employer to show that the hiring practice is job related. Thus, the *employer* must show that the employment practice (in this case, requiring a high school diploma) is needed to perform the job satisfactorily if it has a disparate impact on (unintentionally discriminates against) members of a protected class.

ALBEMARLE PAPER COMPANY V. MOODY In the *Griggs* case, the Supreme Court decided that a screening tool (such as a test) had to be job related or valid—that is, performance on the test must be related to performance on the job. The 1975 *Albemarle* case is important because it helped to clarify what the employer had to do to prove that the test or other screening tools are related to or predict performance on the job. For example, the Court ruled that before using a test to screen job candidates, the performance standards for the job in question should be clear and unambiguous, so the employer can identify which employees were performing better than others (and thus whether the screening tools were effective).

In arriving at its decision, the Court also cited the EEOC guidelines concerning acceptable selection procedures and made these guidelines the "law of the land."[32]

The Civil Rights Act of 1991

Subsequent Supreme Court rulings in the 1980s actually had the effect of limiting the protection of women and minority groups under equal employment laws; this prompted Congress to pass a new Civil Rights Act. President George H. W. Bush signed the

Civil Rights Act of 1991 (CRA 1991)
It places burden of proof back on employers and permits compensatory and punitive damages.

disparate impact
An unintentional disparity between the proportion of a protected group applying for a position and the proportion getting the job.

Civil Rights Act of 1991 (CRA 1991) into law in November 1991. The effect of CRA 1991 was to roll back the clock to where it stood before the 1980s decisions, and in some respects to place even more responsibility on employers.

First, CRA 1991 addressed the issue of *burden of proof*. Today, after CRA 1991, the process of filing and responding to a discrimination charge goes something like this. The plaintiff (say, a rejected applicant) demonstrates that an employment practice (such as a test) has a disparate impact on a particular group. (**Disparate impact** means that "an employer engages in an employment practice or policy that has a greater adverse impact [effect] on the members of a protected group under Title VII than on other employees, regardless of intent."[33]) Requiring a college degree for a job would have an adverse impact on some minority groups, for instance. Disparate impact claims do not require proof of discriminatory intent. Instead, the plaintiff must show two things. First, he or she must show that a significant disparity exists between the proportion of (say) women in the available labor pool and the proportion hired. Second, he or she must show that an apparently neutral employment practice, such as word-of-mouth advertising or a requirement that the job holder "be able to lift 100 pounds," is causing the disparity.[34]

Then, once the plaintiff shows such disparate impact, the *employer* has the *burden of proving* that the challenged practice is job related for the position in question. For example, the employer has to show that lifting 100 pounds is actually required for the position in question, and that the business could not run efficiently without the requirement—that it is a business necessity.

CRA 1991 also makes it easier to sue for *money damages*. It provides that an employee who is claiming *intentional discrimination* (which is called **disparate treatment**) can ask for both compensatory damages and punitive damages, if he or she can show the employer engaged in discrimination "with malice or reckless indifference to the federally protected rights of an aggrieved individual." (See also the *Global Issues in HR* feature.)

disparate treatment
An intentional disparity between the proportion of a protected group and the proportion getting the job.

Finally, CRA 1991 also states:

> An unlawful employment practice is established when the complaining party demonstrates that race, color, religion, sex, or national origin was a motivating factor for any employment practice, even though other factors also motivated the practice.[35]

In other words, an employer generally can't avoid liability by proving it would have taken the same action—such as terminating someone—even without the discriminatory motive. If there is any such motive, the practice may be unlawful.

The Americans with Disabilities Act

Americans with Disabilities Act (ADA)
The act requiring employers to make reasonable accommodations for disabled employees; it prohibits discrimination against disabled persons.

WHAT IS THE ADA? The **Americans with Disabilities Act (ADA)** of 1990 prohibits employment discrimination against qualified disabled individuals.[36] It aims to reduce or eliminate serious problems of discrimination against disabled individuals. And it requires that employers make "reasonable accommodations" for physical or mental limitations, unless doing so imposes an "undue hardship" on the business. On February 1, 2001, President George W. Bush announced his New Freedom Initiative to promote the full participation of people with disabilities in all areas of society.

The ADA's pivotal terms are important in understanding its impact. They provide that "impairment" includes any physiological disorder or condition, cosmetic disfigurement, or anatomical loss affecting one or more of several body systems, or any mental or psychological disorder.[37] However, the act doesn't list specific disabilities. Instead, the EEOC's implementing regulations provide that an individual is disabled if he or she has a physical or mental impairment that substantially limits one or more major life activities. On the other hand, the act does set forth certain conditions that are not to be regarded as disabilities, including homosexuality, bisexuality, voyeurism, compulsive gambling, pyromania, and certain disorders resulting from the person currently using illegal drugs.[38] The ADA does protect employees with intellectual disabilities, including those with IQs below 70–75.[39] The types of disabilities alleged in ADA charges have been somewhat surprising. Mental disabilities account for the greatest number of claims brought under the ADA.[40]

Simply being disabled does not qualify someone for a job, of course. Instead, the act prohibits discrimination against qualified individuals—those who, with (or without) a reasonable accommodation, can carry out the essential functions of the job. This means that the individual must have the requisite skills, educational background, and experience to do the essential functions of the position. A job function is essential when, for instance, it is the reason the position exists, or because the function is so highly specialized that the person doing the job is hired for his or her expertise or ability to perform that particular function.[41]

REASONABLE ACCOMMODATION If the individual can't perform the job as currently structured, the employer is required to make a reasonable accommodation, unless doing so would present an undue hardship. *Reasonable accommodation* might include redesigning the job, modifying work schedules, or modifying or acquiring equipment or other devices to assist the person in performing the job. Court cases illustrate what "reasonable accommodation" means. For example, a Wal-Mart door greeter was diagnosed with and treated for back problems. When she returned to work she asked if she could sit on a stool while on duty. Wal-Mart said no, contending that standing was an essential part of the greeter's job. She sued, but the federal district court agreed with the employer that the door greeters must act in an "aggressively hospitable manner," which can't be done sitting on a stool.[42]

THE ADA IN PRACTICE By most measures, workplace disabilities are on the rise, and employers need to accommodate increasing numbers of heavier and disabled employees.[43] It's thus not surprising that ADA complaints continue to flood the courts.

However, employers typically prevail in about 96% of federal circuit court ADA decisions. A main reason is that employees are failing to show that they're disabled.[44] The employee must establish that he or she has a disability that fits under the ADA's definition. Doing so is more complicated than proving that one is a particular age, race, or gender.

A U.S. Supreme Court decision illustrates what plaintiffs face. An assembly-line worker sued Toyota, arguing that carpal tunnel syndrome and tendonitis prevented her from doing her job (*Toyota Motor Manufacturing of Kentucky, Inc.* v. *Williams*). The U.S. Supreme Court ruled that the ADA covers carpal tunnel syndrome and tendonitis if the impairments affect not only job performance but also daily living activities. Here, the employee admitted that she could perform personal tasks and chores such as washing her face, brushing her teeth, tending her flower garden, and fixing breakfast and doing laundry. The court said the disability must be central to the employee's daily living (not just job) to qualify under the ADA. The court will therefore look at each case (for instance, of carpal tunnel syndrome) individually.[45]

Many other decisions similarly denied the plaintiff's claim. A federal judge held that Home Depot did not violate the ADA by barring a totally deaf worker from receiving training to operate a forklift. The firm's policies prohibit those who can't hear store associates' warnings from holding such positions.[46] On the other hand, one U.S. Circuit Court of Appeals held that punctuality was not an essential job function for a disabled laboratory assistant who was habitually tardy. (The court decided he could perform the job's 7 1/2 hours of data entry even if he arrived late.[47]) And Wal-Mart had to reinstate hearing-impaired workers and pay a $750,000 fine for discrimination under the ADA.[48]

LEGAL OBLIGATIONS The ADA imposes numerous legal obligations on employers. These include (but are not limited to) the following:

■ Employers may not make preemployment inquiries about a person's disability, although employers may ask questions about the person's ability to perform specific job functions. Offers should be made prior to any required medical exam.
■ The timing and nature of any offer are important. The central issue is this: In the event the hiring employer rescinds an offer after the medical exam, the applicant

must be able to identify the specific reason for the rejection. For example, in one case the courts found that American Airlines had violated the ADA by not making a "real" offer to three candidates before requiring them to take their medical exams, because American still hadn't checked their background references. In this case, the medical exams showed the candidates had HIV and American rescinded their offers, thus violating the ADA.[49]

- Employers should review job application forms, interview procedures, and job descriptions for potentially discriminatory items, and identify the essential functions of the jobs in question.
- Employers must make a reasonable accommodation, unless doing so would result in undue hardship.

PRACTICAL IMPLICATIONS FOR MANAGERS The manager should also keep several practical implications in mind when dealing with ADA-related matters.[50]

First, courts will tend to define "disabilities" quite *narrowly*. Employers may therefore require that the employee provide documentation of the disorder and assess what effect that disorder has on the employee's job performance. Employers should also ask questions such as: Does the employee have a disability that substantially limits a major life activity? Is the employee qualified to do the job? Can the employee perform the essential functions of the job? Can any reasonable accommodation be provided without creating an undue hardship on the employer?[51]

Second, it's clear from these decisions that employers generally "do not need to allow *misconduct or erratic performance* (including absences and tardiness), even if that behavior is linked to the disability."[52]

Third, the employer does not have to *create a new job* for the disabled worker nor reassign that person to a light-duty position for an indefinite period, unless such a position exists.[53]

Fourth, one expert advises, "*don't treat employees* as if they are disabled." If they can control their conditions (for instance, through medication), they usually won't be considered disabled. However, if they are treated as disabled by their employers (for instance, with respect to the jobs they're assigned), they'll normally be "regarded as" disabled and protected under the ADA.[54]

Improving Productivity Through HRIS: Accommodating Disabled Employees

Technological innovations make it easier today for employers to accommodate disabled employees. For example, many employees with mobility impairments benefit from voice recognition software that allows them to input information into their computers and interactively communicate (for instance, via e-mail) without touching a keyboard. Others use alternative input devices (such as sticks held in the mouth) to strike keyboard keys. Special typing aids including word prediction software suggest words based on context and on just one or two letters typed.[55] The Firefox Web browser incorporates special IBM software that enables people to use the keyboard arrows rather than the mouse to access pull-down menus, aiding some disabled people.[56]

Employees with hearing and/or speech impairments benefit from the teletypewriter, which lets people communicate by typing and reading messages on a keyboard connected to a phone line. Real-time translation captioning enables them to participate in lectures and meetings. Vibrating text pagers let them know when messages arrive. Employees with vision impairments benefit from add-on computer devices that, among other things, allow adjustments in font size, display color, and screen magnification for specific portions of the computer screen. Voice recognition software transcription devices transcribe and speak out the written word for the employee. Special word processor software provides spoken instructions to aid the employee. Arizona had IBM Global Services create a disability-friendly Web site, "Arizona@YourService," to help link prospective employees and others to various agencies.[57]

Technological innovations make it easier today for employers to accommodate disabled employees.

State and Local Equal Employment Opportunity Laws

In addition to the federal laws, all states and many local governments also prohibit employment discrimination.

In most cases, the effect of the state and local laws is to further restrict employers regarding their treatment of job applicants and employees. In many cases, they cover employers that are not covered by federal legislation (such as those with fewer than 15 employees). Similarly, some local governments extend the protection of age discrimination laws to young people as well as to those over 40. For instance, it would be illegal to advertise for "mature" applicants because that might discourage some teenagers from applying.

State and local equal employment opportunity agencies (often called *human resources commissions, commissions on human relations,* or *fair employment commissions*) also play a role in the equal employment compliance process. When the EEOC receives a discrimination charge, it usually defers it for a limited time to the state and local agencies that have comparable jurisdiction. Then, if satisfactory remedies are not achieved, the charges are referred back to the EEOC for resolution. The *Global Issues in HR* explains international aspects of equal employment.

Global Issues in HR

Applying Equal Employment Law in a Global Setting

Globalization complicates the task of complying with equal employment laws. For example, Dell recently announced big additions to its workforce in India. Are U.S. citizens working for Dell abroad covered by U.S. equal opportunity laws? Are non-U.S. citizens covered? Are non-U.S. citizens working for Dell in the United States covered?

In practice, the answers depend on U.S. laws, international treaties, and the laws of the countries in which the U.S. firms are doing business. For example, the Civil Rights Act of 1991 specifically covers U.S. employees of U.S. firms working abroad. But in practice, the laws of the country in which the U.S. citizen is working may take precedence.[58]

Summary

Table 2.1 summarizes these and selected other equal employment opportunity legislation, executive orders, and agency guidelines.

DEFENSES AGAINST DISCRIMINATION ALLEGATIONS

What Is Adverse Impact?

2 Explain the basic defenses against discrimination allegations.

adverse impact
The overall impact of employer practices that result in significantly higher percentages of members of minorities and other protected groups being rejected for employment, placement, or promotion.

To understand how employers defend themselves against employment discrimination claims, we should first briefly review some basic legal theory.

Adverse impact plays a central role in discriminatory practice allegations. Under the Civil Rights Act of 1991, a person who believes he or she has been unintentionally discriminated against need only establish a prima facie case of discrimination; this means showing that the employer's selection procedures had an *adverse impact* on a protected minority group. **Adverse impact** "refers to the total employment process that results in a

TABLE 2.1   Summary of Important Equal Employment Opportunity Actions

Action	What It Does
Title VII of 1964 Civil Rights Act, as amended	Bars discrimination because of race, color, religion, sex, or national origin; instituted EEOC
Executive orders	Prohibit employment discrimination by employers with federal contracts of more than $10,000 (and their subcontractors); established office of federal compliance; require affirmative action programs
Federal agency guidelines	Indicate policy covering discrimination based on sex, national origin, and religion, as well as on employee selection procedures; for example, require validation of tests
Supreme Court decisions: *Griggs* v. *Duke Power Company*, *Albemarle Paper Company* v. *Moody*	Ruled that job requirements must be related to job success; that discrimination need not be overt to be proved; that the burden of proof is on the employer to prove the qualification is valid
Equal Pay Act of 1963	Requires equal pay for men and women for performing similar work
Age Discrimination in Employment Act of 1967	Prohibits discriminating against a person 40 or over in any area of employment because of age
State and local laws	Often cover organizations too small to be covered by federal laws
Vocational Rehabilitation Act of 1973	Requires affirmative action to employ and promote qualified disabled persons and prohibits discrimination against disabled persons
Pregnancy Discrimination Act of 1978	Prohibits discrimination in employment against pregnant women, or related conditions
Vietnam Era Veterans' Readjustment Assistance Act of 1974	Requires affirmative action in employment for veterans of the Vietnam War era
Wards Cove v. *Atonio*, *Patterson* v. *McLean Credit*	Made it more difficult to prove a case of unlawful discrimination against an employer
Union Martin v. *Wilks*	Allowed consent degrees to be attacked and could have had a chilling effect on certain affirmative action programs
Americans with Disabilities Act of 1990	Strengthens the need for most employers to make reasonable accommodations for disabled employees at work; prohibits discrimination
Civil Rights Act of 1991	Reverses *Wards Cove, Patterson,* and *Martin* decisions; places burden of proof back on employer and permits compensatory and punitive money damages for discrimination

significantly higher percentage of a protected group in the candidate population being rejected for employment, placement, or promotion."[59] "Employers may not institute an employment practice that causes a disparate impact on a particular class of people unless they can show that the practice is job related and necessary."[60]

What does this mean? If a minority or other protected group applicant for the job feels he or she has been discriminated against, the applicant need only show that the selection procedures resulted in an adverse impact on his or her minority group. (There are several ways to do this, for example, by showing that 80% of the white applicants passed the test, but only 20% of the black applicants passed; if this is the case, a black applicant has a prima facie case proving adverse impact.) Then, once the employee has proven his or her point, the burden of proof shifts to the employer. It becomes the employer's task to prove that its test, application form, interview, or the like, is a valid predictor of performance on the job, and that it was applied fairly and equitably to both minorities and non-minorities.

By the way, don't be lulled into thinking that such cases are ancient history. For example, a U.S. Appeals Court recently upheld a $3.4 million jury verdict against Dial Corp. Dial allegedly rejected 52 women for entry-level jobs at a meat processing plant because they failed strength tests, although strength was not a job requirement.[61]

Discrimination law distinguishes between disparate *treatment* and disparate *impact*. *Disparate treatment* means intentional discrimination. It "requires no more than a finding that women (or protected minority group members) were intentionally treated differently . . . because of their gender (or minority status)." *Disparate impact* claims do not require proof of discriminatory intent. Instead, the plaintiff must show that there is a significant disparity between the proportion of (say) women in the available labor pool and the proportion hired, and that there's an apparently neutral employment practice (such as word-of-mouth advertising) causing the disparity.[62] Proving that there was a business necessity for the practice is usually the defense for disparate impact claims.

BRINGING A CASE OF DISCRIMINATION: SUMMARY Assume that an employer turns down a member of a protected group for a job based on a test score (or some other employment practice, such as interview questions or application blank responses). Further assume that the person believes that he or she was discriminated against due to being in a protected class and decides to sue the employer.

All he or she has to do is show (to the court's satisfaction) that the employer's test had an adverse impact on members of his or her minority group. The burden of proof then shifts to the employer, which has the burden of defending itself against the charges of discrimination.

There are two defenses that the employer can use: the bona fide occupational qualification (BFOQ) defense and the business necessity defense. Either can be used to justify an employment practice that has been shown to have an adverse impact on the members of a minority group. (A third defense is that the decision was made on the basis of legitimate nondiscriminatory reasons, such as poor performance, having nothing to do with the alleged prohibited discrimination.)

Bona Fide Occupational Qualification

One approach an employer can use to defend against charges of discrimination is to claim that the employment practice is a **bona fide occupational qualification** for performing the job. Specifically, Title VII provides that

> it should not be an unlawful employment practice for an employer to hire an employee . . . on the basis of religion, sex, or national origin in those certain instances where religion, sex, or national origin is a bona fide occupational qualification reasonably necessary to the normal operation of that particular business or enterprise.

bona fide occupational qualification (BFOQ)
Requirement that an employee be of a certain religion, sex, or national origin where that is reasonably necessary to the organization's normal operation. Specified by the 1964 Civil Rights Act.

For example, an employer can use age as a BFOQ to defend itself against a disparate treatment (intentional discrimination) charge when federal requirements impose a compulsory age limit, such as when the Federal Aviation Agency sets a ceiling of age 65 for pilots. Actors required for youthful or elderly roles or persons used to advertise or promote the sales of products designed for youthful or elderly consumers suggest other instances when age may be a BFOQ, although the courts set the bar high: The reason for the discrimination must go to the essence of the business.

Yet Supreme Court decisions such as *Western Airlines, Inc.* v. *Criswell* seem to be narrowing BFOQ exceptions under ADEA. Here the Court held that the airline could not impose a mandatory retirement age (of 60) for flight engineers, even though they could for pilots. The BFOQ defense is not explicitly allowed for race or color.

Business Necessity

business necessity
Justification for an otherwise discriminatory employment practice, provided there is an overriding legitimate business purpose.

The **business necessity** defense requires showing that there is an overriding business purpose for the discriminatory practice and that the practice is therefore acceptable.

It's not easy to prove that a practice is a business necessity. The Supreme Court has made it clear that business necessity does not encompass such matters as avoiding inconvenience or expense. The Second Circuit Court of Appeals held that *business necessity* means an "irresistible demand" and that to be retained the practice "must not only directly foster safety and efficiency," but also be essential to these goals.[63]

Thus, it is not easy to prove that a practice is required for business necessity. For example, an employer cannot generally discharge employees whose wages have been garnished merely because garnishment (requiring the employer to divert part of the person's wages to pay his or her debts) creates an inconvenience for the employer. On the other hand, many employers have used this defense successfully. In *Spurlock* v. *United Airlines,* a minority candidate sued United Airlines, stating that its requirements that a pilot candidate have 500 flight hours and a college degree were unfairly discriminatory. The Court agreed that these requirements did have an adverse impact on members of the person's minority group. However, the Court held that in light of the cost of the training program and the tremendous human and economic risks involved in hiring unqualified candidates, the selection standards were required by business necessity and were job related.[64]

Attempts by employers to show that their selection tests or other screening practices are valid represent one example of the business necessity defense. Where such validity can be established, the courts have often supported the use of the test or other practice as a business necessity. Used in this context, the word *validity* means the degree to which the test or other employment practice is related to or predicts performance on the job. We discuss validation in chapter 5.

ILLUSTRATIVE DISCRIMINATORY EMPLOYMENT PRACTICES

❸ Present a summary of what employers can and cannot legally do with respect to recruitment, selection, and promotion and layoff practices.

A Note on What You Can and Cannot Do

In this section, we present several illustrations of what managers can and cannot do under equal employment laws. But before proceeding, keep in mind that most federal laws, such as Title VII, do not expressly ban preemployment questions about an applicant's race, color, religion, sex, age, or national origin. Similarly:

> With the exception of personnel policies calling for outright discrimination against the members of some protected group, it is not really the intrinsic nature of an employer's personnel policies or practices that the courts object to. Instead, it is the result of applying a policy or practice in a particular way or in a particular context that leads to an adverse impact on some protected group.[65]

For example, it is not illegal to ask a job candidate about marital status (although at first glance such a question might seem discriminatory). You can ask such a question as long as you can show either that you do not discriminate or that the practice can be defended as a BFOQ or business necessity.

In other words, illustrative inquiries and practices such as those summarized on the next few pages are not illegal per se. But, in practice, there are two good reasons to avoid such questionable practices. First, although federal law may not bar such questions, many state and local laws do. Second, the EEOC has said that it disapproves of such practices as asking women their marital status or applicants their age. Employers who use such practices thus increase their chances of having to defend themselves against charges of discriminatory employment practices.

Recruitment

WORD OF MOUTH You cannot rely on word-of-mouth dissemination of information about job opportunities when your workforce is all (or substantially all) white or all members of some other class such as all female, all Hispanic, and so on. Doing so might reduce the likelihood that others will become aware of the jobs and thus apply for them.

MISLEADING INFORMATION It is unlawful to give false or misleading information to members of any group or to fail to refuse to advise them of work opportunities and the procedures for obtaining them.

HELP WANTED ADS "Help wanted—male" and "Help wanted—female" advertising classifieds are violations of laws forbidding sex discrimination in employment unless sex is a BFOQ for the job advertised.[66] Also, you cannot advertise in any way that suggests that applicants are being discriminated against because of their age. For example, you cannot advertise for a "young" man or woman.

Selection Standards

EDUCATIONAL REQUIREMENTS An educational requirement may be held illegal when (1) it can be shown that minority groups are less likely to possess the educational qualifications (such as a high school diploma), and (2) such qualifications are also not job related. Unnecessary prerequisites (such as requiring a high school diploma where one is not required to perform the job) reportedly remains a problem today.[67]

TESTS According to former Chief Justice Burger:

> Nothing in the [Title VII] act precludes the use of testing or measuring procedures; obviously they are useful. What Congress has forbidden is giving these devices and mechanisms controlling force unless they are demonstrating a *reasonable measure of job performance.*

Tests that disproportionately screen out minorities or women and are not job related are deemed unlawful by the courts. But remember that a test or other selection standard that screens out a disproportionate number of minorities or women is not *by itself* sufficient to prove that the test *unfairly* discriminates. It must also be shown that the tests or other screening devices/results are not job related.

PREFERENCE TO RELATIVES You cannot give preference to relatives of your current employees with respect to employment opportunities if your current employees are substantially nonminority.

HEIGHT, WEIGHT, AND PHYSICAL CHARACTERISTICS Maximum weight rules for employees don't usually trigger adverse legal rulings. However, some minority groups have a higher incidence of obesity, so employers must ensure that their weight rules aren't adversely impacting those groups. Similarly, "few applicants or employees will be able to demonstrate an actual weight-based disability" (in other words, they are 100% above their ideal weight or there is a physiological cause for their disability). Few are thus entitled to reasonable accommodations under the ADA.

However, managers should be vigilant against stigmatizing obese people. Studies leave little doubt that obese individuals are less likely to be hired, less likely to receive promotions, more likely to get less desirable sales assignments, and more likely to receive poor customer service as customers.[68]

HEALTH QUESTIONS Under the ADA, "employers are generally prohibited from asking questions about applicants' medical history or requiring preemployment physical examinations." However, such questions and exams can be used once the job offer has been extended to determine that the applicant can safely perform the job.[69]

ARREST RECORDS You cannot ask about or use a person's arrest record to disqualify him or her automatically for a position because there is always a presumption of innocence until proof of guilt. In addition, arrest records in general have not been shown valid for predicting job performance, and a higher percentage of minorities than nonminorities have been arrested.

APPLICATION FORMS Employment applications generally shouldn't contain questions pertaining, for instance, to applicants' disabilities, workers' compensation history, age, arrest record, marital status, or U.S. citizenship. Personal information required for legitimate reasons (such as who to contact in case of emergency) are best collected after the person has been hired. Note that while equal employment laws discourage employers from asking for such information, no such laws prohibit the applicants from providing such information. One study examined 107 resumes from Australian managerial applicants. It found that many provided information, regarding marital status, ethnicity, age, and gender.[70]

Sample Discriminatory Promotion, Transfer, and Layoff Procedures

Fair employment laws protect not just job applicants but current employees as well.[71] Therefore, any employment practices regarding pay, promotion, termination, discipline, or benefits that (1) are applied differently to different classes of persons (2) have the effect of adversely affecting members of a protected group and (3) cannot be shown to be required as a BFOQ or business necessity may be held to be illegally discriminatory. For example, the EEOC issued an enforcement guidance making it clear that employers may not discriminate against employees in connection with their benefits plans.[72]

UNIFORMS When it comes to discriminatory uniforms and suggestive attire, courts have frequently sided with the employee. For example, requiring female employees (such as waitresses) to wear sexually suggestive attire as a condition of employment has been ruled as violating Title VII in many cases.[73]

THE EEOC ENFORCEMENT PROCESS

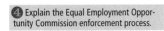
Explain the Equal Employment Opportunity Commission enforcement process.

Processing a Charge

FILE CLAIM The EEOC enforcement process begins with someone filing a claim. Under CRA 1991, the discrimination claim must be filed within 300 days (when there is a similar state law) or 180 days (no similar state law) after the alleged incident took place (two years for the Equal Pay Act). The filing must be in writing and under oath, by (or on behalf of) either the aggrieved person or by a member of the EEOC who has reasonable cause to believe that a violation occurred. In practice the EEOC typically defers a person's charge to the relevant state or local regulatory agency; if the latter waives jurisdiction or cannot obtain a satisfactory solution to the charge, they refer it back to the EEOC.

Litigants must watch the clock. In a recent equal pay decision, the U.S. Supreme Court held (in *Ledbetter* v. *Goodyear Tire & Rubber Company*) that the employee must file a complaint within 180 (or 300) days of the employer's decision to pay the allegedly unfair wage. The clock starts with that first pay decision, not with the subsequent pay checks that the employee receives.[74]

EEOC INVESTIGATION After a charge has been filed (or the state or local deferral period has ended), the EEOC has 10 days to serve notice of the charge on the employer. The EEOC then investigates the charge to determine whether there is reasonable cause to believe it is true; it is expected to make this determination within 120 days. If no reasonable cause is found, the EEOC must dismiss the charge, in which case the person who filed the charge has 90 days to file a suit on his or her own behalf. If reasonable cause for the charge is found, the EEOC must attempt to conciliate. If this conciliation is not satisfactory, the EEOC may bring a civil suit in a federal district court or issue a notice of right to sue to the person who filed the charge. Figure 2.2 summarizes important questions an employer should ask after receiving notice from the EEOC of a bias complaint.

The Equal Employment Opportunity Commission voted unanimously in 2006 to focus more on big, "systemic" cases—ones that reflect a pattern or practice of alleged discrimination.[75] In a suit apparently prompted by its subsequent "Eradicating Racism from Employment" campaign, the U.S. Equal Employment Opportunity Commission (EEOC) recently claimed that Walgreens discriminated against managers and pharmacists. It said

FIGURE 2.2

Questions to Ask When an Employer Receives Notice that EEOC Has Filed a Bias Claim

Sources: Fair Employment Practices Summary of Latest Developments, January 7, 1983: 3, Bureau of National Affairs, Inc. (800–372–1033); Kenneth Sovereign, *Personnel Law* (Upper Saddle River, NJ: Prentice Hall, 1999): 36–37; "EEOC Investigations—What an Employer Should Know." Equal Employment Opportunity Commission www.eeoc.gov/employmers/investigations.html, accessed May 6, 2007.

1. Exactly what is the charge and is your company covered by the relevant statutes? (For example, Title VII and the American with Disabilities Act generally apply only to employees with 15 or more employees; the Age Discrimination in Employment Act applies to employers with 20 or more employees; but the Equal Pay Act applies to virtually all employers with one or more employees.) Did the employee file his or her charge on time, and was it processed in a timely manner by the EEOC?

2. What protected group does the employee belong to? Is the EEOC claiming disparate impact or disparate treatment?

3. Are there any obvious bases upon which you can challenge and/or rebut the claim? For example, would the employer have taken the action if the person did not belong to a protected group? Does the person's personnel file support the action taken by the employer?

4. If it is a sexual harassment claim, are there offensive comments, calendars, posters, screensavers, and so on, on display in the company?

5. In terms of the practicality of defending your company against this claim, who are the supervisors who actually took the allegedly discriminatory actions and how effective will they be as potential witnesses? Have you received an opinion from legal counsel regarding the chances of prevailing? Even if you do prevail, what do you estimate will be the out-of-pocket costs of taking the charge through the judicial process? Would you be better off settling the case, and what are the prospects of doing so in a way that will satisfy all parties?

Walgreens used race to determine who to assign to low-performing stores in African-American communities.[76] The EEOC's systemic task force recently issued specific recommendations the EEOC can use to uncover and remedy systemic discrimination.[77]

VOLUNTARY MEDIATION The EEOC refers about 10% of its charges to a voluntary mediation mechanism. If the plaintiff agrees to mediation, the employer is asked to participate. A mediation session usually lasts up to 4 hours. If no agreement is reached or one of the parties rejects participation, the charge is then processed through the EEOC's usual mechanisms.

Faced with an offer to mediate, three responses are generally possible: Agree to mediate the charge, make a settlement offer without participating in mediation, or prepare a "position statement" for the EEOC. If the employer does not mediate or make an offer, the position statement is required. It should include information relating to the company's business and the charging party's position, a description of any rules or policies and procedures that are applicable, and the chronology of the offense that led to the adverse action.[78]

The EEOC is expanding its mediation program. For example, it signed more than 18 nationwide agreements and 300 local agreements for mediation with participating employers. Under this program, the EEOC refers all eligible discrimination charges filed against these employers to the commission's mediation unit, rather than to the usual charge processing system.[79]

How to Respond to Employment Discrimination Charges

There are several things to keep in mind when confronted by a charge of illegal employment discrimination; some of the more important items can be summarized as follows:

1. Be methodical. Is the charge signed and dated and notarized by the person who filed it? Was it filed within the time allowed? Does the charge name the proper employer?

Is it filed against a company that is subject to federal antidiscrimination statutes (for instance, only companies with 15 or more employees are subject to Title VII and the ADA)? Company records and persons with first-hand knowledge of the facts then should be scoured.[80]

2. Remember that EEOC investigators are not judges and aren't empowered to act as courts. They cannot make findings of discrimination on their own but can merely make recommendations. If the EEOC eventually determines that an employer may be in violation of a law, its only recourse is to file a suit or issue a notice of right to sue to the person who filed the charge.

3. Some experts advise meeting with the employee who made the complaint to determine all relevant issues. For example, ask: *What happened? Who was involved? When did the incident take place? Was the employee's ability to work affected? Were there any witnesses?* Then prepare a written statement summarizing the complaints, facts, dates, and issues involved and request that the employee sign and date this.[81]

4. Give the EEOC a position statement based on your own investigation of the matter. Say something like, "Our company has a policy against discrimination and we would not discriminate in the manner outlined in the complaint." Support your case with some statistical analysis of the workforce, copies of any documents that support your position, and an explanation of any legitimate business justification for the actions you took.

5. Ensure that there is information in the EEOC's file demonstrating lack of merit of the charge. Often the best way to do that is by not answering the EEOC's questionnaire but by providing a detailed statement (as in #4) describing the firm's defense in its most persuasive light.

6. Limit the information supplied as narrowly as possible to only those issues raised in the charge itself. For example, if the charge only alleges sex discrimination, do not invite further scrutiny by responding to the EEOC's request for a breakdown of employees by age and sex.

7. Seek as much information as possible about the charging party's claim in order to ensure that you understand the claim and its ramifications.

8. Prepare for the EEOC's *fact-finding conferences*. These are supposed to be informal meetings held early in the investigatory process aimed at determining whether there is a basis for negotiation. However, the EEOC's emphasis is often on settlement. Its investigators therefore use the conferences to find weak spots in each party's position. Therefore, thoroughly prepare witnesses who are going to testify, especially supervisors.

9. Finally, keep in mind that preventing such claims is usually better than litigating them. Racism's causes are many and complex. However, studies support the commonsense observation that when people with racist attitudes work in companies where there's a climate supporting racism, there is a significantly higher likelihood of racial discrimination.[82]

DIVERSITY MANAGEMENT AND AFFIRMATIVE ACTION PROGRAMS

⑤ List five strategies for successfully increasing diversity of the work force.

To some extent demographic changes and globalization are rendering moot the goals of equitable and fair treatment driving equal employment legislation. Today, as we've seen, white males no longer dominate the labor force, and women and minorities will represent the lion's share of labor force growth over the foreseeable future. Furthermore, globalization requires employers to hire minority members with the cultural and language skills to deal with customers abroad. This means two things for employers. First, companies are increasingly striving for demographic balance, not just because the law says they must, but due to self-interest.[83] Second, since many American workplaces are already diverse, the focus increasingly is on managing diversity rather than on "justifying" it. [84]

Managing diversity has numerous obvious and not-so-obvious benefits. Of course, effectively managing diversity generally means reduced conflict and increased cooperation.

Perhaps not so obvious, one survey of 113 MBA job seekers concluded that women and ethnic minorities considered diversity management important when accepting job offers.[85] Another study found that groups whose members were diverse in their beliefs and perspectives were more likely to perform better than non-diverse groups when solving certain types of problems.[86]

Managing Diversity

In general, race, sex, culture, national origin, handicap, age, and religion comprise the demographic building blocks of diversity at work and are what people often think of when asked what employers mean by *diversity*.[87]

managing diversity
Maximizing diversity's potential benefits while minimizing the potential barriers that can undermine the company's performance.

  Managing diversity means maximizing diversity's potential advantages while minimizing the potential barriers—such as prejudices and bias—that can undermine the functioning of a diverse workforce. In practice, diversity management involves both compulsory and voluntary management actions. We've seen that there are many legally mandated actions employers must take to minimize employment discrimination.

  However, while such compulsory actions can reduce the more blatant diversity barriers, blending a diverse workforce into a close-knit and thriving community isn't easy. For example, one study, in a large British retailer, found that diversity prescriptions like "recognize and respond to individual differences" conflicted with the supervisor's inclination to avoid unequal treatment.[88] Diversity management therefore requires a multi-pronged approach.

  One diversity expert concluded that five sets of voluntary organizational activities are at the heart of any diversity management program. We can summarize these as follows:

  Provide strong leadership. Companies with exemplary reputations in managing diversity typically have CEOs who champion the cause of diversity. Leadership means, for instance, becoming a role model for the behaviors required for the change.

  Assess the situation. One study found that the most common tools for measuring a company's diversity include equal employment hiring and retention metrics, employee attitude surveys, management and employee evaluations, and focus groups.[89]

  Provide diversity training and education. The most common starting point for a diversity management effort is usually some type of employee education program.

  Change culture and management systems. Combine education programs with other concrete steps aimed at changing the organization's culture and management systems. For example, change the performance appraisal procedure to appraise supervisors based partly on their success in reducing intergroup conflicts.

  Evaluate the diversity management program. For example, do employee attitude surveys now indicate any improvement in employees' attitudes toward diversity?

Boosting Workforce Diversity

Employers use various means to increase workforce diversity. Many companies, such as Baxter Healthcare Corporation, start by adopting strong company policies advocating the benefits of a culturally, racially, and sexually diverse workforce: "Baxter International believes that a multi-cultural employee population is essential to the company's leadership in healthcare around the world." Baxter then publicizes this philosophy throughout the company.

  Next, Baxter takes concrete steps to foster diversity at work. These steps include evaluating diversity program efforts, recruiting minority members to the board of directors, and interacting with representative minority groups and networks. Diversity training is another concrete activity. It aims at sensitizing all employees about the need to value differences, build self-esteem, and generally create a more smoothly functioning and hospitable environment for the firm's diverse workforce.

STRATEGY AND HR Workforce diversity makes strategic sense. Consider IBM's diversity programs. With strong top-management support, IBM created several minority task forces focusing on groups such as women and Native Americans. One effect of these teams has

With strong top-management support, IBM created several minority task forces focusing on groups such as women and Native Americans.

been internal: In the 10 or so years since forming them, IBM has boosted the number of U.S.-born ethnic minority executives by almost 2 1/2 times.[90]

However, the firm's diversity program also had profound effects on IBM's strategy of expanding its markets and business results. For example, the task forces have been active in identifying and expanding IBM's multicultural markets. One task force decided to focus on expanding IBM's market among multicultural and women-owned businesses. They did this in part by providing "much-needed sales and service support to small and midsize businesses, a niche well populated with minority and female buyers."[91] As a direct result, this market grew from $10 million to more than $300 million in revenue in just 3 years.

Equal Employment Opportunity Versus Affirmative Action

Equal employment opportunity aims to ensure that anyone, regardless of race, color, disability, sex, religion, national origin, or age, has an equal chance for a job based on his or her qualifications. *Affirmative action* goes beyond equal employment opportunity by requiring the employer to make an extra effort to hire and promote those in a protected group. Affirmative action thus includes specific actions (in recruitment, hiring, promotions, and compensation) to eliminate the present effects of past discrimination.

Steps in an Affirmative Action Program

According to the EEOC, in an affirmative action program the employer ideally takes eight steps:

1. Issues a written equal employment policy indicating that it is an equal employment opportunity employer, as well as a statement indicating the employer's commitment to affirmative action.
2. Appoints a top official with responsibility and authority to direct and implement the program.
3. Publicizes the equal employment policy and affirmative action commitment.
4. Surveys present minority and female employment to determine locations where affirmative action programs are especially desirable.[92]
5. Develops goals and timetables to improve utilization of minorities, males, and females in each area where need for improved utilization has been identified.

6. Develops and implements specific programs to achieve these goals. Here, review the entire human resource management system (including recruitment, selection, promotion, compensation, and disciplining) to identify barriers to equal employment opportunity and to make needed changes.

7. Establishes an internal audit and reporting system to monitor and evaluate progress in each aspect of the program.

8. Develops support for the affirmative action program, both inside the company (among supervisors, for instance) and outside the company in the community.[93]

AFFIRMATIVE ACTION TODAY Affirmative action is still a significant workplace issue today. The incidence of major court-mandated programs is down. However, many employers still engage in voluntary programs. For example, Executive Order 11246 (issued in 1965) requires federal contractors to take affirmative action to improve employment opportunities for women and racial minorities. It covers about 26 million workers—about 22% of the U.S. workforce.

Avoiding an employee backlash to affirmative action programs is important. A review of 35 years of research suggests several steps employers can take to increase employee support. Current employees need to see that the program is fair. *Transparent selection procedures* help in this regard. *Communication* is also crucial. Make clear that the program doesn't involve preferential selection standards. Provide details on the qualifications of all new hires (both minority and nonminority). *Justifications* for the program should emphasize redressing past discrimination and the practical value of diversity, not underrepresentation.[94]

VOLUNTARY PROGRAMS Some employers try to better manage diversity through voluntary affirmative action programs. This means they voluntarily make an extra effort to hire and promote those in protected (such as female or minority) groups. This is in contrast to the involuntary affirmative action programs courts have imposed on some employers since enactment of the 1964 Civil Rights Act.

In implementing voluntary programs, the employer should ensure that its program does not conflict with the Civil Rights Act of 1991, which two experts say may "bar employers from giving any consideration whatsoever to an individual's status as a racial or ethnic minority or as a woman when making an employment decision."[95] This does not seem to be much of a problem, as long as employers emphasize the external recruitment and internal development of better qualified minority and female employees, "while basing employment decisions on legitimate criteria."[96]

IMPROVING PRODUCTIVITY THROUGH HRIS The HR manager who wants to assess the efficiency and effectiveness of his or her company's EEOC and diversity efforts has numerous measures or metrics from which to choose. These might include, for example, the number of EEOC claims per year, the cost of HR-related litigation, percentage of minority/women promotions, and various measures for analyzing the survival and loss rate among new diverse employee groups.

Even for a company with just several hundred employees, keeping track of metrics like these is expensive. The HR manager may therefore want to rely on various computerized solutions. One package called *Measuring Diversity Results* provides several diversity-related software options aimed at boosting accuracy of the information at the manager's disposal and reducing the costs of collecting and compiling it. Among other things, this vendor's diversity management packages let the manager more easily calculate the cost-per-diversity hire, a workforce profile index, the numeric impact of voluntary turnover among diverse employee groups, the effectiveness of the firm's [employment] supplier diversity initiatives, current diversity measures, and such things as direct and indirect replacement cost per hire.

Review

SUMMARY

1. Legislation barring discrimination is not new. For example, the Fifth Amendment to the U.S. Constitution (ratified in 1791) states that no person shall be deprived of life, liberty, or property without due process of law.

2. Legislation barring employment discrimination includes Title VII of the 1964 Civil Rights Act (as amended), which bars discrimination because of race, color, religion, sex, or national origin; various executive orders; federal guidelines (covering procedures for validating employee selection tools, etc.); the Equal Pay Act of 1963; and the Age Discrimination in Employment Act of 1967. In addition, various Court decisions (such as *Griggs* v. *Duke Power Company*) and state and local laws bar various aspects of discrimination.

3. The EEOC was created by Title VII of the Civil Rights Act. It is empowered to try conciliating discrimination complaints, but if this fails, the EEOC has the power to go directly to court to enforce the law.

4. The Civil Rights Act of 1991 had the effect of revising several Supreme Court equal employment decisions and "rolling back the clock." For example, it placed the burden of proof back on employers and held that a nondiscriminatory reason was insufficient to let an employer avoid liability for an action that also had a discriminatory motive.

5. The Americans with Disabilities Act prohibits employment discrimination against the disabled. Specifically, qualified persons cannot be discriminated against if the firm can make reasonable accommodations without undue hardship on the business.

6. A person who believes he or she has been discriminated against by a personnel procedure or decision must prove either that he or she was subjected to unlawful disparate treatment (intentional discrimination) or that the procedure in question has a disparate impact (unintentional discrimination) on members of his or her protected class. Once a prima facie case of disparate treatment is established, an employer must produce evidence that its decision was based on legitimate reasons (such as BFOQ). If the employer does that, the person claiming discrimination must prove that the employer's reasons are only a pretext for letting the company discriminate. Once a prima facie case of disparate impact has been established, the employer must produce evidence that the allegedly discriminatory

practice or procedure is job related and is based on a substantial business reason.

7. An employer should avoid various specific discriminatory human resource management practices:
    a. *In recruitment.* An employer usually should not rely on word-of-mouth advertising or give false or misleading information to minority group members. Also (usually), an employer should not specify the desired sex in advertising or in any way suggest that applicants might be discriminated against.
    b. *In selection.* An employer should avoid using any educational or other requirements where (1) it can be shown that minority-group members are less likely to possess the qualification and (2) such requirement is also not job related. Tests that disproportionately screen out minorities and women and that are not job related are deemed unlawful. Remember that you can use various tests and standards, but you must prove that they are job related or show that they are not used to discriminate against protected groups.

8. In practice, a person's charge to the EEOC is often first referred to a local agency. When the EEOC finds reasonable cause to believe that discrimination occurred, it may suggest the parties try to work out a conciliation. Important points for the employer to remember include (1) EEOC investigators can only make recommendations, (2) you cannot be compelled to submit documents without a court order, and (3) you may limit the information you do submit. Also, make sure you clearly document your position (as the employer).

9. An employer can use three basic defenses in the event of a discriminatory practice allegation. One is *business necessity*. Attempts to show that tests or other selection standards are valid is one example of this defense. *Bona fide occupational qualification* is the second defense. This is applied when, for example, religion, national origin, or sex is a bona fide requirement of the job (such as for actors or actresses). A third is that the decision was made on the basis of legitimate nondiscriminatory reasons (such as poor performance) having nothing to do with the prohibited discrimination alleged.

10. Eight steps in an affirmative action program (based on suggestions from the EEOC) are (1) issue a written equal employment policy,

(2) appoint a top official, (3) publicize the policy, (4) survey present minority and female employees, (5) develop goals and timetables, (6) develop and implement specific programs to achieve goals, (7) establish an internal audit and reporting system, and (8) develop support of in-house and community programs.

11. Recruitment is one of the first activities to which EEOC laws and procedures are applied. We turn to this in Chapter 4.

KEY TERMS

public policy   46
Equal Pay Act of 1963   47
Title VII of the 1964 Civil Rights Act   47
Equal Employment Opportunity Commission
   (EEOC)   47
affirmative action   47
Office of Federal Contract Compliance Programs
   (OFCCP)   47
Age Discrimination in Employment Act (ADEA) of
   1967   48
Vocational Rehabilitation Act of 1973   48
Pregnancy Discrimination Act (PDA)   48
federal agency guidelines   48

sexual harassment   48
Federal Violence Against Women Act of 1994   49
gender harassment   50
Griggs v. *Duke Power Company*   53
protected class   53
Civil Rights Act of 1991 (CRA 1991)   54
disparate impact   54
disparate treatment   54
Americans with Disabilities Act (ADA)   54
adverse impact   57
bona fide occupational qualification (BFOQ)   59
business necessity   59
managing diversity   65

DISCUSSION QUESTIONS AND EXERCISES

1. What is Title VII? What does it state?
2. What important precedents were set by the *Griggs* v. *Duke Power Company* case? The *Albemarle* v. *Moody* case?
3. What is adverse impact? How can it be proven?
4. Assume that you are a supervisor on an assembly line; you are responsible for hiring, supervising, and recommending subordinates for promotion.

Compile a list of discriminatory management practices that you should avoid.
5. Explain the defenses and exceptions to discriminatory practice allegations.
6. What is the difference between affirmative action and equal employment opportunity?
7. Explain how you would set up an affirmative action program.

Application Exercises

HR in Action
Case Incident 1 — An Accusation of Sexual Harassment in Pro Sports

The jury in a sexual harassment suit brought by a former high-ranking New York Knicks basketball team executive recently awarded her over $11 million in punitive damages. They did so after hearing testimony during what the *New York Times* called a "sordid four-week trial." Officials of the Madison Square Garden (which owns the Knicks) said they would appeal the verdict. However, even if they were to win on appeal (which one University of Richmond Law School professor said was unlikely), the case still exposed the organization and its managers to a great deal of unfavorable publicity.

The federal suit pitted Anucha Browne Sanders, the Knicks' senior vice president of marketing and business operations (and former Northwestern University basketball star), against the team's owner, Madison Square Garden, and its president, Isiah Thomas. The suit charged them with sex discrimination and retaliation. Ms. Browne Sanders accused Mr. Thomas of verbally abusing and sexually harassing her over a two-year period, and says the Garden fired her about a month after she complained to top management about the harassment. "My pleas and complaints about Mr. Thomas' illegal and offensive actions fell on deaf ears," she said. At the trial, the Garden cited numerous explanations for the dismissal, saying she had "failed to fulfill professional responsibilities." At a news conference, Browne Sanders said that Thomas "refused to stop his demeaning and repulsive behavior and the Garden refused to intercede." For his part, Mr. Thomas vigorously insisted he was innocent, and said, "I will not allow her or anybody, man or woman, to use me as a pawn for their financial gain." According to one report of the trial her claims of harassment and verbal abuse had little corroboration from witnesses, but neither did the Garden's claims that her performance had been sub-par. After the jury decision came in favor of the Plaintiff, Browne Sanders' lawyers said, "this [decision] confirms what we've been saying all along, that [Browne Sanders] was sexually abused and fired for complaining about it." The Garden's statement said, in part, that "We look forward to presenting our arguments to an appeals court and believe they will agree that no sexual harassment took place."

Questions

1. Do you think Ms. Browne Sanders had the basis for a sexual harassment suit? Why or why not?

2. From what you know of this case, do you think the jury arrived at the correct decision? If not, why not? If so, why?

3. Based on the few facts that you have, what steps if any could Garden management have taken to protect themselves from liability in this matter?

4. Aside from the appeal, what would you do now if you were the Garden's top management?

5. "The allegations against the Madison Square Garden in this case raise ethical questions with regard to the employer's actions". Explain whether you agree or disagree with this statement, and why.

Sources: "Jury Awards $11.6 Million to Former Executive of Pro Basketball Team in Harassment Case", *BNA Bulletin to Management* (October 9, 2007): 323; Richard Sandomir, "Jury Finds Knicks and Coach Harassed a Former Executive," *The New York Times*, www.nytimes.com/2007/ 10/03/sports/basketball/03garden.html?em&ex=1191556800&en=41d47437f805290d&ei=5087%0A, accessed November 13, 2007; "Thomas Defiant in Face of Harassment Claims," http://espn.com, accessed November 13, 2007.

HR in Action Case Incident 2 — Carter Cleaning Company

A Question of Discrimination

One of the first problems Jennifer faced at her father's Carter Cleaning Centers concerned the inadequacies of the firm's current HR management practices and procedures.

One problem that particularly concerned her was the lack of attention to equal employment matters. Virtually all hiring was handled independently by each store manager, and the managers themselves had received no training regarding such fundamental matters as the types of questions that should not be asked of job applicants. It was therefore not unusual—in fact, it was routine—for female applicants to be asked questions such as, "Who's going to take care of your children while you are at work?" and for minority applicants to be asked questions about arrest records and credit histories. Nonminority applicants—three store managers were white males and three were white females, by the way—were not asked these questions, as Jennifer discerned from her interviews with the managers. Based on discussions with her father, Jennifer deduced that part of the reason for the laid-back attitude toward equal employment stemmed from (1) her father's lack of sophistication regarding the legal requirements and (2) the fact that, as Jack Carter put it, "Virtually all our workers are women or minority members anyway, so no one can really come in here and accuse us of being discriminatory, can they?"

Jennifer decided to mull that question over, but before she could, she was faced with two serious equal rights problems.

Two women in one of her stores privately confided to her that their manager was making unwelcome sexual advances toward them, and one claimed he had threatened to fire her unless she "socialized" with him after hours. And during a fact-finding trip to another store, an older man—he was 73 years old—complained of the fact that although he had almost 50 years of experience in the business, he was being paid less than people half his age who were doing the very same job. Jennifer's review of the stores resulted in the following questions.

Questions

1. Is it true, as Jack Carter claims, that "we can't be accused of being discriminatory because we hire mostly women and minorities anyway"?

2. How should Jennifer and her company address the sexual harassment charges and problems?

3. How should she and her company address the possible problems of age discrimination?

4. Given the fact that each of its stores has only a handful of employees, is her company in fact covered by equal rights legislation?

5. And finally, aside from the specific problems, what other human resource management matters (application forms, training, and so on) have to be reviewed given the need to bring them into compliance with equal rights laws?

EXPERIENTIAL EXERCISE

The Interplay of Ethics and Equal Employment

If one accepts the proposition that equal employment is at least partly an ethical matter, then we should expect that real employers recognize and emphasize that fact, for instance on their Web sites. Some do. For example, the Duke Energy Company (which, when known as Duke Power many years ago, lost one of the first and most famous equal employment cases) posts the following on its Web site:

Equal Employment Opportunity: Duke Energy's Code of Business Ethics[*]

Duke Energy seeks and values diversity. The dignity of each person is respected, and everyone's contributions are recognized. We expect Duke Energy employees to act with mutual respect and cooperation toward one another. We do not tolerate discrimination in the workplace.

We comply with laws concerning discrimination and equal opportunity that specifically prohibit discrimination on the basis of certain differences. We will recruit, select, train and compensate based on merit, experience and other work-related criteria.

Our Responsibilities

Duke Energy employees are expected to treat others with respect on the job and comply with equal employment opportunity laws, including those related to discrimination and harassment.

Duke Energy employees must not:

- Use any differences protected by law as a factor in hiring, firing or promotion decisions.
- Use any differences protected by law when determining terms or conditions of employment, such as work assignments, employee development opportunities, vacation or overtime.

- Retaliate against a person who makes a complaint of discrimination in good faith, reports suspected unethical conduct, violations of laws, regulations, or company policies, or participates in an investigation.

[*]*Source:* www.duke-energy.com/corporate-governance/code-of-business-ethics/equal-employment-opportunity.asp, accessed November 13, 2007. © Duke Energy Corporation. All Rights Reserved.

Purpose: Ethical decision-making is an important HR-related personal competency.

The purpose of this exercise is to increase your understanding of how ethics and equal employment are interrelated.

Required Understanding:

Be thoroughly familiar with the material presented in this chapter.

How to Set Up the Exercise/Instructions:

1. Divide the class into groups of three to five students.
2. Each group should use the Internet to identify and access at least five more companies that emphasize how ethics and equal employment are interrelated.
3. Next, each group should develop answers to the following questions:
   a. Based on your Internet research, how much importance do employers seem to place on emphasizing the ethical aspects of equal employment?
   b. What seem to be the main themes these employers emphasize with respect to ethics and equal employment?
   c. Given what you've learned here, explain how you would emphasize the ethical aspects of equal employment if you were creating an equal employment training program for new supervisors.

ENDNOTES

1. "Morgan Stanley Agrees to Settle Proposed Class-Action Suit Alleging Race AND Sex Bias," *BNA Bulletin to Management* 58, no. 3 (August 14, 2007): 257–264.
2. Betsy Morris, "How Corporate America Is Betraying Women," *Fortune* (January 10, 2005): 64–70.
3. Note that private employers are not bound by the U.S. Constitution.
4. Based on or quoted from *Principles of Employment Discrimination Law, International Association of Official Human Rights Agencies,* Washington, D.C. See also Bruce Feldacker, *Labor Guide to Labor Law* (Upper Saddle River, NJ: Prentice Hall, 2000); and www.eeoc.gov Web site. Employment discrimination law is a changing field, and the appropriateness of the rules, guidelines, and conclusions in this chapter and book may also be affected by factors unique to the employer's operation. They should be reviewed by the employer's attorney before implementation.
5. James Higgins, "A Manager's Guide to the Equal Employment Opportunity Laws," *Personnel Journal* 55, no. 8 (August 1976): 406.
6. Ibid.
7. The Equal Employment Opportunity Act of 1972, Subcommittee on Labor or the Committee of Labor and Public Welfare, United States Senate, March 1972, p. 3. In general, it is not discrimination, but unfair discrimination against a person merely because of that person's race, age, sex, national origin, or religion that is forbidden by federal statutes. In the federal government's *Uniform Employee Selection Guidelines,* unfair discrimination is defined as follows: "unfairness is demonstrated through a showing that

members of a particular interest group perform better or poorer on the job than their scores on the selection procedure (test, etc.) would indicate through comparison with how members of the other groups performed." For a discussion of the meaning of fairness, see James Ledvinka, "The Statistical Definition of Fairness in the Federal Selection Guidelines and Its Implications for Minority Employment," *Personnel Psychology* 32 (August 1979): 551–62. In summary, a selection device (such as a test) may discriminate—for example, between low performers and high performers. However, unfair discrimination—discrimination that is based solely on the person's race, age, sex, national origin, or religion—is illegal.

8. Note that the U.S. Supreme Court (in *General Dynamics Land Systems Inc.* v. *Cline, 2004*) held that the ADEA does *not* protect younger workers from being treated worse than older ones. "High Court: ADEA Does Not Protect Younger Workers Treated Worse Than Their Elders," *BNA Bulletin to Management* 55, no. 10 (March 4, 2004): 73–80.

9. John Kohl, Milton Mayfield, and Jacqueline Mayfield, "Recent Trends in Pregnancy Discrimination Law," *Business Horizons* 48, no. 5 (September 2005): 442–429.

10. Nancy Woodward, "Pregnancy Discrimination Grows," *HR Magazine* (July 2005): 79.

11. www.uniformguidelines.com/uniformguidelines.html, accessed November 23, 2007.

12. Ibid.

13. See, for example, Gillian Flynn, "The Maturing of the ADEA," *Workforce Management* (October 2002): 86–87.

14. Larry Drake and Rachel Moskowitz, "Your Rights in the Workplace," *Occupational Outlook Quarterly* (Summer 1997): 19–20.

15. Richard Wiener et al., "The Fit and Implementation of Sexual Harassment Law to Workplace Evaluations," *Journal of Applied Psychology* 87, no. 4 (2002): 747–764.

16. Congress and the president renewed this in 2005. http://www.ilw.com/immigdaily/news/2005,0802-crs.pdf, accessed April 12, 2008.

17. Edward Felsenthal, "Justice's Ruling Further Defines Sexual Harassment," *Wall Street Journal* (March 5, 1998): B1, B5. Similarly, a series of compliments and "requests for a hug" were not sufficient to rise to the level of sexual harassment in one case involving a female supervisor and her female subordinate. ["Compliments, Request for Hug Were Not Harassment by Female Supervisor, Court Says," *Human Resources Report, BNA* (November 20, 2003): 1193].

18. Hilary Gettman and Michele Gelfand, "When the Customer Shouldn't Be King: Antecedents and Consequences of Sexual Harassment by Clients and Customers," *Journal of Applied Psychology* 92, no. 3 (2007): 757–770.

19. See Mindy D. Bergman et al., "The (Un)reasonableness of Reporting: Antecedents and Consequences of Reporting Sexual Harassment," *Journal of Applied Psychology* 87, no. 2 (2002): 230–242; See also W. Kirk Turner and Christopher Thrutchley, "Employment Law and Practices Training: No Longer the Exception—It's the Rule," *Society for Human Resource Management Legal Report* (July–August 2002): 1–2.

20. Chelsea Willness, et al., "A Meta-Analysis of the Antecedents and Consequences of Workplace Sexual Harassment," *Personnel Psychology* 60, no. 60 (2007): 127–162.

21. Jennifer Berdahl and Celia Moore, "Workplace Harassment: Double Jeopardy for Minority Women," *Journal of Applied Psychology* 91, no. 2 (2006): 426–436.

22. Jennifer Berdahl, "The Sexual Harassment of Uppity Women," *Journal of Applied Psychology* 92, no. 2 (2007): 425–437.

23. Lilia Cortina and S. Arzu Wasti, "Profile to Coping: Response to Sexual Harassment Across Persons, Organizations, and Cultures," *Journal of Applied Psychology* 90, no. 1 (2005): 182–192.

24. Maria Rotundo et al., "A Meta-Analytic Review of Gender Differences in Perceptions of Sexual Harassment," *Journal of Applied Psychology* 86, no. 5 (2001): 914–922. See also Nathan Bowling and Terry Beehr, "Workplace Harassment from the Victim's Perspective: A Theoretical Model and Meta Analysis," *Journal of Applied Psychology*, 91, no. 5 (2006): 998–1012.

25. See the discussion in "Examining Unwelcome Conduct in Sexual Harassment Claim," *BNA Fair Employment Practices* (October 19, 1995): 124. See also Molly Bowers et al., "Just Cause in the Arbitration of Sexual Harassment Cases," *Dispute Resolution Journal* 55, no. 4 (November 2000): 40–55.

26. Mindy D. Bergman et al., op cit., p. 237.

27. www.eeoc.gov/, accessed November 11, 2007.

28. Shereen Bingham and Lisa Scherer, "The Unexpected Effects of a Sexual Education Program," *Journal of Applied Behavioral Science* 37, no. 2 (June 2001): 125–153.

29. Manuel Velasquez, *Business Ethics: Concepts and Cases* (Upper Saddle River, NJ: Prentice Hall, 1992): 9. See also Kate Walter, "Ethics Hot Lines Tap Into More Than Wrongdoing," *HR Magazine* (September 1995): 79–85; Skip Kaltenheuser, "Bribery Is Being Outlawed Virtually Worldwide," *Business Ethics* (May 1998): 11.

30. Lauren Weber, "Jury Awards Worker $7.5 Million in Wal-Mart Disability Discrimination," *Knight-Ridder/Tribune Business News* (February 25, 2005).

31. *Griggs* v. *Duke Power Company,* 3FEP cases 175.

32. IOFEP cases 1181.

33. Bruce Feldacker, *Labor Guide to Labor Law* (Upper Saddle River, NJ: Prentice Hall, 2000): 513.

34. "The Eleventh Circuit Explains Disparate Impact, Disparate Treatment," *BNA Fair Employment Practices* (August 17, 2000): 102. See also Kenneth York, "Disparate Results in Adverse Impact Tests: The 4/5ths Rule and the Chi Square Test," *Public Personnel Management* 31, no. 2 (Summer 2002): 253–262.

35. www.eeoc.gov/policy/cra91.html, accessed November 11, 2007.

36. Elliot H. Shaller and Dean Rosen, "A Guide to the EEOC's Final Regulations on the Americans with Disabilities Act," *Employee Relations* 17, no. 3 (Winter 1991–1992), and www.eeoc.gov/ada/, accessed November 20, 2007.

37. Elliot H. Shaller and Dean Rosen, "A Guide to the EEOC's Final Regulations on the Americans with Disabilities Act," *Employee Relations* 17, no. 3 (Winter 1991–1992): 408. The ADEA does not just protect against intentional discrimination (disparate treatment). Under the Supreme Court's *Smith* v. *Jackson, Miss* decision, it also covers employer practices that seem neutral but which actually bear more heavily on older workers (disparate impact). "Employees Need Not

Show Intentional Bias to Bring Claims under ADEA, High Court Says," *BNA Bulletin to Management* 56, no. 14 (April 5, 2005): 105.

38. Ibid., 409.

39. "EEOC Guidance on Dealing with Intellectual Disabilities," *Workforce Management* (March 2005): 16.

40. James McDonald, Jr., "The Americans with Difficult Personalities Act," *Employee Relations Law Journal* 25, no. 4 (Spring 2000): 93–107.

41. See, for example, Paul Starkman, "The ADA's 'Essential Job Function' Requirements: Just How Essential Does an Essential Job Function Have to Be?" *Employee Relations Law Journal* 26, no. 4 (Spring 2001): 43–102.

42. "No Sitting for Store Greeter," *BNA Fair Employment Practices* (December 14, 1995): 150.

43. M. P. McQueen, "Workplace Disabilities Are on the Rise," *Wall Street Journal* (May 1, 2007): A1.

44. "Odds Against Getting Even Longer in ADA Cases," *BNA Bulletin to Management* (August 20, 2000): 229. See also Barbara Lee, "The Implications of ADA Litigation for Employers: A Review of Federal Appellate Court Decisions," *Human Resource Management* 40, no. 1 (Spring 2001): 35–50.

45. "Supreme Court Says Manual Task Limitation Needs Both Daily Living, Workplace Impact," *BNA Fair Employment Practices* (January 17, 2002): 8.

46. "Home Depot Did Not Violate ADA by Barring Deaf Worker from a Forklift Training Program," *BNA Human Resources Report* (November 10, 2003): 1192.

47. "Differing Views: Punctuality as Essential Job Function," *BNA Fair Employment Practices* (April 27, 2000): 56.

48. www.eeoc.gov/press/5–10–01-b.html, accessed January 8, 2008.

49. "Airline Erred in Giving Test Before Making Formal Offer," *BNA Bulletin to Management* (March 15, 2005): 86.

50. Barbara Lee, "Implications of ADA Litigation for Employers: A Review of Federal Appellant Court Decisions", Human Resource management, 40, no.1, pp. 35–50.

51. "Determining Employers' Responsibilities Under ADA," *BNA Fair Employment Practices*, May 16, 1996, p.57.

52. Lee, "Implications of ADA Litigation for Employers."

53. Ibid.

54. Timothy Bland, "The Supreme Court Focuses on the ADA," *HR Magazine* (September 1999): 42–46. See also James Hall and Diane Hatch, "Supreme Court Decisions Require ADA Revision," *Workforce* (August 1999): 60–66.

55. Joe Mullich, "Hiring Without Limits," *Workforce Management* (June 2004): 52–58.

56. Chris Reiter, "New Technology Aims to Improve Internet Access for the Impaired," *Wall Street Journal* (September 22, 2005): 4–6.

57. IOFEP cases 1181. See also Joe Mullich, "Hiring Without Limits," *Workforce Management* (June 2004): 52–58.

58. "Expansion of Employment Laws Abroad Impacts US Employers," *BNA Bulletin to Management* (April 11, 2006): 119; Richard Posthuma, Mark Roehling, and Michael Campion, "Applying US Employment Discrimination Laws to International Employers: Advice for Scientists and Practitioners," *Personnel Psychology* 59 (2006): 705–739.

59. John Klinefelter and James Thompkins, "Adverse Impact in Employment Selection," *Public Personnel Management* (May/June 1976): 199–204. For a recent discussion, see, for example, www.hr-guide.com/data/G702.htm, accessed November 21, 2007.

60. John Moran, *Employment Law* (Upper Saddle River, NJ: Prentice Hall, 1997): 168. A recent study found that using the so-called 4/5ths rule often resulted in false-positive ratings of adverse impact, and that incorporating tests of statistical significance could improve the accuracy of applying the 4/5ths rule. See Philip Roth, Philip Bobko, and Fred Switzer, "Modeling the Behavior of the 4/5ths Rule for Determining Adverse Impact: Reasons for Caution," *Journal of Applied Psychology* 91, no, 3 (2006): 507–522.

61. "Eighth Circuit OKs $3.4 Million EEOC Verdict Relating to Pre-Hire Strength Testing Rules," *BNA Bulletin to Management* (November 28, 2006): 377.

62. "The Eleventh Circuit Explains Disparate Impact, Disparate Treatment," *BNA Fair Employment Practices* (August 17, 2000): 102.

63. *U.S.* v. *Bethlehem Steel Company,* 3FEP cases 589.

64. *Spurlock* v. *United Airlines,* 5FEP cases 17.

65. James Ledvinka and Robert Gatewood, "EEO Issues with Preemployment Inquiries," *Personnel Administrator*, 22, no. 2 (February 1997), 22–26.

66. Howard Anderson and Michael D Levin-Epstein, *Primer of Equal Employment Opportunity* (Washington, D.C.: The Bureau Of National Affairs, 1982), p 28.

67. "Many Well-Intentioned HR Policies Hold Legal Headaches, Consultant Says," *BNA Bulletin to Management* (February 17, 2000): 47.

68. Jenessa Shapiro, et al., "Expectations of Obese Trainees: How Stigmatized Trainee Characteristics Influence Training Effectiveness," *Journal of Applied Psychology* 92, no. 1 (2007): 239–249. See also Lisa Finkelstein et al., "Bias Against Overweight Job Applicants: Further Explanations of When and Why," *Human Resource Management* 46, no. 2 (Summer 2007): 203–222.

69. "American Airlines, Worldwide Flight Sued by EEOC Over Questioning of Applicants," *BNA Fair Employment Practices* (October 12, 2000): 125.

70. Lynn Bennington and Ruth Wein, "Aiding and Abetting Employer Discrimination: The Job Applicant's Role," *Employee Responsibilities and Rights* 14, no. 1 (March 2002): 3–16.

71. This is based on *Anderson* and *Levin-Epstein, Primer of Equal Opportunity*, 93–97.

72. "EEOC Issues New Enforcement Guidance on Discrimination in Employee Benefits," *BNA Fair Employment Practices* (October 12, 2000): 123.

73. Matthew Miklaue, "Sorting Out a Claim of Bias," *Workforce* 80, no. 6 (June 2001): 102–103.

74. "Justices Rule 5–4 Claim-Filing Period Applies to Pay Decision, Not Subsequent Paycheck," *BNA Bulletin to Management* 58, no. 23 (June 5, 2007): 177–184.

75. "EEOC Turning Attention to Broader Cases," *Workforce Management* (April 24, 2006): 6; "EEOC's Focus on Systemic Cases Increases Need for Preventing Bias," *BNA Human Resources Report* (May 22, 2006): 533.

76. Mark Schoef, "Walgreens Suit Reflects EEOC's Latest Strategies," *Workforce Management* (March 26, 2007): 8.

77. Jonathan Segal, "Land Executives, Not Lawsuits," *HR Magazine* 51, no. 10 (October 2006): 123–130.

78. Timothy Bland, "Sealed Without a Kiss," *HR Magazine* (October 2000): 85–92.

79. "EEOC Has 18 Nationwide, 300 Local Accords with Employers to Mediate Job Bias Claims Charges," *BNA Human Resources Report* (October 13, 2003): H-081; http://www.eeoc.gov/mediate/index.html, accessed April 12, 2008.

80. Bland, "Sealed Without a Kiss," 85–92.

81. "Conducting Effective Investigations of Employee Bias Complaints," *BNA Fair Employment Practices* (July 13, 1995): 81.

82. Jonathan Zeigert and Paul Hangies, "Employment Discrimination: The Role of Implicit Attitudes, Motivation, and a Climate for Racial Bias," *Journal of Applied Psychology* 90, no. 3 (2005): 553–562.

83. See, for example, "Diversity Is Used as Business Advantage by Three Fourths of Companies, Survey Says," *BNA Bulletin to Management* (November 7, 2006): 355.

84. Brian O'Leary and Bart Weathington, "Beyond the Business Case for Diversity in Organizations," *Employee Responsibilities and Rights* 18, no. 4 (December 2006): 283–292.

85. Eddy Ng and Ronald Burke, "Person–Organization Fit and the War for Talent: Does Diversity Management Make a Difference?" *International Journal of Human Resource Management* 16, no. 7 (July 2005): 1195–1210.

86. Astrid Homan et al., "Bridging Faultlines by Valuing Diversity: Diversity Beliefs, Informational Elaboration, and Performance in Diverse Work Groups," *Journal of Applied Psychology* 92, no. 5 (2007): 1189–1199.

87. Michael Carrell and Everett Mann, "Defining Work-Force Diversity in Public Sector Organizations," *Public Personnel Management* 24, no. 1 (Spring 1995): 99–111. See also Richard Koonce, "Redefining Diversity," *Training and Development Journal* (December 2001): 22–33.

88. Carly Foster and Lynette Harris, "Easy to Say, Difficult to Do: Diversity Management in Retail," *Human Resource Management Journal* 15, no. 3 (2005): 4–17.

89. Patricia Digh, "Creating a New Balance Sheet: The Need for Better Diversity Metrics," *Mosaics*, Society for Human Resource Management (September/ October 1999): 1. For diversity management steps see Taylor Cox, Jr., *Cultural Diversity in Organizations: Theory, Research and Practice* (San Francisco: Berrett-Koehler, 1993): 236; See also Richard Bucher, *Diversity Consciousness* (Upper Saddle River, NJ: Prentice Hall, 2004): 109–137.

90. David Thomas, "Diversity as Strategy," *Harvard Business Review* (September 2004): 98–104. See also J. T. Childs Jr., "Managing Global Diversity at IBM: A Global HR Topic that Has Arrived," *Human Resource Management* 44, no. 1 (Spring 2005): 73–77.

91. David Thomas, Op. cit., 99.

92. Frank Jossi, "Reporting Race," *HR Magazine* (September 2000): 87–94.

93. U.S. Equal Employment Opportunity Commission, *Affirmative Action and Equal Employment* (Washington, D.C.: January 1974). See also David Kravitz and Steven Klineberg, "Reactions to Two Versions of Affirmative-Action Among Whites, Blacks, and Hispanics," *Journal of Applied Psychology* 85, no. 4 (2000): 597–611.

94. David Harrison et al., "Understanding Attitudes toward Affirmative Action Programs in Employment: Summary and Meta-Analysis of 35 Years of Research," *Journal of Applied Psychology* 91, no. 5 (2006): 1031–1036.

95. James Coil, 3d and Charles Rice, "Managing work-force diversity in the nineties: the impact of the Civil Rights Act of 1991", Employee Relations Law Journal, v18 Spring 1993, p. 548. See also Norma Carr-Ruffino, Making Diversity Work (Upper Saddle River, NJ: 2006) pp 2–28.

96. Coil and Rice, 562–63.

Mergers, Acquisitions, and Strategic Human Resource Management

3

When you finish studying this chapter, you should be able to:

1. *Outline the steps in the strategic management process.*

2. *Explain and give examples of each type of companywide and competitive strategy.*

3. *Explain how employers create competitive advantage through human resource management.*

4. *Define and give several examples of strategic human resource management.*

5. *Learn how to devise human resource practices to support the employer's business strategy.*

Introduction

In the late 1990s, Shanghai's Portman Shangri-La Hotel was a very good but not extraordinary property. Employee and guest satisfaction ratings averaged around 75%. Financial results were not exceptional.[1] When it took over managing the hotel in 1998, The Ritz-Carlton Hotel Company installed a new general manager, and the hotel was renamed The Portman Ritz-Carlton, Shanghai. Together the new management team set out to turn the hotel into a premier property. They built their strategy for doing so in large part around providing superior customer service. A Ritz-Carlton Company motto is, "We are Ladies and Gentlemen serving Ladies and Gentlemen." Management therefore knew the hotel's employees were crucial to their effort: "We're a service business, and service comes only from people." Management introduced the Ritz-Carlton Company's human resource system, including new employee selection standards and training. The efforts paid off. Customer service is exceptional. Since then, The Portman Ritz-Carlton, Shanghai was named the "Best Employer in Asia" and the "best business hotel in China," and the China National Tourism Administration recognized it as Shanghai's only Platinum Five-Star winner. ■

WHAT IS STRATEGIC HUMAN RESOURCE MANAGEMENT?

strategic human resource management
Formulating and executing human resource policies and practices that produce the employee competencies and behaviors the company needs to achieve its strategic aims.

The turnaround of the Portman Hotel in Shanghai (now The Portman Ritz-Carlton, Shanghai) illustrates what managers mean by "strategic human resource management." We'll see in this chapter that **strategic human resource management** means *formulating and executing human resource policies and practices that produce the employee competencies and behaviors the company needs to achieve its strategic aims.* The basic idea behind strategic human resource management is simple but easily missed. The basic idea is this: "in formulating human resource management policies and activities, the manager's goal must be to produce the employee skills and behaviors that the company needs to achieve its strategic aims." We can summarize the process as follows: First, *decide what the strategic goals are,* then *identify the employee skills and behaviors that achieving these goals require,* and then *formulate human resource management policies and practices that will produce these required employee skills and behaviors.*

THE PORTMAN RITZ-CARLTON, SHANGHAI EXAMPLE In turning around the former Portman Shangri-La, the hotel's new management team followed this strategic human resource management process. Here's how:

- *Strategically,* they set out to make the renamed Portman Ritz-Carlton, Shanghai an outstanding property by offering superior customer service.
- To achieve this, the hotel's employees would have to exhibit new *skills and behaviors.* For example, they would have to be trained and motivated to be proactive about providing superior customer service.
- To produce these employee skills and behaviors, management introduced the Ritz-Carlton Company's *human resource system.* For example, the hotel's managers, including its top executive, personally interviewed each candidate. They delved deeply into each candidate's values, selecting only employees who cared for and respected others: "our selection focuses on talent and personal values because these are things that can't be taught . . . it's about caring for and respect and others."[2]

As we noted, their efforts paid off. In the years since it became the Portman Ritz-Carlton, Shanghai, the hotel was named the "best employer in Asia," "overall best business hotel in Asia," and "best business hotel in China", and the China National Tourism Administration recognized it as Shanghai's only Platinum Five-Star winner.

Profits rose. A number of major changes, including a $40 million renovation and effective strategic human resource management helped turn the Portman Ritz-Carlton, Shanghai into an extraordinary hotel.

Again, the basic idea is that "in formulating human resource management policies and activities, the manager's goal must be to produce the employee skills and behaviors that the company needs to achieve its strategic aims." To institute human resource policies and practices—selection practices, incentive plans, union relations polices, for instance—without taking the strategic aims and context into account is pointless. (For example, focusing on customer service practices might make less sense for a deep-discount motel chain.) In this chapter we'll therefore focus on what managers need to know about strategic planning and its relationship to human resource management policies and practices. We start with the strategic management process.

THE STRATEGIC MANAGEMENT PROCESS

American automaker Ford Motor Company, facing huge losses and hemorrhaging market share to Toyota and Nissan, needed a new strategic plan. Competition was fierce, Ford's costs were too high, and Ford's unused plant capacity was draining profits. Ford's managers devised "The Way Forward." This new strategic plan entailed closing a dozen plants, terminating 20,000 employees, and selling off its Jaguar and Land Rover brands. As at Ford, a **strategic plan** is the company's plan for how it will match its internal strengths and weaknesses with external opportunities and threats in order to maintain a competitive advantage. The essence of **strategic planning** is to ask, "Where are we now as a business, where do we want to be, and how should we get there?" The manager then formulates specific (human resources and other) strategies to take the company from where it is now to where he or she wants it to be. A **strategy** is a course of action. Ford's strategies included closing plants, terminating employees, and selling off Jaguar and Land Rover. Strategic planning is part of *strategic management*. **Strategic management** is the process of identifying and executing the organization's strategic plan, by matching the company's capabilities with the demands of its environment.

Steps in Strategic Management

Strategic management entails both strategic planning and strategy execution. Strategic planning comprises (see Figure 3.1) the first five of seven strategic management tasks: (1) defining the business and developing a mission; (2) evaluating the firm's internal and external strengths, weaknesses, opportunities, and threats; (3) formulating new

---

strategic plan
The company's plan for how it will match its internal strengths and weaknesses with external opportunities and threats in order to maintain a competitive advantage.

strategic planning
Manager formulates specific strategies to take the company from where it is now to where he or she wants it to be.

strategy
The company's long-term plan for how it will balance its internal strengths and weaknesses with its external opportunities and threats to maintain a competitive advantage.

strategic management
The process of identifying and executing the organization's mission by matching its capabilities with the demands of its environment.

FIGURE 3.1

The Strategic Management Process

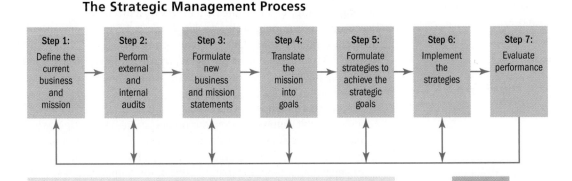

business and mission statements; (4) translating the mission into strategic goals; and (5) formulating strategies or courses of action. Steps (6) and (7) then entail implementing and then evaluating the strategic plan. We can summarize the seven-step strategic management process as follows:

STEP 1: DEFINE THE CURRENT BUSINESS Strategic planning starts with asking, "What business are we in now, and what business do we want to be in, given the threats and opportunities we face and our company's strengths and weaknesses?" Managers then choose strategies—courses of action such as buying competitors or expanding overseas— to get the company from where it is today to where it wants to be tomorrow.

Therefore, a logical place to start is by defining one's current business. Specifically, what products do we sell, where do we sell them, and how do our products or services differ from our competitors? For example, Rolex and Swatch are both in the wristwatch business. However, Rolex sells a limited product line of expensive watches. Swatch sells a variety of relatively inexpensive but innovative specialty watches.

Strengths	**W**eaknesses
Example: strong research group	Example: aging machinery
Opportunities	**T**hreats
Example: expanding China markets	Example: merger of two competitors to form single strong one

FIGURE 3.2

A SWOT Chart

SWOT analysis
The use of a SWOT chart to compile and organize the process of identifying company **S**trengths, **W**eaknesses, **O**pportunities, and **T**hreats.

STEP 2: PERFORM EXTERNAL AND INTERNAL AUDITS No company can risk not adapting its business to changing competitive pressures. Barnes & Noble adapted to Amazon by opening its own online bookstore and by expanding its stores to include coffee shops. Ford is adapting by downsizing and selling off Land Rover and Jaguar.

Adapting means adjusting the company's business to the situation's realities. The manager's strategic plan should provide a direction for the firm that makes sense, in terms of the external opportunities and threats the firm faces and the internal strengths and weaknesses it possesses. To do such a situational audit, managers use SWOT analysis. **SWOT analysis** means using a SWOT chart (as in Figure 3.2) to compile and organize the company's Strengths, Weaknesses, Opportunities, and Threats.

STEP 3: FORMULATE NEW BUSINESS AND MISSION STATEMENTS Based on the SWOT analysis, what should our new business be, in terms of what products we will sell, where we will sell them, and how our products or services will differ from competitors?

America's Safeway Stores, sensing increased competition from competitors like Wal-Mart, redefined its business several years ago. It started Blackhawk Network, Inc. This wholly-owned Safeway subsidiary sells discount gift cards in Safeway stores for purchases at companies like Home Depot and American Airlines. By some estimates, Blackhawk revenues reached about $170 million in 2007. By expanding beyond groceries, Safeway redefined its business, and hopes to shield itself from some of the brutal competition in the food store industry.[3]

Managers sometimes use a *vision statement* to summarize how they see their business down the road. The **vision statement** is a general statement of the firm's intended direction and shows, in broad terms, "what we want to become."[4] Rupert Murdoch, chairman of News Corporation (which owns MySpace.com, the Fox network, and newspapers and satellite TV operations), has a vision of an integrated, global satellite-based news-gathering, entertainment, and multimedia firm. WebMD launched its business based on a vision of a Web site supplying everything one might want to know about medical-related issues. One eye care company says, "Our vision is caring for your vision."[5] Two management gurus, Warren Bennis and Bert Manus, say this about the vision statement:

vision statement
A general statement of its intended direction that evokes emotional feelings in organization members.

> To choose a direction, a leader must first have developed a mental image of a possible and desirable future state for the organization. This image, which we call a vision, may be as vague as a dream or as precise as a goal or mission statement. The critical point is that a vision articulates a view of a realistic, credible, attractive future for the organization, a condition that is better in some important ways than what now exists.[6]

mission statement
Spells out who the company is, what it does, and where it's headed.

Whereas vision statements usually describe in broad terms what the business should be, the company's **mission statement** describes in broad terms what the company's main

WebMD launched its business based on a vision of a Web site supplying everything one might want to know about medical-related issues.

tasks are now. Before their more recent downturn, Ford pursued and then strayed from a remarkably successful mission, summed up by the phrase, "Where Quality is Job One." The mission of the Royal Dutch/Shell Group is "to meet the energy needs of society, in ways that are economically, socially, and environmentally viable, now and in the future." In the movie *Saving Private Ryan*, the team's mission was, of course, to save private Ryan.

STEP 4: TRANSLATE THE MISSION INTO GOALS Saying the mission is "to make quality job one" is one thing; operationalizing that mission for your managers is another.

The company and its managers need strategic goals. For Ford, what exactly did "quality is job one" mean for each department, in terms of how to boost quality? Similarly, WebMD's sales director needs goals regarding the number of new vitamin firms, hospitals, and HMOs it must sign up per year as advertisers. Its business development manager needs goals regarding the number of new businesses—such as using WebMD to help manage doctors' offices online—he or she is to develop and sign.

STEP 5: FORMULATE STRATEGIES TO ACHIEVE THE STRATEGIC GOALS Next, the manager chooses strategies—courses of action—that he or she believes will enable the company to achieve its strategic goals. The new strategies (such as Safeway diversifying into also selling discount gift cards) bridge where the company is now with where it wants to be tomorrow.

The best strategies are usually concise enough for the manager to express in an easily communicated phrase that resonates with employees. Tesco's strategy boils down to "Every Little Helps." Dell's is "be direct."

STEP 6: IMPLEMENT THE STRATEGIES Strategy implementation (or execution) means translating the strategic plan into actions and results. This involves actually hiring (or firing) people, building (or closing) plants, and adding (or eliminating) products and product lines. Safeway management had to create a new company (Blackhawk), hire for it a management and employee team, and develop the retail partners and marketing and other programs to make its new business succeed.

STEP 7: EVALUATE PERFORMANCE Things don't always turn out as planned. For example, Ford originally bought Jaguar and Land Rover to move away from reliance on lower-profit cars. With auto industry competition brutal in 2008, Ford announced it was selling Jaguar and Land Rover to the Indian company Tata. Ford wants to focus its scarce resources on modernizing and turning around its struggling North American operations.

Managing strategy is thus an ongoing process. Competitors introduce new products, technological innovations make production processes obsolete, and social trends reduce demand for some products or services while boosting demand for others. **Strategic control** keeps the company's strategy up to date. It is the process of assessing progress toward strategic goals and taking corrective action as needed. Management monitors the extent to which the firm is meeting its strategic goals, and asks why deviations exist. Management simultaneously scans the firm's strategic situation (competitors, technical advances, customer demographics, and so on) to see if it should make any adjustments. Strategic evaluation addresses several important questions, for example, "Are all the resources of our firm contributing as planned to achieving our strategic goals?" "What is the reason for any discrepancies?" and, "Do changes in our situation suggest that we should revise our strategic plan?"

strategic control
The process of assessing progress toward strategic goals and taking corrective action as needed.

Improving Productivity Through HRIS: Using Computerized Business Planning Software

There are several business planning software packages available to assist the manager in writing strategic and business plans. For example, Business Plan Pro from Palo Alto software contains all the information and planning aids you need to create a business plan. It contains 30 sample plans, step-by-step instructions (with examples) for creating each part of a plan (executive summary, market analysis, and so on), financial planning spreadsheets, easy-to-use tables (for instance, for making sales forecasts), and automatic programs for creating color 3-D charts for showing things like monthly sales and yearly profits.

Business Plan Pro's planning wizard helps the manager or small business owner develop a business plan, step-by-step. The result is an integrated plan, complete with an overall strategic plan, and charts, tables, and professional formatting. For example, click "start a plan" and the planning wizard presents a series of questions, including "Does your Company sell products, services, or both?" "Would you like a detailed or basic business plan?" and, "Does your Company sell on credit?" Then, as you go to each succeeding part of the plan, the planning wizard shows you instructions with examples, making it easier to create your own executive summary (or other plan section, including the strategic plan). As you move into the quantitative part of your plan, such as making sales and financial forecasts, the planning wizard translates your numbers into tables and charts.

Types of Strategies

Managers engage in three types of strategic planning, depending on the level of their companies for which they are formulating plans (see Figure 3.3). There is corporate-wide planning, business unit (or competitive) planning, and functional (or departmental) planning. We'll look at each.

CORPORATE STRATEGY First, every company needs a *corporate strategy*. A company's **corporate-level strategy** identifies the sorts of businesses that will comprise the company and the ways in which these businesses relate to each other. For example, PepsiCo doesn't just make Pepsi. Instead, PepsiCo is comprised of four main businesses: Frito-Lay North America, PepsiCo Beverages North America, PepsiCo International, and Quaker Oats North America.[7] PepsiCo thus bases its corporate strategy on expanding abroad, and on diversifying into businesses related to its famous Pepsi brand beverages.

Companies can pursue several generic (or standard) corporate strategic options when deciding on what basis to build their business portfolio:

corporate-level strategy
Identifies the sorts of businesses that will comprise the company and the ways in which these businesses relate to each other.

- A *diversification* corporate strategy implies that the firm will expand by adding new product lines.
- A *vertical integration* strategy means the firm expands by, perhaps, producing its own raw materials, or selling its products direct.
- A *consolidation* strategy means reducing the company's size.
- *Geographic expansion* means expanding the firm into new locations, for example, taking the business abroad.
- A *concentration* strategy means the firm opts to limit itself to one line of business—McDonald's is an example of such a "one business" business.

FIGURE 3.3

Relationships Among Strategies in Multiple-Business Firms

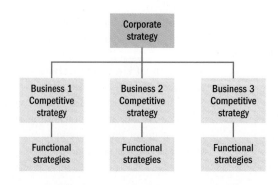

competitive strategy
Identifies how to build and strengthen the business's long-term competitive position in the marketplace.

competitive advantage
Any factors that allow an organization to differentiate its product or service from those of its competitors to increase market share.

COMPETITIVE STRATEGY At the next level down, each of these businesses (such as Frito-Lay) needs its own *business-level/competitive strategy.* A **competitive strategy** identifies how to build and strengthen the business's long-term competitive position in the marketplace.[8] It identifies, for instance, how Carrefour will compete with Tesco or how Dixons competes with Comet. Companies try to achieve competitive advantages for each business they are in. We can define **competitive advantage** as any factors that allow a company to differentiate its product or service from those of its competitors to increase market share. Companies use several generic competitive strategies to achieve competitive advantage:

- *Cost leadership* means the enterprise aims to become the low-cost leader in an industry. Dell is a classic example. It maintains its competitive advantage through its Internet-based sales-processing and distribution system, and by selling direct.
- *Differentiation* is a second example of a competitive strategy. In a differentiation strategy, a firm seeks to be unique in its industry along dimensions that are widely valued by buyers.[9] Thus, Volvo stresses the safety of its cars, Papa John's Pizza stresses fresh ingredients, Marks & Spencer sells somewhat more upscale brands than NEXT, and Mercedes-Benz emphasizes reliability and quality. Like Mercedes-Benz, firms can usually charge a premium price if they successfully stake a claim to being substantially different from competitors in some coveted way.
- *Focusers* carve out a market niche (like Ferrari), and compete by providing a product or service customers can get in no other way.

functional strategies
Identify the basic courses of action that each department will pursue in order to help the business attain its competitive goals.

FUNCTIONAL STRATEGY Finally, each individual business (like Frito-Lay, or Quaker Oats) is composed of departments, such as manufacturing, sales, and human resource management. **Functional strategies** identify the basic courses of action that each department will pursue in order to help the business attain its competitive goals.

The firm's functional strategies should make sense in terms of its business/competitive strategy. For example, the Portman Ritz-Carlton (Shanghai) Hotel's human resource management strategies aim to support management's efforts to offer premier customer service as the hotel's competitive advantage. The accompanying *Business in Action* feature illustrates how managers tie their corporate, competitive, and functional strategies together.

Business in Action   Achieving Strategic Fit

Strategic planning expert Michael Porter says managers should ensure that their firms' functional strategies align with and support their competitive strategies. For example, Southwest Airlines, much like EasyJet in Europe, pursues a low-cost leader strategy. Southwest tailors its functional departmental strategies and activities to deliver low-cost, convenient service on its short-haul routes. It gets fast, 15-minute turnarounds at the gate, so it can keep its planes flying longer hours than rivals and have more departures with fewer aircraft. It generally shuns the frills like meals, assigned seats, and premium classes of service on which other full-service airlines build their competitive strategies.

Figure 3.4 illustrates this. The larger circles represent the activities at the heart of Southwest's low-cost activity system:

limited passenger services; frequent, reliable departures; lean, highly productive ground and gate crews; high aircraft utilization; very low ticket prices; and short-haul, point-to-point routes. Various functional subactivities and decisions support each of these activities. For example, limited passenger service means things like no meals, no seat assignments, no baggage transfers, and limited use of travel agents. Highly productive ground crews mean high compensation, flexible union contracts, and a high level of employee stock ownership. Southwest's successful low-cost strategy reflects a well-managed system in which each functional component fits each other component. Southwest's human resource function strategies in turn support the airline's need for high compensation, flexible union contracts, and a high level of employee stock ownership *(continued)*

FIGURE 3.4

The Southwest Airlines´ Activity System

Note: Companies like Southwest tailor all their activities so that they fit and contribute to making their strategies a reality.

Source: Reprinted by permission of *Harvard Business Review*. From "What Is Strategy?" by Michael E. Porter, November–December 1996. Copyright © 1996 by the President and Fellows of Harvard College. All Rights Reserved.

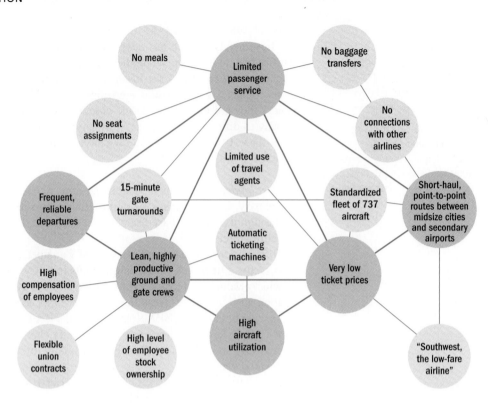

The Importance of Leverage

Strategic fit is a useful concept, but in practice managers can't always get a perfect match between what they can do and what they should do. For example, their situational analysis may reveal that there are opportunities they could pursue, but that they don't have the requisite corporate assets. Or, they may face great competitive threats for which the firm hasn't the strengths to respond.

Strategy experts Hamel and Prahalad agree that every company "must ultimately synchronize" its opportunities and its resources. However, they argue that being too preoccupied with fit can limit growth. Basically, they say there are times when, to pursue opportunities, the manager must underplay the firm's weaknesses, and instead capitalize on some unique core company strength.

leveraging
Supplementing what you have and doing more with what you have.

Put another way, they say that **leveraging** resources—supplementing what you have and doing more with what you have—can be more important than just fitting the strategic plan to current resources. For example, "If modest resources were an insurmountable deterrent to future leadership, American automaker General Motors would not have found itself on the defensive with Honda." Dell—competing with giant IBM at the time—focused its relatively limited resources on building a direct sales operation and highly efficient order processing and distribution system. Apple—competing against relative giants like Microsoft and IBM—capitalized on its competitive strengths in innovating new products, introducing items like the IPhone. All these companies cultivated unique competitive advantages, and then leveraged or built on these advantages to outmaneuver their rivals. And in most of these cases, the skills and knowledge of their employees were a big part of those competitive advantages.

HOW HUMAN RESOURCE MANAGEMENT CREATES COMPETITIVE ADVANTAGE

Every successful company has one or more competitive advantages—factors that enable the company to differentiate its product or service from those of its competitors to increase market share. Apple has creative employees producing innovative products. Southwest

Longo's human resources policies and practices encourage hiring and developing salespeople who speak everything from Spanish and Korean to Tagalog.

Airlines achieves its low-cost leader goals with employment policies that produce the motivated workforce it needs to turn planes in 15 minutes.

Types of Competitive Advantage

Competitive advantages can take many forms. For a pharmaceuticals company, like GlaxoSmithKline it may be the quality of its research team, and its patents. For Google or MySpace, it is their proprietary software systems.

LONGO TOYOTA EXAMPLE Some managers assume that workforce diversity creates conflict and higher cost. But the owners of Longo Toyota in El Monte, California, use diversity as a competitive advantage. Longo's human resources policies and practices encourage hiring and developing salespeople who speak everything from Spanish and Korean to Tagalog.

Because of that human resource strategy, Longo is a top-grossing auto dealer. With a 60-person sales force that speaks more than 20 languages, Longo's staff provides it with a powerful competitive advantage for serving El Monte's highly diverse customer base. While other dealerships lose half of their salespeople each year, Longo retains 90% of its staff, in part by emphasizing a promotion-from-within policy (more than two-thirds of its managers are minorities). It has also taken steps to attract more women. For instance, Longo assigned a sales management staff person to spend time providing the training that inexperienced salespeople need. In a business in which competitors can easily imitate products, showrooms, and most services, Longo has built a competitive advantage based on employee diversity.

Why Human Resources Are Important

In today's global business environment, it's hard to have machinery, technology, or processes that aren't also available to your competitors. For example, Longo Toyota's sales, maintenance, finance, and advertising systems are basically similar to those shared by all Toyota dealers. How then can Longo set itself apart? Longo opted for having a skilled, competent, motivated, diverse workforce, one committed to using their expertise for the company's benefit. As another example, Toyota Motor Manufacturing does not have manufacturing equipment that's unavailable to Ford. Why then is Toyota so much more efficient, and its cars of such high quality? At Toyota's Burnaston, Derbyshire, Corolla plant, a visitor would find small teams of carefully selected and highly trained assembly workers inspecting and assessing their own work, selecting their own team members, interacting with engineers and suppliers to improve components, meeting with the plant's top managers, and spending several weeks each year being trained. Costs are low and quality is high because the self-managing teams have the capacity and commitment to do their best. Toyota's human resource strategies—a full week of employee screening and testing, three weeks per year of training, and team-based rewards that incentivize the assembly teams to self-manage their own performance, for instance—ensure they do.

In other words, even in the most technologically automated facilities, it's the employees' skills and commitment (and the management system that produces the skills and commitment) that create the competitive advantage. A production expert from Harvard University studied manufacturing firms that installed computer-integrated manufacturing systems to boost efficiency and flexibility. He summed it up this way:

All the data in my study point to one conclusion: Operational flexibility is determined primarily by a plant's operators and the extent to which managers cultivate, measure, and communicate with them. Equipment and computer integration are secondary.[10]

Strategic Human Resource Management

Longo and Southwest Airlines and Toyota use strategic human resource management to cultivate the employee skills and behaviors that they need to achieve their strategic goals. We said that strategic human resource management means *formulating and executing human resource policies and practices that produce the employee competencies and behaviors the company needs to achieve its strategic aims.* The basic process of strategic human resource management is simple. First, *decide what the strategic goals are,* then *identify the employee skills and behaviors that achieving these goals require,* and then, *formulate human resource management policies and practices that will produce these required employee skills and behaviors.*

HUMAN RESOURCE STRATEGIES Managers use the term "human resource strategies" to refer to the specific human resource management policies and practices the company uses to help achieve its strategic aims.[11] For example, one of FedEx's strategic aims is to achieve superior levels of customer service and high profitability through a highly committed workforce. FedEx's human resource strategies stem from this aim. They include building two-way communications, screening out potential managers whose values are not people-oriented, guaranteeing to the greatest extent possible fair treatment and employee security for all employees, and utilizing various promotion-from-within activities to give employees every opportunity to fully realize their potential. Figure 3.5 illustrates the interplay between human resource strategy and the company's strategic plans and results.

SOUTHWEST AIRLINES STRATEGIC HR EXAMPLE Most of the passengers boarding Southwest Airlines' flight 172 from Orlando to Louisville probably aren't thinking about how Southwest keeps its prices low. Those who are may assume it's Southwest's young fleet of planes or fuel-buying policies—but those aren't the main reasons. If they were, other U.S.-based airlines United and Delta could just copy Southwest.

Southwest's real secret is its human resource management strategy. Strategic human resource management means formulating and executing human resource management policies and practices *that produce the employee competencies and behaviors the company needs to achieve its strategic aims.* What are Southwest's aims? Its basic aim is to deliver low-cost, convenient service on short-haul routes. How does it do this? One big way is by getting fast, 15-minute turnarounds at the gate, thus keeping planes flying longer hours than rivals. What employee competencies and skills does Southwest need

FIGURE 3.5

Linking Company–Wide and HR Strategies

Source: © Gary Dessler, Ph.D., 2007.

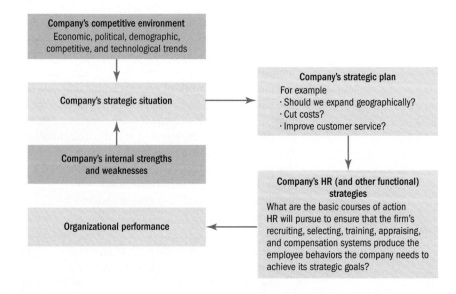

for these fast turnarounds? Ground crews, gate employees, and even pilots who all pitch in and do whatever it takes to get planes turned around. And what human resource management policies and practices would produce such employee competencies and behaviors? An HR strategy built on high compensation, flexible job assignments, cross training, and employee stock ownership. We can outline this as follows: (1) high compensation, flexible work assignments, and so forth, *lead to* (2) motivated flexible ground crews and employees, *who do whatever it takes to* (3) turn the planes around in 15 minutes, *so that* (4) Southwest achieves its strategic aims of delivering low-cost, convenient service.

DELL STRATEGIC HR EXAMPLE Dell's competitive strategy is to be a low-cost leader.

Dell's human resource managers use various HR strategies to support Dell's low-cost aims. For example, Dell's human resource management team delivers most of its human resources services via the Web. A Manager Tools section on Dell's intranet contains about 30 automated Web applications (including executive search reports, hiring tools, and automated employee referrals). This allows managers to perform human resource tasks that previously required costly participation by human resource personnel. The intranet also lets Dell employees administer their own 401(k) plans, check job postings, and monitor their total compensation statements. This dramatically reduces the number of human resource people required to administer these activities, and thus the cost of doing so.[12]

FOUR IMPORTANT STRATEGIC HUMAN RESOURCE ISSUES Examples like Southwest and Dell suggest four issues employers should keep in mind when deciding how to design their strategic human resource management policies:

1. First, global competition requires continually improving quality and performance, and this in turn requires that most firms *build their competitive advantages in whole or part around their employees*. For example, all the elements we associate with high-performance companies like Toyota—such as high-technology team based production—depend on motivated and skilled employees.
2. Second, with employee performance the centerpiece of many employers' performance-improvement efforts, employers expect their human resource managers to *improve employee and organizational performance in measurable ways*.
3. Third, with employee performance so critical, *human resource units must be more involved in designing—not just executing—the company's strategic plan.* It used to be just the company's operating (line) managers who helped design the company's strategic plan. Now, top management needs the human resource team's input, since HR does the hiring, training, and compensating of the firm's employees.
4. Fourth, numbers 1–3 have implications for the training and skills that HR managers need. They need *"an in-depth understanding of the value-creating proposition of the firm [in other words, a basic functional understanding of how the firm makes money]."*[13] Human resource managers should understand the basics of strategic planning, and of accounting, finance, production, and sales. They need to understand things like, "What company activities and processes are most critical for value creation as defined by customers and capital markets?" And, "Who in the firm executes these activities successfully?" HR managers with these skills will (as human resource gurus put it) get their "seat at the table" when top management designs the strategic plan.

HUMAN RESOURCE MANAGEMENT'S STRATEGIC ROLES

When it comes to how involved human resource managers should be in strategic planning, there is often a disconnect between what CEOs say and do. Some employers lean heavily on their human resource management teams. Many don't.

How Involved Is HR in Strategic Management?

Some CEOs do work on the assumption that human resource managers' input is crucial.[14] For example, General Motors CEO Rick Wagner:

> . . . organized a senior executive committee (the "Automotive Strategies Board"). It included GM's chief financial officer, chief information officer, and vice president of global human resources. As Wagner says, "I seek [the HR vice president's] counsel and perspective constantly. She has demonstrated a tremendous capacity to think and act strategically, which is essential to our HR function and what we want to achieve in making GM a globally competitive business."[15]

Some studies support the wisdom of such an approach. A study from the University of Michigan concluded that high-performing companies' human resource professionals should be part of the firm's strategic planning team. They help the team identify the human issues that are vital to business strategy. They help conceptualize and execute the organizational changes that companies need to execute their strategic plans. Another study, by Mercer Consulting, concluded that 39% of CEOs surveyed see human resources as more of a partner than a cost center.[16]

However, surveys suggest that only about half of employers said senior human resource managers are involved in developing their companies' business plans.[17] A survey by the Society for Human Resource Management demonstrates the current situation regarding employers' use of strategic human resource management.[18] Overall, about 75% of the human resource managers surveyed said their companies had strategic plans in place. However, only about 56% of those in firms with strategic plans in place said their human resources departments had their own (departmental) strategic plans.

Table 3.1 summarizes these latter results. As you can see, 56% of the HR managers say "to a large extent" they work closely with senior management in creating strategic plans; 68% say they do so with respect to actually implementing the plans.

TABLE 3.1   Extent of HR's Involvement in Strategic Planning (According to HR Managers)

(n = 236)	To a Large Extent	To Some Extent	To No Extent
HR works closely with senior management in *implementing* organizational strategies	68%	29%	3%
HR works closely with senior management in *creating* organizational strategies	56%	38%	6%
HR has achieved a level of respect that is comparable with other departments in the organization	49%	45%	6%
Senior management realizes that investments in HR make financial sense	47%	47%	6%
HR *implements* strategies and processes to drive business results	46%	49%	6%
HR is involved in the communication of the business goals	46%	41%	14%
The role of HR is increasingly more focused on strategic interests	43%	49%	8%
HR is involved in the alignment of the business goals	42%	49%	10%
HR involvement is essential in all major business activities and decisions	36%	57%	7%
HR *creates* strategies and processes to drive business results	36%	54%	10%
HR is involved in the development of the business goals	31%	55%	14%
HR is involved in monitoring the achievement of business goals	30%	49%	21%

Note: Sample size is based on the actual number of respondents who answered this question using the response options provided. Percentages within each category may not total 100% due to rounding.

Source: Adapted from Society for Human Resource Management, 2006. www.shrm.org, accessed May 10, 2007.

Global Issues in HR

Offshoring

offshoring
Having local employees abroad do jobs that the firm's domestic employees previously did in-house.

Offshoring increasingly plays a role in employers' competitive and human resource strategies. **Offshoring** "is the exporting of jobs from developed countries to countries where labor and other costs are lower."[19] When a pharmaceuticals company decides to have its drugs produced in China, or you find yourself on the phone with a call center employee in Bangalore India, offshoring is taking place.

Historically, offshoring involved mostly lower-skilled manufacturing jobs, as when clothing manufacturers chose to assemble their garments abroad. Increasingly however, employers—seeking to reduce costs and stay competitive—are offshoring thousands of higher-skilled jobs, for instance in financial, legal, and security analysis.

It's advisable to involve the human resource team in the earliest stages of gathering information about things like the educational and pay levels of the countries to which the firm is thinking of offshoring. However, HR's main involvement occurs usually once the decision is made. For example, the human resource management team needs to establish policies governing things like compliance with ethical safety and work standards, and pay levels. HR's involvement at home may be even more crucial. Current, home-country employees and their unions may well resist the transfer of work. Maintaining employee commitment, and maintaining open communications with employees, is therefore important.[20]

In practice, human resource managers can play roles in both *strategy execution* and in *strategy formulation (strategic planning)*. Offshoring (see *Global Issues in HR*) is one area requiring both.

HR's Strategy Execution Role

Strategy execution is traditionally the heart of the human resource manager's strategic job. Top management formulates the company's corporate and competitive strategies. Then, the human resource manager formulates human resource management policies and practices that make sense in terms of what the company is trying to accomplish strategically.

We've already discussed several examples. Shanghai Portman's new human resource policies and practices help improve customer service and thus make the hotel a premier property. Dell's human resource policies and activities—the Web-based help desk, its centralized intranet service bureau—help the firm better execute Dell's low-cost strategy. FedEx's human resources strategies—supporting communication and employee development, for instance—help FedEx differentiate itself from its competitors by offering superior customer service.

HR's Strategy Formulation Role

We've seen that employers are expanding human resource management's traditional strategy execution role to include working with top management to actually help formulate the employer's strategic plan.

This reflects the reality employers face today. Globalization means more competition. More competition means more performance. And, most employers (such as Ritz-Carlton, Dell, and Toyota) pursue improved performance (in whole or part) by boosting the competence and commitment levels of their employees. That makes human resource management's knowledge and expertise (in issues such as, "How can we boost employee productivity?") vital at the strategy formulation stage.

The human resource manager supports strategy formulation in several ways, most notably at the situational, SWOT analysis, stage as follows.

EXTERNAL OPPORTUNITIES AND THREATS The human resource manager is in a unique position to supply competitive intelligence that may be useful in strategic planning. Details regarding competitors' incentive plans, opinion survey data from employees that elicit information about customer complaints, and information about pending legislation such as labor laws and mandatory health insurance are some examples. Furthermore:

> From public information and legitimate recruiting and interview activities, you ought to be able to construct organization charts, staffing levels, and group missions for the various organizational components of each of your major competitors. Your knowledge of how brands are sorted among sales divisions and who reports to whom can give important clues as to a competitor's strategic priorities. You may even know the track record and characteristic behavior of the executives.[21]

INTERNAL STRENGTHS AND WEAKNESSES Human resource management is ideally positioned to offer insights regarding the company's own human strengths and weaknesses.

For example, several years ago, a Great Britain-based metal fabrication company decided that to compete effectively, it had to move its operations to a new highly automated plant. However, doing so required that production workers grasp a whole new set of skills: using computers, reading technical manuals, working in teams, and so on. Therefore, before the CEO could move far along in his strategic planning, he needed input from HR on his employees' competencies and skills. How many were computer literate? How many had the educational background to assimilate the new training? What math competencies did they have? And could the company provide the necessary training, on time, or would they have to turn to outside vendors—or to hiring all new workers?

Some firms, thanks to such input, even build new strategies around human resource strengths. For example, in the process of automating its factories, U.S. farm equipment manufacturer John Deere developed a workforce that was exceptionally expert in factory automation. This prompted the firm to start a new-technology division to offer automation services to other companies. The *HR in Practice* summarizes the strategic HR process.

HR in Practice

How to Translate Strategy into Human Resource Policy and Practice

Let us step back and review, with an example, how the human resource manager translates the company's strategic plan into HR policies and practices.[22] Figure 3.6 outlines the basic process.

- Management (hopefully with HR's input) formulates a *strategic plan*.
- The strategic plan implies certain *workforce requirements*, in terms of the employee skills, attributes, and behaviors that the human resource management team must deliver to enable the business to achieve its strategic goals. (For example, must our employees dramatically improve the level of customer service?[23] Do we need more computer-literate employees to run our new machines?)

- Given these workforce requirements, human resource management formulates *HR strategies, policies, and practices* it believes will produce the desired workforce skills, attributes, and behaviors. (These may take the form of new selection, training, and compensation policies and practices, for instance.)[24]
- Finally, the human resource manager identifies measures he or she can use to gauge the extent to which its new policies and practices are actually producing the required employee competencies and skills, and thus supporting management's strategic goals. For example, how many weeks of training per year do our employees receive?

FIGURE 3.6

How to Align HR Strategy and Actions with Business Strategy

Source: Adapted from Garrett Walker and J. Randal MacDonald, "Designing and Implementing an HR Scorecard," *Human Resources Management* 40, no. 4 (2001): 370.

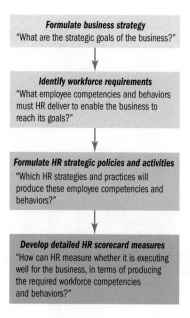

Strategic Human Resource Management: Einstein Medical Example

When he took over in the 1990s, it was apparent to Einstein Medical Hospital's new CEO that things had to change. Intense competition, technological changes, the growth of managed care, and significant cuts in U.S. health care programs Medicare and Medicaid meant that his company needed a new strategic plan. At the time, Einstein Medical was a single acute-care hospital, treating the seriously ill.[25]

EINSTEIN MEDICAL'S NEW STRATEGY AND GOALS The essence of the CEO's new strategy plan was to redefine its business—specifically, to turn Einstein Medical into a comprehensive health care network, one with multiple facilities offering a full range of health care services in various local markets.

Executing a massive change like that is never easy. The CEO knew that achieving this change from a single acute-care hospital to a far-flung network of full-care facilities would require numerous changes in how Einstein Medical and its employees did things. For one thing, he felt that executing such a huge change would require a much more flexible, adaptable, and professional approach to delivering services. Based on that, he summarized the employee-related strategic goals of his change program in three words: "initiate," "adapt," and "deliver." To achieve Einstein Medical's strategic aims, its human resource and other strategies would have to help the medical center and its employees to *produce new services (initiate), capitalize on opportunities (adapt),* and offer consistently *high-quality services (deliver).*

NEW EMPLOYEE COMPETENCIES AND BEHAVIORS The CEO then turned to the question, "What employee competencies, skills, and behaviors will Einstein Medical need to produce these three outcomes?" He worked with the head of human resources to identify four critical employee skills and behaviors: Einstein employees would need to be "dedicated, accountable, generative, and resilient."

1. They would have to be *dedicated* to Einstein's focus on initiate, adapt, and deliver.
2. They would have to take personal *accountability* for their results.
3. They would have to be *generative,* which means able and willing to apply new knowledge and skills in a constant search for innovative solutions.
4. And they would have to be *resilient,* for instance, in terms of moving from job to job as the company's needs changed.

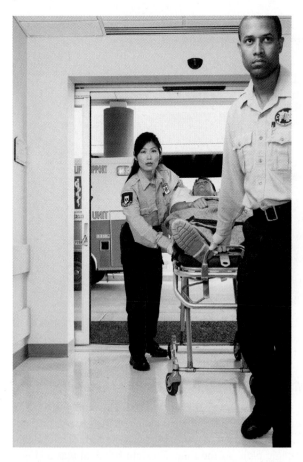

NEW HUMAN RESOURCE POLICIES AND PRACTICES Then, Einstein Medical's human resource manager could ask, "What specific HR policies and practices will enable Einstein to create a dedicated, accountable, generative, and resilient workforce?" The answer was to implement several new human resource programs:

- New *training and communications programs* aimed at ensuring that employees clearly understood the company's new vision and what it would require of all employees.
- *Enriching work* involved providing employees with more challenge and responsibility through flexible assignments and team-based work.
- New *training and benefits programs* promoted *personal growth,* which meant helping employees take personal responsibility for their own improvement and personal development.
- Providing *commensurate returns* involved tying employees' rewards to organizationwide results and providing nonmonetary rewards (such as more challenging jobs).
- *Improved selection, orientation, and dismissal procedures* also helped Einstein build a more dedicated, resilient, accountable, and generative workforce.

Supporting top management in planning and executing mergers, acquisitions, and similar restructurings is an increasingly important part of the human resource manager's strategic management role. We turn to this next.

Einstein Medical's human resource manager had to ask, "What specific HR policies and practices will enable Einstein to create a dedicated, accountable, generative, and resilient workforce?"

STRATEGIC HR IN ACTION: HUMAN RESOURCE MANAGEMENT'S ROLE IN MERGERS AND ACQUISITIONS

Mergers, acquisitions, and restructurings are ubiquitous today. In one recent year giant corporations or private equity firms acquired 42 of the Fortune 1000 corporations. (Private equity firms attract investor capital, which they then use to buy and improve companies, so as to sell them in several years at a profit.) For example, in 2007 the private equity firm Cerberus purchased Chrysler Corporation from Daimler Corporation. Thousands of smaller firms were similarly merged or acquired.[26]

The Logic and Effectiveness of Mergers and Acquisitions

The logic driving most of these acquisitions is fairly simple, and is summed up by the word *synergy.* Basically, synergy means cutting costs or boosting revenues (or both) by combining operations. Thus, when Hewlett-Packard merged with Compaq, the idea, in part, was to enable the new HP to sell the same or more computers than did HP and Compaq alone (boost revenues), and to do so by eliminating duplicate ("redundant") accounting, advertising, sales, and other departments (cut expenses). Management gurus therefore sometimes define the synergy idea by saying it means "2 + 2 = 5."

The plan is often to achieve such results by reducing the workforce. The U.S. economy has thus experienced continuing waves of layoffs and downsizings in recent years. For example, in April 2007 alone, Citigroup announced it was eliminating 17,000 positions, while the financial sector as a whole (including Citigroup) announced plans to eliminate over 50,000 jobs. In just one month, February 2007, employers discharged about 1.2 million workers from their jobs involuntarily.[27]

Unfortunately, even with such layoffs (or, some would say, because of them), many mergers and acquisitions ("M&As") fail to achieve their financial goals. Estimates vary, but, until recently, it appears that only about half of all mergers and acquisitions achieved their anticipated outcomes.[28] Some put the success rate at 40% or less.[29]

Why a Human Resource Management Role in Mergers and Acquisitions?

When mergers and acquisitions fail, it's often not due to financial or technical issues (like inadequate financing) but to personnel-related ones. These may include, for example, employee resistance, mass exits by high-quality employees, declining morale and productivity, inadequate financial incentives, and unexpectedly high benefits expenses. People problems can also manifest themselves in other, tangible ways. These include, for instance, product development delays, losing respected employees, declining sales productivity, and customer defections.[30] As one study concluded some years ago, mergers and acquisitions often fail due to "a lack of adequate preparation of the personnel involved and a failure to provide training which fosters self-awareness, cultural sensitivity, and a spirit of cooperation."[31]

INVOLVEMENT BY HR It's therefore ironic that until recently top executives rarely involved their human resource managers in planning the merger or acquisition. Surveys by consultants Towers Perrin found that prior to 2000, HR executives tended to play relatively limited roles in M&A planning and due diligence, getting more involved only at the formal merger integration stage. Today, by contrast, "close to two-thirds of the [survey] participants are involved in M&A due diligence now, and fully three-quarters expect a high degree of involvement in due diligence and future deals."[32]

Even private equity firms, known for their hard-nosed financial approach to deals, increasingly tap human resource management expertise early on. For example, "because they are looking to sell the company for a profit within a few years, private equity investors turn to HR to create incentive plans with short-term goals of generating cash." HR can also provide critical early information (for instance, regarding which employees and executives to keep), as well as guidance in installing employee retention plans and instituting new compensation and incentive plans.[33] As the head of the M&A practice at one consulting firm put it, "there is a growing understanding that people issues can make or break a deal."[34] This means involving the human resource team in the earliest M&A planning stages.

HR AND M&A RESULTS So, while it may be a coincidence, it's probably not surprising that there's been (1) a rise in M&A success as (2) employers have involved their human resource experts earlier. Prior to 2000, HR tended to be less involved, and (as noted) about half of all mergers and acquisitions failed to meet their shareholders expectations.[35] In contrast, a more recent survey concluded that almost 80% of recent mergers and acquisitions had satisfactory results; the reason, in part, "is that HR functions now have far greater involvement in the process than in the past—at earlier stages as well—and believe they are increasingly well-prepared to identify and address the many."[36] Another survey of 1,310 human resource management professionals found that mergers in which top management asked human resource management to apply its expertise consistently outperformed those in which human resources was less involved.[37] Figure 3.7 summarizes the findings.

FIGURE 3.7

Percent of Successful Mergers in Which HR Manager Was Involved

Source: HR Magazine by Jeffrey Schmidt. Copyright 2001 by Society for Human Resource Management (S H R M). Reproduced with permission of Society for Human Resource Management (S H R M) in the format Textbook via Copyright Clearance Center.

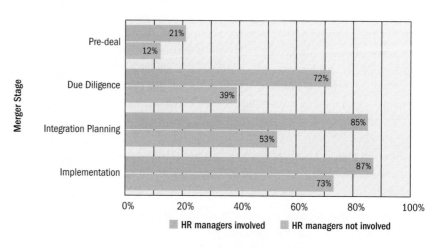

Percent of Successful Mergers

Human Resource Management's Specific Merger and Acquisition Roles

In general, top management requires human resource management expertise at the M&A *planning, due diligence, and integration* stages. In *planning* its initial offer, for example, the acquiring team will benefit from having information about the acquisition target on matters such as total headcount, benefits and pension obligations, and pending litigation—all matters generally accessible via public sources.

DUE DILIGENCE STAGE Before finalizing a deal, its usual for the acquirer (or merger partners) to perform due diligence reviews, to ensure it (or they) know what they're getting into. For the human resource teams, such due diligence reviews include reviewing, for instance, organizational culture and structure, employee compensation and benefits, industrial relations, pending employee litigation, human resource policies and procedures, and key talent analysis.[38]

Employee benefits are one obvious area for personnel due diligence and analysis. For example, do the target firm's health insurance contracts have termination clauses that could eliminate coverage for all employees if too many are laid off after the acquisition? If the acquired company's employee benefits are higher than yours, will you maintain those, lower them, or raise yours? How much do you estimate it will cost in separation benefits—severance, continuing health benefits, and higher unemployment compensation charges, for instance? And who will pay any COBRA health insurance benefits, the seller or the buyer?[39]

INTEGRATION STAGE The human resource team has numerous responsibilities as the merger or acquisition moves into the integration stage. Critical human resource management team issues during the first few months of a merger, acquisition, or restructuring include ensuring effective top management leadership, choosing the top team, communicating effectively with employees, retaining key talent, and aligning the cultures of the organizations.[40] The accompanying *Personal Competencies* feature explains how to size up organizational cultures.

organizational culture
The characteristic values, traditions, and behaviors a company's employees share.

Personal Competencies

Building Your *Organizational Culture* Skills

Sometimes, the most challenging aspect of the merger is blending the two firms' **organizational cultures**—the *basic values its employees share and the ways in which these values manifest themselves in the companies' ways of doing things and in their employees' behavior.* For example, some attribute Motorola's lackluster performance in the early 2000s to the company's culture, which one writer described as "stifling bureaucracy, snail-paced decision making . . . and internal competition so fierce that [former CEO] Galvin himself has referred to it as a 'culture of warring tribes.'"[41]

The first step in changing or merging the cultures is to understand what they are now. Suggestions for doing so include:[42]

- *Observe the physical surroundings.* Look at how the employees dress, the openness among offices, the furniture and its placement, and any signs (such as a long list of activities that are "prohibited here").

- *Sit in on a team meeting.* How do the employees treat each other? Are the communications open or one-sided?

- *Listen to the language.* Is there a lot of talk about "quality," "perfection," and "going the extra mile"? Or is there more emphasis on "don't rock the boat," or "don't tell those people what we're doing."

- *Note to whom you are introduced and how they act.* Is the person casual or formal, laid-back or serious?

- *Get the views of outsiders, including vendors, customers, and former employees.* What do they think of the firm? Do you get responses like "they're so bureaucratic that it takes a year to get an answer"?

CREATING AND SUSTAINING THE RIGHT CORPORATE CULTURE The new CEO takes over a merged but struggling company. Backbiting, bureaucratic behavior, and disdain for clients are rampant. Having sized up the situation, what should the CEO do to change the culture? The thing to keep in mind is that it is the manager's behavior, not just what he or she says, that molds what employees come to see as the firm's real values. Experts suggest taking the following actions:[43]

1. *Make it clear to your employees what you pay attention to, measure, and control.* For example, direct your employees' attention toward controlling costs or serving customers if those are the values you want to emphasize. At Toyota, "quality and teamwork" are desirable values. Toyota's selection and training processes therefore focus on the candidate's orientation toward quality and teamwork.
2. *React appropriately* to critical incidents and organizational crises. For example, if you want to emphasize the value that "we're all in this together," don't react to declining profits by saying "it's their fault."
3. *Use signs, symbols, stories, rites, and ceremonies* to signal your values. JC Penney prides itself on loyalty and tradition. To support this, the firm inducts new management employees into the "Penney Partnership" at conferences where they commit to Penney's values of "honor, confidence, service, and cooperation."
4. *Deliberately role model, teach, and coach the values you want to emphasize.* For example, Wal-Mart founder Sam Walton lived the values "hard work, honesty, neighborliness, and thrift." He explained driving a pickup truck by saying, "If I drove a Rolls-Royce, what would I do with my dog?"
5. *Communicate your priorities by how you appraise employees and allocate rewards.* For example, General Foods reoriented its strategy from cost control to diversification and sales growth. It supported these new priorities by linking bonuses to sales volume and new-product development, rather than just increased earnings.

As an example, Lawrence Weinbach, chairman and CEO of Unisys, took many steps to change his firm's culture. His main aim was to focus employees on performance and execution. As he said, "We've moved to a pay-for-performance approach, to make sure that we're properly recognizing the people who are doing things right. . . . in some cases, we've needed to tell people to seek opportunities elsewhere . . . we've invested in training and education and created Unisys University, where employees can find courses and programs on a range of . . . business-related topics. We've also spent a lot of time communicating and educating people about the importance of execution."[44]

OUTLINE OF SPECIFIC M&A ROLES Several global human resource consulting companies provide M&A-related human resource management services. A review of these services provides a useful outline of the sorts of practical M&A issues employers expect their human resource experts to be able to address. For example, consultant Towers Perrin's HR Services unit provides the following mergers, acquisitions, and restructuring services:

- *Manage the deal price:* For example, identify and quantify people-related costs, risks, and potential synergies. These range from purely pension issues to items such as redundancy costs and stock options.
- *Manage the messages:* "We support our clients in rapidly developing and deploying an employee communication strategy."
- *Secure the top team and key talent:* Help clients to identify key talent, and then develop suitable retention strategies.
- *Prioritize and manage activities:* Insofar as the integration of the two businesses is a project, Towers Perrin provides project management support, for instance, with respect to staffing a dedicated project management office for the restructuring.
- *Define and implement an effective HR service delivery strategy:* Towers Perrin helps its clients plan out how they're going to implement the delivery of HR services, such as in combining payroll systems.

- *Develop a workable change management plan:* "Especially in cross-border transactions, we assist companies in understanding and managing the cultural differences they face as part of the deal."
- *Design and implement the right staffing model:* Help companies design the organization structure and determine which employee is best for which role.
- *Align total rewards:* "When integration is desirable, we help companies' benchmarking and integration of compensation and benefit programs."
- *Measure synergies:* Based on the synergy goals and targets the company identified during due diligence, Towers Perrin helps them deliver on those targets and track their progress.[45]

TWO EXAMPLES Several examples can further illustrate human resource managers' M&A responsibilities. When HP and Compaq merged in 2001, HP charged its top human resource officer with taking the lead in tasks such as blending the two firms' cultures, designing the new organization, and helping select the executive team, along with calculating cost considerations regarding health care plans, pensions, and the number of employees the combined company can afford.[46]

Several years ago Shaws Supermarkets acquired Star Markets. At the time, Shaws had 126 stores and Star had 54.[47] The activities the two firms' human resource management teams addressed included developing preliminary organizational designs and identifying the top three levels of management; assessing critical players and critical managers and employees in the new company; retention of key people, and planning for and executing the separation of redundant staff; developing a total rewards strategy for the combined company; developing and implementing a communication strategy to inform employees about the acquisition; and integration of payroll benefits and human resource information systems.[48]

Review

SUMMARY

1. In formulating their human resource strategies, HR managers must address several issues, such as: the need to support corporate productivity and performance improvement efforts, the fact that employees play an expanded role in the employer's performance improvement efforts, and the fact that HR must be more involved in designing—not just executing—the company's strategic plan.

2. There are seven basic steps in the strategic management process: Define the business and its mission, perform an external and internal audit, formulate new business and mission statements, translate the mission into strategic goals, formulate a strategy to achieve the strategic goals, implement the strategy, and evaluate performance.

3. There are three main types of strategic plans. The company's corporate-level strategy identifies the portfolio of businesses that in total comprise the company and includes diversification, vertical integration, consolidation, and geographic expansion. Each business needs a business level/competitive strategy: Differentiation and cost leadership are two examples. Finally, each individual business is composed of departments that require functional strategies. The latter identify the basic courses of action each department will pursue in order to help the business attain its strategic goals.

4. A strategy is a course of action. It shows how the enterprise will move from the business it is in now to the business it wants to be in, given its opportunities and threats and its internal strengths and weaknesses.

5. Strategic human resource management means formulating and executing HR systems that produce the employee competencies and behaviors the company requires to achieve its strategic aims.

6. The basic process of aligning human resources strategies and actions with business strategy entails four steps: Formulate the business strategy, identify the workforce (employee) behaviors needed to produce the outcomes that will help the company achieve its strategic goals, formulate human resources strategic policies and actions to produce these employee behaviors, and develop measures (metrics) to evaluate the human resources department's performance.

7. There's been (1) a rise in M&A success as (2) employers have involved their human resource experts earlier. Prior to 2000, HR tended to be less involved. In contrast, a more recent survey concluded that almost 80% of recent mergers and acquisitions had satisfactory results; the reason, in part, "is that HR functions now have far greater involvement in the process than in the past.

8. Top management requires HR expertise at the M&A *planning, due diligence, and integration* stages. In *planning* its initial offer, for example, the acquiring team will benefit from having information about the acquisition target on matters such as total headcount. Before finalizing a deal, HR due diligence reviews include reviewing, for instance, employee compensation and benefits, industrial relations, and pending employee litigation. As the merger or acquisition moves into the integration stage, critical HR team issues include ensuring effective top management leadership.

KEY TERMS

strategic human resource management   76
strategic plan   77
strategic planning   77
strategy   77
strategic management   77
SWOT analysis   78
vision statement   78
mission statement   78

strategic control   79
corporate-level strategy   80
competitive strategy   81
competitive advantage   81
functional strategies   81
leveraging   82
offshoring   87
organizational cultures   92

DISCUSSION QUESTIONS AND EXERCISES

1. What is the difference between a strategy, a vision, and a mission? Please give one example of each.
2. Define and give at least two examples of the cost leadership competitive strategy and the differentiation competitive strategy.
3. Explain how human resource management can be instrumental in helping a company create a competitive advantage.
4. What is meant by "HR adding value"? Provide several examples of how HR managers add value to their companies.
5. With three or four other students, form a strategic management group for your college or university. Your assignment is to develop the outline of a strategic plan for the college or university. This should include such things as mission and vision statements; strategic goals; and corporate, competitive, and functional strategies. In preparing your plan, make sure to show the main strengths, weaknesses, opportunities, and threats the college faces, and which prompted you to develop your particular strategic plans.
6. Using the Internet or library resources, analyze the annual reports of five companies. Bring to class examples of how those companies say they are using their HR processes to help the company achieve its strategic goals.
7. Interview an HR manager and write a short report on the topic "The strategic roles of the HR manager at XYZ Company."

Application Exercises

HR in Action Case Incident 1

Is There Such a Thing as a *Socially Responsible* Acquisition?

Cerberus Buys Chrysler

Can an acquisition that entails dismissing hundreds or thousands of employees still be "socially responsible"? That's a question some are asking about the purchase by private equity firm Cerberus of Chrysler Corporation.

Corporate social responsibility refers to the extent to which companies should and do direct resources toward improving segments of society other than the firm's owners. In essence, "theories of corporate social responsibility suggest that there needs to be a balance between what business takes from society and what it gives back in return."[49] Socially responsible behavior might include creating jobs for minorities, controlling pollution, improving working conditions for one's employees abroad, or supporting educational facilities or cultural events, for example.[50]

The topic of social responsibility continues to provoke lively debate. On one point all or most agree: Acting in a socially responsible manner means being ethical, doing the right thing with respect to issues such as pollution or charitable contributions. The question is: Is a company that tries to do its best only for its owners any less ethical than one that tries to help customers, vendors, and employees, too? The answer depends on what you believe is the purpose of a business. Many perfectly ethical people believe that a company's only social responsibility is to its stockholders. Others disagree.

That's why, when Cerberus announced on May 14, 2007, that it was buying Chrysler, most observers believed the purchase didn't bode well for the United Auto Workers' union, or Chrysler's workers. "Everyone knows that private equity firms' primary objective is to make money," said a law professor at St. John's University in New York. "Cerberus is going to be ruthless in seeking out major concessions."[51] Several months earlier, DaimlerChrysler said it was laying off 13,000 workers. Most assumed the new owners would make even deeper cuts.[52] Chrysler's management had made several mistakes, including focusing too much on vans and trucks, just as the trend toward small cars was gaining speed. Cost cuts seemed inevitable.

However, Cerberus has a record of dealing well with unions.[53] For example, in an earlier purchase, Cerberus won the support of the United Food and Commercial Workers union. Another union head said, "Our union has a good relationship with Cerberus. . . . They worked with us to get things done."[54]

Still, it's clear that Cerberus must make changes, and these will impact Chrysler's employees. Cerberus has approached you for advice on several specific issues.

Questions

1. Assuming we want to make Chrysler more competitive, what strategy should we pursue and specifically what implications does that have for Chrysler's new human resource management strategy?
2. Before we hire you, give us a one-page explanation of how human resource management practices can help us with this acquisition at the planning, due diligence, and integration stages.
3. Is reducing the workforce necessarily socially irresponsible? Why?
4. Could Cerberus quickly reduce Chrysler's workforce by several thousand employees, but do so in a socially responsible manner? How?

HR in Action Case Incident 2 — The Carter Cleaning Company: The High-Quality Work System

As a recent graduate and person who keeps up with the business press, Jennifer is familiar with the benefits of programs such as total quality management and high-performance work systems.

Jack has installed a total quality program of sorts at Carter, and it has been in place for about five years. This program takes the form of employee meetings. Jack holds employee meetings periodically, but particularly when there is a serious problem in a store—such as poor-quality work or machine breakdowns. When problems like these arise, instead of trying to diagnose them himself or with Jennifer, he contacts all the employees in that store and meets with them as soon as the store closes. Hourly employees get extra pay for these meetings. The meetings have been fairly useful in helping Jack to identify and rectify several problems. For example, in one store all the fine white blouses were coming out looking dingy. It turned out that the cleaner-spotter had been ignoring the company rule that required cleaning ("boiling

down") the perchloroethylene cleaning fluid before washing items like these. As a result, these fine white blouses were being washed in cleaning fluid that had residue from other, earlier washes.

Jennifer now wonders whether these employee meetings should be expanded to give the employees an even bigger role in managing the Carter stores' quality. "We can't be everywhere watching everything all the time," she said to her father. "Yes, but these people only earn about $8 per hour. Will they really want to act like mini-managers?" he replied.

Questions

1. Would you recommend that the Carters expand their quality program? If so, specifically what form should it take?
2. Assume the Carters want to institute strategic human resource management practices as a test program in one of their stores. Write a one-page outline summarizing what such a program would consist of.

EXPERIENTIAL EXERCISE

Developing an HR Strategy for Starbucks

In 2008, Starbucks was facing serious challenges. Sales per store were stagnant or declining, and its growth rate and profitability were down. Many believed that its introduction of breakfast foods had diverted its "baristas" from their traditional jobs as coffee-preparation experts. McDonalds and Dunkin Donuts were introducing lower priced but still high-grade coffees. Starbucks' former CEO stepped back into the company's top job. You need to help him formulate a new direction for his company.

Purpose:

The purpose of this exercise is to give you experience in developing an HR strategy, in this case by developing one for Starbucks.

Required Understanding:

You should be thoroughly familiar with the material in this chapter, including the "Einstein Medical" HR strategy example, and Figure 3.6.

How to Set the Exercise/Instructions:

Set up groups of three or four students for this exercise. You are probably already quite familiar with what it's like to have a cup of coffee or tea in a Starbucks coffee shop, but if not, spend some time in one prior to this exercise. Meet in groups and develop an outline for an HR strategy for Starbucks Corp. Your outline should include four basic elements, as follows: A basic business/competitive strategy for Starbucks, workforce requirements (in terms of employee competencies and behaviors) this strategy requires, specific HR policies and the activities necessary to produce these workforce requirements, and suggestions for metrics to use to measure the success of the HR strategy.

Part I Video Cases Appendix

VIDEO 1: INTRODUCTION TO HUMAN RESOURCE MANAGEMENT, AND STRATEGIC HUMAN RESOURCE MANAGEMENT

Video Title: Showtime

Showtime Networks operates cable networks and pay-per-view cable channels across the United States and in several countries abroad. As this video illustrates, its HR function supports corporate strategy by helping to determine what kind of employees are needed to keep the company in peak performance, and then by providing the company and its employees with the HR activities that these employees need to do their jobs. For example, you'll see that Showtime offers many development and training programs, as well as personal development–type activities including mentoring programs and career-oriented development activities. The firm's performance management process (which the employees helped develop) focuses specifically on the work activities and results that help achieve departmental and corporate goals. In this video, Matthew, the firm's CEO, emphasizes that it's essential to use human resources as a strategic partner, and the video then goes on to provide something of a summary of the basic human resource management functions.

Discussion Questions

1. What concrete evidence do you see in this video that HR at Showtime helps the company achieve its strategic goals?
2. What specific HR functions does the video mention, at least in passing?
3. Why do you think management at Showtime places such a heavy emphasis on personal development and quality of work issues such as open door policies, mentoring programs, and allowing employees to swap jobs?

VIDEO 2: MANAGING EQUAL OPPORTUNITY AND DIVERSITY

Video Title: IQ Solutions

IQ Solutions is in the business of providing health-care system services. It says one of its aims is lessening the inequality that it believes exists in America's health-care system, and the company uses its diverse employee base to better serve and attract a broad client base. Employees at IQ Solutions work together in teams to achieve the company's goals. As we see in this video, the company itself is indeed very diverse: for example, employees speak about 18 languages. The company capitalizes on this diversity in many ways. For example, it lets its employees share their ethnically unique holidays, and provides special training and other benefits that support diversity.

Discussion Questions

1. To what extent does diversity management at IQ Solutions contribute to the company achieving its strategic goals?
2. Based upon what you read in this part of the book, which diversity management programs can you identify in use at IQ Solutions?

ENDNOTES

1. Arthur Yeung, "Setting Up for Success: How the Portman Ritz-Carlton Hotel Gets the Best from Its People," *Human Resource Management* 45, no. 2 (Summer 2006): 67–75.
2. Ibid.
3. David Kesmodel, "New Safeway Business Takes Root," *Wall Street Journal* (December 3, 2007): A15.
4. Fred David, *Strategic Management* (Upper Saddle River, NJ: Prentice Hall, 2007): 11.
5. Ibid.

6. Warren Bennis and Bert Manus, *Leaders: The Strategies for Taking Charge* (New York: Harper & Row, 1985), quoted in Andrew Campbell and Sally Yeung, "Mission, Vision and Strategic Intent," *Long-Range Planning* 24, no. 4 (1991): 145.

7. www.pepsico.com/PEP_Company/Overview, accessed December 7, 2007.

8. Paul Nutt, "Making Strategic Choices," *Journal of Management Studies* (January 2002): 67–96.

9. Michael Porter, *Competitive Strategy* (New York: The Free Press, 1980): 14.

10. David Upton, "What Really Makes Factories Flexible?" *Harvard Business Review* (July–August 1995): 75.

11. See for example, Evan Offstein, Devi Gnyawali, and Anthony Cobb, "A Strategic Human Resource Perspective of Firm Competitive Behavior," *Human Resource Management Review* 15 (2005): 305–318.

12. "Human Resource Goes High-Tech: The 1999 HR Technology Conference and Exposition," *BNA Bulletin to Management* (October 14, 1999): S1–S2; and Ann Pomeroy, "Agent of Change: At a Company that Thrives on Growth, No One Is More Adept at Change Management Than Dell's HR Head Paul McKinnon," *HR Magazine* 50, no. 5 (May 2005): 52(5).

13. "The New HR Agenda: 2002 Human Resource Competencies Study, Executive Summary," University of Michigan Business School (May 2003): 6. See also Brian Becker and Mark Huselid, "Strategic Human Resources Management: Where Do We Go from Here?" *Journal of Management* 32, no. 6 (December 2006): 898–925.

14. "More on What CEOs Want from HR," *HR Focus* 80, no. 4 (April 2003): 5.

15. Bill Leonard, "GM Drives HR to the Next Level," *HR Magazine* (March 2002): 48.

16. "The New HR Agenda: 2002 Human Resource Competencies Study, Executive Summary," University of Michigan Business School (May 2003).

17. "Strategic HR Means Translating Plans into Action," *HR Magazine* 48, no. 3 (March 2003): 8; and "Closer to Becoming a Strategic Partner? HR Moves Forward but Faces Obstacles," *BNA Bulletin to Management* (July 15, 2005): 225.

18. SHRM Research, "2006 Strategic HR Management," *Society for Human Resource Management,* (2006): 5–19, www.SHRM.org, accessed May 10, 2007.

19. SHRM Research, "Offshoring," *Workplace Visions,* no. 2 (2004): 1

20. Ibid., 7.

21. Samuel Greengard, "You're Next! There's No Escaping Merger Mania!" *Workforce* (April 1997): 52–62.

22. See, for example, Maria Fleurie and Lenne Fleurie, "In Search of Competence: Aligning Strategy and Competencies in the Telecommunications Industry," *International Journal of Human Resource Management* 16, no. 9 (September 2005): 1640–1655.

23. Garrett Walker and J. Randal MacDonald, "Designing and Implementing an HR Scorecard," *Human Resource Management* 40, no. 4 (2001): 365–377.

24. See, for example, James Werbel and Samuel DeMarie, "Aligning Strategic Human Resource Management and Person–Environment Fit," *Human Resource Management Review* 15 (2005): 247–262.

25. Richard Shafer et al., "Crafting a Human Resource Strategy to Foster Organizational Agility: A Case Study," *Human Resource Management* 40, no. 3 (Fall 2001): 197–211.

26. http://www.marketwatch.com/news/story/layoff-plans-rise-16-november/story.aspx?guid=%7BC201E82C%2DCAA3%2D4 6BE%2D952D%2D4985C49E4F8A%7D&dist=msr_10, accessed December 5, 2007, and http://Money.CNN.com/magazines/fortune, accessed December 5, 2007.

27. Ibid.

28. Bou-Wen Lin et al., "Mergers and Acquisitions as a Human Resource Strategy," *International Journal of Manpower* 27, no. 2 (2006): 127.

29. "Mergers & Acquisitions—Managing the HR Issues," *The M&A Spotlight* (January 1, 2007), http://www.accessmylibrary.com/coms2/summary_0286–29 399891_ITM, accessed December 3, 2007.

30. Andy Cook, "Make Sure You Get a Prenup," *EVCJ* (December/January 2007): 76.

31. Bou-Wen Lin et al, "Mergers & Acquisitions as a Human Resource Strategy, *International Journal of Management* 27, no.2 (2006): 135–142.

32. www.towersPerrin.com, accessed December 4, 2007.

33. Jessica Marquez, "HR's Rising Equity," *Workforce Management* (September 24, 2007): 16–22.

34. Ann Pomeroy, "A Fitting Role: HR Is Helping Businesses Puzzle Through the Difficult Process of a Successful Merger or Acquisition," *HR Magazine* 50, no. 6 (June 2005): 54–61.

35. Ibid.

36. www.towersPerrin.com, accessed December 4, 2007.

37. Jeffrey Schmidt, "The Correct Spelling of M&A Begins with HR," *HR Magazine* (June 2001): pp. 102–108. See also Wendy Boswell, "Aligning Employees with the Organization's Strategic Objectives: Out of Line of Sight, Out of Mind," *International Journal of Human Resource Management* 17, no. 9 (September 2006): 1014–1041.

38. "Mergers & Acquisitions—Managing the HR Issues," *The M&A Spotlight* (January 1, 2007), http://www.accessmy library.com/coms2/summary_0286–29399891_ITM, accessed December 3, 2007.

39. Leah Carlson, "Smooth Transition: HR Input Can Prevent Benefits Blunders During M&A's, *Employee Benefit News* (June 1, 2005).

40. www.towersPerrin.com, accessed December 4, 2007. See also Ingmar Bjorkman, "The HR Function in Large-Scale Mergers and Acquisitions: The Case of Nordea," *Personnel Review* 35, no. 6 (2006): 654–671, and Elina Antila, "The Role of HR Managers in International Mergers and Acquisitions: A Multiple Case Study," *The International Journal of Human Resource Management* 17, no. 6, issue 6 (June 2006): 999–1020.

41. John Kador, "Shall We Dance?" *Electronic Business* 28, no. 2 (February 2002): 56.

42. This checklist is based on Philip Hunsaker, *Training in Management Skills* (Upper Saddle River, NJ: Prentice Hall, 2001): 323.

43. Edgar Schein, *Organizational Culture and Leadership* (San Francisco: Jossey-Bass, 1985): 224–237. Peter Wright, Mark Kroll, and John Parnell, *Strategic Management Concepts* (Upper Saddle River, NJ: Prentice Hall, 1996): 233–236; and Benjamin Schneider et al., "Creating a Climate and Culture for Sustainable Organizational

Change," *Organizational Dynamics* 24, no. 4 (1996): 7–19. See also John S. Oakland and Steve J. Tanner "Quality Management in the 21st Century: Implementing Successful Change," *International Journal of Productivity and Quality Management* 1, no. 1/2 (December 12, 2005): 69.

44. Peter N. Haapaniemi, "How Companies Transformed Themselves," *Chief Executive* (November 2001): 2–5. See also "Unisys to Get New CEO," *Client Server News* (November 1, 2004).

45. This is paraphrased or quoted from "HR Services, Service Offerings: Mergers, Acquisitions and Restructuring," www.towersperrin.com, accessed December 4, 2007.

46. Ann Pomeroy, "Orchestrating a Megamerger," *HR Magazine* 50, no. 6 (June 2005).

47. "Mergers & Acquisitions—Managing the HR Issues," *The M&A Spotlight* (January 1, 2007).

48. Ibid; See also Ruth Bramson, "HR's Role in Mergers and Acquisitions," *Training and Development* 54, no. 10 (October 2000): 59–66.

49. Dennis Patton, "Give or Take on the Internet: An Examination of the Disclosure Practices of Insurance Firm Web Innovators," *Journal of Business Ethics* 36, no. 3 (March 15, 2002): 247–260.

50. Ibid.

51. Jessica Marquez, "Chrysler Sale Could Put UAW in Tough Spot," *Workforce Management* 86, no. 10 (May 21, 2007): 8.

52. Jerry Flint, "Advice for New Owners," *Ward's Auto World* 43, no. 6 (June 2007): 48.

53. Katie Benner and Adam Lashinsky, "The Dog That Ate Detroit," *Fortune* 155, no. 11 (June 11, 2007): 21–22.

54. Ibid.

Personnel Planning and Recruiting

4

When you finish studying this chapter, you should be able to:

1. *Describe the basic methods of collecting job analysis information.*

2. *Conduct a job analysis.*

3. *Explain the process of forecasting personnel requirements.*

4. *Compare eight methods for recruiting job candidates.*

5. *Explain how to use application forms to predict job performance.*

Introduction

With 110 restaurants open, and adding 20 new ones per year, The California-based Cheesecake Factory must hire about 24,000 people per year. For Ed Eynon, the firm's senior vice president for human resources, that means casting a wide net when it comes to recruiting—"You don't find all the people you need from one source," he says. Having the right recruiting sources is crucial to The Cheesecake Factory's success.[1] ∎

JOB ANALYSIS

Staffing means planning the company's personnel needs, and then recruiting candidates and selecting the best for its positions. We'll focus on workforce planning and recruiting in this chapter, and on selection in chapter 5. Before deciding what jobs need to be filled and how to recruit applicants for them, employers typically want to know the duties and worker skills each job requires. Job analysis provides that information.

What Is Job Analysis?

job analysis
The procedure for determining the duties and skill requirements of a job and the kind of person who should be hired for it.

Organizations consist of jobs that have to be staffed. **Job analysis** is the procedure through which you determine the duties of these jobs, and the characteristics of the people who should perform them. The manager then uses this information for developing **job descriptions** (what the job entails) and **job specifications** (what kind of people to hire for the job).[2]

A supervisor or HR specialist normally does the job analysis, perhaps using a questionnaire like the one in the chapter Appendix (Figure A 4.3, page 141). The questionnaire typically includes information on the work activities performed (such as cleaning, selling, teaching, or painting) and about matters like physical working conditions and work schedule.

job description
A list of a job's duties, responsibilities, reporting relationships, working conditions, and supervisory responsibilities—one product of a job analysis.

Job analysis information is the basis for many human resource management decisions. For example, you'll use information about the human traits required to do the job to decide what sorts of people to recruit and hire. And you'll need information about the job's duties to create training programs and to compute pay rates. Because job analysis plays a central role in human resource management, the U.S. Federal Agencies' *Uniform Guidelines on Employee Selection* stipulate that job analysis is crucial for validating all major personnel activities.

job specification
A list of a job's "human requirements," that is, the requisite education, skills, personality, and so on—a product of a job analysis.

JOB ANALYSIS AND EQUAL EMPLOYMENT OPPORTUNITY (EEO) Job analysis therefore plays a central role in equal employment compliance. We discussed U.S. EEO issues in chapter 2. Employers must be able to show that their screening tools and appraisals are related to performance on the job in question. To do this, of course, the manager must know what duties and skills the job entails—which in turn requires a competent job analysis.

Methods of Collecting Job Analysis Information

① Describe the basic methods of collecting job analysis information.

Managers use various techniques to do a job analysis (in other words, to collect information on the duties, responsibilities, and activities of the job). Some of the more popular techniques are as follows.

INTERVIEWS Job analysis interviews involve interviewing job incumbents or one or more supervisors who are thoroughly knowledgeable about the job. Typical interview questions include "What is the job being performed?" "What are the major duties of your position?" "What exactly do you do?" and "What activities do you participate in?"

Interviews are probably the most widely used method for determining a job's duties and responsibilities, and their wide use reflects their advantages. Most importantly, this is a simple and straightforward method. Interviewing also lets workers report activities and behavior that might not otherwise surface. For example, a skilled interviewer could unearth important duties that occur only occasionally, or informal communication (between, say, a production supervisor and the sales manager) that would not be obvious from the organization chart.

Interviewing's major problem is distortion of information. A job analysis is often a prelude to changing a job's pay rate. Employees therefore sometimes view them as affecting their pay, and so exaggerate some responsibilities and minimize others. Obtaining valid information can be a slow process.

For example, in one experiment the researchers listed duties either as simple task statements ("record phone messages and other routine information") or as ability statements ("ability to record phone messages and other routine information").[3] Respondents were much more likely to report the ability-based versions of the statements. Perhaps there's a tendency to inflate one's job's importance when abilities are involved, to impress others.[4]

QUESTIONNAIRES Many firms ask employees to fill out questionnaires to describe their job-related duties and responsibilities.

Some questionnaires are very structured checklists. Each employee is presented with an inventory of perhaps hundreds of specific tasks (such as "change and splice wire"). Each employee must indicate whether he or she performs each task and, if so, how much time is normally spent on each. At the other extreme, the questionnaire can be open-ended and simply ask the employee to "describe the major duties of your job."

In practice, the best questionnaire often falls between these two extremes. As illustrated in Figure A4.3, page 141, a typical job analysis questionnaire might have several open-ended questions (such "Is the incumbent performing duties he/she considers unnecessary?") as well as structured questions (concerning, for instance, previous experience required).

OBSERVATION Managers use direct observation when jobs consist mainly of observable physical activity. Jobs such as janitor, assembly-line worker, and accounting clerk are examples. On the other hand, observation is usually not appropriate when the job entails a lot of unmeasurable mental activity (lawyer, design engineer). Nor is it useful if the employee engages in important activities that might occur only occasionally, such as a nurse who handles emergencies.

PARTICIPANT DIARY/LOGS Another approach is to ask workers to keep a diary/log or list of what they do during the day. For every activity the employee engages in, he or she records the activity (along with the time) in a log. This can produce a very complete picture of the job, especially when supplemented with subsequent interviews with the worker and his or her supervisor. Some employees may try to exaggerate some activities and underplay others. However, the detailed, chronological nature of the log tends to

Managers use direct observation with jobs, such as assembly-line worker, that consist mainly of observable physical activity.

mediate against this. Some employees may compile their logs by periodically dictating what they're doing into a handheld dictating machine.

USING THE INTERNET Face-to-face interviews and observations can be time-consuming. Collecting the information from internationally dispersed employees is particularly challenging.[5]

Internet-based job analysis is a good solution.[6] The human resource department distributes the job analysis questionnaires to dispersed employees via the company intranet, with instructions to complete and return them by a particular date.

EXPEDITING THE JOB ANALYSIS PROCESS Employers usually collect job analysis data from several job incumbents, using questionnaires and interviews. Then they average data from employees from different departments to determine how much time, for example, a typical sales assistant spends on each of several specific tasks.

The process might take several days, to explain the job analysis process and the reason for it, and then to interview several employees and their managers. However, it's possible to reduce the process to just 3 or 4 hours.[7] The abbreviated steps include:

1. greet participants and conduct very brief introductions;
2. briefly explain the job analysis process and the participants' roles in this process;
3. spend about 15 minutes determining the scope of the job you're about to analyze, by getting agreement on the job's basic summary;
4. identify the job's broad functional or duty areas, such as "administrative" and "supervisory";
5. identify tasks within each duty area, using a flip chart or collaboration software; and
6. print the task list and get the group to sign off on it.

Note that job analysis data self-reported by job incumbents display the lowest reliability or consistency, while those collected by job analysts are usually more reliable.[8]

OTHER JOB ANALYSIS METHODS You may encounter several other job analysis methods, most notably those in the chapter Appendix.

Writing Job Descriptions

2 Conduct a job analysis.

The job analysis should provide the information required for writing a job description. A job description is a written statement of *what* the jobholder does, *how* he or she does it, and under *what conditions* the job is performed. The manager in turn uses this information to write a job specification that lists the knowledge, abilities, and skills needed to perform the job satisfactorily. Figure 4.1 presents a typical job description. As is usual, it contains several types of information.

JOB IDENTIFICATION As in Figure 4.1, the job identification section contains the job title; this specifies the title of the job, such as marketing manager, sales manager, or inventory control clerk. It also usually contains department, date, and similar information.

JOB SUMMARY The job summary should describe the general nature of the job, listing only its major functions or activities.

RELATIONSHIPS A relationships statement may show the jobholder's relationships with others inside and outside the organization, and might look like this for a human resource manager:

Reports to: Vice president of employee relations

Supervises: Human resource clerk, test administrator, labor relations director, and one secretary

Works with: All department managers and executive management

Outside the company: Employment agencies, executive recruiting firms, union representatives, state and federal employment offices, and various vendors

FIGURE 4.1 Sample Job Description, Pearson Education

JOB TITLE: Telesales Representative	**JOB CODE:** 100001
RECOMMENDED SALARY GRADE:	**EXEMPT/NONEXEMPT STATUS:** Nonexempt
JOB FAMILY: Sales	**EEOC:** Sales Workers
DIVISION: Higher Education	**REPORTS TO:** District Sales Manager
DEPARTMENT: In-House Sales	**LOCATION:** Boston
	DATE: April 2008

SUMMARY (Write a brief summary of job.)

The person in this position is responsible for selling college textbooks, software, and multimedia products to professors, via incoming and outgoing telephone calls, and to carry out selling strategies to meet sales goals in assigned territories of smaller colleges and universities. In addition, the individual in this position will be responsible for generating a designated amount of editorial leads and communicating to the publishing groups product feedback and market trends observed in the assigned territory.

SCOPE AND IMPACT OF JOB

Dollar responsibilities (budget and/or revenue)

The person in this position is responsible for generating approximately $2 million in revenue, for meeting operating expense budget of approximately $4000, and a sampling budget of approximately 10,000 units.

Supervisory responsibilities (direct and indirect)

None

Other

REQUIRED KNOWLEDGE AND EXPERIENCE (Knowledge and experience necessary to do job)

Related work experience

Prior sales or publishing experience preferred. One year of company experience in a customer service or marketing function with broad knowledge of company products and services is desirable.

Formal education or equivalent
Bachelor's degree with strong acedemic performance or work equivalent experience.

Skills
Must have strong organizational and persuasive skills. Must have excellent verbal and written communications skills and must be PC proficient.

Other

Limited travel required (approx 5%)

(continued)

RESPONSIBILITIES AND DUTIES This section is the heart of the job description and presents a full list of the job's responsibilities and duties. Here, list and describe in sentences each of the job's major duties. For instance, you might further define the duty "selects, trains, and develops subordinate personnel" as follows: "develops spirit of cooperation and understanding," "ensures that work group members receive specialized training as necessary," and "directs training involving teaching, demonstrating, and/or advising."

FIGURE 4.1 Continued

PRIMARY RESPONSIBILITIES (List in order of importance and list amount of time spent on task.)

Driving Sales (60%)
- Achieve quantitative sales goal for assigned territory of smaller colleges and universities.
- Determine sales priorities and strategies for territory and develop a plan for implementing those strategies.
- Conduct 15–20 professor interviews per day during the academic sales year that accomplishes those priorities.
- Conduct product presentations (including texts, software, and Web site); effectively articulate author's central vision of key titles; conduct sales interviews using the PSS model; conduct walk-through of books and technology.
- Employ telephone selling techniques and strategies.
- Sample products to appropriate faculty, making strategic use of assigned sampling budgets.
- Close class test adoptions for first edition products.
- Negotiate custom publishing and special packaging agreements within company guidelines.
- Initiate and conduct in-person faculty presentations and selling trips as appropriate to maximize sales with the strategic use of travel budget. Also use internal resources to support the territory sales goals.
- Plan and execute in-territory special selling events and book-fairs.
- Develop and implement in-territory promotional campaigns and targeted email campaigns.

Publishing (editorial/marketing) 25%
- Report, track, and sign editorial projects.
- Gather and communicate significant market feedback and information to publishing groups.

Territory Management 15%
- Track and report all pending and closed business in assigned database.
- Maintain records of customer sales interviews and adoption situations in assigned database.
- Manage operating budget strategically.
- Submit territory itineraries, sales plans, and sales forecasts as assigned.
- Provide superior customer service and maintain professional bookstore relations in assigned territory.

Decision-Making Responsibilities for This Position:
Determine the strategic use of assigned sampling budget to most effectively generate sales revenue to exceed sales goals.
Determine the priority of customer and account contacts to achieve maximum sales potential.
Determine where in-person presentations and special selling events would be most effective to generate most sales.

Submitted By: Jim Smith, District Sales Manager	Date: April 10, 2008
Approval:	Date:
Human Resources:	Date:
Corporate Compensation:	Date:

Source: Courtesy of HR Department, Pearson Education.

AUTHORITY This section defines the limits of the jobholder's authority. For example, the jobholder might have authority to approve purchase requests up to $5,000, grant time off or leaves of absence, discipline department personnel, recommend salary increases, and interview and hire new employees.[9]

STANDARDS OF PERFORMANCE Some job descriptions also contain a standards of performance section. This lists the standards the employee is to achieve in each of the job description's main duties and responsibilities.

WORKING CONDITIONS AND PHYSICAL ENVIRONMENT The job description also lists the general working conditions involved in the job. These might include noise level, hazardous conditions, heat, and other conditions.

INTERNET-BASED JOB DESCRIPTIONS Most employers write their job descriptions based wholly or in part on Internet-based services. One site, www.jobdescription.com, illustrates why. The process is simple. Search by alphabetical title, key word, category, or industry to find the desired job title. This leads you to a generic job description for that title—say, "computers & EDP systems sales representative." You can then use the wizard to customize the generic description for this position. For example, you can add specific information about your organization, such as job title, job codes, department, and preparation date. And you can indicate whether the job has supervisory abilities, and choose from a number of possible desirable competencies and experience levels.

The U.S. Department of Labor's *Occupational Information Network*, or O*NET (http://onetonline.gov) is an invaluable (and free) resource. Its wizards allow users to see the duties and responsibilities of thousands of jobs, as well as the training, experience, and education and knowledge each job requires. Figure 4.2 presents part of one O*NET job description.

WRITING JOB DESCRIPTIONS THAT COMPLY WITH THE ADA The Americans with Disabilities Act (ADA)—similar to the United Kingdom's Disability Discrimination Act—does not require employers to have job descriptions. However, most ADA lawsuits revolve around the question, "What are the essential functions of the job?" *Essential job functions* are those job duties that employees must be able to perform, with or without reasonable accommodation. Without a job description listing these functions, it is difficult to convince a court that the functions were essential.[10] The job description should identify and list the essential functions as "essential."[11]

Writing Job Specifications

The job specification starts with the job description and then answers the question, "What human traits and experience are required to do this job well?" It shows what kind of person to recruit and for what qualities that person should be tested. The job specification may be a separate section on the job description (as at the end of the first page of Figure 4.1) or a separate document entirely.

TRAINED EMPLOYEES It's usually not too difficult to determine the human requirements for placing already trained and experienced people on a job. You may reasonably assume that past performance is a good predictor of how the person will do. For example, suppose you want to fill a position for a trained bookkeeper. Your job specifications might focus mostly on traits such as education, length of previous service, quality of relevant training, and previous job performance.

UNTRAINED EMPLOYEES It's not as simple when you're filling jobs with untrained people. Here you must specify qualities such as physical traits or sensory skills that imply some potential for performing the job or for having the ability to be trained for the job. For example, suppose the job requires detailed manipulation on a circuit board assembly line. You might want to ensure that the person scores high on a test of finger dexterity. Your goal, in other words, is to identify those personal traits—or human requirements—that predict which candidate will do well on the job. Identifying these human requirements for a job is accomplished either through a subjective, judgmental approach or through statistical analysis.

Common sense is important when listing a job's human requirements. Certainly job-specific human traits such as manual dexterity and education are important. However, there are also general work behaviors (such as industriousness, thoroughness, good attendance, and honesty) that seem to apply to almost any job, but might not normally be unearthed through a job analysis.[12]

FIGURE 4.2 O*NET Job Description

Summary Report for:
11-2022.00 — Sales Managers

Direct the actual distribution or movement of a product or service to the customer. Coordinate sales distribution by establishing sales territories, quotas, and goals and establish training programs for sales representatives. Analyze sales statistics gathered by staff to determine sales potential and inventory requirements and monitor the preferences of customers.

Sample of reported job titles: Sales Manager, Director of Sales, District Sales Manager, Regional Sales Manager, Sales Supervisor, General Manager, Sales and Marketing Vice President, Sales Representative, Store Manager

Tasks

- Resolve customer complaints regarding sales and service.
- Monitor customer preferences to determine focus of sales efforts.
- Direct and coordinate activities involving sales of manufactured products, services, commodities, real estate or other subjects of sales.
- Determine price schedules and discount rates.
- Review operational records and reports to project sales and determine profitability.
- Direct, coordinate, and review activities in sales and service accounting and recordkeeping, and in receiving and shipping operations.
- Confer or consult with department heads to plan advertising services and to secure information on equipment and customer specifications.
- Advise dealers and distributors on policies and operating procedures to ensure functional effectiveness of business.
- Prepare budgets and approve budget expenditures.
- Represent company at trade association meetings to promote products.

Source: http://onetonline.gov, accessed December 20, 2007. Reprinted by permission of O*NET Online.

O*NET JOB SPECIFICATIONS The O*NET system provides valuable job specification information, both for trained and untrained personnel. As an example, the O*NET sales manager report lists required sales manager skills such as "Active Listening—Giving full attention to what other people are saying, taking time to understand the points being made, asking questions as appropriate, and not interrupting at inappropriate times"; and "Mathematics—Using mathematics to solve problems."[13]

Job Analysis in a "Jobless" World

A *job* is a set of closely related activities carried out for pay, but over the past few years, the concept of *job* has been changing quite dramatically. Globalized competition means more pressure for performance. Firms are therefore instituting high-performance workplace policies and practices. These include management systems (such as "just-in-time production methods") based on flexible, multiskilled job assignments, and on teamwork and participative decision making.

In turn, flexible jobs and teamwork assume that job assignments may change frequently. Changes like these have blurred the meaning of *job* as a set of well-defined and clearly delineated responsibilities. Employers want employees to define their jobs more broadly and flexibly. Therefore job descriptions tend to be less structured and restrictive. The trend is toward newer ways to analyze and describe jobs. One of these is competency-based job analysis.

FIGURE 4.3

The Skills Matrix for One Job at BP

Note: The shaded boxes (D, C, B, E, D, D, C) indicate the minimum level of skill required for the job.

	Technical expertise	Business awareness	Communication and interpersonal	Decision making and initiative	Leadership and guidance	Planning and organizational ability	Problem solving
H	H	H	H	H	H	H	H
G	G	G	G	G	G	G	G
F	F	F	F	F	F	F	F
E	E	E	E	**E**	E	E	E
D	**D**	D	D	D	**D**	**D**	D
C	C	**C**	C	C	C	C	**C**
B	B	B	**B**	B	B	B	B
A	A	A	A	A	A	A	A

Competency-Based Job Analysis

WHAT ARE COMPETENCIES? *Competencies* are demonstrable characteristics of the person that enable performance. Job competencies are always observable and measurable behaviors comprising part of a job (such as, "ability to record phone messages"). We can say that *competency-based job analysis* means describing the job in terms of measurable, observable, behavioral competencies (knowledge, skills, and/or behaviors) that an employee doing that job must exhibit to do the job well. This contrasts with the traditional way of describing the job in terms of job duties and responsibilities.[14]

Traditional job analysis focuses on "what" a job is in terms of job duties and responsibilities. *Competency analysis* focuses more on "how" the worker actually does the work, in terms of required behaviors like being able to answer phones, analyze blueprints, and write computer code.[15] Traditional job analysis is more job focused. Competency-based analysis is more worker focused—specifically, what must he or she be competent to do?

AN EXAMPLE In practice, competency-based analysis often comes down to specifying the basic skills an employee needs to do the job. For example, British Petroleum's exploration division managers wanted a more efficient, faster acting, flatter organization and empowered employees. To help accomplish this, senior managers wanted to shift employees from a job description–oriented "that's-not-my-job" attitude to one that motivated them to obtain the new skills they needed to accomplish their broader responsibilities.

The solution was a skills matrix as in Figure 4.3. BP created skills matrices for various jobs within two groups of employees: those on a management track and those whose aims lay elsewhere (such as to stay in engineering). HR prepared a matrix for each job or job family (such as drilling managers). As in Figure 4.3, the matrix listed (1) the basic skills needed for that job (such as technical expertise) and (2) the minimum level of each skill required for that job or job family. This way, the focus is no longer on job duties. Instead, the focus is on developing the skills the employees need to be more self-directed, and to do other, more demanding jobs if the situation requires it.

The skills matrix method prompted other HR changes in this division. For example, management instituted a new skills-based pay plan that awards raises based on skills improvement. Performance appraisals now focus more on skills employees acquire. And training emphasizes developing broad skills like leadership and planning—skills applicable across a wide range of responsibilities and jobs.

THE RECRUITMENT AND SELECTION PROCESS

The most familiar use for job descriptions is for deciding what types of people to recruit and select for the company's jobs.

This *recruitment and selection process* is a series of steps, as follows:

1. Do workforce planning and forecasting to determine the positions to be filled.
2. Build a pool of candidates for these jobs by recruiting internal or external candidates.
3. Have the applicants fill out application forms and perhaps undergo an initial screening test and interview.
4. Utilize various selection techniques such as tests, background investigations, and physical exams to identify viable job candidates.
5. Send one or more viable job candidates to the supervisor responsible for the job.
6. Have the candidate(s) go through one or more selection interviews with the supervisor and other relevant parties for the purpose of finally determining to which candidate(s) an offer should be made.

Workforce planning and recruiting (steps 1 through 3) are the subjects of the remainder of this chapter. Chapter 5 then focuses on employee selection techniques including tests, background checks, and physical exams.

WORKFORCE PLANNING AND FORECASTING

3️⃣ Explain the process of forecasting personnel requirements.

When Dan Hilbert became staffing manager at the San Antonio, Texas-based Valero Energy Corp., the company was doing no employment planning. After analyzing the firm's demographic and turnover data, he discovered that Valero would soon face employment shortages in its oil refineries. The projected shortfalls were four times higher than Valero could fill with its current recruitment procedures. The solution was to start developing specific employment plans.[16]

workforce planning
The process of formulating plans to fill the employer's future openings, based on (1) projecting open positions, and (2) deciding whether to fill these with inside or outside candidates.

Workforce (or personnel, or employment) **planning** is the process of formulating plans to fill the employer's future openings, based on (1) projecting open positions, and (2) deciding whether to fill these with inside or outside candidates. It therefore refers to planning to fill any or all of the firm's future positions, from maintenance clerk to CEO. However, most firms use *succession planning* to refer to the process of planning how to fill the company's most important top executive positions.

STRATEGY AND WORKFORCE PLANNING Personnel plans should flow from the firm's strategic planning processes, but personnel planning cannot be mechanical. The heart of personnel planning involves predicting the skills and competencies the employer will need to execute its strategy. Personnel planning therefore can't just involve extrapolating the past. Instead, it must be a collaborative process. At IBM and Hewlett-Packard, for instance, human resource executives routinely discuss with their firm's finance and other executives the personnel ramifications of their company's strategic plans, for instance, in terms of the employee capabilities the firms will need to achieve their goals.[17]

INSIDE OR OUTSIDE CANDIDATES? We'll see that one big question is always whether to fill projected openings with current employees or by recruiting from outside.

Each option produces its own set of human resource management plans. Current employees may require training, development, and coaching before they're ready to fill new jobs—and, thus, development plans. Going outside requires deciding what recruiting sources to use, and what the availability will be. For example, unemployment rates of over 5% in much of the United States in 2008 signaled, to many human resource managers, that they'd probably be able to be more selective in their hiring. Just a year earlier, a tight job market had recruiters ramping up their recruiting efforts.[18]

How does a manger like Dan Hilbert at Valero Energy decide how many employees he or she needs over the next few years? In planning for employment requirements, you'll need to forecast three things: personnel needs, the supply of inside candidates, and the supply of outside candidates. We'll start with personnel needs.

How to Forecast Personnel Needs

As a first approximation, managers traditionally use simple tools like *trend analysis* or *ratio analysis* to estimate staffing needs, based on sales projections and on past sales-to-personnel relationships.

Knowing your product's or service's expected demand is paramount. The usual process is therefore to forecast revenues first. Then estimate the size of the staff required to achieve this volume, for instance, by using historical ratios.

trend analysis
Study of a firm's past employment needs over a period of years to predict future needs.

TREND ANALYSIS While some firms use sophisticated computerized personnel forecasting tools, there are several simple ways for a manager to estimate future personnel needs. **Trend analysis** involves studying your firm's employment levels over the past 5 years or so to predict future needs. Thus, you might compute the number of employees in your firm at the end of each of the past 5 years, or perhaps the number in each subgroup (such as salespeople, production people, secretarial, and administrative) at the end of each of those years. The aim is to identify employment trends you think might continue into the future.

ratio analysis
A forecasting technique that involves analyzing and extrapolating the ratio of a dependent variable, such as sales persons required, with an independent variable, such as sales.

RATIO ANALYSIS Another approach, **ratio analysis**, means making forecasts based on the ratio between some causal factor (such as sales volume) and the number of employees required (for instance, number of salespeople). For example, suppose you find that a salesperson traditionally generates $500,000 in sales. Then, if the sales revenue-to-salespeople ratio remains the same, you would require six new salespeople next year (each of whom produces an extra $500,000 in sales) to produce, say, the desired extra $3 million in sales.

scatter plot
A graphical method used to help identify the relationship between two variables.

SCATTER PLOTS The **scatter plot** method shows graphically how two variables are related. If they are related, then if you can forecast the level of one variable (for example, hospital size) you should also be able to estimate your personnel requirements (for example, nurses).

For example, assume a 1,000-bed hospital expects to expand to 1,500 beds over the next 5 years. The director of nursing and the human resource director want to forecast the requirement for registered nurses. The human resource director decides to determine the relationship between *size of hospital* (in terms of number of beds) and *number of nurses required*. She calls several hospitals of various sizes and gets the following figures:

Size of Hospital (Number of Beds)	Number of Registered Nurses
200	240
300	260
400	470
500	500
600	620
700	660
800	820
900	860

Figure 4.4 on the next page shows the hospital size (in beds) on the horizontal axis. The number of nurses is on the vertical axis. If the two factors are related, then the points will tend to fall along a straight line, as they do here. If you carefully draw a line to minimize the squared distances between the line and each of the plotted points, you will be able to estimate (forecast) the number of nurses needed for each given hospital size. Thus, for a 1,500-bed hospital, the human resource director would assume she needs about 1,100 nurses.

Managerial judgment always plays a role in employment planning. It's rare that any historical trend will continue unchanged. Important factors that may influence your forecasts include:

1. Projected turnover (as a result of resignations or terminations)
2. Quality and skills of your employees (in relation to what you see as the changing needs of your organization)

FIGURE 4.4

Using a Scatter Plot to Estimate Relationship between Hospital Size and Number of Nurses

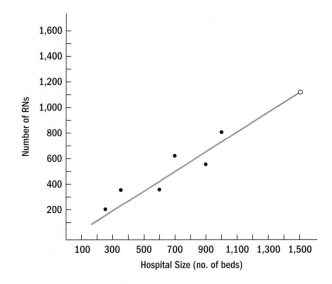

3. Strategic decisions to upgrade the quality of products or services or enter into new markets
4. Technological and other changes resulting in increased productivity
5. The financial resources available to your department

Forecasting the Supply of Outside Candidates

The preceding forecast provides only half the staffing equation, by answering the question, "How many employees will we need?" Next, the manager must estimate the projected *supply* of both internal and external candidates.

If there will not be enough qualified inside candidates to fill anticipated openings, employers may want to project supplies of outside candidates—those not currently employed by your organization. This may require forecasting general economic conditions, local market conditions, and occupational market conditions. (Then, faced with, say, a projected undersupply of people to fill specific projected needs, managers like Dan Hilbert at Valero Energy may investigate other options, such as encouraging employees of retirement age not to leave, or working with local schools to create special training programs.)

In any case, the first step here is often to forecast general economic conditions and the expected prevailing rate of unemployment. Usually, the lower the rate of unemployment the lower the labor supply and the harder it is to recruit personnel. For the United Kingdom, look for economic projections online, for example, from private sources such as London's Deloitte & Touche, www.deloitte.com.

Local labor market conditions are also important. For example, the growth of computer and semiconductor firms recently prompted low unemployment in U.S. cities like Seattle, quite aside from general economic conditions in the country.

Finally, forecast the availability of potential job candidates in specific occupations for which you will be recruiting. Recently, for instance, there has been an undersupply of registered nurses nationally. The British Department of Work and Pensions prepares excellent occupational projections (available at www.dwp.gov.uk/asd/asd5/).

Forecasting the Supply of Inside Candidates

In practice, as at Valero Energy, forecasting the supply of a firm's inside candidates requires analyzing demographic, turnover, and other data. The manager asks questions such as "How many current employees are due to retire?" and "What is our usual yearly turnover?"

A qualifications inventory can facilitate forecasting internal candidates. **Qualifications inventories** contain summary data such as each current employee's performance record, educational background, age, and promotability, compiled either manually or in a computerized system. **Personnel replacement charts** (see Figure 4.5) show the present performance and

qualifications inventories
Manual or computerized records listing employees' education, career and development interests, languages, special skills, and so on to be used in identifying inside candidates for promotion.

personnel replacement charts
Company records showing present performance and promotability of inside candidates for the firm's most important positions.

FIGURE 4.5

Management Replacement Chart Showing Development Needs of Potential Future Divisional Vice Presidents

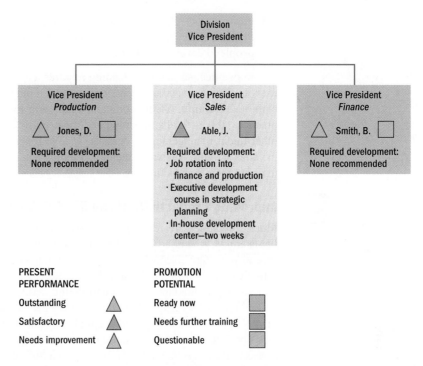

promotability for each potential replacement for important positions. As an alternative, you can develop a *position replacement card* for each position, showing possible replacements as well as present performance, promotion potential, and training required by each possible candidate.

COMPUTERIZED INFORMATION SYSTEMS Employers can't maintain qualifications inventories on hundreds or thousands of employees manually. Many firms computerize this information, and a number of packaged systems are available for accomplishing this task.

Typically, employees fill out a Web-based survey in which they describe their background and experience. The system also typically includes records of performance appraisals. When a manager needs a qualified person to fill a position, he or she describes the position (for instance, in terms of key words like education and skills) and then enters this information online. After scanning its database, the program presents the manager with a list of candidates.

SUCCESSION PLANNING Forecasting the availability of inside candidates is particularly important in succession planning. Succession planning refers to the plans a company makes to fill its most important executive positions.

In practice, the process often involves a fairly complicated and integrated series of steps. For example, the company might route potential successors for top management through the top jobs at several key divisions as well as overseas, and through Oxford University's Said Business School's Advanced Management Program. So, a more comprehensive definition of *succession planning* is "the process of ensuring a suitable supply of successors for current and future key jobs arising from business strategy, so that the careers of individuals can be planned and managed to optimize the organization's needs and the individuals' aspirations."[19] Succession planning includes these activities:

- Analysis of the demand for managers and professionals by company level, function, and skill
- Audit of existing executives and projection of likely future supply from internal and external sources
- Planning of individual career paths based on objective estimates of future needs and drawing on performance appraisals and assessments of potential
- Career counseling in the context of a realistic understanding of the future needs of the firm, and of the individual
- Accelerated promotions, with development targeted against the future needs of the business

■ Performance-related training and development to prepare individuals for future roles
■ Planned strategic recruitment, not only to fill short-term needs but also to provide people to develop to meet future needs[20]

In practice, succession planning requires a coordinated approach. It's obviously futile to try to plan managerial successions without input on things like performance reviews and employee training. Of the companies planning to change their succession management practices, three-fourths recently cited the need to "integrate succession management with other talent management processes."[21] (We'll see in a moment that *talent management* includes activities such as screening, training, and appraising employees.) Information systems are therefore useful here.

Improving Productivity Through HRIS: Succession Planning Systems

More companies are relying on software to facilitate the succession planning process. For example, when Larry Kern became president of the California-based Dole Food Co. Inc. several years ago, each of its separate operating companies handled most of their own HR activities and succession planning. Kern's strategy involved improving financial performance by reducing redundancies and centralizing certain activities, including succession planning.[22] Technology helped Dole do this. Dole decided to use special software from Pilat NAI. Pilat NAI runs the software and keeps all the data on its own servers for a monthly fee.

The Pilat succession planning system is easy for Dole's managers to use. They get access to the program via the Web using a password. They fill out online résumés for themselves, including career interests, and note special considerations such as geographic restrictions. The managers also assess themselves on four competencies. When the manager completes his or her succession planning input, the program automatically notifies the manager's boss. The latter then assesses his or her subordinate and indicates whether the person should be promoted. The person's manager also assesses his or her overall potential. This assessment, plus the online résumés, then goes automatically to the division head and the divisional HR director. Dole's senior vice president for HR for North America then uses the information to create a career development plan for each manager, including seminars and other programs.[23]

Talent Management

For most employers today, succession planning can't ensure they have all the talent that they need. Succession planning tends to focus just on the firm's top positions. But with employers competing vigorously for talent at all organizational levels, no one wants to lose any current high-potential employees, or fail to attract top-caliber ones. It's therefore not surprising that a recent survey of human resource executives found that for about 62% of respondents, "talent management" issues were the most pressing ones they faced.[24]

talent management
The end to end process of planning, recruiting, developing, managing, and compensating employees throughout the organization.

WHAT IS TALENT MANAGEMENT? In simple terms, talent management means attracting, developing, and retaining key talent.[25] It therefore involves coordinating several human resource activities, in particular workforce acquisition, assessment, development, and retention.[26] **Talent management** "is the end to end process of planning, recruiting, developing, managing, and compensating employees throughout the organization."[27] Talent management involves instituting, in a planned and thoughtful way, a coordinated process for identifying, recruiting, hiring, and developing high-potential employees. One survey of CEOs of the largest companies said they typically spent between 20% and 40% of their time on talent management.[28]

There are two main reasons for talent management's growing popularity. One, as noted, is that with employers now competing vigorously for talent, no one wants to lose high-potential employees, or fail to attract top-caliber ones. The second reason is the availability of new talent management information systems; these integrate talent management system components like succession planning, recruitment, learning, and employee pay, enabling seamless updating of data among them.

TALENT MANAGEMENT'S FOUR CHARACTERISTICS Four characteristics set talent management apart from traditional human resource management processes (such as staffing):

1. Taking a talent management approach recognizes that in a competitive world, acquiring, developing, and retaining talent are critical tasks. Viewing the various talent management activities (such as recruiting, learning, and paying employees) as parts of a single integrated process helps ensure that managers *consciously focus on all the tasks required for managing the company's talent.*

2. An effective talent management process should *integrate the underlying talent management activities* such as succession planning, recruiting, developing, and compensating employees. For example, performance appraisals should prompt training assignments for employees.

3. Talent management is *goal directed.* The aim is to align the employees' efforts and the firm's talent management activities with the company's strategic goals. For example, the employer's strategic goals drive how, where, and who the employer recruits, the training and development each employee receives, and how he or she is compensated. Figure 4.6 summarizes this idea.

4. Integrating the talent management functions means that effective talent management systems are almost always *information technology–based.* Several software providers offer specialized talent management software suites.

   • For example, Talent Management Solutions' (www.talentmanagement101.com) talent management suite includes e-recruiting software, employee performance management, a learning management system, and compensation management. Among other things, Talent Management Solutions' suite of programs "relieves the stress of writing employee performance reviews by automating the task," and ensures "that all levels of the organization are aligned—all working for the same goals."[29]

   • SilkRoad Technology's talent management solution includes applicant tracking, on-boarding, performance management, compensation, and employee Internet. Its talent management "Life Suite" "helps you recruit, manage, and retain your best employees."[30]

   • Info HCM Talent Management "includes several upgrades including tracking and monitoring performance metrics, interactive online training via WebEx, support for e-commerce integration to enable training . . . , and full localization for additional languages including Spanish, French, and Chinese."[31]

   • Workstream's new talent management suite includes "industry leading compensation, performance, development, competencies, knowledge management and rewards applications."[32]

FIGURE 4.6

The Talent Management Process

RECRUITING JOB CANDIDATES

Once authorized to fill a position, the next step is to develop an applicant pool, either from internal or external sources. Recruiting is important because the more applicants you have, the more selective you can be in your hiring. With baby boomers now retiring and fewer teenagers entering the labor pool, recruitment will be a challenge in the years ahead. By several estimates, the shortage of workers will grow from almost nothing today to about 20 million workers by 2020. At that point, the U.S. labor force will only be able to fill about 90% of the available jobs.[33]

④ Compare eight methods for recruiting job candidates.

THE COMPLEX JOB OF RECRUITING EMPLOYEES   Effective recruiting is more complex than just placing ads and calling agencies. For one thing, recruitment should *make sense in terms of your company's strategic plans.* For example, BASF Group found that successfully executing a new plant-expansion strategy required thinking through what employees they'd need and how they'd do the recruiting.

Second, *some recruiting methods are superior* to others, depending on who you're recruiting. Figure 4.7 summarizes the sources of new hires, based on one survey. Overall, employers most often used employee referrals and large job boards (such as Monster).[34]

Third, recruiting results reflect various *nonrecruitment issues.* For example, paying 10% more than competitors should make recruiting easier. As another example, Cummins Engine Company's "Dream it, Do it," program goes to U.S. schools to show local state school seniors the challenging nature of Cummins's work. The program prompted more local state school graduates to apply for jobs at Cummins.[35]

Finally, there are legal constraints. For example, the U.S. EEOC's compliance manual says that with a nondiverse workforce, relying on word-of-mouth referrals may be a barrier to equal employment opportunity.[36] The *HR in Practice* feature explains another issue to be aware of.

HR in Practice

The Hiring Manager's Obligations

The hiring manager needs to be careful not to interfere with applicants' obligations to their current employers. In general, even without a written contract, courts generally hold that employees have a duty of loyalty to their current employers during their employment.[37] Asking job candidates about their current employers' plans can thus prompt serious legal consequences. In recruiting, interviewing, and negotiating with a candidate, keep these points in mind:

- Courts generally expect employees to maintain the confidentiality of confidential employer information such as customer lists.

- In general, the hiring manager has both an ethical and legal obligation to respect the prospective employee's duty of loyalty.
- To the extent that the hiring manager participates in any breach of that loyalty—for instance, inquiring about customers' buying patterns or about new products under development—the hiring manager may share in the liability for the breach.
- One way to handle this is to make it clear at the outset that you expect applicants to honor their duty of loyalty to their current employers.[38]

RECRUITING EFFECTIVENESS   Given all this, it's important to assess how effectively the employer is spending its recruiting dollars. Is it more cost effective for us to advertise for applicants on the Web or in Sunday's paper? Should we use this employment agency or that one?

Logically, one would expect most employers to try to assess which of their recruiting tactics are working best. Yet, one survey found that only about 44% of the 279 firms surveyed make formal attempts to evaluate the outcomes of their recruitment efforts.[39]

Internal Sources of Candidates

Although *recruiting* may bring to mind employment agencies and classified ads, filling open jobs with current employees (internal recruiting) is often an employer's best bet. To

FIGURE 4.7

Relative Recruiting Source Effectiveness Based on New Hires

Note: Internet job boards continue to be the most effective sources, followed by employee referral programs and professional and trade media and associations.

Source: © Staffing.org, Inc., 2007. All Rights Reserved. The 2007 Recruiting Metrics and Performance Benchmark Report, 2nd Ed., is sponsored by NAS Recruitment Communications.

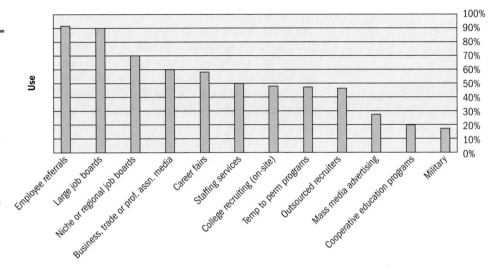

job posting

Posting notices of job openings on company bulletin boards as a recruiting method.

be effective, this approach requires using **job posting**, personnel records, and skill banks.[40] *Job posting* means "posting the open job—on company bulletin boards and/or on the Web—and listing its attributes, such as qualifications, supervisor, working schedule, and pay rate." Some union contracts require such postings to ensure that union members get first choice of better positions. Yet posting is also good practice in nonunion firms, if it facilitates the transfer and promotion of qualified inside candidates. Personnel records are useful here. An examination of personnel records (including qualifications inventories) may reveal persons who have potential for further training or those who already have the right background for the open jobs in question.

Recruiting via the Internet

Internal candidates may not be sufficient to fill your recruiting needs. In that case, the manager turns to outside sources. Most firms start by placing Internet ads.

HOME PAGES Many firms attract employment applications via their own Web sites. Unilever's home page (www.unilever.com) includes useful information about working for Unilever but also includes numerous useful job-seeker aids. The accounting firm Deloitte & Touche created one global recruitment site, thus eliminating the need to maintain 35 separate local recruiting Web sites.[41]

To improve recruitment prospects, Cummins Engine Company's "Dream it, Do it" U.S. program goes to schools to show local state school seniors the challenging nature of Cummins's work—here, assembling a diesel engine.

Some estimate employers have only about 4 minutes "before online applicants will turn their attention elsewhere."[42] Making the employer's Web site user-friendly for prospective job applicants can help boost the number of online recruits. There are several ways to do this. Make it easy to get from the homepage to the career section in just one or two clicks; keep any pre-employment screening questions simple; allow job seekers to apply online and via fax or e-mail if they prefer; and include a tool that lets visitors register and receive notices about new jobs to their e-mail.[43]

JOB BOARDS Others post positions on Internet job boards such as CareerBuilder.com and Monster.com, or on the sites of professional associations (such as the European Federation of Chemical Engineering) or the sites of their local newspapers. Figure 4.8 lists some top online recruiting job sites.

FIGURE 4.8

Some Top Online Recruiting Job Sites

Source: Adapted from www.quintcareers.com, accessed January 18, 2008.

America's Job Bank—Almost a million job leads in their database. Job seekers can search for jobs or post your resumes. Free.

BilingualCareer.com—Bilingual job seekers (English and at least one other language) can search job listings, post resume, and find job interviewing and resume preparation advice.

Careerbuilder—Claims to have the largest assortment of job listings on the Net—a combination of help wanted ads of the nation's leading newspapers and job listings from the Web sites of leading employers.

Career.com—Lots of job opportunities, searchable by company, location, and discipline. Also lists jobs for new college graduates.

College Recruiter—Jobs for college students, grads, and recent graduates. Entry-level work and career opportunities. Part-time and full-time. A great resource for job seekers.

Futurestep—An executive recruiting service from Korn/Ferry International that focuses on filling mid-level positions in professional services, information technology, human resources, accounting, sales and marketing, public relations, production, engineering, and planning across all industries.

Job.com—Where job seekers can post your resume and search thousands of jobs by industry, city, state, job title, and keywords. Job listings show posted date. Free to job seekers.

JobBank USA—Specializes in providing employment and resume information services to job candidates, employers, and recruitment firms. One of the largest employment Web sites.

Jobcentral—A national employment network formed by an alliance between two nonprofit associations to provide job seekers in all industries and occupations, entry level to chief executive officer.

Monster.com—One of the oldest job sites on the Web, with several hundred thousand jobs worldwide. Also includes career advice and relocation services for job seekers.

Quintcareers—Now startling its 12th year of operations, and with more than 3,500 pages of free college, career, and job-search content to empower your success in life.

Truecareers—Find job listings, company research, and other career information (articles, advice, etc.). Search for jobs (by keywords, location, salary, employers), post resume, and use a job search agent.

Yahoo! HotJobs—Candidates create a personalized career management page called *My HotJobs,* which provides the tools needed for an easy, simple, and confidential job search.

Employers seem to be shifting from national generalist job board sites to niche sites. For example, in August 2007, the unique visitors to CareerBuilder.com dropped about 2%, while those to technology site Dice.com jumped 34%.[44]

New job board sites capitalize on social networking. Users register and supply their name, location, and the kind of work they do on social networking/recruitment sites like Monster Network and LinkIn.com. These sites enable members to developing personal relationships for networking, hiring, and employee referrals.[45] To benefit from YouTube-type networking sites, the accounting firm Deloitte & Touche asked employees to make short videos describing their experiences with the firm. Deloitte then took the 14 best (of the 400 videos that employees submitted) and posted them on YouTube.[46]

THE DOT-JOBS DOMAIN The new .jobs domain gives job seekers a simple, one-click conduit for finding jobs at the employers who registered at .jobs (employers register at www.goto.jobs). For example, applicants seeking a job at Disneyland can go to www.Disneyland.jobs. This takes them to Disney's recruiting Web site for Disneyland.

VIRTUAL JOB FAIRS Virtual (fully online) job fairs are another option. For example, the U.S. magazine *PR Week* recently organized a virtual job fair for about a dozen public relations employers. At a virtual job fair, "online visitors see a very similar setup to a regular job fair. They can listen to presentations, visit booths, leave résumés and business cards, participate in live chats, and get contact information from recruiters, HR managers, and even hiring managers."[47] At *PR Week's* fair, one employer included short videos in its virtual "booth" introducing its company culture and talking about the firm. Several of its recruiters were online from 9 a.m. to 9 p.m. to virtually chat in real time with the hundreds of prospective applicants who visited its virtual job booth.[48] McDonald's Corp. posted a series of employee testimonials on social networking sites like Second Life as a way to attract applicants.[49]

INTERNET RECRUITING PROS AND CONS Internet recruiting's wide use reflects its advantages. Newspapers may charge employers up to several thousand dollars for one large print ad, while job listings on one's own Web site are essentially free. Newspaper ads might have a life span of perhaps 10 days, whereas the Internet ad may attract applications for 30 days or more. Internet recruiting can also be fast, since responses to electronic job listings often start coming in at once. Most employers also report great success in using the Web to generate applications. It's not unusual to start receiving numerous e-mailed applications minutes after posting an open job on Monster, for instance.

Yet some employers cite a flood of responses as one downside of Internet recruiting. The problem is that the relative ease of responding to Internet ads encourages unqualified or geographically remote job seekers to apply. On the whole, though, more applicants are usually better than fewer, and we will see in a moment that more companies are using special software to scan, digitize, and process applicant résumés automatically.

E-recruiting also has some potential legal pitfalls. For example, if fewer minorities use the Internet, then automated online application gathering and screening might mean the employer inadvertently excludes higher numbers of minority applicants. Furthermore, employers need to track applicants' race, sex, and ethnic group. But the Internet makes it so easy to submit résumés that many applicants are unsolicited and not aimed at specific jobs. However, in the case of U.S. EEOC law, an "applicant" must meet three conditions: he or she must express interest in employment; the employer must have taken steps to fill a specific job; and the individual must have followed the employer's standard application procedure.[50]

applicant tracking systems
Online systems that help employers attract, gather, screen, compile, and manage applications.

APPLICANT TRACKING SYSTEMS Employers often install *applicant tracking systems* to support their on- and off-line recruiting efforts. **Applicant tracking systems** are software systems that help employers keep track of their applicants by performing various services such as collecting application information, prescreening applicants, scheduling interviews, and letting employers easily do searches (such as by skill or degree) to match candidates with positions. The systems also help employers reports.[51]

The applicant tracking system should also (but often doesn't) help the employer identify and compare recruiting sources. Employers reportedly spent about $6.4 billion on help wanted advertising in the United States in one recent year, but about 30% of applicant tracking systems "lack the necessary tools to effectively pinpoint source of hire."[52] If the employer can't identify which recruiting sources are producing which hires, it's impossible to determine which source is most effective, or to efficiently allocate the recruitment budget.

APPLICATION SERVICE PROVIDERS   While many employers use their own applicant tracking software to process applications via their recruitment sites, others farm out that processing work to *application service providers* (ASPs). When applicants log on to the "jobs" page of the employer's Web site, they actually go to the servers of the **application service provider**, which then uses its own systems to compile application information, prescreen applicants, and help the employer rank applicants and set interview appointments.

> **application service provider**
> An online vendor that uses its own servers and systems to manage tasks for employers, such as recruitment or training. In recruitment, they compile application information, prescreen applicants, and help the employer rank applicants and set interview appointments.

Advertising as a Source of Candidates

To use help wanted ads successfully, you need to address two issues: the media and the ad's construction. The selection of the best medium (be it your local paper, the Web, the *Financial Times,* or a technical journal) depends on the type of positions for which you're recruiting. Because you're drawing from a local market, your local newspaper is usually a good source of blue-collar help, clerical employees, and lower-level administrative employees. For specialized employees or professionals, you can advertise in trade and professional journals such as the *British Association of Occupational Therapists Sales Management, Chemical Engineering,* and *Recruit.* One drawback to print advertising is that there may be a week or more between insertion of the ad and publication of the journal.

Help wanted ads in papers such as the *Financial Times* can be good sources of middle- or senior-management personnel. Other employers turn to the Internet for faster turnaround.

Business in Action Building Your *Marketing* Knowledge

Attracting applicants is more important than most managers realize. As we said, the more applicants you have, the more selective you can be in your hiring. The converse is that with, say, just one or two applicants for one or two positions, your only real decision is to "take them or leave them." You can't be very selective.

That's why attracting applicants relies (or should rely) on good marketing skills. *Marketing* doesn't just mean selling. Marketing means enabling people to get what they need and want by creating something that's of value to them.[53] Employers can therefore view recruiting partly in terms of marketing. You want to attract applicants. You do this by signaling that working for you will create value for them. And you do that by appealing, with your recruitment efforts, to their *needs* (for things like security, affection, camaraderie, or self expression) or to their *wants* for culturally determined things like particular items such as designer clothes. It's therefore no accident that some high-fashion retail stores like Saks prominently emphasize employee shopping discounts when they write their help wanted ads! The bottom line is, take a marketing, "how can we create value for prospective applicants" approach when creating your recruitment campaign.

CONSTRUCTING THE AD   Experienced advertisers use a four-point guide labeled AIDA (attention, interest, desire, action) to construct ads. You must, of course, attract attention to the ad, or readers may just miss or ignore it. Figure 4.9 shows an ad from one paper's classified section. Why does this ad attract *attention*? The words "next key player" certainly help. Employers usually advertise key positions in separate display ads like this one. The *Business in Action* shows recruiting's marketing aspects.

FIGURE 4.9

Help Wanted Ad that Draws Attention

Source: As published in *The New York Times*, May 13, 2007, Business p. 18. Reprinted by permission of Giombetti Associates.

Are You Our Next Key Player?

PLANT CONTROLLER — Northern New Jersey

Are you looking to make an impact? Can you be a strategic business partner and team player, versus a classic, "bean counter"? Our client, a growing **Northern New Jersey** manufacturer with two locations, needs a high-energy, self-initiating, technically competent Plant Controller. Your organizational skills and strong understanding of general, cost, and manufacturing accounting are a must. We are not looking for a delegator, this is a hands-on position. If you have a positive can-do attitude and have what it takes to drive our accounting function, read oh!

Responsibilities and Qualifications:
- Monthly closings, management reporting, product costing, and annual budget.
- Accurate inventory valuations, year-end physical inventory, and internal controls.
- 4-year Accounting degree, with 5–8 years experience in a manufacturing environment.
- Must be proficient in Microsoft Excel and have general computer skills and aptitude.
- Must be analytical and technically competent, with the leadership ability to influence people, situations, and circumstances.

If you have what it takes to be our next key player, tell us in your cover letter, *"Beyond the beans, what is the role of a Plant Controller?"* **Only cover** letters addressing that question will be considered. Please indicate your general salary requirements in your cover letter and email or fax your resume and cover letter to:

Rich Frigon
Giombetti Associates
2 Allen Street, P.O. Box 720
Hampden, MA 01036
Email: rfrigon@giombettiassoc.com
Fax: (413) 566-2009

Next, develop *interest* in the job. You can create interest by the nature of the job itself, with lines such as "Are you looking to make an impact?" You can also use other aspects of the job, such as its location, to create interest.

Create *desire* by spotlighting the job's interest factors with words such as *travel* or *challenge*. As an example, having a graduate school nearby may appeal to engineers and professional people.

Finally, the ad should prompt *action*, with a statement like "Call today," or "Please forward your résumé." (And, of course, as explained earlier in this chapter, the ad should comply with equal employment laws, avoiding features like, "man wanted.")

Employment Agencies as a Source of Candidates

There are three basic types of employment agencies: (1) those operated by government; (2) those associated with nonprofit organizations; and (3) privately owned agencies.

Public agencies typically maintain a nationwide computerized job bank and are a major source of blue-collar and often white-collar workers.

These agencies' usefulness is on the rise. Under a single roof, employers and job seekers can access an array of services such as recruitment services, employee training programs, and access to local and national labor market information.

Other employment agencies are associated with *nonprofit organizations*. For example, most professional and technical societies have units that help their members find jobs. Similarly, many public welfare agencies try to place people who are in special categories, such as those who are physically disabled or who are war veterans.

Private employment agencies are important sources of clerical, white-collar, and managerial personnel. They charge a fee for each applicant they place. These fees are usually set by law and are posted in their offices. The trend is toward "fee-paid jobs," in which the employer pays the fees.

Some specific reasons you might want to use an agency include the following:

- Your firm does not have its own human resource department.
- Your firm found it difficult in the past to generate a pool of qualified applicants.
- You must fill an opening quickly.
- You want to attract a greater number of minority or female applicants.
- The recruitment effort is aimed at reaching individuals who are currently employed and who might feel more comfortable dealing with employment agencies than with competitors directly.

However, employment agencies are no panacea. For example, the employment agency's screening may let unqualified applicants go directly to the supervisors responsible for the hiring, who may in turn naïvely hire them.

TEMPORARY WORKERS Many employers supplement their permanent employee base by hiring contingent or temporary workers, often through temporary help agencies. Also called *part-time* or *just-in-time* workers, the *contingent workforce* is big and growing. The contingent workforce is not limited to clerical or maintenance staff. Each year, more than 100,000 people find temporary work in engineering, science, or management support occupations. The *Personal Competencies* explains managing the agency vendor relationship.

Staffing with contingent workers owes its popularity to several things. First, employers have always used "temps" to fill in for the days or weeks that permanent employees were out sick or on vacation. Second, today's desire for ever-higher productivity contributes to temp workers' growing popularity. For one thing, you pay temp workers only for hours worked, not for the hours that some non-temp workers may spend sitting around. Contingent workers often aren't paid benefits, which is another saving for the employer. Third, using temp workers lets employers readily expand and contract with changes in demand. Many firms also use temporary hiring to give prospective employees a trial run before hiring them as regular employees.[54]

Employers hire temp workers either through direct hires or through temporary staff agencies. Direct hiring involves simply hiring workers and placing them on the job. The employer usually pays these people directly, as it does all its employees, but classifies them separately from regular employees.[55] The employer generally classifies these workers as casual, seasonal, or temporary employees, and often awards few if any benefits (such as pension benefits). If hired through agencies, the agency usually pays the employees' salaries and (any) benefits. Nike Inc. recently signed a multimillion dollar deal with Kelly Services to manage Nike's contingent workforce (temporary hires).[56]

Several years ago, U.S. government agents rounded up about 250 illegal "contract" workers in 60 Wal-Mart stores. The case underscores the need for employers to understand the status and source of the contract employees who work on their premises under the auspices of outside contingent staffing firms. These workers often handle activities like security, food service, or, as in Wal-Mart's case, after-hours store cleaning.[57]

ALTERNATIVE STAFFING Temporary employees are examples of alternative staffing—basically, the use of nontraditional recruitment sources. The use of alternate staffing sources is widespread and growing. Many British employees are employed in some alternative work arrangement. Alternative staffing arrangements include, for example, "in-house temporary employees" (people employed directly by the company, but on an explicit short-term basis) and "contract technical employees" (highly skilled workers like engineers, who are supplied for long-term projects under contract from an outside technical services firm). Dealing with firms like these requires special vendor management skills.

Personal Competencies

Building Your *Vendor Management* Skills

Vendor management is an important competency when dealing with suppliers like employment and temp agencies. Delegating too much authority to them, without retaining sufficient oversight, can lead to problems, such as bringing employees on board who don't meet your firm's normal screening standards. When working with temporary agencies, ensure that basic policies and procedures are in place, including:

- *Invoicing.* Get a sample copy of the agency's invoice. Make sure it fits your company's needs.
- *Time sheets.* With temps, the time sheet is not just a verification of hours worked. Once the worker's supervisor signs it, it's usually an agreement to pay the agency's fees.
- *Temp-to-perm policy.* What is the policy if the client wants to hire one of the agency's temps as a permanent employee?

- *Recruitment of and benefits for temp employees.* Find out how the agency plans to recruit employees and what sorts of benefits it pays.
- *Dress code.* Specify the appropriate attire at each of your offices or plants.
- *Equal employment opportunity statement.* Get a document from the agency stating that it is not discriminating when filling temp orders.
- *Job description information.* Have a procedure whereby you can ensure the agency understands the job to be filled and the sort of person, in terms of skills and so forth, you want to fill it.
- *Selection standards.* Make sure you and the agency fully understand and agree on the selection procedures and standards the agency will use in selecting employees for your positions.[58]

Executive Recruiters as a Source of Candidates

Executive recruiters (also called *headhunters*) are special employment agencies retained by employers to seek out top-management talent for their clients. They fill jobs in the $80,000 and up category, although $120,000 is often the lower limit. The percentage of your firm's positions filled by these services might be small. However, these jobs include the most crucial executive and technical positions. For top executive positions, headhunters may be your *only* source. The employer pays their fees.

Top headhunter firms once took months to complete a big search. Much of that time went into shuffling chores between headhunters and the researchers who develop the initial "long list" of candidates. This approach takes too long in today's fast-moving environment. Most of these firms now have Internet-linked databases, which can help create a list of potential candidates at the push of a button. Top recruiters include Heidrick & Struggles, Egon Zehnder International, Russell Reynolds Associates, and Spencer Stuart.[59]

PROS AND CONS Headhunters are useful. They have many contacts and are especially adept at contacting qualified candidates who are not actively looking to change jobs. They can also keep your firm's name confidential until late in the search process. The recruiter can save top management time by doing the preliminary work of advertising for the position and screening what could turn out to be dozens of applicants. The recruiter's fee might actually turn out to be insignificant compared to the cost of the executive time saved.

But there are pitfalls. As an employer, you must explain fully what sort of candidate is required and why. Some recruiters may be more interested in persuading you to hire a candidate than in finding one who will do the best job. Sometimes, what clients say or think they want is not really what they need. Therefore, be prepared for some in-depth dissecting of your request. Also make sure to meet the person who will be handling your search, nail down exactly what the charges will be, and always make sure to check (or re-check) the final candidates' references yourself.

CANDIDATES' CAVEATS As a job candidate, keep several things in mind when dealing with executive search firms. Some of these firms may present an unpromising candidate to a client simply to make their other one or two proposed candidates look better. Some eager clients may also jump the gun, checking your references and undermining your present position prematurely. Finally, do not confuse executive search firms with the many executive assistance firms that help out-of-work executives find jobs. The latter charge the job seekers handsome fees to assist with things like résumé preparation and interview skills. They rarely actually reach out to prospective employers to find their clients jobs.

College Recruiting and Interns as a Source of Candidates

Many promotable candidates originally get hired through college recruiting. Such recruiting is thus an important source of management trainees, as well as of professional and technical employees.

There are two main problems with on-campus recruiting. First, recruiting is relatively expensive and time-consuming. Schedules must be set, company brochures printed, records of interviews kept, and much time spent on campus. Second, recruiters themselves are sometimes ineffective. Some recruiters are unprepared, show little interest in candidates, and act superior. Others don't effectively screen their student candidates.

Campus recruiters should have two goals. The main goal is determining whether a candidate is worthy of further consideration. Exactly which traits you look for depends on your specific recruiting needs. However, the traits to assess usually include motivation, communication skills, education, appearance, and attitude.

While the main goal is to find good candidates, the other is to attract them to your firm. A sincere and informal attitude, respect for the applicant, and prompt follow-up letters can help to sell the employer to the interviewee.

Job seekers should know that recruiters are usually coy when it comes to revealing the full amount they're willing to pay. For example, one researcher found that 9 out of 10 recruiters say they do not reveal, during hiring interviews, the full amount they're willing to pay to hire good employees for the job. Thus, there's often more flexibility at the top than applicants may realize.[60] Recruiting is increasingly global, as the *Global Issues in HR* explains.

INTERNSHIPS Many college students get their jobs through college internships, a recruiting approach that has grown dramatically in recent years.

Internships can be win-win situations for both students and employers. For students, an internship may mean being able to hone business skills, check out potential employers, and learn more about their career likes (and dislikes). Employers can use the interns to make useful contributions while they're being evaluated as possible full-time employees. One survey found that employers offer jobs to over 70% of their interns.[61]

Partnering with a college or university's career center can thus be useful. It provides recruiters with relatively quick and easy access to a good source of applicants. And it can provide useful advice to recruiters regarding things like labor market conditions and the effectiveness of one's recruiting ads.[62] The Shell Group of companies reduced the list of schools its recruiters visit, using factors such as quality of academic program, number of students enrolled, and student body diversity.[63]

Global Issues in HR

The Global Talent Search

As companies expand across national borders, they must increasingly tap overseas recruiting sources. For example, Gillette International has an international graduate training program aimed at identifying and developing foreign nationals. Gillette subsidiaries overseas hire outstanding business students from top local universities. These foreign nationals are then trained for 6 months at the Gillette facility in their home countries.

However, you don't have to be a multinational to have to recruit abroad. Desperate for qualified nurses, many hospitals (such as Sinai and Northwest hospitals in the Baltimore, Maryland, area) are recruiting in countries like the Philippines, India, and China.[64]

Furthermore, when employers hire "global" employees, they're not just hiring employees who will be sent to work abroad. Employers recognize today that with business increasingly multinational, all employees need a certain level of global awareness. As one article recently put it, "Cube dwellers increasingly need to work, often virtually, across borders with people whose first language is not English, who don't have the same cultural touch points as U.S. employees do, and who don't approach business in the same way that Americans do."[65]

As a result, many employers want their recruiters to look for evidence of global awareness early in the interview process. For example, at Tetra PAK, Inc., recruiters look for expatriate potential every time they hire. International experience (including internships and considerable travel abroad) as well as language proficiency are two of the things employers such as these often look for.

Referrals and Walk-ins as a Source of Candidates

With *employee referrals* campaigns, the firm posts announcements of openings and requests for referrals on its intranet and bulletin boards. It may offer prizes for referrals that end in hirings.

Employee referral programs have pros and cons. Current employees can and usually do provide accurate information about the job applicants they are referring, because they're putting their reputations on the line. The new employees may also have more realistic views of what working in the firm is really like. Referral programs may also result in higher quality candidates, insofar as employees are reluctant to refer less qualified candidates.

But the success of the campaign depends a lot on your employees' morale. And the campaign can backfire if an employee's referral is rejected and the employee becomes dissatisfied. Using referrals exclusively may also be discriminatory if most of your current employees (and their referrals) are male or white.

Employee referral programs are popular. Employee referrals have been the source of almost half of all hires at AmeriCredit since the firm kicked off its "you've got friends, we want to meet them" employee referrals program. Employees making a referral receive $1,000 awards, with the payments spread over a year. As the head of recruiting said, "Quality people know quality people. If you give employees the opportunity to make referrals, they automatically suggest high-caliber people because they are stakeholders."[66]

WALK-INS Particularly for hourly workers, *walk-ins*—direct applications made at your office—are a major source of applicants, one you can even encourage by posting "Hiring" signs on your property.

Treat all walk-ins courteously and diplomatically. Many employers give every walk-in a brief interview with someone in the HR office, even if it is only to get information on the applicant in case a position should open in the future. Good business practice also requires answering all letters of inquiry from applicants promptly and courteously.

CUSTOMERS AS CANDIDATES The Texas-based Container Store uses a successful variant of the employee referrals campaign. It trains its employees to recruit new employees from among the firm's customers. For example, if an employee sees that a customer seems interested in the Container Store, the employee might say, "If you love shopping here, you'd love working here."[67]

TELECOMMUTERS Hiring telecommuters is another option. For example, JetBlue Airways uses at-home agents who are JetBlue employees to handle its reservation needs. These "crewmembers" all live in the Salt Lake City area, and work out of their homes. They use JetBlue-supplied computers and technology, and receive JetBlue training.[68]

CHEESECAKE EXAMPLE To support its fast-growth strategy, The Cheesecake Factory uses four recruiting sources: employee referrals, promotions of current employees, search

The Container Store trains its employees to recruit new employees from among the firm's customers.

firms, and online job postings. The firm's head of HR, Ed Eynon, says the Web has become "our No. 1 source of recruitment, with between 30% and 35% of our new managers coming through it." The company also does not just post short print-type help wanted ads on the Web. For most jobs it includes the entire job description. This helps provide potential applicants with a realistic picture of the job, and helps to screen out people who see that the job is not for them. The server's description on CareerBuilder.com includes a 765 word list of duties, for instance.[69]

Summary of Current Recruitment Practices

An SHRM survey provides a useful overview of current recruitment practices:[70]

- More employees are using newer recruiting tools such as niche (specialist) job boards, social networking sites, and the new .jobs domain.
- Many employers use so-called passive job candidate recruiting methods—in other words, seeking out candidates who aren't actively seeking jobs. Popular methods here include reviewing associations and trade groups' membership directories, scanning social networking sites, and mining industry-specific sites such as discussion forums, newsgroups, and blogs.
- Employers most frequently use "the time to fill outstanding job vacancies," "cost per hire," "number of outstanding job vacancies," and "first-year turnover" to measure their recruiting efforts' effectiveness.
- For most employers, the Internet was their primary recruiting method.
- Between 50% and 60% of employers surveyed use applicant tracking systems, and about 22% more intend to implement one shortly.
- For most employers, national online job boards produced the *most* applicants, followed by employee referrals, and the employer's own Web site. Employee referrals, followed by national online job boards and internal job postings, generated by far the highest *quality* of job candidates. Employee referrals, national online job boards, and internal job postings produced the *best return* on these employers' recruiting dollars.

Recruiting a More Diverse Workforce

In countries like the United Kingdom, France, Australia and the U.S., the workforce is becoming more diverse. This means taking special steps to recruit older workers, minorities, and women.

Many factors contribute to successful minority/female recruiting. For example, flexible hours make it easier to attract and keep single parents. However, the important point is to take the steps that "say" this is a good place for diverse employees to work. Doing so might include using minority-targeted media outlets; highly diverse ads; emphasizing inclusiveness in policy statements; and using minority, female, and/or older recruiters.[71]

OLDER WORKERS AS A SOURCE OF CANDIDATES Employers increasingly turn to older workers as a source of recruits, for several reasons. Because of buyouts and downsizing-related early retirements, many workers retired early and want to reenter the workforce.[72] Furthermore, the number of baby boom generation workers in the U.S. aged 55–64 is growing faster than just about all other demographic groups.[73] As many of these workers retire, employers are having difficulty replacing them with younger workers. A survey by the American Association of Retired Persons (AARP) concluded that about 70% of the baby boomers expect to work after retirement, at least part-time.[74]

Recruiting and attracting older workers involves any or all of the sources we described earlier (advertising, employment agencies, and so forth), but with one big difference. Recruiting and attracting older workers generally requires a comprehensive effort before the recruiting begins, in part because older workers may have some special preferences. The effort's aim is to make the company an attractive place in which the older worker can work. AARP published its list of "The Top 15" best companies for older workers. A sampling of what sets these employers apart for older workers follows:[75]

- Baptist Health System South Florida, Stanley Group, and Hartford Financial Services Group offer flexible work arrangements including phased retirement. Hartford actually offers eight flexible work arrangements.
- New York Life Insurance Company opens its child care center to grandchildren.
- Ultratech Stepper and Baptist Health have "age-friendly cultures."
- The most effective ads for attracting older workers emphasize schedule flexibility and accentuate the firm's equal opportunity employment statement.[76]

RECRUITING SINGLE PARENTS About two-thirds of all single parents are in the workforce, and this group thus represents an important source of candidates.

Formulating an intelligent program for attracting (and keeping) single parents starts with understanding the problems they encounter balancing work and family life. In one early survey, working single parents (the majority single mothers) stated that their work responsibilities interfered significantly with their family life. They described as a no-win situation the challenge of having to do a good job at work and being a good parent, and many expressed disappointment at feeling like failures in both endeavors.

The respondents generally viewed themselves as having "less support, less personal time, more stress, and greater difficulty balancing job and home life" than other working parents.[77] However, most were hesitant to dwell on their single-parent status at work for fear that such a disclosure would affect their jobs adversely.[78]

Given such concerns, the first step in attracting (and keeping) single parents is to make the workplace as user-friendly for single parents as practical. Organizing regular, ongoing support groups and other forums at which single parents can share their concerns is useful. The financial firm Barclaycard organized a "buddy" system in which the firm teamed members of its HR group with single parents out of work, to mentor them in skills like interviewing and résumé writing.[79]

However, the main aim should be to make the workplace more family friendly. Many firms have instituted family friendly programs but these may not be extensive enough for single parents. For example, *flextime* programs provide employees some flexibility (such as 1-hour windows at the beginning or end of the day) around which to build their workdays. The problem is that for many single parents this limited flexibility may not be enough to really make a difference in the face of the "patchwork child care" and conflicting work–home pressures that many face.[80]

Flexible work schedules and child care benefits are thus two main single-parent magnets. In addition, supervisors play a central role. Surveys suggest that a supportive attitude on the supervisor's part can go far towards making the single parent's work–home balancing act more bearable.

RECRUITING MINORITIES AND WOMEN   The same prescriptions that apply to recruiting single parents apply to recruiting minorities and women. In other words, employers have to formulate comprehensive plans for attracting minorities and women. These plans may include reevaluating personnel policies, developing flexible work options, redesigning jobs, and offering flexible benefit plans.

An employer can do many specific things to become more attractive to minorities. To the extent that many minority applicants may not meet the educational or experience standards for a job, many companies offer remedial training in basic arithmetic and writing. Online diversity data banks or minority-focused recruiting publications are another option.

Sometimes the easiest way to recruit women and minorities is to make sure that they don't quit in the first place. For example, the accounting firm KPMG works hard to make sure that female employees who take maternity leave will want to return. When an expectant mother tells HR that she's going to take maternity leave, the company sends her a basket containing a description of its parental leave benefits as well as a baby bottle, a rattle, and a tiny T-shirt that says, "My mom works at KPMG."[81]

THE DISABLED   The U.S. EEOC estimates that nearly 70% of the disabled are jobless, but it certainly doesn't have to be that way.[82] In Germany, for instance, customers visiting Volkswagen's Wolfsburg plant are met by receptionist Mr. Janz. If they don't check the sign on his counter, they might assume he's ignoring them. In fact, Mr. Janz is blind, and the sign tells visitors to speak directly to him so he knows they are there.[83] Volkswagen recruited Mr. Janz because the company has a policy of integrating people with disabilities into its workforce.

Doing so involves several initiatives. For some managers it may require a new mindset, one that welcomes disabled employees as an excellent and largely untapped source of competent, efficient labor for jobs ranging from information technology to creative advertising to receptionist. Complying with a country's disability laws is another sensible strategy, but it's also important to go beyond this. For instance, actively seek out and make available the sorts of voice recognition and other technologies that can ensure the disabled worker is a productive one.

DEVELOPING AND USING APPLICATION FORMS

⑤ Explain how to use application forms to predict job performance.

Purpose of Application Forms

application form
The form that provides information on education, prior work record, and skills.

Once you have a pool of applicants, the selection process can begin, and for most employers the application form is the first step in this process. (Some firms first require a brief, prescreening interview.) The **application form** is a good way to quickly collect verifiable and therefore fairly accurate historical data from the candidate. It usually includes information about such areas as education, prior work history, and hobbies.

A filled-in form provides at least four types of information. First are data on substantive matters, such as does the applicant have the education and experience to do the job? Second, you can draw some conclusions about the applicant's career progress. Third, you can draw tentative conclusions regarding the applicant's stability based on previous work record. (However, be careful not to assume that an unusual number of job changes necessarily reflects on the applicant's stability; for example, the person's two most recent employers may have had to lay off large numbers of employees.) Fourth, it provides information you can use to check references and to assess the veracity of the applicant's answers.

In practice, most organizations need several application forms. For technical and managerial personnel, for example, the form may require detailed answers to questions concerning such areas as the applicant's education. The form for hourly factory workers might focus on such areas as the tools and equipment the applicant has used.

Equal Opportunity and Application Forms

Employers should carefully review their application forms to ensure that they comply with equal employment laws. Questions concerning race, religion, age, sex, or national origin are generally not illegal per se under U.S. government laws, but are illegal under certain state laws. However, in the U.S. the EEOC views them with disfavor. If the applicant shows that a disproportionate number of protected group applicants gets screened out, then the burden of proof will be on the employer to prove that the potentially discriminatory items are both related to success or failure on the job and not unfairly discriminatory.

Perhaps due to their proliferation, online application forms may be particularly susceptible to illegal or inadvisable questions. One survey of 41 Internet-based applications found that over 97% contained at least one inadvisable question. There were an average of just over four inappropriate questions per form. Questions regarding the applicant's past salary, age, and driver's license information led the list.[84]

Figure 4.10 presents the approach one employer—the U.S. Federal Bureau of Investigation—uses to collect application form information. The Employment History section requests detailed information on each prior employer, including job title, duties, name of supervisor, and whether the employment was involuntarily terminated. Also note that in signing the application, the applicant certifies his or her understanding of several things: that falsified statements may be cause for dismissal; that investigation of credit, employment, and driving records is authorized; that a medical examination may be required; that drug screening tests may be required; and that employment is for no definite period of time.

VIDEO RÉSUMÉS More candidates are submitting video résumés, a practice replete with benefits and threats. About half of responding employers in one survey thought video résumés might give employers a better feel for the candidate's professional demeanor, presentation skills, and job experience. The danger is that a video résumé makes it more likely rejected candidates may claim discrimination.[85]

MANDATORY DISPUTE RESOLUTION Increasingly today, many employers are requiring applicants to sign mandatory alternative dispute resolution forms as part of the application process. For example, the employment application package for an electronics firm requires applicants to agree to arbitrate certain legal disputes related to their application for employment or employment with the company.

While mandatory arbitration is on the rise, it is also under attack. In the U.S., courts, government agencies, and even arbitrators are concerned that binding arbitration strips away too many employees' rights (*voluntary* arbitration is not under attack).[86] Mandatory arbitration can also inhibit recruiting. In one study, making employment arbitration mandatory had a significantly negative impact on the attractiveness to the subjects of the company as a place to work.[87]

After You Receive the Application

After you receive the application, the job of screening the applicants begins, so we turn to selection and screening in chapter 5. Before turning to selection, however, there are two points to keep in mind.

COURTESY First, some employers develop expensive recruiting programs and then drop the ball by treating candidates discourteously. A survey by Monster.com illustrates this. What interviewer behaviors most annoyed job seekers? Seventy percent of job seekers listed "acting as if there is no time to talk to me." Fifty-seven percent listed "withholding information about position." About half listed "turning interview into cross examination" and "showing up late."[88]

STAYING IN TOUCH Second, some employers maintain contact with candidates who, while not hirable today, may be of interest tomorrow. Some employers use "candidate relationship management" systems for this. Similar to the customer relationship management systems companies use to decide which customer should receive which coupon offers, *candidate relationship management* systems aim to nurture relationships with prospective candidates. They do this by periodically informing past candidates about potentially interesting job openings, and by collecting data on each candidate's evolving skills.[89]

FIGURE 4.10 Employment Application

FEDERAL BUREAU OF INVESTIGATION

Preliminary Application for
Special Agent Position
(Please Type or Print in Black Ink)

Date: _____

<table>
<tr><td colspan="2">FIELD OFFICE USE ONLY
Right Thumb Print</td></tr>
<tr><td>Div:</td><td>Program:</td></tr>
</table>

I. PERSONAL HISTORY

Name in Full (Last, First, Middle)	List College Degree(s) Already Received or Pursuing, Major, School, and Month/Year:

Marital Status: ☐ Single ☐ Engaged ☐ Married ☐ Separated ☐ Legally Separated ☐ Widowed ☐ Divorced

Birth Date (Month, Day, Year) Birth Place:	Social Security Number: (Optional)	Do you understand FBI employment requires availability for assignment anywhere in the U.S.?

Current Address

Street _____ Apt. No. _____

Home Phone _____
Area Code _____ Number _____

City _____ State _____ Zip Code _____
Work Phone _____
Area Code _____ Number _____

Are you: CPA ☐ Yes ☐ No   Licensed Driver ☐ Yes ☐ No   U. S. Citizen ☐ Yes ☐ No

Have you served on active duty in the U. S. Military? ☐ Yes ☐ No If yes, indicate branch of service and dates (month/year) of active duty. Include military school attendance (month/year):

How did you learn or become interested in FBI employment as a Special Agent?	Have you previously applied for FBI employment? ☐ Yes ☐ No If yes, location and date:

Do you have a foreign language background? ☐ Yes ☐ No List proficiency for each language on reverse side.

Have you ever been arrested for any crime (include major traffic violations such as Driving Under the Influence or While Intoxicated, etc.)? ☐ Yes ☐ No If so, list all such matters on a continuation sheet, even if not formally charged, or no court appearance or found not guilty, or matter settled by payment of fine or forfeiture of collateral. Include date, place, charge, disposition, details, and police agency on reverse side.

II. EMPLOYMENT HISTORY

Identify your most recent three years FULL-TIME work experience, after high school (excluding summer, part-time and temporary employment).

From Month/Year	To Month/Year	Title of Position and Description of Work	# of hrs. Per week	Name/Location of Employer

III. PERSONAL DECLARATIONS

Persons with a disability who require an accommodation to complete the application process are required to notify the FBI of their need for the accommodation.

Have you used marijuana during the last three years or more than 15 times? ☐ Yes ☐ No

Have you used any illegal drug(s) or combination of illegal drugs, other than marijuana, more than 5 times or during the last 10 years? ☐ Yes ☐ No

All Information provided by applicants concerning their drug history will be subject to verification by a preemployment polygraph examination.

Do you understand all prospective FBI employees will be required to submit to an urinalysis for drug abuse prior to employment? ☐ Yes ☐ No

Please do not write below this line.

I am aware that willfully withholding information or making false statements on this application constitutes a violation of Section 1001. Title 18, U.S. Code and if appointed, will be the basis for dismissal from the Federal Bureau of Investigation. I agree to these conditions and I hereby certify that all statements made by me on this application are true and complete, to the best of my knowledge.

_____
Signature of applicant as usually written (**Do Not Use Nickname**)

Review

SUMMARY

1. Developing an organization structure results in jobs that have to be staffed. Job analysis is the procedure through which you find out (1) what the job entails and (2) what kinds of people should be hired for the job. It involves six steps: (1) Determine the use of the job analysis information, (2) collect background information, (3) select the positions to be analyzed, (4) collect job analysis data, (5) review information with participants, and (6) develop a job description and job specification.

2. The job description should portray the work of the position so well that the duties are clear without reference to other job descriptions. Always ask yourself: Will the new employee understand the job if he or she reads the job description?

3. The job specification supplements the job description to answer the question "What human traits and experience are necessary to do this job well?" It tells what kind of person to recruit and for what qualities that person should be tested. Job specifications are usually based on the educated guesses of managers; however, a more accurate statistical approach to developing job specifications can also be used.

4. *Traditional job analysis* focuses on "what" a job is in terms of job duties and responsibilities. *Competency analysis* focuses more on "how" the worker meets the job's objectives or actually accomplishes the work. Traditional job analysis is more job focused. Competency-based analysis is more worker focused—specifically, what must he or she be competent to do?

5. Developing personnel plans requires three forecasts: one for personnel requirements, one for the supply of outside candidates, and one for the supply of inside candidates. To predict the need for personnel, first project the demand for the product or service. Next project the volume of production required to meet these estimates. Finally, relate personnel needs to these production estimates.

6. Once personnel needs are projected, the next step is to build a pool of qualified applicants. We discussed several sources of candidates, including internal sources (or promotion from within), advertising, employment agencies, executive recruiters, college recruiting, the Internet, and referrals and walk-ins. Remember that it is unlawful to discriminate against any individual with respect to employment because of race, color, religion, sex, national origin, or age (unless these are bona fide occupational qualifications).

7. Once you have a pool of applicants, the work of selecting the best can begin. We turn to employee selection in the following chapter.

KEY TERMS

job analysis   102
job description   102
job specification   102
workforce planning   110
trend analysis   111
ratio analysis   111
scatter plot   111

qualifications inventories   112
personnel replacement charts   112
talent management   114
job posting   117
application tracking systems   119
application service provider   120
application form   128

DISCUSSION QUESTIONS AND EXERCISES

1. What items are typically included in a job description? What items are not shown?

2. What is job analysis? How can you make use of the information it provides?

3. We discussed several methods for collecting job analysis data. Compare these methods, explain what each is useful for, and list the pros and cons of each.

4. Explain how you would conduct a job analysis.

5. Working individually or in groups, obtain copies of job descriptions for clerical positions at the college or university you attend or the firm where you work. What types of information do they contain? Do they give you enough information to explain what the job involves and how to do it? How would you improve the descriptions?

6. Compare five sources of job candidates.

7. What types of information can an application form provide?

8. Working individually or in groups, bring to class several classified and display ads from this Sunday's help wanted ads. Analyze the effectiveness of these ads.

9. Working individually or in groups, visit your local office of your country's employment agency. Come back to class prepared to discuss the following questions: What types of jobs seemed to be available through this agency, predominantly? To what extent do you think this particular agency would be a good source of professional, technical, and/or managerial applicants? What sort of paperwork are applicants to the state agency required to complete before their applications are processed by the agency? What other opinions did you form about the state agency?

10. Working individually or in groups, review help wanted ads placed over the past few Sundays by local employment agencies. Do some employment agencies seem to specialize in certain types of jobs? If you were an HR manager seeking a relationship with an employment agency for each of the following types of jobs, which local agencies would you turn to first, based on their help wanted ad history: engineers, secretaries, data-processing clerks, accountants, and factory workers?

Application Exercises

HR in Action Case Incident 1 — Finding People Who Are Passionate About What They Do

Trilogy Enterprises Inc., of Austin, Texas, is a fast-growing software company, and provides software solutions to giant global firms for improving sales and performance. It prides itself on its unique and unorthodox culture. Many of its approaches to business practice are unusual, but in Trilogy's fast-changing and highly competitive environment they seem to work.

There is no dress code and employees make their own hours, often very long. They tend to socialize together (the average age is 26), both in the office's well-stocked kitchen and on company-sponsored events and trips to places like local dance clubs and retreats in Las Vegas and Hawaii. An in-house jargon has developed, and the shared history of the sixteen-year-old firm has taken on the status of legend. Responsibility is heavy and comes early, with a "just do it now" attitude that dispenses with long apprenticeships. New recruits are given a few weeks of intensive training, known as Trilogy University and described by participants as "more like boot camp than business school." Information is delivered as if with "a fire hose," and new employees are expected to commit their expertise and vitality to everything they do. Jeff Daniel, director of college recruiting, admits the intense and unconventional firm is not the employer for everybody. "But it's definitely an environment where people who are passionate about what they do can thrive."

The firm employs about 700 such passionate people. Trilogy's managers know the rapid growth they seek depends on having a staff of the best people they can find, quickly trained and given broad responsibility and freedom as soon as possible. Founder and CEO Joe Liemandt says, "At a software company, people are everything. You can't build the next great software company, which is what we're trying to do here, unless you're totally committed to that. Of course, the leaders at every company say, 'People are everything.' But they don't act on it."

Trilogy makes finding the right people (it calls them "great people") a companywide mission. Recruiters actively pursue the freshest, if least experienced, people in the job market, scouring college career fairs and computer science departments for talented overachievers with ambition and entrepreneurial instincts. Top managers conduct the first rounds of interviews, letting prospects know they will be pushed to achieve but will be well rewarded. Employees take top recruits and their significant others out on the town when they fly into Austin for the standard, three-day preliminary visit. A typical day might begin with grueling interviews but end with mountain biking, rollerblading, or laser tag. Executives have been known to fly out to meet and woo hot prospects who couldn't make the trip.

One year, Trilogy reviewed 15,000 résumés, conducted 4,000 on-campus interviews, flew 850 prospects in for interviews, and hired 262 college graduates, who account for over a third of its current employees. The cost per hire was $13,000; recruiter Jeff Daniel believes it was worth every penny.

Questions

1. Identify some of the established recruiting techniques that underlie Trilogy's unconventional approach to attracting talent.
2. What particular elements of Trilogy's culture most likely appeal to the kind of employees it seeks? How does it convey those elements to job prospects?
3. Would Trilogy be an appealing employer for you? Why or why not? If not, what would it take for you to accept a job offer from Trilogy?
4. What suggestions would you make to Trilogy for improving its recruiting processes?

Sources: Chuck Salter, "Insanity, Inc.," *Fast Company* (January 1999): 101–108; and www.trilogy.com/sections/careers/work, accessed August 24, 2007.

HR in Action *Case Incident 2*	Carter Cleaning Company: A Tight Labor Market for Cleaners—Applying Your Marketing Skills

While most of the publicity about "tight" labor markets usually revolves around systems engineers, nurses, and chemical engineers, some of the tightest markets are found in some surprising places. For example, if you were to ask Jennifer Carter, the head of her family's chain of dry-cleaning stores, what the main problem was in running their firm, the answer would be quick and short: hiring good people. The typical dry-cleaning store is heavily dependent on hiring good managers, cleaner-spotters, and pressers. Employees generally have no more than a high school education (many have less), and the market is very competitive. Over a typical weekend, literally dozens of want ads for cleaner-spotters or pressers can be found in area newspapers. These people are generally paid about $12 an hour, and they change jobs frequently.

Why so much difficulty finding good help? The work is hot and uncomfortable; the hours are often long; the pay is often the same or less than the typical applicant could earn working in an air-conditioned environment, and the fringe benefits are usually nonexistent, unless you count getting your clothes cleaned for free.

Complicating the problem is the fact that Jennifer and other cleaners are usually faced with the continuing task of recruiting and hiring qualified workers out of a pool of individuals who are almost nomadic in their propensity to move around. The turnover in her stores and the stores of many of their competitors is often 400% per year. The problem,

Jennifer says, is maddening: "On the one hand, the quality of our service depends on the skills of the cleaner-spotters, pressers, and counter staff. People come to us for our ability to return their clothes to them spotless and crisply pressed. On the other hand, profit margins are thin and we've got to keep our stores running, so I'm happy just to be able to round up enough live applicants to be able to keep my stores fully manned."

Questions

1. Recruiting for cleaning store employees obviously presents quite a challenge to one's marketing skills. Review what we discussed earlier in this chapter about using marketing to create value in terms of peoples' needs and wants. Then, provide a detailed list of recommendations concerning how Jennifer should go about increasing the number of acceptable job applicants, so that her company need no longer hire just about anyone who walks in the door. Specifically, your recommendations should include:
   - Completely worded classified ads
   - Recommendations concerning any other recruiting strategies you would suggest she use.
2. What practical suggestions could you make that might help reduce turnover and make the stores an attractive place in which to work, thereby reducing recruiting problems?

EXPERIENTIAL EXERCISE

The Nursing Shortage

As of March 2008, U.S. unemployment was beginning to drift up, and employers were obviously holding back on their hiring. However, while many people were unemployed, that was not the case with nurse professionals. Virtually every hospital was aggressively recruiting nurses. Many were turning to foreign-trained nurses, for example, by recruiting nurses in the Philippines. Experts expected nurses to be in very short supply for years to come. The same trend has held true for the United Kingdom, where a nursing shortage has been tracked for much of this decade.

Purpose:

The purpose of this exercise is to give you experience creating a recruitment program.

Required Understanding:

You should be thoroughly familiar with the contents of this chapter, and with the nurse recruitment program of a hospital

such as St. George's Hospital in London (see for example www.stgeorges.nhs.uk/workingindex.asp).[90]

How to Set Up the Exercise/Instructions:

Set up groups of four to five students for this exercise. The groups should work separately and should not converse with each other. Each group should address the following tasks:

1. Based on information available on the hospital's Web site, create a hard-copy ad for the hospital to place in the Sunday edition of *The Times of London*. Which (geographic) editions of the *Times* would you use and why?
2. Analyze and critique the hospital's current online nurses' ad. How would you improve it?
3. Prepare in outline form a complete nurses' recruiting program for this hospital, including all recruiting sources your group would use

ENDNOTES

1. "Help Wanted—and Found," *Fortune* (October 2, 2006): 40.

2. Frederick Morgeson and Michael Campion, "Accuracy in Job Analysis: Toward an Inference Based Model," *Journal of Organizational Behavior* 21, no. 7 (November 2000): 819–827. See also Frederick Morgeson and Stephen Humphrey, "The Work Design Questionnaire (WDQ): Developing and Validating a Comprehensive Measure for Assessing Job Design and the Nature of Work," *Journal of Applied Psychology* 91, no. 6 (2006): 1321–1339.

3. Frederick Morgeson et al., "Self Presentation Processes in Job Analysis: A Field Experiment Investigating Inflation in Abilities, Tasks, and Competencies," *Journal of Applied Psychology* 89, no. 4 (November 4, 2004): 674–686.

4. Ibid., 674.

5. Roni Reiter-Palmon et al., "Development of an O*NET Web Based Job Analysis and Its Implementation in the U.S. Navy: Lessons Learned," *Human Resource Management Review* 16 (2006): 294–309.

6. Ibid., 294.

7. Darin Hartley, "Job Analysis at the Speed of Reality," *Training and Development* (September 2004): 20–22.

8. Erik Dirdorff and Mark Wilson, "A Meta Analysis of Job Analysis Reliability," *Journal of Applied Psychology* 88, no. 4 (2003): 635–646.

9. Op. sit., 18.

10. Deborah Kearney, *Reasonable Accommodations: Job Descriptions in the Age of ADA, OSHA, and Workers Comp* (New York: Van Nostrand Reinhold, 1994): 9.

11. Ibid.

12. Steven Hunt, "Generic Work Behavior: An Investigation into the Dimensions of Entry-Level, Hourly Job Performance," *Personnel Psychology* 49 (1996): 51–83.

13. http://online.onetcenter.org/link/summary/11–2022.00, accessed April 18, 2008.

14. Jeffrey Shippmann et al., "The Practice of Competency Modeling," *Personnel Psychology* 53, no. 3 (2000): 703.

15. Ibid.

16. Carolyn Hirschman, "Putting Forecasting in Focus," *HR Magazine* (March 2007): 44–49.

17. "More Companies Turn to Workforce Planning to Boost Productivity and Efficiency," The Conference Board, press release/news, August 7, 2006; Carolyn Hirschman, "Putting Forecasting in Focus," *HR Magazine* (March 2007): 44–49.

18. "Demands of Tight Labor Market Will Test HR in 2007," *BNA Bulletin to Management* (January 23, 2007): 31.

19. This is a modification of a definition found in Peter Wallum, "A Broader View of Succession Planning," *Personnel Management* (September 1993): 45. See also Michelle Harrison et al., "Effective Succession Planning," *Training and Development* (October 2006): 22–23.

20. Wallum op cit., 43–44.

21. "Succession Planning: A Never-Ending Process that Must Mesh with Talent Management," *HR Focus* 84, no. 5 (May 2007): 8.

22. Bill Roberts, "Matching Talent with Tasks," *HR Magazine* (November 2002): 91–96.

23. Ibid.

24. "Survey: Talent Management a Top Concern," *CIO Insight* (January 2, 2007).

25. Paul Loftus, "Tackle Talent Management to Achieve High Performance," *Plant Engineering* 61, no. 6 (June 15, 2007): 29.

26. "Talent Management Is on HR's Agenda for 2007 and Beyond," *HR Focus* 84, no. 4 (April 2007): 8.

27. www.talentmanagement101.com, accessed December 10, 2007.

28. Michael Laff, "Talent Management: From Hire to Retire," *Training and Development* (November 2006): 42–48.

29. www.talentmanagement101.com, accessed December 10, 2007.

30. www.silkroadtech.com, accessed December 10, 2007.

31. "Software Facilitates Talent Management," *Product News Network* (May 18, 2007).

32. "Work Stream to Announce 'Project X.'—Their Next-Generation Talent Management Solutions—at HR Technology Conference & Exposition, October 10, 2007, in Chicago, Illinois," *CNW Group* (September 26, 2007).

33. Tony Carnevale, "The Coming Labor and Skills Shortage," *Training and Development* (January 2005): 36–41. "Report Says More Companies Focus on Workforce Planning to Heighten Productivity," *Training and Development* (October 2006): 10–12. See also "Employers Responding to a Potential Exodus with Recruitment, Retention, Training," *BNA Bulletin to Management* 58, no. 31 (July 31, 2007): 241.

34. Gina Ruiz, "Special Report: Talent Acquisition," *Workforce Management* (July 23, 2007): 39.

35. Paul Loftus, "Tackle Talent Management to Achieve High Performance," *Plant Engineering* 61, no. 6 (June 15, 2007): 29.

36. Jonathan Segal, "Land Executives, Not Lawsuits," *HR Magazine* (October 2006): 123–130.

37. Jonathan Segal, "Strings Attached," *HR Magazine* (February 2005): 119–123.

38. Ibid., 120.

39. Kevin Carlson et al., "Recruitment Evaluation: The Case for Assessing the Quality of Applicants Attracted," *Personnel Psychology* 55 (2002): 461–490. For a recent survey of recruiting source effectiveness, see, "The 2007 Recruiting Metrics and Performance Benchmark Report, 2nd ed.," Staffing.org, Inc., 2007.

40. Arthur R. Pell, *Recruiting and Selecting Personnel* (New York: Regents, 1969): 10–12.

41. Jessica Marquez, "A Global Recruiting Site Helps Far-Flung Managers at the Professional Services Company Acquire the Talent They Need—and Saves One Half-Million Dollars a Year," *Workforce Management* (March 13, 2006): 22.

42. Dawn Onley, "Improving Your Online Application Process," *HR Magazine* 50, no. 10 (October 2005): 109.

43. Martha Frase-Blunt, "Make a Good First Impression," *HR Magazine* (April 2004): 81–86. See also "Corporate Recruiting Web Sites Luring Workers, But Could Be Improved, Experts Say," *BNA Bulletin to Management* (March 14, 2006): 81–82.

44. Emily Steel, "Job Search Sites Face a Nimble Threat," *Wall Street Journal*, http://online.wsj.com/public/article/SB119189368160253014-ZQlBizIzas3h1_yL_eRq5Yc4_kI_20071108.html?mod=tff_main_tff_top, accessed April 18, 2008.

45. Jennifer Berkshire, "Social Network Recruiting," *HR Magazine* (April 2005): 95–98.

46. Josee Rose, "Recruiters Take Hip Path to Fill Accounting Jobs," *Wall Street Journal* (September 18, 2007): 38. See also Karen Donovan, "Law Firms Go a Bit Hollywood to Recruit the YouTube Generation," *New York Times* (September 28, 2007).

47. Elizabeth Agnvall, "Job Fairs Go Virtual," *HR Magazine* (July 2007): 85.

48. Ibid.

49. "Innovative HR Programs Cultivate Successful Employees," *Nation's Restaurant News* 41, no. 50 (December 17, 2007): 74.

50. "EEOC Issues Much Delayed Definition of 'Applicant'," *HR Magazine* (April 2004): 29; Valerie Hoffman and Greg Davis, "OFCCP's Internet Applicant Definition Requires Overhaul of Recruitment and Hiring Policies," legal report, the Society for Human Resource Management (January/February 2006): 2.

51. Jim Meade, "Where Did They Go?" *HR Magazine* (September 2000): 81–84.

52. Gino Ruiz, "Special Report: Talent Acquisition," *Workforce Management* (July 23, 2007): 39.

53. See, for example, Phillip Kotler and Gary Armstrong, *Principles of Marketing* (Upper Saddle River, NJ: 2001): 6–8.

54. "John Zappe, "Temp-to-Hire Is Becoming a Full-Time Practice at Firms," *Workforce Management* (June 2005): 82–86.

55. Robert Bogner Jr. and Elizabeth Salasko, "Beware the Legal Risks of Hiring Temps," *Workforce* (October 2002): 50–57.

56. Fay Hansen, "A Permanent Strategy for Temporary Hires," *Workforce Management* (February 26, 2007): 27.

57. Carolyn Hirschman, "Are Your Contractors Legal?" *HR Magazine* (March 2004): 59–63.

58. This is adapted from Nancy Howe, "Match Temp Services to Your Needs," *Personnel Journal* (March 1989): 45–51. See also Richard Vosburgh, "The Evolution of HR: Developing HR as an Internal Consulting Organization," *Human Resource Planning* 30, no. 3 (September 2007): 11–12; and Stephen Miller, "Collaboration Is Key to Effective Outsourcing," *HR Magazine* 58 (supp Trendbook 2008): 60–61.

59. "Leading Executive Search Firms," *Workforce Management* (June 25, 2007): 24.

60. "In Negotiating Game, Most Recruiters Hold Back, Knowing Few Candidates Hold Out for Better Offer," *BNA Bulletin to Management* (2000): 291.

61. "Internships Growing in Popularity Among Companies Seeking Fresh Talent and Ideas," *BNA Bulletin to Management* (March 20, 2007): 89–90.

62. Lisa Munniksma, "Career Matchmakers," *HR Magazine* (February 2005): 93–96.

63. Joel Mullich, "Finding the Schools that Yield the Best Job Applicant ROI," *Workforce Management* (March 2004): 67–68.

64. Scott Graham, "Hospitals Recruiting Overseas," *Baltimore Business Journal* (June 1, 2001): 1.

65. Martha Frase, "Show All Employees a Wider World," *HR Magazine* (June 2007): 99–102.

66. Michelle Martinez, "The Headhunter Within," *HR Magazine* (August 2001): 48–56.

67. Jennifer Taylor Arnold, "Customers as Employees," *HR Magazine* (April 2007): 77–82.

68. Martha Frase-Blunt, "Call Centers Come Home," *HR Magazine* (January 2007): 85–90.

69. "Help Wanted—and Found," *Fortune* (October 2, 2006): 40.

70. "2007 Advances in E-Recruiting: Leveraging the .jobs Domain," Society for Human Resource Management, June 2007.

71. Derek Avery and Patrick McKay, "Target Practice: An Organizational Impression Management Approach to Attracting Minority and Female Job Applicants," *Personnel Psychology* 59 (2006): 157–87.

72. Sandra Block and Stephanie Armour, "Many Americans Retire Years Before They Want To," *USA Today* (July 26, 2006), http://usatoday.com, accessed December 23, 2007.

73. "Workforce Trends," *AARP*, www.AARP.org/money/careers, accessed December 23, 2007.

74. Ibid.

75. Ed Shanahan, "The Top 15," www.aarpmagazine.org/lifestyle, accessed December 23, 2007.

76. Gary Adams and Barbara Rau, "Attracting Retirees to Apply: Desired Organizational Characteristics of Bridge Employment," *Journal of Organizational Behavior* 26, no. 6 (September 2005): 649–660.

77. Judith Casey and Marci Pitt-Catsouphes, "Employed Single Mothers: Balancing Job and Home Life," *Employee Assistance Quarterly* 9, no. 3/4 (1994): 37–53.

78. Ibid., 45.

79. "Barclaycard Helps Single Parents to Find Employment," *Personnel Today* (November 7, 2006).

80. Susan Glairon, "Single Parents Need More Flexibility at Work, Advocates in Denver Says," *Daily Camera* (February 8, 2002).

81. Allison Wellner, "Welcoming Back Mom," *HR Magazine* (June 2004): 77–78.

82. Linda Moore, "Firms Need to Improve Recruitment, Hiring of Disabled Workers, EEO Chief Says," *Knight Ridder/Business News* (November 2003): Item 03309094. See also "Recruiting Disabled More than Good Deed, Experts Say," *BNA Bulletin to Management* (February 27, 2007): 71.

83. Richard Donkin, "Making Space for a Wheelchair Worker," *Financial Times* (November 13, 2003): 9.

84. J. Craig Wallace et al., "Applying for Jobs Online: Examining the Legality of Internet-Based Application Forms," *Public Personnel Management* 20, no. 4 (Winter 2000): 497–504.

85. Kathy Gurchiek, "Video Resumes Spark Curiosity, Questions," *HR Magazine* (May 2007): 28–30; and "Video Resumes Can Illuminate Applicants Abilities, But Pose Discrimination Concerns," *BNA Bulletin to Management* (May 20, 2007): 169–170.

86. *Ryan's Family Steakhouse Inc.* v. *Floss*, "Supreme Court Let Stand Decision Finding Prehire Arbitration Agreements Unenforceable," *BNA Bulletin to Management* (January 11, 2001): 11.

87. Douglas Mahoney et al., "The Effects of Mandatory Employment Arbitration Systems on Applicants' Attraction to Organizations," *Human Resource Management* 44, no.4 (Winter 2005): 449–470.

88. Scott Erker, "What Does Your Hiring Process Say About You?" *Training and Development* (May 2007): 67–70.

89. Martha Frase, "Stocking Your Talent Pool," *HR Magazine* (April 2007): 67–74.

90. Accessed Aug. 5, 2008.

Appendix

ENRICHMENT TOPICS IN JOB ANALYSIS

Additional Job Analysis Methods

Job Analysis Record Sheet

You may encounter several other job analysis methods. For example, the U.S. Civil Service Commission has a standardized procedure for comparing and classifying jobs. Information here is compiled on a *job analysis record sheet* (see Figure A4.1). Identifying information (such as job title) and a brief summary of the job are listed first. Next the job's specific tasks are listed in order of importance. Then, for each task, the analyst specifies such things as the knowledge required (for example, the facts or principles the worker must be acquainted with to do his or her job), skills required (for example, the skills needed to operate machines or vehicles), and abilities required (for example, mathematical, reasoning, problem solving, or interpersonal abilities).

Position Analysis Questionnaire

The *position analysis questionnaire (PAQ)* is a very structured job analysis questionnaire.[1] The PAQ is filled in by a job analyst, a person who should be acquainted with the particular job to be analyzed. The PAQ contains 194 items, each of which (such as "written materials") represents a basic element that may or may not play an important role in the job. The job analyst decides whether each item plays a role on the job and, if so, to what extent. In Figure A4.2, for example, "Written materials" might receive a rating of 4, indicating that written materials (such as books, reports, and office notes) play a considerable role in this job.

The advantage of the PAQ is that it provides a quantitative score or profile of any job in terms of how that job rates on five basic job traits such as "having decision-making/communications/social responsibilities." The PAQ lets you assign a single quantitative score or value to each job. You can therefore use the PAQ results to compare jobs relative to one another; this information can then be used to assign pay levels for each job.

U.S. Department of Labor Procedure

The *U.S. Department of Labor (DOL) procedure* also aims to provide a standardized method by which different jobs can be quantitatively rated, classified, and compared. Although largely displaced by the Department of Labor's newer O*NET system, it still provides a useful approach.[2] The heart of this analysis is a rating of each job in terms of an employee's specific functions with respect to *data, people,* and *things*. As illustrated in Table A4.1, a set of basic activities called *worker functions* describes what a worker can do with respect to data, people, and things. With respect to *data*, for instance, the basic functions include synthesizing, coordinating, and copying. Note also that each worker function has been assigned an importance level. Thus, "coordinating" is 1, and "copying" is 5. If you were analyzing the job of a receptionist/clerk, for example, you might label the job 5, 6, 7, which would represent copying data, speaking-signaling people, and handling things.

A Practical Job Analysis Method

Without their own job analysts or (in many cases) HR managers, many small-business owners and managers face two hurdles when doing job analyses and job descriptions. First, they often need a more streamlined approach than those provided by questionnaires like the one shown in Figure A4.3. Second, there is always the reasonable fear that in writing their job descriptions, they will overlook duties that subordinates should be assigned, or assign duties not usually associated with such positions. What they need is an encyclopedia listing all or most positions they might encounter, including a detailed listing of the duties normally assigned to these positions.

FIGURE A4.1 Portion of a Completed Civil Service Job Analysis Record Sheet

JOB ANALYSIS RECORD SHEET

IDENTIFYING INFORMATION

Name of Incumbent:	A. Adler
Organization/Unit:	Welfare Services
Title:	Welfare Eligibility Examiner
Date:	11/12/08
Interviewer:	E. Jones

BRIEF SUMMARY OF JOB

Conducts interviews, completes applications, determines eligibility, provides information to community sources regarding food stamp program; refers noneligible food stamp applicants to other applicable community resource agencies.

TASKS

1. Decide (determine) eligibility of applicant in order to complete client's application for food stamps using regulatory policies as guide.

Knowledge Required

—Knowledge of contents and meaning of items on standard application form
—Knowledge of Social-Health Services food stamp regulatory policies
—Knowledge of statutes relating to Social-Health Services food stamp program

Skills Required

—None

Abilities Required

—Ability to read and understand complex instructions such as regulatory policies
—Ability to read and understand a variety of procedural instructions, written and oral, and convert these to proper actions
—Ability to use simple arithmetic: addition and subtraction
—Ability to translate requirements into language appropriate to laypeople

Physical Activities

—Sedentary

Environmental Conditions

—None

Typical Work Incidents

—Working with people beyond giving and receiving instructions

Interest Areas

—Communication of data
—Business contact with people
—Working for the presumed good of people

(continued)

FIGURE A4.1 Continued

2. Decides upon, describes, and explains other agencies available for client to contact in order to assist and refer client to appropriate community resources using worker's knowledge of resources available and knowledge of client's needs.

Knowledge Required

—Knowledge of functions of various assistance agencies
—Knowledge of community resources available and their locations
—Knowledge of referral procedures

Skills Required

—None

Abilities Required

—Ability to extract (discern) persons' needs from oral discussion
—Ability to give simple oral and written instructions to persons

Physical Activities

—Sedentary

Environmental Conditions

—None

Typical Work Incidents

—Working with people beyond giving and receiving instructions

Interest Areas

—Communication of data
—Business contact with people
—Abstract and creative problem solving
—Working for the presumed good of people

Note: This job might typically involve five or six tasks. For *each* task, list the knowledge, skill abilities, physical activities, environmental conditions, typical work incidents, and interest areas.

Help is at hand: The small-business owner has at least three options. The U.S. Department of Labor's *Dictionary of Occupational Titles* provides detailed descriptions of thousands of jobs and their human requirements. (Although largely replaced by the DOL's O*NET system, you can still find the *Dictionary*, online, at http://www.oalj.dol.gov/libdot.htm).[3] Web sites like www.jobdescription.com provide customizable descriptions by title and industry. And the Department of Labor's O*NET is a third alternative. We'll focus on using O*NET for creating job descriptions in this section.

Step 1. **Decide on a Plan** Start by developing at least the broad outline of a corporate plan. What do you expect your sales revenue to be next year, and in the next few years? What products do you intend to emphasize? What areas or departments in your company do you think will have to be expanded, reduced, or consolidated, given where you plan to go with your firm over the next few years? What kinds of new positions do you think you'll need in order to accomplish your strategic goals?

FIGURE A4.2 Portions of a Completed Page from the Position Analysis Questionnaire

The PAQ Answer Sheet

The PAQ answer sheet is a two-sided computer-scorable answer sheet designed for optical scanning. The first side is for administrative use and should be filled out by the job analyst, simply coding in the information requested and providing in the upper left corner a brief job description of the job being analyzed. Refer to the PAQ *Job Analysis Manual* for explicit instructions on completing the information fields shown on side 1. The second side is reserved for item responses. Use only a No. 2 pencil for marking responses, filling in response bubbles completely and erasing carefully any changed responses and/or stray marks. Please do not fold or staple the answer sheet.

When entering responses to PAQ items, make sure to use the response scale that is clearly indicated in the outer narrow margin. After deciding which is the most appropriate response, darken the corresponding response bubble for the item on the answer sheet. Once you have responded to all of the items on the PAQ, please review the answer sheet to ensure that all information entered is complete and accurate. Refer to the PAQ *Job Analysis Manual* for specific instructions regarding the completion of the Pay or Income items found in section F10.

A. Information Input

A1. Visual Sources of Job Information

Using the response scale at the left, rate each of the following items on the basis of the extent to which it is used by the worker as a source of information in performing the job.

Extent of Use

0 Does not apply
1 Nominal/very infrequent
2 Occasional
3 Moderate
4 Considerable
5 Very substantial

1. Written materials
E.g., books, reports, office notes, articles, job instructions, or signs

2. Quantitative materials
Materials that deal with quantities or amounts, e.g., graphs, accounts, specifications, or tables of numbers

3. Pictorial materials
Pictures or picture-like materials used as sources of information, e.g., drawings, blueprints, diagrams, maps, tracings, photographic films, x-ray films, or TV pictures

4. Patterns or related devices
E.g., templates, stencils, or patterns used as sources of information when observed during use (Do not include materials described in item 3.)

5. Visual displays
E.g., dials, gauges, signal lights, radarscopes, speedometers, or clocks

6. Measuring devices
E.g., rules, calipers, tire pressure gauges, scales, thickness gauges, pipettes, thermometers, or protractors used to obtain visual information about physical measurements (Do not include devices described in item 5.)

7. Mechanical devices
E.g., tools, equipment, or machinery that are sources of information when observed during use or operation

Source: Reprinted by permission of PAQ Services, Inc.

Step 2.   Develop an Organization Chart Next, develop a company organization chart. Show who reports to the president and to each of his or her subordinates. Complete the chart by showing who reports to each of the other managers and supervisors in the firm. Start by drawing up the organization chart as it is now. Then, depending on how far in advance you're planning, produce a chart showing how you'd like your chart to look in the immediate future (say, in 2 months) and perhaps two or three other charts showing how you'd like your organization to evolve over the next 2 or 3 years.

TABLE A4.1   Basic Department of Labor Worker Functions

	Data	People	Things
	0 Synthesizing	0 Mentoring	0 Setting up
	1 Coordinating	1 Negotiating	1 Precision working
	2 Analyzing	2 Instructing	2 Operating/controlling
	3 Compiling	3 Supervising	
Basic Activities	4 Computing	4 Diverting	3 Driving/operating
	5 Copying	5 Persuading	4 Manipulating
	6 Comparing	6 Speaking/signaling	5 Tending
		7 Serving	6 Feeding/offbearing
		8 Taking instructions/helping	7 Handling

Note: Determine employee's job "score" on data, people, and things by observing his or her job and determining, for each of the three categories, which of the basic functions illustrates the person's job. "0" is high; "6," "8," and "7" are lows in each column.

You can use several tools here. For example, MSWord includes an organization charting function: On the Insert menu, click Object, then Create New. In the Object type box, click MS Organization Chart, and then OK. Software packages such as OrgPublisher for Intranet 3.0 from TimeVision of Irving, Texas, are another option.[4]

Step 3. Use a Job Analysis/Description Questionnaire   Next, use a job analysis questionnaire to determine what each job entails. You can use one of the more comprehensive questionnaires (see Figure A4.3); however, the job description questionnaire in Figure A4.4 is a simpler and often satisfactory alternative. Fill in the required information, then ask the supervisors and/or employees to list the job's duties (on the bottom of the page), breaking them into daily duties, periodic duties, and duties performed at irregular intervals. You can distribute a sample of one of these duties (see Figure A4.5) to supervisors and/or employees to facilitate the process.

Step 4. Obtain Lists of Job Duties from O*NET   The list of job duties you uncovered in the previous step may or may not be complete. We'll therefore use O*NET to compile a more comprehensive list. (Refer to Figure A4.6 for a visual example as you read along.) Start by going to http://online.onetcenter.org (top). Here, click on Find Occupations to continue, which brings you to http://online.onetcenter.org/find/, the Find Occupations Search Result (middle). Type in Retail Sales under find occupations in the keyword box. Clicking on Retail Salespersons produces the job summary and specific occupational duties for retail salespersons (bottom, http://online.onetcenter.org/link/summary/41–2031.00). For a small company or department, you might want to combine the duties of the retail salesperson with those of first-line supervisors/managers of retail salespeople.

Step 5. Compile the Job's Specification from O*NET   Next, return to the Snapshot for Retail Salesperson (bottom). Here, note the knowledge, skills, and abilities on the page. You can use this information to develop a job specification for recruiting, selecting, and training the employees.

Step 6. Complete Your Job Description   Finally, using Figure A4.4, write an appropriate job summary for the job. Then use the information obtained in Steps 4 and 5 to create a complete listing of the tasks, duties, and human requirements of each of the jobs you will need to fill.

FIGURE A4.3 Job Analysis Questionnaire for Developing Job Descriptions. *Use a questionnaire like this to interview job incumbents, or have them fill it out.*

Job Analysis Information Sheet

Job Title _____ **Date** _____

Job Code _____ **Dept.** _____

Superior's Title _____

Hours worked _____ **AM to** _____ **PM**

Job Analyst's Name _____

1. **What is the job's overall purpose?**
_____

2. **If the incumbent supervises others,** list them by job title; if there is more than one employee with the same title, put the number in parentheses following the title.
_____

3. **Check those activities** that are part of the incumbent's supervisory duties.

☐ Training

☐ Performance appraisal

☐ Inspecting work

☐ Budgeting

☐ Coaching and/or counseling

☐ Others (please specify) _____

4. **Describe the type and extent of supervision** received by the incumbent.
_____

5. **JOB DUTIES:** Describe briefly WHAT the incumbent does and, if possible, HOW he/she does it. Include duties in the following categories:

   a. Daily duties (those performed on a regular basis every day or almost every day)
   _____

   b. Periodic duties (those performed weekly, monthly, quarterly, or at other regular intervals)
   _____

   c. Duties performed at irregular intervals
   _____

6. Is the incumbent performing duties he/she considers unnecessary? If so, describe.
_____

7. Is the incumbent performing duties not presently included in the job description? If so, describe.
_____

8. **EDUCATION:** Check the box that indicates the educational requirements for the job (not the educational background of the incumbent).

☐ No formal education   ☐ Eighth grade education

☐ High school diploma (or equivalent)   ☐ 2-year college degree (or equivalent)

☐ 4-year college degree (or equivalent) (specify)   ☐ Graduate work or advanced degree

☐ Professional license (specify)

9. **EXPERIENCE:** Check the amount of experience needed to perform the job.

☐ None   ☐ Less than one month

☐ One to six months   ☐ Six months to one year

☐ One to three years   ☐ Three to five years

☐ Five to ten years   ☐ More than ten years

(continued)

FIGURE A4.3 Continued

10. **LOCATION:** Check location of job and, if necessary or appropriate, describe briefly.

☐ Outdoor   ☐ Indoor

☐ Underground   ☐ Pit

☐ Scaffold   ☐ Other (specify)

11. **ENVIRONMENTAL CONDITIONS:** Check any objectionable conditions found on the job and note afterward how frequently each is encountered (rarely, occasionally, constantly, etc.).

☐ Dirt   ☐ Dust

☐ Heat   ☐ Cold

☐ Noise   ☐ Fumes

☐ Odors   ☐ Wetness/humidity

☐ Vibration   ☐ Sudden temperature changes

☐ Darkness or poor lighting   ☐ Other (specify)

12. **HEALTH AND SAFETY:** Check any undesirable health and safety conditions under which the incumbent must perform and note how often they are encountered.

☐ Elevated workplace   ☐ Mechanical hazards

☐ Explosives   ☐ Electrical hazards

☐ Fire hazards   ☐ Radiation

☐ Other (specify)

13. **MACHINES, TOOLS, EQUIPMENT, AND WORK AIDS:** Describe briefly what machines, tools, equipment, or work aids the incumbent works with on a regular basis.

14. Have concrete work standards been established (errors allowed, time taken for a particular task, etc.)? If so, what are they?

15. Are there any personal attributes (special aptitudes, physical characteristics, personality traits, etc.) required by the job?

16. Are there any exceptional problems the incumbent might be expected to encounter in performing the job under normal conditions? If so, describe.

17. Describe the successful completion and/or end results of the job.

18. What is the seriousness of error on this job? Who or what is affected by errors the incumbent makes?

19. To what job would a successful incumbent expect to be promoted?

[**Note:** This form is obviously slanted toward a manufacturing environment, but it can be adapted quite easily to fit a number of different types of jobs.]

Source: Reprinted from HR.BLR.com with the permission of BLR. © 2007. Business & Legal Reports, Inc., 141 Mill Rock Rd East, Old Saybrook, CT 06475.

FIGURE A4.4 Job Description Questionnaire

Background Data for Job Description

Job Title _____   Department _____

Job Number _____   Written By _____

Today's Date _____   Applicable Codes _____

I. Applicable job titles from O*NET:

II. Job Summary:
(List the more important or regularly performed tasks)

III. Reports To:

IV. Supervises: _____

V. Job Duties: _____
(Briefly describe, for each duty, what employee does and, if possible, how employee does it. Show in parentheses at end of each duty the approximate percentage of time devoted to duty.)

A. Daily Duties:

B. Periodic Duties:
(Indicate whether weekly, monthly, quarterly, etc.)

C. Duties Performed at Irregular Intervals:

FIGURE A4.5

Background Data for Examples

Example of Job Title: Customer Service Clerk

Example of Job Summary: Answers inquiries and gives directions to customers, authorizes cashing of customers' checks, records and returns lost charge cards, sorts and reviews new credit applications, works at customer-service desk in department store.

Example of One Job Duty: Authorizes cashing of checks: authorizes cashing of personal or payroll checks (up to a specified amount) by customers desiring to make payment by check. Requests identification, such as driver's license, from customers, and examines check to verify date, amount, signature, and endorsement. Initials check and sends customer to cashier.

FIGURE A4.6

Shown in the Three Screen Captures, O*NET Easily Allows the User to Develop Job Descriptions

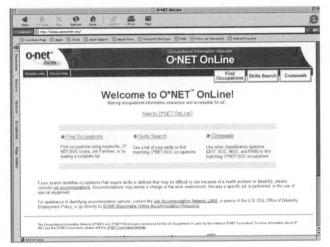

Reprinted by permission of O*NET OnLine.

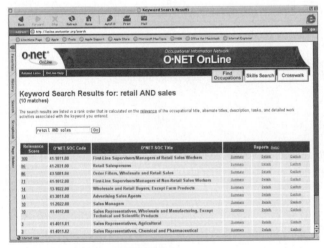

Reprinted by permission of O*NET OnLine.

(continued)

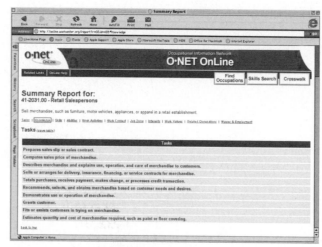

Reprinted by permission of O*NET OnLine.

Endnotes

1. Note that the PAQ (and other quantitative techniques) can also be used for job evaluation, which is explained in chapter 8.
2. See for example, Sidney A. Fine, "Fifty Years of Things, Data, People: Whither Job Analysis?" http://www.siop.org/TIP/backissues/Oct04/07fiine.aspx, accessed April 18, 2008.
3. Accessed April 18, 2008.
4. David Shair, "Wizardry Makes Charts Relevant," *HR Magazine* (April 2000): 127.

Selecting Employees

5

When you finish studying this chapter, you should be able to:

1. *Define basic testing concepts, including validity and reliability.*

2. *Discuss at least four basic types of personnel tests.*

3. *Explain the factors and problems that can undermine an interview's usefulness, and techniques for eliminating them.*

4. *Explain the pros and cons of background investigations, reference checks, and preemployment information services.*

Introduction

Google, Inc. recently changed its employee screening process. A few years ago, candidates sometimes spent months going through a dozen or more personal interviews. The firm's hiring team would then routinely reject candidates with years of experience if they had just-average college grades. But, as Google's new head of human resources says, "Everything works if you're trying to hire 500 people a year, or 1000." Now Google is hiring thousands of people per year, and can't let slow hiring bog it down. So Google reduced the number of interviews (to about five, on average) and no longer puts as much weight on GPA. Other selection changes are in store.[1] ■

THE BASICS OF TESTING AND SELECTING EMPLOYEES

With a pool of applicants, your next step is to select the best person for the job. This usually means whittling down the applicant pool by using screening tools explained in this chapter, including tests, interviews, and background and reference checks.

Why Careful Selection Is Important

Selecting the right employees is important for four main reasons.

- First, we'll see that the evidence clearly shows that carefully testing and screening job candidates leads to *improved employee and organizational performance*.
- Second, *your own performance* always depends partly on your subordinates. Employees with the right skills and attributes will do a better job for you and the company. Employees without these skills or who are abrasive or obstructionist won't perform effectively, and your own performance and the firm's will suffer.
- Third, screening can help reduce *dysfunctional behaviors* at work. By some estimates, 75% of employees have stolen from their employers at least once; 33% to 75% have engaged in behaviors such as theft, vandalism, and voluntary absenteeism; almost 25% say they've had knowledge of illicit drug use among coworkers; and 7% of a sample of employees reported being victims of coworkers' physical threats.[2] The time to screen out such undesirables is before they are in the door, not after.
- Fourth, effective screening is important because it's *costly* to recruit and hire employees. Hiring and training even a clerk can cost $10,000 or more in fees and supervisory time. The total cost of hiring a manager could easily be 10 times as high, after search fees, interviewing time, reference checking, and travel and moving expenses are tallied.

LEGAL IMPLICATIONS AND NEGLIGENT HIRING Fifth, careful selection is important because of the *legal implications* of incompetent selection. For example (as we saw in chapter 2), U.S. Equal Employment Opportunity laws and court decisions require you to ensure that you're not unfairly discriminating against any protected group.

negligent hiring
Hiring workers with criminal records or other such problems without proper safeguards.

Negligent hiring is another legal issue. Courts will find employers liable when employees with criminal records or other problems use their access to customers' homes or similar opportunities to commit crimes. Hiring workers with such backgrounds without proper safeguards is called *negligent hiring*. For example, after lawyers sued U.S.-based Wal-Mart alleging that several of its employees with criminal convictions for sexually-related offenses had assaulted young girls, Wal-Mart instituted a new program of criminal background checks.[3]

Avoiding negligent hiring claims requires taking "reasonable" action to investigate the candidate's background. Among other things, employers "must make a systematic effort to gain relevant information about the applicant, verify documentation, follow up on missing records or gaps in employment, and keep a detailed log of all attempts to obtain information, including the names and dates for phone calls or other requests."[4]

reliability
The characteristic that refers to the consistency of scores obtained by the same person when retested with the identical or equivalent tests.

Reliability

Effective screening is therefore important, and depends to a large degree on the basic testing concepts of reliability and validity. **Reliability** refers to the test's consistency. It is "the consistency of scores obtained by the same person when retested with the identical tests or

1 Define basic testing concepts, including validity and reliability.

with an equivalent form of a test."[5] Test reliability is essential: If a person scored 90 on an intelligence test on Monday and 130 when retested on Tuesday, you probably wouldn't have much faith in the test.

There are several ways to estimate a test's consistency or reliability. You could administer the same test to the same people at two different points in time, comparing their test scores at Time 2 with their scores at Time 1; this would be a *retest estimate*. Or you could administer a test and then administer what experts believe to be an equivalent test at a later date; this would be an *equivalent-form estimate*. The Scholastic Aptitude Test is an example of the latter.

A test's internal consistency is another measure of its reliability. For example, assume you have 10 items on a test of vocational interest. These items are supposed to measure in various ways the person's interest in working outdoors. You administer the test and then statistically analyze the degree to which responses to these items vary together. This would provide a measure of the internal reliability of the test and is referred to as an *internal comparison estimate*. Internal consistency is one reason you often find questions that apparently are repetitive on some test questionnaires.

Validity

Any test is a sample of a person's behavior, but some tests more clearly reflect the behavior you're sampling. For example, a typing test clearly corresponds to an on-the-job behavior—typing. At the other extreme, there may be no apparent relationship between the items on the test and the behavior. For example, in the Thematic Apperception Test item in Figure 5.1, the person is asked to explain how he or she interprets the blurred picture. Is the young woman daydreaming of her affectionate mother, or hoping that a rival will grow old before her time? The psychologist then uses that interpretation to draw conclusions about the person's personality and behavior. In such tests, it is harder to "prove" that the tests are measuring what they are purported to measure—that they are *valid*.

Test validity answers the question, Does this test measure what it's supposed to measure? Stated differently, "validity refers to the confidence one has in the meaning attached to the scores."[6] With respect to employee selection tests, the term *validity* often refers to evidence that the test is job related, in other words, that performance on the test is a *valid predictor* of subsequent performance on the job. A selection test must be valid because, without proof of its validity, there is no logical or legally permissible reason to continue using it to screen job applicants.

In employment testing, there are two main ways to demonstrate a test's validity: **criterion validity** and **content validity**. Demonstrating *criterion validity* means demonstrating that those who do well on the test also do well on the job, and that those who do poorly on the test do poorly on the job. In psychological measurement, a predictor is the measurement (in this case, the test score) that you are trying to relate to a criterion, such as performance on the job. In criterion validity, the two should be closely related. The term *criterion validity* comes from that terminology.

test validity
The accuracy with which a test, interview, and so on measures what it purports to measure or fulfills the function it was designed to fill.

criterion validity
A type of validity based on showing that scores on the test (*predictors*) are related to job performance (*criterion*).

content validity
A test that is *content valid* is one in which the test contains a fair sample of the tasks and skills actually needed for the job in question.

FIGURE 5.1

Sample Picture from Thematic Apperception Test

Source: Reprinted by permission of the publishers from Henry A. Murray, THEMATIC APPERCEPTION TEST, Card 12F, Cambridge, Mass.: Harvard University Press, Copyright © 1943 by the President and Fellows of Harvard College, © 1974 by Henry A. Murray.

The employer demonstrates the *content validity* of a test by showing that the test constitutes a fair sample of the content of a job. A typing test illustrates this. If the content of the typing test is a representative sample of the typist's job, then the test is probably content valid.

How to Validate a Test

For example, what makes a test such as the Graduate Record Examination (GRE) useful for U.S. college admissions directors? What makes a mechanical comprehension test useful for managers trying to hire machinists?

The answer to both questions is usually that people's scores on these tests have been shown to be predictive of how people perform. Thus, other things being equal, students who score high on the GRE also do better in graduate school. Applicants who score higher on a mechanical comprehension test perform better as machinists.

Strictly speaking, an employer should be fairly sure that scores on the tests are related in a predictable way to performance on the job before using that test to screen employees. In other words, it is important that you validate the test before using it. You generally do this by ensuring that test scores are a good predictor of some criterion such as job performance. In other words, you should demonstrate the test's criterion validity. This validation process usually requires the expertise of an industrial psychologist, and is summarized in Figure 5.2.

FIGURE 5.2

How to Validate a Test

Step 1: Analyze the Job. First, analyze the job descriptions and specifications. Specify the human traits and skills you believe are required for adequate job performance. For example, must an applicant be aggressive? Must the person be able to assemble small, detailed components? These requirements become your predictors. They are the human traits and skills you believe to be predictive of success on the job.

In this first step, you must also define what you mean by "success on the job" because it is this success for which you want predictors. The standards of success are called *criteria*. You could focus on production-related criteria (quantity, quality, and so on), personnel data (absenteeism, length of service, and so on), or judgments (of worker performance by persons such as supervisors). For an assembler's job, predictors for which to test applicants might include manual dexterity and patience. Criteria that you would hope to predict with your test might then include quantity produced per hour and number of rejects produced per hour.

Step 2: Choose the Tests. Next, choose tests that you think measure the attributes (predictors) important for job success. This choice is usually based on experience, previous research, and best guesses, and you usually won't start off with just one test. Instead, you choose several tests, combining them into a test battery aimed at measuring a variety of possible predictors, such as aggressiveness, extroversion, and numeric ability.

Step 3: Administer Tests. Administer the selected test(s) to employees. *Predictive validation* is the most dependable way to validate a test. The test is administered to applicants before they are hired. Then these applicants are hired using only existing selection techniques, not the results of the new test you are developing. After they have been on the job for some time, you measure their performance and compare it to their performance on the earlier test. You can then determine whether their performance on the test could have been used to predict their subsequent job performance.

Step 4: Relate Scores and Criteria. Next, determine whether there is a significant relationship between scores (the predictor) and performance (the criterion). The usual way to do this is to determine the statistical relationship between scores on the test and performance through correlation analysis, which shows the degree of statistical relationship.

Step 5: Cross-Validate and Revalidate. Before putting the test into use, you may want to check it by cross-validating, by again performing steps 3 and 4 on a new sample of employees. At a minimum, an expert should validate the test periodically.

Business in Action   Building Your *Business Law* Knowledge in Testing

We've seen that various governmental laws bar discrimination on the basis of race, color, age, religion, sex, disability, and national origin. With respect to testing, these laws boil down to two things: (1) You must be able to prove that your tests were related to success or failure on the job, and (2) you must be able to prove that your tests don't unfairly discriminate against either minority or nonminority subgroups. If confronted by a legitimate discrimination charge, the burden of proof rests with you. Once the plaintiff shows that one of your selection procedures has an adverse impact on his or her protected class, you must demonstrate the validity and selection fairness of the allegedly discriminatory test or item.[7] *Adverse impact* means there is a significant discrepancy between rates of rejection of members of the protected groups and others. For example, a U.S. federal court ruled that Dial Corp. discriminated against female job applicants at a meatpacking facility by requiring employees to take a preemployment strength test. The test had an adverse impact on women. Furthermore, there appeared to be no compelling need for strength on the job.[8]

In the U.S., EEO laws can't be avoided by not using tests, by the way. EEO guidelines and laws apply to any and all screening or selection devices, including interviews, applications, and references. The same burden of proving job relatedness that falls on interviews and other techniques (including performance appraisals) also falls on tests.

INDIVIDUAL RIGHTS OF TEST TAKERS AND TEST SECURITY Test takers have various privacy and information rights in most countries. They have the right to the confidentiality of the test results and the right to informed consent regarding the use of these results. They have the right to expect that only people qualified to interpret the scores will have access to them or that sufficient information will accompany the scores to ensure their appropriate interpretation. They have the right to expect that the test is secure; no person taking the test should have prior information concerning the questions or answers.

USING TESTS AS SUPPLEMENTS Do not use tests as your only selection technique; instead, use them to supplement other techniques such as interviews and background checks. Tests are not infallible. Even in the best cases, the test score usually accounts for only about 25% of the variation in the measure of performance. The *Business in Action* reviews legal aspects of testing and selection.

USING TESTS AT WORK

Employers have long used tests to predict behavior and performance, and they can be effective. For example, researchers administered an aggression questionnaire to high school hockey players prior to the season. Preseason aggressiveness as measured by the questionnaire predicted the amount of minutes they subsequently spent in the penalty box for penalties such as fighting, slashing, and tripping.[9] Try the short test in Figure 5.3 to see how prone you might be to on-the-job accidents.

How Are Tests Used at Work?

Employers use tests to measure a wide range of candidate attributes, including cognitive (mental) abilities, motor and physical abilities, personality and interests, and achievement. Many firms such as FedEx Kinko's have applicants take online or offline computerized tests—sometimes online, and sometimes by phone using the touchtone keypad—to quickly prescreen applicants prior to more in-depth interviews and background checks. Barclays Capital gives graduate and undergraduate job candidates aptitude tests instead of first-round interviews.[10]

FIGURE 5.3 Sample Selection Test

CHECK YES OR NO   YES   NO

1. You like a lot of excitement in your life.

2. An employee who takes it easy at work is cheating on the employer.

3. You are a cautious person.

4. In the past three years you have found yourself in a shouting match at school or work.

5. You like to drive fast just for fun.

Analysis: According to John Kamp, an industrial psychologist, applicants who answered no, yes, yes, no, no to questions 1, 2, 3, 4, and 5 are statistically likely to be absent less often, to have fewer on-the-job injuries, and, if the job involves driving, to have fewer on-the-job driving accidents. Actual scores on the test are based on answers to 130 questions.

Source: Courtesy of *The New York Times.*

EXAMPLE Florida-based Outback Steakhouse has used preemployment testing since just after the company started. Outback is looking for employees who are highly social, meticulous, sympathetic, and adaptable. It uses a special personality assessment test as part of a preemployment interview process. Applicants take the test, and the company then compares the results to the profile for Outback Steakhouse employees. Those who score low on certain traits (like compassion) don't move to the next step. Those who score high get interviewed by two managers. The latter focus on asking "behavioral" questions, such as, "What would you do if a customer asked for a side dish we don't have on the menu?"[11]

The basic types of tests are as follows.

Outback Steakhouse has used preemployment testing since just after the company started.

❷ Discuss at least four basic types of personnel tests.

TESTS OF COGNITIVE ABILITIES Employers often want to assess a candidate's cognitive or mental abilities. For example, you may be interested in determining whether a supervisory candidate has the intelligence to do the job's paperwork or a bookkeeper candidate has the required numeric aptitude.

Intelligence tests, such as IQ tests, are tests of general intellectual abilities. They measure not a single intelligence trait, but rather a range of abilities, including memory, vocabulary, verbal fluency, and numeric ability. Today, psychologists often measure intelligence with individually administered tests such as the Stanford–Binet test or the Wechsler Adult Intelligence Scale. Employers use other IQ tests such as the Wonderlic to provide quick measures of IQ for both individuals and groups of people.

There are also measures of specific mental abilities. Tests in this category are often called *aptitude tests* because they aim to measure the applicant's aptitudes for the job in question. For example, consider the Test of Mechanical Comprehension illustrated in Figure 5.4. It tests the applicant's understanding of basic mechanical principles. It may therefore reflect a person's aptitude for jobs—such as engineer—that require mechanical comprehension.

TESTS OF MOTOR AND PHYSICAL ABILITIES There are many motor or physical abilities you might want to measure, such as finger dexterity, strength, manual dexterity, and reaction time (for instance, for machine operators or police candidates). The Stromberg Dexterity Test is an example. It measures the speed and accuracy of simple judgment as well as the speed of finger, hand, and arm movements.

MEASURING PERSONALITY A person's mental and physical abilities alone seldom explain his or her job performance. Other factors, such as motivation and interpersonal skills, are important, too. Employers often use personality and interests tests (or "inventories") to measure and predict such intangibles. As one consultant put it, most people are hired based on qualifications, but most are fired for nonperformance. And *nonperformance* (or *performance*) "is usually the result of personal characteristics, such as attitude, motivation, and especially, temperament."[12]

FIGURE 5.4

Two Problems from the Test of Mechanical Comprehension

Source: Bennett Mechanical Comprehension Test. Copyright © 1942, 1967–1970, 1980 by Harcourt Assessment, Inc. Reproduced with permission. All rights reserved.

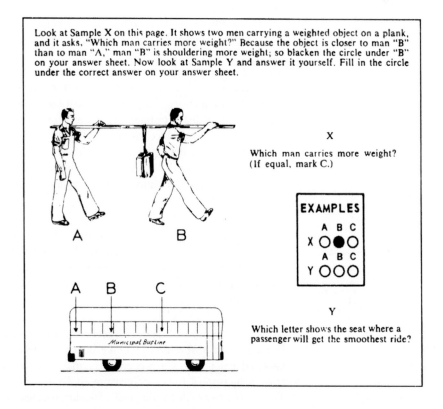

Personality tests measure basic aspects of an applicant's personality, such as introversion, stability, and motivation. A sample personality inventory item is:

It does not make sense to work hard on something if no one will notice:
  a. Definitely true.
  b. Somewhat true.
  c. Neither true nor false.
  d. Somewhat false.
  e. Definitely false.[13]

Of course personality testing isn't limited to employment settings. Some online dating services, like eHarmony.com, have prospective members take online personality tests, and reject those applicants its software judges as unmatchable. Figure 5.5 shows a sample page from one online personality inventory.

Many personality tests are projective, meaning that the person taking the test must interpret or react to an ambiguous stimulus such as an inkblot or clouded picture. Because the pictures are ambiguous, the person supposedly projects into the picture his or her own emotional attitudes about life. Thus, a security-oriented person might describe the woman in Figure 5.1 as "Me worrying about my mother worrying about what I'll do if I lose my job."

Personality tests—particularly the projective type—are the most difficult to evaluate and use. An expert must analyze the test taker's interpretations and reactions and infer from them his or her personality. The usefulness of such tests for selection then assumes that you find a relationship between a measurable personality trait (such as extroversion) and success on the job. Because they are personal in nature, employers should always use personality tests with caution, particularly where the focus is on aberrant behavior. Rejected candidates may (validly) claim that the results are false, or that they violate worker disability laws.

PERSONALITY TEST EFFECTIVENESS The difficulties notwithstanding, studies confirm that personality tests can help companies hire more effective workers. Industrial psychologists often study the "big five" personality dimensions as they apply to personnel testing: extroversion, emotional stability, agreeableness, conscientiousness, and openness to experience.[14]

One study focused on how these five personality dimensions predicted performance (for instance, in terms of job and training proficiency) for professionals, police officers, managers, sales workers, and skilled/semiskilled workers. Conscientiousness showed a consistent relationship with all job performance criteria for all the occupations. Extroversion was a valid predictor of performance for managers and sales employees—two of the occupations involving the most social interaction. Openness to experience and extroversion predicted training proficiency for all occupations.[15]

Overall, the evidence on personality testing suggests the following: Employers are increasingly using personality tests. The weight of evidence is that personality measures (particularly the big five) contribute to predicting job performance. And, employers can reduce personality test faking by warning applicants that faking may reduce the chances of being hired.[16]

INTEREST INVENTORIES *Interest inventories* compare one's interests with those of people in various occupations. Thus, when a person takes the Strong–Campbell Interest Inventory, he or she receives a report comparing his or her interests to those of people already in occupations such as accounting, engineering, management, and medical technology.

ACHIEVEMENT TESTS An *achievement test* is basically a measure of what a person has learned. Most of the tests you take in school are achievement tests. They measure your knowledge in areas such as economics, marketing, or accounting. In addition to job knowledge, achievement tests can measure applicants' abilities; a typing test is one example.[17] The *Global Issues in HR* on page 156 addresses testing for assignments abroad.

FIGURE 5.5 Sample Page from Online Personality Inventory

Your Personality Profile

Please Note
To maintain the accuracy of the assessment, it is important that you:

- complete the test in one session
- make sure that you don't skip any questions

I work best:

☐ In a group/ team
☐ On my own

Given the choice, I would:

☐ Choose the job that is stable and financially secure
☐ Choose the job that offers variety/ travel, although slightly unstable/ insecure

My emotional response is usually quite:

☐ Stable - not affected by mood swings often
☐ Varied - my response can vary according to the mood I am in at the time

It is important to me to:

☐ Understand my feelings; I spend a lot of time looking inward
☐ Move onward; I don't spend much time reflecting/ looking inward

Choosing the Right Answer
In some of the questions you may find it difficult to choose an answer. It may feel like neither option describes you perfectly or that more than one option suits you. If this happens, guess which option suits you better. We are able to detect patterns in your responses, even if some of your answers feel like guesses.

If I were a car, I would most resemble a:

☐ VW Beetle: Carefree, enthusiastic, easy-going
☐ VW Passat/Jetta: Detailed, reliable, quality-oriented

I trust strangers:

☐ Easily - on the whole, people have good intentions
☐ Not easily - trust needs to be earned

Clutter in my workspace is something I:

☐ Feel the urge to straighten up
☐ Am not bothered by

Philosophical debates ("What is the meaning of existence?") interest me:

☐ Very much
☐ Little

(continued)

FIGURE 5.5 Continued

I tend to be more:

☐ Factual than speculative
☐ Speculative than factual

When faced with a decision, I am most likely to:

☐ Pick/choose quickly, often on an impulse
☐ Analyze all options with care, so as to make the best choice
☐ Tend to become indecisive

I am most interested in:

☐ Causes (What created the situation?)
☐ Effects (What was the result of the situation?)
☐ Correlations (How does this situation connect or relate to other situations?)

When assessing other people, I usually:

☐ Have a rational explanation for my judgment
☐ Rely more on a 'gut feeling'

It would be more accurate to say:

☐ I probably don't spend enough time worrying about problems.
☐ I probably spend too much time worrying about problems.

A hallway in a friend's apartment has been redecorated. You:

☐ Didn't notice - your attention is directed elsewhere
☐ Notice, but don't much care - not of that much interest to you
☐ Notice, take in all the details - you are interested in such things

You are invited to go sky diving. Your response?

☐ "Count me in!" - you are immediately excited
☐ "Probably" - Sounds a little scary, you will have to talk yourself into it.
☐ "Probably not" - it's a little out of your range, but you will think about it.
☐ "No way" - You will cheer and watch, but from safely upon the ground.

Source: http://www.personality100.com/page/registration/userreg.xml?sessioni.

Global Issues in HR

Testing for Assignments Abroad

Living and working abroad requires some special talents. Not everyone can easily adapt to having one's friends and family far away, and to dealing with colleagues whose cultural values may be strikingly different from one's own. Doing so requires high levels of adaptability and interpersonal skills.[18]

Employers often use special inventories such as the Global Competencies Inventory (GCI) to assess the likelihood someone can work effectively where cultural norms are different from one's own. The report focuses on three aspects of intercultural adaptability.

- The Perception Management Factor examines the way a person cognitively approaches cultural differences. This factor assesses people's tendency to be rigid in their view of cultural differences, their tendency to be judgmental about those differences, and their ability to deal with complexity and uncertainty.
- The Relationship Management Factor scales assess a person's orientation toward the importance of relationships, and one's awareness of the impact he or she is having on others.
- The Self Management Factor takes into account one's strength of identity. It assumes that to be successful in an assignment abroad starts with having a stable sense of self, and being mentally and emotionally healthy.

Computerized and Online Testing

Computerized and online testing (see, for example, Figure 5.6, a sample of the Wonderlic personnel test) is increasingly replacing conventional paper-and-pencil and manual tests. Most of the types of tests we described are available in both computerized and paper form. Studies of tests like the Test of Workplace Essential Skills (a test of adult literacy) suggest that paper and computerized test version scores are equivalent.[19]

Consider these computerized and/or online testing examples:

- As noted earlier, many firms such as FedEx Kinko's have applicants take online or offline computerized tests to prescreen applicants prior to more in-depth interviews and background checks.[20] The applicant tracking programs we discussed in chapter 3

FIGURE 5.6 Sample Items from Wonderlic Personnel Test

Sample Questions for WPT-R
The following questions are similar, but not identical, to those presented on the actual WPT-R forms.

Question 1
Which of the following is the earliest date?

A) Jan. 16, 1898   B) Feb. 21, 1889   C) Feb. 2, 1898   D) Jan. 7, 1898   E) Jan. 30, 1889

Question 2
LOW is to HIGH as EASY is to_____?

J) SUCCESSFUL   K) PURE   L) TALL   M) INTERESTING   N) DIFFICULT

Question 3
One word below appears in color. What is the OPPOSITE of that word?

She gave a complex answer to the question and we all agreed with her.

A) long   B) better   C) simple   D) wrong   E) kind

Answers
1. E   2. N   3. C

Source: http://www.wonderlic.com/products/selection/wptr/sampleQuestions.asp.

often include an online prescreening test,[21] and applications service provider firms process and score online preemployment tests from employers' applicants.

■ CapitalOne's online system eliminates the bank's previous time-consuming paper-and-pencil test process.[22] Applicants for call center jobs complete an online application and online math and biodata tests. They also take an online role-playing call simulation. For the latter, they use a headset, and watch seven different customer situations. Applicants (playing the role of operators) answer multiple-choice questions online regarding how they would respond.

■ Automated in-basket tests require job candidates to deal with a "virtual inbox" comprised of e-mails, phone calls, and documents and folders to assess the candidates' decision-making and problem-solving skills. Candidates for architectural certification solve online architectural problems, for instance, designing building layouts to fit specified space constraints.[23]

CITY GARAGE COMPUTERIZED TESTING EXAMPLE One fast-growing U.S. auto repair chain, City Garage, knew they'd never be able to implement their growth strategy without a dramatic change in how they tested and hired employees.[24] Their old hiring process consisted of a paper-and-pencil application and one interview, immediately followed by a hire/don't hire decision. While that might work for a slow-growth operation, it was unsatisfactory for a fast-growing operation like City Garage. For one thing, local shop managers didn't have the time to evaluate every applicant, so "if they had been shorthanded too long, we would hire pretty much anybody who had experience," said training director Rusty Reinoehl. Complicating the problem was that City Garage competitively differentiates itself with an "open garage" arrangement, where customers interact directly with technicians. Therefore, finding mechanics who not only tolerate but also react positively to customer inquiries is essential.

City Garage's solution was to purchase the Personality Profile Analysis (PPA) online test from Dallas-based Thomas International USA. Now, after a quick application and background check, likely candidates take the 10-minute, 24-question PPA. City Garage staff then enter the answers into the PPA Software system and receive test results in less than 2 minutes. These show whether the applicant is high or low in four personality characteristics. It also produces follow-up questions about areas that might cause problems. For example, applicants might be asked how they've handled possible weaknesses such as lack of patience. If candidates answer those questions satisfactorily, they're asked back for extensive, all-day interviews, after which hiring decisions are made.

Management Assessment Centers

management assessment center
A facility in which management candidates are asked to make decisions in hypothetical situations and are scored on their performance.

In a **management assessment center**, management candidates take tests and make decisions in simulated situations while observers grade their performance. The time at the assessment center is usually 2 or 3 days. It involves 10 to 12 management candidates performing realistic management tasks (such as making presentations) under the observation of expert assessors. The center may be a plain conference room, but often it is a special room with a one-way mirror to facilitate unobtrusive observations. Examples of the simulated but realistic exercises included in a typical assessment center are as follows:

■ *The in-basket.* In this exercise, the candidate is faced with an accumulation of reports, memos, notes of incoming phone calls, letters, and other materials collected in the in-basket of the simulated job he or she is to take over. The candidate takes appropriate action on each of these materials.

■ *The leaderless group discussion.* A leaderless group is given a discussion question and told to arrive at a group decision. The raters then evaluate each group member's interpersonal skills, acceptance by the group, leadership ability, and individual influence.

■ *Individual presentations.* A participant's communication skills and persuasiveness are evaluated by having the person make an oral presentation on an assigned topic.

In practice, employers use assessment centers for selection, promotion, and development. Supervisor recommendations usually play a big role in choosing center participants.

Line managers usually act as assessors and typically arrive at their ratings through consensus.[25] Centers are expensive to set up, but at least one study (of 40 police candidates) found that such centers are worth the extra cost. The researchers concluded: "assessment center performance shows a unique and substantial contribution to the prediction of future police work success, justifying the usage of such method."[26]

GOOGLE EXAMPLE Having to add thousands of new employees each year, Google's top managers revamped their employee selection process. Google no longer requires most candidates to endure multiple interviews. They've streamlined the process. They did this in part by testing all their current employees to see what makes them successful. Then Google tests job candidates to see if they have these "Google success" traits.

INTERVIEWING CANDIDATES

⬤ Explain the factors and problems that can undermine an interview's usefulness, and techniques for eliminating them.

interview
A procedure designed to solicit information from a person's oral responses to oral inquiries.

While not all companies use tests or assessment centers, it's very unusual for a manager not to interview a prospective employee; interviewing is thus an indispensable management tool. An **interview** is a procedure designed to solicit information from a person's oral responses to oral inquiries. A *selection interview,* which we'll focus on in this chapter, is "a selection procedure designed to predict future job performance on the basis of applicants' oral responses to oral inquiries."[27]

Types of Selection Interviews

As you probably know from your own experience, there are several ways to conduct selection interviews. For example, some interviewers are completely open-ended and perhaps even rambling in what they cover, while others basically follow a checklist of questions. Some approaches are more useful than others, so you should understand the basic approaches.

STRUCTURE First, we can distinguish between *nonstructured* and *structured interviews.* In the former, you ask questions as they come to mind, and there is generally no set format to follow. In a more structured or directive interview, the questions and perhaps even acceptable responses are specified in advance, and the responses may be rated for appropriateness of content. Figure 5.7 presents one example of a structured interview.

TYPE OF QUESTIONS Interviewers can also ask different types of questions. *Situational* questions focus on the candidate's ability to project what his or her behavior *would be* in a given situation.[28] For example, you might ask a candidate for a supervisor position how he or she would respond to a subordinate coming to work late 3 days in a row. With *behavioral* questions you ask interviewees how they behaved *in the past* in some situation. Thus, an interviewer might ask, "Did you ever have a situation in which a subordinate came in late? If so, how did you handle the situation?" For example, when a banking corporation found that 31 of the 50 people in its call center quit in 1 year, the call center's head switched to behavioral interviews. Many of those who left did so because they didn't enjoy fielding questions from occasionally irate clients. So Wilson no longer tries to predict how candidates will act based on asking them if they want to work with angry clients. Instead, she asks behavioral questions like, "Tell me about a time you were speaking with an irate person, and how you turned the situation around." Wilson says this makes it much harder to fool the interviewer, and, indeed, only four people left her center in the following year.[29] *Knowledge and background* questions probe candidates' job-related knowledge and experience, as in, "What math courses did you take in college?"

HOW TO ADMINISTER We can also classify interviews based on how we administer them. For example, most interviews are administered *one-on-one:* Two people meet alone and one interviews the other by seeking oral responses to oral inquiries. Most selection processes are also sequential. In a *sequential interview* several people interview the applicant in sequence before a selection decision is made. In a *panel interview* the candidate is interviewed simultaneously by a group (or panel) of interviewers, rather than sequentially.

FIGURE 5.7

Structured Interview Guide

Source: Copyright 1992. The Dartnell Corporation, Chicago, IL. Adapted with permission.

What did you do before you took your last job? _____

Where were you employed? _____

Location _____ Job title _____

Duties _____

Did you hold the same job throughout your employment with that company? _____ Yes _____ No. If not, describe the jobs you held, when you held them, and the duties of each. _____

_____

What was your starting salary? _____ What was your final salary? _____

Name of your last supervisor _____

May we contact that company? _____ Yes _____ No

What did you like most about that job? _____

What did you like least about that job? _____

Why did you leave that job? _____

Would you consider working there again? _____

Interviewer: If there is any gap between the various periods of employment, the applicant should be asked about them. _____

Interviewer's comments or observations _____

_____

What did you do prior to the job with that company? _____

What other jobs or experience have you had? Describe them briefly and explain the general duties of each.

_____

Have you been unemployed at any time in the last five years? _____ Yes _____ No. What efforts did you make to find work? _____

What other experience or training do you have that would help qualify you for the job applied for? Explain how and where you obtained this experience or training. _____

_____

Educational Background

What education or training do you have that would help you in the job for which you have applied? _____

_____

Describe any formal education you have had. (Interviewer may substitute technical training, if relevant.) _____

_____

Off-Job Activities

What do you do in your off-hours? ___ Part-time job ___ Athletics ___ Spectator sports ___ Clubs ___ Other

Please explain. _____

Interviewer's Specific Questions

Interviewer: Add any questions to the particular job for which you are interviewing, leaving space for brief answers.

(Be careful to avoid questions that may be viewed as discriminatory.)

_____

_____

_____

Personal

Would you be willing to relocate? _____ Yes _____ No

Are you willing to travel? _____ Yes _____ No

Some interviews are done by *video* or *phone*. Phone interviews can actually be more accurate than face-to-face ones for judging an applicant's conscientiousness, intelligence, and interpersonal skills. Perhaps because neither side need worry about things like clothing or handshakes, the telephone interview may let both focus more on substantive answers. In a typical study, interviewers tended to evaluate applicants more favorably in telephone versus face-to-face interviews, particularly where the interviewees were less physically attractive. The interviewers came to about the same conclusions regarding the interviewees whether the interview was face-to-face or by videoconference. Applicants themselves preferred the face-to-face interviews.[30]

How Useful Are Interviews?

While virtually all employers use interviews, the statistical evidence regarding their validity is quite mixed. Much of the early research gave selection interviews low marks for reliability and validity.[31] However, recent studies confirm that the "validity of the interview is greater than previously believed."[32] The key is that the interview's usefulness depends on how you do the interview itself. We can make the following generalizations, based on interview validity studies:

- With respect to predicting job performance, *situational interviews* yield a higher mean (average) validity than do behavioral interviews.
- *Structured interviews*, regardless of content, are more valid than unstructured interviews for predicting job performance. They are more valid party because they are more reliable—for example, the same interviewer administers the interview more consistently from candidate to candidate.[33]
- Both when they are structured and when they are unstructured, *one-on-one interviews* tend to be more valid than are panel interviews, in which multiple interviewers provide ratings in one setting.[34]

In summary, structured situational interviews (in which you ask the candidates what they would do in a particular situation) conducted one-on-one seem to be the most useful for predicting job performance. However, whether you are an effective interviewer also depends on avoiding common interviewing mistakes, a subject to which we now turn.

How to Avoid Common Interviewing Mistakes

Most people tend to think they're better interviewers than they really are. In one study, less than 34% of interviewers had formal interview training. However, these "interviewers were confident that they could identify the best candidates regardless of the amount of interview structure employed."[35] Actually, several common interviewing mistakes can undermine an interview's usefulness. Some of these common mistakes—and suggestions for avoiding them—follow.

SNAP JUDGMENTS One consistent finding is that interviewers tend to jump to conclusions— make snap judgments—about candidates during the first few minutes of the interview. In fact, this often occurs even before the interview begins, based on test scores or résumé data. One London-based psychologist interviewed the chief executives of 80 top companies. She came to this conclusion about snap judgments in selection interviews: "Really, to make a good impression, you don't even get time to open your mouth. . . . An interviewer's response to you will generally be preverbal—how you walk through the door, what your posture is like, whether you smile, whether you have a captivating aura, whether you have a firm, confident handshake. You've got about half a minute to make an impact and after that all you are doing is building on a good or bad first impression. . . . It's a very emotional response."[36]

For interviewees, such findings underscore why it's important to start off right. Interviewers usually make up their minds about you during the first few minutes of the interview, and prolonging the interview past this point usually adds little to change their decisions. From the interviewer's point of view, the findings underscore the importance of consciously delaying a decision, and keeping an open mind until the interview is over.

NEGATIVE EMPHASIS Jumping to conclusions is especially troublesome given the fact that interviewers also tend to have a consistent negative bias. They are generally more influenced by unfavorable than favorable information about the candidate. Furthermore, their impressions are much more likely to change from favorable to unfavorable than from unfavorable to favorable. Often, in fact, interviews are mostly searches for negative information.

What are the implications? As an interviewer, remember to keep an open mind and consciously work against being preoccupied with negative impressions. As an interviewee, remember the old saying that "You only have one chance to make a good first impression." If you start with a poor initial impression, you'll find it almost impossible to overcome that first, bad impression during the interview.

NOT KNOWING THE JOB Interviewers who don't know precisely what the job entails and what sort of candidate is best suited for it usually form incorrect stereotypes about what makes a good applicant. They then erroneously match interviewees against these incorrect stereotypes. Studies therefore have long shown that more job knowledge on the part of interviewers translates into better interviews.[37] Interviewers should know as much as possible about the nature of the position for which they're interviewing, and about the human requirements (e.g., interpersonal skills, job knowledge) that the job requires.

PRESSURE TO HIRE Being under pressure to hire undermines an interview's usefulness. In one study, a group of managers were told to assume that they were behind in their recruiting quota. A second group was told that they were ahead of their quota. Those behind evaluated the same recruits much more highly than did those ahead.[38]

CANDIDATE ORDER (CONTRAST) ERROR Candidate order (or contrast) error means that the order in which you see applicants affects how you rate them. In one study, researchers asked managers to evaluate a candidate who was "just average" after first evaluating several "unfavorable" candidates. The average candidate was evaluated more favorably than he might otherwise have been, because in contrast to the unfavorable candidates the average one looked better than he actually was.[39]

INFLUENCE OF NONVERBAL BEHAVIOR Not just what the candidate says but how he or she looks and behaves can influence the interviewer's ratings. For example, studies show that interviewers rate applicants who demonstrate more eye contact, head moving, smiling, and similar nonverbal behaviors higher. Such behaviors often account for over 80% of the applicant's rating.[40] In another study, vocal cues (such as the interviewee's pitch, speech rates, and pauses) and visual cues (such as physical attractiveness, smile, and body orientation) correlated with the evaluator's judgments of whether the interviewees could be liked and trusted, and were credible.[41] In one study of 99 graduating college seniors, the interviewee's apparent level of extroversion influenced whether he or she received follow-up interviews and job offers.[42] Extroverted applicants seem particularly prone to self-promotion, and self-promotion is strongly related to the interviewer's perceptions of candidate job fit.[43]

ATTRACTIVENESS An applicant's attractiveness and sex also play a role.[44] In general, studies find that individuals ascribe more favorable traits and more successful life outcomes to attractive people.[45] In one study, researchers asked subjects to evaluate candidates for promotability based on photographs. Men were perceived to be more suitable for hire and more likely to advance to the next executive level than were equally qualified women, and more attractive candidates, especially men, were preferred over less attractive ones.[46] These stereotypes are changing. However, women still account for only about 16% of corporate officers and 1% of CEOs at Fortune 500 companies.[47]

INGRATIATION Interviewees also boost their chances for job offers through self-promotion and ingratiation. *Ingratiation* involves, for example, agreeing with the recruiter's opinions and thus signaling that they share similar beliefs. *Self-promotion* means promoting one's own skills and abilities to create the impression of competence.[48]

NONVERBAL IMPLICATIONS With respect to nonverbal behavior (such as eye contact), it seems apparent that otherwise inferior candidates who are trained to "act right" in interviews often get appraised more highly than do more competent applicants without the right nonverbal interviewing skills. Interviewers should thus, first, endeavor to look beyond the behavior to who the person is and what he or she is saying. Second, demographic and physical attributes, such as attractiveness, sex, or race, may influence your decisions as an interviewer. Because such attributes are generally irrelevant to job performance, interviewers should anticipate the potential impact of such biases and guard against letting them influence their ratings.

The accompanying *Personal Competencies* feature explains how cross-cultural sensitivity can help further reduce employee selection errors.

Personal Competencies

Building Your Cross-Cultural Sensitivity: Skills to Reduce Employee Selection Errors

GENDER ISSUES IN TESTING   Employers using selection tests should know that gender issues may distort the results. TV commercials for children's toys attest to the fact that gender-role socialization is a continuing reality. Parents and others often socialize girls into traditionally female roles and boys into traditionally male roles. Thus there is a continuing underrepresentation of women in traditional male areas such as top management and in engineering and the sciences. Such stereotypes are changing. One recent study found that both male and female managers "are rating women more as leaders than they did 15 and 30 years ago."[49]

Yet gender-role socialization does influence men's and women's test results. For example, it can influence the occupational interests for which candidates express a preference. Males tend to score higher on aptitude tests in what some view as male fields (such as mechanical reasoning). The test results may thus ironically perpetuate the narrowing of females' career options.

RACE   Race also plays a role. One study examined racial differences in ratings of black and white interviewees when the interviewees appeared before three interview panels: panels in which the racial composition was primarily black (75% black, 25% white), racially balanced (50% black, 50% white), and primarily white (75% white, 25% black).[50] On the primarily black panels, black and white raters judged black and white candidates similarly. On the other hand, in the primarily white panels or in those in which black and white interviewers were equally represented, white candidates were rated higher by white interviewers, and black candidates were rated higher by black interviewers.

APPLICANT DISABILITY AND THE EMPLOYMENT INTERVIEW   A study by the Research and Evaluation Center at the National Center for Disability Services provides some insight into what disabled people who use "assistive technology" (such as word recognition software) at work expect and prefer from interviewers.[51]

Researchers surveyed 40 disabled people from various occupations to arrive at their conclusions. The basic finding was that, from the disabled person's point of view, interviewers tend to avoid directly addressing the disability, and therefore make their decisions without getting all the facts. What the disabled people prefer is an open discussion, one that would allow the employer to fully clarify his or her concerns and reach a knowledgeable conclusion. Among the questions disabled persons said they would like interviewers to ask were these:

- Is there any kind of setting or special equipment that will facilitate the interview process for you?
- Is there any specific technology that you currently use or have used in previous jobs that assists the way you work?
- Provide an example of how you would use technology to carry out your job duties.
- Is there any technology that you don't currently have that would be helpful in performing the duties of this position?
- Other than technology, what other kind of support did you have in previous jobs? If none, is there anything that would benefit you?

In interviewing physically disabled applicants, structured interviews seem less biased. In one study where raters used unstructured interviews, the raters evaluated disabled candidates more positively than equally qualified nondisabled ones. Structured interviews reduced this effect.[52]

In Summary: Steps in Conducting an Effective Interview

Steps to follow in designing and conducting an effective interview include:

STRUCTURE THE INTERVIEW Structuring the interview assures greater consistency and also helps ensure that you ask questions that provide real insight into how the person will perform on the job—and that, of course, is the main point of the interview. There are several ways to increase the standardization (structure) of the interview or otherwise assist the interviewer to ask more consistent and job-relevant questions.[53] They include:[54]

1. Study the job description and base questions on actual job duties. Minimize irrelevant questions based on inaccurate beliefs about the job's requirements.
2. Use job knowledge, background, situational or behavioral questions for sizing up the candidate. Questions that ask for opinions and attitudes, goals and aspirations, and self-descriptions and self-evaluations encourage self-promotion and allow candidates to avoid revealing weaknesses. Examples of structured questions include (1) *situational* questions like "Suppose you were giving a sales presentation and a difficult technical question arose that you could not answer. What would you do?" (2) *past behavior* questions like "Can you provide an example of a specific instance where you developed a sales presentation that was highly effective?" (3) *background* questions like "What work experiences, training, or other qualifications do you have for working in a teamwork environment?" and (4) *job knowledge* questions like "What factors should you consider when developing a TV advertising campaign?"
3. Train interviewers. For example, review employment laws with prospective interviewers and train them to avoid irrelevant or potentially discriminatory questions. Studies show training interviewers boosts their effectiveness.[55]
4. Use the same questions with all candidates. Using the same questions with all candidates can also reduce bias by giving all the candidates the exact same opportunity.
5. Use rating scales to rate answers, if possible. For each question, provide a range of sample ideal answers, and a quantitative score for each. Then rate each candidate's answers against this scale.
6. Use multiple interviewers. Doing so can reduce bias by diminishing the importance of one interviewer's idiosyncratic opinions, and by bringing in more points of view.
7. If possible, use a structured interview form. Interviews based on structured guides, like the one in Figure 5.7, usually result in superior interviews.[56] At the very least, list your questions before the interview.

PLAN FOR THE INTERVIEW Conduct the interview in a private room where telephone calls are not accepted and where you can minimize interruptions. Begin by reviewing the candidate's application and résumé, and note any areas that are vague or that may indicate strengths or weaknesses. Review the job specification and plan to start the interview with a clear picture of the traits of an ideal candidate.

ESTABLISH RAPPORT The main reason for the interview is to find out about the applicant. To do this, start by putting the person at ease. Greet the candidate and start the interview by asking a noncontroversial question, perhaps about the weather or the traffic conditions that day. As a rule, all applicants—even unsolicited drop-ins—should receive friendly, courteous treatment, not only on humanitarian grounds but also because your reputation is on the line.

ASK QUESTIONS Try to follow your structured interview guide or the questions you wrote out ahead of time. You'll find a menu of questions to choose from (such as "Describe a situation which best illustrates your leadership ability.") in Figure 5.8.

One way to get more candid answers is to make it clear you're going to conduct reference checks. Ask, "If I were to ask your boss, and if the boss were very candid with me, what's your best guess as to what he or she would say are your strengths, weaker points, and overall performance?"[57] The *HR in Practice* feature on page 166 presents some guidelines.

FIGURE 5.8 Sample Interview Questions

Organization and Planning Skills

1. Describe a specific situation which illustrates how you set objectives to reach a goal.
2. Tell me about a time when you had to choose between two or more important opportunities. How did you go about deciding which was most important to you?
3. Tell me how you normally schedule your time in order to accomplish your day-to-day tasks.
4. Describe a situation where you had a major role in organizing an important event. How did you do it?
5. Think about a lengthy term paper or report that you have written. Describe how you organized, researched and wrote that report.
6. Give an example of how you organized notes and other materials in order to study for an important exam.
7. Describe a time when you reorganized something to be more efficient. How did you do it?
8. Think of a time when you made important plans that were fouled up. How did you react? What did you do?

Interaction and Leadership

1. Tell me about an event in your past which has greatly influenced the way you relate to people.
2. Give a specific example that best illustrates your ability to deal with an uncooperative person.
3. Some people have the ability to "roll with the punches." Describe a time when you demonstrated this skill.
4. Tell me when you had to work with someone who had a negative opinion of you. How did you overcome this?
5. Recall a time when you participated on a team. Tell me an important lesson you learned that is useful to you today.
6. Describe an instance when you reversed a negative situation at school, work, or home. How did you do it?
7. Describe a situation which best illustrates your leadership ability.
8. Think about someone whose leadership you admire. What qualities impress you?

Assertiveness and Motivation

1. Describe several work standards that you have set for yourself in past jobs. Why are these important to you?
2. Tell me a time when you have experienced a lack of motivation. What caused this? What did you do about it?
3. Describe a situation where you had to deal with someone whom you felt was dishonest. How did you handle it?
4. Describe a situation that made you extremely angry. How did you react?
5. Tell me about a time that best illustrates your ability to "stick things out" in a tough situation.
6. Describe a time when you motivated an unmotivated person to do something you wanted them to do.
7. Give me an example of a time when you were affected by organizational politics. How did you react?
8. Give me an example of when someone tried to take advantage of you. How did you react?

Decision Making and Problem Solving

1. Give an example that illustrates your ability to make a tough decision.
2. Tell me about a decision you made even though you did not have all the facts.
3. Describe a situation where you have had to "stand up" for a decision you made, even though it was unpopular.
4. Describe a situation where you changed your mind, even after you publicly committed to a decision.
5. Describe a situation that illustrates your ability to analyze and solve a problem.
6. Tell me about a time where you acted as a mediator to solve a problem between two other people.
7. Describe a problem that seemed almost overwhelming to you. How did you handle it?
8. Tell me about a time where you have used a creative or unique approach to solve a tough problem.

The following general questions will also help you prepare for employment interviews:

1. Tell me a little about yourself.
2. Why did you attend Indiana State University?
3. What led you to choose your major or career field?
4. What college subjects did you like best/least? What did you like/dislike about them?
5. What has been your greatest challenge in college?
6. Describe your most rewarding college experience?
7. Do you think that your grades are a good indication of your academic abilities?
8. If you could change a decision you made while at college, what would you change? Why?
9. What campus involvements did you choose? What did you gain/contribute?
10. What are your plans for continued or graduate study?
11. What interests you about this job? What challenges are you looking for in a position?
12. How have your educational and work experiences prepared you for this position?
13. What work experiences have been most valuable to you and why?
14. Why are you interested in our organization? In what way do you think you can contribute to our company?
15. How would you describe yourself?
16. What do you consider to be your greatest strengths? Weaknesses? Give examples.
17. If I asked the people who know you for one reason why I shouldn't hire you, what would they say?
18. What accomplishments have given you the most satisfaction? Why?
19. What are your long-range career objectives? How do you plan to achieve these?
20. How would you describe your ideal job?
21. What two or three things are most important to you in your job?
22. Do you have a geographical preference? Why?

Source: Used with permission of the Indiana State University Career Center. All rights reserved.

HR in Practice

Dos and Don'ts of Interview Questions

- **Don't** ask questions that can be answered yes or no.
- **Don't** put words in the applicant's mouth or telegraph the desired answer, for instance, by nodding or smiling when the right answer is given.
- **Don't** interrogate the applicant as if the person is a criminal, and don't be patronizing, sarcastic, or inattentive.
- **Don't** monopolize the interview by rambling, nor let the applicant dominate the interview so you can't ask all your questions.

- **Do** ask open-ended questions.
- **Do** listen to the candidate to encourage him or her to express thoughts fully.
- **Do** draw out the applicant's opinions and feelings by repeating the person's last comment as a question (e.g., "You didn't like your last job?").
- **Do** ask for examples.[58] For instance, if the candidate lists specific strengths or weaknesses, follow up with, "What are specific examples that demonstrate each of your strengths?"

TAKE BRIEF NOTES DURING THE INTERVIEW. Doing so may help to overcome "the recency effect" (putting too much weight on the last few minutes of the interview). It may also help you keep an open mind rather than making a snap judgment early in the interview, and may also help jog your memory once the interview is complete. The research suggests that the interviewer should take notes, but not copious ones, instead noting just the key points of what the interviewee says.[59]

CLOSE THE INTERVIEW Toward the close of the interview, leave time to answer any questions the candidate may have and, if appropriate, to advocate your firm to the candidate.

Try to end all interviews on a positive note. Tell the applicant whether there is an interest and, if so, what the next step will be. Similarly, make rejections diplomatically (for instance, with a statement such as "Thank you but there are other candidates whose experience is closer to our requirements").

REVIEW THE INTERVIEW After the candidate leaves, review your interview notes, fill in the structured interview guide (if this was not done during the interview), and review the interview while it's fresh in your mind.

USING OTHER SELECTION TECHNIQUES

4 Explain the pros and cons of background investigations, reference checks, and preemployment information services.

Background Investigations and Reference Checks

About 82% of HR managers report checking applicants' backgrounds; 80% do criminal convictions searches, and 35% do credit history reports.[60]

There are two key reasons for checking backgrounds. One is to verify the accuracy of factual information the applicant provided; the other is to uncover damaging background information such as criminal records and suspended drivers' licenses. In Chicago, for instance, a pharmaceutical firm discovered that it had hired gang members in mail delivery and computer repair. The gang members were stealing close to a million dollars per year in computer parts and then using the mail department to ship them to a nearby computer store they owned.[61]

WHAT TO VERIFY The most commonly verified background areas are legal eligibility for employment (to comply with immigration laws), dates of prior employment, military service (including discharge status), education, and identification (including date of birth and address). Other items should include county criminal records (current residence, last residence), motor vehicle record, credit, licensing verification, Social Security number, and reference checks.[62]

The position determines how deeply you search. For example, a credit and education check is more important for hiring an accountant than a groundskeeper. In any case, do not limit your background checks only to new hires. For example, also periodically check, say, the credit ratings of employees who have easy access to company assets, and the driving records of employees who routinely use company cars.

COLLECTING BACKGROUND INFORMATION There are several ways to collect background information. Most employers at least try to directly verify an applicant's current position, salary, and employment dates with his or her current employer by phone (assuming that the candidate cleared doing so). Others call the applicant's current and previous supervisors to try to discover more about the person's motivation, technical competence, and ability to work with others.

Many employers get background reports from commercial credit rating companies or employment screening services. These can provide information about an applicant's credit standing, indebtedness, reputation, character, lifestyle, and the truthfulness of the person's application data. There are also thousands of online databases and sources for obtaining background information, including sex offender registries; workers compensation histories; nurses aid registries; and sources for criminal, employment, and educational histories.[63] Top employee background providers include Kroll (*www.Krollworldwide.com*) and First Advantage (*www.FADV.com*).[64]

CHECKING SOCIAL NETWORKING SITES More employers are checking candidates' social networking sites' postings. One employer went to Facebook.com and found that a top candidate described his interests as smoking marijuana and shooting people. The student may have been joking, but did not get the offer.[65] After conducting such informal online reviews, recruiters found that 31% of applicants had lied about their qualifications and 19% had posted information about their drinking or drug use, according to a CareerBuilder.com survey.[66] Similarly, social networking sites can also help prospective employers identify an applicant's former colleagues, and thus contact them.[67]

REFERENCE CHECK EFFECTIVENESS Handled correctly, background checks are an inexpensive and straightforward way to verify factual information (such as current and previous job titles) about applicants. However, reference checking can also backfire. For one thing, it is not easy for the reference to prove that the bad reference he or she gave an applicant was warranted. The rejected applicant thus has various legal remedies, including suing the reference for defamation of character, a fact that can understandably inhibit former employers and supervisors from giving candid references.[68] In one case, a man was awarded $56,000 after being turned down for a job because, among other things, a former employer called him a "character."

It is not just the fear of legal reprisal that can lead to useless or misleading references. Many supervisors don't want to diminish a former employee's chances for a job. Others rather give an incompetent employee good reviews if it will get rid of him or her. Even when checking references via the phone, therefore, be careful. Ask the right questions, and judge whether the reference's answers are evasive and, if so, why.

MAKING REFERENCE CHECKS MORE PRODUCTIVE You can do several things to make your reference checking more productive.

First, remember to have the candidate sign a release authorizing the background check. If he or she won't sign a release, have former employers just verify the applicant's name, dates of employment, position, and salary (or find another candidate).[69]

Second, always get at least two forms of identification and make applicants fill out job applications. Always compare the application to the résumé (people tend to be more creative on their résumés than on their application forms, where they must certify the information).[70]

Third, use a structured reference-checking form as in Figure 5.9. The form helps ensure that you don't overlook important questions.

Fourth, use the references offered by the applicant as merely a source for other references who may know of the applicant's performance. Thus, you might ask each of the

(Verify that the applicant has provided permission before conducting reference checks.)

Candidate Name _____

Reference Name _____

Company Name _____

Dates of Employment
From: _____   To: _____

Position(s) Held _____

Salary History _____

Reason for Leaving _____

Explain the reason for your call and verify the above information with the supervisor (including the reason for leaving)
_____
_____
_____

1. Please describe the type of work for which the candidate was responsible.
_____
_____
_____

2. How would you describe the applicant's relationships with coworkers, subordinates (if applicable), and with superiors?
_____
_____
_____

3. Did the candidate have a positive or negative work attitude? Please elaborate.
_____
_____
_____

4. How would you describe the quantity and quality of output generated by the former employee?
_____
_____
_____

5. What were his/her strengths on the job?
_____
_____

6. What were his/her weaknesses on the job?
_____
_____

7. What is your overall assessment of the candidate?
_____
_____
_____

8. Would you recommend him/her for this position? Why or why not?
_____
_____
_____

9. Would this individual be eligible for rehire? Why or why not?
_____
_____

Other comments?
_____
_____
_____

applicant's references, "Could you please give me the name of another person who might be familiar with the applicant's performance?" In that way, you begin getting information from references who may be more objective because they weren't referred directly by the applicant. Try to contact two superiors, two peers, and two subordinates from each job previously held by the candidate to form a reliable picture of the candidate. Fifth, also ask open-ended questions, such as "How much direction does the applicant need in his or her work?" in order to get the references to talk more about the candidate.

Finally, companies fielding reference requests should ensure that only authorized managers give them. Centralize the task within HR. Former employees may understandably hire reference checking firms and take legal action for defamatory references. There are dozens of reference-checking firms like Allison & Taylor Reference Checking Inc. in Jamestown, New York.[71] Charging as little as $80, many use certified court reporters to manually transcribe what the reference is saying.[72] One supervisor, describing a former city employee, reportedly "used swear words, said he was incompetent and said that he almost brought the city down on its knees."[73]

USING PREEMPLOYMENT INFORMATION SERVICES Online databases make it easier to check background information about candidates. As a result, numerous employment screening services such as Powerchex (see www.powerchex.co.uk) now use databases to conduct background checks for employers. They access dozens of databases, by county, to quickly compile background information for employers.

Although they are valuable, the employer should make sure the screening service does not take any actions that run afoul of employment laws. For example, as we discussed in chapter 2, under the U.S. Americans With Disabilities Act, employers should avoid preemployment inquiries into the existence, nature, or severity of a disability.

In choosing a screening firm, the employer should make sure the firm requires an applicant-signed release authorizing the background check, complies with relevant laws, and uses only legal data sources. A basic criminal check might cost $25, while a comprehensive background check costs about $200.[74]

Honesty Testing

POLYGRAPH TESTS The *polygraph* (or "*lie detector*") machine is a device that measures physiological changes such as increased perspiration. The assumption is that such changes reflect changes in the emotional stress that accompanies lying. The usual procedure is to attach the applicant or current employee to the machine with painless electronic probes. He or she is then asked a series of neutral questions by the polygraph expert. Once the person's emotional reactions to giving truthful answers to neutral questions has been ascertained, questions such as "Have you ever taken anything without paying for it?" can be asked. In theory, the expert can determine with some accuracy whether the applicant is lying.

In the U.S., complaints about offensiveness as well as grave doubts about the polygraph's accuracy culminated in signing the Employee Polygraph Protection Act into law in 1988. With few exceptions, the law prohibits most employers from conducting polygraph examinations of all applicants and most employees. Even in the case of ongoing investigations of theft, the employer's right to use polygraphs is quite limited under the act.

PAPER-AND-PENCIL HONESTY TESTS The virtual elimination of the polygraph as a screening device triggered a burgeoning market for other honesty testing devices. Paper-and-pencil honesty tests are psychological tests designed to predict job applicants' proneness to dishonesty. Most of these tests measure attitudes regarding things such as tolerance of others who steal, acceptance of rationalizations for theft, and admission of theft-related activities.

Psychologists have some concerns about paper-and-pencil honesty tests. For example, integrity tests may be prone to producing a high percentage of false positives, and are susceptible to coaching.[75] However, studies tend to support these tests' validity. One focused on 111 employees hired by a major retail convenience store chain to work at convenience store or gas station outlet counters.[76] "Shrinkage" was estimated to

The polygraph (or "lie detector") machine is a device that measures physiological changes such as increased perspiration.

equal 3% of sales, and internal theft was believed to account for much of this. The researchers found that scores on an honesty test successfully predicted theft, as measured by termination for theft.

In practice, detecting dishonest candidates (see *HR in Practice*) involves not only paper-and-pencil tests but also a comprehensive screening procedure.

HR in Practice

How to Spot Dishonesty

One expert suggests following these steps.

- **Ask blunt questions.**[77] You can ask very direct questions in the face-to-face interview. For example, there is probably nothing wrong with asking the applicant, "Have you ever stolen anything from an employer?", "Have you recently held jobs other than those listed on your application?", and "Is any information on your application misrepresented or falsified?"
- **Listen, rather than talk.** Allow the applicant to do the talking so you can learn as much as possible about the person.
- **Ask for a credit check.** Include a clause in your application form that gives you the right to certain background checks on the applicant, including credit checks and motor vehicle reports.
- **Check all references.** Rigorously pursue employment and personal references.
- **Consider using a paper-and-pencil test.** Consider utilizing paper-and-pencil honesty tests and psychological tests as part of your honesty screening.
- **Test for drugs.** Devise a drug testing program and give each applicant a copy of the policy.

- **Conduct searches.** Establish a search-and-seizure policy. Give each applicant a copy of the policy and require each to return a signed copy. The policy should state that all lockers, desks, and similar property remain the property of the company and may be inspected routinely.
- **Communicate with employees.** Don't rely on testing or interviews to weed out dishonesty. Continuing close supervision, retraining, and employee competency checks are essential. "Meet personally with all your staff members to let them know of the deficiency. Make clear that any future failures to follow protocols or falsification of records will not be tolerated and will result in disciplinary action that may include immediate dismissal."[78]
- **Use caution.** Being rejected for dishonesty carries with it more stigma than does being rejected for, say, poor mechanical comprehension. Furthermore, some governmental laws limit the use of paper-and-pencil honesty tests. Therefore, ensure that you are protecting your candidates' and employees' rights to privacy and that you are adhering to the law in using honesty tests.

Graphology

The use of graphology (handwriting analysis) is based on the assumption that the writer's basic personality traits will be expressed in his or her handwriting. Handwriting analysis thus has some resemblance to projective personality tests.

Although some writers estimate that more than 1,000 U.S. companies use handwriting analysis to assess applicants for certain positions, the validity of handwriting analysis is questionable. In general, the evidence suggests that graphology does not predict job performance.[79] Why so many employers use it is thus a matter of some debate. Perhaps it's because it seems, to many people, to have face validity. Or perhaps in some specific situations it can be shown to predict performance.[80]

Medical Exams

Medical examinations are often the next step in the selection process, and there are several reasons for requiring them. Such exams can confirm that the applicant qualifies for the physical requirements of the position and can unearth any medical limitations that should be taken into account in placing the applicant. The examination can also detect communicable diseases that may be unknown to the applicant. Under some employment laws, a person with a disability can't be rejected for the job if he or she is otherwise qualified and if the person could perform the essential job functions with reasonable accommodation. According to some employment laws, a medical exam is permitted during the period *between the job offer and the commencement of work*, but only if such exams are standard for all applicants for that job.

Drug Screening

Employers generally conduct drug tests. The most common practice is to test new applicants just before they are formally hired. Many firms also test current employees when there is reason to believe an employee has been using drugs after a work accident, or when there are obvious behavioral symptoms like high absenteeism. Some firms administer drug tests on a random basis, while others do so when transferring an employee.[81] Most employers that conduct such tests use urine sampling. Numerous local, national, and international vendors provide workplace drug testing services.[82]

PROBLEMS Unfortunately, drug testing in general doesn't always correlate closely with actual impairment levels.[83] Although Breathalyzers and blood tests for alcohol (like those police give roadside to inebriated drivers) do correlate closely with impairment levels, urine and blood tests for other drugs only show whether drug residues are present. They can't measure impairment or, for that matter, habituation or addiction.[84] Furthermore, "there is a swarm of products that promise to help employees (both male and female) beat [urine analysis] drug tests."[85] (However, hair follicle testing and newer oral fluid samples are much less subject to tampering.)

In any case, drug testing raises several issues. Without strong evidence linking blood or urine drug levels to impairment, some argue that drug testing violates citizens' rights to privacy and due process, and that the procedures themselves are degrading and intrusive. Others argue that workplace drug testing might identify one's use of drugs during leisure hours, but have little or no relevance to the job itself.[86] Furthermore, some employees will claim that drug tests violate their rights to privacy.

In fact, it is not clear that drug testing improves either safety or performance. At least one study, reported by a committee of the U.S. National Academy of Sciences, concluded that other than alcohol, there is no clear evidence that drugs diminish safety or job performance.[87] Another study, conducted in three hotels, concluded that preemployment drug testing seemed to have little or no effect on workplace accidents. However, a combination of preemployment and random ongoing testing was associated with a significant reduction in workplace accidents.[88]

LEGAL ISSUES In the U.S., several laws impact workplace drug testing. Under the ADA, courts might well view a former drug user (one who no longer uses illegal drugs

U.S. Department of
Transportation workplace
regulations require firms
with more than 50 eligible
employees in transportation
industries to conduct
alcohol testing on workers
with sensitive or safety-
related jobs.

and successfully completed or is participating in a rehabilitation program) as a qualified applicant with a disability.[89] U.S. Department of Transportation workplace regulations require firms with more than 50 eligible employees in transportation industries to conduct alcohol testing on workers with sensitive or safety-related jobs. These include mass-transit workers, air traffic controllers, train crews, and school-bus drivers.[90] Particularly where safety-sensitive jobs are concerned, courts appear to side with employers when questions arise.

Realistic Job Previews

Sometimes, a dose of realism makes the best screening tool. For example, Wal-Mart found that associates who quit within the first 90 days often did so because of conflict in their schedules or because they preferred to work in another geographic area. The firm then began explicitly explaining and asking about work schedules and work preferences.[91] One study even found that some applicants accepted jobs with the intention to quit, a fact that more realistic interviewing might have unearthed.[92]

Complying with Immigration Law

HOW TO COMPLY There are two basic ways prospective employees can show their eligibility for employment. One is to show a document such as a passport or alien registration card containing a photograph that proves both identity and employment eligibility. However, many prospective employees do not have either of these documents. Therefore, the other way to verify employment eligibility is to see a document that proves the person's identity, along with a separate document showing the person's employment eligibility, such as a work permit.

Employers run the risk of accepting fraudulent documents, and here they can protect themselves in several ways. Systematic background checks are the most obvious. Preemployment screening should include employment verification, criminal record checks, drug screens, and reference checks. Employers can avoid accusations of discrimination by verifying the documents of all applicants, not just those they think may be suspicious.[93]

Evaluating the Selection Process

More employers today take the time to evaluate just how effective their recruitment and screening processes are. General Electric, for example, compares its various recruiting sources to the performances of the employees they produce, and in that way fine-tunes what recruiting sources it uses. Some firms use "mystery shoppers" to help evaluate their recruitment and staffing processes. Thus, one consulting firm worked with a client to create phantom applicants, complete with résumés. These phantoms then applied to the client employer and reported back on the effectiveness of the employer's recruitment and selection processes.[94] Table 5.1 summarizes the validity, cost, and potential adverse impact of some popular selection methods.

Improving Productivity Through HRIS: Comprehensive Automated Applicant Tracking and Screening Systems

The applicant tracking systems we introduced in chapter 4 (recruiting) do more than compile incoming Web-based résumés and track applicants during the hiring process. The new systems also do three things to help companies screen applicants.

First, most employers also use their applicant tracking systems (ATSs) to "knock out" applicants who do not meet minimum, nonnegotiable job requirements, like submitting to drug tests or holding driver's licenses.

Second, employers use these advanced ATSs to test and screen applicants online. This includes Web-based skills testing (in accounting, for instance), cognitive skills testing (such as for mechanical comprehension), and even psychological testing. Some design their ATSs to screen for intangibles. For example, U.S.-based Recreation Equipment, Inc., needed a system that would match applicant skills with the company's culture, and in

TABLE 5.1 Evaluation of Assessment Methods on Four Key Criteria

Assessment Method	Validity	Adverse Impact	Costs (Develop/ Administer)	Applicant Reactions
Cognitive ability tests	High	High (against minorities)	Low/low	Somewhat favorable
Job knowledge test	High	High (against minorities)	Low/low	More favorable
Personality tests	Low to moderate	Low	Low/low	Less favorable
Biographical data inventories	Moderate	Low to high for different types	High/low	Less favorable
Integrity tests	Moderate to high	Low	Low/low	Less favorable
Structured interviews	High	Low	High/high	More favorable
Physical fitness tests	Moderate to high	High (against females and older workers)	High/high	More favorable
Situational judgment tests	Moderate	Moderate (against minorities)	High/low	More favorable
Work samples	High	Low	High/high	More favorable
Assessment centers	Moderate to high	Low to moderate, depending on exercise	High/high	More favorable
Physical ability tests	Moderate to high	High (against females and older workers)	High/high	More favorable

Note: There was limited research evidence available on applicant reactions to situational judgment tests and physical ability tests. However, because these tests tend to appear very relevant to the job, it is likely that applicant reactions to them would be favorable.

Source: Elaine Pulakos, *Selection Assessment Methods,* SHRM Foundation (2005): 17. Reprinted by permission of Society for Human Resource Management via Copyright Clearance Center.

particular, identify applicants who were naturally inclined to work in teams. The company worked with its applicant tracking system vendor to customize its system to do that.[95]

Third, the newer systems don't just screen out candidates, but discover "hidden talents." Thanks to the Internet, applicants often send their résumés out across a wide range of job openings, hoping a shotgun approach will help them hit a match between their résumé-based qualifications and the listed job requirements. For most employers, this is simply a screening nuisance. But for those who design their ATS to do so, the ATS can identify talents in the candidate pool that lend themselves to job matches at the company that even the applicant didn't know existed when he or she applied.[96]

Review

SUMMARY

1. In this chapter we discuss several techniques for screening and selecting job candidates: The first is testing.

2. Test validity answers the question "What does this test measure?" Criterion validity means demonstrating that those who do well on the test do well on the job. Content validity is demonstrated by showing that the test constitutes a fair sample of the content of the job.

3. As used by psychologists, the term *reliability* always means "consistency." One way to measure reliability is to administer the same (or equivalent) tests to the same people at two different points in time. Or you could focus on internal consistency, comparing the responses to roughly equivalent items on the same test.

4. There are many types of personnel tests in use, including intelligence tests, tests of physical skills, tests of achievement, aptitude tests, interest inventories, and personality tests.

5. Under equal opportunity legislation, an employer may have to prove that his or her tests are predictive of success or failure on the job. This usually requires a predictive validation study, although other means of validation are often acceptable.

6. Management assessment centers are screening devices that expose applicants to a series of real-life exercises. Performance is observed and assessed by experts, who then check their assessments by observing the participants when they are back at their jobs. Examples of such real-life exercises include a simulated business game, an in-basket exercise, and group discussions.

7. Several factors and problems can undermine the usefulness of an interview: making premature decisions, letting unfavorable information predominate, not knowing the requirements of the job, being under pressure to hire, not allowing for the candidate order effect, and nonverbal behavior.

8. The five steps in the interview include plan, establish rapport, question the candidate, close the interview, and review the data.

9. Other screening tools include reference checks, background checks, physical exams, and realistic previews.

10. Once you've selected and hired your new employees, they must be trained. We turn to training in the following chapter.

KEY TERMS

negligent hiring   148
reliability   148
test validity   149
criterion validity   149

content validity   149
management assessment center   158
interview   159

DISCUSSION QUESTIONS AND EXERCISES

1. Explain what is meant by *reliability* and *validity*. What is the difference between them? In what respects are they similar?

2. Write a short essay discussing some of the ethical and legal considerations in testing.

3. Working individually or in groups, check online information for a standardized test such as the SAT and obtain written information regarding the test's validity and reliability. Present a short report in class discussing what the test is

supposed to measure and the degree to which you think the test does what it is supposed to do, based on the reported validity and reliability scores.

4. Give some examples of how interest inventories could be used to improve employee selection. In doing so, suggest several examples of occupational interests that you believe might predict success in various occupations, including college professor, accountant, and computer programmer.

5. Why is it important to conduct preemployment background investigations? How would you go about doing so?
6. For what sorts of jobs do you think computerized interviews are most appropriate? Why?
7. Give a short presentation titled "How to Be Effective as an Interviewer."
8. Briefly discuss and give examples of at least five common interviewing mistakes. What recommendations would you give for avoiding these interviewing mistakes?

Application Exercises

HR in Action Case Incident 1 — Ethics and the Out-of-Control Interview

Ethics are "the principles of conduct governing an individual or a group"—they are the principles people use to decide what their conduct should be.[97]

Fairness is important in employee selection. For example, "If prospective employees perceive that the hiring process does not treat people fairly, they may assume that ethical behavior is not important in the company, and that 'official' pronouncements about the importance of ethics can be discounted."[98]

That's one reason why the situation Maria Fernandez ran into is disturbing. Maria is a bright, popular, and well-informed mechanical engineer who graduated with an engineering degree from State University in June 2008. During the spring preceding her graduation, she went out on many job interviews, most of which she thought were conducted courteously and were reasonably useful in giving both her and the prospective employer a good impression of where each of them stood on matters of importance to both of them. It was, therefore, with great anticipation that she looked forward to an interview with the one firm where she most wanted to work: Apex Environmental. She had always had a strong interest in cleaning up the environment and firmly believed she could best use her training and skills in a firm like Apex, where she thought she could have a successful career while making the world a better place.

The interview, however, was a disaster. Maria walked into a room in which a panel of five men—the president of the company, two vice presidents, the marketing director, and another engineer—began throwing questions at her that she felt were aimed primarily at tripping her up rather than finding out what she could offer through her engineering skills. The questions ranged from unnecessarily discourteous ("Why would you take a job as a waitress in college if you're such an intelligent person?") to irrelevant and sexist ("Are you planning on settling down and starting a family anytime soon?"). Then, after the interview, she met with two of the gentlemen individually (including the president), and the discussions focused almost exclusively on her technical expertise. She

thought that these later discussions went fairly well. However, given the apparent aimlessness and even mean-spiritedness of the panel interview, she was astonished when several days later she received a job offer from the firm.

The offer forced her to consider several matters. From her point of view, the job itself was perfect—she liked what she would be doing, the industry, and the firm's location. And in fact, the president had been quite courteous in subsequent discussions, as had been the other members of the management team. She was left wondering whether the panel interview had been intentionally tense to see how she'd stand up under pressure, and, if so, why they would do such a thing.

Questions

1. How would you explain the nature of the panel interview Maria had to endure? Specifically, do you think it reflected a well-thought-out interviewing strategy on the part of the firm or carelessness (or worse) on the part of the firm's management? If it was carelessness, what would you do to improve the interview process at Apex Environmental?
2. Do you consider the managers' treatment of Maria ethical? Why? If not, what specific steps would you take to make sure the interview process is ethical from now on?
3. Would you take the job offer if you were Maria? If you're not sure, is there any additional information that would help you make your decision, and if so, what is it?
4. The job of applications engineer for which Maria was applying requires (a) excellent technical skills with respect to mechanical engineering, (b) a commitment to working in the area of pollution control, (c) the ability to deal well and confidently with customers who have engineering problems, (d) a willingness to travel worldwide, and (e) a very intelligent and well-balanced personality. List 10 questions you would ask when interviewing applicants for the job.

HR in Action Case Incident 2

Honesty Testing at Carter Cleaning Company

Jennifer Carter, president of Carter Cleaning Centers, and her father have what the latter describes as an easy but hard job when it comes to screening job applicants. It is easy because for two important jobs—the people who actually do the pressing and those who do the cleaning–spotting—the applicants are easily screened with about 20 minutes of on-the-job testing. As with typists, as Jennifer points out, "Applicants either know how to press clothes fast enough or how to use cleaning chemicals and machines, or they don't, and we find out very quickly by just trying them out on the job." On the other hand, applicant screening for the stores can also be frustratingly hard because of the nature of some of the other qualities that Jennifer would like to screen for.

Two of the most critical problems facing her company are employee turnover and employee honesty. Jennifer and her father sorely need to implement practices that will reduce the rate of employee turnover. If there is a way to do this through employee testing and screening techniques, Jennifer would like to know about it because of the management time and money that are now being wasted by the never-ending need to recruit and hire new employees. Of even greater concern to Jennifer and her father is the need to institute new practices to screen out those employees who may be predisposed to steal from the company.

Employee theft is an enormous problem for Carter Cleaning Centers, and one that is not just limited to employees who handle the cash. For example, the cleaner–spotter and/or the presser often open the store themselves, without a manager present, to get the day's work started, and it is not unusual to have one or more of these people steal supplies or "run a route." Running a route means that an employee canvasses his or her neighborhood to pick up people's clothes for cleaning and then secretly cleans and presses them in the Carter store, using the company's supplies, gas, and power. It would also not be unusual for an unsupervised person (or his or her supervisor, for that matter) to accept a one-hour rush order for cleaning or laundering, quickly clean and press the item, and return it to the customer for payment without making out a proper ticket for the item posting the sale. The money, of course, goes into the worker's pocket instead of into the cash register.

The more serious problem concerns the store manager and the counter workers who actually handle the cash.

According to Jack Carter, "You would not believe the creativity employees use to get around the management controls we set up to cut down on employee theft." As one extreme example of this felonious creativity, Jack tells the following story: "To cut down on the amount of money my employees were stealing, I had a small sign painted and placed in front of all our cash registers. The sign said: YOUR ENTIRE ORDER FREE IF WE DON'T GIVE YOU A CASH REGISTER RECEIPT WHEN YOU PAY. CALL 552–0235. It was my intention with this sign to force all our cash-handling employees to place their receipts into the cash register where they would be recorded for my accountants. After all, if all the cash that comes in is recorded in the cash register, then we should have a much better handle on stealing in our stores, right? Well, one of our managers found a diabolical way around this. I came into the store one night and noticed that the cash register this particular manager was using just didn't look right, although the sign was dutifully placed in front of it. It turned out that every afternoon at about 5:00 P.M. when the other employees left, this character would pull his own cash register out of a box that he hid underneath our supplies. Customers coming in would notice the sign and of course the fact that he was meticulous in ringing up every sale. But unknown to them and us, for about five months the sales that came in for about an hour every day went into his cash register, not mine. It took us that long to figure out where our cash for that store was going."

Jennifer would like you to answer the following questions.

Questions

1. What would be the advantages and disadvantages to Jennifer's company of routinely administering honesty tests to all its employees?
2. Specifically, what other screening techniques could the company use to screen out theft-prone and turnover-prone employees, and how exactly could these be used?
3. How should her company terminate employees caught stealing, and what kind of procedure should be set up for handling reference calls about these employees when they go to other companies looking for jobs?

EXPERIENTIAL EXERCISE

The Most Important Person You'll Ever Hire

Purpose:

The purpose of this exercise is to give you practice using some of the interview techniques you learned from this chapter.

Required Understanding:

You should be familiar with the information presented in this chapter, and read this: For parents, children are precious. It's therefore interesting that parents who hire "nannies" to take care of their children usually do little more than ask several interview questions and conduct what is often, at best, a perfunctory reference check. Given the often questionable validity of interviews, and the (often) relative inexperience of the father or mother doing the interviewing, it's not surprising that many of these arrangements end in disappointment. You know from this chapter that it is difficult to conduct a valid interview unless you know exactly what you're looking for and, preferably, also structure the interview. Most parents simply aren't trained to do this.

How to Set Up the Exercise/Instructions:

1. Set up groups of five or six students. Two students will be the interviewees, while the other students in the group will serve as panel interviewers. The interviewees will develop a form for assessing the interviewers, and the panel interviewers will develop a structured situational interview for a "nanny."

2. Instructions for the interviewees: The interviewees should leave the room for about 20 minutes. While out of the room, the interviewees should develop an "interviewer assessment form" based on the information presented in this chapter regarding factors that can undermine the usefulness of an interview. During the panel interview, the interviewees should assess the interviewers using the interviewer assessment form. After the panel interviewers have conducted the interview, the interviewees should leave the room to discuss their notes. Did the interviewers exhibit any of the factors that can undermine the usefulness of an interview? If so, which ones? What suggestions would you (the interviewees) make to the interviewers on how to improve the usefulness of the interview?

3. Instructions for the interviewers: While the interviewees are out of the room, the panel interviewers will have 20 minutes to develop a short structured situational interview form for a "nanny." The panel interview team will interview two candidates for the position. During the panel interview, each interviewer should be taking notes on a copy of the structured situational interview form. After the panel interview, the panel interviewers should discuss their notes. What were your first impressions of each interviewee? Were your impressions similar? Which candidate would you all select for the position and why?

ENDNOTES

1. Kevin Delaney, "Google Adjusts Hiring Process as Needs Grow," *Wall Street Journal* (October 23, 2006): B1, B8.
2. See Rebecca Bennett and Sandra Robinson, "Development of a Measure of Workplace Deviance," *Journal of Applied Psychology* 85, no. 3 (2000): 349.
3. "Wal-Mart to Scrutinize Job Applicants," *CNN Money* (August 12, 2004), http://money.cnn.com/2004/08/12/News/fortune500/walmart_jobs/index.htm, accessed August 8, 2005.
4. Fay Hansen, "Taking 'Reasonable' Action to Avoid Negligent Hiring Claims," *Workforce Management* (September 11, 2006): 31.
5. Anne Anastasi, *Psychological Patterns* (New York: Macmillan, 1968). See also Kevin Murphy and Charles David Shafer, *Psychological Testing* (Upper Saddle River, NJ: Prentice Hall, 2001): 108–124.
6. Robert M. Guion, "Changing Views for Personnel Selection Research," *Personnel Psychology* 40, no. 2 (Summer 1987): 199–213.
7. Note that the U.S. Department of Labor recently reminded federal contractors that even if they use a third party to prepare an employment test, the contractors themselves are "ultimately responsible" for ensuring the tests' job relatedness and EEO compliance. "DOL Officials Discuss Contractors' Duties on Validating Tests," *BNA Bulletin to Management* (September 4, 2007): 287.
8. "Hiring Based on Strength Test Discriminates Against Women," *BNA Bulletin to Management* (February 22, 2005): 62.
9. Brad Bushman and Gary Wells, "Trait Aggressiveness and Hockey Penalties: Predicting Hot Tempers on the Ice," *Journal of Applied Psychology* 83, no. 6 (1998): 969–974.
10. For some other examples see William Shepherd, "Increasing Profits by Assessing Employee Work Styles," *Employment Relations Today*, 32, no.1 (Spring 2005): 19–23; and Eric Krell, "Personality Counts," *HR Magazine* (November 2005): 47–52.
11. Sarah Gale, "Three Companies Cut Turnover with Tests," *Workforce* (April 2002): 66–69.
12. William Wagner, "All Skill, No Finesse," *Workforce* (June 2000): 108–16. See also, for example, James Diefendorff and Kajal Mehta, "The Relations of Motivational Traits with Workplace Deviance," *Journal of Applied Psychology* 92, no. 4 (2007): 967–977.
13. Elaine Pulakos, *Selection Assessment Methods*, SHRM Foundation (2005): 9.

14. See, for example, Douglas Cellar et al., "Comparison of Factor Structures and Criterion-Related Validity Coefficients for Two Measures of Personality Based on the Five Factor Model," *Journal of Applied Psychology* 81, no. 6 (1996): 694–704; Jesus Salgado, "The Five Factor Model of Personality and Job Performance in the European Community," *Journal of Applied Psychology* 82, no. 1 (1997): 30–43; Joyce Hogan et al., "Personality Measurement, Faking, and Employee Selection," *Journal of Applied Psychology* 92, no. 5 (2007): 1270–1285.

15. Murray Barrick and Michael Mount, "The Big Five Personality Dimensions and Job Performance: A Meta Analysis," *Personnel Psychology* 44, no. 1 (Spring 1991): 1–26. See also Robert Schneider, Leatta Hough, and Marvin Dunnette, "Broad-Sided by Broad Traits: How to Sink Science in Five Dimensions or Less," *Journal of Organizational Behavior* 17, no. 6 (November 1996): 639–655, and Paula Caligiuri, "The Big Five Personality Characteristics as Predictors of Expatriate's Desire to Terminate the Assignment and Supervisor Rated Performance," *Personnel Psychology* 53 (2000): 67–68.

16. Mitchell Rothstein and Richard Goffin, "The Use of Personality Measures in Personnel Selection: What Does Current Research Support?" *Human Resource Management Review* 16 (2006): 155–180.

17. Kathryn Tyler, "Put Applicants' Skills to the Test," *HR Magazine* (January 2000): 75–79.

18. Adapted from www.kozaigroup.com/inventories.php, accessed March 3, 2008.

19. Hal Whiting and Theresa Kline, "Assessment of the Equivalence of Conventional versus Computer Administration of the Test of Workplace Essential Skills," *International Journal of Training and Development* 10, no. 4 (December 2006): 285–290.

20. Scott Hayes, "Kinko's Dials into Automated Applicants Screening," *Workforce* (November 1999): 71–73; Gilbert Nicholson, "Automated Assessments for Better Hires," *Workforce* (December 2000): 102–107. Proctored Web-based and paper-and-pencil tests of applicants produce similar results, for instance on personality and judgment tests. However, a timed test may take longer for applicants on the Web, due to downloading problems and the fact that there are fewer items presented on the viewable page. Similarly, tests takers generally find it more difficult to go back and review their results on the Web-based tests. Proctoring is another problem. There is "currently no way to completely prevent [online] test takers from cheating or copying items during testing" or to ensure there's not someone looking over the test taker's shoulder. See Robert Plyhart et al., "Web-Based and Paper-and-Pencil Testing of Applicants in a Proctored Setting: Are Personality, Biodata and Situational Judgment Tests Comparable?" *Personnel Psychology* 56 (2003): 733–752; Denise Potosky and Philip Bob Bobko, "Selection Testing Via the Internet: Practical Considerations and Exploratory Empirical Findings," *Personnel Psychology* 57 (2004) 1025.

21. Requiring job seekers to complete prescreening questionnaires and screening selected applicants out on this basis carries legal and business consequences. See, for example, Lisa Harpe, "Designing an Effective Employment Prescreening Program," *Employment Relations Today* 32, no. 3 (Fall 2005): 43–41.

22. Gilbert Nicholson, "Automated Assessments for Better Hires," *Workforce* (December 2000): 102–107.

23. Brian O'Leary et al., "Selecting the Best and Brightest," *Human Resource Management* 41, no. 3 (Fall 2002): 25–34.

24. Gilbert Nicholson, "Automated Assessments for Better Hires," *Workforce* (December 2000): 102–107.

25. Annette Spychalski, Miguel Quinones, Barbara Gaugler, and Katja Pohley, "A Survey of Assessment Center Practices in Organizations in the United States," *Personnel Management* 50, no. 10 (Spring 1997): 71–90. See also Winfred Arthur Jr. et al., "A Meta Analysis of the Criterion Related Validity of Assessment Center Data Dimensions," *Personnel Psychology* 56 (2003): 124–154.

26. Kobi Dayan et al., "Entry-Level Police Candidate Assessment Center: An Efficient Tool or a Hammer to Kill a Fly?" *Personnel Psychology* 55 (2002): 827–848.

27. Michael McDaniel et al., "The Validity of Employment Interviews: A Comprehensive Review and Meta-Analysis," *Journal of Applied Psychology* 79, no. 4 (1994): 599. See also Richard Posthuma et al., "Beyond Employment Interview Validity: A Comprehensive Narrative Review of Recent Research and Trends over Time," *Personnel Psychology* 55 (2002): 1–81.

28. Michael McDaniel et al., "The Validity of Employment Interviews: A Comprehensive Review and Meta-Analysis," *Journal of Applied Psychology* 79, no. 4 (1994): 601. See also Allen Huffcutt et al., "Comparison of Situational and Behavior Description Interview Questions for Higher Level Positions," *Personnel Psychology* 54 (Autumn 2001): 619–644; Stephen Maurer, "A Practitioner Based Analysis of Interviewer Job Expertise and Scale Format as Contextual Factors in Situational Interviews," *Personnel Psychology* 55 (2002): 307–327.

29. Bill Stoneman, "Matching Personalities with Jobs Made Easier with Behavioral Interviews," *American Banker* 165, no. 229 (November 30, 2000): 8a.

30. Susan Strauss et al., "The Effects of Videoconference, Telephone, and Face-to-Face Media on Interviewer and Applicant Judgments in Employment Interviews," *Journal of Management* 27, no. 3 (2001): 363–381. If the employer records a video interview with the intention of sharing it with hiring managers who don't participate in the interview, it's advisable to first obtain the candidate's written permission. Matt Bolch, "Lights, Camera . . . Interview!" *HR Magazine* (March 2007): 99–102.

31. See, for example, M. M. Harris, "Reconsidering the Employment Interview: A Review of Recent Literature and Suggestions for Future Research," *Personnel Psychology* 42 (1989): 691–726; Richard Posthuma et al., "Beyond Employment Interview Validity: A Comprehensive Narrative Review of Recent Research and Trends Over Time," *Personnel Psychology* 55, no. 1 (Spring 2002): 1–81.

32. Timothy Judge et al., "The Employment Interview: A Review of Recent Research and Recommendations for Future Research," *Human Resource Management* 10, no. 4 (2000): 392. There is disagreement regarding the relative superiority of individual versus panel interviews. See, for example, Marlene Dixon et al., "The Panel Interview: A Review of Empirical Research and Guidelines

for Practice," *Public Personnel Management* (Fall 2002): 397–428.

33. Frank Schmidt and Ryan Zimmerman, "A Counterintuitive Hypothesis About Employment Interview Validity and Some Supporting Evidence," *Journal of Applied Psychology* 89, no. 3 (2004): 553–561.

34. The validity discussion and these findings are based on Michael McDaniel et al., "The Validity of Employment Interviews: A Comprehensive Review and Meta-Analysis," *Journal of Applied Psychology* 79, no. 4 (1994): 607–610. See also Robert Dipboye et al., "The Validity of Unstructured Panel Interviews," *Journal of Business & Strategy* 16, no. 1 (Fall 2001): 35–49, and Marlene Dixon et al., "The Panel Interview: A Review of Empirical Research and Guidance," *Public Personnel Management* 3, no. 3 (Fall 2002): 397–428. See also Todd Maurer and Jerry Solomon, "The Science and Practice of a Structured Employment Interview Coaching Program," *Personnel Psychology* 59 (2006): 433–456.

35. Derek Chapman and David Zweig, "Developing a Nomological Network for Interview Structure: Antecedents and Consequences of the Structured Selection Interview," *Personnel Psychology* 58 (2005): 673–702.

36. Anita Chaudhuri, "Beat the Clock: Applying for a Job? A New Study Shows That Interviewers Will Make Up Their Minds about You Within a Minute," *The Guardian* (June 14, 2000): 2–6.

37. Don Langdale and Joseph Weitz, "Estimating the Influence of Job Information on Interviewer Agreement," *Journal of Applied Psychology* 57 (1973): 23–27.

38. R. E. Carlson, "Selection Interview Decisions: The Effects of Interviewer Experience, Relative Quota Situation, and Applicant Sample on Interview Decisions," *Personnel Psychology* 20 (1967): 259–280.

39. R. E. Carlson, "Effects of Applicant Sample on Ratings of Valid Information in an Employment Setting," *Journal of Applied Psychology* 54 (1970): 217–222.

40. See, for example, Scott Fleischmann, "The Messages of Body Language in Job Interviews," *Employee Relations* 18, no. 2 (Summer 1991): 161–176. See also James Westpall and Ithai Stern, "Flattery Will Get You Everywhere (Especially if You're a Male Caucasian): How Ingratiation, Board Room Behavior, and a Demographic Minority Status Affect Additional Board Appointments at US Companies," *Academy of Management Journal* 50, no. 2 (2007): 267–288.

41. Tim DeGroot and Stephen Motowidlo, "Why Visual and Vocal Interview Cues Can Affect Interviewer's Judgments and Predicted Job Performance," *Journal of Applied Psychology* (December 1999): 968–984.

42. David Caldwell and Jerry Burger, "Personality Characteristics of Job Applicants and Success in Screening Interviews," *Personnel Psychology* 51 (1998): 119–136.

43. Amy Kristof-Brown et al., "Applicant Impression Management: Dispositional Influences and Consequences for Recruiter Perceptions of Fit and Similarity," *Journal of Management* 28, no. 1 (2002): 27–46. See also Linda McFarland et al., "Impression Management Use and Effectiveness Across Assessment Methods," *Journal of Management* 29, no. 5 (2003): 641–661.

44. See, for example, Cynthia Marlowe, Sondra Schneider, and Carnot Nelson, "Gender and Attractiveness Biases in Hiring Decisions: Are More Experienced Managers Less Biased?" *Journal of Applied Psychology* 81, no. 1 (1996): 11–21; see also Shari Caudron, "Why Job Applicants Hate HR," *Workforce* (June 2002): 36.

45. Marlowe et al., "Gender and Attractiveness Biases in Hiring Decisions," 11.

46. Ibid., 18.

47. Emily Duehr and Joyce Bono, "Men, Women, and Managers: Are Stereotypes Finally Changing?" *Personnel Psychology* 59 (2006): 837.

48. Chad Higgins and Timothy Judge, "The Effect of Applicant Influence Tactics on Recruiter Perceptions of Fit and Hiring Recommendations: A Field Study," *Journal of Applied Psychology* 89, no. 4 (2004): 622–632.

49. Dirk Steiner and Stephen Gilliland, "Fairness Reactions to Personnel Selection Techniques in France and the United States," *Journal of Applied Psychology* 81, no. 2 (1996): 134–141; Emily Duehr and Joyce Bono, "Men, Women, and Managers: Are Stereotypes Finally Changing?" *Personnel Psychology* 59 (2006): 815–846.

50. Amelia J. Prewett-Livingston et al., "Effects of Race on Interview Ratings in a Situational Panel Interview," *Journal of Applied Psychology* 81, no. 2 (1996): 178–186; see also Richard White Jr., "Ask Me No Questions, Tell Me No Lies: Examining the Uses and Misuses of the Polygraph," *Public Personnel Management* 30, no. 4 (Winter 2001): 483–493.

51. Andrea Rodriguez and Fran Prezant, "Better Interviews for People with Disabilities," *Workforce,* downloaded from workforce.com on November 14, 2003.

52. Ellyn Brecher et al., "The Structured Interview: Reducing Biases toward Job Applicants with Physical Disabilities," *Employee Responsibilities and Rights* 18, no. 3 (September 2006): 155–170.

53. Laura Gollub Williamson et al., "Employment Interview on Trial: Linking Interview Structure with Litigation Outcomes," *Journal of Applied Psychology* 82, no. 6 (1996): 901; Michael Campion, David Palmer, and James Campion, "A Review of Structure in the Selection Interview," *Personnel Psychology* 50 (1997): 655–702.

54. Unless otherwise specified, the following are based on Williamson et al., "Employment Interview on Trial," 901–902.

55. Todd Maurer and Jerry Solamon, "The Science and Practice of a Structured Employment Interview Coaching Program," *Personnel Psychology* 59 (2006): 433–456.

56. R. E. Carlson, "Selection Interview Decisions: The Effects of Interviewer Experience, Relative Quota Situation, and Applicant Sample on Interview Decisions," *Personnel Psychology* 20 (1967): 259–280.

57. "Looking to Hire the Very Best? Ask the Right Questions. Lots of Them," *Fortune* (June 21, 1999): 192–194.

58. Panel Kaul, "Interviewing Is Your Business," *Association Management* (November 1992): 29. See also Nancy Woodward, "Asking for Salary Histories," *HR Magazine* (February 2000): 109–112. Gathering information about specific interview dimensions such as social ability, responsibility, and independence (as is often done with structured interviews) can improve interview accuracy, at least for more complicated jobs. See also Andrea Poe, "Graduate Work: Behavioral Interviewing Can Tell You If an Applicant

Just Out of College Has Traits Needed for the Job," *HR Magazine* 48, no. 10 (October 2003): 95–96.

59. Catherine Middendorf and Therese Macan, "Note Taking in the Employment Interview: Effects on Recall and Judgment," *Journal of Applied Psychology* 87, no. 2 (2002): 293–303.

60. "Are Your Background Checks Balanced? Experts Identify Concerns Over Verifications," *BNA Bulletin to Management* (May 13, 2004): 153.

61. Based on Samuel Greengard, "Have Gangs Invaded Your Workplace?" *Personnel Journal* (February 1996): 47–57; See also, Carroll Lachnit, "Protecting People and Profits with Background Checks," *Workforce* (February 2002): 52.

62. Carroll Lachnit, "Protecting People and Profits with Background Checks," *Workforce* (February 2002): 52. See also Robert Howie and Lawrence Shapero, "Preemployment Criminal Background Checks: Why Employers Should Look Before They Leap," *Employee Relations Law Journal* (Summer 2002): 63–77.

63. Ibid., 50ff.

64. "Top Employee Background Checking and Screening Providers," *Workforce Management* (November 7, 2005): 14.

65. Alan Finder, "When A Risqué Online Persona Undermines a Chance for a Job," *New York Times* (June 11, 2006): 1.

66. "Vetting via Internet Is Free, Generally Legal, but Not Necessarily Smart Hiring Strategy," *BNA Bulletin to Management* (February 20, 2007): 57–58.

67. Anjali Athavaley, "Job References You Can't Control," *Wall Street Journal* (September 27, 2007): B1.

68. For example, see Lawrence Dube Jr., "Employment References and the Law," *Personnel Journal* 65, no. 2 (February 1986): 87–91. See also Mickey Veich, "Uncover the Resume Ruse," *Security Management* (October 1994): 75–76; Mary Mayer, "Background Checks in Focus," *HR Magazine* (January 2002): 59–62.

69. Diane Cadrain, "Job Detectives Dig Deep for Defamation," *HR Magazine* 49, no. 10 (October 2004): 34FF.

70. Carroll Lachnit, "Protecting People and Profits with Background Checks," *Workforce* (February 2002): 54; Shari Caudron, "Who Are You Really Hiring?" *Workforce* (November 2002): 31.

71. Kris Maher, "Reference Checking Firms Flourish, but Complaints About Some Arise," *Wall Street Journal* (March 5, 2002): B8.

72. Diane Cadrain, "Job Detectives Dig Deep for Defamation," *HR Magazine* 49, no. 10 (October 2004): 34FF.

73. "Undercover Callers Tip Off Job Seekers to Former Employers' Negative References," *BNA Bulletin to Management* (May 27, 1999): 161.

74. Carroll Lachnit, "Protecting People and Profits with Background Checks," *Workforce* (February 2002): 52.

75. Ronald Karren and Larry Zacharias, "Integrity Tests: Critical Issues," *Human Resource Management Review* 17 (2007): 221–234.

76. John Bernardin and Donna Cooke, "Validity of an Honesty Test in Predicting Theft Among Convenience Store Employees," *Academy of Management Journal* 36, no. 5 (1993): 1097–1108. *HR in Practice* suggestions adapted from "Divining Integrity Through Interviews," *BNA Bulletin to Management* (June 4, 1987): 184; and "Ideas and Trends," *Commerce Clearing House* (December 29, 1998): 222–223. Note that some suggest that by possibly signaling mental illness, integrity tests may conflict with the Americans with Disabilities Act, but one review concludes that such tests pose little legal risk to employers. Christopher Berry et al., "A Review of Recent Developments in Integrity Test Research," *Personnel Psychology* 60 (2007): 271–301.

77. Based on "Divining Integrity Through Interviews," *BNA Bulletin to Management* (June 4, 1987), and "Ideas and Trends," Commerce Clearing House (December 29, 1998): 222–223.

78. Christopher S. Frings, "Testing for Honesty," *Medical Laboratory Observer* 35, no. 12 (December 2003): 27(1).

79. Anthony Edwards, "An Experiment to Test the Discrimination Ability of Graphologists," *Personality and Individual Differences B,* no. 1 (January 1992): 69–74; George Langer, "Graphology in Personality Assessment: A Reliability and Validity Study," *Dissertation Abstracts International: Section B: The Sciences and Engineering* 54, no. 7-B (1994): 38–56.

80. Steven L. Thomas and Steve Vaught, "The Write Stuff: What the Evidence Says About Using Handwriting Analysis in Hiring," *Advanced Management Journal* 66. No. 4 (August 2001): 31–35; Kevin Murphy and Charles David Shafer, Op cit, 438–9.

81. Peter Cholakis, "How to Implement a Successful Drug Testing Program," *Risk Management* 52, no. 11 (November 2005): 24–28; Elaine Davis and Stacie Hueller, "Strengthening the Case for Workplace Drug Testing: The Growing Problem of Methamphetamines," *Advanced Management Journal* 71, no 3 (Summer 2006): 4–10.

82. For example, http://www.infolinkscreening.com/InfoLink/DrugTesting/DrugTesting. aspx?s=buscom3a, accessed April 19, 2008.

83. Scott MacDonald et al., "The Limitations of Drug Screening in the Workplace," *International Labor Review* 132, no. 1 (1993): 100.

84. Ibid., 103.

85. Diane Cadrain, "Are Your Employees' Drug Tests Accurate?" *HR Magazine* (January 2003): 40–45. See also Ari Nattle, "Drug Testing Impaired," *Traffic World* 271, no. 45 (November 12, 2007): 18.

86. MacDonald et al., "The Limitations of Drug Screening in the Workplace," 105–106.

87. Lewis Maltby, "Drug Testing: A Bad Investment," *Business Ethics* 15, no. 2 (March 2001): 7.

88. Frank Lockwood et al., "Drug Testing Programs and Their Impact on Workplace Accidents: A Time Series Analysis," *Journal of Individual Employment Rights* 8, no. 4 (2000): 295–306.

89. O'Neill, "Legal Issues Presented by Hair Follicle Testing," 411.

90. Richard Lisko, "A Manager's Guide to Drug Testing," *Security Management* 38, no. 8 (August 1994): 92; http://www.dol.gov/dol/topic/safety-health/drugfreeworkplace.htm, accessed April 19, 2008; and http://www.fmcsa.dot.gov/rules-regulations/topics/drug/engtesting.htm, accessed April 19, 2008.

91. Coleman Peterson, "Employee Retention: The Secrets Behind Wal-Mart's Successful Hiring Policies," *Human Resource Management* 44, no. 1 (Spring 2005): 85–88.

92. Murray Barrick and Ryan Zimmerman, "Reducing Voluntary, Avoidable Turnover Through Selection," *Journal of Applied Psychology* 90, no. 1 (2005): 159–166.

93. Russell Gerbman, "License to Work," *HR Magazine* (June 2000): 151–160.

94. Diane Cadrain, "Mystery Shoppers Can Improve Recruitment," *HR Magazine* (November 2006): 26.
95. Note that unproctored Internet tests raise serious questions in employment settings. Nancy Tippins et al., "Unproctored Internet Testing in Employment Settings," *Personnel Psychology* 59 (2006): 189–225.
96. From Bob Neveu, "Applicant Tracking's Top 10: Do You Know What to Look for in Applicant Tracking Systems?" *Workforce* (October 2002): 10.
97. Manuel Velasquez, *Business Ethics: Concepts and Cases* (Upper Saddle River, NJ: Prentice Hall, 1992): 9. See also O. C. Ferrell, John Fraedrich, and Linog Ferrell, *Business Ethics* (Boston: Houghton Mifflin, 2008).
98. Gary Weaver and Linda Trevino, "The Role of Human Resources in Ethics/Compliance Management: A Fairness Perspective," *Human Resource Management Review* 11 (2001): 123. See also Linda Andrews, "The Nexus of Ethics," *HR Magazine* (August 2005): 53–58.

Training and Developing Employees

6

When you finish studying this chapter, you should be able to:

1. *Describe the basic training process.*

2. *Discuss at least two techniques used for assessing training needs.*

3. *Explain the pros and cons of at least five training techniques.*

4. *Explain what management development is and why it is important.*

5. *Describe the main development techniques.*

employee orientation
A procedure for providing new employees with basic background information about the firm.

Introduction

With 32,000 restaurants and a strategy based on consistency, McDonald's must train its employees if the firm is to prosper. As McDonald's president said, "Our success is because of the training and replication systems we put in place that allowed us to change our menu and deliver operations at a higher level than before." The question is, "What type of training to put in place?"[1] ■

ORIENTING EMPLOYEES

After selecting new employees, management turns to orienting and training them on their new jobs. **Employee orientation** provides new employees with the basic background information they need to perform their jobs satisfactorily, such as information about company rules. Orientation is one component of the employer's new-employee socialization process. *Socialization* is the continuing process of instilling in all employees the attitudes, standards, values, and patterns of behavior that the organization and its departments expect.[2] For example, the Mayo Clinic, based in Rochester, Minnesota, recently revised its orientation program to embrace the clinic's history, values, and culture. It's new "heritage and culture" orientation session covers things like Mayo's core principles, history, work atmosphere, teamwork, personal responsibility, innovation, integrity, diversity, customer service, and mutual respect.[3]

TYPES OF PROGRAMS Orientation programs range from brief, informal introductions to lengthy, formal programs of a half day or more. In either case, new employees usually receive printed or Web-based handbooks covering matters such as working hours, performance reviews, getting on the payroll, and vacations, as well as a facilities tour. Other information might cover employee benefits, personnel policies, the employee's daily routine, company organization and operations, and safety measures and regulations.[4] Because there is a possibility that courts will find that your employee handbook's contents represent a contract with the employee, employers should include disclaimers. These should make it clear that statements of company policies, benefits, and regulations do not constitute an employment contract, either expressed or implied.

PURPOSES A successful orientation should accomplish four things. The new employee should feel welcome. He or she should understand the organization in a broad sense (its past, present, culture, and vision of the future), as well as key facts such as policies and procedures. The employee should be clear about what the firm expects in terms of work and behavior. And, hopefully, the employee should begin the process of becoming socialized into the firm's preferred ways of acting and doing things.[5]

The HR specialist usually performs the initial orientation and explains such matters as working hours and vacation. The employee then meets his or her new supervisor. The latter continues the orientation by explaining the exact nature of the job, introducing the person to his or her new colleagues, and familiarizing the new employee with the workplace and the job.

TECHNOLOGY Technology improves the orientation process. For example, some firms provide incoming managers with preloaded personal digital assistants. These contain information the new managers need to better adjust to their new jobs, such as key contact information, main tasks to undertake, and even digital images of employees the new manager needs to know.[6] Some firms provide all new employees with disks containing discussions of corporate culture, videos of corporate facilities, and welcoming addresses from top managers. Others create orientation Web sites. Particularly for new managers, these include information such as the company's approaches to hiring, ethics, procurement policies, and performance management.

VIRTUAL ORIENTATION Employers including IBM use virtual environments like Second Life to support their orientation efforts. They particularly do this for employees, like those in India and China, who are separated from IBM headquarters by great distances. The new employees choose virtual avatars to represent themselves. They then interact via their avatars with other company avatars, for instance, to learn how to sign up for benefits.[7]

TRAINING'S PURPOSE AND PROCESS

training
The process of teaching new employees the basic skills they need to perform their jobs.

Training is next. **Training** refers to the methods employers use to give new or present employees the knowledge and skills they need to perform their jobs.

Training Today

Three things characterize training today. First, we'll see that training is increasingly technology based. Most employees today get at least some of their training online and/or via computers.

Second, trainers generally focus more explicitly on improving organizational performance than they have in the past. A survey by IBM and the American Society for Training and Development (ASTD) found that "establishing a linkage between learning and organizational performance" was the number one issue facing training professionals.[8] As one trainer said, "We sit down with management and help them identify strategic goals and objectives and the skills and knowledge needed to achieve them. Then we work together to identify whether our staff has the skills and knowledge, and when they don't, that's when we discuss training needs."[9] Training experts today sometimes use the phrase "workplace learning and performance" in lieu of training. This underscores training's dual aims of improving both employee learning and organizational performance.[10] Training does have an impressive record of influencing organizational effectiveness. One study found it scored higher than "appraisal and feedback" and just below "goal setting" in its effect on productivity.[11] The *Business in Action* feature elaborates on this.

Third, training's focus is broader today than it was years ago. People used to associate training with teaching technical skills, such as training assemblers to solder wires. Today's team-based and empowered companies demand a different type of employee and a different type of training. For example, employees today may require team-building, decision-making, and communication skills training. And, with most firms technologically advanced, employees require training in computer skills, such as computer-aided design and manufacturing.[12]

Business in Action   Building Your *Strategic Management* Knowledge

Wisconsin-based Signicast produces metal parts from a casting process. The basic process is very old, although Signicast has improved it dramatically. For Signicast to vie with world-class competitors, it needs a new, automated plant. Many of its employees have little formal education, and lack the mathematical and computer skills the new plant will require of its employees. The question is, how should Signicast train the new plant's employees, so the computerized plant will have the tech-friendly employees it requires to succeed?[13] The firm's president, Terry Lutz, knew his plans for growing his company hinged on human resource management.

Terry Lutz's experience illustrates why managers say that human resource management needs to be "strategic." Computerized machines like Signicast's are useless without competent employees to run them. The purpose of human resource management is for the company's human resource processes—

screening, training, and appraising, for instance—*to produce the employee behaviors the company needs to achieve its strategic goals.* It is in this way that the employer ensures that the company's human resource management policies and practices *add value to the company.* Signicast needs employees who can run the automated, computerized equipment for its new plant. With jobs increasingly knowledge- and technology-based, selecting the right employees, and getting them trained and performing satisfactorily, is more crucial and demanding then ever.

We discussed strategic planning in chapter 3. Strategic human resource management means aligning the firm's human resource management policies and practices with the company's strategic goals, so that the company's HR policies and practices produce the employee behaviors the company needs to achieve its strategic goals.

(continued)

Signicast's HR group helped the company execute its plant expansion strategy. For example, the new plant would produce parts almost five times faster than the old plant. The employees would thus have to assume more responsibility, so selection standards were tighter. At the old plant, the only hiring requirements were a high school diploma and a good work ethic. The new plant would require the same high school degree and work ethic plus team orientation, good trainability, good communication skills, and a willingness to do varied jobs over a 12-hour shift. HR also created a cross-training program, so employees could do each other's jobs. This ensured the employees could easily switch from job to job, as needed. At Signicast, training played a strategic role in executing the company's new high-tech plant strategy.[14]

---

❶ Describe the basic training process.

The Training and Development Process

As you can see in Figure 6.1, we can visualize a training and development program as consisting of five steps: needs analysis, instructional design, validation, implementation, and evaluation.

❷ Discuss at least two techniques used for assessing training needs.

TRAINING NEEDS—TASK ANALYSIS The first step in training is to determine what training, if any, the employee requires. Some call this the "skills gapping" process. Employers determine the skills each job requires, and the skills of the job's current or prospective employees. Then they design a training program to eliminate the skills gap.[15]

There are two traditional needs analysis methods. Assessing *new* employees' training needs usually involves *task analysis*—breaking the job into subtasks and teaching each to the new employee. Needs analysis for *current* employees is more complex: Is training the solution, or is performance down because the person isn't motivated? Here *performance analysis* is required. We'll look at each.

task analysis

A detailed study of a job to identify the skills required so that an appropriate training program may be instituted.

Managers use *task analysis* for determining new employees' training needs. With inexperienced personnel, your aim is to provide the new employees with the skills and knowledge required for effective performance. **Task analysis** is a detailed study of the job to determine what specific skills—like Java (in the case of a Web developer) or interviewing (in the case of a supervisor)—the job requires. Job descriptions and job specifications are helpful here. These list the job's specific duties and skills and thus provide the basic reference point in determining the training required. You can also uncover training needs by reviewing performance standards, performing the job, and questioning current job holders and their supervisors.[16]

performance analysis

Verifying that there is a performance deficiency and determining whether that deficiency should be rectified through training or through some other means (such as transferring the employee).

TRAINING NEEDS—PERFORMANCE ANALYSIS For current employees whose performance is deficient, task analysis is usually not enough. **Performance analysis** means verifying that there is a performance deficiency and determining whether that deficiency should be rectified through training or through some other means (such as transferring the employee or changing the compensation plan).

FIGURE 6.1

Steps in the Training and Development Process

1. The first, or *needs analysis* step, identifies the specific job performance skills needed, assesses the prospective trainees' skills, and develops specific, measurable knowledge and performance objectives based on any deficiencies.
2. In the second step, *instructional design,* you decide on, compile, and produce the training program content, including workbooks, exercises, and activities. Here, you'll use techniques like those discussed in this chapter, such as on-the-job training and computer-assisted learning.
3. There may be a third, *validation* step, in which the bugs are worked out of the training program by presenting it to a small representative audience.
4. The fourth step is to *implement* the program, by actually training the targeted employee group.
5. The fifth step is *evaluation,* where management assesses the program's successes or failures.

Employers identify employees' performance deficiencies and training needs in several ways. These include:[17]

- supervisor, peer, self-, and 360-degree performance reviews;
- job-related performance data (including productivity, absenteeism and tardiness, accidents, short-term sickness, grievances, waste, late deliveries, product quality, downtime, repairs, equipment utilization, and customer complaints);
- observation by supervisors or other specialists;
- interviews with the employee or his or her supervisor;
- tests of things like job knowledge, skills, and attendance;
- attitude surveys;
- individual employee daily diaries;
- devised situations such as role playing and case studies and other types of tests;
- assessment centers; and
- management-by-objective evaluations.

The first step is usually to appraise the employee's performance. Examples of specific performance deficiencies are:

"I expect each salesperson to make 10 new contracts per week, but John averages only six." "Other plants our size average no more than two serious accidents per month; we're averaging five."

Distinguishing between "can't do" and "won't do" problems is the heart of performance analysis. First, determine whether it's a "can't do" problem and, if so, its specific causes. Training won't solve all "can't do" problems. For example, perhaps the employees don't know what to do or what your standards are, or there are obstacles such as lack of tools or supplies. Perhaps job aids are needed, such as color-coded wires that show assemblers what wire goes where; or poor screening results in hiring people who haven't the skills to do the job; or, inadequate training may be the issue.

On the other hand, it might be a "won't do" problem, in which employees *could* do a good job if they wanted to. Training won't help here. Instead, the manager may have to change the reward system, perhaps by implementing an incentive plan.

SHARP'S COMPETENCY MODELS Instead of conventional training needs analysis, many firms, like Sharp Electronics of Japan, develop generic "competency models" for jobs or closely related groups of jobs. Then they design the training to develop these competencies. In this context, *competency* means knowledge, skills, and behaviors that enable employees to effectively perform their jobs. Sharp's approach is to create a set of guidelines (a "competency model") listing each job's required competencies.

Sharp's process for identifying a job's competencies begins with interviews with senior executives. The aim here is for the training team to better understand the firm's strategic objectives. From that, they can get a better picture of what competencies the firm's employees will need. (For example, the *Business in Action* feature explained how Signicast's training program helped the firm execute its expansion into a new high-tech factory.) Sharp human resource specialists then interview the top performers in the job in question. Their aim is to identify the competencies (such as "demonstrates creativity," and "focuses on the customer") that together will comprise the job's list of required competencies. Subsequent training and development then focuses on developing these competencies.[18]

SETTING TRAINING OBJECTIVES After uncovering the training needs, trainers set concrete, measurable training objectives. Training, development, or (more generally) *instructional objectives* "specify the employee and organizational outcomes that should be achieved as a result of the training."[19] The objectives should specify what the trainee should be able to accomplish after successfully completing the training program. They thus provide a focus for the efforts of both the trainee and the trainer and a benchmark for evaluating the success of the training program. For example:

> The technical service representative will be able to adjust the color guidelines on this HP Officejet All-in-One printer copier within 10 minutes according to the device's specifications.

MOTIVATION Training is futile if the trainee lacks the ability or motivation to benefit from it.[20] The employer can take several steps to increase the trainee's motivation to learn. Providing a graphic illustration of what can go wrong is one technique—for instance, ticketed drivers attending driving school often start class by watching filmed accidents. Other useful techniques to improve motivation include building in opportunities for active practice and letting the trainee make errors and explore alternate solutions.[21] Feedback—including periodic performance assessments and more frequent verbal critiques—is also important.[22] Also, make the material meaningful. For example, provide an overview of the material, and ensure that the program uses familiar examples and concepts to illustrate key points.[23]

TRADITIONAL TRAINING TECHNIQUES

❸ Explain the pros and cons of at least five training techniques.

After you verify the employees' training needs, create a perceived need, and set training goals, you can design, validate, and implement a training program. Most employers can choose training materials from packaged on-and-offline programs already available from vendors like the American Management Association[24] or at the American Society for Training and Development's *Infoline,* at *www.astd.org*.[25]

We can conveniently classify training techniques as either traditional techniques (like on-the-job training) or as computer and Internet-based techniques. We'll look first at traditional techniques.

On-the-Job Training

Every employee gets some on-the-job training when starting a new job. The most familiar on-the-job training (OJT) technique is the coaching or understudy method. Here an experienced worker or supervisor trains the employee on the job. At lower levels, trainees may acquire skills for, say, running a machine by observing the supervisor. But this technique is also widely used at top-management levels. Some firms use the position of "assistant to" to train and develop the company's future top managers. Job rotation, in which an employee (usually a management trainee) moves from job to job at planned intervals, is another on-the-job technique. Special assignments similarly give lower-level executives firsthand experience in working on actual problems.

The Men's Wearhouse has a formal process of "cascading" responsibility for training.

The Houston, Texas-based company Men's Wearhouse uses on-the-job training. It has few full-time trainers. Instead, the Men's Wearhouse has a formal process of "cascading" responsibility for training: Every manager is formally accountable for the development of his or her direct subordinates.[26]

Informal Learning

Surveys from the American Society for Training and Development estimate that as much as 80% of what employees learn on the job they learn not through formal training programs but through informal means, including performing their jobs in collaboration with their colleagues.[27]

Although managers don't arrange informal learning, there's a lot they can do to ensure that it occurs. Most of the steps are simple. For example, at some Siemens Power Transmission and Distribution offices in Australia, tools are placed in cafeteria areas to take advantage of the work-related discussions taking place. Even simple things like installing whiteboards and keeping them stocked with markers can facilitate informal learning.

Apprenticeship Training

More employers are going "back to the future" by implementing apprenticeship training programs, an approach to training that began in the Middle Ages. Apprenticeship training is a structured process by which individuals become skilled workers through a combination of formal instruction and on-the-job training, usually under the guidance of someone who's already an expert. It's especially popular for learning professional trades, such as plumber.

However, employers use it too. When Canadian steelmaker Dofasco discovered that many of its employees would be retiring during the next 5 to 10 years, the company decided to revive its apprenticeship training program. Applicants are prescreened; new recruits then spend about 32 months in an internal training program that emphasizes apprenticeship training, learning various jobs under the tutelage of experienced craftspersons.[28] The Siemens Stromberg-Carlson plant in Florida has apprenticeships for adults and high school students training for jobs as electronics technicians. Here:

> Adults work on the factory floor, receive classroom instruction at Seminole Community College, and also study at the plant's hands-on apprenticeship lab. Graduates receive Associates Degrees in telecommunications and electronics engineering. High school students spend two afternoons per week at the apprenticeship lab.[29]

Vestibule Training

vestibule/simulated training
A method in which trainees learn on the actual or on simulated equipment they would use on the job, but are actually trained off the job.

With **vestibule/simulated training,** trainees learn on the actual or simulated equipment they will use on the job but receive their training off the job. Such training is necessary when it's too costly or dangerous to train employees on the job. Putting new assembly-line workers right to work could slow production, for instance, and when safety is a concern—as with pilots—simulated training may be the only practical alternative.

Vestibule training (other words for vestibule are "foyer" or "entrance hall") may just occur in a separate room using the equipment the trainees will actually be using on the job. However, it often involves the use of equipment simulators. In pilot training, for instance, simulators let crews practice flight maneuvers in a controlled environment. Some computerized training methods like those we'll address below are modern versions of simulated training.

Behavior Modeling

behavior modeling
A training technique in which trainees are first shown good management techniques in a film, are then asked to play roles in a simulated situation, and are then given feedback and praise by their supervisor.

Behavior modeling involves (1) showing trainees the right (or "model") way of doing something, (2) letting trainees practice that way, and then (3) giving feedback on the trainees' performance. This is "one of the most widely used, well researched, and highly regarded psychologically based training interventions."[30] The procedure is as follows:

1. *Modeling.* First, trainees watch live or video examples that show models behaving effectively in a problem situation. The video might show a supervisor effectively disciplining a subordinate, if teaching how to discipline is the aim of the training program.
2. *Role playing.* Next, the trainees are given roles to play in a simulated situation; here they practice and rehearse the effective behaviors demonstrated by the models.

3. *Social reinforcement.* The trainer provides reinforcement in the form of praise and constructive feedback based on how the trainee performs in the role-playing situation.
4. *Transfer of training.* Finally, trainees are encouraged to apply their new skills when they are back on their jobs.

Behavior modeling is quite popular. By one estimate, firms spend more of their training dollars on behavioral computer skills training than they do on sales training, supervisory training, or communication training.[31] Studies suggest that behavioral modeling results in significant improvements in knowledge and skill learning, but its effect on actual job behavior is less clear.[32]

Videoconference Distance Learning

Videoconferencing allows people in one location to communicate live with people in another location or with groups in several other locations. It's an effective way to simultaneously train employees at remote and/or multiple locations. Some firms, like Harrods, have used conventional TV broadcasts for this purpose. Others, like Management Recruiters International (MRI), use PC-based systems such as "ConferView" to train hundreds of employees—each in their individual offices—simultaneously. Today, videoconferencing will generally involve Internet transmissions, compressed audio and video signals over cable lines, satellite, or, increasingly, broadband connections.[33] Keypad systems allow for audience–trainer interactivity.

COMPUTER AND INTERNET-BASED TRAINING

In a Stanford University hospital training room in California, medical students wearing virtual reality headsets control computer screen avatars. The avatars are computerized simulations dressed in medical scrubs. Each avatar plays a different role, such as nurse or emergency room technician. The residents and medical students use their keypads to control their avatar's every move in the virtual reality trauma center. One avatar props up the patient; another rushes to clear his airway. On the screen, the patient's vital signs react appropriately to the medical students' and residents' decisions. Later, instructors replay the scenario, showing trainees what they did right and wrong.[34] As at Stanford's hospital, training today increasingly is computer-based.

computer-based training (CBT)
Trainees use a computer-based system to interactively increase their knowledge or skills.

In **computer-based training (CBT),** trainees use a computer-based system to interactively increase their knowledge or skills. As at Stanford, this may mean presenting trainees with computerized simulations, and using multimedia to help the trainees learn the job.[35] But often, computer-based training is less complex. For example, it may simply involve reviewing PowerPoint slides online and passing a quiz.

As another example, in one computer-based training program, a trainee for a job as a recruiter sits before a computer screen. The screen shows the "applicant's" employment application, as well as information about the job. The trainee then begins a simulated interview by typing in questions that a pre-recorded video-based "applicant" answers, using responses to dozens of questions experts previously programmed into the computer. At the end of the session, the computer tells the trainee where he or she went wrong (perhaps in asking discriminatory questions, for instance) and offers further instructional material to correct these mistakes.

DVD-Based Training

McDonald's developed a number of computer disk–based courses for its franchises' employees. The programs consist of graphics-supported lessons, and require trainees to make choices to show their understanding.[36] Specialist multimedia software houses produce much of the content for CBT programs like these. They produce both custom titles and generic programs, like a package for teaching workplace safety.

Simulated Learning

"Simulated learning" means different things to different people. A recent survey asked training professionals what experiences qualified as simulated learning experiences. The percentages of trainers choosing each experience were:

- Virtual reality–type games, 19%
- Step-by-step animated guide, 8%
- Scenarios with questions and decision trees overlaying animation, 19%
- Online role-play with photos and videos, 14%
- Software training including screenshots with interactive requests for responses, 35%
- Other, 6%[37]

As at Stanford, employers increasingly rely on computerized simulations to inject more realism into their training programs. For example, Orlando-based Environmental Tectonics Corporation created an Advanced Disaster Management simulation for emergency medical response trainees. One of the simulated scenarios involves a passenger plane crashing onto an airport runway. So realistic that it's "unsettling," trainees including firefighters and airport officials respond to the simulated crash's sights and sounds via pointing devices and radios.[38] IBM created a new training effort called *IBM At Play*. This uses videogame technology and three-dimensional virtual environments to facilitate training.[39] When Cisco Systems decided it needed a better way to train the thousands of Cisco trainees around the world sitting for Cisco certification exams it turned to gaming. For example, to help trainees learn the binary system, Cisco hired a game developer. That person embedded the necessary learning within a videogame-like atmosphere that included music, graphics, and sound effects.[40]

Training simulations are expensive, but, particularly for larger companies, the cost per employee is usually reasonable. For example, a "branching story" simulation challenges students to make a series of decisions as they move through a multiple-choice interface. Such a simulation usually ranges in costs from $30,000 to $500,000.[41]

Internet-Based Training

Internet or Web-based learning is rapidly replacing other types of training. Many firms simply let their employees take online courses offered by online course providers. Others use their intranets to facilitate such training. Thus, Delta Airlines' customer service personnel receive about 70% of their annual required FAA training via their intranet.

Orlando-based Environmental Tectonics Corporation created an Advanced Disaster Management simulation for emergency medical response trainees.

Delta likes it because "prior to online training, employees had to travel to one of five training centers, keeping them away from their jobs for at least the day."[42]

There are basically two ways to make online courses available to employees. First, the employer can encourage and/or facilitate having its employees take relevant online courses from its own online (intranet) offerings, or from the hundreds of online training vendors on the Web. For example, an employer in England might arrange with The Royal Society for the Prevention of Accidents to let its employees take one or more occupational safety courses from those the organization offers. The second main approach is to arrange with an online training vendor to make its courses available via the employer's intranet-based learning portal.

LEARNING PORTALS A *learning portal* is a section of an employer's Website that offers employees online access to many or all of the training courses they need to succeed at their jobs. Most often, the employer contracts with applications service providers (ASP) like those we list in Figure 6.2. When employees go to their firm's learning portal, they actually access the server and menu of courses that the ASP company contracted with the employer to offer.

FIGURE 6.2

Partial List of E-Learning Vendors

Source: Google. http://www.google.com/permissions/index.html, accessed January 19, 2008.

E-learning Companies
Reference > Education > Distance Learning > Online Teaching and Learning > E-learning Companies   Go to Directory Home

Categories

Course Authoring (71)
E-learning Portals (60)
E-learning Research (23)
Learning Management Systems (73)
Online Classrooms (18)

Related Categories:
Computers > Education > Commercial Services > Training Companies > Self-Study (49)
Reference > Education > Distance Learning > Online Courses (281)
Reference > Education > Distance Learning > Services (34)
Reference > Knowledge Management > Business and Companies (124)

Web Pages   Viewing in Google PageRank order   View in alphabetical order

Skillsoft - http://www.skillsoft.com
Providers of enterprise e-learning, a fully integrated student environment and courseware to support e-Learning initiatives in enterprises.

Plateau Systems - http://www.plateau.com
Corporate learning solutions deployed at enterprises across the world enabling global organizations to increase productivity and save millions of training dollars.

Academee - http://www.academee.com
Integrated learning programmes, blending consultancy, online e-learning and face-to-face classroom courses for management and professional development.

Enspire Learning - http://www.enspire.com
Enspire Learning develops custom e-learning courses that include interactive multimedia, simulations, and engaging scenarios.

Ninth House Network - http://www.ninthhouse.com
A leading e-learning broadband environment for organizational development, delivering to the desktop experiential, interactive programs that leverage the world's foremost business thinkers.

Futurate Ltd - http://www.futurate.com
Developers of eLearning content and systems that are engaging and accessible to all. They offer a 'full service' from consultancy to implementation and maintenance.

PrimeLearning - http://www.primelearning.com
E-learning company that specialises in business and professional skills courses provided off the self or can be custom made.

Intellinex - http://www.intellinex.com
Provider of e-Learning solutions for workers in Global 2000 companies, government, and educational institutions. Courseware covers PC and business skills applications.

Allen Communication - http://www.allencomm.com
Provides e-Learning solutions including learning portals, strategic planning for training, courseware development and authoring / design tools.

The Learning House, Inc. - http://www.learninghouse.com
Learning House, Inc. is an eLearning services company that creates off the shelf and custom online degree and professional development courses.

DefinITion - http://www.definition.be
DefinITion design and development e-learning courses for companies. The company is based in Belgium and their services include consultancy and support.

Intrac Design Inc - http://www.intrac.biz
The development and delivery of customizable training programs for live classroom and e-learning delivery.

Seward, Inc. - http://www.sewardinc.com
Seward, Inc. provide engaging, instructionally sound, cost-effective training solutions ranging from soft skills involved in sales to the most technically exacting fields of medicine, engineering, and finance.

Silverchair Learning Systems - http://www.silverchairlearning.com
Online employee education exclusively for the Senior Care industry.

Tata Interactive Systems - http://www.tatainteractivesystems.com
Developer of custom e-learning solutions for corporate, educational and governmental organizations.

Little Planet Learning - http://www.littleplanet.com
Provides design and development of learning experiences delivered live and through elearning, computer and web based training (CBT and WBT), and multimedia programs.

Employment Law Learning Technologies - http://www.elt-inc.com
Online compliance training for managers and employees on critical US employment law / HR topics, including harassment, discrimination, privacy and diversity.

Improving Productivity Through HRIS: Learning Management Systems

Learning management systems (LMS) play an important role in helping employers identify training needs, and in scheduling, delivering, and assessing and managing the online training itself. For example, General Motors uses a new LMS to help its dealers in Africa and the Middle East deliver high-quality training programs. The Internet-based LMS includes a course catalog, two-step enrollment (supervisor approved self enrollment), facilities and training schedule management, and assessment systems (including pre-and post-course tests). Dealers, supervisors, and employees can review the list of courses on the LMS. They then choose courses based upon their needs, for instance in specific areas such as automobile transmissions and sales management. The system then automatically schedules the individual's training.[43]

The movement today is toward integrating the e-learning system with the company's overall, enterprisewide information systems. In that way, for instance, employers can automatically update skills inventory and succession plans as employees complete their training.[44]

The Virtual Classroom

Conventional Web-based learning tends to be limited to the sorts of online learning with which many college students are already familiar—reading PowerPoint presentations, participating in instant message–type chat rooms, and taking online exams, for instance.

virtual classroom
Special collaboration software used to enable multiple remote learners, using their PCs or laptops, to participate in live audio and visual discussions, communicate via written text, and learn via content such as PowerPoint slides.

The virtual classroom takes online learning to a new level. A **virtual classroom** uses collaboration software to enable multiple remote learners, using their PCs or laptops, to participate in live audio and visual discussions, communicate via written text, and learn via content such as PowerPoint slides.

The virtual classroom combines the best of Web-based learning offered by companies like Leeds-based Cubik. For example, Elluminate Inc. makes one popular virtual classroom system, Elluminate Live! It enables learners to communicate with clear, two-way audio; build communities with user profiles and live video; collaborate with chat and shared whiteboards; and learn with shared applications such as PowerPoint slides.[45]

Improving Web-Based Learning

Having already had some experience with Web-learning, most students know it can be an effective way to learn, when used appropriately. In one review of the evidence, Web-based instruction was a bit more effective than classroom instruction for teaching memory of facts and principles; Web-based instruction and classroom instruction were equally effective for teaching information about how to perform a task or action; trainees were equally satisfied with Web-based instruction and classroom instruction; and Web-based instruction was much more effective than classroom instruction when the trainees could use the Web program to control the pace and selection of the content.[46] Of course, the need to teach large numbers of students remotely, or to enable students to study at their leisure, often makes e-learning so much more efficient that the small differences in Web-based versus classroom learning become somewhat meaningless.

STEPS TO TAKE In establishing e-learning programs, there are three things to keep in mind. First, there are still many learning situations where conventional in-class work is usually preferable—a chemical engineering lab session, for instance. Second, the employer needs to balance the extra cost of creating the online learning against the advantages of being able to use it to offer courses 24/7, and remotely.

Third, the trainer should keep e-learning's limitations in mind. From a practical point of view, allow for the fact that learners tend to be slower taking online exams than they are paper-and-pencil ones. (This is because the Web page tends to have fewer questions in a larger font than do paper quizzes, and because going back and reviewing one's answers tends to take longer online.) It's also important to make sure that the trainee can actually use the extra control that Web-based learning should provide. For example, a Web-based program may give learners the opportunity to choose the content they'll focus on, and its sequence and pacing.[47] Therefore, make sure to explain to trainees the control that they have and how they can use it, such as how to change the learning sequence.

In practice, the trend is toward blended learning, wherein the trainee uses several delivery methods (for instance, manuals, in-class lectures, self-guided e-learning programs, and Web-based seminars or "webinars") to learn the material.[48] Intuit (which makes software such as TurboTax) uses instructor-led classroom training for bringing in new distributors and getting them up to speed. Then, they use their virtual classroom systems to provide additional training, for monthly meetings with distributors, and for short classes on special software features.[49]

Mobile Learning

Mobile learning (or "on-demand learning") means delivering learning content on demand via mobile devices like cell phones, laptops, and iPhones, wherever and whenever the learner has the time and desire to access it.[50] Employers use it to deliver "corporate training and downloads on everything from how to close an important sales deal to optimizing organizational change to learning business Spanish . . . you can be on an airplane, you can be taking a walk or riding your bike" while listening to the training program.[51] Financial services firm CapitalOne purchased 3,000 iPods for trainees who had enrolled in one of 20 instructor-led courses at its CapitalOne University. The training department then had an Internet audio book provider create an audio learning site within CapitalOne's firewall. Employees used it to download the instructor-requested books and other materials to their iPods.[52] IBM uses mobile learning to deliver just in time information (for instance about new product features) to its sales force. To increase such learning's accessibility, IBM's training department often breaks up, say, an hour program into 10-minute pieces. That way employees needn't put away a full hour to listen.

Mobile learning isn't for everyone. Many types of training, such as in human relations, may require more interaction than mobile learning provides. Similarly, any training that requires a lot of graphics isn't appropriate. On the other hand, mobile learning is excellent for some things, like giving a traveling salesperson a quick update that helps him or her make a sale.

INSTANT MESSAGING   Some employers, including Deutsche Bank Group encourage employees to use instant messaging as a quick learning device. Employers also use instant messaging to supplement classroom training, for instance by using IM for online office hours, and for coaching and group chats.

Training for Special Purposes

Training today does more than just prepare employees to perform their jobs effectively. Training for special purposes—dealing with diversity, for instance—is required, too. A sampling of such special-purpose training programs follows.

lifelong learning
Providing employees with continuing learning experiences over their tenure with the firm, with the aim of ensuring they have the opportunity to obtain the knowledge and skills they need to do their jobs effectively.

PROVIDING LIFELONG LEARNING   **Lifelong learning** means providing employees with continuing learning experiences over their tenure with the firm, with the aim of ensuring they have the opportunity to obtain the knowledge and skills they need to do their jobs effectively. Such training may range from basic remedial skills to advanced decision-making techniques throughout employees' careers. Programs typically contain several elements, including training, as appropriate, in such things as English as a second language, basic literacy, arithmetic, and computer literacy; in-house college course work; and job-related training sessions.

Many employers embrace lifelong learning because they're not satisfied with the basic learning skills their employees got in elementary and high school. Functional illiteracy—the inability to handle basic reading, writing, and arithmetic—is a serious problem at work. By one estimate, about 39 million people in the United States have a learning disability that makes it challenging for them to read, write, or do arithmetic.[53] Yet literacy is crucial. Today's emphasis on teamwork and quality requires employees to have the ability to adequately read, write, and understand numbers. Employers often turn to private firms like Education Management Corporation to provide the requisite postsecondary education.[54]

Another simple approach is to have supervisors teach basic skills by giving employees writing and speaking exercises. One way to do this is to convert materials used in the employee's job into instructional tools. For example, if an employee needs to use a manual to find out how to change a part, teach that person how to use an index to locate the relevant section. Another approach is to bring in outside professionals (such as teachers from a local high school) to teach, say, remedial reading or writing. Having employees attend adult education or high school evening classes is another option.

DIVERSITY TRAINING With an increasingly diverse workforce, many firms employ diversity training programs. *Diversity training* refers to "techniques for creating better cross-cultural sensitivity among supervisors and nonsupervisors with the aim of creating more harmonious working relationships among a firm's employees." For example, Adams Mark Hotel & Resorts conducted a diversity training seminar for about 11,000 employees. It combined lectures, video, and employee role-playing to emphasize sensitivity to race and religion.[55]

There are a variety of training programs aimed at counteracting potential problems associated with a diverse workforce. These include programs for improving interpersonal skills, understanding/valuing cultural differences, improving technical skills, socializing into corporate culture, indoctrinating recent immigrants into the United Kingdom work ethic, and improving bilingual skills for English-speaking employees.

TRAINING FOR TEAMWORK AND EMPOWERMENT Teamwork—at least at work—is apparently not something that always comes naturally. Toyota therefore devotes many hours to training new employees to listen to each other and to cooperate. Toyota's training process stresses dedication to team work. For example, the program uses short exercises to illustrate examples of good and bad teamwork, and to mold new employees' attitudes regarding good teamwork.

Some firms use outdoor training such as Outward Bound programs to build teamwork. Outdoor training usually involves taking a firm's management team out into rugged, mountainous terrain. For example, Howard Atkins, chief financial officer for a large banking company, helped organize a retreat for 73 of his firm's financial officers and accountants. While all his participants were already top performers, Atkins' goal was something more: "they are very individualistic in their approach to their work. . . . What I have been trying to do is get them to see the power of acting more like a team."[56]

Global Issues in HR

Exporting Values

Sometimes, supervisory training programs address special issues when implemented abroad. For example, Gap Inc. asked a World Bank affiliate to provide supervisory training for line managers in Gap's vendors' Cambodian garment factories.[57] Gap was not just aiming to improve these managers' supervisory skills. The firm's broader goal was to improve labor relations of their vendors abroad. Gap's supervisory training program therefore covers matters such as how to handle worker complaints, human resource management, personal productivity, and conflict resolution.

MANAGERIAL DEVELOPMENT AND TRAINING

management development
Any attempt to improve current or future management performance by imparting knowledge, changing attitudes, or increasing skills.

Management development is any attempt to improve managerial performance by imparting knowledge, changing attitudes, or increasing skills. It thus includes in-house programs such as courses, coaching, and rotational assignments; professional programs such as SHRM seminars; and university programs such as executive MBA programs.

The ultimate aim of such development programs is, of course, to enhance the future performance of the organization itself. For this reason, the overall management development process consists of *assessing* the company's needs (for instance, to fill future executive openings, or to make the firm less bureaucratic), *appraising* the managers' performance, and then *developing* the managers themselves.

④ Explain what management development is and why it is important.

Trends in Management Development

Globalization and increased competitiveness mean it's more important today for leadership development programs to be organizationally relevant. This means three things. The program should make sense in terms of the company's *strategy and goals*. This means involving the top management team in formulating the program's aims, and also specifying concrete competencies and knowledge outcomes, rather than just attitudes. Second, there is more emphasis on supplementing traditional development methods (such as lectures, case discussion groups, and simulations) with *realistic methods* like action learning projects where trainees solve actual company problems.[58] Third, *trainee assessment* usually precedes manager development programs. For example, at frozen foods manufacturer Schawn, a committee of senior executives first whittles 40 or more candidates down to 10 or less. Then the program begins with a one-day assessment by outside consultants of each manger's leadership strengths and weaknesses. This assessment becomes the basis for each manager's individual development plan. Action-learning projects then supplement individual and group training activities.[59]

Several principles for designing leadership development programs (such as "involve top management") are summarized in Figure 6.3.

Development methods (many equally useful for first-line supervisors, too) are described on the next few pages.

FIGURE 6.3

Management and Leadership Development Guidelines

1. Design the program so that it flows from and makes sense in terms of the company's strategy and goals.
2. Involve the top management team in formulating the program's aims.
3. Make sure to design the program to improve managers' deficiencies and needs that you identify ahead of time.
4. Aim for practicality rather than just theory.
5. Specify concrete competencies and skills outcomes, not just knowledge and attitude changes, and use realistic learning methods like action learning projects where trainees solve real company problems.
6. Aim for short, high-involvement, 3–4 day programs rather than longer immersion programs.

Sources: Adapted from P. Nick Blanchard and James Thacker, *Effective Training* (Upper Saddle River, NJ: Pearson, 2007): 439–467; Jack Zenger, Dave Ulrich, and Norm Smallwood. "The New Leadership Development," *Training & Development* (March 2000): 22–27: W. David Patton and Connie Pratt, "Assessing the Training Needs of High Potential Managers," *Public Personnel Management* 31, no. 4 (Winter 2002): 465–474: and Ann Locke and Arlene Tarantino, "Strategic Leadership Development," *Training & Development* (December 2006): 53–55.

⑤ Describe the main development techniques.

job rotation
A management training technique that involves moving a trainee from department to department to broaden his or her experience and identify strengths and weaknesses.

coaching/understudy method
An experienced worker or supervisor trains the employee on the job.

action learning
A training technique by which management trainees are allowed to work full time analyzing and solving problems in other departments.

case study method
A development method in which the manager is presented with a written description of an organizational problem to diagnose and solve.

management game
A development technique in which teams of managers compete by making computerized decisions regarding realistic but simulated situations.

improvisation
A form of management training in which the trainees learn skills such as openness and creativity by playing games that require that they improvise answers and solutions.

Managerial On-the-Job Training

On-the-job training is not just for nonsupervisory employees. It is also a popular manager development method. Important variants include *job rotation*, the *coaching/understudy method*, and *action learning*. **Job rotation** means moving management trainees from department to department to broaden their understanding of all parts of the business. The trainee may spend several months in each department; this helps not only broaden his or her experience but also discover the jobs he or she prefers. The person learns the department's business by actually doing it, whether it involves sales, production, finance, or some other function. With the **coaching/understudy method,** the new manager, of course, receives ongoing advice, often from the person he or she is scheduled to replace.

Action Learning

Action learning programs give groups of managers released time to work full-time analyzing and solving problems in departments other than their own. The basics include carefully selected teams of 5 to 25 members, assigning the teams real-world business problems that extend beyond their usual areas of expertise, and structured learning through coaching and feedback. The employer's senior managers usually choose the projects and decide whether to accept the teams' recommendations.[60] Many major firms around the world, from General Electric to Samsung and Deutsche Bank, use action learning.[61]

The Case Study Method

The **case study method** presents a trainee with a written (or sometimes video) description and history of an organizational problem. The trainee reads and analyzes the case, diagnoses the problem, and presents his or her findings and solutions in an interactive discussion with other trainees. The basic idea is to simulate an actual managerial situation, and to thereby give trainees realistic experience in identifying and analyzing complex problems in an environment in which a trained discussion leader guides their progress.

The usefulness of the case study method depends largely on the trainer's (or professor's) case analysis skills. The trainer should at least:[62]

- Guide the trainees in examining the possible alternatives and consequences.
- Avoid stating his or her opinions on what those alternatives and consequences are.
- Keep in mind that his or her own analysis of the case situation and action plan are irrelevant and may hinder the group's discussion and learning.
- Keep the aim of the training in mind; for instance, if the overall aim is building decision-making skills, it's appropriate to interject in the discussion practical suggestions about decision-making skills.
- Make sure to facilitate the group discussion, for instance, by encouraging everyone to participate, maintaining an open and supportive climate (for instance, by discouraging harsh criticism), and by encouraging everyone to consider each other's suggestions with an open mind.

Management Games

In computerized **management games,** trainees split into five- or six-person companies, each of which has to compete with the others in a simulated marketplace. Each company can make several decisions. For example, the group may be allowed to decide how much to spend on advertising, how much to produce, how much inventory to maintain, and how many of which product to produce. Usually, the game compresses a 2- or 3-year period into days, weeks, or months. As in the real world, each company usually can't see what decisions the other firms have made, although these decisions affect their own sales. For example, if a competitor decides to increase its advertising expenditures, that firm may end up increasing its sales at the expense of the others.[63]

Improvisation is a recent variant. For example, Nike Corporation asked Second City Communications, the consulting arm of the comedy improvisational group Second City, to help prepare some Nike engineers for an assignment. The engineers were to spend a month

Second City trainers put Nike engineers through an improvisational game called "word ball."

watching kids in playgrounds, so as to design new Nike shoes. Second City trainers put the engineers through an improvisational game called "word ball." In this game, trainees pass a make-believe ball to one another, each time calling out one word. (Thus, the first person might pass the ball and call out "cat," the second catches and then passes on the make-believe ball and calls out "furry," and so on.) The aim was to get the Nike engineers "to instantly react without thinking . . . to be unafraid to look foolish."[64]

Outside Seminars

Many organizations offer management development seminars and conferences. The American Management Association for instance, provides thousands of courses in areas such as general management, human resources, sales and marketing, and international management. Courses cover topics such as how to sharpen business writing skills, strategic planning, and assertiveness training for managers. SHRM—the Society for Human Resource Management—offers numerous courses for HR professionals.

Most such programs offer continuing education units (CEUs) for course completion. CEUs generally can't be used to obtain degree-granting credit at most colleges or universities, but they provide a record of the fact that the trainee participated in and completed a conference or seminar and may count toward professional certification.

University-Related Programs

Many universities provide executive education and continuing education programs in leadership, supervision, and the like. These can range from 1- to 4-day programs to executive development programs lasting 1 to 4 months. An increasing number of these are online.

The Advanced Management Program at Oxford University's Said Business School is an example. Students here consist of experienced managers from around the world. It uses cases and lectures to provide top-level management talent with the latest management skills, and with practice analyzing complex organizational problems.

University-based executive education is becoming more realistic, relying more on active learning, business simulations, and experiential learning.[65] Employers are also becoming more sophisticated in how they select and manage university-related development programs. For example, Home Depot created a "preferred network" of university partners. Home Depot arranges for employees who take courses at an in-network university to get discount course prices.[66]

EXAMPLES Joint employer/university management development partnerships can be effective. For example, when Hasbro Inc. needed to improve the creativity skills of its top executives, it turned to the Amos Tuck business school at Dartmouth University. It wanted "a custom approach to designing a program that would be built from the ground up to suit Hasbro's specific needs."[67]

Hasbro and Tuck's executive program faculty directors designed a special version of Tuck's 1-week Global Leadership Development Program, with four basic elements. First, when participants first arrive, they receive sealed envelopes containing their confidential performance assessment reports. Second, managers receive both group and individual coaching from special "executive coaches." The goal is to help Hasbro executives identify "blind spots" that may be hampering their performance and to develop plans to address these issues. Third, they participate in "MBA-type" courses, selected to be relevant for them, based on their and Hasbro's needs. Finally, the executives work in action learning project teams, under the guidance of Hasbro's in-house coaches.

In-House Learning and Development Centers

in-house development centers
A company-based facility for exposing current or prospective managers to exercises to develop improved management skills.

Many firms have **in-house development centers,** or "universities," which usually combine classroom learning (lectures and seminars, for instance) with other techniques such as assessment centers and online learning opportunities to help develop employees and other managers. For example, at General Electric's Leadership Institute, the courses range from entry-level programs in manufacturing and sales to a business course for English majors. However, perhaps because so many more training vendors are offering catalogues of courses online, corporate universities seem to be moving from offering large catalogs of courses to more focused offerings on topics like strategy and performance management.[68]

LEARNING PORTALS For many firms, their online learning portals are becoming their virtual in-house development centers. Bain & Company, a management consulting firm based in Boston, Massachusetts, is one example. Its Web-based virtual university provides a means for conveniently coordinating all the company's training efforts, and also for delivering Web-based modules on topics from strategic management to mentoring.[69]

LEARNING ACCOUNTS IBM recently established 401(k)-type "learning accounts" to encourage its employees to further their training. An employee can put up to $1,000 a year into his or her account, and IBM contributes an additional $0.50 for every dollar the employee contributes. The accounts are interest-bearing, and the employees can use the funds as they prefer, or take the funds with them if and when they leave IBM.[70]

EXECUTIVE COACHES Many firms use executive coaches to develop their top managers' effectiveness. An *executive coach* is an outside consultant who questions the executive's boss, peers, subordinates, and (sometimes) family in order to identify the executive's strengths and weaknesses, and to counsel the executive so he or she can capitalize on those strengths and weaknesses. Coaches come from a variety of backgrounds, including teaching and counseling. Some firms, including Becton Dickinson & Co., encourage professional and management employees to coach each other.[71]

Executive coaching can be effective. Participants in one study included about 1,400 senior managers who had received "360-degree" performance feedback from bosses, peers, and subordinates. About 400 worked with an executive coach to review the feedback. Then, about a year later, these 400 managers and about 400 who did not receive coaching again received multiscore feedback. Managers who received executive coaching were more likely to set more effective, specific goals for their subordinates, and to have received improved ratings from subordinates and supervisors.[72] Because executive coaching can cost as much as $50,000 per executive, experts recommend using formal assessments prior to coaching, to uncover strengths and weaknesses to provide more focus for the coaching.[73]

Organizational Development

organizational development (OD)
A development method aimed at changing the attitudes, values, and beliefs of employees so that employees can improve the organization.

Organizational development (OD) aims to change the attitudes, values, and beliefs of employees so that the employees can identify and implement changes (such as reorganizations), usually with the aid of an outside change agent, or consultant.

survey feedback
A method that involves surveying employees' attitudes and providing feedback to facilitate problems being solved by the managers and employees.

sensitivity training
A method for increasing employees' insights into their own behavior through candid discussions in groups led by special trainers.

team building
Improving the effectiveness of teams through the use of consultants and team-building meetings.

Action research is the foundation of most OD programs (or "interventions"). It means gathering data about the organization and its operations and attitudes, with an eye toward solving a particular problem (for example, conflict between the sales and production departments); feeding back these data to the employees involved; and then having them team-plan solutions to the problems.

Specific examples of OD programs include survey feedback, sensitivity training, and team building. **Survey feedback** uses questionnaires to survey employees' attitudes and to provide feedback. Its aim is usually to crystallize for the managers the fact that there is a problem that must be addressed. Then the department managers can use the results to turn to the job of discussing and solving it.

Sensitivity training aims to increase participants' insights into their behavior and the behavior of others by encouraging an open expression of feelings in the trainer-guided "T-group laboratory" (the "T" is for training). Sensitivity training seeks to accomplish its aim of increasing interpersonal sensitivity by requiring frank, candid discussions in the small, off-site T-group, specifically discussions of participants' personal feelings, attitudes, and behavior. As a result, it is a controversial method surrounded by heated debate and is used much less today than in the past.

Finally, **team building** refers to a group of OD techniques aimed at improving the effectiveness of teams at work. The typical team-building program begins with the consultant interviewing each of the group members prior to the group meeting. He or she asks them what their problems are, how they think the group functions, and what obstacles are in the way of the group performing better.[74] The consultant usually categorizes the interview or attitude survey data into themes and presents the themes to the group at the beginning of the meeting. They might include, for example, "Not enough time to get my job done," or "I can't get any cooperation around here." The group then ranks the themes by importance. The most important ones form the agenda for the meeting. The group examines and discusses the issues, examines the underlying causes of the problem, and begins work on a solution to the problems.

WEB-BASED TOOLS There are many Web-based tools one can use to facilitate organizational development programs. For example, there are Web-based organizational surveys, including ones at *http://surveymonkey.com, http://Zoomerang.com,* and *http://brainbench.com.* The manager will also find OD-related self-assessment tools at Web sites such as *http://CPP.com.*[75]

Organizational Change

Today, intense international competition means companies have to change fast, perhaps changing their strategies to enter new businesses, or their organization charts, or their employees' attitudes and values.

Major organizational changes like these are never easy, but perhaps the hardest part of leading a change is overcoming the resistance to it. Individuals, groups, and even entire organizations may resist the change, perhaps because they are accustomed to the usual way of doing things or because of perceived threats to their power and influence, or some other reason.

Lewin's Process for Overcoming Resistance

German-born psychologist Kurt Lewin formulated a model of change to summarize what he believed was the basic process for implementing a change with minimal resistance. To Lewin, all behavior in organizations was a product of two kinds of forces: those striving to maintain the status quo and those pushing for change. Implementing change thus meant either reducing the forces for the status quo or building up the forces for change. Lewin's process consisted of three steps:

1. *Unfreezing* means reducing the forces that are striving to maintain the status quo, usually by presenting a provocative problem or event to get people to recognize the need for change and to search for new solutions.
2. *Moving* means developing new behaviors, values, and attitudes, sometimes through organizational structure changes and sometimes through the other management development techniques (such as team building).
3. *Refreezing* means building in the reinforcement to make sure the organization doesn't slide back into its former ways of doing things. Use new incentive plants, for instance.

HR in Practice

A Process for Leading Organizational Change[76]

Unfreezing Stage

1. Establish a sense of urgency. Most CEOs start by creating a sense of urgency. This often takes creativity. For example, the CEO might present executives with an analyst's report describing the firm's lack of competitiveness.

2. Mobilize commitment through joint diagnosis of problems. Having established a sense of urgency, the leader may then create one or more task forces to diagnose the problems facing the company. Such teams can produce a shared understanding of what they can and must improve, and thereby mobilize commitment.

Moving Stage

3. Create a guiding coalition. No one can really implement major organizational changes alone. Most CEOs create a guiding coalition of influential people. They work together as a team to act as missionaries and implementers.

4. Develop and communicate a shared vision. Organizational renewal requires a new leadership vision, "a general statement of the organization's intended direction that evokes emotional feelings in organization members." For example, when Barry Gibbons became CEO of Spec's Music some years ago, his vision of a leaner Spec's offering a diversified blend of concerts and retail music helped provide this direction.

5. Help employees make the change. Are there impediments to change? Does a lack of skills stands in the way? Do policies, procedures, or the firm's organization make it difficult to act? Do intransigent managers discourage employees from acting? If so, address these impediments.

6. Consolidate gains and produce more change. Aim for attainable short-term accomplishments, and use the credibility from these to change all the systems, structures, and policies that don't fit well with the company's new vision. Leaders continue to produce more change by hiring and promoting new people, by identifying selected employees to champion the continuing change, and by providing additional opportunities for short-term wins by employees.[77]

Refreezing Stage

7. Reinforce the new ways of doing things with changes to the company's systems and procedures. Use new appraisal systems and incentives to reinforce the desired behaviors. Change the culture by ensuring that the firm's managers take steps to role-model and communicate the company's new values.

8. Finally, the leader must monitor and assess progress. In brief, this involves comparing where the company is today with where it should be, based on measurable milestones. For example, several years ago, Avon's CEO knew the firm had to dramatically increase its new products. She instituted many changes, and then asked how many new products has the company introduced? How many new door-to-door sales reps has the firm added? See the *Personal Competencies* feature below for a discussion of the role of leadership in managing change.

Of course, the challenge is in the details. Actually finding the right techniques that will help you accomplish each of those three steps and then using them is the difficult part. You'll find an 8-step process for leading organizational change in the *HR in Practice* feature, above.

Personal Competencies

Building Your *Leadership* Skills

Effective leadership is often the "secret ingredient" in successful organizational changes. For example, several years ago Avon Products was in trouble. Few people were signing on as Avon sales reps. It was taking the firm's research and development department three years to develop new products. The firm's whole "back end" operation—buying from suppliers, taking orders, and distributing products to local sales reps—lacked automation. The sales rep still took orders by hand. The company's board of directors knew it had to do something. What it did was appoint Andrea Jung as CEO. In 20 months, Avon's new CEO had turned her company

(continued)

around. She did it by overhauling "everything about the way Avon does business: how it advertises, manufactures, packages, and even sells its products."[78]

Major Avon-type transformations require special leaders. James McGregor Burns wrote a book in which he addressed this issue. He argued for a new type of leadership style.[79] Burns said all leadership behavior is either "transactional" or "transformational." Leaders act *transactional* when they focus on accomplishing the tasks at hand and at maintaining good relations.[80] Burns said that Avon-type changes require transformational leaders.[81] *Transformational* leaders inspire their followers to want to make the change and to throw themselves into doing so. They encourage and obtain performance beyond expectations, by formulating visions and inspiring subordinates to pursue them. Transformational leaders come across as charismatic, inspirational, considerate, and stimulating. Specifically, they are:[82]

- **Charismatic.** Employees often idolize and develop strong emotional attachments to these leaders. A typical transformational leadership questionnaire answer is, "I am ready to trust him or her to overcome any obstacle."
- **Inspirational** transformational leaders have the knack for passionately communicating a future idealistic organization that can be shared.
- **Considerate** transformational leaders treat employees as individuals. They stress helping these employees become all that they are capable of becoming.
- **Stimulating** transformational leaders encourage employees to approach familiar problems in new ways.

EVALUATING THE TRAINING AND DEVELOPMENT EFFORT

There are two basic issues in evaluating a training program. The first is how to design the evaluation study and, in particular, whether to use controlled experimentation. The second is what training effect to measure.

controlled experimentation
Formal methods for testing the effectiveness of a training program, preferably with before-and-after tests and a control group.

Controlled experimentation is the best method to use in evaluating a training program. A controlled experiment uses both a training group and a control group (which receives no training). Data (for instance, on quantity of production or quality of soldered junctions) are obtained both before and after the training effort in the group exposed to training, and before and after a corresponding work period in the control group. In this way it is possible to determine the extent to which any change in performance in the training group resulted from the training itself rather than from some organizationwide change such as a raise in pay; we assume that the latter would have equally affected employees in both groups. This controlled approach is feasible and is sometimes used.[83] In terms of current practices, however, few firms use this approach. Most simply measure trainees' reactions to the program; some also measure the trainees' job performance before and after training.

Training Effects to Measure

Four basic categories of training outcomes can be measured:

1. *Reaction.* First, evaluate trainees' reactions to the program. Did they like the program? Did they think it worthwhile?
2. *Learning.* Second, test the trainees to determine whether they learned the principles, skills, and facts they were supposed to learn.
3. *Behavior.* Next, ask whether the trainees' behavior on the job changed because of the training program. For example, are employees in the store's complaint department more courteous toward disgruntled customers than previously?
4. *Results.* Finally, but most importantly, ask what final results were achieved in terms of the training objectives previously set. Did the number of customer complaints about employees drop? Did the reject rate improve? Did scrappage cost decrease? Was turnover reduced?

EVALUATION IN PRACTICE In today's metrics-oriented business environment, employers increasingly demand quantified training evaluations, either of reactions, learning, behavior, results, or some combination of these. In one survey, most responding employers said they set formal response-rate goals (in terms of number of trainees responding) for end-of-training class evaluations. In general, the actual response rate depended on the method the employer used to obtain the response. The response rate of trainees was about 82% with paper-and-pencil end-of-class evaluation surveys, 59% with online surveys, and 53% with e-mail surveys. Response rates for delayed, follow-up surveys were only about 38%. Most firms collecting end-of-class evaluation data—about 90%—use paper-and-pencil surveys.[84] Figure 6.4 shows one online survey.

FIGURE 6.4 Online Training Evaluation Form

Online Training Evaluation Form

Questions marked with an asterisk (*) are mandatory.

Required Fields

1. * Date of Training Session:

_____ Month _____ Day _____ Year _____ Time

2. * Location of Training:

_____

3. * Name of Trainer:

_____

4. * Select the category that best describes your position:

_____

5. * Was your training?

☐ a Web Conference -or-

☐ On-Site

6. * Was your training?

☐ Lecture Style -or-

☐ Hands On

Optional Fields

7. Name:

_____

8. Email Address:

_____

9. Telephone Number:

_____

Please evaluate the emphasis of each topic listed as it was covered in your training session.

Program Content

10. * The content was relevant to my needs/job.

☐ Strongly Agree   ☐ Agree   ☐ Not Sure   ☐ Disagree   ☐ Strongly Disagree   ☐ Not Applicable

---

(continued)

FIGURE 6.4 Continued

11. * I can use the product(s) more effectively than I could before I attended today's training.

☐ Strongly Agree ☐ Agree ☐ Not Sure ☐ Disagree ☐ Strongly Disagree ☐ Not Applicable

12. If trained via Web Conference, the Web Conference technology was easy to use and an effective way for me to receive training.

☐ Strongly Agree ☐ Agree ☐ Not Sure ☐ Disagree ☐ Strongly Disagree ☐ Not Applicable

13. * The length of the training session was appropriate.

☐ Strongly Agree ☐ Agree ☐ Not Sure ☐ Disagree ☐ Strongly Disagree ☐ Not Applicable

Instructor

14. * The instructor was well organized and prepared.

☐ Strongly Agree ☐ Agree ☐ Not Sure ☐ Disagree ☐ Strongly Disagree ☐ Not Applicable

15. * The instructor presented the material in a logical sequence.

☐ Strongly Agree ☐ Agree ☐ Not Sure ☐ Disagree ☐ Strongly Disagree ☐ Not Applicable

16. * The instructor was knowledgeable about the course material.

☐ Strongly Agree ☐ Agree ☐ Not Sure ☐ Disagree ☐ Strongly Disagree ☐ Not Applicable

17. * The instructor answered questions effectively.

☐ Strongly Agree ☐ Agree ☐ Not Sure ☐ Disagree ☐ Strongly Disagree ☐ Not Applicable

Satisfaction

18. * Please rate your overall satisfaction with this training session.

☐ Extremely Satisfied ☐ Satisfied ☐ Not Sure ☐ Dissatisfied ☐ Extremely Dissatisfied

Written Comments:

19. What was the most useful thing that you learned in today's training session?

20. What suggestions do you have to improve the functionality and/or content of Gale databases?

21. What suggestions do you have to improve this training?

22. If you identified areas for improvement, may we follow-up with you personally? If yes, please make sure to enter your name and contact information at the start of this form.

☐ Yes   ☐ No

Computerization is facilitating the evaluation process. For example, Bovis Lend Lease in New York City offers its 625 employees numerous courses in construction and other subjects. The firm uses learning management software to monitor which employees are taking which courses, and the extent to which employees are improving their skills.[85]

TRANSFER OF TRAINING Only about 10% to 35% of trainees are transferring what they learned to their jobs a year after training. Managers can improve this. *Prior to training*, get trainee and supervisor input in designing the program, institute a training attendance policy, and encourage employees to participate. *During training*, provide trainees with training experiences and conditions (surroundings, equipment) that resemble the actual work environment. *After training* reinforce what trainees learned, for instance, by appraising and rewarding employees for using new skills, and by ensuring they have the tools and materials they need to use their new skills.[86]

MCDONALD'S EXAMPLE To support McDonald's strategy of consistency, its managers attend its famous Hamburger University. Employees at "seed stores" in each local area provide employees from surrounding stores with hands-on training. These seed store–trained employees then train their own stores' teams.

McDonald's measures training effectiveness in several ways. They ask trainees to evaluate classes, and test them on what they've learned. McDonald's also speaks with the employees' supervisors about how the trainees did before and after the training, to try to determine the extent to which the trainees changed their behavior.[87]

Review

SUMMARY

1. The training process consists of five steps: needs analysis, instructional design, validation, implementation, and evaluation.

2. Vestibule training combines the advantages of on- and off-the-job training.

3. On-the-job training might take the form of the coaching/understudy method, job rotation, or special assignments and committees. Other training methods include audiovisual techniques, lectures, and apprenticeship training.

4. Computer-based training includes simulated training, DVD/CD-ROM- and Internet-based training, and learning portals. *Mobile learning* (or "on-demand learning") means delivering learning content on demand via mobile devices like cell phones, laptops, and iPhones, wherever and whenever the learner has the time and desire to access it.

5. Management development is aimed at preparing employees for future managerial jobs with the organization, or at solving organizationwide problems concerning, for instance, inadequate interdepartmental communication.

6. On-the-job experience is the most popular form of management development.

7. Managerial on-the-job training methods include job rotation, coaching, and action learning. Case studies, management games, outside seminars, university-related programs, behavior modeling, and in-house development centers are other methods.

8. Organizational development is an approach to instituting change in which employees themselves play a major role in the change process by providing data, obtaining feedback on problems, and team-planning solutions. There are several OD methods, including sensitivity training, team development, and survey feedback.

9. Overcoming employee resistance is a crucial aspect of implementing organizational change.

KEY TERMS

employee orientation   184

training   185

task analysis   186

performance analysis   186

vestibule/simulated training   189

behavior modeling   189

computer-based training (CBT)   190

virtual classroom   193

lifelong learning   194

management development   196

job rotation   197

coaching/understudy method   197

action learning   197

case study method   197

management game   197

improvisation   197

in-house development centers   199

organizational development (OD)   199

survey feedback   200

sensitivity training   200

team building   200

controlled experimentation   202

DISCUSSION QUESTIONS AND EXERCISES

1. A well-thought-out orientation program is especially important for employees (such as recent graduates) who have had little or no work experience. Explain why you agree or disagree with this statement.

2. You're the supervisor of a group of employees whose task is to assemble devices that go into cell phones. You find that quality is not what it should be and that many of your group's devices have to be brought back and reworked; your own boss says, "You better start doing a better job of training your workers."
   a. What are some of the staffing factors that could be contributing to this problem?
   b. Explain how you would go about assessing whether it is, in fact, a training problem.

3. Explain how you would go about developing a training program for teaching this course.

4. John Santos is an undergraduate business student majoring in accounting. He has just failed the first accounting course, Accounting 101, and is understandably upset. Explain how you would use performance analysis to identify what, if any, are Santos's training needs.

5. What are some typical on-the-job training techniques? What do you think are some of the main drawbacks of relying on informal on-the-job training for helping new employees become accustomed to their jobs?

6. Experts argue that one reason for implementing special global training programs is the need to avoid lost business "due to cultural insensitivity." What sort of cultural insensitivity do you think is referred to and how might that translate into lost business? What sort of training program would you recommend to avoid such cultural insensitivity?

7. Do you think job rotation is a good method to use for management trainees? Why or why not?

8. Working individually or in groups, obtain, perhaps via the Web, copies of management development seminars from a vendor such as the American Management Association. At what levels of managers do they aim their seminar offerings? What seems to be the most popular type of development program? Why do you think that's the case?

9. Working individually or in groups, discuss whether you think the college you are currently attending is or is not a learning organization. On what do you base your conclusion?

10. Since at least 2003, the U.S. has been sending hundreds of trainers to that country to train new cadres of Iraqi workers, from teachers to police officers. Perhaps no training task was more pressing than that involved in creating the country's new police force. These were the people who were to help the coalition bring security to Iraq at that time. However, many new officers had no experience in police work. There were language barriers between trainers and trainees. And some trainees found themselves quickly under fire from insurgents when they went as trainees out into the field. Based on what you have learned about training from this chapter, list the five most important things you would tell the officer in charge of training (a former U.S. big-city police chief) to keep in mind as he designs the training program.

Application Exercises

| HR in Action Case Incident 1 | Reinventing the Wheel at Apex Door Company |

Jim Delaney, president of Apex Door Company, has a problem. No matter how often he tells his employees how to do their jobs, they invariably "decide to do things their way," as he puts it, and arguments ensue between Delaney, the employee, and the employee's supervisor. One example is in the door-design department. The designers are expected to work with the architects to design doors that meet the specifications. Although it's not "rocket science," as Delaney puts it, the designers often make mistakes, such as designing in too much steel—a problem that can cost Apex tens of thousands of wasted dollars, especially considering the number of doors in, say, a 30-story office tower.

The order processing department is another example. Although Jim has a specific, detailed way he wants each order written up, most of the order clerks don't understand how to use the multipage order form, and they improvise when it comes to a question such as whether to classify a customer as "industrial" or "commercial."

The current training process is as follows. None of the jobs have training manuals per se, although several have somewhat out-of-date job descriptions. The training for new employees is all on the job: Usually, the person leaving the company trains the new person during the 1- or 2-week overlap period, but if there's no overlap, the new person is trained as well as possible by other employees who have occasionally filled in on the job in the past. The training is basically the same throughout the company—for machinists, secretaries, assemblers, and accounting clerks, for example.

Questions

1. What do you think of Apex's training process? Could it help explain why employees "do things their way," and if so, how?
2. What role do job descriptions play in training?
3. Explain in detail what you would do to improve the training process at Apex. Make sure to provide specific suggestions.

| HR in Action Case Incident 2 | Carter Cleaning Company: The New Training Program |

At the present time Carter Cleaning Centers have no formal orientation or training policies or procedures, and Jennifer believes this is one reason why the standards to which she and her father would like employees to adhere are generally not followed.

The Carters would prefer that certain practices and procedures be used in dealing with the customers at the front counters. For example, all customers should be greeted with what Jack refers to as a "big hello." Garments they drop off should immediately be inspected for any damage or unusual stains so these can be brought to the customer's attention, lest the customer later return to pick up the garment and erroneously blame the store. The garments are then supposed to be immediately placed together in a nylon sack to separate them from other customers' garments. The ticket also has to be carefully written up, with the customer's name and telephone number and the date precisely and clearly noted on all copies. The counterperson is also supposed to take the opportunity to try to sell the customer additional services such as waterproofing, or simply notify the customer that "Now that people are doing their spring cleaning, we're having a special on drapery cleaning all this month." Finally, as the customer leaves, the counterperson is supposed to make a courteous comment like "Have a nice day" or "Drive safely." Each of the other jobs in the stores—pressing, cleaning and spotting, periodically maintaining the coin laundry equipment, and so forth—similarly contain certain steps, procedures, and most importantly, standards the Carters would prefer to see upheld.

The company has had problems, Jennifer feels, because of a lack of adequate employee training and orientation. For example, two new employees became very upset last month when they discovered that they were not paid at the end of the week, on Friday, but instead were paid (as are all Carter employees) on the following Tuesday. The Carters use the extra two days in part to give them time to obtain everyone's hours and compute their pay. The other reason they do it, according to Jack, is that "frankly, when we stay a few days behind in paying employees it helps to ensure that they at least give us a few days' notice before quitting on us. While we are certainly obligated to pay them anything they earn, we find that psychologically they seem to be less likely to just walk out on us Friday evening and not show up Monday morning if they still haven't gotten their pay from the previous week. This way they at least give us a few days' notice so we can find a replacement."

Other matters that could be covered during orientation and training, says Jennifer, include company policy regarding paid holidays, lateness and absences, health and hospitalization benefits (there are none, other than workers' compensation), and general matters like the maintenance of a clean and safe work area, personal appearance and cleanliness, time sheets, personal telephone calls and mail, company policies regarding matters like substance abuse, and eating or smoking on the job (both forbidden).

Jennifer believes that implementing orientation and training programs would help to ensure that employees know how to do their jobs the right way. And she and her father further believe that it is only when employees understand the right way to do their jobs that there is any hope their jobs will in fact be accomplished the way the Carters want them to be accomplished.

Questions

1. Specifically what should the Carters cover in their new employee orientation program and how should they convey this information?
2. In the HR management course Jennifer took, the book suggested using a job description sheet to identify tasks performed by an employee. Should Carter use a form like this for the counterperson's job, and if so, what would the filled-in form look like?
3. Which specific training techniques should Jennifer use to train her pressers, her cleaner–spotters, her managers, and her counterpeople, and why?

EXPERIENTIAL EXERCISE

The Interplay of Strategy and Training

Flying the Friendlier Skies

Purpose:

The purpose of this exercise is to give you practice in developing a training program for the job of airline reservation clerk for a major airline.

Required Understanding:

You should be fully acquainted with the material in this chapter and should read the following introduction and description of an airline reservation clerk's duties.

Its founders started U.S.-based JetBlue Airlines with a unique combination of competitive strategies: JetBlue would (1) pursue a low-cost strategy by hiring non-union employees and having many reservations and clerical people work from their homes, while (2) providing high-quality service, for instance, by emphasizing clean new planes, free in-flight food, and very friendly service. JetBlue knew that just low cost was not enough. Passengers wanted and demanded high-quality service, too. That obviously had implications for JetBlue's reservations clerk training programs.

Customers contact JetBlue's airlines reservation clerks to obtain flight schedules, prices, and itineraries. The reservation clerks use their online access tools to look up the requested information on our airline's online flight schedule

system, which are updated continuously. The reservation clerk must deal courteously and expeditiously with the customer and be able to quickly find alternative flight arrangements in order to provide the customer with the itinerary that fits his or her needs. Alternative flights and prices must be found quickly, so that the customer is not kept waiting, and so that the reservations operations group maintains its efficiency standards. It is often necessary to look under various routings, since there may be a dozen or more alternative routs between the customer's starting point and destination.

You may assume that we just hired 30 new clerks, and that you must create a 3-day training program. Just about all clerks work out of their homes, although they meet periodically at local JetBlue centers.

How to Set Up the Exercise/Instructions:

Divide the class into teams of five or six students. Airline reservation clerks obviously need numerous skills to perform their jobs. JetBlue Airlines has asked you to quickly develop the outline of a training program for its new reservation clerks. You may want to start by listing the job's main duties. In any case, please produce the requested outline, making sure to be very specific about (1) what you want to teach the new clerks, (2) what the trainees should keep in mind regarding why they should do things in a particular way, and (3) specifically what methods and aids you suggest using to train them.

ENDNOTES

1. Tony Bingaman and Pat Galagan, "Training: They're Lovin' It," *Training and Development* (November 2006): 30.
2. For a good discussion of socialization see, for example, George Chao et al., "Organizational Socialization: Its Content and Consequences," *Journal of Applied Psychology* 79, no. 5 (1994): 730–743. See also Talya Bauer et al., "Newcomer Adjustment During Organizational Socialization: A Meta-analytic Review of Antecedents, Outcomes, and Methods," *Journal of Applied Psychology* 92, no. 3 (2007): 707–721.
3. Sheila Hicks et al., "Orientation Redesign," *Training and Development* (July 2006): 43–46.
4. John Kammeyer-Mueller and Connie Wanberg, "Unwrapping the Organizational Entry Process: Disentangling Multiple Antecedents and Their Pathways to Adjustments," *Journal of Applied Psychology* 88, no. 5 (2003): 779–794.
5. Sabrina Hicks, "Successful Orientation Programs," *Training & Development* (April 2000): 59. See also Howard Klein and Natasha Weaver, "The Effectiveness of an Organizational

Level Orientation Program in the Socialization of New Hires," *Personnel Psychology* 53 (2000): 47–66; and Laurie Friedman, "Are You Losing Potential New Hires at Hello?" *Training and Development* (November 2006): 25–27.

6. This section based on Darin Hartley, "Technology Kicks Up Leadership Development," *Training and Development* (March 2004): 22–24.

7. Ed Frauenheim, "IBM Learning Programs Get a 'Second Life,'" *Workforce Management* (December 11, 2006): 6.

8. Nancy DeViney and Brenda Sugrue, "Learning Outsourcing: A Reality Check," *Training and Development* (December 2004): 41.

9. Christine Ellis and Sarah Gale, "A Seat at the Table," *Training* (March 2001): 90–96.

10. Brenda Sugrue et al., "What in the World Is WLP?" *Training and Development* (January 2005): 51–54.

11. Winfred Alfred Jr. et al., "Effectiveness of Training in Organizations: A Meta Analysis of Design and Evaluation Features," *Journal of Applied Psychology* 88, no. 2 (2003): 242.

12. Harley Frazis, Diane Herz, and Michael Horrigan, "Employer-Provided Training: Results from a New Survey," *Monthly Labor Review* (May 1995): 3–17. See also Anders Gronstedt, "The Changing Face of Workplace Learning," *Training and Development* (January 2007): 20–24.

13. Ben Nagler, "Recasting Employees Into Teams," *Workforce* (January 1998): 101–106.

14. Ibid., p. 103.

15. Marcia Jones, "Use Your Head When Identifying Skills Gaps," *Workforce* (March 2000): 118.

16. P. Nick Blanchard and James Thacker, *Effective Training: Systems, Strategies and Practices* (Upper Saddle River, NJ: Prentice Hall, 2007): 100–143.

17. Ibid., 106.

18. Richard Montier et al., "Competency Models Develop Top Performance," *Training and Development* (July 2006): 47–50.

19. P. Nick Blanchard and James Thacker, *Effective Training: Systems, Strategies, and Practices* (Upper Saddle River, NJ: Prentice Hall, 2007): 8.

20. Kenneth Wexley and Gary Latham, *Development and Training Human Resources in Organizations* (Upper Saddle River, NJ: Prentice Hall, 2002): 107.

21. Ibid., 82.

22. Ibid., 87.

23. Ibid., 90.

24. The American Society for Training & Development (ASTD) offers thousands of packaged training programs, such as "Be a Better Manager," "Strategic Planning 101," "12 Habits of Successful Trainers," "Mentoring," and "Using Job Aids." American Society for Training & Development, Spring and Fall Line Catalog (2007); American Society for Training & Development, 1640 King St. Box 1443, Alexandria, VA 22313.

25. See, for example. "Infoline," American Society for Training and Development (2007 Fall catalog): 3.

26. Donna Goldwaser, "Me a Trainer?" *Training* (April 2001): 60–66.

27. Robert Weintraub and Jennifer Martineau, "The Just in Time Imperative," *Training and Development* (June 2002): 52.

28. Cindy Waxer, "Steelmaker Revives Apprentice Program to Address Graying Workforce, Forge Next Leaders," *Workforce Management* (January 30, 2006): 40.

29. David Finegold and Karin Wagner, "Are Apprenticeships Still Relevant in the 21st Century? The Case Study of Changing Youth Training Arrangements in German Banks," *Industrial and Labor Relations Review* (July 2002): 667–685.

30. Paul Taylor et al., "A Meta-Analytic Review of Behavior Modeling Training," *Journal of Applied Psychology* 90, no. 4 (2005): 692–719.

31. See Tom Barron, "The Link Between Leadership Development and Retention," *Training and Development* (April 2004): 58–65.

32. Paul Taylor et al., "A Meta-Analytic Review of Behavior Modeling Training," *Journal of Applied Psychology* 90, no. 4 (2005): 692–719.

33. See, for example, "Larta Institute Announces Selection of Israeli Companies in US-Israel Life Sciences Bridge Program, Entrepreneurs to Receive Videoconference Training Starting April 15; Three Candidates Will Come to L.A. for One-Month Incubation Visit," *Internet Wire* (April 20, 2004).

34. David Raths, "Virtual Reality in the OR," *Training and Development* (August 2006): 36–43.

35. See, for example, Kim Kleps, "Virtual Sales Training Scores a Hit," *Training and Development* (December 2006): 63–64.

36. Dina Berta, "Computer-Based Training Clicks with Both Franchisees and Their Employees," *Nation's Restaurant News* (July 9, 2001): 1, 18; See also Daniel Cable and Charles Parsons, "Socialization Tactics and Person-Organization Fit," *Personnel Psychology* 54 (2001): 1–23.

37. Michael Laff, "Simulations: Slowly Proving Their Worth," *Training and Development* (June 2007): 30–34.

38. Jenni Jarventaus, "Virtual Threat, Real Sweat," *Training and Development* (May 2007): 72–78.

39. Ed Frauenheim, "IBM Learning Programs Get a 'Second Life,'" *Workforce Management* (December 11, 2006): 6.

40. Clark Aldrich, "Engaging Mini-Games Find Niche in Training," *Training and Development* (July 2007): 22–24.

41. "What Do Simulations Cost?" *Training and Development* (June 2007): 88.

42. Ellen Zimmerman, "Better Training Is Just a Click Away," *Workforce* (January 2001): 36–42.

43. John Zonneveld, "GM Dealer Training Goes Global," *Training and Development* (December 2006): 47–51.

44. "The Next Generation of Corporate Learning," *Training & Development* (June 2003): 47.

45. Traci Sitzmann et al., "The Comparative Effectiveness of Web-Based and Classroom Instruction: A Meta-Analysis," *Personnel Psychology* 59 (2006): 623–664.

46. Ibid.

47. Renee DeRouin et al., "Optimizing E-Learning: Research-Based Guidelines for Learner Controlled Training," *Human Resource Management* 43, no. 2 (Summer/Fall 2004): 147–162.

48. "The Next Generation of Corporate Learning," *Training and Development* (June 2004): 47.

49. Ruth Clark, "Harnessing the Virtual Classroom," *Training and Development* (November 2005): 40–46.

50. Jennifer Taylor Arnold, "Learning On-the-Fly," *HR Magazine* (September 2007): 137.

51. Elizabeth Agnvall, "Just-In-Time Training," *HR Magazine* (May 2006): 67–78.

52. Ibid.

53. Paula Ketter, "The Hidden Disability," *Training and Development* (June 2006): 34–40.

54. Jennifer Salopek, "The Growth of Succession Management," *Training and Development* (June 2007): 22–24; and Kermit Kalleba, "Businesses Continue to Push for Lifelong Learning," *Training and Development* (June 2007): 14.

55. "Adams Mark Hotel & Resorts Launches Diversity Training Program," *Hotel and Motel Management* 216, no. 6 (April 2001): 15.

56. Douglas Shuit, "Sound of the Retreat," *Workforce Management* (September 2003): 40.

57. "For Gap, Management Training Doesn't Stop at the Border," *BNA Bulletin to Management* (February 2005): 63.

58. Jack Zenger, Dave Ulrich, and Norm Smallwood, "The New Leadership Development," *Training and Development* (March 2000): 22–27. See also W. David Patton and Connie Pratt, "Assessing the Training Needs of High Potential Managers," *Public Personnel Management* 31, no. 4 (Winter 2002): 465–474; and Ann Locke and Arlene Tarantino, "Strategic Leadership Development," *Training and Development* (December 2006): 53–55.

59. Ann Pomeroy, "Head of the Class," *HR Magazine* (January 2005): 57.

60. "Thrown into Deep End, Workers Surface as Leaders," *BNA Bulletin to Management* (July 11, 2002): 223.

61. Michael Marquardt, "Harnessing the Power of Action Learning," *Training and Development* (June 2004): 26–32.

62. Following quoted or paraphrased from P. Nick Blanchard and James Thacker, *Effective Training: Systems, Strategies and Practices* (Upper Saddle River, NJ: Prentice Hall, 2007): 233–234.

63. See, for example, Michael Laff, "Serious Gaming: The Trainer's New Best Friend," *Training and Development* (January 2007): 52–56.

64. Jean Thilmany, "Acting Out," *HR Magazine* (January 2007): 95–100.

65. Chris Musselwhite, "University Executive Education Gets Real," *Training and Development* (May 2006): 57.

66. Jeanne Meister, "Universities Put to the Test," *Workforce Management* (December 11, 2006): 27–30.

67. Ann Pomeroy, "Head of the Class," *HR Magazine* (January 2005): 57.

68. "Corporate Universities Getting a Refresher," *Workforce Management* (June 11, 2007): 23.

69. Russell Gerbman, "Corporate Universities 101," *HR Magazine* (February 2000): 101–106. Before creating an in-house university, the employer needs to ensure that the corporate university's vision, mission, and programs support the company's strategic goals. See Michael Laff, "Centralized Training Leads to Nontraditional Universities," *Training and Development* (January 2007): 27–29.

70. "Corporate Universities Getting a Refresher," *Workforce Management* (June 11, 2007): 23.

71. Joseph Toto, "Untapped World of Peer Coaching," *Training and Development* (April 2006): 69–72.

72. James Smither et al., "Can Working with an Executive Coach Improve Multiscore Feedback Ratings Over Time?" *Personnel Psychology* 56, no. 1 (Spring 2003): 23–44.

73. "As Corporate Coaching Goes Mainstream, Keyed Prerequisite Overlooked: Assessment," *BNA Bulletin to Management* (May 16, 2006): 153.

74. Wendell French and Cecil Bell Jr., *Organization Development* (Upper Saddle River, NJ: Prentice Hall, 1999): 155–190. See also P. Nick Blanchard and James Thacker, *Effective Training* (Upper Saddle River NJ: Pearson, 2007): 38–46.

75. Darin Hartley, "OD Wired," *Training and Development* (August 2004): 20–24.

76. The steps are based on Michael Beer, Russell Eisenstat, and Burt Spector, "Why Change Programs Don't Produce Change," *Harvard Business Review* (November–December 1990): 158–166; Thomas Cummings and Christopher Worley, *Organization Development and Change* (Minneapolis, MN: West Publishing Company, 1993); John P. Kotter, "Leading Change: Why Transformation Efforts Fail," *Harvard Business Review* (March–April 1995): 59–66; and John P. Kotter, *Leading Change* (Boston: Harvard Business School Press, 1996). Change doesn't necessarily have to be painful. See, for example, Eric Abrahamson, "Change Without Pain," *Harvard Business Review* (July–August 2000): 75–79; and Michael Beer and Nitin Nohria, "Cracking the Code of Change," *Harvard Business Review* (June 2000): 133–141. See also David Herold et al., "Beyond Change Management: A Multilevel Investigation of Contextual and Personal Influences on Employee's Commitment to Change," *Journal of Applied Psychology* 92, no. 4 (2007): 949.

77. Michael Beer, Russell Eisenstat, and Burt Spector, "Why Change Programs Don't Produce Change," *Harvard Business Review* (November–December 1990): 164.

78. "Avon Sees China Operation as a Sole Business Unit," *China Business Daily News* (December 13, 2005): 1; and "Avon, the Net, and Glass Ceiling," *Business Week* (February 6, 2005): 104; Katrina Brooker, "It Took a Lady to Save Avon," *Fortune* (October 15, 2001): 203–208.

79. J. M. Burns, *Leadership* (New York: Harper, 1978).

80. See, for example, Bernard Bass, "Theory of Transformational Leadership Redux," *Leadership Quarterly* (Winter 1995): 463–478.

81. Gary Yukl, *Leadership in Organizations* (Upper Saddle River, NJ: Prentice Hall, 1998): 324.

82. Bernard Bass, *Leadership and Performance Beyond Expectations* (New York: The Free Press, 1985); and Gary Yukl, *Leadership in Organizations* (Upper Saddle River, NJ: Prentice Hall, 1998): 298–299.

83. See, for example, Charlie Morrow, M. Quintin Jarrett, and Melvin Rupinski, "An Investigation of the Effect and Economic Utility of Corporate-Wide Training," *Personnel Psychology* 50 (1997): 91–119. See also Antonio Aragon-Sanchez et al., "Effects of Training on Business Results," *International Journal of Human Resource Management* 14, no. 6 (September 2003): 956–980.

84. Jeffrey Berk, "Training Evaluations," *Training and Development* (September 2004): 39–45.

85. Todd Raphel, "What Learning Management Reports Do for You," *Workforce* 80, no. 6 (June 2001): 56–58.

86. Alan Saks and Monica Belcourt, "An Investigation of Training Activities and Transfer of Training in Organizations," *Human Resource Management* 45, no. 4 (Winter 2006): 629–648.

87. Tony Bingaman and Pat Galagan, "Training: They're Lovin' It," *Training and Development* (November 2006): 30.

Performance Management and Appraisal

7

When you finish studying this chapter, you should be able to:

1. *Explain the purpose of performance appraisal.*

2. *Answer the question, "Who should do the appraising?"*

3. *Discuss the pros and cons of at least eight performance appraisal methods.*

4. *Explain how to conduct an appraisal feedback interview.*

5. *Give examples of five potential appraisal problems.*

6. *Explain how to install a performance management program.*

7. *Explain how to design a career management program.*

performance appraisal
Evaluating an employee's current and/or past performance relative to his or her performance standards.

performance management
The process through which companies ensure that employees are working toward organizational goals. It includes practices through which the manager defines the employee's goals and work, develops the employee's skills and capabilities, evaluates the person's goal-directed behavior, and then rewards him or her in a fashion consistent with the company's and the person's needs.

Introduction

With more than 100,000 employees in 36 countries, administering employee appraisals and managing performance is a complicated process in a company like TRW.[1] A few years ago, the firm was deeply in debt, and the company's heavy investment in the automotive business was draining its profits. TRW's top managers knew they had to take steps to make the firm more performance driven. To do that, they needed to focus employees' attention on performance, in part by instituting a new performance management and appraisal system. The question was how to do this. ∎

BASIC CONCEPTS IN PERFORMANCE MANAGEMENT

Performance appraisal means evaluating an employee's current and/or past performance relative to his or her performance standards. Although "appraising performance" usually brings to mind filling out an appraisal form like the one in Figure 7.1, the actual appraisal and form are only part of the appraisal process. Appraising performance also requires that the supervisor set performance standards. And it requires that the employee get the training, feedback, and incentives required to eliminate performance deficiencies or to continue to perform above par.

There's nothing new about the idea that the actual appraisal is just one step in improving employee performance. However, managers generally take the integrated nature of that process—of setting goals, training employees, and then appraising, counseling, and (if need be) retraining and rewarding them—more seriously today than they have in the past. They've also given this whole process a new name.

Performance Management

Managers call the entire, integrated process *performance management*. **Performance management** is the continuous process of identifying, measuring, and developing the performance of individuals and teams and aligning their performance with the organization's goals.[2]

PERFORMANCE MANAGEMENT VS. PERFORMANCE APPRAISAL Performance management is a very important process. Managers use performance management to ensure that employees are working toward organizational goals and accomplishing what they're supposed to be accomplishing.[3] In comparing performance management and performance appraisal, one compensation expert says "the distinction is the contrast between a year-end event—the completion of the appraisal form—and a process that starts the year with performance planning and is integral to the way people are managed throughout the year."[4] So, what distinguishes performance management from performance appraisal is the former's focus on *continuously* monitoring and aligning employees' *performance* with their *goals*. We'll see that in practice, performance management systems generally use sophisticated information technology to help managers automatically track employee performance and take immediate corrective action as required. Performance *appraisal* systems usually rely on paper forms, or perhaps online or computerized appraisal forms.

Defining the Employee's Goals and Work Efforts

You can neither manage nor appraise employees' performance if they don't know what their performance standards or goals are.[5] In practice (and ideally), there is a hierarchy or chain of goals in the company. The CEO may have a goal to double sales this year. Then her vice president of sales has his or her own sales goals, and each salesperson has their sales goal. This has two practical implications for performance appraisal and management. First, the employee's performance standards should make sense in terms of the company's broader goals. Second, the manager should appraise the employee based on how that person did with respect to achieving the specific goals by which he or she expected to be measured.

FIGURE 7.1 Online Departmental Teaching Appraisal Form

Faculty Evaluation Form

INSTRUCTIONS FOR COMPLETING STUDENT EVALUATION FORM

Today you are being asked to evaluate this course and the instructor. Please read and answer each question thoughtfully and honestly.

Evaluations are helpful to faculty in improving their teaching and their courses. They are also an important element in the College's ongoing evaluation of faculty for tenure and promotion.

Your answers are anonymous and confidential. Comments will be typed so that the instructor cannot identify your handwriting. Your answers will be returned to the instructor only after final grades for this course have been recorded.

Your written comments on the last page are especially helpful.

CRN _____   Course _____

Instructor _____   Term _____

STUDENT EVALUATION OF INSTRUCTION

Student Information: (Please circle your answers).

1. I had completed the recommended preparation (prerequisites) for this course before beginning the course. (Select NA if the course has no prerequisites.)

   All   Most   Some   Very Few   Don't Know   NA

2. I attended classes.

   All   Most   Some   Very Few   NA

3. To be adequately prepared for this class, I feel I need to spend this many hours per week outside of class, studying and preparing assignments:

   15+ hours   12-14 hours   9-11 hours   7-8 hours   4-6 hours   1-3 hours

4. For this course, I expect to receive a grade of:

   A   B   C   D   F

Evaluation of Instruction: (7 = strongly agree .... 1 = strongly disagree).

1. The learning objectives (competencies) of this course have been made clear.

   7   6   5   4   3   2   1

2. The course activities are related to the learning objectives (competencies).

   7   6   5   4   3   2   1

3. The instructor is well-prepared for class.

   7   6   5   4   3   2   1

4. The instructor is available during posted office hours or by appointment.

   7   6   5   4   3   2   1

5. Feedback on my work is timely, constructive, and clear enough to benefit my learning.

   7   6   5   4   3   2   1

6. My grades accurately measure my learning in this class.

   7   6   5   4   3   2   1

(continued)

FIGURE 7.1 Continued

---

7. The instructor creates a learning environment in which diverse points of view are respected and can be freely expressed.

          7   6   5   4   3   2   1

8. Based on what I have learned, I would recommend this course to other students.

          7   6   5   4   3   2   1

COMMENTS

Your written comments are especially helpful. Comments will be typed so that the instructor cannot identify your handwriting. Your answers will be returned to the instructor only after final grades for this course have been recorded.

1. What are the most valuable aspects of this course and/or the way the course was taught?

2. Even excellent courses can be improved. Can you give some constructive suggestions for making the course better?

3. Do you wish to comment on any of your ratings in the "Evaluation of Instruction" section on the Previous page? If so, please state the item number to which your comment refer

---

Source: Copyright © COCC 2007 Central Oregon Community College, http://employees.cocc.edu/Faculty+Resources/Fac_Guides/Fac_Eval_Standards/Eval_Form/default.aspx.

TWO ISSUES In practice, two things stand in the way of this ideal process. First, while comparing performance to previously set numerical targets is certainly the preferred approach, many managers haven't the time or inclination to set measurable goals for all employees. Job descriptions are rarely helpful when it comes to specific goals. Your sales manager's job description may list duties like "supervise sales force." However, you may also expect your sales manager to personally sell at least $600,000 worth of products per year by handling the division's two largest accounts. Unfortunately, some supervisors are lax when it comes to setting goals for their employees. The bottom line is that it's not uncommon to have supervisors appraise employees, not relative to goals, but by using generic, subjective (but still *carefully defined* and *previously discussed*) standards such as "teamwork" and "quality." But again, with or without numerical goals, employees should always know ahead of time how and on what basis you're going to appraise them.[6]

The second issue is that setting useful goals is not as simple as it may appear. The supervisor must first decide what to measure. The most straightforward way to do this (for the sales manager job, for instance) is to set measurable standards for each expectation. You might measure the "personal selling" activity in terms of how many dollars of sales the manager is to generate personally. Perhaps measure "keeping the sales force happy" in terms of turnover (on the assumption that less than 10% of the sales force will quit in any given year if morale is high). The *Business in Action* feature explains how to use behavioral science to improve your goal-setting effectiveness.

Business in Action — Improving Your *Organizational Behavior/Goal-Setting* Knowledge

Setting goals is one thing; setting effective goals is another. One way to think of this is to remember that the goals you set should be "SMART." They are specific, and clearly state the desired results. They are measurable, and answer the question "How much?" They are attainable. They are relevant, and clearly derive from what the manager and company want to achieve. And they are timely, and reflect deadlines and milestones.[7]

Behavioral science research studies provide useful insights into setting motivational goals. These studies suggest four things:

1. Assign Specific Goals. Employees who receive specific goals usually perform better than those who do not.
2. Assign Measurable Goals. Put goals in quantitative terms and include target dates or deadlines. Goals set in

absolute terms (such as "an average daily output of 300 units") are less confusing than goals set in relative terms (such as "improve production by 20%"). If measurable results will not be available, then "satisfactory completion"—such as "satisfactorily attended workshop" or "satisfactorily completed his or her degree"—is the next best thing. In any case, target dates or deadlines should always be set.

3. Assign Challenging but Doable Goals. Goals should be challenging, but not so difficult that they appear impossible or unrealistic.

4. Encourage Participation. Throughout your management career (and often several times a day) you'll be faced with this question: Should I just tell my employees what their goals are, or should I let them participate with me in setting their goals? The evidence suggests that participatively set goals do not consistently result in higher performance than assigned goals, nor do assigned goals consistently result in higher performance than participatively set ones. It is only when the participatively set goals are more difficult (are set higher) than the assigned ones that the participatively set goals produce higher performance. Because it tends to be easier to set higher standards when your employees participate in the process, participation tends to facilitate standards setting and performance.[8]

Why Appraise Performance?

❶ Explain the purpose of performance appraisal.

There are three main reasons to appraise subordinates' performance. First, appraisals provide important data the supervisor then uses to make *promotion and salary raise* decisions.[9] Second, the appraisal lets the boss and subordinate develop *a plan* for correcting any deficiencies the appraisal might have unearthed, and to reinforce the things the subordinate does correctly. Finally, appraisals can serve a useful *career-planning* purpose, by providing the opportunity to review the employee's career plans in light of his or her apparent strengths and weaknesses.

Who Should Do the Appraising?

❷ Answer the question, "Who should do the appraising?"

Appraisals by the immediate supervisor are still the heart of most appraisal processes.

Getting a supervisor's appraisal is relatively straightforward and also makes sense. The supervisor should be and usually is in the best position to observe and evaluate his or her subordinate's performance. The supervisor is also responsible for that person's performance.

Yet, although widely used, supervisors' ratings are no panacea, and relying only on them is not always advisable. For example, an employee's supervisor may not understand or appreciate how customers and colleagues who interact with the employee rate his or her performance. Furthermore, there is always some danger of bias for or against the employee. If so, managers have several appraisal options.

Appraisals by the immediate supervisor are still the heart of most appraisal processes.

PEER APPRAISALS With more firms using self-managing teams, appraisal of an employee by his or her peers—peer appraisal—is more popular. At one Australian electronics manufacturer for example, an employee due for an annual appraisal chooses an appraisal chairperson. The latter then selects one supervisor and three peers to evaluate the employee's work.

Research indicates that peer appraisals can be effective. One study involved undergraduates placed into self-managing work groups. The researchers found that peer appraisals had "an immediate positive impact on [improving] perception of open communication, task motivation, social loafing, group viability, cohesion, and satisfaction."[10]

RATING COMMITTEES Some companies use rating committees. A rating committee is usually composed of the employee's immediate supervisor and three or four other supervisors.

Using multiple raters is advantageous. It can help cancel out problems such as bias on the part of individual raters. It can also provide a way to include in the appraisal the different facets of an employee's performance observed by different appraisers. At a minimum, most appraisal processes require that the supervisor's boss sign off on any appraisals done by the supervisor.

It usually makes sense to have more than one supervisor appraise an employee. Multiple raters often see different facets of an employee's performance. Studies often find that the ratings obtained from different sources rarely match.[11] It's therefore advisable to obtain ratings from the supervisor, his or her boss, and perhaps another manager who is familiar with the employee's work.[12]

SELF-RATINGS Some employers collect employees' self-ratings, usually in conjunction with supervisors' ratings. The basic problem, of course, is that employees usually rate themselves higher than their supervisors or peers would rate them.[13] One study found that, when asked to rate their own job performances, 40% of employees in jobs of all types placed themselves in the top 10%, and virtually all remaining employees rated themselves at least in the top 50%.[14] In another study, subjects' self-ratings actually correlated negatively with their subsequent performance in an assessment center—the higher they appraised themselves, they worse they did in the center. In contrast, an average of the person's supervisor, peer, and subordinate ratings predicted the subjects' assessment center performance.[15]

APPRAISAL BY SUBORDINATES Anonymity affects upward feedback. Managers who get feedback from subordinates who identify themselves view the upward feedback process more positively than do managers who get anonymous feedback. However, subordinates are more comfortable giving anonymous responses, and those who must identify themselves tend to give inflated ratings.[16]

Upward feedback can improve a manager's performance. One study focused on 252 managers during five annual administrations of an upward feedback program. Managers who were initially rated poor or moderate "showed significant improvements in [their] upward feedback ratings over the five-year period." And, managers who met with their subordinates to discuss their upward feedback improved more than the managers who did not.[17]

360-DEGREE FEEDBACK With 360-degree feedback, the employer collects performance information all around an employee, from his or her supervisors, subordinates, peers, and internal or external customers, generally for developmental rather than pay purposes.[18] The usual process is to have the raters complete online appraisal surveys on the ratee. Computerized systems then compile all this feedback into individualized reports to ratees (see sample in Figure 7.2). The person may then meet with his or her supervisor to develop a self-improvement plan.

Results are mixed. Participants seem to prefer this approach, but one study concluded that multisource feedback led to "generally small" improvements on subsequent ratings by supervisors, peers, and subordinates. Improvement was most likely to occur when the feedback the person received indicated that change was necessary, and when the recipients believed that change was necessary and had a positive view of the change process.[19] Three-sixty degree appraisals are also more helpful when it's clear they're developmental

FIGURE 7.2 Online 360 Coworker Feedback

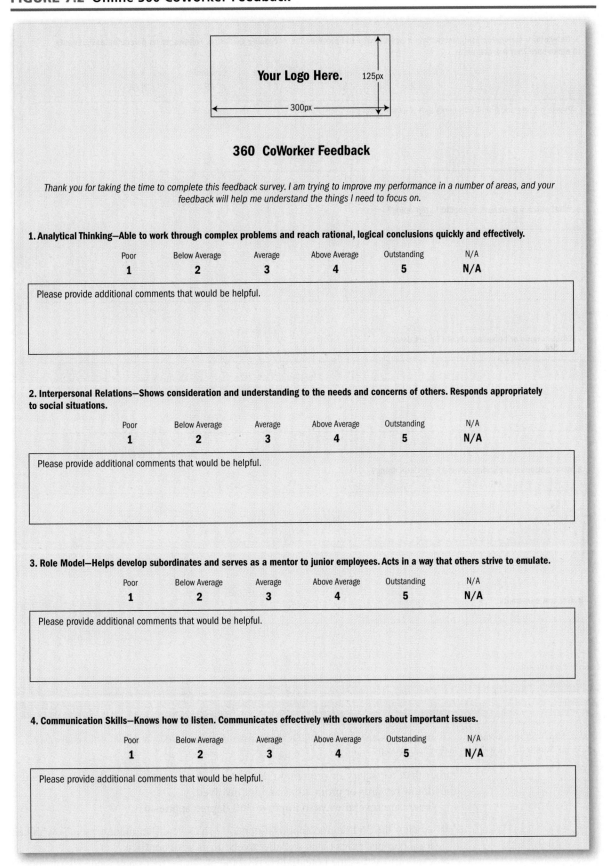

(continued)

FIGURE 7.2 Continued

5. Delegation—Delegates assignments when appropriate and provides the necessary guidance. Follows up on delegated assignments to make sure they are complete.

Poor	Below Average	Average	Above Average	Outstanding	N/A
1	2	3	4	5	N/A

Please provide additional comments that would be helpful.

6. What actions or behaviors should I stop doing?

7. What actions or behaviors should I start doing?

8. What actions or behaviors should I continue doing?

9. General comments:

Source: https://360.grapevinesurveys.com/evaluation.asp?sid=20066291246736, accessed January 10, 2008. Reprinted with permission of Grapevine Solutions, www.GrapevineEvaluations.com.

rather than for salary or promotion decisions; subordinates tend to be more candid when they know rewards or promotions are not involved.

There are several ways to improve 360-degree appraisals.

- Anchor the 360-degree appraisal items (such as "conflict management") with behavioral competencies (such as "effectively deals with conflicts").[20]
- Carefully assess the potential costs of the program, focus any feedback on specific goals, carefully train the people who are giving and receiving the feedback, and do not rely solely on 360-degree feedback for performance appraisal.[21]

■ With so many appraisers involved, make sure that the feedback the person receives is productive, unbiased, and development oriented.[22]

■ Reduce the administrative costs associated with collecting multisource feedback by using a Web-based system such as Visual 360 from SumTotal. This lets the rater log in, open a screen with a rating scale, and rate the person along a series of competencies with ratings such as "top five percent."[23]

APPRAISAL METHODS

The manager usually conducts the appraisal using one or more of the formal methods we describe in this section.

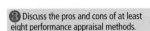

Graphic Rating Scale Method

A graphic rating scale lists a number of traits and a range of performance for each. As in Figure 7.3, a typical scale lists traits (such as teamwork) and a range of performance standards (in Figure 7.3 Below Expectations, Meets Expectations, and Role Model) for each trait. The supervisor rates each subordinate by circling or checking the score that best describes the subordinate's performance for each trait, then totals the scores for all traits.

Alternation Ranking Method

Ranking employees from best to worst on a trait or traits is another popular appraisal method. Because it is usually easier to distinguish between the worst and best employees than to rank them, an alternation ranking method is useful. With this method the supervisor uses a form like that in Figure 7.4 to specify the employee who is highest on the trait being measured and also the one who is the lowest, alternating between highest and lowest until all employees to be rated have been addressed.

Paired Comparison Method

With the paired comparison method, every subordinate to be rated is paired with and compared to every other subordinate on each trait.

For example, suppose there are five employees to be rated. With this method, a chart such as that in Figure 7.5 shows all possible pairs of employees for each trait. Then for each trait, the supervisor indicates (with a plus or minus) who is the better employee of the pair. Next, the number of times an employee is rated better is added up. In Figure 7.5 employee Maria ranked highest (has the most plus marks) for "quality of work," and Art ranked highest for "creativity."

Forced Distribution Method

With the forced distribution method, the manager places predetermined percentages of subordinates in performance categories, as when a professor "grades on a curve." About a fourth of Fortune 500 companies, including Sun Microsystems, Microsoft, ConcoPhillips, and Intel, use forced distribution.[24] General Electric popularized forced ranking, but now tells managers not to adhere to its famous 20/70/10 split. The advantages are that forced distribution prevents supervisors from leniently rating most employees "satisfactory," and makes top and bottom performers stand out.

EXAMPLES At California-based Sun Microsystems managers appraise employees in groups of about 30. There is a top 20%, a middle 70%, and a bottom 10%. The bottom 10% can either take a quick exit package or embark on a 90-day performance improvement action plan. If they're still in the bottom 10% in 90 days, they get a chance to resign and take severance pay. Some decide to stay, but "if it doesn't work out" the firm fires them without severance.[25] GE, which first popularized forced ranking, has been injecting more flexibility into its system. For instance, it no longer strictly adheres to its famous 20/70/10 split, and tells managers to use more common sense in assigning rankings.[26]

FIGURE 7.3 Sample Graphic Rating Form with Behavioral Examples

Sample Performance Rating Form

Employee's Name _____   Level: Entry-level employee

Manager's Name _____

Key Work Responsibilities   Results/Goals to be Achieved
1. _____   1. _____
2. _____   2. _____
3. _____   3. _____
4. _____   4. _____

Communication

1	2	3	4	5

Below Expectations	Meets Expectations	Role Model
Even with guidance, fails to prepare straight-forward communications, including forms, paperwork, and records, in a timely and accurate manner; products require minimal corrections. Even with guidance, fails to adapt style and materials to communicate straightforward information.	With guidance, prepares straightforward communications, including forms, paperwork, and records, in a timely and accurate manner; products require minimal corrections. With guidance, adapts style and materials to communicate straightforward information.	Independently prepares communications, such as forms, paperwork, and records, in a timely, clear, and accurate manner; products require few, if any, corrections. Independently adapts style and materials to communicate information.

Organizational Know-How

1	2	3	4	5

Below Expectations	Meets Expectations	Role Model
<performance standards appear here>	<performance standards appear here>	<performance standards appear here>

Personal Effectiveness

1	2	3	4	5

Below Expectations	Meets Expectations	Role Model
<performance standards appear here>	<performance standards appear here>	<performance standards appear here>

Teamwork

1	2	3	4	5

Below Expectations	Meets Expectations	Role Model
<performance standards appear here>	<performance standards appear here>	<performance standards appear here>

Achieving Business Results

1	2	3	4	5

Below Expectations	Meets Expectations	Role Model
<performance standards appear here>	<performance standards appear here>	<performance standards appear here>

FIGURE 7.3 Continued

Results Assessment

Accomplishment 1: _____

1	2	3	4	5
Low Impact		**Moderate Impact**		**High Impact**
The efficiency or effectiveness of operations remained the same or improved only minimally. The quality of products remained the same or improved only minimally.		The efficiency or effectiveness of operations improved quite a lot. The quality of products improved quite a lot.		The efficiency or effectiveness of operations improved tremendously. The quality of products improved tremendously.

Accomplishment 2: _____

1	2	3	4	5
Low Impact		**Moderate Impact**		**High Impact**
The efficiency or effectiveness of operations remained the same or improved only minimally. The quality of products remained the same or improved only minimally.		The efficiency or effectiveness of operations improved quite a lot. The quality of products improved quite a lot.		The efficiency or effectiveness of operations improved tremendously. The quality of products improved tremendously.

Narrative

_____

_____

_____

_____

_____

Areas to be Developed	Actions	Completion Date

Manager's Signature _____ Date _____

Employee's Signature _____ Date _____

The above employee signature indicates receipt of, but not necessarily concurrence with, the evaluation herein.

Source: Sample Performance Rating Form from Elaine D. Pulakos, *Performance Management: A Roadmap for Developing, Implementing and Evaluating Performance Management Systems* (SHRM Foundation, 2004), pp. 16–17.

FIGURE 7.4

Alternation Ranking Method

ALTERNATION RANKING SCALE

Trait: _____

For the trait you are measuring, list all the employees you want to rank. Put the highest-ranking employee's name on line 1. Put the lowest-ranking employee's name on line 20. Then list the next highest ranking on line 2, the next lowest ranking on line 19, and so on. Continue until all names are on the scale.

Highest-ranking employee

1. _____ 11. _____
2. _____ 12. _____
3. _____ 13. _____
4. _____ 14. _____
5. _____ 15. _____
6. _____ 16. _____
7. _____ 17. _____
8. _____ 18. _____
9. _____ 19. _____
10. _____ 20. _____

Lowest-ranking employee

DRAWBACKS While widely used, some balk at forced distribution appraisals. As most students know, forced distribution grading is unforgiving. With forced distribution, you're either in the top 5% or 10% (and thus get that "A"), or you're not. And, if you're in the bottom 5% or 10%, you get an "F," no questions asked. Your professor hasn't much wiggle room. Some must fail. In one survey 77% of responding employers were at least "somewhat satisfied" with forced ranking, while the rest were dissatisfied with it. The biggest complaints: 44% said it damages morale, and 47% said it creates interdepartmental inequities, since "high-performing teams must cut 10% of their workers while low-performing teams are still allowed to retain 90% of theirs."[27] Some writers refer unkindly to forced ranking as "Rank and Yank."[28]

FIGURE 7.5

Paired Comparison Method

Note: + means "better than," − means "worse than." For each chart, add up the number of +'s in each column to get the highest ranked employee.

FOR THE TRAIT "QUALITY OF WORK"

Employee rated:

As Compared to:	A Art	B Maria	C Chuck	D Diane	E José
A Art		+	+	−	−
B Maria	−		−	−	−
C Chuck	−	+		+	−
D Diane	+	+	−		+
E José	+	+	+	−	

↑ Maria ranks highest here

FOR THE TRAIT "CREATIVITY"

Employee rated:

As Compared to:	A Art	B Maria	C Chuck	D Diane	E José
A Art		−	−	−	−
B Maria	+		−	+	+
C Chuck	+	+		−	+
D Diane	+	−	+		−
E José	+	−	−	+	

↑ Art ranks highest here

Given this, employers need to be doubly careful to protect these appraisal plans from managerial abuse. Office politics and managerial bias can taint ratings. To protect against bias claims, employers should take several steps.[29] Appoint a review committee to review any employee's low ranking. Train raters to be objective. And consider using multiple raters in conjunction with the forced distribution approach.

Critical Incident Method

The critical incident method entails keeping a record of uncommonly good or undesirable examples of an employee's work-related behavior and reviewing it with the employee at predetermined times.

Employers often compile critical incidents to supplement a rating or ranking method. Keeping a running list of critical incidents provides concrete examples of what specifically the subordinates can do to eliminate any performance deficiencies, and provides opportunities for mid-year corrections if required. Compiling incidents all year also helps reduce supervisors' tendencies to unduly focus on just the last few weeks when appraising subordinates' performance.

Behaviorally Anchored Rating Scales

A behaviorally anchored rating scale (BARS) is an appraisal method that combines the benefits of critical incidents and quantitative ratings by anchoring a quantified scale with specific narrative examples of good and poor performance.

Figure 7.6 is an example. It shows the behaviorally anchored rating scale for the trait "salesmanship skills" used for armed forces recruiters. Note how the various performance levels, from 9 (high) to 1 (low), are anchored with specific behavioral examples such as "When a prospect states an objection to being in the Navy, the recruiter ends the conversation."

Appraisal Forms in Practice

In practice, appraisal forms often blend several approaches. For example, Figure 7.3 is basically a graphic rating scale supported with specific behavioral competency expectations. These expectations pinpoint what raters should look for. Even without using the more elaborate behaviorally anchored appraisal approach, behaviorally anchoring a graphic scale, as in Figure 7.3, can improve the reliability and validity of the appraisal scale.

The Management by Objectives Method

The term management by objectives (MBO) usually refers to a multi-step organization-wide goal-setting and appraisal program. MBO requires the manager to set specific measurable organizationally relevant goals with each employee, and then periodically discuss the latter's progress toward these goals. The steps are:

1. Set the organization's goals. Establish an organizationwide plan for next year and set goals.
2. Set departmental goals. Department heads and their superiors jointly set goals for their departments.
3. Discuss departmental goals. Department heads discuss the department's goals with all subordinates in the department and ask them to develop their own individual goals. In other words, how can each employee contribute to the department attaining its goals?
4. Define expected results (set individual goals). Department heads and their subordinates set short-term performance targets.
5. Conduct performance reviews and measure the results. Department heads compare the actual performance of each employee with expected results.
6. Provide feedback. Department heads hold periodic performance review meetings with subordinates to discuss and evaluate the subordinates' progress in achieving expected results.

FIGURE 7.6

Behaviorally Anchored Rating Scale

Source: Berk, Ronald A., *Performance Assessment: Methods and Applications.* Figure 3.2, p. 103. Copyright © 1986. Reproduced with permission of The Johns Hopkins University Press.

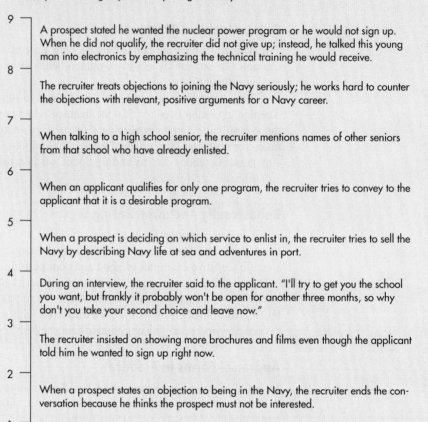

SALESMANSHIP SKILLS

Skillfully persuading prospects to join the Navy; using Navy benefits and opportunities effectively to sell the Navy; closing skills; adapting selling techniques appropriately to different prospects; effectively overcoming objectives to joining the Navy.

9 — A prospect stated he wanted the nuclear power program or he would not sign up. When he did not qualify, the recruiter did not give up; instead, he talked this young man into electronics by emphasizing the technical training he would receive.

8 — The recruiter treats objections to joining the Navy seriously; he works hard to counter the objections with relevant, positive arguments for a Navy career.

7 — When talking to a high school senior, the recruiter mentions names of other seniors from that school who have already enlisted.

6 — When an applicant qualifies for only one program, the recruiter tries to convey to the applicant that it is a desirable program.

5 — When a prospect is deciding on which service to enlist in, the recruiter tries to sell the Navy by describing Navy life at sea and adventures in port.

4 — During an interview, the recruiter said to the applicant. "I'll try to get you the school you want, but frankly it probably won't be open for another three months, so why don't you take your second choice and leave now."

3 — The recruiter insisted on showing more brochures and films even though the applicant told him he wanted to sign up right now.

2 — When a prospect states an objection to being in the Navy, the recruiter ends the conversation because he thinks the prospect must not be interested.

1

Computerized and Web-Based Performance Appraisals

Appraisals today are most often Web- or PC-based. For example, Employee Appraiser presents a menu of more than a dozen evaluation dimensions, including dependability, initiative, communication, decision making, leadership, judgment, and planning and productivity.[30] Within each dimension are various performance factors, again in menu form. For example, under "Communication" are separate factors for things like writing, verbal communication, and receptivity to feedback and criticism.

When the user clicks on a performance factor, he or she is presented with a sophisticated version of a graphic rating scale. However, instead of numbers, Employee Appraiser uses behaviorally anchored examples. For example, for *verbal communication* there are six choices, ranging from "presents ideas clearly" to "lacks structure." The manager chooses the phrase that most accurately describes the worker. Then Employee Appraiser generates an appraisal with sample text. The eAppraisal system from Halogen Software is another example.[31] Figure 7.7 presents an example of its online appraisal tool.

California-based Seagate Technology uses "Enterprise Suite" for managing the performance of its 39,000 employees.[32] Early in Seagate's first fiscal quarter, employees enter the system and set goals and development plans for themselves that make sense in terms of

FIGURE 7.7 Online Appraisal Tool

Seagate's corporate objectives. Employees update their plans quarterly, and then do self-evaluations at the end of the year, with follow-up reviews by their supervisors.

Electronic Performance Monitoring

Electronic performance monitoring (EPM) systems use computer network technology to allow managers access to their employees' computers and telephones. They thus allow managers to monitor the employees' rate, accuracy, and time spent working online.[33]

EPM can improve productivity in certain circumstances. For example, for more routine, less complex jobs, highly skilled and monitored subjects keyed in more data entries than did highly skilled unmonitored participants. However, EPM can also backfire. In this same study, low-skilled but highly monitored participants did more poorly than low-skilled, unmonitored participants. EPM also seems to raise employee stress.[34]

The accompanying *Global Issues in HR* feature discusses some special challenges in appraising employees abroad.

Global Issues in HR

Appraising Employees Abroad

Appraising someone with whom you work everyday is challenging enough. Installing a process for appraising expatriate employees (who move temporarily abroad) is even more challenging. For example, do you use the same appraisal process as the local subsidiary, or the one by which you would have appraised the person if he or she was still working at the home office?

One study found that, at least for large multinational companies, employers used the same forms and procedures abroad that they do at headquarters. The researchers interviewed expatriate employees and human resource managers of five MNE (multinational enterprise) subsidiaries of information technology firms Applied Material (American), Philips (Dutch), Hitachi (Japanese), Samsung (Korean), and Winbond (Taiwan). In brief, the researchers found that different firms used different forms and procedures. As they put it, "Divergent practices in goal setting, performance appraisal, and performance-related pay were largely attributed to the parent company's culture."[35] On the other hand, each of the five firms used standardized performance forms set by headquarters, and did not adapt them to local operating situations. They therefore apparently tried to maintain some consistency in both the appraisals and thus in the conclusions they could draw from those appraisals.

THE APPRAISAL FEEDBACK INTERVIEW

4 Explain how to conduct an appraisal feedback interview.

An appraisal usually culminates in an appraisal interview. Here the supervisor and subordinate review the appraisal and make plans to remedy deficiencies and reinforce strengths. Interviews like these can be uncomfortable because few people like to receive—or give—negative feedback.[36] Adequate preparation and effective implementation are therefore essential.

Preparing for the Appraisal Interview

Adequate preparation involves three steps. First, give the subordinate at least a week's notice to review his or her work, and to read over his or her job description, analyze problems, and compile questions and comments. Next, study his or her job description, compare the employee's performance to his or her standards, and review the files of the person's previous appraisals. Finally, choose the right place for the interview and schedule enough time for it. Conduct the interview in a private area where you won't be interrupted by phone calls or visitors. Find a mutually agreeable time for the interview and leave enough time—perhaps one-half-hour for lower-level personnel such as clerical workers and maintenance staff, and an hour or so for management employees.

Conducting the Interview

There are several things to keep in mind when actually conducting appraisal interviews.

■ First, the interview's main aim is to reinforce satisfactory performance or to diagnose and improve unsatisfactory performance. Probably the best way to help do this is to be direct and specific. Talk in terms of objective work data, using examples such as absences, quality records, inspection reports, and tardiness.

■ Second, get agreement before the subordinate leaves on how things will be improved and by when. An action plan showing steps and expected results can be useful. If a formal written warning is required, it should identify the standards under which the employee is judged, make it clear that the employee was aware of the standard, specify any violation of the standard, and show that the employee had an opportunity to correct his or her behavior.

■ Third, ensure that the process is fair. Letting the employee participate in the appraisal process by at least letting his or her opinions be heard is therefore essential.[37]

■ Fourth, deal with defensiveness. For example, when a person is accused of poor performance, the first reaction is usually denial. Such defensiveness is normal. It is prudent not to attack the person's defenses (for instance, by trying to "explain someone to themselves" by saying things like, "You know the real reason you're using that excuse is that you can't bear to be blamed for anything"). Another approach is to postpone action—for instance, by giving the person a few minutes to cool down after being informed of unsatisfactory performance.

■ Finally, keep in mind that (just as job candidates try to influence recruiters by ingratiating themselves) subordinates try to influence their ratings by using "impression management" tactics during appraisal interviews (for instance nodding agreement and looking attentive).[38] Therefore, focus on the employee's performance.

The *Personal Competencies* feature provides additional advice.

Personal Competencies

Building Your *Communications* Skills

Few supervisory situations demand better interpersonal communication skills than does appraising employees' performance. People don't like giving or receiving negative feedback, and appraisals thus tend to be tense, unproductive affairs. Clear, unambiguous, effective, communication is vital.

BARRIERS TO EFFECTIVE COMMUNICATION   Start by understanding the barriers to effective communication. These include:

■ Ambiguous, muddled messages. "Say what you mean, and mean what you say" is good advice. Few things cause more communication breakdowns than do ambiguous, muddled messages. For instance, don't say, "as soon as you can" if you mean "tomorrow."

■ Physical barriers. Make sure physical barriers like street noise, frequent interruptions, and the clattering of machines don't reduce your comments' impact.

■ Emotions. Emotions influence what you say and how you do things. An angry or frustrated person may ignore even the most persuasive argument. Someone in a good mood may be more agreeable.

■ Perception. Misperceptions can ruin communications. This is because people's needs and situation shape how they see and hear things. If you're concerned about losing your job, you may be jumpy if your boss schedules an appraisal interview with you.

METHODS FOR IMPROVING INTERPERSONAL COMMUNICATIONS   Methods for improving interpersonal communications include:

■ Pay attention. Communication means "exchanging information in such a way that you create a common basis of understanding and feeling." You are unlikely to create such a common understanding if you don't listen attentively, and make it clear that the person has your undivided attention.

(continued)

- Make yourself clear. For example, if you mean immediately, say "immediately," not "as soon as you can."
- Be an active listener. Communication pioneer Carl Rogers says that *active listeners* don't just listen to what the speaker says; they also try to understand and respond to the feelings underlying the words. They try to understand the person from his or her point of view and to convey the message, "I understand." Suggestions include *listen for total meaning* (try to understand the feelings underlying what the person is saying), *reflect feelings* (for instance, by replying with something like "they're pushing you pretty hard, aren't they?"), and watch for *all cues* (not all communication is verbal; facial expressions and gestures reveal feelings too).

APPRAISAL PROBLEMS

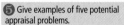 Give examples of five potential appraisal problems.

Recently a long-term U.S. National Aeronautics and Space Administration employee smuggled a revolver into the space center and, after speaking with his former supervisor for several minutes, said, "You're the one who's going to get me fired" and murdered him. The supervisor had apparently given the shooter a poor job review, and the person feared dismissal.[39]

While such reactions are not the norm, few supervisory tasks are fraught with more peril than appraising subordinates' performance.[40] Employees tend to be overly optimistic about what their ratings are, and also know that their raises, career progress, and peace of mind may hinge on how you rate them. This alone should make it somewhat difficult to rate performance. Even more problematic, however, are the numerous structural problems (discussed next) that can cast doubt on just how fair the process is.[41] Fortunately, as explained in this section, there are also ways to avoid or solve these problems.

Unclear Standards

The unclear standards appraisal problem means the appraisal scale is too open to interpretation. As in Figure 7.8, the rating scale may seem objective, but would probably result in unfair appraisals because the traits and degrees of merit are open to interpretation. For example, different supervisors would probably define "good" performance differently. The same is true of traits such as "quality of work." The best way to rectify this problem is to develop and include descriptive phrases that define each trait and degree of merit.

Halo Effect

The halo effect means that the rating you give a subordinate on one trait (such as "gets along with others") influences the way you rate the person on other traits (such as "quantity of work"). Thus, an unfriendly employee might be rated unsatisfactory for all

FIGURE 7.8 A Graphic Rating Scale with Unclear Standards

	Excellent	Good	Fair	Poor
Quality of work				
Quantity of work				
Creativity				
Integrity				

Note: For example, what exactly is meant by "good," "quantity of work," and so forth?

traits rather than just for the trait "gets along with others." Being aware of this problem is a major step toward avoiding it.

Central Tendency

The central tendency problem refers to a tendency to rate all employees about average. For example, if the rating scale ranges from 1 to 7, a supervisor may tend to avoid the highs (6 and 7) and lows (1 and 2) and rate most of his or her employees between 3 and 5. Such restriction can distort the evaluations, making them less useful for promotion, salary, and counseling purposes. Ranking employees instead of using a graphic rating scale can eliminate this problem because all employees must be ranked and thus can't all be rated average.

Leniency or Strictness

Conversely, some supervisors tend to rate all their subordinates consistently high or low, a problem referred to as the strictness/leniency problem. Again, one solution is to insist on ranking subordinates, because that forces the supervisor to distinguish between high and low performers.

The appraisal you do may be less objective than you realize. One study focused on how personality influenced the peer evaluations students gave their peers. Raters who scored higher on "conscientiousness" tended to give their peers lower ratings; those scoring higher on "agreeableness" gave higher ratings.[42]

Bias

Indeed, appraisees' (and appraisers') personal characteristics (such as age, race, and gender) can affect their ratings, often quite apart from each ratee's actual performance. Appraisals often say more about the appraiser than about the appraised.[43] Studies suggest that "rater idiosyncratic biases account for the largest percentage of the observed variances in performance ratings."[44]

EXAMPLE   For example, one study found that raters penalized successful women for their success.[45] Earlier studies had found that raters tend to demean women's performance, particularly when they excel at what seems like male-typical tasks, and that's exactly what happened here. In this new study, the researchers told the subject-raters that they'd view information about someone who was one of 30 people who had just finished a year-long management training program. The researchers were careful to make it seem that the training program was mostly for male employees, for instance, by emphasizing that most of the trainees were men. The researchers found,

> "there are many things that lead an individual to be disliked, including obnoxious behavior, arrogance, stubbornness, and pettiness, [but] it is only women, not men, for whom a unique propensity toward dislike is created by success in a nontraditional work situation."[46]

Table 7.1 summarizes the pros and cons of the most popular rating methods.

Legal Issues in Performance Appraisal

Performance appraisals play a central role at work. They affect raises, promotions, training opportunities, and other HR actions. If the manager is inept or biased in making the appraisal, how can one defend the promotion decisions that stem from the appraisal? In one case, a 36-year-old supervisor ranked a 62-year-old subordinate at the bottom of the department's rankings, and then terminated him. The U.S. Court of Appeals for the 10th Circuit determined that the appraisal and termination might have been influenced by the discriminatory motives of the younger boss.[47] The accompanying *HR in Practice* feature on page 230 summarizes some steps to make appraisals more legally defensible.

TABLE 7.1 Important Similarities and Differences, and Advantages and Disadvantages of Appraisal Tools

Tool	Similarities/Differences	Advantages	Disadvantages
Graphic rating scale	These are both absolute scales aimed at measuring an employee's *absolute* performance based on objective criteria as listed on the scales.	Simple to use; provides a quantitative rating for each employee.	Standards may be unclear; halo effect, central tendency, leniency, bias can also be problems.
BARS		Provides behavioral "anchors." BARS is very accurate.	Difficult to develop.
Alternation ranking	These are both methods for judging the *relative* performance of employees relative to each other, but still based on objective criteria.	Simple to use (but not as simple as graphic rating scales); avoids central tendency and other problems of rating scales.	Can cause disagreements among employees and may be unfair if all employees *are*, in fact, excellent.
Forced distribution method		End up with a predetermined number of people in each group.	Appraisal results depend on the adequacy of your original choice of cutoff points.
Critical incident method	These are both more subjective, narrative methods for appraising performance, generally based, however, on the employee's absolute performance.	Helps specify what is "right" and "wrong" about the employee's performance; forces supervisor to evaluate subordinates on an ongoing basis.	Difficult to rate or rank employees relative to one another.
MBO		Tied to jointly agreed-upon performance objectives.	Time consuming.

HR in Practice

Making Appraisals More Defensible

Steps to take to ensure your appraisals are legally defensible include:

- Base the performance appraisal criteria on a documented job analysis.
- At the start of the period, communicate performance standards to employees in writing.
- Base appraisals on separate evaluations of each of the job's performance dimensions. Use of a single "overall" rating of performance or ranking of employees is not acceptable to the courts.[48] Courts often characterize such systems as vague. Courts generally require that separate ratings along each performance dimension be combined through some formal weighting system to yield a summary score.

- Include an employee appeals process. Employees should have the opportunity to review and make comments, written or verbal, about their appraisals before they become final and should have a formal appeals process through which to appeal their ratings.
- One appraiser should never have absolute authority to determine a personnel action.
- Document all information bearing on a personnel decision in writing. "Without exception, courts condemn informal performance evaluation practices that eschew documentation."[49]
- Train supervisors to use the appraisal instruments. If formal rater training is not possible, at least provide raters with written instructions on how to use the rating scale.[50]

PERFORMANCE MANAGEMENT

What Is Performance Management?

If you were to spend several days in Toyota's Burnaston, Derbyshire, Corolla plant, the absence of "appraisal" as most of us know it would soon be apparent. Supervisors don't sit down with individual employees to fill out forms and appraise them. Instead, teams of employees monitor their own results, continuously adjusting how they and their team members do things, to align those results with the work team's standards and with the plant's overall quality and productivity needs. Team members who need further training receive it, and procedures that need changing get changed. This is *performance management* in action. Recall that performance management is a *continuous* process of identifying, measuring, and developing the performance of individuals and teams and *aligning* their performance with the organization's *goals*.[51]

PERFORMANCE APPRAISAL VS. PERFORMANCE MANAGEMENT Four things distinguish a performance management program from performance appraisal.

1. First, unlike performance appraisal, performance management never just means meeting with a subordinate once or twice a year to "review your performance." It means *continuous, daily, or weekly* interactions and feedback to ensure continuous improvement in the employee's and team's capacity and performance.[52]
2. Second, performance management is always *goal directed*. The ongoing performance reviews involve explicitly comparing the employee's or team's actual performance against goals that make sense in terms of the company's strategic goals.
3. Third, performance management therefore also means the company has in place a *strategic plan*, and that each employee's and team's goals make sense and *flow from* that strategic plan.
4. Fourth, performance management means *continuously reevaluating and (if need be) modifying* how the employee and team get their work done. Depending on the issue, this may mean providing additional training, changing work procedures, or instituting new incentive plans, for instance.

Why Performance Management?

Employers are migrating from performance appraisal to performance management for three main reasons: *total quality, appraisal issues, and strategic planning.*

TOTAL QUALITY First, performance management is a quality-oriented process. More managers today are adapting the total quality management (TQM) philosophy advocated by management experts like W. Edwards Deming. Basically, Deming argued that if things go wrong, it's not the employee, it's the system.

Specifically, he said an employee's performance is more a function of things like training, communication, tools, and supervision than of his or her own motivation. Performance appraisals tend to focus more on problems—what's the employee doing wrong? In line with Deming's philosophy, performance management focuses on using continuous collegial feedback and (when necessary) changes to the management system (training, incentives, procedures, and so on) to improve performance.

APPRAISAL ISSUES Second, we've seen that traditional performance appraisals are subject to numerous problems, and are often not just useless but tense and counterproductive.[53] Indeed, there is an obvious flaw in appraising employees just once or twice per year: If things need improving, why wait 6 months to do something about it? Performance management requires continuous feedback.

STRATEGIC PLANNING Third, employers know that the challenge in strategic planning isn't just designing good strategies; it is getting employees to execute them. For example, researchers studied 1,800 large companies. About 90% had detailed strategic plans with strategic goals. However, only about one in eight achieved their strategic goals.[54]

Several things account for this. Some managers don't even *keep track of performance*. In one study, consultants found that most of the 200 firms they surveyed didn't bother comparing performance with goals: "In our experience, less than 15% of the companies make it a regular practice to go back and compare the business's results with the performance forecast for each unit."[55] Other managers do a poor job of *communicating goals to employees*. Others fail to show employees how their goals relate to the *company's broader strategies*.

In a nutshell, many managers spend a lot of time formulating strategic plans and then drop the ball. They do so by not communicating their plans to employees, by not assigning each employee clear goals and responsibilities, and by not monitoring and feeding back to employees their actual progress.

Performance management programs aim to avoid such strategic miscommunications. With performance management, employees get goals that flow from and make sense in terms of the company's strategy. And, managers and employees continuously compare the team's actual performance against its goals, taking corrective action as needed.

Information Technology-Supported Performance Management

⑥ Explain how to install a performance management program.

The availability of new information technology-based tools provides a new and powerful way to manage employee performance. These tools are *strategy maps, balanced scorecards, digital dashboards,* and *performance management software*. The basic idea is to assign goals to each team, and then to use the information technology tools to continuously monitor, on PC displays, how each team is doing. This gives management a real-time bird's-eye view of how the company is doing in terms of (1) carrying out the tasks required to achieve its strategic goals, and (2) actually achieving those goals.

Figure 7.9 summarizes this process. It starts with the strategy map.

strategy map
Diagram that summarizes the chain of major activities that contribute to a company's success.

THE STRATEGY MAP The **strategy map** is a graphical tool that summarizes the chain of activities that contribute to a company's success. It thus shows the "big picture" of how each department's or team's performance contributes to achieving the company's overall strategic goals.

Figure 7.10 presents a strategy map for EasyJet airlines. EasyJet pursues a low-cost leader competitive strategy. It therefore tailors all its activities to delivering low-cost, convenient service. The strategy map for EasyJet succinctly lays out the hierarchy of big activities required for EasyJet to succeed. At the top is achieving company-wide, strategic financial goals. The strategy map shows the chain of activities that help EasyJet achieve these goals. To boost revenues and profitability, EasyJet needs to fly fewer planes (to keep costs down), attract and keep customers, maintain low prices, and maintain on-time flights. In turn (further down the strategy map), on-time flights and low prices require fast turnaround. And, fast turn around requires motivated, committed ground and flight crews.

FIGURE 7.9

Summary of Performance-Management Process

Source: From Dessler. *Managing Now,* 1e. © 2008 South-Western, a part of Cengage Learning, Inc. All rights reserved. Reproduced by permission. Text/images may not be modified or reproduced in any way without prior written permission of the publisher. www.cengage.com/permissions.

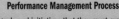

Performance Management Process
A system that focuses employees on the goals and initiatives that they must execute for the company to succeed, and that gives managers a timely way to monitor performance and take corrective action.

Strategy Map	Balanced Scorecard	Digital Dashboard
Graphical tool that summarizes the chain of activities that contribute to a company's success, and so shows employees the "big picture" of how their performance contributes to achieving the company's overall strategic goals.	A process for managing employees' performance and for aligning all employees with key objectives, by assigning financial and non-financial goals, monitoring and assessing performance, and quickly taking corrective action.	Presents the manager with desktop graphs and charts, so he or she gets a picture of where the company has been and where it's going, in terms of each activity in the strategy map.

FIGURE 7.10 Strategy Map for EasyJet Airlines

The strategy map enables management to see at a glance each of the activities that contribute to EasyJet's success. It also helps employees understand how their efforts mesh with the big picture. For example, each ground crew employee can see that by working hard to turn planes around fast, he or she is contributing to a chain of activities that help make EasyJet profitable. And, it shows EasyJet's human resource managers the sorts of employee skills and behaviors its HR policies need to promote (like building employee commitment).

THE BALANCED SCORECARD Once the manager outlines the activities with the strategy map, he or she can attach measurable targets to each activity. For example, "What do we mean by faster turnaround time?" and "what do we mean by on-time flights?"

The *balanced scorecard process* helps the manager do this. The **balanced scorecard** is not a scorecard; it refers to a process for assigning financial and nonfinancial goals to the chain of activities required for achieving the company's strategic aims, and for continuously monitoring results. In particular, the balanced scorecard process involves:

balanced scorecard
Refers to a process for assigning financial and nonfinancial goals to the chain of activities required for achieving the company's strategic aims, and for continuously monitoring results.

- Assigning financial and nonfinancial goals to the activities in the strategy map,
- Informing all employees of their goals,
- Monitoring and assessing performance, and
- Taking corrective action as required. The "balanced" in balanced scorecard refers to a balance of goals. It includes a balance of financial and nonfinancial goals or measures,

of short-term and long-term goals, and of external goals (for instance, what the customer thinks) and internal goals (for instance, airplane turnaround time). For example, EasyJet might measure turnaround time in terms of "improve turnaround time from an average of 30 minutes per plane to 26 minutes per plane this year." It might measure customer satisfaction with periodic surveys.

The great advantage of the balanced scorecard process is that it is predictive. Financial goals such as budgets are better at telling managers how they've done than how they'll do tomorrow. Continuously monitoring a balanced set of measures can signal problems ahead. Thus, it might prompt a EasyJet Airlines manager to say, "Our customer service ratings dipped, and, since good customer service leads to more customers and in turn to future revenues, we should take corrective action now."

PERFORMANCE MANAGEMENT SOFTWARE The balanced scorecard process produces objectives, targets, and initiatives for each activity in the strategy map. Therefore, even a simple strategy map produces dozens of objectives, measures, and initiatives. How is the manager to monitor, integrate, and analyze information on the performance for all employees and activities on all these measures?

Managers now use special performance management software systems to do this. These systems integrate and store information from hundreds or thousands of sources (for instance, feedback from customer surveys, daily airplane turnaround statistics, employee performance measures, and on-time flights). They employ built-in analytical tools to provide managers with continuous, real-time updates regarding the company's performance. These systems also enable managers to analyze the causal linkages among strategy map activities. For example, EasyJet's managers might use such a system to better understand how much of an effect airplane turnaround time has on profitability. The performance management systems then generally present the summarized information the managers need in computerized "digital dashboards."

digital dashboard
Presents the manager with desktop graphs and charts, so he or she gets a picture of where the company has been and where it's going, *in terms of each activity in the strategy map.*

THE DIGITAL DASHBOARD The saying "a picture is worth a thousand words" explains the purpose of the digital dashboard. A **digital dashboard** (like that in Figure 7.11) presents the manager with desktop graphs and charts, so he or she gets a picture of where the company has been and where it's going, *in terms of each activity in the strategy map.* It is, in effect, the "scoreboard" in the balanced scorecard process. The dashboard takes all the results of the number-crunching by the company's performance management software, and presents it to the manager in an intelligible form. For example, a top manager's dashboard for EasyJet might display daily trends for strategy map activities such as fast turnaround, attracting and keeping customers, and on-time flights. This gives the manager time take to corrective action. For example, if ground crews are turning planes around slower today, financial results tomorrow may decline unless the manager takes action.[56]

Like a car's dashboard, a digital dashboard also presents information so it grabs the manager's attention (perhaps a graph blinking red if turnaround time is rising). For example, SAS Software's Strategic Performance Management package is a Web-based system that produces alerts "that call employees to action when performance is not meeting targets."[57]

Performance management software systems like these help managers make better decisions. For example, Oracle's Balanced Scorecard package lets management compare performance against industry peers, as well as against internal budgets and historical data. Managers, from their desktops, can click on any display to perform more detailed analyses. As the managing director of a Danish mortgage company says, "When I turn on my computer in the morning, our scorecard is the first thing I see. . . . If I discover any deviations of the key figures I contact the person responsible for the specific area."[58]

The accompanying Improving Productivity feature describes how one employer created an information technology-based performance management system.

FIGURE 7.11 Digital Dashboard

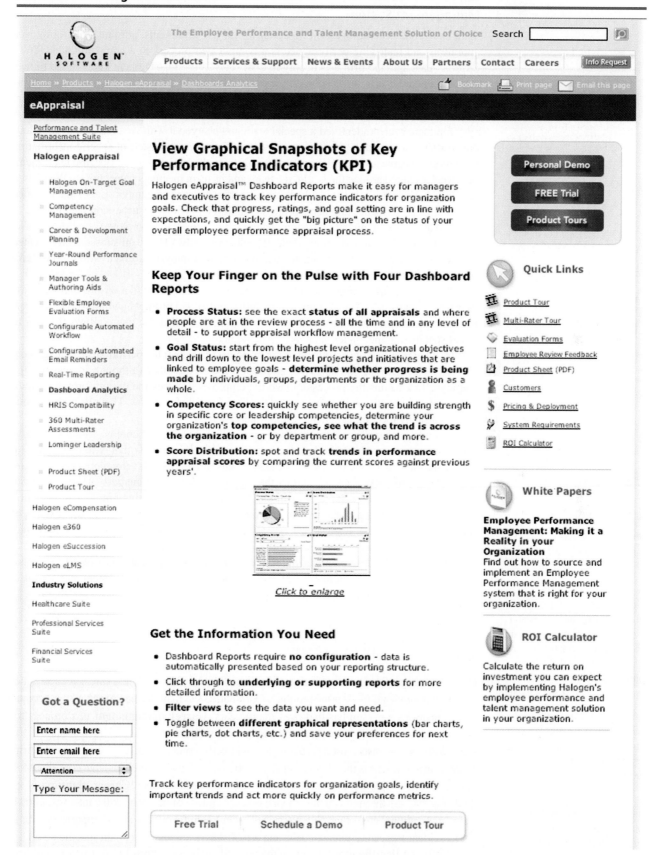

Improving Productivity Through HRIS: RW's New Performance Management System

With over 100,000 employees in 36 countries on five continents, administering employee appraisals and managing performance is a complicated process in a company like TRW.[59] Several years ago, the firm was deeply in debt. TRW's top management knew it had to take steps to make the firm more competitive and performance driven. At the time, most of the firm's far-flung departments used their own paper-based appraisal systems. Top management decided that a company-wide performance management system was a top priority.

Top management identified a special team and charged it with creating a "one company, one system" performance management system. The team consisted of several information technology experts, and key HR representatives from the business units. Because team members were scattered around the world, the team and its team meetings were entirely Web-based and virtual. Their aim was to quickly develop a performance management system that included goal setting, performance appraisal, professional development, and succession planning.

The team created an online system, one in which most TRW employees and supervisors worldwide could input and review their data electronically. (The team subsequently created an equivalent paper-based system, for use by certain employees abroad, who did not have easy access to the Web.)

To facilitate filling in the online form's pages, the team created a wizard that leads the user from step to step. The system also includes embedded prompts and pull-down menus. For example, in the "demonstrated strengths" area, the pull-down menu allows the user to select specific competencies such as "financial acumen."

In practice, either the employee or the manager can trigger the performance management process by completing the appraisal and sending it to the other (although it's usually the employee that begins the process). Once the employee finishes the online form, a system-generated e-mail notifies the manager that the form is ready for review. Then the two fine-tune the appraisal by meeting in person, and by interacting online.

The new performance management system produced many benefits. It focuses everyone's attention on goal-oriented performance, specifically on what that employee needs to do to contribute to achieving TRW's strategic goals. It identifies development needs that are both relevant to TRW's needs, and to the employee. It gives managers instant access to employee performance data. (For example, by clicking a "managing employees" function on the online system, a manager can see an onscreen overview of the assessment status of each of his or her subordinates.) It gives all managers access to an employee database (so, for instance, a search for an engineer with Chinese language skills takes just a few minutes). And, the system lets the manager quickly review the development needs of all his or her employees. The result is an integrated, goal-oriented employee development and appraisal performance management process.

CAREER MANAGEMENT

career
The occupational positions a person has had over many years.

career management
A process for enabling the employees to better understand and develop their career skills and interests, and to use the skills and interests most effectively both within the company and, if necessary, after they leave the firm.

career development
The lifelong series of activities that contribute to a person's career exploration, establishment, success, and fulfillment.

career planning
The deliberate process through which someone becomes aware of personal skills, interests, knowledge, motivations, and other characteristics; and establishes action plans to attain specific goals.

Once you've appraised their performance, it's usually advisable to address career-related issues and to communicate these issues to the subordinates. We may define **career** as the occupational positions a person has had over many years. **Career management** is a process for enabling employees to better understand and develop their career skills and interests, and to use these skills and interests most effectively both within the company and after they leave the firm. **Career development** is the lifelong series of activities (such as workshops) that contribute to a person's career exploration, establishment, success, and fulfillment. **Career planning** is the deliberate process through which someone becomes aware of personal skills, interests, knowledge, motivations, and other characteristics; acquires information about opportunities and choices; identifies career-related goals; and establishes action plans to attain specific goals.

We'll see that the employee's manager and employer should play roles in guiding and developing the employee's career. However, the employee must always accept full responsibility for his or her own career development and career success.

The Employee's Role

7 Explain how to design a career management program.

For the employee, career planning means matching individual strengths and weaknesses with occupational opportunities and threats. The person wants to pursue occupations, jobs, and a career that capitalizes on his or her interests, aptitudes, values, and skills. He or she also wants to choose occupations, jobs, and a career that makes sense in terms of projected future demand for various types of occupations. There is a wealth of sources people can turn to.

SKILLS AND APTITUDES The process logically starts with identifying one's occupational strengths, weaknesses, preferences, aptitudes, and skills. As an example, career-counseling expert John Holland says that personality (including values, motives, and needs) is one career choice determinant. For example, a person with a strong social orientation might be attracted to careers that entail interpersonal rather than intellectual or physical activities and to occupations such as social work. Based on research with his Vocational Preference Test (VPT), Holland found six basic personality types or orientations. Individuals can use his Self Directed Search (SDS) test (available at www.self-directed-search.com) to assess their occupational orientations and preferred occupations.

The SDS has an excellent reputation, but the career seeker needs to be somewhat wary of some of the other online career assessment sites. One study of 24 no-cost online career assessment Web sites concluded that they were easy to use, but suffered from insufficient validation and confidentiality. However, a number of online career assessment instruments such as Career Key (www.careerkey.org) do reportedly provide validated and useful information.[60]

IDENTIFY HIGH-POTENTIAL OCCUPATIONS Learning about yourself is only half the job of choosing an occupation. You also have to identify those occupations that are right (given your occupational orientations, skills, career anchors, and occupational preferences) as well as those that will be in high demand in the years to come.

Sometimes, there's no good substitute for actually trying a variety of jobs. Another useful way to learn about and compare and contrast occupations is through the Internet. For example, the United Kingdom's Department for Work and Pensions (www.dwp.gov.uk) provides detailed descriptions and information on hundreds of occupations.

SHOULD THE PERSON CHANGE JOBS? An employee unhappy with his or her job can do several things short of changing occupations. First, if you are satisfied with your occupation and where you work, but not with your job as it now is, *reconfigure your job*. For example, consider alternative work arrangements such as part-time work, flexible hours, or telecommuting; delegate or eliminate the job functions that you least prefer; and seek out a "stretch assignment" that will let you work on something that you find challenging.[61] Second, *enhance your networks*. For instance, discuss your career goals with role models or become a board member for a nonprofit organization so you can interact with new people.

MENTORING Having a mentor—a senior person who is a sounding board for career questions and concerns, and who provides career-related guidance and support—can significantly enhance career satisfaction and success.[62] Suggestions for finding and using a mentor include:

- Choose an appropriate potential mentor. The mentor should be able to remain objective to offer good career advice.
- Make it easier for a potential mentor to agree to your request by clarifying what you expect in terms of time and advice.
- Have an agenda. Bring an agenda to your first mentoring meeting that lays out key issues and topics for discussion.
- Respect the mentor's time. Be selective about the work-related issues that you bring to the table.
- Mandatory mentoring is OK. Studies suggest that mandatory participation is no less effective than voluntary participation in a mentoring program.[63]

Having a mentor can significantly enhance career satisfaction and success.

- Match mentors. However, having input into the mentor matching is important. Both the mentor and a protégé should have some influence on who the company matches them with.[64]
- Provide training. Finally, provide participants with training aimed at enabling them to get the most out of the mentoring relationship.[65]

Many employers, like Charles Schwab and Bank of America, offer formal mentoring programs.[66] The accounting firm KPMG made an online mentoring program part of its "employer of choice" initiative. This program also includes shared time off, flexible work schedules, and community volunteer opportunities with pay and benefits.[67] Dow Chemical Co. has a Web-based mentor technology similar to a Google search. It enables Dow employees who are seeking mentors to screen lists of potential Dow mentors online.[68]

The Employer's Role in Career Management

The employer's career development tasks depend partly on how long the employee has been with the firm. *Before hiring*, realistic job interviews can help prospective employees more accurately gauge whether the job is a good fit with a candidate's skills and interests.

Especially for recent college graduates, *the first job* can be crucial for building confidence and a more realistic picture of what he or she can and cannot do: Providing challenging first jobs (rather than relegating new employees to "jobs where they can't do any harm") and having an experienced mentor who can help the person learn the ropes are important. Some refer to this as preventing reality shock, a phenomenon that occurs when a new employee's high expectations and enthusiasm confront the reality of a boring, unchallenging job.

After the person has been *on the job* for a while, new employer career management roles arise. Career-oriented appraisals—in which the manager is trained not just to appraise the employee but also to match the person's strengths and weaknesses with a feasible career path and required development work—is one important step. Similarly, providing periodic job rotation can help the person develop a more realistic picture of what he or she is (and is not) good at, and thus the sort of future career moves that might be best. Some innovative career development activities include:[69]

1. Provide each employee with an individual career development budget. He or she can use this budget for learning about career options and personal development.

2. Offer online career centers. These might include career development materials, career workshops, and also provide individual career coaches for career guidance.
3. Encourage role reversal. Have employees temporarily work in different positions in order to develop a better appreciation of their occupational strengths and weaknesses.

Figure 7.12 lists HR activities that can impact and support employee career planning and development

Gender Issues in Career Development

Women and men face different challenges as they advance through their careers. In one study, promoted women had to receive higher performance ratings than promoted men to get promoted, "suggesting that women were held to stricter standards for promotion."[70] Women report greater barriers (such as being excluded from informal networks) than do men, and more difficulty getting developmental assignments and geographic mobility opportunities. Women have to be more proactive than men just to be considered for such assignments, and employers therefore need to focus on breaking down the barriers that impede women's career progress. One study concluded that three corporate career development activities—fast-track programs, individual career counseling, and career planning workshops—were less available to women than to men.[71] Many call this combination of subtle and not-so-subtle barriers to women's progress the *glass ceiling*.

MINORITY WOMEN In these matters, minority women may be particularly at risk. Women of color hold only a small percentage of professional and managerial private-sector positions. The minority women in one survey several years ago reported that the main barriers to advancement included not having an influential mentor (47%), lack of informal networking

FIGURE 7.12

List of Employer HR Actions that Can Impact Career Planning and Development

Source: Adapted from "Career Development in Organizations and Beyond: Balancing Traditional and Contemporary Viewpoints," *Human Resource Management Review* 16 (2006): 131.

- Job postings
- Formal education/tuition reimbursement
- Performance appraisal for career planning
- Counseling by manager
- Lateral moves/job rotations
- Counseling by HR
- Pre-retirement programs
- Succession planning
- Formal mentoring
- Dual ladder programs (options for non-managers to move up)
- Career booklets/pamphlets
- Written individual career plans
- Career workshops
- Assessment center
- Peer appraisal
- Upward appraisal
- Appraisal committees
- Training programs for managers
- Orientation/induction programs
- Diversity management
- Expatriation/repatriation

In one study, promoted women had to receive higher performance ratings than promoted men to get promoted.

with influential colleagues (40%), lack of company role models for members of the same racial or ethnic group (29%), and a lack of high-visibility assignments (28%).[72]

Adding to the problem is the fact that some corporate career development programs may actually be inconsistent with the needs of minority and nonminority women. For example, such programs may assume that career paths are sequential and continuous; yet the need to stop working for a time to attend to family needs often characterizes the career paths of many people of color and women (and perhaps men).[73]

Managing Promotions and Transfers

Promotions are one of the more significant career decisions to result from the performance appraisal. In developing promotion policies, employers need to address several issues.

A main issue concerns seniority versus competence. Competence is normally the basis for promotions. However, in many organizations civil service or union requirements and similar constraints still give an edge to more senior applicants.

Furthermore, if competence is to be the basis for promotion, how should we measure it? Defining past performance is usually straightforward. Managers use performance appraisals for this. However, sizing up how even a high-performing employee will do in a new, more challenging job is not so easy. Innumerable great salespeople turn out to be dreadful managers, for instance. Many employers therefore use formal selection devices like tests and (particularly) assessment centers to supplement performance appraisals.

With firms downsizing and flattening their organizations, "promotions" today often mean lateral moves or transfers. In such situations, the promotional aspect is not so much a higher level job or more pay. Instead, it's the opportunity to assume new, same-level responsibilities (such as a salesperson moving into HR) or increased, enriched decision-making responsibilities within the same job.

A transfer is a move from one job to another, usually with no change in salary or grade. Employees may seek transfers not just for advancement but also for noncareer reasons, such as better hours, location of work, and so on.

Retirement Counseling

For many employees, years of appraisals and career planning end with retirement.

Retirement planning is a significant issue for employers. In the United States, the number of 25- to 34-year-olds is growing relatively slowly, and the number of 35- to 44-year-olds is declining. Furthermore, "In the past few years, companies have been so focused on downsizing to contain costs that they largely neglected a looming threat to their competitiveness. A severe shortage of talented workers."[74]

So, with many older employees moving towards traditional retirement age, employers face a labor shortage. Many have wisely chosen to fill their staffing needs in part with current or soon-to-be in which "shorter hours, lighter duties and other perks entice older workers to stay on the job."[75]

Therefore, "retirement planning" is no longer just for helping current employees slip into retirement.[76] It can also enable the employer to retain, in some capacity, the skills and brain power of those who would normally retire and leave the firm. Fortuitously, 78% of employees in one survey said they expect to continue working in some capacity after normal retirement age (64% said they want to do so part-time). Only about a third said they plan to continue work for financial reasons; about 43% said they just wanted to remain active.[77]

Employers should conduct the necessary numerical analyses of pending retirements. This should include a demographic analysis (including a census of the company's employees), a determination of the average retirement age for the company's employees, and a review of how retirement is going to impact the employer's health care and pension benefits. The employer can then determine the extent of the "retirement problem," and take fact-based steps to address it.[78]

METHODS Employers seeking to recruit and/or retain retirees should take several steps. The general idea is to institute human resource policies that encourage and support older workers' employment. Suggestions include:

- Create a culture that honors experience. For example, in addition to traditional help-wanted ads, the CVS pharmacy chain works through The National Council on Aging, city agencies, and community organizations to find new employees. They also make it clear to retirees that they welcome older workers: "I'm too young to retire. [CVS] is willing to hire older people. They don't look at your age but your experience" said one dedicated older worker.[79]
- Modify selection procedures. For example, one Australian bank stopped using psychometric tests, replacing them with role-playing exercises to gauge how candidates deal with customers.
- Offer flexible work. Companies "need to design jobs such that staying on is more attractive than leaving." One of the simplest ways to do this is through flexible work, specifically, making *where* one works (as with telecommuting) and *when* the work is performed flexible.[80]
- Phased retirement. Many employers are implementing phased retirement programs. These combine reduced work hours, job change, reduced responsibilities, and sometimes transitioning to independent contractor status.

Review

SUMMARY

1. Performance appraisal means evaluating an employee's current or past performance relative to his or her performance standards. Performance management is the process through which companies ensure that employees are working toward organizational goals, and includes defining goals, developing skills, appraising performance, and rewarding the employee.

2. Managers appraise their subordinates' performance to obtain input on which promotion and salary raise decisions can be made, to develop plans for correcting performance deficiencies, and for career planning purposes. Supervisory ratings are still at the heart of most appraisal processes.

3. The appraisal is generally conducted using one or more popular appraisal methods or tools. These include graphic rating scales, alternation ranking, paired comparison, forced distribution, critical incidents, behaviorally anchored rating scales, MBO, computerized performance appraisals, and electronic performance monitoring.

4. An appraisal typically culminates in an appraisal interview. Adequate preparation, including giving the subordinate notice, reviewing his or her job description and past performance, choosing the right place for the interview, and leaving enough time for it, are essential. In conducting the interview, the aim is to reinforce satisfactory perfor-

mance or to diagnose and improve unsatisfactory performance. A concrete analysis of objective work data and development of an action plan are therefore advisable. Employee defensiveness is normal and needs to be dealt with.

5. The appraisal process can be improved, first, by eliminating chronic problems that often undermine appraisals and graphic rating scales in particular. These common problems include unclear standards, halo effect, central tendency, leniency or strictness, and bias.

6. Care should also be taken to ensure that the performance appraisal is legally defensible. For example, appraisal criteria should be based on documented job analyses, employees should receive performance standards in writing, and multiple performance dimensions should be rated.

7. Performance management is a *continuous* process of identifying, measuring, and developing the performance of individuals and teams and *aligning* their performance with the organization's *goals*. Unlike performance appraisal, performance management never just means meeting with a subordinate once or twice a year to "review your performance." It means *continuous, daily, or weekly* interactions and feedback to ensure continuous improvement in the employee's and team's capacity and performance.

8. Career management is the process for enabling employees to better understand and develop their career skills and interests, and to use these most effectively, both within the company and after they leave the firm.

KEY TERMS

performance appraisal   212
performance management   212
strategy map   232
balanced scorecard   233
digital dashboard   234

career   236
career management   236
career development   236
career planning   236

DISCUSSION QUESTIONS AND EXERCISES

1. Discuss the pros and cons of at least four performance appraisal tools.
2. Working individually or in groups, develop a graphic rating scale for the following jobs: secretary, engineer, and directory assistance operator.
3. Working individually or in groups, evaluate the rating scale in Figure 7.1. Discuss ways to improve it.
4. Explain how you would use the alternation ranking method, the paired comparison method, and the forced distribution method.
5. Working individually or in groups, develop a set of critical incidents covering the classroom performance of one of your instructors.
6. Explain the problems to be avoided in appraising performance.
7. Discuss the pros and cons of using various potential raters to appraise an employee's performance.
8. Explain how to conduct an appraisal interview.
9. Compare and contrast performance appraisal and performance management, using specific examples.

Application Exercises

HR in Action Case Incident 1   Appraising the Secretaries at Sweetwater U

Rob Winchester, newly appointed vice president for administrative affairs at Sweetwater University, faced a tough problem shortly after his university career began. Three weeks after he came on board in September, Sweetwater's president, Rob's boss, told Rob that one of his first tasks was to improve the appraisal system used to evaluate secretarial and clerical performance at Sweetwater U. Apparently, the main difficulty was that the performance appraisal was traditionally tied directly to salary

increases given at the end of the year. So most administrators were less than accurate when they used the graphic rating forms that were the basis of the clerical staff evaluation. In fact, what usually happened was that each administrator simply rated his or her clerk or secretary as "excellent." This cleared the way for all support staff to receive a maximum pay increase every year.

But the current university budget simply did not include enough money to fund another "maximum" annual increase for every staffer. Furthermore, Sweetwater's president felt that the custom of providing invalid feedback to each secretary on his or her year's performance was not productive, so he had asked the new vice president to revise the system. In October, Rob sent a memo to all administrators telling them that in the future no more than half the secretaries reporting to any particular administrator could be appraised as "excellent." This move, in effect, forced each supervisor to begin ranking his or her secretaries for quality of performance. The vice president's memo met widespread resistance immediately—from administrators, who were afraid that many of their secretaries would begin leaving for more lucrative jobs in private industry; and from secretaries, who felt that the new system was unfair and reduced each secretary's chance of receiving a maximum salary increase. A handful of secretaries had begun quietly picketing outside the president's home on the university campus. The picketing, caustic remarks by disgruntled administrators, and rumors of an impending slowdown by the secretaries (there were about 250 on campus) made Rob Winchester wonder whether he had made the right decision by setting up forced ranking. He knew, however, that there were a few performance appraisal experts in the School of Business, so he decided to set up an appointment with them to discuss the matter.

He met with them the next morning. He explained the situation as he had found it: The present appraisal system had been set up when the university first opened 10 years earlier, and the appraisal form had been developed primarily by a committee of secretaries. Under that system, Sweetwater's administrators filled out forms similar to the one shown in Figure 7.8. This once-a-year appraisal (in March) had run into problems almost immediately, since it was apparent from the start that administrators varied widely in their interpretations of job standards, as well as in how conscientiously they filled out the forms and supervised their secretaries. Moreover, at the end of the first year it became obvious to everyone that each secretary's salary increase was tied directly to the March appraisal. For example, those rated "excellent" received the maximum increases, those rated "good" received smaller increases, and those given neither rating received only the standard across-the-board, cost-of-living increase. Since universities in general—and Sweetwater in particular—have paid secretaries somewhat lower salaries than those prevailing in private industry, some secretaries left in a huff that first year. From that time on, most administrators simply rated all secretaries excellent in order to reduce staff turnover, thus ensuring each a maximum increase. In the process, they also avoided the hard feelings aroused by the significant performance differences otherwise highlighted by administrators.

Two Sweetwater School of Business experts agreed to consider the problem, and in two weeks they came back to the vice president with the following recommendations. First, the form used to rate the secretaries was grossly insufficient. It was unclear what "excellent" or "quality of work" meant, for example. They recommended instead a form like that in Figure 7.3. In addition, they recommended that the vice president rescind his earlier memo and no longer attempt to force university administrators to arbitrarily rate at least half their secretaries as something less than excellent. The two consultants pointed out that this was, in fact, an unfair procedure since it was quite possible that any particular administrator might have staffers who were all or virtually all excellent—or conceivably, although less likely, all below standard. The experts said that the way to get all the administrators to take the appraisal process more seriously was to stop tying it to salary increases. In other words, they recommended that every administrator fill out a form like that in Figure 7.3 for each secretary at least once a year and then use this form as the basis of a counseling session. Salary increases would have to be made on some basis other than the performance appraisal, so that administrators would no longer hesitate to fill out the rating forms honestly.

Rob thanked the two experts and went back to his office to ponder their recommendations. Some of the recommendations (such as substituting the new rating form for the old) seemed to make sense. Nevertheless, he still had serious doubts as to the efficacy of any graphic rating form, particularly if he were to decide in favor of his original forced ranking approach. The experts' second recommendation—to stop tying the appraisals to automatic salary increases—made sense but raised at least one very practical problem: If salary increases were not to be based on performance appraisals, on what were they to be based? He began wondering whether the experts' recommendations weren't simply based on ivory tower theorizing.

Questions

1. Do you think that the experts' recommendations will be sufficient to get most of the administrators to fill out the rating forms properly? Why? Why not? What additional actions (if any) do you think will be necessary?
2. Do you think that Vice President Winchester would be better off dropping graphic rating forms, substituting instead one of the other techniques discussed in this chapter, such as a ranking method? Why?
3. What performance appraisal system would you develop for the secretaries if you were Rob Winchester? Defend your answer.

HR in Action Case Incident 2   Carter Cleaning Company: The Performance Appraisal

After spending several weeks on the job, Jennifer was surprised to discover that her father had not formally evaluated any employee's performance for all the years that he had owned the business. Jack's position was that he had "a hundred higher-priority things to attend to," such as boosting sales and

lowering costs, and, in any case, many employees didn't stick around long enough to be appraisable anyway. Furthermore, contended Jack, manual workers such as those doing the pressing and the cleaning did periodically get positive feedback in terms of praise from Jack for a job well done, or criticism, also from Jack, if things did not look right during one of his swings through the stores. Similarly, Jack was never shy about telling his managers about store problems so that they, too, got some feedback on where they stood.

This informal feedback notwithstanding, Jennifer believes that a more formal appraisal approach is required. She believes that there are criteria such as quality, quantity, attendance, and punctuality that should be evaluated periodically even if a worker is paid on piece rate. Furthermore, she feels quite strongly that

the managers need to have a list of quality standards for matters such as store cleanliness, efficiency, safety, and adherence to budget on which they know they are to be formally evaluated.

Questions

1. Is Jennifer right about the need to evaluate the workers formally? The managers? Why or why not?
2. Develop a performance appraisal method for the workers and managers in each store.

EXPERIENTIAL EXERCISE

Setting Goals For and Appraising an Instructor

Purpose:

The purpose of this exercise is to give you practice in developing and using a performance appraisal form.

Required Understanding:

You are going to develop a performance appraisal form for an instructor and should therefore be thoroughly familiar with the discussion of performance appraisals in this chapter.

How to Set Up the Exercise/Instructions:

Divide the class into groups of four or five students.

1. First, based on what you now know about performance appraisals, do you think Figure 7.1 is an

effective scale for appraising instructors? Why or why not?

2. Next, your group should develop its own tool for appraising the performance of an instructor. Decide which of the appraisal tools (graphic rating scales, alternation ranking, and so on) you are going to use, and then design the instrument itself. Apply what you learned in this chapter about goal-setting to provide the instructor with practical goals.

3. Next, have a spokesperson from each group put his or her group's appraisal tool on the board. How similar are the tools? Do they all measure about the same factors? Which factor appears most often? Which do you think is the most effective tool on the board? Can you think of any way of combining the best points of several of the tools into a new performance appraisal tool?

ENDNOTES

1. D. Bradford Neary, "Creating a Company-Wide, Online, Performance Management System: A Case Study at TRW Inc.," *Human Resource Management* 41, no. 4 (Winter 2002): 495. For some insight into the TRW culture, see http://www.trw.com/careers/main/0,1005,7_478_485%5E3%5E485%5E485,00.html accessed April 20, 2008.
2. Herman Aguinis, *Performance Management* (Upper Saddle River NJ: Pearson, 2007): 2.
3. Peter Glendinning, "Performance Management: Pariah or Messiah," *Public Personnel Management* 31, no. 2 (Summer 2002): 161–178. See also Howard Risher, "Refocusing Performance Management for High Performance," *Compensation and Benefits Review* (September/October 2003): 20–30.
4. Howard Risher, "Getting Serious about Performance Management," *Compensation and Benefits Review* (November/December 2005): 19.
5. Vesa Suutari and Marja Tahbanainen, "The Antecedents of Performance Management among Finnish Expatriates," *Journal of Human Resource Management* 13, no. 1 (February 2002): 53–75.

6. See, for example, Doug Cederblom and Dan Pemerl, "From Performance Appraisal to Performance Management: One Agency's Experience," *Personnel Management* 31, no. 2 (Summer 2002): 131–140.
7. "Get SMART about Setting Goals," *Asia Africa Intelligence Wire* (May 22, 2005).
8. See, for example, Robert Renn, "Further Examination of the Measurement of Properties of Leifer & McGannon's 1996 Goal Acceptance and Goal Commitment Scales," *Journal of Occupational and Organizational Psychology* (March 1999): 107–114.
9. Experts debate the pros and cons of tying appraisals to pay decisions. One side argues that doing so distorts the appraisals. A recent study concludes the opposite. Based on an analysis of surveys from over 24,000 employees in more than 6,000 workplaces in Canada, the researchers concluded: (1) linking the employees' pay to their performance appraisals contributed to improved pay satisfaction; (2) even when appraisals are not directly linked to pay, they apparently contributed to pay satisfaction, "probably through mechanisms related to perceived organizational justice"; and (3) whether or not the employees received

performance pay, "individuals who do not receive performance appraisals are significantly less satisfied with their pay." Mary Jo Ducharme et al., "Exploring the Links between Performance Appraisals and Pay Satisfaction," *Compensation and Benefits Review* (September/October 2005): 46–52. See also Robert Morgan, "Making the Most of Performance Management Systems," *Compensation and Benefits Review* (September/October 2006): 22–27.

10. Vanessa Druskat and Steven Wolf, "Effects and Timing of Developmental Peer Appraisals in Self-Managing Work-Groups," *Journal of Applied Psychology* 84, no. 1 (1999): 58–74.

11. Jeffrey Facteau and S. Bartholomew Craig, "Performance Appraisal Ratings from Different Rating Scores," *Journal of Applied Psychology* 86, no. 2 (2001): 215–227.

12. See also Kevin Murphy et al., "Raters Who Pursue Different Goals Give Different Ratings," *Journal of Applied Psychology* 89, no. 1 (2004): 158–164.

13. Such findings may be culturally related. One study compared self and supervisor ratings in "other-oriented" cultures (as in Asia, where values tend to emphasize teams). It found that self and supervisor ratings were related. M. Audrey Korsgaard et al., "The Effect of Other Orientation on Self: Supervisor Rating Agreement," *Journal of Organizational Behavior* 25, no. 7 (November 2004): 873–891.

14. Forest Jourden and Chip Heath, "The Evaluation Gap in Performance Perceptions: Illusory Perceptions of Groups and Individuals," *Journal of Applied Psychology* 81, no. 4 (August 1996): 369–379. See also Sheri Ostroff, "Understanding Self-Other Agreement: A Look at Rater and Ratee Characteristics, Context, and Outcomes," *Personnel Psychology* 57, no. 2 (Summer 2004): 333–375.

15. Paul Atkins and Robert Wood, "Self versus Others Ratings as Predictors of Assessment Center Ratings: Validation Evidence for 360 Degree Feedback Programs," *Personnel Psychology* 55, no. 4 (Winter 2002): 871–904.

16. David Antonioni, "The Effects of Feedback Accountability on Upward Appraisal Ratings," *Personnel Psychology* 47 (1994): 349–355.

17. Alan Walker and James Smither, "A Five-Year Study of Upward Feedback: What Managers Do with Their Results Matters," *Personnel Psychology* 52 (1999): 393–423.

18. See, for example, "360-Degree Feedback on the Rise Survey Finds," *BNA Bulletin to Management* (January 23, 1997): 31; Leanne Atwater et al., "Multisource Feedback: Lessons Learned and Implications for Practice," *Human Resource Management* 46, no. 2 (Summer 2007): 285.

19. James Smither et al., "Does Performance Improve Following Multi-Score Feedback? A Theoretical Model, Meta Analysis, and Review of Empirical Findings," *Personnel Psychology* 58 (2005): 33–36.

20. Christine Hagan et al., "Predicting Assessment Center Performance with 360 Degree, Top-Down, and Customer-Based Competency Assessments," *Human Resource Management* 45, no. 3 (Fall 2006): 357–390.

21. Bruce Pfau, "Does a 360-Degree Feedback Negatively Affect the Company Performance?" *HR Magazine* (June 2002): 55–59.

22. Jim Meade, "Visual 360: A Performance Appraisal System That's 'Fun,'" *HR Magazine* (July 1999): 118–119.

23. http://www.sumtotalsystems.com/performance/index.html?e=001&sitenbr=156896193&keys=visual+360&submit.x=11&submit.y=11&submit=submit, accessed April 20, 2008.

24. Steven Scullen et al., "Forced Distribution Rating Systems and the Improvement of Workforce Potential: A Baseline Simulation," *Personnel Psychology* 58 (2005): 1; Jena McGregor, "The Struggle to Measure Performance," *Business Week* (January 9, 2006): 26.

25. Del Jones, "More Firms Cut Workers Ranked at Bottom to Make Way for Talent," *USA Today* (May 30, 2001): B1; "Straight Talk about Grading on a Curve," *BNA Bulletin to Management* (November 1, 2001): 351; Steve Bates, "Forced Ranking," *HR Magazine* (June 2003): 63–68.

26. Herman Aguinis, *Performance Management* (Upper Saddle River, NJ: Pearson, 2007): 179.

27. "Survey Says Problems with Forced Ranking Include Lower Morale and Costly Turnover," *BNA Bulletin to Management* (September 16, 2004): 297.

28. Steve Bates, "Forced Ranking: Why Grading Employees on a Scale Relative to Each Other Forces a Hard Look at Finding Keepers, Losers May Become Weepers," *HR Magazine* 48, no. 6 (June 2003): 62.

29. "Straight Talk about Grading Employees on a Curve," *BNA Bulletin to Management* (November 1, 2001): 351.

30. www.employeeappraiser.com/index.php, accessed January 10, 2008.

31. www.halogensoftware.com/products/halogen-eappraisal/, accessed January 10, 2008.

32. Drew Robb, "Building a Better Workforce," *HR Magazine* (October 2004): 87–94.

33. See, for example, Stoney Alder and Maureen Ambrose, "Towards Understanding Fairness Judgments Associated with Computer Performance Monitoring: An Integration of the Feedback, Justice, and Monitoring Research," *Human Resource Management Review* 15, no. 1 (March 2005): 43–67.

34. See, for example, John Aiello and Y. Shao, "Computerized Performance Monitoring," paper presented at the Seventh Conference of the Society for Industrial and Organizational Psychology, Montreal, Quebec, Canada, May 1992.

35. Hsi-An Shih, Yun-Hwa Chiang, and In-Sook Kim, "Expatriate Performance Management from MNEs of Different National Origins," *International Journal of Manpower* 26, no. 2 (February 2005): 157–175.

36. Donald Fedor and Charles Parsons, "What Is Effective Performance Feedback?" in Gerald Ferris and M. Ronald Buckley, *Human Resources Management*, 3rd ed. (Upper Saddle River, NJ: Prentice Hall, 1996): 265–270. See also Herman Aguinis, *Performance Management* (Upper Saddle River, NJ: Pearson, 2007): 196–219.

37. Brian Cawley et al., "Participation in the Performance Appraisal Process and Employee Reactions: A Meta-Analytic Review of Field Investigations," *Journal of Applied Psychology* 83, no. 4 (1998): 615–633.

38. Lynne McFarland et al., "Impression Management's Use and Effectiveness Across Assessment Methods," *Journal of Management* 29, no. 5 (2003): 641–661.

39. Rasha Madkour, "NASA Shooting Suspect Received Poor Job Review and Feared Being Fired, Police Say," *Associated Press* (April 21, 2007).

40. See, for example, "Communicating Beyond the Ratings Can Be Difficult," *Workforce Management* (April 24, 2006): 35.

41. See, for example, Manuel London, Edward Mone, and John C. Scott, "The Contributions of Psychological Research to HRM: Performance Management and Assessment—Methods for Improved Rater Accuracy and Employee Goal Setting," *Human Resource Management* 43, no. 4 (Winter 2004): 319–336.

42. H. John Bernardin et al., "Conscientiousness and Agreeableness as Predictors of Rating Leniency," *Journal of Applied Psychology* 85, no. 2 (2000): 232–234.

43. Clinton Wingrove, "Developing a New Blend of Process and Technology in the New Era of Performance Management," *Compensation and Benefits Review* (January/February 2003): 25–30.

44. Gary Gregures et al., "A Field Study of the Effects of Rating Purpose on the Quality of Multiscore Ratings," *Personnel Psychology* 56 (2003): 1–21.

45. Madeleine Heilman et al., "Penalties for Success: Reactions to Women Who Succeed at Male Gender Type Tasks," *Journal of Applied Psychology* 89, no. 3 (2004): 416–427.

46. Ibid., 426. Another study found that successful female managers didn't usually suffer such a fate when those rating them saw them as supportive, caring, and sensitive to their needs. Madeleine Heilmann and Tyler Okimoto, "Why Are Women Penalized for Success at Male Tasks?: The Implied Communality Deficit," *Journal of Applied Psychology*, 92, no. 1 (2007): 81–92.

47. "Flawed Ranking System Revives Workers Bias Claim," *BNA Bulletin to Management* (June 28, 2005): 206.

48. James Austin, Peter Villanova, and Hugh Hindman, "Legal Requirements and Technical Guidelines Involved in Implementing Performance Appraisal Systems," in Gerald Ferris and M. Ronald Buckley, *Human Resources Management*, 3rd ed. (Upper Saddle River, NJ: Prentice Hall, 1996): 271–288.

49. Ibid., 282.

50. But beware: one problem with training raters to avoid rating errors is that, sometimes, what appears to be an error—such as leniency—isn't an error at all, as when all subordinates really are superior performers. Manuel London, Edward Mone, and John Scott, "Performance Management and Assessment: Methods for Improved Rater Accuracy and Employee Goal Setting," *Human Resource Management* 43, no. 4 (Winter 2004): 319–336.

51. Herman Aguinis, *Performance Management* (Upper Saddle River, NJ: Pearson, 2007): 2.

52. Clinton Wingrove, "Developing an Effective Blend of Process and Technology in the New Era of Performance Management," *Compensation and Benefits Review* (January/February 2003): p. 27.

53. Mushin Lee and Byoungho Son, "The Effects of Appraisal Review Content on Employees' Reactions and Performance," *International Journal of Human Resource Management* 1 (February 1998): 283; David Antonioni, "Improve the Management Process Before Discontinuing Performance Appraisals," *Compensation and Benefits Review* (May–June 1994): 29; Jonathan Siegel, "86 Your Appraisal Process?" *HR Magazine* (October 2000): 199–206; Steve Bates, "Performance Appraisals: Some Improvement Needed," *HR Magazine* (April 2003): 12.

54. Robert Kaplan and David Norton, "The Office of Strategy Management," *Harvard Business Review* (October 2005): 72–80.

55. Michael Mankin and Richard Steele, "Turning Great Strategy Into Great Performance," *Harvard Business Review* (July/August 2005): 65–72.

56. See, for example, Wendy Boswell et al., "Aligning Employees Through 'Line of Sight,' " *Business Horizons* 49, no. 6 (November/December 2006): 499–509.

57. www.SAS.com, accessed January 2006.

58. www.SAS.com/success, accessed, January 10, 2006.

59. D. Bradford Neary, "Creating a Company-Wide, Online, Performance Management System: A Case at TRW, Inc.," *Human Resource Management* 41, no. 4 (Winter 2002): 491–498.

60. Edward Levinson et al., "A Critical Evaluation of the Web-Based Version of the Career Key," *Career Development Quarterly* 50, no. 1 (September 1, 2002): 26–36.

61. Deb Koen, "Revitalize Your Career," *Training and Development* (January 2003): 59–60.

62. Michael Doody, "A Mentor Is a Key to Career Success," *Health-Care Financial Management* 57, no. 2 (February 2003): 92–94.

63. Tammy Allen et al., "The Relationship between Formal Mentoring Program Characteristics and Perceived Program Effectiveness," *Personnel Psychology* 59 (2006): 125–153.

64. Ibid.

65. Ibid.

66. Ibid.

67. Donna Owens, "Virtual Mentoring," *HR Magazine* (March 2006): 15–17.

68. Eve Tahmincioglu, "Looking for a Mentor? Technology Can Help Make the Right Match," *Workforce Management* (December 2004): 863–865.

69. Barbara Greene and Liana Knudsen, "Competitive Employers Make Career Development Programs a Priority," *San Antonio Business Journal* 15, no. 6 (July 20, 2001): 27. See also Yehuda Baruch, "Career Development in Organizations and Beyond: Balancing Traditional and Contemporary Viewpoints," *Human Resource Management Review* 16 (2006): 131.

70. Karen Lyness and Madeline Heilman, "When Fit Is Fundamental: Performance Evaluations and Promotions of Upper-Level Female and Male Managers," *Journal of Applied Psychology* 91, no. 4 (2006): 777(9).

71. Jan Selmer and Alicia Leung, "Are Corporate Career Development Activities Less Available to Female than to Male Expatriates?" *Journal of Business Ethics* (March 2003): 125–137.

72. "Minority Women Surveyed on Career Growth Factors," *Community Banker* 9, no. 3 (March 2000): 44.

73. In Ellen Cook et al., "Career Development of Women of Color and White Women: Assumptions, Conceptualization, and Interventions from an Ecological Perspective," *Career Development Quarterly* 50, no. 4 (June 2002): 291–306.

74. Ken Dychtwald et al., "It's Time to Retire Retirement," *Harvard Business Review* (March 2004): 49.

75. Claudia Deutsch, "A Longer Goodbye," *The New York Times* (April 21, 2008): H1, 10.

76. See, for example, Matt Bolch, "Bidding Adieu," *HR Magazine* (June 2006): 123–127.

77. "Employees Plan to Work Past Retirement, but not Necessarily for Financial Reasons," *BNA Bulletin to Management* (February 19, 2004): 57–58. See also Mo Wang, "Profiling Retirees in the Retirement Transition and Adjustment Process: Examining the Longitudinal Change Patterns of Retirees' Psychological Well-Being,"

Journal of Applied Psychology 92, no. 2 (2007): 455–474.

78. Luis Fleites and Lou Valentino, "The Case for Phased Retirement," *Compensation & Benefits Review* (March/April 2007): 42–46.

79. Ken Dychtwald et al., "It's Time to Retire Retirement," *Harvard Business Review* (March 2004): 52.

80. Ibid.

Compensating Employees

8

When you finish studying this chapter, you should be able to:

1. *Discuss four basic factors determining pay rates.*

2. *Explain each of the five basic steps in establishing pay rates.*

3. *Compare and contrast piecework and team or group incentive plans.*

4. *List and describe each of the basic benefits most employers might be expected to offer.*

employee compensation
All forms of pay or rewards going to employees and arising from their employment.

① Discuss four basic factors determining pay rates.

Fair Labor Standards Act
Congress passed this act in 1938 to provide for minimum wages, maximum hours, overtime pay, and child labor protection. The law has been amended many times and covers most employees.

Introduction

The retail grocery business has very low profit margins. So when Wal-Mart moves into a grocery's area, the knee-jerk reaction is usually to cut wage rates and benefits. For example, several years ago, Safeway Stores cut employee health care benefits, precipitating a strike by its California employees. As Wegman's Food Markets Inc. adds more stores and increasingly confronts competition from Wal-Mart, its management similarly needs to decide what to do about pay. Should they cut pay to better compete based on cost?[1]

Employee compensation refers to all forms of pay or rewards going to employees and arising from their employment. It has two main components: *direct financial payments* (in the form of wages, salaries, incentives, commissions, and bonuses) and *indirect payments* (in the form of financial benefits like employer-paid insurance and vacations). We'll discuss both in this chapter. ∎

WHAT DETERMINES HOW MUCH YOU PAY?

Four basic factors determine what people are paid: legal, union, policy, and equity factors. We'll look at each, starting with legal considerations.

Some Important Compensation Laws

Numerous laws stipulate what employers can or must pay in terms of minimum wages, overtime rates, and benefits. For example:[2]

1938 FAIR LABOR STANDARDS ACT The U.S. **Fair Labor Standards Act,** passed in 1938 and since amended many times, contains minimum wage, maximum hours, overtime pay, equal pay, record-keeping, and child labor provisions covering most U.S. workers— virtually anyone engaged in producing or selling goods for interstate and foreign commerce.

One well-known provision governs overtime pay. It states that employers must pay overtime at a rate of at least one and a half times normal pay for any hours worked over 40 in a workweek.

The act also sets a minimum wage, which sets a floor for employees covered by the act (and usually bumps up wages for practically all workers when Congress raises the minimum). The minimum wage will rise for the majority of those covered by the act from $6.55 in July 2008 to $7.25 per hour in July 2009.[3] (In the U.S., several states and about 80 municipalities have their own, higher, minimum wages.)

The act also contains child labor provisions. These provisions prohibit employing minors between 16 and 18 years of age in hazardous occupations (such as mining), and further restrict employment of those under 16.

EXEMPT/NON-EXEMPT Specific categories of employees are *exempt* from the act or certain provisions of the act, and particularly from the act's overtime provisions—they are "exempt employees." A person's exemption depends on his or her responsibilities, duties, and salary. Bona fide executive, administrative (like office managers), and professional (like architects) employees are generally exempt from the act's minimum wage and overtime requirements.[4] A white-collar worker earning more than $100,000 and performing any one exempt administrative, executive, or professional duty is automatically ineligible for overtime pay. Other employees can generally earn up to $23,660 per year and still automatically get overtime pay. (So, most employees earning less than $455 per week are non-exempt and earn overtime.)[5]

If an employee is exempt from the FLSA's minimum wage provisions, then he or she is also exempt from its overtime pay provisions. However, certain employees are always exempt from overtime pay provisions. They include, among others, agricultural employees, live-in household employees, taxicab drivers, outside sales employees, and motion picture theater employees.[6]

As noted, some jobs—for example, top managers and lawyers—are clearly exempt, while others—such as office workers earning less than $23,660 per year—are non-exempt. Unfortunately, beyond the obvious categorizations, it's generally advisable to do some analyses before classifying a job as exempt or non-exempt. Figure 8.1 presents a procedure for making this decision. Note that in all but the clearest situations, it's advisable to carefully review the person's job description. Make sure, for instance, that the job does in fact require that the person perform, say, a supervisory duty.[7]

Violating this act's provisions is a bad idea, but even giant firms make errors. Wal-Mart voluntarily told the U.S. Department of Labor that it had failed to pay some management trainees overtime pay, and had not included incentive pay in some employees' overtime pay calculations. Wal-Mart settled with the Department of Labor for $33 million.[8] Other firms try to evade the law by claiming that some employees—say, those who are doing computer programming—aren't employees but rather "independent contractors" (who are more like consultants than employees); this tactic rarely works when challenged.

Equal Pay Act of 1963
An amendment to the Fair Labor Standards Act designed to require equal pay for women doing the same work as men.

1963 EQUAL PAY ACT The U.S. **Equal Pay Act,** an amendment to the Fair Labor Standards Act, states that employees of one sex may not be paid wages at a rate lower than that paid to employees of the opposite sex for doing roughly equivalent work. Specifically, if the work requires equal skills, effort, and responsibility and is performed under similar working conditions, employees of both sexes must receive equal pay unless the differences in pay are based on a seniority system, a merit system, the quantity or quality of production, or any factor other than sex.

Civil Rights Act of 1964, Title VII
Law that makes it unlawful practice for an employer to discriminate against any individual with respect to hiring, compensation, terms, conditions, or privileges of employment because of race, color, religion, sex, or nation.

1964 CIVIL RIGHTS ACT Title VII of the U.S. **Civil Rights Act** makes it an unlawful practice for an employer to discriminate against any individual with respect to hiring, compensation, terms, conditions, or privileges of employment because of race, color, religion, sex, or national origin.

OTHER DISCRIMINATION LAWS Various other discrimination laws influence compensation decisions. For example, the Age Discrimination in Employment Act prohibits age

FIGURE 8.1 Who Is Exempt? Who Is Not Exempt?

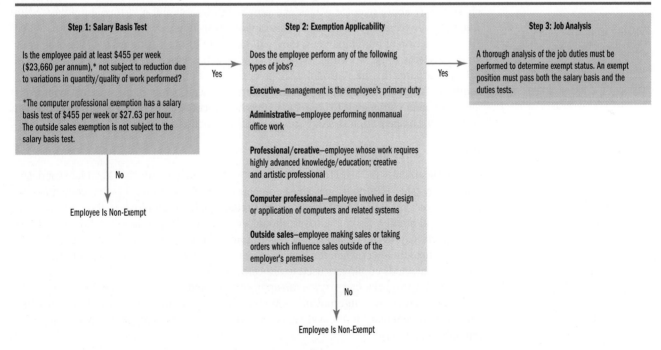

discrimination against employees who are 40 years of age and older in all aspects of employment, including compensation. The Americans with Disabilities Act similarly prohibits discrimination against qualified persons with disabilities in all aspects of employment, including compensation. The Family and Medical Leave Act entitles eligible employees, both men and women, to take up to 12 weeks of unpaid, job-protected leave for the birth of a child or for the care of a child, spouse, or parent. Employers that are U.S. government contractors or subcontractors are required by various executive orders not to discriminate and to take affirmative action in various areas of employment, including compensation.

How Unions Influence Compensation Decisions

For unionized companies, union-related issues also influence pay plan design. The U.S. National Labor Relations Act (NLRA) of 1935 granted employees the right to organize, to bargain collectively, and to engage in concerted activities for the purpose of collective bargaining or other mutual aid or protection. Historically, the wage rate is the main issue in collective bargaining. However, other pay-related issues including time off with pay, income security (for those in industries with periodic layoffs), cost-of-living adjustments, and various benefits such as health care are also important.[9]

Compensation Policies

As at Wegman's, an employer's strategy and compensation policies significantly influence the wages and benefits it pays. For example, a hospital might have a pay policy of starting nurses at a wage at least 20% above the prevailing market wage. Other important pay policies include the basis for salary increases, foreign pay differentials, and overtime pay. Geographic pay differentials are another issue. For example, the average base pay recently for an executive secretary ranged from $37,300 in Albuquerque, New Mexico; to $41,900 in Tampa, Florida; $59,800 in New York, New York; and $60,100 in San Francisco, California.[10]

Distinguishing between high and low performers is another important pay policy. For example, for many years Payless ShoeSource hardly distinguished in pay among high and low performers. However, after seeing its market share drop over several years, management decided to embark on a turnaround plan. The plan included revising its compensation policies. It now differentiates more aggressively between top performers and others.[11]

WEGMAN'S EXAMPLE With competition from Wal-Mart and other chains, Wegman's chose to pay above-average wages and provide all its full and part-time employees with free health coverage. Management's assumption, as its human resources head put it, is that "if we take care of our employees, they will take care of our customers."[12] Wegman's pay strategy seems to be working. Its larger stores each average about $950,000 a week in sales, compared to the national U.S. average of about $361,564 for grocery stores. Similarly, Wegman's employee turnover figures are well below retail store national averages. Wegman's strategy is to compete with other grocery chains based on productivity and service. Its compensation strategy supports that competitive strategy.

Equity and Its Impact on Pay Rates

Equity, specifically the need for external equity and internal equity, is a key factor in determining pay rates. Externally, pay must compare favorably with rates in other companies, or an employer will find it hard to attract and retain qualified employees. Pay must also be equitable internally: Each employee should view his or her pay as equitable given other employees' pay in the organization. For example, in one study turnover of retail buyers was significantly lower when the buyers perceived fair treatment in the amount or rewards and in the methods employers used to allocate rewards.[13]

Salary inequities can trigger disappointment and conflict. Some firms therefore maintain secrecy over internal pay matters. However, online pay forums on sites like salaryexpert.com make it relatively easy today for employees to judge if they're being paid equitably externally.

HOW EMPLOYERS ESTABLISH PAY RATES

In practice, setting pay rates while ensuring external and internal equity usually entails five steps:

② Explain each of the five basic steps in establishing pay rates.

1. Conduct a salary survey of what other employers are paying for comparable jobs (to price benchmark jobs and help ensure external equity).
2. Determine the worth of each job in your organization through job evaluation (to help ensure internal equity). An employee evaluation committee (possibly including an HR specialist) usually does the evaluation.
3. Group similarly paid jobs into pay grades.
4. Price each pay grade by using wage curves.
5. Develop rate ranges.

We explain each of these steps in this section, starting with salary surveys.

Step 1: Conduct the Salary Survey

salary (or compensation) survey

A survey aimed at determining prevailing pay rates. Provides specific wage rates for specific jobs.

Salary (or compensation) surveys—formal or informal surveys of what other employers are paying for similar jobs—play a central role in pricing jobs. Most employers therefore conduct such surveys for pricing one or more jobs.

Employers use salary surveys in three ways. First, they use them to price *benchmark jobs.* These anchor the employer's pay scale. The manager slots other jobs around them, based on their relative worth to the firm. (*Job evaluation,* explained next, is the technique used to determine the relative worth of each job.) Second, employers usually price 20% or more of their positions directly in the marketplace (rather than relative to the firm's benchmark jobs), based on a formal or informal survey of what comparable firms are paying for comparable jobs. (This is particularly true for pricing fast-changing high-tech jobs, for instance.) Finally, surveys also collect data on benefits such as insurance, sick leave, and vacation time.

Finding salary data and negotiating raises are not as mysterious as they used to be, thanks to the Internet. Figure 8.2 summarizes some popular salary Web sites. The U.S. Bureau of Labor Statistics organized its various pay surveys into a new National Compensation Survey, and publishes this information on the Web. The Internet site is *http://stats.bls.gov.*[14]

Step 2: Determine the Worth of Each Job: Job Evaluation

After conducting a salary survey, the employer turns to job evaluation.

FIGURE 8.2 Some Pay Data Web Sites

Sponsor	Internet Address	What It Provides	Downside
Salary.com	www.Salary.com	Salary by job and post code, plus job and description, for hundreds of jobs	Adapts national averages by applying local cost-of-living differences
Wageweb	www.wageweb.com	Average salaries for more than 150 clerical, professional, and managerial jobs	Charges $169 for breakdowns by industry, location, etc.
Job Smart	http://jobstar.org/tools/salary/sal-prof.php	Profession-specific salary surveys	Necessary to review numerous salary surveys for each profession
moving.com	www.moving.com	Median salaries for thousands of jobs, by city	Doesn't consider factors like company size or benefits
cnnmoney.com	http://money.cnn.com	Input your current salary and city, and this gives you comparable salary in destination city	Based on national averages adapted to cost of living differences

Note: All sites accessed May 2007.

job evaluation
A formal and systematic comparison of jobs to determine the worth of one job relative to another.

compensable factors
Fundamental, compensable elements of a job, such as skills, effort, responsibility, and working conditions.

ranking method
The simplest method of job evaluation that involves ranking each job relative to all other jobs, usually based on a job's overall difficulty.

PURPOSE OF JOB EVALUATION **Job evaluation** is a formal and systematic comparison of jobs to determine the worth of one job relative to another. The basic job evaluation procedure is to compare the content of jobs in relation to one another, for example, in terms of their effort, responsibility, and skills. Suppose you know (based on your salary survey and compensation policies) how to price key benchmark jobs, and can use job evaluation to determine the relative worth of all the other jobs in your firm relative to these key jobs. Then you are well on your way to being able to equitably price all the jobs in your organization.

COMPENSABLE FACTORS There are two basic approaches to comparing the worth of several jobs. First, you could take an intuitive approach. You might decide that one job is more important than another and not dig any deeper into why in terms of specific job-related factors.

As an alternative, you could compare the jobs based on certain basic factors they have in common. In compensation management, these basic factors are called **compensable factors.** They are the factors that determine your definition of job content. They also establish how the jobs compare to each other, and set the compensation paid for each job.

JOB EVALUATION METHODS The simplest job evaluation method ranks each job relative to all other jobs, usually based on some overall compensable factor such as job difficulty. There are several steps in this *job* **ranking method,** as the *HR in Practice* feature summarizes. *Job classification* is another simple, widely used method. Here the manager categorizes jobs into groups based on their similarity in terms of compensable factors such as skills and responsibility. The groups are called *classes* if they contain similar jobs, or *grades* if they contain jobs that are similar in difficulty but otherwise different. The *point method* is a quantitative job evaluation technique. It involves identifying several compensable factors, each having several degrees, and then assigning points based on the number of degrees so as to come up with a total number of points for each job.

HR in Practice

Steps in the Ranking Method of Job Evaluation

1. ***Obtain job information.*** Job analysis is the first step in the ranking method. Job descriptions for each job are prepared, and these are usually the basis on which the rankings are made. (Sometimes job specifications also are prepared, but the job ranking method usually ranks jobs according to the whole job rather than a number of compensable factors. Therefore, job specifications—which provide an indication of the demands of the job in terms of problem solving, decision making, and skills, for instance—are not as necessary with this method as they are for other job evaluation methods.)

2. ***Select raters and jobs to be rated.*** It is often not practical to make a single ranking of all jobs in an organization. The more usual procedure is to rank jobs by department or in clusters (such as factory workers and clerical workers). This eliminates the need for having to compare directly, say, factory jobs and clerical jobs.

3. ***Select compensable factors.*** In the ranking method, it is common to use just one factor (such as job difficulty) and to rank jobs on the basis of the whole job. Regardless of the number of factors you choose, it's advisable to explain the definition of the factor(s) to the evaluators carefully so that they evaluate the jobs consistently.

4. ***Rank jobs.*** Next the jobs are ranked. The simplest way is to give each rater a set of index cards, each of which contains a brief description of a job. These cards are then ranked from lowest to highest. Some managers use an

alternation ranking method for making the procedure more accurate; they use the cards to first choose the highest and the lowest, and then the next highest and next lowest, and so forth until all the cards have been ranked. Because it is usually easier to choose extremes, this approach facilitates the ranking procedure. Table 8.1

illustrates a job ranking. Jobs in this small health facility are ranked from maid up to office manager. The corresponding pay scales are shown on the right.

5. **Combine ratings.** Usually several raters rank the jobs independently. Then the rating committee (or employer) can average the rankings.

TABLE 8.1 Job Ranking at Olympia Health Care

Ranking Order	Annual Pay Scale
1. Office manager	$48,000
2. Chief nurse	47,500
3. Bookkeeper	39,000
4. Nurse	37,500
5. Cook	36,000
6. Nurse's aide	33,500
7. Maid	30,500

Note: After ranking, it becomes possible to slot additional jobs between those already ranked and to assign each an appropriate wage rate.

Step 3: Group Similar Jobs into Pay Grades

Once a job evaluation method has been used to determine the relative worth of each job, the evaluation committee can start assigning pay rates to each job; it usually first groups jobs into pay grades. A *pay grade* comprises jobs of approximately equal difficulty or importance as determined by job evaluation. If the point method were used, the pay grade would consist of jobs falling within a range of points. If the ranking plan were used, the grade would consist of all jobs that fall within two or three ranks. If the classification system were used, then the jobs are already categorized into classes or grades. Ten to 16 grades per job cluster (or logical grouping such as factory jobs, clerical jobs, etc.) are common.

Step 4: Price Each Pay Grade: Wage Curves

wage curve
Shows the relationship between the relative value of the job and the average wage paid for this job.

The next step is to assign average pay rates to each of the pay grades. (Of course, if you choose not to slot jobs into pay grades, an individual pay rate has to be assigned to each individual job.) Assigning pay rates to each pay grade (or to each job) is usually accomplished with the help of a **wage curve,** which shows the average pay rates currently being paid for jobs in each pay grade, relative to the points or rankings assigned to each job or grade by the job evaluation. Figure 8.3 illustrates a wage curve. The purpose of a wage curve is to show the relationship between (1) the value of the job as determined by one of the job evaluation methods and (2) the current average pay rates for the grades. The wage line then becomes the target for wages or salary rates for the jobs in each pay grade.

Step 5: Develop Rate Ranges

Finally, most employers do not just pay one rate for all jobs in a particular pay grade. Instead, they develop rate ranges for each grade. Thus there might be 10 levels or steps within each pay grade, and 10 corresponding pay rates within each pay grade. The employer may then fine-tune pay rates to account for individual circumstances.

FIGURE 8.3

Plotting a Wage Curve

Note: The average pay rates for jobs in each grade (Grade I, Grade II, Grade III, etc.) are plotted, and the wage curve is fitted to the resulting points.

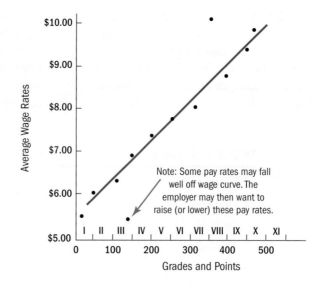

Note: Some pay rates may fall well off wage curve. The employer may then want to raise (or lower) these pay rates.

Pricing Managerial and Professional Jobs

For managerial and professional jobs, job evaluation provides only a partial answer to the question of how to pay these employees. Managerial and professional jobs tend to emphasize nonquantifiable factors like judgment and problem solving more than do production and clerical jobs. There is also more of a tendency to pay managers and professionals based on their performance, on what competitors are paying, or on what they can do, rather than on intrinsic job demands such as working conditions. For top executive jobs (especially the CEO), job evaluation typically has little or no relevance. One study concluded that three main factors, *job complexity* (span of control, the number of functional divisions over which the executive has direct responsibility, and management level), the employer's *ability to pay* (total profit and rate of return), and the executive's *human capital* (educational level, field of study, work experience) accounted for about two-thirds of executive compensation variance.[15]

ELEMENTS For a company's top executives, the compensation plan generally consists of four main components: base salary, short-term incentives, deferred long-term incentives, and executive benefits and perks.[16]

- *Base salary* includes the obvious fixed compensation paid regularly as well as, often, guaranteed bonuses such as "10% of pay at the end of the fourth fiscal quarter, regardless of whether the company makes a profit," and discretionary bonuses which the board may elect to give the executive for exceptional results.
- *Short-term incentives* are usually paid in cash or stock for achieving short-term goals, such as year-to-year increases in sales revenue. Companies like Nucor Corp. also have annual profit sharing and/or gainsharing plans in which their executives participate. Incentives equal 31% or more of a typical executive's base pay in many countries, including the United States, United Kingdom, France, and Germany.[17]
- *Deferred long-term incentives* include such things as stock options, which generally give the executive the right to purchase stock at a specific price for a specific period of time and are aimed at encouraging the executive to take actions that will drive up the value of the company's stock. They are "deferred" insofar as they reflect a contractual agreement between the executive and employer to make payments at a later date. The deferred compensation may also include a "golden parachute" clause, aimed at giving the executive special pay and benefits in the event the firm is sold or taken over.
- Finally, *executive benefits and perks* might include supplemental executive retirement plans, supplemental life insurance, and health insurance without a deductible or coinsurance. Supplemental retirement plans generally head the list of executive perks. Other popular executive perks include leased automobiles, automobile allowance, and free medical examinations.

STRATEGY AND EXECUTIVE PAY As with any pay plans, those for managers and professionals should make sense in terms of what the company wants to accomplish strategically. To help accomplish this:

- Formulate the company's strategic plan, and translate this into specific business goals.
- List the competencies and behaviors your firm's managerial and professional employees should exhibit to accomplish these goals.
- Evaluate the extent to which the existing pay plan promotes these skills, competencies, and behaviors. For example, ask: Does the pay plan motivate managers to achieve their goals? Do we now provide competitive pay and incentives for those who demonstrate the required competencies and skills? Does the pay plan motivate employees to acquire these skills?[18]
- Finally, design and implement the new pay plan. Make sure it "communicates to employees what's important about performance and what is not important."[19]

CURRENT TRENDS IN COMPENSATION

How employers pay employees has been evolving.[20] Overall, there is less emphasis on basing pay on seniority and more on the employee's contribution, performance, and value to the business; less emphasis on the job's duties and more on the person's skills and competencies and on how his or her contribution fits with the firm's overall strategic needs; finally, there's less emphasis on narrowly defined pay ranges and jobs and more on broader jobs and pay ranges. This section looks at three important trends: competency-based pay, broadbanding, and board oversight of executive pay.[21] We'll discuss performance-based pay later in this chapter.

Competency- and Skill-Based Pay

Some question whether job evaluation's tendency to slot jobs into narrow cubbyholes (consisting, say, of "Grade I," "Grade II," and so on) might not actually be counterproductive in today's high-performance work systems. Systems like these depend on flexible, multiskilled job assignments and on high-involvement techniques like teamwork and participative decision making. There's thus no place for employees who say, "That's not my job." Yet if you want someone in Grade I to do a Grade II job for a while, that's actually what the response may be. Competency-based pay (and broadbanding, explained later) aim to avoid this problem.[22]

With competency- or skill-based pay, you pay the employee for the skills and knowledge he or she is capable of using rather than for the responsibilities of the job currently held.[23] *Competencies* are demonstrable personal characteristics such as knowledge, skills, and behaviors.

Why pay employees based on the skill levels they achieve, rather than based on the jobs they're assigned to? The answer is to encourage the person to become more multiskilled. With more companies organizing around project teams, employers expect employees to be able to rotate among jobs. Doing so requires having more skills.

ELEMENTS Skill-based pay programs generally contain five main elements. The employer *defines* specific skills, and chooses a *method* for tying the person's pay to his or her skill competencies. A *training* system lets employees seek and acquire skills. There is a formal competency *testing* system. And, the work is *designed* in such a way that employees can easily move among jobs of varying skill levels.

In practice, competency-based pay usually comes down to pay for knowledge or skill-based pay.[24] Pay-for-knowledge plans reward employees for learning organizationally relevant knowledge—for instance, you might pay a new waiter more once he or she memorizes the menu. With skill-based pay, the employee earns more after developing organizationally relevant skills—Microsoft pays programmers more as they master the skill of writing new programs.

Broadbanding

Most firms end up with pay plans that slot jobs into classes or grades, each with its own vertical pay rate range.

The question is how wide should the salary grades be, in terms of the number of job evaluation points or rankings they include? There is a downside to having narrow grades. Again, for instance, if you want someone whose job is in grade 2 to fill in for a time in a job that happens to be in grade 1, it's difficult to reassign that person without lowering his or her salary. Similarly, if you want the person to learn about a job that happens to be in grade 3, the employee might object to the reassignment without a corresponding raise to grade 3 pay. Traditional grade pay plans thus breed inflexibility.

That is why some firms are broadbanding their pay plans. Broadbanding means collapsing salary grades and ranges into just a few wide ranges, or bands, each of which contains a relatively wide range of jobs and salary levels. Figure 8.4 illustrates this. In this figure, the company's previous six pay grades are consolidated into two broadbands.

WHAT TO BROADBAND A company may create broadbands for all its jobs, or for specific groups such as managers or professionals. The pay rate range of each broadband is relatively large, since it ranges from the minimum pay of the lowest grade the firm merged into the broadband up to the maximum pay of the highest merged grade. Thus, for example, instead of having 10 salary grades, each of which contains a salary range of $15,000, the firm might collapse the 10 grades into three broadbands, each with a set of jobs such that the difference between the lowest and highest paid jobs might be $40,000 or more. For the jobs that fall in each broadband, there is therefore a much wider range of pay rates. You can move employees from job to job within the broadband more easily, without worrying about the employees moving outside the relatively narrow rate range associated with a traditional narrow pay grade. Broadbanding therefore breeds flexibility. The *Global Issues in HR* feature addresses one global aspect of pay policy.

FIGURE 8.4

Broadbanded Structure and How It Relates to Traditional Pay Grades and Ranges

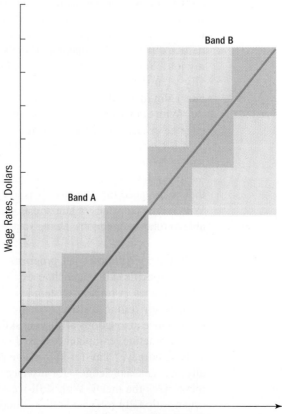

Global Issues in HR

Compensating Expatriate Employees

With dramatically different costs of living among countries, compensating managers who are sent to work abroad is never easy. Many companies use what experts call the *balance sheet method* to compute the expatriate manager's pay. The aim here is to make sure the person's compensation remains consistent with what it would have been if he or she had stayed home. The person's base salary reflects the salaries in his or her home country. Then the employer layers on additional payments to cover things like housing costs, tax differences, and other living expenses (such as private schools for the person's children).[25] At the other extreme, some employers pay the manager based on what people are earning in the host country. This is known as the "host-country-based" or "going-rate" approach.

Each approach has pros and cons. The balance sheet approach makes it easier to repatriate employees, and generally elicits less resistance from the employees themselves (who might object to having their salaries slashed just because they're moving from high-cost London to low-cost Bangalore). On the other hand, paying the expatriate more can lead to tensions between the manager and his or her host-country peers. The country-based approach has the advantage of integrating the expatriate better, since he or she is earning what his or her host country peers are earning. But it can mean slashing an employee's salary, hardly a practical option.

Board Oversight of Executive Pay

For 15 years, the Board of Directors of UnitedHealth Group Inc. supported its CEO with almost $2 billion in compensation. Recently, the board ousted him, allegedly because, as the *Wall Street Journal* put it, "his explanation for a pattern of unusually well-timed stock option grants didn't add up."[26]

There are various reasons why boards are clamping down on executive pay. In the U.S., the Financial Accounting Standards Board now requires that most public companies recognize as an expense the fair value of the stock options they grant.[27] The U.S. Securities and Exchange Commission (SEC) now requires filing more compensation-related information. The Sarbanes-Oxley Act makes executives personally liable, under certain conditions, for corporate financial oversight lapses.[28] The net result is that lawyers specializing in executive pay suggest that boards of directors ask themselves these questions:

- Has our compensation committee thoroughly identified its duties and processes?
- Is our compensation committee being appropriately advised? (Government regulators and commentators strongly encourage this.)
- Are there particular executive compensation issues that our committee should address?
- Do our procedures demonstrate diligence and independence? (This demands careful deliberations and records.)
- Is our committee appropriately communicating its decisions? How will shareholders react?[29]

③ Compare and contrast piecework and team or group incentive plans.

INCENTIVE PLANS

Many—perhaps most—employees don't just earn a salary or hourly wage. They also earn some type of incentive. Indeed, "paying for performance" may be the most significant compensation trend today.

incentive plan
A compensation plan that ties pay to performance.

This section addresses some popular **incentive plans**. *Individual incentive programs* give performance-based pay to individual employees. *Variable pay* refers to group pay plans that tie payments to productivity or to some other measure of the firm's profitability.[30]

Traditionally, all incentive plans are pay-for-performance plans. They pay all employees based on the employee's performance. Several incentive plan examples follow.

Piecework Plans

piecework
A system of incentive pay tying pay to the number of items processed by each individual worker.

Piecework is the oldest incentive plan and still the most commonly used. Pay is tied directly to what the worker produces: The person is paid a "piece rate" for each unit he or she produces. Thus, if Tom Smith gets $0.40 for each address he finds on the Web, then he would make $40 for finding 100 addresses a day and $80 for 200.

Incentives for Managers and Executives

Managers and executives play a central role in influencing divisional and corporate profitability, and most firms therefore put considerable thought into how to reward them.

As noted previously, in addition to salary, most managers get short-term bonuses and incentives (for reporting purposes, employers often lump short term bonuses and incentives into one "bonus" category), as well as deferred long-term incentives.[31] The size of the bonus (in terms of percentage of salary) is usually greater for top-level executives. A recent Mercer Consultants survey found that the recent average CEO pay mix was 16% salary, 22% bonus, and 62% long-term incentives.[32] Employers generally pay out bonus and short-term incentive awards in cash. Long-term incentives more often take the form of company stock, sometimes stock options.

stock option
The right to purchase a stated number of shares of company stock at a set price at some time in the future.

STOCK OPTIONS A **stock option** is the right to purchase a specific number of shares of company stock at a specific price during a period of time. The executive hopes to profit by exercising his or her option to buy the shares in the future, but at today's price. The firm's profitability and growth affects its stock price, and because the executive can affect these factors, the stock option supposedly is an incentive.

The chronic problem with stock options is that they often don't motivate performance. For example, some firms awarded stock options to new executives when they started their jobs. They then discovered that the managers could subsequently profit from their options because the stock prices of all the firms in the industry rose due to favorable economic trends.

There are other issues with options. Many blame stock options for contributing to numerous corporate scandals. For example, some executives allegedly manipulated the dates they received their options to maximize their returns. Furthermore, until recently, most companies did not treat stock options as an expense. This made the firm's expenses look less than they really were. With more companies trying to emphasize accuracy and transparency in financial statements, more are now expensing stock options. This in turn makes options less attractive to employers.

In Germany, the government of chancellor Angela Merkel set up a working group in the summer of 2008 to offer proposals aimed at cracking down on what the government considered "excessive" executive pay. The move, according to the *Financial Times*, could curtail the use of stock options and could include a tightening of corporate governance rules and corporate taxation.

In any case, there is a trend toward using new types of deferred compensation, tied more explicitly to performance goals. Instead of stock options, more firms are granting various types of deferred "performance shares" such as performance-contingent restricted stock; the executive receives his or her shares only if he or she meets the pre-set performance targets.[33]

SARBANES-OXLEY The U.S. Sarbanes-Oxley Act of 2002 affects how employers formulate their executive incentive programs and was meant to inject a higher level of responsibility into executives' and board members' decisions. It makes them personally liable for violating their fiduciary responsibilities to their shareholders. The act also requires that CEOs and CFOs of a public company repay any bonuses, incentives, or equity-based compensation received from the company during the 12-month period following the issuance of a financial statement that the company must restate due to material noncompliance with a financial reporting requirement as a result of misconduct.[34]

Incentives for Salespeople

Most companies pay their salespeople a combination of salary and commissions, usually with a sizable salary component. Typical is a 70% base salary/30% incentive mix. This cushions both the downside risk from the salesperson's point of view and limits the risk that the rewards would be too great from the firm's point of view.

Setting effective quotas is an art. Questions to ask include: Are quotas communicated to the sales force within 1 month of the start of the period? Does the sales force know how their quotas are set? Do you combine bottom-up information (like account forecasts) with top-down requirements (like the company business plan)? Are quotas stable through the performance period? Are returns and debookings reasonably low? And, has your firm generally avoided compensation-related lawsuits?[35] One expert suggests the following as a rule of thumb as to whether the sales incentive plan is effective: 75% or more of the sales force achieving quota or better; 10% of the sales force achieving higher performance level (than previously); 5% to 10% of the sales force achieving below-quota performance and receiving performance development coaching.[36]

Some salespeople respond more positively to fixed salary plans while others prefer incentives. As a result, human resource and sales managers need to carefully select salespeople at least partly based on whether the job is commission or salary-based.[37]

AN EXAMPLE: AUTO DEALERS Commission rates vary by industry, but a look at how auto dealers set their salesperson's commission rates provides some interesting insights. Compensation for car salespeople ranges from a high of 100% commission to a small base salary with commission accounting for most of the total compensation. Commission is generally based on the net profit on the car when it's delivered to the buyer. This promotes precisely the sorts of behaviors the car dealers want to encourage. For example, it encourages the salesperson to hold firm on the retail price, and to push "after-sale products" like floor mats, side moldings, and car alarms. Car dealers also use short-term incentives. For helping sell slow-moving vehicles, the salesperson may be offered a "spiff"—a car dealer term for an extra incentive bonus over commission.[38]

Non-Tangible and Recognition-Based Awards

Recognition is one of several types of non-tangible incentives. The term *recognition program* usually refers to formal programs, such as employee-of-the-month programs. *Social*

Compensation for car salespeople ranges from a high of 100% commission to a small base salary with commission accounting for most of the total compensation.

recognition program refers to more informal manager-employee exchanges such as praise, approval, or expressions of appreciation for a job well-done. *Performance feedback* is similar to social recognition, but means "providing quantitative or qualitative information on task performance for the purpose of changing or maintaining performance and specific ways."[39] The *HR in Practice* feature explains how supervisors use these methods.

Studies show that recognition has a positive impact on performance, either alone or in conjunction with financial rewards.[40] It's therefore not surprising that in one survey, 78% of CEOs and 58% of HR vice presidents said their firms were using performance recognition programs.[41] At American Skandia, which provides insurance and financial planning products and services, customer service reps who exceed standards receive a plaque, a $500 check, their photo and story on the firm's internal Web site, and a dinner for them and their teams.[42] One survey of 235 managers found that the most-used rewards to motivate employees (top-down from most used to least) were:[43]

- Employee recognition
- Gift certificates
- Special events
- Cash rewards
- Merchandise incentives
- E-mail/print communications
- Training programs
- Work/life benefits
- Variable pay
- Group travel
- Individual travel
- Sweepstakes

HR in Practice

Incentives Supervisors Can Use

As you can see, the individual line manager should not rely just on the employer's incentive plans for motivating subordinates. Those plans may not be very complete, and there are simply too many opportunities to motivate employees every day to let those opportunities pass. There are three guides to follow.

First, the best option for motivating employees is also the simplest—*make sure the employee has a doable goal* and that he or she agrees with that. It makes little sense to try to motivate employees with financial incentives if they don't know their goals or don't agree with them. Many psychologists have consistently found that specific, challenging goals lead to higher task performance than specific, unchallenging goals, or vague goals or no goals.

Second, *recognizing an employee's contribution* is a powerful motivation tool. Studies show that recognition has a positive impact on performance, either alone or in combination with financial rewards. For example, in one study, combining financial rewards with recognition produced a 30% performance improvement in service firms, almost twice the effect of using each reward alone.

Third, remember that there are numerous *positive reinforcement rewards* you can use on a day-to-day basis. A short list would include:[44]

- Challenging work assignments
- Freedom to choose own work activity
- Having fun built into work
- More of preferred task
- Role as boss's stand-in when he or she is away
- Role in presentations to top management
- Job rotation
- Encouragement of learning and continuous improvement
- Being provided with ample encouragement
- Being allowed to set own goals
- Compliments
- Expression of appreciation in front of others
- Note of thanks
- Employee-of-the-month award
- Special commendation
- Bigger desk
- Bigger office or cubicle

Online Award Programs

If there's a downside to financial recognition programs like prizes and rewards, it's that they're expensive to administer. Many firms—including GlaxoSmithKline, Barnes and Noble, Citibank, and Wal-Mart—therefore partner with online incentive firms to expedite the process. Internet incentive/recognition sites include www.bravanta.com, and www.incentivecity.com. They enable a client firm's supervisors to easily make awards.

Merit Pay as an Incentive

merit pay (merit raise)
Any salary increase awarded to an employee based on his or her individual performance.

team
A small number of people with complementary skills who are committed to a common purpose, set of performance goals, and approach for which they hold themselves mutually accountable.

Merit pay, or a **merit raise**, is any salary increase awarded to an employee based on his or her individual performance. It is different from a bonus in that it usually becomes part of the employee's base salary, whereas a bonus is a one-time payment. Although the term *merit pay* can apply to the incentive raises given to any employee—exempt or nonexempt, office or factory—the term is more often used with respect to white-collar employees and particularly professional, office, and clerical employees.

Merit pay has both advocates and detractors. Advocates argue that only rewards like these that are tied directly to performance can motivate improved performance. Detractors say it can undermine teamwork, and that, since the merit pay typically depends on the performance appraisal, unfair appraisals will lead employees to perceive the pay as unfair, too.

Instead of incentivizing individual employees, many employers create team incentive plans. The *Personal Competencies* feature addresses this.

Personal Competencies

Building Your *Team-Building* Skills and Team Incentives

Businesses increasingly organize their efforts around teams. For instance, work teams basically run the General Mills cereal plant in Lodi, California. At Johnsonville foods, similar self-managing teams recruit, hire, evaluate, and (if necessary) fire on their own. Because teams are so important at work today, all managers need a working knowledge of what teams are, and how to organize and incentivize them. A **team** is "a small number of people with complementary skills who are committed to a common purpose, set of performance goals, and approach for which they hold themselves mutually accountable."[45]

WHY TEAMS ARE IMPORTANT   Teams are important at work for several reasons. One reason is that for better or worse teams influence their members' behavior. They exert their influence largely through *group norms*. These are informal rules that teams adopt to regulate and regularize their members' behavior. Researchers, during a classic project known as the Hawthorne studies, described, for instance, how production levels that exceeded the group norms triggered a slap on the hand for the team members producing too much. The other side of the coin is that teams with positive attitudes can have a positive effect. In companies like Mercedes-Benz, highly motivated work teams make sure that team members have the training and values necessary to keep production and quality high.

MIXED RESULTS   Unfortunately, the evidence regarding work team productivity is mixed. After Kodak's consumer film finishing division instituted a team-based structure, the division's costs declined by 6% per year and productivity rose by over 200% in six years. On the other hand, experts generally blame an ill-conceived team incentive plan instituted at Levi Strauss' American factories with hastening the closure of those factories.

Team Incentive Plans

Given results like these, experts argue against assuming that team incentives themselves are a panacea. Motivating the team should start with organizing the team properly—in terms of membership, leadership, and training. One compensation expert says, "the best advice I can give is to get the [team] set up right; pay comes later, if at all, to reward team members for performance."[46]

There are several ways to design team incentives. One company created a pool of money such that if the company

(continued)

reached 100% of its overall goal, the employees would share in about 5% of this. That 5% pool was then divided by the number of employees, to arrive at the value of a share. Each *work team* then received two goals. If the team achieved both of its goals, each employee would earn one full share (in addition to his or her base pay). Employees on teams that reached only one goal would earn a half-share. Those on teams reaching neither goal earned no shares.[47]

A group incentive plan's main disadvantage is that each worker's rewards are not based just on his or her own efforts. If the person does not see his or her effort translating directly into proportional rewards, a group plan may be less effective than an individual plan.

Nucor Team Incentive Example   Nucor Corp. is the largest steel producer in the United States; it also has the highest productivity, highest wages, and lowest labor cost per ton in the American steel industry.[48] Its bonus plans help explain this.

Nucor employees earn bonuses of 100% or more of base salary. All participate in one of four performance-based incentive plans. With the *production incentive plan,* plant operating and maintenance employees and supervisors get weekly bonuses based on their workgroup's productivity. The *department manager incentive plan* pays department managers annual incentive bonuses based mostly on the ratio of net income to dollars of assets employed for their division. With the *professional and clerical bonus plan,* employees who are not in one of the two previous plans get bonuses based on their division's net income return on assets. Finally, under the *senior officers incentive plan,* Nucor senior managers (whose base salaries are lower than those of executives in comparable firms) get bonuses based on Nucor's annual overall percentage of net income to stockholder's equity.[49] Including bonuses, a typical Nucor steel mill worker earns about $72,000 a year, not counting the profit sharing plan that recently paid out an additional $18,000 per employee.[50]

Profit-Sharing Plans

profit-sharing plan
A plan whereby most employees share in the company's profits.

In a **profit-sharing plan**, most employees receive a share of the company's annual profits, usually at the end of the fiscal year. With *current profit sharing* plans, employees share in a portion of the employer's profits quarterly or annually. With *deferred profit sharing* plans, the employer puts cash awards into trust accounts for the employees' retirement. In general, employers base the pool of profit sharing funds on a fixed or graduated percentage of the firm's profits. They then distribute the profit sharing awards to employees based on a percentage of the employee's salary, or some measure of the employee's contribution to company profits.[51]

Research on the effectiveness of such plans is sketchy. One early study concluded that there was "ample" evidence that profit sharing plans boost productivity, but that their effect on profits is insignificant, once you factor in the costs of the plans' payouts.[52]

Employee Stock Ownership Plans

employee stock ownership plan (ESOP)
A corporation contributes shares of its own stock to a trust to purchase company stock for employees. The trust distributes the stock to employees upon retirement or separation from service.

Employee Retirement Income Security Act (ERISA)
Signed into law by President Ford in 1974 to require that pension rights be vested, and protected by a government agency, Pension Benefits Guarantee Corporation.

Employee stock ownership plans (ESOPs) are company-wide plans in which a corporation contributes shares of its own stock—or cash to be used to purchase such stock—to a trust established to purchase shares of the firm's stock for employees. The firm generally makes these contributions annually in proportion to total employee compensation, with a limit of 15% of compensation. The trust holds the stock in individual employee accounts. It then distributes it to employees upon retirement (or other separation from service), assuming the person has worked long enough to earn ownership of the stock. (Traditional stock options, as discussed elsewhere in this chapter, go directly to the employees individually to use as they see fit, rather than into a retirement trust.) Trustees and possibly top management can and have been held responsible for ESOP trust problems, as when funds are lost.[53]

ESOPs have several advantages. In the U.S., the corporation receives a tax deduction equal to the fair market value of the shares that it transfers to the trustee. It can also claim an income tax deduction for dividends paid on stock the ESOP owns. Employees are not taxed until they receive a distribution from the trust, usually at retirement when they normally have a reduced tax rate. And the **Employee Retirement Income Security Act (ERISA)** allows a firm to borrow against employee stock held in trust. The employer can then repay the loan in pretax rather than in after-tax dollars, another ESOP tax incentive.

BROAD-BASED STOCK OPTIONS For many years, some employers awarded stock options to all or most employees (not just executives) as part of the employers' profit sharing plans. One study compared performance of 229 "new economy" (technology, Internet, and so forth) firms offering broad-based stock options to that of their non-stock-option counterparts. Those offering stock options had higher shareholder returns than those not offering the options.[54]

Recently, however, a number of large companies announced they were discontinuing distributing stock options to most employees. Some of them, including Microsoft, are instead awarding stock. With companies now having to show the options as an expense when awarded, firms like Microsoft apparently feel awarding stock instead of stock options is a more direct and immediate way of linking pay to performance.[55]

Scanlon/Gainsharing Plans

Scanlon plan

An incentive plan developed in 1937 by Joseph Scanlon and designed to encourage cooperation, involvement, and sharing of benefits.

gainsharing plan

An incentive plan that engages employees in a common effort to achieve productivity objectives and share the gains.

The **Scanlon plan** is an incentive plan developed in 1937 by Joseph Scanlon, a United Steel Workers Union official;[56] it is remarkably progressive considering that it was developed so long ago. It is one of many **gainsharing plans**, the aim of which are to encourage improved employee productivity by sharing resulting financial gains with employees. Other popular types of gainsharing plans include the Rucker and Improshare plans.

FEATURES Scanlon plans have five basic features.[57] The first is the *philosophy of cooperation* on which it is based. This philosophy assumes that managers and workers should rid themselves of the "us" and "them" attitudes that normally inhibit employees from developing a sense of ownership in the company. It substitutes instead a climate in which everyone cooperates because he or she understands that economic rewards are contingent on honest cooperation.

A second feature of a Scanlon plan is *identity*. This means that to focus employee efforts, the company's mission or purpose must be clearly articulated, and employees must understand how the business operates in terms of customers, prices, and costs, for instance. *Competence* is a third basic feature. The plan, say three experts, "explicitly recognizes that a Scanlon plan demands a high level of competence from employees at all levels."[58]

The fourth feature is the *involvement system*.[59] This takes the form of two levels of committees—the departmental level and the executive level. Employees present productivity-improving suggestions to the appropriate departmental-level committees, which transmit the valuable ones to the executive-level committee. The latter then decides whether to implement the suggestions.

The fifth feature of the plan is the *sharing of benefits formula*. The Scanlon plan assumes that employees should share directly in any extra profits resulting from their cost-cutting suggestions. For example, if a suggestion is implemented and successful, all employees might share in 75% of the savings.

Earnings-at-Risk Pay Plans

The basic characteristic of an earnings-at-risk pay plan is that some portion of the employee's base salary is at risk. For example, suppose in one department the employees' at-risk pay is 6%. This means that each employee's base pay will be 94% of his or her counterpart's salary in other (not-at-risk) departments. If the department achieves its goals, the employees get their full pay; if it exceeds its goals, they may receive a bonus exceeding the 6%.

One study concluded that the employees they studied were dissatisfied with their lower base salary, but that this dissatisfaction seemed to motivate them to work harder to earn the incentive and thereby raise their total pay.[60]

Improving Productivity Through HRIS: Incentive Management Systems

Incentives are becoming ever more complicated. For one thing, as we've seen, more employees—not just salespeople—now get incentives. Furthermore, the range of behaviors for which employers pay incentives is now quite broad, from better service to cutting costs to answering more calls per hour.[61]

Tracking performance of dozens or hundreds of measures like these and then computing individual employees' incentives can be very time consuming. Several companies therefore provide software known as Enterprise Incentive Management (EIM) systems to automate the planning and management of plans like these. As one expert says, "EIM software automates the planning, calculation, modeling, and management of incentive compensation plans, enabling companies to align their employees with corporate strategy and goals."[62]

For a large business with thousands of sales reps, employee incentive management (EIM) systems can cost between $1 million and $10 million to install. But when you consider that it costs an average of $1,500 a year per employee to manage a manual system, an EIM system can pay for itself in the first year or two.[63] The market for EIM systems now probably exceeds a billion dollars.[64]

Employers also increasingly use the Web to support their sales and other incentive programs. For example, SalesDriver, in Maynard, Massachusetts, runs Web-based, sales performance–based incentive programs. Firms like these create online sales incentive programs. SalesDriver can help a company launch a campaign Web template in a day or less. Using the template, the sales manager can select from a catalog of 1,500 reward items, and award these to sales and marketing reps for meeting quotas for things like lead generation and total sales.[65]

EMPLOYEE BENEFITS

benefits
Indirect financial payments given to employees. They may include health and life insurance, vacation, pension, education plans, and discounts on company products, for instance.

Benefits represent an important part of just about every employee's pay. They are "indirect monetary and nonmonetary payments an employee receives for continuing to work for the company." Benefits include such things as time off with pay, health and life insurance, and child care facilities.

Most full-time employees in the United States receive benefits. Virtually all employers—99%—offer some health insurance coverage.[66]

In the U.S., benefits are a major expense for most employers. Employee benefits account for 33% to 40% of wages and salaries (or about 28% of total payrolls); legally required benefits (like unemployment insurance) are the most expensive single benefit cost, followed by health insurance. Consultants Towers Perrin estimate that the recent cost of medical coverage alone was about $888 per month for family coverage.[67]

There are many benefits and various ways to classify them. In the remainder of this section we classify benefits as pay for time not worked, insurance benefits, retirement benefits, and employee services benefits.

Pay for Time Not Worked

4 List and describe each of the basic benefits most employers might be expected to offer.

Supplemental pay benefits, or pay for time not worked, are typically one of an employer's most expensive benefits because of all the time off that employees receive. Common time-off-with-pay benefits include holidays, vacations, jury duty, bereavement leave, military duty, sick leave, sabbatical leave, maternity leave, and unemployment insurance payments for laid-off or terminated employees.

UNEMPLOYMENT INSURANCE All states in the U.S. have unemployment insurance or compensation acts, which provide for weekly benefits if a person is unable to work through some fault other than his or her own. The benefits derive from an unemployment tax on employers that can range from 0.1% to 5% of taxable payroll in most states. States each have their own unemployment laws, which follow federal guidelines. An organization's unemployment tax reflects its experience with personnel terminations.

Unemployment benefits are not meant for all dismissed employees, only for those terminated through no fault of their own. Thus, strictly speaking, a worker fired for chronic lateness has no legitimate claim to benefits. But in practice, many managers take a lackadaisical attitude toward protecting their employers against unwarranted claims. Therefore, employers spend thousands of dollars more per year on unemployment taxes than would be necessary if they protected themselves—for instance, by keeping careful records of lateness and absences, and by warning employees whose performance is inadequate.[68]

VACATIONS AND HOLIDAYS Most firms offer vacation leave benefits. Eighty-four percent of human resource professionals said their firms offered paid holiday for employees, and more than half (51%) reported offering paid personal days.[69] On average, American workers get 8.9 days of leave after one year's employment. Days off rises to about 11 after 3 years, 14 after 5 years, and 16 after 10 years.[70] The average number of annual vacation days varies around the world. For example, vacation allowances vary from 6 days in Mexico to 10 days in Japan, 25 in Sweden, 25 in France, and 33 in Denmark.

More firms are moving to a somewhat more flexible vacation leave approach. For example, all of IBM's 350,000 plus employees are eligible for at least 3 weeks vacation. However, IBM doesn't formally track how much vacation each person takes, or when they take it. Instead, employees simply make informal vacation arrangements with their direct supervisors.[71]

SICK LEAVE Sick leave provides pay to employees when they are out of work because of illness. In the U.S., sick leave policies grant full pay for a specified number of permissible sick days, usually up to about 12 per year. The sick days often accumulate at the rate of approximately 1 day per month of service.

Sick leave pay causes consternation for many employers. The problem is that although many employees use their sick days only when they are legitimately sick, others (in the eyes of some employers) take advantage of sick leave by using it as if it's extra holiday time, whether they are sick or not. One survey a few years ago found that the average cost of absenteeism per employee per year in the U.S. was about $789, with personal illness accounting for about a third of the absences.[72]

Employers utilize several tactics to eliminate or reduce this problem:

■ Many use *pooled paid leave* plans. These plans—which lump together days off for sick leave, vacation, and holidays into a single leave pool—have grown from 21% of firms surveyed 5 years ago to 66% recently.[73]

■ Other firms buy back unused sick leave at the end of the year by paying their employees a daily equivalent pay for each sick leave day not used. The drawback is that the policy can encourage legitimately sick employees to come to work despite their illness.

■ Others hold monthly lotteries in which only employees with perfect attendance are able to participate; those who participate are eligible to win a cash prize.

■ Still others aggressively investigate all unplanned absences, for instance, by calling the absent employees at their homes when they are taking sick days.

FMLA Sick leave policy depends to some extent on the U.S. Family and Medical Leave Act of 1993 (FMLA). Among its provisions, the law stipulates that:

1. Private employers of 50 or more employees must provide eligible employees up to 12 weeks of unpaid leave for their own serious illness, the birth or adoption of a child, or the care of a seriously ill child, spouse, or parent.
2. Employers may require employees to take any unused paid sick leave or annual leave as part of the 12-week leave provided in the law.
3. Employees taking leave are entitled to receive health benefits while they are on unpaid leave under the same terms and conditions as when they were on the job.
4. In most cases, employers must guarantee employees the right to return to their previous or equivalent position with no loss of benefits at the end of the leave.

severance pay
A one-time payment employers provide when terminating an employee.

SEVERANCE PAY Many employers provide **severance pay**—a one-time separation payment—when terminating an employee. Other firms provide "bridge" severance pay by keeping employees (especially managers) on the payroll for several months, until they find new jobs. About half of employers surveyed give white-collar and exempt employees one week of severance pay per year of service, and about one-third do the same for blue-collar workers. It is most common to award severance pay as part of a reduction in workforce. It is somewhat less common to award it when dismissing someone for poor performance. It is uncommon to pay severance when employees quit or are fired for cause (though some employers do, to head off lawsuits).[74]

Severance pay makes sense on several grounds. It is a humanitarian gesture as well as good public relations. In addition, most managers expect employees to give them at least 1 or 2 weeks' notice if they plan to quit; it is therefore appropriate (and in some states mandatory) to provide at least one pay period's severance pay if an employee is terminated. Such payments can also reduce the possibility that a terminated employee will litigate.

Things to keep in mind when crafting the severance plan include:[75]

- List the situations for which the firm will pay severance, such as layoffs resulting from internal reorganizations. Indicate that action regarding other situations will be determined by management as necessary.
- Require signing of a waiver/general release prior to remittance of any severance pay, absolving the employer from employment-related liability. To be an effective release, the signing of the release must be knowing and voluntary, and there are additional legal requirements.
- Reserve the right to terminate or alter the policy.
- Remember that as with all personnel actions, the employer must make severance payments, if any, equitably.

Plant closings and downsizings have put thousands of employees out of work, often with little or no notice or severance pay. *The Worker Adjustment and Retraining ("plant closing") Act* of 1989 requires covered employers to give employees 60 days' written notice of plant closures or mass layoffs.

Insurance Benefits

workers' compensation
Provides income and medical benefits to work-related accident victims or their dependents regardless of fault.

WORKERS' COMPENSATION **Workers' compensation** laws are aimed at providing sure, prompt income and medical benefits to work-related accident victims or their dependents, regardless of fault. Every state has its own workers' compensation law, and some states offer their own insurance programs. However, most require employers to purchase workers' compensation insurance through private state-approved insurance companies. These firms then charge the employer an annual premium based in part on the employer's accident and claims rates.

Workers' compensation benefits can be either monetary or medical. In the event of a worker's death or disablement, the person or his or her beneficiary gets a cash benefit based on prior earnings—usually one-half to two-thirds of the worker's average weekly wage, per week of employment. In most states there is a set time limit—such as 500 weeks—for which an employee can receive benefits. If the injury causes a specific loss (such as loss of an arm), the employee may receive additional benefits based on a statutory list of losses, even though he or she may return to work. In addition to these cash benefits, employers must furnish accident-related medical, surgical, and hospital services needed by the employee.

For an injury or illness to be covered by workers' compensation, the employee need only prove that it arose while he or she was on the job. It does not matter that the employee may have been at fault or disregarded instructions. If he or she was on the job when the injury occurred, he or she is entitled to workers' compensation.

Many, or most, workers' compensation claims are legitimate, but some are not. Supervisors should be aware of typical red flags of fraudulent claims, such as vague accident details and minor accidents resulting in major injuries.

Hospitalization, Medical, and Disability Insurance

Health care benefits top employees' desired benefits. Seventy-five percent of respondents in one recent survey said they considered health care benefits their most important benefits.[76]

Most employers therefore offer their employees some type of hospitalization, medical, and prescription insurance (see Table 8.2). Many offer membership in a health maintenance organization (HMO) as a hospital/medical option. The HMO is a medical organization consisting of numerous specialists (surgeons, psychiatrists, etc.) operating out of a community-based health care center. Preferred provider organizations (PPOs) let employees select providers (such as participating physicians) who agree to provide price discounts and submit to certain utilization controls, such as the number of diagnostic tests that can be ordered.

THE PREGNANCY DISCRIMINATION ACT The Pregnancy Discrimination Act (PDA) aims to prohibit sex discrimination based on "pregnancy, childbirth, or related medical conditions." Before enactment of this U.S. law in 1978, employers generally paid temporary disability benefits for pregnancies in the form of either sick leave or disability insurance, if at all. However, although most employers provide temporary disability income to their employees for up to 26 weeks for most illnesses, those that provided benefits for pregnancy usually limited benefits to only 6 weeks for normal pregnancies. Many believed that the shorter duration of pregnancy benefits constituted discrimination based on sex.

The act requires employers to treat women affected by pregnancy, childbirth, or related medical conditions the same as any employee not able to work, with respect to all benefits, including sick leave and disability benefits, and health and medical insurance. For example, if an employer provides up to 26 weeks of temporary disability income to employees for all illnesses, it is also required to provide up to 26 weeks for pregnancy and childbirth or related medical conditions.

COBRA REQUIREMENTS The ominously titled COBRA—Consolidated Omnibus Budget Reconciliation Act—requires most private employers to make available to terminated or retired employees and their families continued health benefits for a period of time, generally 18 months. If the former employee chooses to continue these benefits, he or she must pay for them, as well as a small fee for administrative costs.

Take care in administering COBRA, especially with respect to informing employees of their COBRA rights. For example, you do not want a separated uninsured employee to be injured and come back and claim she didn't know her insurance coverage could have been

TABLE 8.2 Percentage of U.S. Employers Offering Various Health Benefits

	Yes (%)	No (%)	Plan to (%)
Prescription drug program coverage	95	5	
Dental insurance	94	5	1
Mail order prescription program	87	12	1
PPO (preferred provider organization)	87	12	1
Mental health insurance	73	27	
Vision insurance	79	20	1
Employee assistance program	73	25	2
Vaccinations onsite (example: flu shots)	62	37	1
Chiropractic insurance	80	20	
Wellness program, resources, and information	68	26	6
CPR training/first aid	55	42	3
HMO (health maintenance organization)	48	51	

Source: Adapted from SHRM/SHRM Foundation 2007 Benefits Survey Report.

Health care benefits top employees' desired benefits.

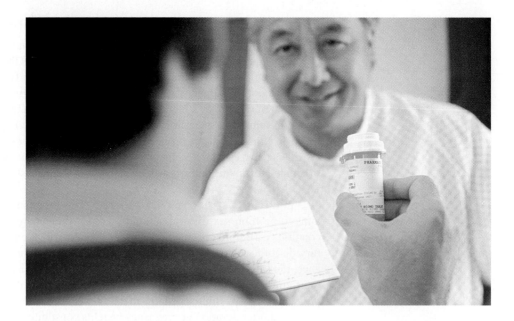

continued. Therefore, when a new employee first becomes eligible for your company's insurance plan, the employee should receive and acknowledge having received an explanation of COBRA rights. More important, all employees separated from the company should sign a form acknowledging that they have received and understand their COBRA rights.

COST CONTROL Health care costs are spiraling. For example (see Figure 8.5), they're projected to grow from about 16% of GNP in 2004 to 20% in 2009. Containing those costs is thus a huge employer concern. Strategies include the following.

Cost containment specialists Many are using cost-containment specialists—companies that specialize in helping employers reduce their health care costs. For example, health care containment companies can use their network of contacts with PPOs to help employers obtain the best PPO coverage for their needs.

Online administration Other big savings come from automating health care plan administration, for instance, by making online enrollment by employees mandatory.

Defined benefits Other employers are moving toward defined contribution health care plans. Under defined contribution health care plans, each employee has a medical allotment that he or she can use for co-payments or discretionary medical costs, rather than a health care benefits package with open-ended costs.

Deductibles Other firms are moving toward offering plans with high deductibles—more than $1,000—for individual coverage.[77]

Outsourcing Outsourcing is another option. For example, 84% of firms in one survey said they were outsourcing employee assistance and counseling, and 53% were outsourcing health care benefits administration.[78]

FIGURE 8.5   U.S. Health Care Cost Increases*

	2004	2009	2015
Total spending on health care	$1.9 trillion	$2.9 trillion	$4 trillion
% of GNP	16%	18%	20%

Note: Figures for 2009 and 2015 estimated. Health care costs rose 7.9% in 2004, about twice the rate of inflation, and are expected to rise at that rate through 2015.

Sources: Eric Perlmenter, "Controlling Health Care Costs," *Compensation & Benefits Review* (September/October 2002): 44; Victoria Colliver, "Health Care Costs Continue Double Digit Increase," *San Francisco Chronicle* (December 8, 2003); The National Coalition on Health Care, www.nchc.org/facts/cost.shtml, accessed March 21, 2007.

Wellness programs Medical experts believe that many illnesses are preventable, and studies show that that controlling health risks can reduce illnesses and health care costs.[79] Most large employers (and many small ones) therefore offer some form of preventive services or "wellness benefits." *Clinical prevention* programs include things like mammograms, immunizations, and routine checkups. *Health promotion and disease prevention* programs include things like seminars and incentives aimed at improving health by changing unhealthy behaviors or modifying lifestyles.[80]

For example, Vaught Aircraft Industries Inc. kicked off its wellness program with health fairs in all its locations. Employees and families could come to the fairs to receive one-on-one health assessments (including blood samples and blood pressure readings). Vaught also offers a 24-hour telephone hotline to answer employees' health and lifestyle questions, as well as workshops and classes on things like stress management.[81]

Claims audits Many employers pay out thousands or millions of dollars in erroneous health claims. The industry standard for percentage of claims dollars actually paid in error is 1%; in two recent years the *actual* percentage of claims dollars paid in error were 3.5% and 3.3%. Setting standards for errors, and then aggressively auditing the claims being paid, may be the most direct way to reduce employer health care expenses.[82]

Medical tourism "Medical tourism" is another option. Here employers encourage employees to have some non-urgent medical procedures done overseas. Hospitals in Brazil or Malaysia may charge half what a U.S. hospital would for shoulder surgery, for instance. The key question is quality of care, but (while many people have successfully used this option) it's still not entirely clear how to assess overseas medical quality.[83]

LONG-TERM CARE Today, there are many types of long-term care—care to support older persons in their old age—for which employers can provide insurance benefits for their employees. For example, adult day-care facilities offer social and recreational activities. Assisted-living facilities offer shared housing and supervision for those who cannot function independently. Home care is care received at home from a nurse, an aide, or another specialist.

U.S. Retirement Benefits

SOCIAL SECURITY There are three types of Social Security benefits. First are the familiar *retirement benefits*, which provide an income if the employee retires at age 62 or thereafter and is insured under the Social Security Act. Second, survivor's or *death benefits* provide monthly payments to dependents regardless of the employee's age at death, again assuming the employee was insured under the Social Security Act. Finally, *disability payments* provide monthly payments to an employee and his or her dependents if the employee becomes totally disabled for work and meets specified work requirements. The Social Security system also administers the Medicare program, which provides a wide range of health services to people 65 and over.

"Full retirement age" traditionally was 65—the usual age for retirement. However, full retirement age to collect Social Security rose gradually, and is now 67 for those born in 1960 or later. Employer and employee generally share equally in paying the social security tax. In 2008, the maximum earnings subject to the 6.2% Social Security tax was $102,000.[84]

PENSION PLANS Pensions provide income to individuals in their retirement, and just over half of full-time workers participate in some type of pension plan at work.

We can classify pension plans in three basic ways: contributory versus noncontributory plans; qualified versus nonqualified plans; and defined contribution versus defined benefit plans.[85] The employee contributes to the contributory pension plan, while the employer makes all contributions to the noncontributory pension plan. Employers derive certain tax benefits from contributing to qualified pension plans, such as tax deductions for contributions (they are "qualified" under IRS regulations); nonqualified pension plans get less favorable tax treatment for employees and employers.[86]

defined benefit plan
A plan that contains a formula for specifying retirement benefits.

defined contribution plan
A plan in which the employer's contribution to employees' retirement or savings funds is specified.

portability
Making it easier for employees who leave the firm prior to retirement to take their accumulated pension funds with them.

With **defined benefit plans**, the employee knows ahead of time the pension benefits he or she will receive. The defined pension benefit itself is usually set by a formula that ties the person's retirement pension to an amount equal to a percentage of the person's pre-retirement pay. For instance, the plan may multiply an average of his or her last 5 years of annual pay by the number of years he or she worked for the company.

Defined contribution plans specify what contribution the employee and employer will make to the employee's retirement or savings fund. Here, the contribution is defined, not the pension. With a defined benefit plan, the employee knows what his or her retirement benefits will be upon retirement. With a defined contribution plan, the person's pension will depend on the amounts contributed to the fund and on the retirement fund's investment earnings. Defined contribution plans are increasingly popular among employers today because of their relative ease of administration, favorable tax treatment, and other factors. **Portability**—making it easier for employees who leave the firm prior to retirement to take their accumulated pension funds with them—is enhanced by switching from defined benefit to defined contribution plans

401(K) PLANS The 401(k) plan is one defined contribution plan. Under the 401(k) plan (based on Section 401(k) of the Internal Revenue Code), employees have the employer place a portion of their compensation, which would otherwise be paid in cash, into a company profit sharing or stock bonus plan. This results in a pretax reduction in salary, so the employee isn't taxed on those set-aside dollars until after he or she retires (or removes the money from the pension fund). Some employers also match a portion of what the employee contributes to the 401(k) plan. One attraction of 401(k) is that employees may have a range of investment options for the 401(k) funds, including mutual stock funds and bond funds.

CASH BALANCE PENSION PLANS In a defined benefit plan, to get the maximum benefit, the person generally must "put in" his or her full 30 or so years with the firm. This approach tends to favor older employees (whose income is often higher and who have been with the firm for a number of years). Younger employees (and/or those who want the option of moving on with their vested pension benefits after a few years) might prefer defined contribution plans. Here the employee receives the full vested value of his or her pension up to when he or she leaves. (The vested funds are those the employee owns.)

Cash balance plans are a hybrid; when they leave or retire, employees have a cash balance in their account (thus similar to a defined benefit), but they also have the portability advantages of defined contribution plans. These plans thus provide the portability of defined contribution plans with the more predictable benefits of defined benefit plans.[87] Employees who retire can get either their account's cash balance, or an annual pension.

ERISA The Employee Retirement Income Security Act (ERISA) aims to protect the pensions of workers and to stimulate pension plan growth. Before enactment of ERISA, pension plans often failed to deliver expected benefits to employees. Many reasons, such as business failure and inadequate funding, could result in employees losing their expected pensions and facing the prospect of being unable to retire.

vested
The proportion of the employers contribution to the employee's pension plan that is guaranteed to the employee and which the employee can therefore take when he or she leaves.

VESTING Under ERISA, pension rights must be **vested**—guaranteed to the employee—under one of three formulas. Today (the rules changed in 2002) employers can choose one of two minimum vesting schedules (employers can allow funds to vest faster if they wish). With *cliff vesting*, the time period for acquiring a nonforfeitable right in employer matching contributions (if any) is 3 years. So, the employee must have nonforfeitable rights to these funds by the end of 3 years. With the second option (*graded vesting*), participants in pension plans must receive nonforfeitable rights to the matching contributions as follows: 20% after 2 years, and then 20% for each succeeding year, with a 100% nonforfeitable right by the end of 6 years.

The Pension Benefits Guarantee Corporation (PBGC) ensures that pensions meet their obligations under ERISA. The PBGC also insures pensions should a plan terminate without sufficient funds. However, the PBGC guarantees only defined benefit, not defined contribution plans. Furthermore, it will only pay someone a pension of up to about $49,000 per year (for someone 65 years of age) with a plan terminating in 2007. So, high-income workers may still end up with reduced pensions if a plan fails.

Employee Services and Family-Friendly Benefits

Although an employer's time off, insurance, and retirement benefits account for the main part of its benefits costs, many employers also provide a range of services, including personal services (such as legal and personal counseling), job-related services (such as subsidized child care facilities), educational subsidies, and executive perquisites (such as company cars and planes for its executives).

Employee Assistance Programs (EAPs) are an example. Originally aimed at supporting employees with alcohol and mental health problems, today's EAPs are generally more wide ranging, addressing matters such as elder care, domestic violence, and legal problems, for instance.[88] EAPs are increasingly popular, with more than 60% of larger firms offering such programs.

Among other benefits, employers may also offer employees full or partial college tuition reimbursement. The idea is to help attract upwardly mobile recruits, retain employees who might otherwise leave, and provide promotable employees with the educations they need to move up. However, enhanced mobility is a double-edged sword. An analysis of the U.S. Navy's tuition assistance program found that those who used the Navy's tuition assistance were also significantly more likely to leave the Navy.[89]

FAMILY-FRIENDLY BENEFITS The term "*family-friendly*" benefits refers to a fairly long list of benefits like child care, the overall aim of which is to make it easier for employees to balance their work life and home life responsibilities. For example, software giant SAS Institute offers preschool child care centers, a gym, a full-time in-house elder care consultant, 3 weeks' paid vacation, a flexible ("flextime") work schedule, and a standard 35-hour workweek.

As you can see in Figure 8.6, the list of possible family-friendly benefits is quite long, but three increasingly popular benefits deserve special note. More employers are offering *emergency child care benefits*, for instance, for when a young child's regular babysitter is a no-show. For example, Canadian financial services company CIBC is expanding its on-site child care center to handle last-minute emergencies.[90] Similarly, with more older workers in the workforce, about 120 million Americans are now or have in the past cared for an adult relative or friend. Employers therefore increasingly offer *adult care support*, including counseling and adult day care centers.[91] Some employers enrich their *parental leave plans* to make it more attractive for mothers to return from maternity leave, for instance, offering meaningful jobs with reduced travel and hours.[92]

WHY FAMILY-FRIENDLY BENEFITS? That employees want and need such benefits seems obvious. For example, about half of 2,586 workers surveyed felt they were working too much and putting too little time into "other things in life that really matter."[93]

For the employer, programs like these produce advantages as well as costs. For example, sick family members and health problems such as depression account for many of the sick-leave days employees take. Employers can reduce these absences with programs that provide advice on issues like elder care referrals and personal counseling.[94]

WORKPLACE FLEXIBILITY Employees are increasingly conducting business from nontraditional office settings (in their cars or on vacation, for instance) using technological means like iPods and Blackberry-type devices.[95] As a result, more employers are introducing workplace flexibility programs. **Workplace flexibility** means arming employees with the information technology tools they need to get their jobs done wherever the employees are. For example, Capital One Financial Corp. has its Future of Work program. Certain Capital One employees received mobile technology tools such as wireless

Employee Assistance Program (EAP)
A formal employer program for providing employees with counseling and/or treatment programs for problems such as alcoholism, gambling, or stress.

workplace flexibility
Arming employees with the information technology tools they need to get their jobs done wherever the employees are.

FIGURE 8.6 Popular U.S. Family-Friendly Benefits

(n = 90) Companies now offering:	Yes	No	Plan to
Dependent care flexible spending account	76%	22%	2%
Life insurance for dependents	65%	34%	1%
Flextime	58%	40%	3%
Telecommuting on an ad-hoc basis	48%	52%	1%
Compressed workweek	38%	60%	2%
Health care benefits for dependent grandchildren	38%	61%	1%
Domestic partner benefits (same-sex partners)	33%	66%	2%
Domestic partner benefits (opposite-sex partners)	33%	66%	2%
Telecommuting on a part-time basis	33%	66%	1%
Paid family leave	33%	67%	*
Bring child to work in emergency	29%	70%	1%
Health care benefits for foster children	29%	70%	1%
Family leave above and beyond required federal FMLA leave	27%	73%	1%
Lactation program/designated area	26%	72%	2%
Family leave above and beyond required state FMLA leave	24%	76%	1%
Eldercare referral service	22%	77%	1%
Childcare referral service	21%	78%	1%
Telecommuting on a full-time basis	21%	78%	1%
Parental leave above and beyond federal FMLA	21%	79%	1%
Adoption assistance	20%	78%	2%
Job sharing	20%	78%	2%
Parental leave above and beyond state FMLA	20%	80%	1%
Scholarships for members of employees' families	20%	80%	1%

Note: Data sorted in descending order by the "Yes" column. Percentages are row percentages and may not total 100% due to rounding.

Source: Adapted from SHRM Foundation 2007 Benefits Survey Report.

access laptops and Blackberry-type cell phone devices. The program seems to have led to about a 41% increase in overall workplace satisfaction, a 31% reduction in time needed to get input from peers, and a 53% increase in those who say their workplace enhances group productivity.[96]

Flexible Benefits

Employees tend to differ in what benefits they want and need. Young workers with families may want more child care. Older workers may want elder care advice and resources.

flexible benefits plan
Individualized plans allowed by employers to accommodate employee preferences for benefits.

Flexible benefits plans are also called *cafeteria plans* because employees can spend their benefits allowances on a choice of benefits options. Either way, the idea is to let the employee put together his or her own benefit package, subject to two constraints. First, the employer must carefully limit total cost for each benefit package. Second, each benefit plan must include certain nonoptional items, including, for example, Social Security, workers' compensation, and unemployment insurance. About 37% of employers offer a flexible benefits plan (ability to select from a variety of benefits).[97]

Workplace flexibility means arming employees with the information technology tools they need to get their jobs done wherever the employees are.

Flexible benefits plans are also subject to U.S. Internal Revenue Service regulations. For example, new IRS regulations require formal written plans describing the employer's cafeteria plan, including benefits and procedures for choosing them.[98]

Benefits and Employee Leasing

Employee leasing firms (also known as professional employer organizations) arrange to have all the employer's employees transferred to the employee leasing firm's payroll. The employee leasing firm becomes the legal employer and handles all the employer's employee-related paperwork. This usually includes recruiting, hiring, paying tax liabilities (Social Security payments, unemployment insurance, etc.), and handling day-to-day details such as performance appraisals (with the assistance of the onsite supervisor). However, it is with respect to benefits management that employee leasing is often most advantageous.

Getting insurance is often the most serious personnel problem smaller employers face. Remember that the leasing firm is the legal employer of the other company's employees. Therefore, the employees are absorbed into a much larger insurable group (along with other employers' former employees). The employee leasing company can therefore often offer benefits smaller companies can't obtain at such a low cost.

Benefits Web Sites

To reduce the costs of administering benefits, many employers enable employees to manage much of their own benefits changes (dependants, 401(k), health plan, and so on) themselves, via the employer's (or an outside vendor's) Web site.

Employers are adding new services to their benefits Web sites. In addition to offering things like self enrollment, the insurance company USAA's Web site helps employees achieve better work–life balance. For example, suppose the employee clicks on the "today, I'm feeling . . . " menu. Here employees can respond to a list of words (such as "stressed"), and from there see suggestions for dealing with (in this case) stress. Go to "my child is behaving badly" and the employee gets access to resources like "guide to addressing child behavior problems."[99] Boeing's Pay & Benefits Profile site draws on data from about 30 different compensation sources. Employees can get real-time information about the status of their salary and bonuses, benefits, pension, and even special services such as child care referrals.[100]

The *Business in Action* feature on page 276 addresses the role of finance and budgeting in compensation management.

Business in Action Building Your *Finance and Budgeting* Knowledge

No manager should formulate pay policies without understanding how total compensation fits within the department's and company's budgets. For example, embarking on a plan to raise wages 5% is probably foolhardy if, given the financial situation, the employer won't be able to afford the extra expenses. Those formulating compensation plans must thus have at least a good working knowledge of budgeting (and of what their own company's budgetary constraints are).

Budgets are formal financial expressions of a manager's plans. They show targets for things like sales, cost of materials, production levels, and profit, expressed in dollars. These planned targets are the standards against which the manager compares and controls the unit's actual performance. Budgets are the most widely used control device. Each manager, from first-line supervisor to company president, usually has an operating budget to use as a standard of comparison.

The first step in budgeting is generally to develop a sales forecast and sales budget. The sales budget shows the planned sales activity for each period (usually in units per month) and the revenue expected from the sales.

The manager can then produce various operating budgets. *Operating budgets* show the expected sales and/or expenses for each of the company's departments for the planning period in question. For example, the *production and materials budget* (or plan) shows what the company will spend for materials, labor, and administration to implement the sales budget. The *personnel budget* shows what executing the plan will cost in terms of employee wages, incentives and benefits.

Profit Planning

The next step is to combine all these departmental budgets into a profit plan for the coming year. This profit plan is the budgeted *income statement* or pro forma income statement. It lists expected sales, then expected expenses, and then expected income or profit (or loss) for the year. In practice, cash from sales usually doesn't flow into the firm so that it coincides precisely with cash disbursements. (Some customers may take 35 days to pay their bills, for instance, but employees expect paychecks every week.) The *cash budget* or plan shows, for each month, the amount of cash the company can expect to receive and the amount it can expect to disperse. The manager can use it to anticipate his or her cash needs, and to arrange for short-term loans, if need be.

The company also has a budgeted *balance sheet*. The budgeted balance sheet shows managers, owners, and creditors what the company's projected financial picture should be at the end of the year. It shows assets (such as cash and equipment), liabilities (such as long-term debt), and net worth (the excess of assets over other liabilities).

The firm's accountants compile the financial information and feed it back to the appropriate managers. A *performance report* shows budgeted or planned targets. Next to these numbers, it shows the department's actual performance numbers. *Variances* show the differences between budgeted and actual amounts. The report may provide a space for the manager to explain any variances. After reviewing the performance report, management can take corrective action.

The firm's outside accountants periodically audit the firm's financial statements. An *audit* is a systematic process that involves three steps: (1) objectively obtain and evaluate evidence regarding important aspects of the firm's performance; (2) judge the accuracy and validity of the data; and (3) communicate the results to interested users, such as the board of directors and the company's banks. The purpose of the audit is to certify that the firm's financial statements accurately reflect its performance.

Review

SUMMARY

1. Establishing pay rates involves five steps: conduct salary survey, evaluate jobs, develop pay grades, use wage curves, and develop pay ranges.
2. Job evaluation is aimed at determining the relative worth of a job. It compares jobs to one another based on their content, which is usually defined in terms of compensable factors such as skills, effort, responsibility, and working conditions.
3. Most managers group similar jobs into wage or pay grades for pay purposes. These grades are composed of jobs of approximately equal difficulty or importance as determined by job evaluation.
4. Developing a compensation plan for executive, managerial, and professional personnel is complicated by the fact that factors such as performance and creativity must take precedence over static factors such as working conditions. Market rates, performance, and incentives and benefits thus play a much greater role than does job evaluation for these employees.

5. Broadbanding means collapsing salary grades and ranges into just a few wide levels or bands, each of which then contains a relatively wide range of jobs and salary levels.

6. Piecework is the oldest type of incentive plan; a worker is paid a piece rate for each unit he or she produces. Team incentives are another option. With team incentives, the employee's team receives an incentive payment (shared by team members) for achieving a target. Unlike individual incentive plans team-based plans pay incentives on how the team does, so that individual workers who do exemplary work may feel underpaid.

7. Profit sharing and the Scanlon plan are examples of organizationwide incentive plans. The problem with such plans is that the link between a person's efforts and rewards is sometimes unclear. Merit plans are other popular incentive plans.

8. Supplemental pay benefits provide pay for time not worked. They include unemployment insurance, vacation and holiday pay, severance pay, and supplemental unemployment benefits.

9. Insurance benefits are another type of employee benefit. Workers' compensation, for example, is aimed at ensuring prompt income and medical benefits to work accident victims or their dependents, regardless of fault. Most employers also provide group life insurance and group hospitalization, accident, and disability insurance.

10. Two types of retirement benefits are Social Security and pensions. Social Security covers not only retirement benefits but also survivors and disability benefits. One of the critical issues in pension planning is vesting the money that the employer has placed in the latter's pension fund, which cannot be forfeited for any reason. ERISA ensures that pension rights become vested and protected after a reasonable amount of time.

KEY TERMS

employee compensation 250
Fair Labor Standards Act 250
Equal Pay Act 251
Civil Rights Act 251
salary (or compensation) surveys 253
job evaluation 254
compensable factors 254
ranking method 254
wage curve 255
incentive plan 260
piecework 260
stock option 260
merit pay (merit raise) 263
team 263
profit-sharing plan 264

employee stock ownership plan (ESOP) 264
Employee Retirement Income Security Act (ERISA) 264
Scanlon plan 265
gainsharing plan 265
benefits 266
severance pay 268
workers' compensation 268
defined benefit plan 272
defined contribution plan 272
portability 272
vested 272
Employee Assistance Programs (EAPs) 273
workplace flexibility 273
flexible benefits plan 274

DISCUSSION QUESTIONS AND EXERCISES

1. What is the difference between exempt and non-exempt jobs?

2. What is the relationship between compensable factors and job specifications?

3. Working individually or in groups, conduct salary surveys for the following positions: entry-level accountant and entry-level chemical engineer. What sources did you use, and what conclusions did you reach? If you were the HR manager for a local engineering firm, what would you recommend that you pay for each job?

4. Working individually or in groups, use published (Internet or other) wage surveys to determine local

area earnings for the following positions: file clerk I, accounting clerk II, and secretary V. How do the published figures compare with comparable jobs listed in your Sunday newspaper? What do you think accounts for any discrepancy?

5. Working individually or in groups, use the ranking method to evaluate the relative worth of the jobs listed in question 4. (You may use The U.S. Department of Labor's O*NET as an aid.) To what extent do the local area earnings for these jobs correspond to your evaluations of the jobs?

6. Working individually or in groups, develop an incentive plan for the following positions: chemical

engineer, plant manager, and used-car salesperson. What factors did you have to consider in reaching your conclusions?

7. A state university system in the Southeast instituted a Teacher Incentive Program for its faculty. Faculty committees within each university's college were told to award $5,000 raises (not bonuses) to about 40% of their faculty members based on how good a job they did teaching undergraduates and how many they taught per year. What are the potential advantages and pitfalls of such an incentive program? How well do you think it was accepted by the faculty? Do you think it had the desired effect?

8. What is merit pay? Do you think it's a good idea to award employees merit raises? Why or why not?

9. Working individually or in groups, research and compile a list of the perks available to the following individuals: the head of your local airport, the president of your college or university, and the president of a large company in your area. Do they all have certain perks in common? What do you think accounts for any differences?

10. You are the HR consultant to a small business with about 40 employees. At the present time the business offers 5 days of vacation, five paid holidays, and legally mandated benefits such as unemployment insurance payments. Develop a list of other benefits you believe the firm should offer, along with your reasons for suggesting them.

11. It was recently reported in the news that the average pay for most university presidents ranged around $250,000 per year, but that a few earned much more. For example, one new president recently received $852,000. Discuss why you would (or would not) pay university presidents as much or more than you would pay many corporate CEOs.

Application Exercises

HR in Action Case Incident 1 — Inserting the Team Concept into Compensation—or Not

One of the first things Sandy Caldwell wanted to do in his new position at Hathaway Manufacturing was improve productivity through teamwork at every level of the firm. As the new human resource manager for the suburban plant, Sandy set out to change the culture to accommodate the team-based approach he had become so enthusiastic about in his most recent position.

Sandy started by installing the concept of team management at the highest level, to oversee the operations of the entire plant. The new management team consisted of manufacturing, distribution, planning, technical, and human resource plant managers. Together they developed a new vision for the 500-employee facility, which they expressed in the simple phrase "Excellence Together." They drafted a new mission statement for the firm that focused on becoming customer driven and team based, and that called upon employees to raise their level of commitment and begin acting as "owners" of the firm.

The next step was to convey the team message to employees throughout the company. The communication process went surprisingly well, and Sandy was happy to see his idea of a "workforce of owners" begin to take shape. Teams trained together, developed production plans together, and embraced the technique of 360-degree feedback, in which an employee's performance evaluation is obtained from supervisors, subordinates, peers, and internal or external customers. Performance and morale improved, and productivity began to tick upward. The company even sponsored occasional celebrations to reward team achievements, and the team structure seemed firmly in place.

Sandy decided to change one more thing. Hathaway's long-standing policy had been to give all employees the same annual pay increase. But Sandy felt that in the new team environment, outstanding performance should be the criterion for pay raises. After consulting with CEO Regina Cioffi, Sandy sent a memo to all employees announcing the change to team-based pay for performance.

The reaction was immediate and 100% negative. None of the employees was happy with the change, and among their complaints, two stood out. First, because the 360-degree feedback system made everyone responsible in part for someone else's performance evaluation, no one was comfortable with the idea that pay raises might also somehow be linked to peer input. Second, there was a widespread perception that the way the change was decided upon, and the way it was announced, put the firm's commitment to team effort in doubt. Simply put, employees felt left out of the decision process.

Sandy and Regina arranged a meeting for early the next morning. Sitting in her office over their coffee, they began a painful debate. Should the new policy be rescinded as quickly as it was adopted, or should it be allowed to stand?

Questions

1. Does the new pay-for-performance plan seem like a good idea? Why or why not?
2. What advice would you give Regina and Sandy as they consider their decision?

3. What mistakes did they make in adopting and communicating the new salary plan? How might Sandy have approached this major compensation change a little differently?

4. Assuming the new pay plan is eventually accepted, how would you address the fact that in the new performance

evaluation system, employees' input affects their peers' pay levels?

Note: The incident in this case is based on an actual event at Frito-Lay's Kirkwood, New York, plant, as reported in C. James Novak, "Proceed with Caution When Paying Teams," *HR Magazine* (April 1997): 73.

HR in Action Case Incident 2 — Carter Cleaning Company: The Incentive Plan

The question of whether to pay Carter Cleaning Centers employees an hourly wage or an incentive of some kind has always intrigued Jack Carter.

His basic policy has been to pay employees an hourly wage, except that his managers receive an end-of-year bonus depending, as Jack puts it, "on whether their stores do well or not that year."

He is, however, considering using an incentive plan in one store. Jack knows that a presser should press about 25 "tops" (jackets, dresses, blouses) per hour. Most of his pressers do not attain this ideal standard, though. In one instance, a part-time presser named Walt was paid $8 per hour, and Jack noticed that regardless of the amount of work he had to do, Walt always ended up going home at about 3 P.M., so he earned about $300 at the end of the week. If it was a holiday week, for instance, and there were a lot of clothes to press, he might average 22 to 23 tops per hour (someone else did pants) and so he'd earn perhaps $300 and still finish up each day in time to leave by 3 P.M. so he could pick up his children at school. But when things were very slow in the store, his productivity would drop to perhaps 12 to 15 pieces an hour, so that at the end of the week he'd end up earning perhaps $280, and in fact not go home much earlier than he did when it was busy.

Jack spoke with Walt several times, and while Walt always promised to try to do better, it gradually became apparent to Jack that Walt was simply going to earn his $300 per week no matter what. While Walt never told him so directly, it dawned on Jack that Walt had a family to support and was not about to earn less than his "target" wage regardless of how busy or slow the store was. The problem was that the longer Walt kept pressing each day, the longer the steam boilers and compressors had to be kept on to power his machines, and the fuel charges alone ran close to $6 per hour. Jack clearly needed

some way short of firing Walt to solve the problem, since the fuel bills were eating up his profits.

His solution was to tell Walt that instead of an hourly $8 wage he would henceforth pay him $0.33 per item pressed. That way, said Jack to himself, if Walt presses 25 items per hour at $0.33 he will in effect get a small raise. He'll get more items pressed per hour and will therefore be able to shut the machines down earlier.

On the whole, the experiment worked well. Walt generally presses 25 to 35 pieces per hour now. He gets to leave earlier, and with the small increase in pay he generally earns his target wage. Two problems have arisen, though. The quality of Walt's work has dipped a bit, plus, his manager has to spend a minute or two each hour counting the number of pieces Walt pressed that hour. Otherwise Jack is fairly pleased with the results of his incentive plan and he's wondering whether to extend it to other employees and other stores.

Questions

1. Should this plan in its present form be extended to pressers in the other stores? Why?

2. Should other employees (cleaner–spotters, counter people) be put on a similar plan? Why? Why not? If so, how, exactly?

3. Is there another incentive plan you think would work better for the pressers?

4. A store manager's job is to keep total wages to no more than 30% of sales and to maintain the fuel bill and the supply bill at about 9% of sales each. Managers can also directly affect sales by ensuring courteous customer service and by ensuring that the work is done properly. What suggestions would you make to Jennifer and her father for an incentive plan for store managers?

EXPERIENTIAL EXERCISE

Job Evaluation at the University

Purpose:

The purpose of this exercise is to give you experience in performing a job evaluation using the ranking method.

Required Understanding:

You should be thoroughly familiar with the ranking method of job evaluation and obtain (or write) job descriptions for your college's dean, department chairperson, and your professor.

How to Set Up the Exercise/Instructions:

Divide the class into groups of four or five students. The groups will perform a job evaluation of the positions of dean, department chairperson, and professor using the ranking method.

1. Perform a job evaluation by ranking the jobs. You may use one or more compensable factors.

2. If time permits, a spokesperson from each group can put his or her group's ratings on the board. Did the groups end up with about the same results? How did they differ? Why do you think they differed?

ENDNOTES

1. Elayne Robertson Demby, "Two Stores Refused to Join the Race to the Bottom for Benefits and Wages," *Workforce Management* (February 2004): 57–59. For a summary of how Wegman's addressed this, see their list of benefits, at http://www.wegmans.com/webapp/wcs/stores/servlet/CategoryDisplay?langId=-1&storeId=10052&catalogId=10002&categoryId=256548 accessed April 21, 2008.

2. Richard Henderson, *Compensation Management* (Reston, VA: Reston 1980); Joseph Martocchio, *Strategic Compensation* (Upper Saddle River, NJ: Prentice Hall, 2006): 67–94.

3. "Senate Passes Minimum Wage Increase that Includes Small-Business Tax Provisions," *BNA Bulletin to Management* (February 6, 2007): 41; www.dol.gov/esa/whd/flsa/, accessed August 12, 2007.

4. For a description of exemption requirements see Jeffrey Friedman, "The Fair Labor Standards Act Today: A Primer," *Compensation* (January/February 2002): 51–54.

5. "Employer Ordered to Pay $2 Million in Overtime," *BNA Bulletin to Management* (September 26, 1996): 308–309. See also "Restaurant Managers Awarded $2.9 Million in Overtime Wages for Nonmanagement Work," *BNA Bulletin to Management* (August 30, 2001): 275.

6. Because the overtime and minimum wage rules only changed in 2004, exactly how to apply these rules is still in a state of flux. If there's doubt about exemption eligibility, it's probably best to check with the local Department of Labor Wage and Hour office. See, for example, "Attorneys Say FLSA Draws a Fine Line Between Exempt/Nonexempt Employees," *BNA Bulletin to Management* (July 5, 2005): 219; "DOL Releases Letters on Administrative Exemption, Overtime," *BNA Bulletin to Management* (October 18, 2005): 335.

7. See, for example, Jeffrey Friedman, "The Fair Labor Standards Act Today: A Primer," *Compensation* (January/February 2002): 53; Andre Honoree, "The New Fair Labor Standards Act Regulations and the Sales Force: Who Is Entitled to Overtime Pay?" *Compensation & Benefits Review* (January/February 2006): 31; www.shrm.org/issues/FLSA, accessed August 12, 2007; www.dol.gov/esa/whd/flsa, accessed August 12, 2007.

8. "Wal-Mart to Pay More Than $33 Million in Settlement with the DOL Involving Overtime," *BNA Bulletin to Management* (January 30, 2007): 33.

9. Richard Henderson, *Compensation Management* (Reston, VA: Reston 1980): 101–127; Arthur Sloane and Fred Witney, Labor Relations (Upper Saddle River, NJ: Prentice Hall, 2004): 273–287.

10. "Salaries for Similar Jobs Vary Significantly across the United States," *Compensation & Benefits Review* (January/February 2006): 9.

11. Jessica Marquez, "Raising the Performance Bar," *Workforce Management* (April 24, 2006): 31–32.

12. Elayne Robertson Demby, "Two Stores Refused to Join the Race to the Bottom for Benefits and Wages," *Workforce Management* (February 2004): 57; and see http://www.wegmans.com/webapp/wcs/stores/servlet/

CategoryDisplay?langId=-1&storeId=10052&catalogId=10002&categoryId=256548, accessed April 21, 2008.

13. James DeConick and Dane Bachmann, "An Analysis of Turnover among Retail Buyers," *Journal of Business Research* 58, no. 7 (July 2005): 874–882.

14. Allison Wellner, "Salaries in Site," *HR Magazine* (May 2001): 89–96. See also "Web Access Transforms Compensation Surveys," *Workforce Management* (April 24, 2006): 34.

15. Syed Tahir Hijazi, "Determinants of Executive Compensation and Its Impact on Organizational Performance," *Compensation & Benefits Review* 39, no. 2 (March/April 2007): 58–59.

16. Mark Meltzer and Howard Goldsmith, "Executive Compensation for Growth Companies," *Compensation & Benefits Review* (November/December 1997): 41–50; Bruce Ellig, "Executive Pay: A Primer," *Compensation & Benefits Review* (January/February 2003): 44–50; Joseph Martocchio, *Strategic Compensation* (Upper Saddle River, NJ: Prentice Hall, 2006): 421–428. See also Martin J. Conyon, "Executive Compensation and Incentives," *The Academy of Management Perspectives* 20, no. 1 (February 2006): 25(20); and "Realities of Executive Compensation—2006/2007 Report on Executive Pay and Stock Options," www.watsonwyatt.com/research/resrender.asp?id=2006-US-0085&page=1), accessed May 20, 2007.

17. "Executive Pay," *Wall Street Journal* (April 11, 1996): R16, R170; and Fay Hansen, "Current Trends in Compensation and Benefits," *Compensation & Benefits Review* 36, no. 2 (March/April 2004): 7–8.

18. Patricia Zingheim and Jay Schuster, "Designing Pay and Rewards in Professional Services Companies," *Compensation & Benefits Review* (January/February 2007): 55–62.

19. Ibid., 60.

20. See, for example, Patricia Zingheim and Jay Schuster, "The Next Decade for Pay and Rewards," *Compensation & Benefits Review* (January/February 2005): 29; and Patricia Zingheim and Jay Schuster, "What Are Key Pay Issues Right Now?" *Compensation & Benefits Review* (May/June 2007): 51–55.

21. Another dubious trend is that U.S. wage disparities are rising. Those with high salaries have seen their pay rise much faster in the past 20 or so years than have those at the bottom. Increased demand for the skills that come through education (for instance, for more skilled workers as manufacturing facilities became computerized) explains much of this. The wage gap has not grown as much in Europe, in part because "unions in Europe were and are still more powerful and able to keep up [workers'] wages." Thomas Atchison, "Salary Trends in the United States and Europe," *Compensation & Benefits Review* (January/February 2007): 36.

22. See, for example, Hai-Ming Chen et al., "Key Trends of the Total Reward System in the 21st Century," *Compensation & Benefits Review* (November/December 2006): 64–70.

23. See, for example, Robert Henneman and Peter LeBlanc, "Development of an Approach for Valuing Knowledge Work," *Compensation & Benefits Review* (July/August 2002): 47.

24. Joseph Martocchio, *Strategic Compensation* (Upper Saddle River, NJ: Prentice Hall, 2006): 168.

25. Bobby Watson Jr. and Gangaram Singh, "Global Pay Systems: Compensation in Support of Multinational Strategy," *Compensation & Benefits Review* (January/February 2005): 33–36.

26. Jamison Bandler and Charles Forelle, "How a Giant Insurer Decided to Oust Hugely Successful CEO," *Wall Street Journal* (December 7, 2006): A1.

27. Mark Poerio and Eric Keller, "Executive Compensation 2005: Many Forces, One Direction," *Compensation & Benefits Review* (May/June 2005): 34–40.

28. The federal government also recently introduced new compensation disclosure rules, and these are affecting executive compensation. For example, corporations must now list a single dollar figure to represent an executive's total pay, including salary, bonus, prerequisites, long-term incentives, and retirement benefits. They must also be more diligent in listing all executive perquisites. The net effect of this greater transparency will probably be to pressure employers to increasingly link their executives' pay with the company's performance. See Brent Longnecker and James Krueger, "The Next Wave of Compensation Disclosure," *Compensation & Benefits Review* (January/February 2007): 50–54.

29. Ibid.

30. Note that the employer needs to beware of instituting so many incentive plans (cash bonuses, stock options, recognition programs, and so on) tied to so many different behaviors that employees don't have a clear picture of the employer's priorities. Stephen Rubenfeld and Jennifer David, "Multiple Employee Incentive Plans: Too Much of a Good Thing?" *Compensation & Benefits Review* (March/April 2006): 35–43.

31. Mark Meltzer and Howard Goldsmith, "Executive Compensation for Growth Companies," *Compensation & Benefits Review* (November/December 1997): 41–50; Barbara Kiviat, "Everyone into the Bonus Pool," *Time* 162, no. 24 (December 15, 2003): A5; Joseph Martocchio, *Strategic Compensation* (Upper Saddle River, NJ: Prentice Hall, 2006): 421–428.

32. www.mercer.com/pressrelease/details.jhtml/dynamic/idContent/1263210, accessed January 2, 2007.

33. Ibid.

34. "Impact of Sarbanes-Oxley on Executive Compensation," downloaded December 11, 2003, from www.thelenreid.com, Thelen, Reid, and Priest, L.L.P. See also Brent Longnecker and James Krueger, "The Next Wave of Compensation Disclosure," *Compensation & Benefits Review* (January/February 2007): 50–54.

35. S. Scott Sands, "Ineffective Quotas: The Hidden Threat to Sales Compensation Plans," *Compensation & Benefits Review* (March/April 2000): 35–42. See also "Driving Profitable Sales Growth: 2006/2007 Report on Sales Effectiveness," www.watsonwyatt.com/research/resrender.asp?id=2006-US-0060&page=1, accessed May 20, 2007.

36. Peter Gundy, "Sales Compensation Programs: Built to Last," *Compensation & Benefits Review* (September/October 2002): 21–28. See also Tara Burnthorne Lopez, Christopher D. Hopkins, and Mary Anne Raymond, "Reward Preferences of Salespeople: How Do Commissions Rate?" *Journal of Personal Selling & Sales Management* 26, no. 4 (Fall 2006): 381(10).

37. James M. Pappas and Karen E. Flaherty, "The Moderating Role of Individual-Difference Variables in Compensation Research," *Journal of Managerial Psychology* 21, no. 1 (January 2006): 19–35.

38. Peter Glendinning, "Kicking the Tires of Automotive Sales Compensation," *Compensation & Benefits Review* (September/October 2000): 47–53. See also "Driving Profitable Sales Growth: 2006/2007 Report on Sales Effectiveness," www.watsonwyatt.com/research/resrender.asp?id=2006-US-0060&page=1, accessed May 20, 2007.

39. Suzanne Peterson and Fred Luthans, "The Impact of Financial and Nonfinancial Incentives on Business Unit Outcomes over Time," *Journal of Applied Psychology* 91, no. 1 (2006): 158.

40. See, for example, Suzanne Peterson and Fred Luthans, "The Impact of Financial and Nonfinancial Incentives on Business Unit Outcomes over Time," *Journal of Applied Psychology* 91, no. 1 (2006): 156–165.

41. Leslie Yerkes, "Motivating Workers in Tough Times," *Incentives* 75, no. 10 (October 2001): 120. See also "Incentives, Motivation and Workplace Performance," Incentive Research Foundation, www.incentivescentral.org/employees/whitepapers, accessed May 19, 2007. For some examples of recognition programs in practice, see http://www.recognition.org, accessed April 21, 2008.

42. Ibid. See also Chris Taylor, "On-the-Spot Incentives," *HR Magazine* (May 2004): 80–85.

43. Charlotte Huff, "Recognition that Resonates," *Workforce Management* (September 11, 2006): 25–29. See also Scott Jeffrey and Victoria Schaffer, "The Motivational Properties of Tangible Incentives," *Compensation & Benefits Review* (May/June 2007): 44–50.

44. Bob Nelson, *1001 Ways to Reward Employees* (New York: Workmen Press, 1994): 19. See also Sunny C. L. Fong and Margaret A. Shaffer, "The Dimensionality and Determinants of Pay Satisfaction: A Cross-cultural Investigation of a Group Incentive Plan," *International Journal of Human Resource Management* 14, no. 4 (June 2003): 559(22).

45. Jack Orsburn et al., *Self-Directed Work Teams: The New American Challenge* (Homewood, IL: Business One Irwin, 1990): 34.

46. Matt Bolch, "Rewarding the Team," *HR Magazine* 52, no.2 (Fall 2007): 91–93.

47. Richard Seaman, "Rejuvenating an Organization with Team Pay," *Compensation & Benefits Review* (September/October 1997): 25–30. See also Sunny C.L. Fong and Margaret A. Shaffer, "The Dimensionality and Determinants of Pay Satisfaction: A Cross-Cultural Investigation of a Group Incentive Plan," *International Journal of Human Resource Management* 14, no. 4 (June 2003): 559(22); and Mark Kroll, Jeffrey A. Krug, Michael Pettus, and Peter Wright, "Influences of Top Management Team Incentives on Firm Risk Taking," *Strategic Management Journal* 28, no. 1 (January 2007): 81–89.

48. Janet Wiscombe, "Can Pay for Performance Really Work?" *Workforce* (August 2001): 30.

49. Susan Marks, "Incentives That Really Reward and Motivate," *Workforce* (June 2001): 108–114.

50. Matt Bolch, "Rewarding the Team," *HR Magazine* 52, no.2 (Fall 2007): 91–93.

51. Joseph Martocchio, *Strategic Compensation* (Upper Saddle River, NJ: Prentice Hall, 2006): 163–165.

52. Seongsu Kim, "Does Profit Sharing Increase Firms' Profits?" *Journal of Labor Research* (Spring 1998): 351–371. See also Jacqueline Coyle-Shapiro et al., "Using Profit-Sharing to Enhance Employee Attitudes: A Longitudinal Examination of the Effects on Trust and Commitment," *Human Resource Management* 41, no. 4 (Winter 2002): 423–449.

53. For instance, see "ESOP Trustees Breached Their Fiduciary Duties under ERISA by Failing to Make Prudent Investigation into Value of Stock Purchased by ESOP," *Tax Management Compensation Planning Journal* 30, no. 10 (October 4, 2002): 301(1); and Jeffery D. Mamorsky, "Court Approves ERISA Action against ENRON Executives, Trustee, and Plan Auditor for Retirement Plan Losses," *Journal of Compensation & Benefits* 20, no. 1 (January/February 2004): 46(7).

54. James Sesil et al., "Broad-Based Employee Stock Options in U.S. New Economy Firms," *British Journal of Industrial Relations* 40, no. 2 (June 2002): 273–294.

55. "Time Warner Stops Granting Stock Options to Most of Staff," *New York Times* (February 19, 2005).

56. Brian Moore and Timothy Ross, *The Scanlon Way to Improved Productivity: A Practical Guide* (New York: Wiley, 1978): 2. For recent research in gainsharing and Scanlon plans, see, for example, James Reynolds and Daniel Roble, "Combining Pay for Performance with Gainsharing," *Healthcare Financial Management* 60, no. 11 (November 2006): 50(6); Max Reynolds and Joane Goodroe, "The Return of Gainsharing: Gainsharing Appears to Be Enjoying a Renaissance," *Healthcare Financial Management* 59 no. 11 (November 2005): 114(6); Dong-One Kim, "The Benefits and Costs of Employee Suggestions under Gainsharing," *Industrial and Labor Relations Review* 58, no. 4 (July 2005): 631(22); Geoffrey B. Sprinkle and Michael G. Williamson, "The Evolution from Taylorism to Employee Gainsharing: A Case Study Examining John Deere's Continuous Improvement Pay Plan," *Issues in Accounting Education* 19, no. 4 (November 2004): 487(17); and Woodruff Imberman, "Are You Ready to Boost Productivity with a Gainsharing Plan? To Survive and Prosper in Our Hyper-Competitive Environment, Board Converters Must Motivate Employees at All Levels," *Official Board Markets* 82, no. 47 (November 25, 2006): 5(2).

57. Based in part on Steven Markham, K. Dow Scott, and Walter Cox Jr., "The Evolutionary Development of a Scanlon Plan," *Compensation & Benefits Review* (March/April 1992): 50–56. See also Geoffrey B. Sprinkle; Michael G. Williamson, "The Evolution from Taylorism to Employee Gainsharing: A Case Study Examining John Deere's Continuous Improvement Pay Plan," *Issues in Accounting Education* 19, no. 4 (November 2004): 487(17).

58. Steven Markham, K. Dow Scott, and Walter Cox Jr., "The Evolutionary Development of a Scanlon Plan," *Compensation & Benefits Review* (March/April 1992): 51.

59. Brian Moore and Timothy Ross, *The Scanlon Way to Improved Productivity: A Practical Guide* (New York: Wiley, 1978): 1–2.

60. Robert Renn et al., "Earnings and Risk Incentive Plans: A Performance, Satisfaction and Turnover Dilemma," *Compensation & Benefits Review* (July/August 2001): 68–72.

61. William Bulkeley, "Incentives System Fine-Tunes Pay/Bonus Plans," *Wall Street Journal* (August 16, 2001): B4.

62. Nina McIntyre, "EIM Technology to Successfully Motivate Employees," *Compensation & Benefits Review* (July/August 2001): 57–60.

63. Jeremy Wuittner, "Plenty of Incentives to use E.I.M. Software Systems," *American Banker* 168, no. 129 (July 8, 2003): 680.

64. Ibid.

65. Kathleen Cholewka, "Tech Tools," *Sales and Marketing Management* 153, no. 7 (July 2001): 24. See also Andrew Perlmutter, "Taking Motivation and Recognition Online," *Compensation & Benefits Review* (March/April 2002): 70–74.

66. "Survey Finds 99 Percent of Employers Providing Health-Care Benefits," *Compensation & Benefits Review* (September/October 2002): 11. See also "National Compensation Survey: Employee Benefits in Private Industry in the United States, March 2006," U.S. Department of Labor, U.S. Bureau of Labor Statistics (August 2006).

67. "Employers Face Fifth Successive Year of Major Heath Cost Increases, Survey Finds," *BNA Human Resources Report* (October 6, 2003): 1050; and "National Compensation Survey: Employee Benefits in Private Industry in the United States, March 2006," U.S. Department of Labor, U.S. Bureau of Labor Statistics (August 2006).

68. See, for example, Laurie Nacht, "Make an Appealing Case: How to Prepare For and Present an Unemployment Insurance Appeal," *Society for Human Resource Management Legal Report* (March/April 2004): 1–8.

69. "2007 Benefits," A Survey Report by the Society for Human Research Management, 2007.

70. "National Compensation Survey: Employee Benefits in Private Industry in the United States, March 2006," U.S. Department of Labor, U.S. Bureau of Labor Statistics (August 2006): 26.

71. Ken Belson, "At IBM, a Vacation Anytime, or Maybe No Vacation at All," *New York Times* (August 31, 2007): A1–A18.

72. "Unscheduled Employee Absences Cost Companies More Than Ever," *Compensation & Benefits Review* (March/April 2003): 19.

73. "SHRM Benefits Survey Finds Growth in Employer Use of Paid Leave Pools," *BNA Bulletin to Management* (March 21, 2002): 89.

74. Terry Baglieri, "Severance Pay," www.SHRM.org, accessed December 23, 2006.

75. Ibid.

76. "Healthcare Tops List of Value Benefits," *BNA Bulletin to Management* (April 24, 2007): 132.

77. "High Deductible Plans Might Catch On," *BNA Human Resource Report* (September 15, 2003): 967.

78. "HR Outsourcing: Managing Costs and Maximizing Provider Relations," *BNA, Inc* 21, no. 11 (Washington, DC: November 2003): 10.

79. Ron Finch, "Preventive Services: Improving the Bottom Line for Employers and Employees," *Compensation & Benefits Review* (March/April 2005): 18.

80. Ibid. See also Josh Cable, "The Road to Wellness," *Occupational Hazards* (April 2007): 23–27.

81. "Employer Partners to Launch a Three-Year Wellness Initiative," *BNA Bulletin to Management* (August 7, 2007): 255.

82. Vanessa Fuhrmanns, "Oops! As Health Plans Become More Complicated, They're Also Subject to a Lot More Costly Mistakes," *Wall Street Journal* (January 24, 2005): R4.

83. Betty Liddick, "Going the Distance for Health Savings," *HR Magazine* (March 2007): 51–55.

84. http://www.socialsecurity.gov/pubs/10003.html, accessed April 21, 2008

85. Joseph Martocchio, *Strategic Compensation* (Upper Saddle River, NJ: Prentice Hall, 2006): 349–355; and Lin Grensing-Pophal, "A Pension Formula That Pays Off," *HR Magazine* (February 2003): 58–62.

86. About half of American employees work for employers who don't offer pension plans. Congress has therefore recently considered legislation that would encourage employees without pensions to save for retirement, for instance, by requiring most firms to offer automatic pay-roll deductions into IRAs. "Automatic IRA Deductions Gain Broad Support," *Workforce Management* (June 25, 2007): 18.

87. "New Pension Law Plus a Recent Court Ruling Doom Age-Related Suits, Practitioners Say," *BNA Bulletin to Management* 57, no. 36 (September 5, 2006): 281–282.

88. Donna Owens, "EAPs for a Diverse World," *HR Magazine* 51, no. 10 (October 2006): 91–96.

89. Richard Buddin and Kanika Kapur, "The Effect of Employer-Sponsored Education on Job Mobility: Evidence from the U.S. Navy," *Industrial Relations* 44, no. 2 (April 2005): 341–363. See also Michael Laff, "US Employers Tighten Reins on Tuition Reimbursement," *Training and Development* (July 2006): 18.

90. Brian O'Connell, "No Baby Sitter? Emergency Child Care to the Rescue," (May 2005): www.SHRM.org/rewards/library, accessed December 23, 2006; Kathy Gurchiek, "Give Us Your Sick," *HR Magazine* (January 2007): 91–93.

91. "Employers Gain from Elder Care Programs by Boosting Workers Morale, Productivity," *BNA Bulletin to Management* 57, no. 10 (March 7, 2006): 73–74.

92. Sue Shellenbarger, "The Mommy Drain: Employers Beef Up Perks to Lure New Mothers Back to Work," *Wall Street Journal* (September 28, 2006,): D1.

93. Sue Shellenbarger, "Companies Retool Time Off Policies to Prevent Burnout, Reward Performance," *Wall Street Journal* (January 5, 2006): D1.

94. "Making Up for Lost Time: How Employers Can Curb Excessive Unscheduled Absences," *BNA Human Resources Report* (October 20, 2003): 1097. Family-friendly benefits may improve a firm's bottom line in some less obvious ways. One study found that when employees experienced work–family conflict, the employees were more likely to exhibit guilt and hostility at work and at home. "Therefore, when work family conflict causes employees to feel guilty and angry, it is likely that the service encounter will be affected negatively." (Timothy Judge et al., "Work Family Conflict and Emotions: Effects at Work and at Home," *Personnel Psychology* 50, no. 9 (2006): 779–814.

95. Farrokh Mamaghani, "Impact of Information Technology on the Workforce of the Future: An Analysis," *International Journal of Management* 23, no. 4 (2006): 845–850.

96. Ann Pomeroy, "The Future Is Now," *HR Magazine* (September 2007): 46–52.

97. "2007 Benefits," A Survey Report by the Society for Human Research Management (2007): 23.

98. "Employers Should Update Cafeteria Plans Now Based on Proposed Regs, Experts Say," *BNA Bulletin to Management* (September 4, 2007): 281–282.

99. Scott Harper, "Online Resources System Boosts Worker Awareness," *BNA Bulletin to Management* (April 10, 2007): 119.

100. Drew Robb, "A Total View of Employee Records," HR Magazine (August 2007): 93–96.

Part 4 Employee and Labor Relations

Ethics, Employee Rights, and Fair Treatment at Work

9

When you finish studying this chapter, you should be able to:

1. *Explain what is meant by ethical behavior.*

2. *Discuss important factors that shape ethical behavior at work.*

3. *Discuss at least four specific ways in which HR management can influence ethical behavior at work.*

4. *Exercise fair disciplinary practices.*

5. *Discuss at least four procedural suggestions for managing dismissals effectively.*

Introduction

Wal-Mart instituted a new employee scheduling system. Formerly, employees had specific work shifts, for instance, Tuesday–Friday, noon–5. With the new system, employees had to list, on "availability forms," what hours all day and night they were willing to work. Then, as the store's customer traffic rose and fell, supervisors called in (or sent home) employees to fit demand. This was good for minimizing the stores' staffing needs. However, some critics felt that by forcing employees to work unpredictable hours, the new system interrupted employees' family lives and was unfair. ■

ETHICS, EMPLOYEE RIGHTS, AND FAIR TREATMENT AT WORK

Anyone who's suffered unfair treatment at work knows it is demoralizing. Studies, some of which we'll discuss in the next few pages, confirm this common sense observation. Unfair treatment reduces morale, increases stress, and has negative effects on performance. Managers, and HR management, can take steps to reduce such unfairness.

Workplace Unfairness

Workplace unfairness can be blatant. For example, some supervisors are workplace bullies, yelling and ridiculing subordinates, humiliating them, and perhaps making threats. Not surprisingly, employees of abusive supervisors are more likely to quit their jobs, and to report lower job and life satisfaction and higher stress if they remain in those jobs.[1]

The employer should always prohibit such behavior, and many firms do have antiharassment policies. For example, Walgreens' mission statement says, "We will treat each other with respect and dignity and do the same for all we serve.[2] At work, fair treatment reflects concrete actions such as "employees are trusted," "employees are treated with respect," and "employees are treated fairly" (see Figure 9.1).[3]

FIGURE 9.1 Perceptions of Fair Interpersonal Treatment Scale

What is your organization like most of the time? Circle YES if the item describes your organization, NO if it does not describe your organization, and ? if you cannot decide.

IN THIS ORGANIZATION . . .

1. Employees are praised for good work	Yes	?	No
2. Supervisors yell at employees (R)	Yes	?	No
3. Supervisors play favorites (R)	Yes	?	No
4. Employees are trusted	Yes	?	No
5. Employees' complaints are dealt with effectively	Yes	?	No
6. Employees are treated like children (R)	Yes	?	No
7. Employees are treated with respect	Yes	?	No
8. Employees' questions and problems are responded to quickly	Yes	?	No
9. Employees are lied to (R)	Yes	?	No
10. Employees' suggestions are ignored (R)	Yes	?	No
11. Supervisors swear at employees (R)	Yes	?	No
12. Employees' hard work is appreciated	Yes	?	No
13. Supervisors threaten to fire or lay off employees (R)	Yes	?	No
14. Employees are treated fairly	Yes	?	No
15. Co-workers help each other out	Yes	?	No
16. Co-workers argue with each other (R)	Yes	?	No
17. Co-workers put each other down (R)	Yes	?	No
18. Co-workers treat each other with respect	Yes	?	No

Note: R = the item is reverse scored.

Source: Michelle A. Donovan et al., "The Perceptions of Their Interpersonal Treatment Scale: Development and Validation of a Measure of Interpersonal Treatment in the Workplace," *Journal of Applied Psychology* 83, no.5 (1998): 692. Copyright © 1997 by Michelle A. Donovan, Fritz Drasgow, and Liberty J. Munson at the University of Illinois at Urbana-Champaign. All rights reserved.

Why Treat Employees Fairly?

There are many reasons that managers should be fair, some more obvious than others. The golden rule is one obvious reason: As management guru Peter Drucker has said, "[T]hey're not employees, they're people," and the manager should treat people with dignity and respect. An increasingly litigious workforce is another reason. The manager wants to be sure to institute disciplinary and discharge procedures that will survive the scrutiny of arbitrators and the courts.

What may not be so obvious is that employees' fairness perceptions also have important organizational ramifications. For example, perceptions of fairness relate to enhanced employee commitment; enhanced satisfaction with the organization, jobs, and leaders; and enhanced organizational citizenship behaviors.[4]

EXAMPLE A study provides an illustration. College instructors first completed surveys concerning the extent to which they saw their colleges as treating them with *procedural* and *distributive justice*. (Procedural justice refers to fair processes; distributive justice refers to fair outcomes.) The procedural justice items included, for example, "In general, the department/college's procedures allow for requests for clarification or for additional information about a decision." The distributive justice items included, "I am fairly rewarded considering the responsibilities I have." Then, the instructors completed organizational commitment questionnaires. These included questions such as "I am proud to tell others that I am part of this department/college." Their students then completed surveys. These contained items such as "the instructor put a lot of effort into planning the content of this course," "the instructor was sympathetic to my needs," and "the instructor treated me fairly."

The results were telling.

- Instructors who perceived high distributive and procedural justice reported higher organizational commitment.
- Furthermore, these instructors' students reported higher levels of instructor effort, prosocial behaviors, and fairness, as well as more positive reactions to their instructors.

"Overall," as the researcher says, "the results imply that fair treatment of employees has important organizational consequences."[5]

The grounds for fair treatment go deeper than the golden rule or unfairness's practical consequences. Treating people fairly at work also has roots in the concepts of ethics, employee rights, and in the law. We'll start with ethics.

The Meaning of Ethics

❶ Explain what is meant by ethical behavior.

People face ethical choices every day. For example, is it wrong to use company e-mail for personal reasons? Is a $50 gift to a boss unacceptable? Compare your answers to those of other Americans by answering the quiz in Figure 9.2.

When it comes to ethics, headlines tend to focus on top management misdeeds, (like whether bank executives who profited from the subprime mortgage fiasco should keep their paychecks). But many ethical blunders actually stem from human resource management–related actions. Two experts say, "[H]iring, performance evaluation, discipline, and terminations can be ethical issues because they all involve honesty, fairness, and the dignity of the individual."[6] For example, one survey found that 6 of the 10 most serious ethical issues—including workplace safety, employee records security, employee theft, and employee privacy rights—were human resource management related.[7]

Of course, human resource activities needn't be breeding grounds for ethical misdeeds. Instead, HR can drive positive ethical behavior. We focus on how in this and the following sections. Let's look first at what *ethics* means.

ethics
The study of standards of conduct and moral judgment; also the standards of right conduct.

Ethics are "the principles of conduct governing an individual or a group"—they are the principles people use to decide what their conduct should be.[8] However, ethical decisions don't include just any type of behavior. For instance, deciding which car to buy would not, in itself, involve ethics. Instead, ethical decisions are always rooted in morality. *Morality* means society's accepted standards of behavior. Like the Ten Commandments, morality involves basic questions of right and wrong, such as stealing, murder, and how to treat other people. As such, how to treat employees who may be a different age, race, gender, or national origin than the manager is almost always as much of an ethical question as it is a purely legal one.[9]

FIGURE 9.2 *The Wall Street Journal* **Workplace–Ethics Quiz**

The spread of technology into the workshop has raised a variety of new ethical questions and many old ones still linger. Compare your answers with those of other Americans surveyed, on page 311.

Office Technology

1. Is it wrong to use company e-mail for personal reasons?
☐ Yes   ☐ No

2. Is it wrong to use office equipment to help your children or spouse do schoolwork?
☐ Yes   ☐ No

3. Is it wrong to play computer games on office equipment during the workday?
☐ Yes   ☐ No

4. Is it wrong to use office equipment to do Internet shopping?
☐ Yes   ☐ No

5. Is it unethical to blame an error you made on a technological glitch?
☐ Yes   ☐ No

6. Is it unethical to visit pornographic Web sites using office equipment?
☐ Yes   ☐ No

Gifts and Entertainment

7. What's the value at which a gift from a supplier or client becomes troubling?
☐ $25   ☐ $50   ☐ $100

8. Is a $50 gift to a boss unacceptable?
☐ Yes   ☐ No

9. Is a $50 gift *from* the boss unacceptable?
☐ Yes   ☐ No

10. Of gifts from suppliers: Is it OK to take a $200 pair of football tickets?
☐ Yes   ☐ No

11. Is it OK to take a $120 pair of theater tickets?
☐ Yes   ☐ No

12. Is it OK to take a $100 holiday food basket?
☐ Yes   ☐ No

13. Is it OK to take a $25 gift certificate?
☐ Yes   ☐ No

14. Can you accept a $75 prize won at a raffle at a supplier's conference?
☐ Yes   ☐ No

Truth and Lies

15. Due to on-the-job pressure, have you ever abused or lied about sick days?
☐ Yes   ☐ No

16. Due to on-the-job pressure, have you ever taken credit for someone else's work or idea?
☐ Yes   ☐ No

Source: Wall Street Journal (October 21, 1999): B1–B4. Ethics Offer Association, Belmont, MA: Ethics Leadership Group.

Ethics and the Law

Perhaps surprisingly, the law is a far-from-perfect guide to what is ethical, because something may be legal but not right, or right but not legal. Firing a 38-year-old employee with 20 years' tenure without notice may be unethical, but still legal, for instance. Patrick Gnazzo, vice president for business practices at United Technologies Corp. (and a former trial lawyer), put it this way: "Don't lie, don't cheat, don't steal. We were all raised with essentially the same values. *Ethics* means making decisions that represent what you stand for, not just what the laws are."[10]

Yet, while not a perfect gauge of right or wrong, laws do have a strong effect on organizational fairness. The *Business in Action* feature addresses this.

Business in Action   Building Your *Employee Rights and Business Law* Knowledge

Most industrial societies don't rely solely on employers' ethical compasses or sense of fair play when it comes to employees. Instead, they also pass laws to codify employees' rights.

What these "rights" are depends on several things. For example, most societies hold that people (workers included) share certain inalienable rights—rights they have just because they are people living in civil societies. Thus, the rights to "life, liberty, and the pursuit of happiness" are ingrained in American culture. For workers everywhere, the International Labor Organization's *Declaration on Fundamental Principles and Rights at Work* lists these workers' rights:[11]

■ The freedom of association and effective recognition of the right to collective bargaining,

■ The elimination of forced or compulsory labor,

- The abolition of child labor, and
- The elimination of discrimination with respect to employment and occupation.

In England, employees also have certain rights under common law—the law that evolved out of court decisions over time.[12] For example, under common law, an employee may have the right to sue the employer whose supervisor published or promulgated embarrassing private and personal information about the employee.[13]

Employee Rights and the Law

Similarly, employment laws don't just list what employers can and can't do in the workplace. Instead, they also give employees (or prospective employees, and sometimes past employees) numerous *rights*. For example, under Title VII of the U.S. Civil Rights Act, employers can't turn someone down for a job based on his or her color. Under the Wage and Hour Act, employers can't hire someone under 16 for a hazardous job. The U.S. Employee Retirement Income Security Act's so-called retaliation provision gives employees who believe they were denied profit sharing or pension benefits due to age the right to seek to redress the violation.[14] The Occupational Safety and Health Act gives employees the right to refuse to work under unsafe conditions.[15] A partial list of legal areas under which workers have rights includes:[16]

- Leave of absence and vacation rights
- Injuries and illnesses rights
- Noncompetition agreement rights
- Employee rights on employer policies
- Discipline rights
- Rights on personnel files
- Employee pension rights

- Employee benefits rights
- References rights
- Rights on criminal records
- Employee distress rights
- Defamation rights
- Employee rights on fraud
- Rights on assault and battery
- Employee negligence rights
- Rights on political activity
- Union/group activity rights
- Whistle-blowing rights
- Workers compensation rights

Notification

Governments in the United Kingdom also don't generally leave informing employees about their legal rights to chance. Most employment laws and regulations require employers to post official notices of employee rights. Many states in the U.S. have similar posting requirements.[17] For example, the required OSHA safety poster lists employees' rights under OSHA, including "the right to notify your employer or OSHA about workplace hazards" and "the right to request an OSHA inspection if you believe that there are unsafe and unhealthful conditions in your workplace."

Expanding Employees' Rights

The trend is to expand employees' legal rights. Over the past century we've seen the introduction of union relations laws, civil rights and equal employment laws, and occupational safety laws, for instance. This trend shows no indication of slowing. For example, 11 states, including Connecticut, Hawaii, New Jersey, and New York, were recently debating legislation that would give victims of verbally abusive bosses the right to sue for damages.[18]

EMPLOYEE RIGHTS ABROAD And the concept of employee rights is not limited to the United States. In fact, in some places, including Europe, employees' rights are, if anything, broader than in the United States. For example, employees in much of Europe have more job security and require more notice for termination than do U.S. employees.[19]

2 Discuss important factors that shape ethical behavior at work.

WHAT SHAPES ETHICAL BEHAVIOR AT WORK?

In many cases people undoubtedly act ethically because they fear breaking the law—they do the right thing because they're afraid they may get caught. But, in practice, whether a person acts ethically at work is more complicated. We'll look first at the factors (like individual traits, and pressures from the boss) that shape ethical behavior. Then we'll discuss the steps managers can take to help ensure that ethical behavior prevails.

Individual Factors

Because people bring to their jobs their own ideas of what is morally right and wrong, each person must shoulder much of the credit (or blame) for his or her ethical choices. Researchers surveyed CEOs to study the CEOs' intentions to engage (or to not engage) in two questionable business practices: soliciting a competitor's technological secrets, and making illegal payments to foreign government officials. The researchers concluded that the CEOs' personal predispositions more strongly affected their decisions than did outside pressures or characteristics of their firms.[20]

TRAITS   It's hard to generalize about the characteristics of ethical or unethical people, but age is a factor. One study surveyed 421 employees to measure the degree to which age, gender, marital status, education, dependent children, region of the country, and years in business influenced responses to ethical decisions. (Decisions included "doing personal business on company time" and "calling in sick to take a day off for personal use.") Older workers generally had stricter interpretations of ethical standards and made more ethical decisions than did younger ones.

Honesty testing (as we discussed in chapter 5) shows that some people are more inclined to make the wrong ethical choice. How would you rate your own ethics? Figure 9.3 presents a short self-assessment survey for helping you answer that question.

FIGURE 9.3 How Do My Ethics Rate?

Instrument

Indicate your level of agreement with these 15 statements using the following scale:

   1 = Strongly disagree
   2 = Disagree
   3 = Neither agree nor disagree
   4 = Agree
   5 = Strongly agree

	1	2	3	4	5
1. The only moral of business is making money.	1	2	3	4	5
2. A person who is doing well in business does not have to worry about moral problems.	1	2	3	4	5
3. Act according to the law, and you can't go wrong morally.	1	2	3	4	5
4. Ethics in business is basically an adjustment between expectations and the ways people behave.	1	2	3	4	5
5. Business decisions involve a realistic economic attitude and not a moral philosophy.	1	2	3	4	5
6. "Business ethics" is a concept for public relations only.	1	2	3	4	5
7. Competitiveness and profitability are important values.	1	2	3	4	5
8. Conditions of a free economy will best serve the needs of society. Limiting competition can only hurt society and actually violates basic natural laws.	1	2	3	4	5
9. As a consumer, when making an auto insurance claim, I try to get as much as possible regardless of the extent of the damage.	1	2	3	4	5
10. While shopping at the supermarket, it is appropriate to switch price tags on packages.	1	2	3	4	5
11. As an employee, I can take home office supplies; it doesn't hurt anyone.	1	2	3	4	5
12. I view sick days as vacation days that I deserve.	1	2	3	4	5
13. Employees' wages should be determined according to the laws of supply and demand.	1	2	3	4	5
14. The business world has its own rules.	1	2	3	4	5
15. A good businessperson is a successful businessperson.	1	2	3	4	5

ANALYSIS AND INTERPRETATION

Rather than specify "right" answers, this instrument works best when you compare your answer to those of others. With that in mind, here are mean responses from a group of 243 management students. How did your responses compare?

1. 3.09	6. 2.88	11. 1.58
2. 1.88	7. 3.62	12. 2.31
3. 2.54	8. 3.79	13. 3.36
4. 3.41	9. 3.44	14. 3.79
5. 3.88	10. 1.33	15. 3.38

Source: Adapted from A. Reichel and Y. Neumann, *Journal of Instructional Psychology* (March 1988):25–53. With permission of the authors.

Organizational Pressures

If people did unethical things at work solely for personal gain, it perhaps would be understandable (though inexcusable). The scary thing about unethical behavior at work is that it's often not driven by personal interests.

Table 9.1 summarizes the results of one ethics survey. In this case the researchers were studying the principal causes of ethical lapses, as reported by six levels of employees and managers.

As you can see, organizational pressures are a big factor. For example, "meeting schedule pressure" was the number one reported factor in causing ethical lapses. For most of these employees, "meeting overly aggressive financial or business objectives" and "helping the company survive" were the two other top causes. "Advancing my own career or financial interests" ranked toward the bottom of the list of principal reported causes of ethical compromises. Thus (at least in this case) most ethical lapses occurred because employees were under the gun to do what they thought was best to help their companies.

EXAMPLES Evidence of this abounds. Several years ago, a judge sentenced WorldCom's former chief financial officer to 5 years in jail, allegedly for helping the firm's former chair mask WorldCom's deteriorating financial situation. Among other things, the U.S. government accused him of instructing underlings to fraudulently book accounting entries, and of filing false statements with the U.S. Securities and Exchange Commission. Why, as a star CFO and someone trained to protect the interest of his shareholders, would the CFO do such a thing? "I took these actions, knowing they were wrong, in a misguided attempt to preserve the company to allow it to withstand what I believed were temporary financial difficulties."[21]

Having rules on the books forbidding such behavior does not, by itself, seem to work. For example, several years ago, New York's attorney general filed charges against Merrill Lynch. He alleged that several of its analysts had issued optimistic ratings on stocks, while privately expressing concerns about those same stocks. The allegation was that they did so to aid and support Merrill Lynch's investment banking relationships with these companies.

TABLE 9.1 Principal Causes of Ethical Compromises

	Senior Mgmt.	Middle Mgmt.	Front Line Supv.	Prof. Non-Mgmt.	Admin. Salaried	Hourly
Meeting schedule pressure	1	1	1	1	1	1
Meeting overly aggressive financial or business objectives	3	2	2	2	2	2
Helping the company survive	2	3	4	4	3	4
Advancing the career interests of my boss	5	4	3	3	4	5
Feeling peer pressure	7	7	5	6	5	3
Resisting competitive threats	4	5	6	5	6	7
Saving jobs	9	6	7	7	7	6
Advancing my own career or financial interests	8	9	9	8	9	8
Other	6	8	8	9	8	9

Note: 1 is high; 9 is low.

Source: O. C. Ferrell and John Fraedrich, *Business Ethics,* 3d ed. (New York: Houghton Mifflin, 1997): 28. Adapted from Rebecca Goodell, *Ethics in American Business: Policies, Programs, and Perceptions* (1994): 54. Permission provided courtesy of the Ethics Resource Center.

Several years ago, a judge sentenced WorldCom's former chief financial officer to 5 years in jail, allegedly for helping the firm's former chair mask WorldCom's deteriorating financial situation.

In making his case, the attorney general released numerous e-mails and other documents written by Merrill analysts. One, for instance, reportedly read:

> Some of the communication with the go-to people and the bankers prior to the initiation may have been a technical violation of the firm's written policies and procedures (which, I have now learned, say the company's bankers should not be told what the proposed rating is or will be, even if the company isn't currently under coverage), so my guess is the lawyers will want to offer this in detail. From what they've told me, however, even if there was a violation, this is not a big deal.[22]

The Boss's Influence

Another factor is the extent to which employees can model their ethical behavior on the ethical behavior of their supervisors. According to one report, for instance, "the level of misconduct at work dropped dramatically when employees said their supervisors exhibited ethical behavior." Only 25% of employees who agreed that their supervisors "set a good example of ethical business behavior" said they had observed misconduct in the last year, compared with 72% of those who did not feel that their supervisors set good ethical examples.[23] Yet, in another poll, only about 27% of employees strongly agreed that their organizations' leadership is ethical.[24]

Examples of how supervisors knowingly (or unknowingly) lead subordinates astray ethically include:

- Tell staffers to do whatever is necessary to achieve results.
- Overload top performers to ensure that work gets done.
- Look the other way when wrongdoing occurs.
- Take credit for others' work or shift blame.[25]

Ethics Policies and Codes

An ethics policy and code is another way to signal that the firm is serious about ethics. For example, IBM's code of ethics has this to say about tips, gifts, and entertainment:

> No IBM employee, or any member of his or her immediate family, can accept gratuities or gifts of money from a supplier, customer, or anyone in a business relationship. Nor can they accept a gift or consideration that could be perceived as having been offered because of the business relationship. "Perceived" simply means this: if you

read about it in the local newspaper, would you wonder whether the gift just might have had something to do with a business relationship? No IBM employee can give money or a gift of significant value to a customer, supplier, or anyone if it could reasonably be viewed as being done to gain a business advantage.[26]

Sometimes ethics codes don't work. Enron Corp. allegedly collapsed in part due to the ethical misdeeds of some executives. Yet Enron's ethical principles were easily accessible on the firm's Web site. It stated, that, "as a partner in the communities in which we operate, Enron believes it has a responsibility to conduct itself according to certain basic principles." Those include, "respect, integrity, communication and excellence."[27]

QUICK TEST   Beyond the code, some firms urge employees to apply a quick "ethics test" to evaluate whether what they're about to do fits the company's code of conduct. For example, Raytheon Co. asks employees who are faced with ethical dilemmas to ask:

Is the action legal?

Is it right?

Who will be affected?

Does it fit Raytheon's values?

How will it "feel" afterwards?

How will it look in the newspaper?

Will it reflect poorly on the company?[28]

ENFORCEMENT   However, codifying the rules without enforcing them is futile. As one study of ethics concludes, "strong statements by managers may reduce the risk of legal and ethical violations by their work forces, but enforcement of standards has the greatest impact."[29] More firms, such as Lockheed Martin Corp., therefore appoint chief ethics officers—in Lockheed's case, Nancy Higgins, executive vice president of ethics and business conduct.[30]

The Organization's Culture

organizational culture
The characteristic values, traditions, and behaviors a company's employees share.

One reason why ethics codes (and what the boss says) do not always have the desired effect is that it is not what the boss or company says but what they do that's important. Organizational psychologists refer to this phenomenon as *organizational culture*. The accompanying *Personal Competencies* feature helps build organizational culture knowledge and skills.

Personal Competencies

Building Your *Organizational Culture* Skills

Organizational culture is the characteristic values, traditions, and behaviors a company's employees share. A *value* is a basic belief about what is right or wrong, or about what you should or shouldn't do. ("Honesty is the best policy" would be a value.) Values are important because they guide behavior. Managing people and shaping their behavior therefore depends on shaping the values they use as behavioral guides. The firm's culture should therefore send unambiguous signals about what is and is not acceptable behavior.

To an outside observer, a company's culture would reveal itself in several ways. You could see it in employees'

patterns of behavior, such as ceremonial events and written and spoken commands. For example, managers and employees may engage in behaviors such as hiding information, politicking, or (more positively) expressing concern when a colleague bends ethical rules. You could also see it in the *physical manifestations* of a company's behavior, such as written rules, office layout, organizational structure, and ethics codes.

In turn, these cultural symbols and behaviors reflect the firm's shared *values*, such as "the customer is always right" or "be honest." If management and employees really believe

(continued)

"honesty is the best policy," the written rules they follow and the things they do should reflect this value. A certain budget-airline founder wanted all employees to get the message that, "we're all in this together." You'd therefore often find him helping out at the gate, or handing luggage up into the plane.

THE MANAGER'S ROLE   A truism about organizational culture is that employees take their signals about what's acceptable not just from what managers say, but from what they do. With respect to ethics, managers therefore have to think through how to send not just accurate but the right signals to their employees. Doing so includes:

■ *Clarifying Expectations.* First, managers should make clear their expectations with respect to the values they want subordinates to follow. One way to do this is to publish a corporate ethics code. For example, the Johnson & Johnson code says "We believe our first responsibility is to the doctors, nurses and patients, to mothers and fathers and all others who use our products and services."

■ *Using Signs and Symbols. Symbolism*—what the manager actually does and thus the signals he or she sends—ultimately does the most to create and sustain the company's culture. Managers need to "walk the talk." They cannot expect to say "don't fudge the financials" and then do so themselves.

■ *Providing Physical Support.* The physical manifestations of the manager's values—the firm's incentive plan, appraisal system, and disciplinary procedures, for instance—send strong signals regarding what employees should and should not do. Does the firm reward ethical behavior or penalize it?

■ *Using Stories.* Stories can illustrate important company values. Express and mail delivery company TNT has such stories, like the one about how TNT employees drove through storms to get parcels customers.

■ *Organizing Rites and Ceremonies.* U.S. retailer JC Penney used to induct new management employees into the "Penney Partnership." Each inductee received an HCSC lapel pin. The letters denote JCPenney's core values of honor, confidence, service, and cooperation.

Research Findings: Important Facts About Cultivating Ethical Behavior at Work

Several experts reviewed the research concerning factors that influence ethical behavior at work. Here's what they found:[31]

■ Ethical behavior starts with *moral awareness*. In other words, does the person even recognize that a moral issue exists in the situation? To sensitize employees, managers need to use training and personal examples to illustrate how typical workplace situations (such as employee dismissals) entail moral issues.
■ *Managers* can do a lot to influence employee ethics by carefully cultivating the right norms, peer behavior, leadership, reward systems, and culture.
■ Problems arise when people undergo "*moral disengagement*." Doing so frees them from the guilt that would normally accompany violating one's ethical standards. For example, people are more likely to harm others when they view the victims as nongroup members.
■ "*Systematic cognitive biases*" affect how people process information. For example, people tend to judge others based on erroneous stereotypes—for instance, "elderly people can't work hard." That then leads them to make unethical decisions about these people.
■ The most powerful morality comes from *within*. In effect, when the moral person asks, "Why be moral?" the answer is, "because that is who I am." Then, failure to act morally creates emotional discomfort and becomes, in effect, a betrayal of oneself.[32]
■ Beware the seductive power of an *unmet goal*. Unmet goals pursued blindly can contribute to unethical behavior, especially when someone is very close to achieving the goal.[33]
■ Offering *rewards* for ethical behavior can backfire. Doing so may actually undermine the intrinsic value of ethical behavior.
■ Make sure no one is rewarded for bad behavior. For example, don't promote someone who got a big sale by bribing the customer. Rewarding *bad behavior* increases that behavior.[34]

■ Employers should *punish unethical behavior*. Employees who observe unethical behavior expect the perpetrators to be disciplined. Weak sanctions can send the wrong signal and be worse for ethical behavior than no sanctions at all.

■ The degree to which employees *openly talk about ethics* is a good predictor of ethical conduct. Conversely, organizations characterized by "moral muteness" suffer more ethically problematic behavior.

■ People tend to shift their *moral compasses* when they join an organization. They then uncritically equate "what's best for this organization" with "what's the right thing to do?"

❸ Discuss at least four specific ways in which HR management can influence ethical behavior at work.

HR MANAGEMENT'S ROLE IN ETHICS AND FAIR TREATMENT

Managers can take several steps to ensure ethical behavior by their employees. Many of these actions are clearly human resource management–based activities.

Staffing and Selection

"The simplest way to tune up an organization, ethically speaking, is to hire more ethical people," says one writer.[35] Screening for ethics can start before applicants even apply, by creating recruitment materials that emphasize the firm's commitment to ethics. (The U.S. Data Trust site in Figure 9.4 is an example.) Employers can then use tools such as honesty tests and meticulous background checks to screen out undesirables.[36] Also, ask behavioral questions such as "Have you ever observed someone stretching the rules at work? What did you do about it?" and, "Have you ever had to go against company guidelines or procedures in order to get something done?"[37]

FIGURE 9.4

U.S. Data Trust Web Site

Source: Reprinted with permission of U.S. Data Trust Corporation. www.USDataTrust.com/company.

The apparent fairness of the selection process is also important. For example, "If prospective employees perceive that the hiring process does not treat people fairly, they may assume that ethical behavior is not important in the company, and that 'official' pronouncements about the importance of ethics can be discounted."[38] The manager can do several things to ensure that others view the firm's assessment methods as fair: [39]

- *Make the procedures fair.* Candidates will tend to view the *formal procedure* (such as the selection interview) as fair to the extent that it tests job-related criteria, provides an opportunity to demonstrate competence, provides a way of redressing an error, and is used consistently with all applicants (or employees).
- *Treat applicants fairly.* The person's *interpersonal treatment* reflects such things as the propriety of the questions, the politeness and respect of the person doing the assessing, and the degree to which there was an opportunity for two-way communication.
- *Provide explanations.* Candidates appreciate employers' *providing explanations*. Individuals see a system as fair to the extent that the employer provides useful knowledge both about the employee's or candidate's own performance and about the employer's assessment procedures.[40]
- *Choose tests carefully.* Applicants or employees tend to view some *selection tools* as fairer than others. For example, they tend to view tools like work sample tests that are clearly job-related as fair. Subjects in several studies preferred honesty tests or urinalysis to personality assessment tests, probably because of the lack of obvious job relevance of personality assessment.
- *Allow for two-way feedback.* Effective interviews that provide for *two-way communication*—that let the applicant display skills, offer feedback, and have high face validity (in terms of measuring what they're purported to measure)—are also viewed as fair.

Training

Ethics training usually involves showing employees how to recognize ethical dilemmas, how to use ethical frameworks (such as codes of conduct) to resolve problems, and how to use personnel activities like interviews and disciplinary practices in ethical ways.[41] In addition to such mechanics, the training should also emphasize the moral underpinnings of the ethical choice and the company's deep commitment to integrity and ethics. Include participation by top managers to underscore that commitment.[42]

For all practical purposes, ethics training is mandatory today. Since 1991, U.S. government sentencing guidelines have prescribed reduced penalties for employers accused of misconduct who implement codes of conduct and ethics training.[43] The Sarbanes–Oxley Act of 2002 makes ethics training even more important.

Improving Productivity Through HRIS: Web-Based Ethics Training

Ethics training is often Internet-based. In one program, Lockheed Martin had its 160,000 employees take ethics and legal compliance training via the firm's intranet. Lockheed's ethics program software also kept track of how well the company and its employees were doing maintaining high ethical standards. For instance, the program helped top managers see that in one year, 4.8% of the company's ethics allegations involved conflicts of interest, and that it took about 30 days to complete an ethics violation internal investigation.[44] Other online ethics training programs include *Business Ethics*, from skillsoft.com, and two online courses, *Ethical Decision Making*, and *Managerial Business Ethics*, both from netG.com.[45]

Figure 9.5 summarizes nuts and bolts of typical ethics training programs. Note that new hire orientation, annual refresher training, and distributing the companies' policies and handbooks are all quite important.

Performance Appraisal

Unfair appraisals send the signal that the employer itself may condone unethical behavior. In fact, some managers do ignore accuracy and honesty in performance appraisals and

FIGURE 9.5

The Role of Training in Ethics

Source: HR Magazine by Susan Wells. Copyright 1999 by Society for Human Resource Management (S H R M). Reproduced with permission of Society for Human Resource Management (S H R M) in the format Other book via Copyright Clearance Center.

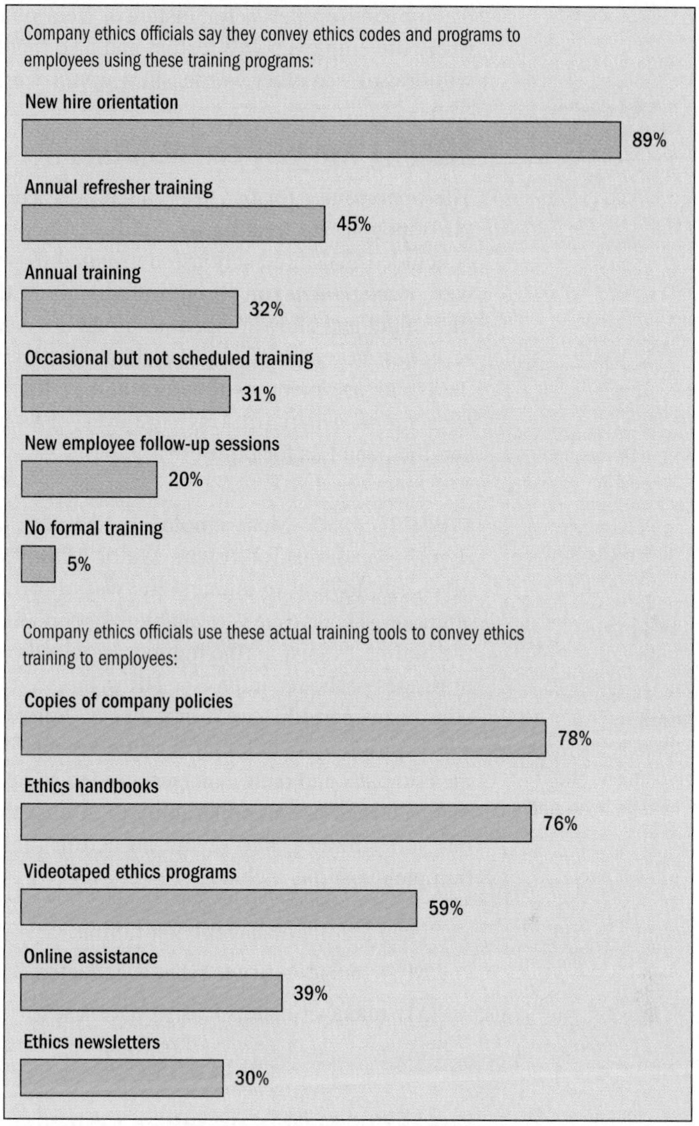

instead misuse the appraisals for political purposes (such as encouraging employees with whom they don't get along to leave the firm).[46] With a fair appraisal process,

- the employees' standards should be clear,
- employees should understand the basis on which they're going to be appraised, and
- the supervisors should perform the appraisals themselves objectively and fairly.[47]

Reward and Disciplinary Systems

Employees expect their employers to dole out relatively harsh punishment for unethical conduct.[48] Where it does not, it's often the ethical employees (not the unethical ones) who feel punished. Similarly, the employer can't have two sets of standards, and, specifically, should discipline executives, not just underlings, who misbehave.[49]

Workplace Aggression and Violence

We'll see in chapter 11 that workplace aggression is a serious problem, as well as one that often stems from real or perceived inequities. Thus, employees who believe that their employers treated them unfairly—for instance underpaid them, or unfairly dismissed them—may well retaliate. Numerous human resource actions, including layoffs, being passed over for promotion, terminations, and discipline, can prompt perceptions of unfair treatment.[50] Counterproductive behaviors here might include employee theft or destruction of company property, for instance. Real or imagined mistreatment also makes it more likely the employee will resign, and also that the person will show higher levels of "work withdrawal" (in other words, show up for work, but not do his or her best).[51]

Building Two-Way Communication

The opportunity for two-way, interactive communication affects our perceptions of how fairly people are treating us. Studies support this commonsense observation. One study concluded that three actions contributed to perceived fairness in business settings. These were *engagement* (involving individuals in the decisions that affect them by asking for their input and allowing them to refute the merits of one another's ideas and assumptions), *explanation* (ensuring that everyone involved and affected should understand why final decisions are made as they are and of the thinking that underlies the decisions), and *expectation clarity* (making sure everyone knows by what standards they will be judged and the penalties for failure).[52]

STEPS TO TAKE Many employers therefore take steps to facilitate two-way communication. For example, at Toyota Motor Manufacturing in Burnaston, Derbyshire, a *hotline* gives employees an anonymous way to bring questions or problems to management's attention. The hotline is available 24 hours per day. Employees can pick up any phone, dial the hotline extension (the number is posted on the plant bulletin boards), and deliver their messages to the recorder. The HR manager reviews and answers all messages. Other firms administer periodic **opinion surveys.** For example, the FedEx Survey Feedback Action (SFA) program includes an anonymous survey. This lets employees express feelings about the company and their managers, and to some extent about service, pay, and benefits. Each manager then has an opportunity to discuss the anonymous department results with his or her subordinates, and create an action plan for improving work group commitment. Sample questions include:

> "I can tell my manager what I think."
> "My manager tells me what is expected."
> "My manager listens to my concerns."
> "My manager keeps me informed."

opinion surveys
Questionnaires that regularly ask employees their opinions about the company, management, and work life.

Other Illustrative HR Ethics Activities

Human resource management supports ethics programs in other ways. For example, one study of Fortune 500 companies concluded that a human resources officer was responsible for the employer's ethics program in 28% of responding firms. Another 28% gave the firm's legal officers responsibility, and 16% established separate ethics or compliance departments. Other firms spread the responsibility among auditing departments, or positions such as public affairs and corporate communications.[53]

WAL-MART EXAMPLE Some people accused Wal-Mart of unfairness after it instituted its new policy requiring employees to come to work at a moment's notice, depending on their stores' last-minute needs. From Wal-Mart's point of view, the change made strategic sense. Their competitive advantage is low costs. The new employee scheduling policy enabled Wal-Mart to minimize labor costs when stores were slow (by sending employees home). Would you consider Wal-Mart's new store staffing policy to be unethical? Why?

EMPLOYEE DISCIPLINE AND PRIVACY

discipline
A procedure that corrects or punishes a subordinate for violating a rule or procedure.

The purpose of **discipline** is to encourage employees to behave sensibly at work (where *sensible* means adhering to rules and regulations). Discipline is necessary when an employee violates one of the rules.[54] The manager builds a fair discipline process on three pillars: rules and regulations, a system of progressive penalties, and an appeals process.

The purpose of discipline is to encourage employees to behave sensibly at work.

④ Exercise fair disciplinary practices.

Three Pillars

RULES A set of clear disciplinary rules and regulations is the first pillar. The rules should address issues such as theft, destruction of company property, drinking on the job, and insubordination. Examples of rules include:

> *Poor performance is not acceptable.* Each employee is expected to perform his or her work properly and efficiently and to meet established standards of quality.

> *Alcohol and drugs do not mix with work.* The use of either during working hours and reporting for work under the influence of either are both strictly prohibited.

> *The vending of anything in the plant without authorization is not allowed; nor is gambling in any form permitted.*

The purpose of the rules is to inform employees ahead of time what is and is not acceptable behavior. Employees should be told, preferably in writing, what is not permitted. This usually occurs during the employee's orientation. The employee orientation handbook should contain the rules and regulations.

PENALTIES A system of progressive penalties is a second pillar of effective discipline. The severity of the penalty is usually a function of the type of offense and the number of times the offense has occurred. For example, most companies issue warnings for the first unexcused lateness. However, for a fourth offense, discharge is the usual disciplinary action. Penalties may range from oral warnings to written warnings to suspension from the job to discharge.

APPEALS PROCESS Third, an appeals process should be part of the disciplinary process. The aim here is to ensure that supervisors mete out discipline fairly.

guaranteed fair treatment
Employer programs aimed at ensuring that all employees are treated fairly, generally by providing formalized, well-documented, and highly publicized vehicles through which employees can appeal any eligible issues.

FedEx's **guaranteed fair treatment** multistep program illustrates this. In *step 1, management review,* the complainant submits a written complaint to a member of management (manager, senior manager, or managing director). Then the manager, senior manager, and managing director of the employee's group review all relevant information; hold a telephone conference and/or meeting with the complainant; make a decision to either uphold, modify, or overturn management's action; and communicate their decision in writing to the complainant and the department's personnel representative.

If not satisfied, then in *step 2, officer complaint,* the complainant submits a written appeal to the vice president or senior vice president of the division.

Finally, in *step 3, executive appeals review,* the complainant may submit a written complaint to the employee relations department. They then investigate and prepare a case

HR in Practice

Fair Discipline Guidelines

Useful discipline guidelines for supervisors to keep in mind include:

- *Make sure the evidence supports the charge of employee wrongdoing.* Arbitrators often cite "The employer's evidence did not support the charge of employee wrongdoing" when reinstating discharged employees or reducing suspensions.
- *Make sure to protect the employees' due process rights.* Arbitrators normally reverse discharges and suspensions when the process that led to them is obviously unfair or violates due process.[55] For example, follow established progressive discipline procedures, and make sure the discipline is in line with what you've meted out to others.
- *Adequately warn the employee of the disciplinary consequences of his or her alleged misconduct.* Have the employee sign a form as in Figure 9.6 (page 301).
- *The rule that allegedly was violated should be "reasonably related"* to the efficient and safe operation of the particular work environment.
- *Fairly and adequately investigate the matter before administering discipline.*
- *The investigation should produce substantial evidence of misconduct.*
- *Apply applicable rules, orders, or penalties without discrimination.*
- *The penalty should be reasonably related to the misconduct and to the employee's past work history.*
- *Maintain the employee's right to counsel.* For example, all union employees generally have the right to bring a representative to an interview that they reasonably believe might lead to disciplinary action.
- *Don't rob your subordinate of his or her dignity.* For example, discipline your subordinate in private.
- *Remember that the burden of proof is on you.* A person is always considered innocent until proven guilty.
- *Get the facts.* Don't base your decision on hearsay evidence or on your general impression.
- *Don't act while angry.* Very few people can be objective and sensible when they are angry.
- *Use ombudsmen.* Some companies establish *ombudsmen,* neutral counselors outside the chain of command to whom employees who believe they were treated unfairly can turn to for confidential advice.[56]

file for the executive review appeals board. The appeals board—the CEO, the COO, the chief HR officer, and three senior vice presidents—then reviews all relevant information and makes a decision to uphold, overturn, or initiate a board of review or to take other appropriate action. The *HR in Practice* feature presents some fair discipline guidelines.

DISCIPLINE WITHOUT PUNISHMENT   Traditional discipline has two main drawbacks. First, no one likes being punished. Second, punishment tends to gain short-term compliance, but not the long-term cooperation employers often prefer.

Discipline without punishment (or alternative or nonpunitive discipline) aims to avoid these drawbacks. It does this by gaining employees' acceptance of the rules and by reducing the punitive nature of the discipline itself. Steps include:[57]

1. *Issue an oral reminder.*
2. *Should another incident arise within 6 weeks, issue a formal written reminder, and place a copy in the employee's personnel file.* Also hold a second private discussion with the employee.
3. *Give a paid, 1-day "decision-making leave."* If another incident occurs in the next 6 weeks or so, tell the employee to take a 1-day leave with pay, and to consider whether he or she wants to abide by the company's rules. When the employee returns to work, he or she meets with you and gives you a decision.
4. *If no further incidents occur in the next year or so, purge the 1-day paid suspension from the person's file.* If the behavior is repeated, the next step is dismissal (see later discussion).

FIGURE 9.6

Report of Employee Discipline

Apex Telecommunications Corporation
Report of Disciplinary Action and Warning

Employee's Name_____
Employee's Department_____
Date of Misconduct_____   Today's Date_____

Description of Incident and misconduct (including witnesses, if any)_____
_____
_____
_____

Witnesses to Incident_____
_____
_____

If the misconduct violated an Apex Co. policy or rule, state the policy or rule_____
_____
_____

Employee's explanation for misconduct, if any_____
_____
_____

Disciplinary action taken, if any_____
_____
_____

The employee was warned today that if misconduct such as this reoccurs at any time during the next_____
weeks, he or she may be subject to the following disciplinary action _____
_____
_____

_____   _____
Supervisor's signature   Employee's signature

_____   _____
Print name   Print name

The process would not apply to exceptional circumstances. Criminal behavior or in-plant fighting might be grounds for immediate dismissal, for instance.

Employee Privacy[58]

Most people probably view invasions of their privacy as both unethical and unfair. At work, four main employee privacy violations are *intrusion* (locker room and bathroom surveillance), *publication* of private matters, *disclosure* of medical records, and *appropriation* of an employee's name or likeness for commercial purposes.[59] Background checks, monitoring off-duty conduct and lifestyle, drug testing, workplace searches, and workplace activities monitoring trigger most privacy violations.[60] We'll look more closely at monitoring.

EMPLOYEE MONITORING A New Jersey court recently found an employer liable when one of its employees used his company computer at work to distribute child pornography. (Someone had previously alerted the employer to the suspicious activity and the employer had not taken action.)[61]

Managing and monitoring company e-mail is an urgent problem for employers. About one-third of U.S. companies recently investigated suspected leaks, via e-mail, of confidential or proprietary information. One hospital found that, to facilitate working at home, some medical staff were e-mailing patients' confidential records to themselves, violating federal privacy laws. Other employers face demands to produce employee e-mail as part of litigation, as when one employee sues another for sexual harassment. It's therefore not surprising that over half of employers say they monitor their employees' incoming and outgoing e-mail; 27% monitor internal e-mail as well.[62] Such monitoring raises privacy issues.

Monitoring today goes far beyond listening in on phone lines. Biometrics—using physical traits such as fingerprints or iris scans for identification—is one example. New York's Bronx Lebanon Hospital uses biometric scanners to ensure that employees that clock in really are who they say they are.[63] Iris scanning tends to be the most accurate authorization device. Some organizations like the U.S. Federal Aviation Authority use it to control employees' access to its network information systems.[64]

Location monitoring is becoming pervasive. As its name implies, this involves monitoring the location and movement of employees.[65] Employers ranging from TNT to cities in the United Kingdom use GPS units to monitor their truckers' and municipal vehicles' whereabouts. Inexpensive GPS technologies will contribute to wider use of location monitoring.

Employee monitoring is widespread. One survey found that about two-thirds of companies monitor e-mail activity, three-quarters monitor employee Internet use, and about 40% monitor phone calls.[66] Employers say they do so mostly to improve productivity and protect themselves from computer viruses, leaks of confidential information, and harassment suits.[67] But as we noted above, employees who use company computers to do things like swap illegal items can also ensnare employers in illegal activities—another reason to clarify what employees can and can't use company computers for.[68]

Employers therefore routinely use software to monitor (usually secretly) what their employees are doing online. When one employer noticed that employees were piling up overtime claims, they installed new software and discovered many employees were spending hours each day shopping online instead of working.

LEGAL ISSUES Electronic eavesdropping is legal—up to a point. For example, U.S. government law and most state laws allow employers to monitor employees' phone calls in the ordinary course of business. However, they must stop listening once it becomes clear that a conversation is personal rather than business related. You can also intercept e-mail service to protect the property rights of the e-mail provider. However, to be safe, employers often issue e-mail and online service usage policies. These warn employees that those systems are meant to be used for business purposes only. Employers also have employees sign e-mail and telephone monitoring acknowledgment statements like that in Figure 9.7.

Videotaped workplace monitoring calls for more legal caution than, for instance, e-mail monitoring. Continuous video surveillance of employees in an office setting may not be a problem. But a Boston employer had to pay over $200,000 to five workers it secretly videotaped in an employee locker room, after they sued.[69]

FIGURE 9.7

Sample Telephone Monitoring Acknowledgment Statement

I understand that XYZ Company periodically monitors any e-mail communications created, sent, or retrieved using this company's e-mail system. Therefore I understand that my e-mail communications may be read by individuals other than the intended recipient. I also understand that XYZ Company periodically monitors telephone communications, for example to improve customer service quality.

Signature   Date

Print Name   Department

MANAGING DISMISSALS

dismissal
Involuntary termination of an employee's employment with the firm.

Because **dismissal** is the most drastic disciplinary step, the manager should ensure that the dismissal is fair and warranted. On those occasions that require immediate dismissal, the manager still needs to ensure that the action is humane.

The best way to "handle" a dismissal is to avoid it in the first place, when possible. Many dismissals start with bad hiring decisions. Using sound selection practices including assessment tests, reference and background checks, drug testing, and clearly defined jobs can reduce the need for dismissals.[70]

terminate at will
The idea, based in law, that the employment relationship can be terminated at will by either the employer or the employee for any reason.

TERMINATION AT WILL For more than 100 years, the prevailing rule in the United States has been that without an employment contract, either the employer or the employee can **terminate at will** the employment relationship. In other words, the employee could resign for any reason, at will, and the employer could similarly dismiss an employee for any reason, at will. Today, however, dismissed employees increasingly take their cases to court, and in many cases employers are finding that they no longer have a blanket right to fire.

TERMINATION AT WILL EXCEPTIONS Three main protections against wrongful discharge eroded the termination-at-will doctrine—*statutory exceptions, common law exceptions,* and *public policy exceptions.*

First, in terms of *statutory exceptions,* federal and state equal employment and workplace laws prohibit specific types of dismissals. For example, Title VII of the U.S. Civil Rights Act of 1964 prohibits discharging employees based on race, color, religion, sex, or national origin.[71]

Second, numerous *common law exceptions* exist. For example, a court may decide that an employee handbook promising termination only "for just cause" may create an exception to the at-will rule.[72]

Finally, under the *public policy exception,* courts have held a discharge to be wrongful when it was against an explicit, well-established public policy (for instance, the employer fired the employee for refusing to break the law).

Grounds for Dismissal

There are four bases for dismissal: unsatisfactory performance, misconduct, lack of qualifications for the job, and changed requirements of (or elimination of) the job. *Unsatisfactory performance* may be defined as a persistent failure to perform assigned duties or to meet prescribed standards on the job.[73] Specific reasons include excessive absenteeism; tardiness; a persistent failure to meet normal job requirements; or an adverse attitude toward the company, supervisor, or fellow employees. *Misconduct* is deliberate and willful violation of the employer's rules and may include stealing, rowdy behavior, and insubordination. *Lack of qualifications for the job* is an employee's inability to do the assigned work, although he or she is diligent. Because in this case the employee may be trying to do the job, it is reasonable for the employer to do what's possible to salvage him or her—perhaps by assigning the employee to another job, or retraining the person. *Changed requirements of the job* is an employee's incapability of doing the work assigned after the nature of the job has been changed. Similarly, you may have to dismiss an employee when his or her job is eliminated. Again, the employee may be industrious, so it is reasonable to retrain or transfer this person, if possible.

insubordination
Willful disregard or disobedience of the boss's authority or legitimate orders.

Insubordination, a form of misconduct, is sometimes the grounds for dismissal. Stealing, chronic tardiness, and poor-quality work are concrete grounds for dismissal, but insubordination is sometimes harder to translate into words. Some acts should be deemed insubordinate whenever and wherever they occur. These include, for instance:[74]

1. Direct disregard of the boss's authority.
2. Direct disobedience of, or refusal to obey, the boss's orders, particularly in front of others.
3. Deliberate defiance of clearly stated company policies, rules, regulations, and procedures.
4. Public criticism of the boss.
5. Blatant disregard of reasonable instructions.

6. Contemptuous display of disrespect.

7. Disregard for the chain of command.

8. Participation in (or leadership of) an effort to undermine and remove the boss from power

FAIRNESS IN DISMISSALS   Dismissing employees is never easy, but at least the employer can try to ensure the employee views the process as fair. Communication is important here. One study found that "individuals who reported that they were given full explanations of why and how termination decisions were made were more likely to (1) perceive their layoff as fair, (2) endorse the terminating organization, and (3) indicate that they did not wish to take the past employer to court."[75]

Avoiding Wrongful Discharge Suits

In what *Business Week* magazine recently referred to as a "fear of the firing," the magazine described how some employers—even when faced with employee theft—were reluctant to terminate disruptive employees, for fear of lawsuits. In practice, plaintiffs (the dismissed employees) only win a tiny fraction of such suits. However, the cost of defending the suits is still huge.[76]

wrongful discharge
An employee dismissal that does not comply with the law or does not comply with the contractual arrangement stated or implied by the firm via its employment application forms, employee manuals, or other promises.

Wrongful discharge occurs when an employee's dismissal does not comply with the law or with the contractual arrangement stated or implied by the firm via its employment application forms, employee manuals, or other promises. (In a *constructive discharge* claim, the plaintiff argues that he or she quit, but had no choice because the employer made the situation so intolerable at work.[77]) The time to protect against such suits is before the manager errs and suits are filed.

Protecting against wrongful discharge suits requires a two-stage strategy: procedural steps, and fairness safeguards.

5 Discuss at least four procedural suggestions for managing dismissals effectively.

PROCEDURAL STEPS   *First,* lay the groundwork, starting with the employment application, that will help avoid such suits. Procedural steps include:[78]

- Have applicants sign the employment application. Make sure it contains a statement that the employer can terminate at any time.
- Review your employee manual to look for and delete statements that could undermine your defense in a wrongful discharge case. For example, delete any reference to "employees can be terminated only for just cause."
- Have written rules listing infractions that may require discipline and discharge, and then follow the rules.
- If a rule is broken, get the worker's side of the story in front of witnesses, and preferably get it signed. Then check out the story.
- Be sure that employees get a written appraisal at least annually. If an employee shows evidence of incompetence, give that person a warning and provide an opportunity to improve.
- Keep careful confidential records of all actions such as employee appraisals, warnings or notices, and so on.
- Finally, ask the questions in Figure 9.8.

FAIRNESS SAFEGUARDS   Terminated employees are less likely to sue if they walk away feeling you treated them fairly. *Second,* therefore, employ practices (like those in this chapter) that help ensure the fairness of the dismissal.[79] People who are fired and who walk away feeling that they've been embarrassed, stripped of their dignity, or treated unfairly financially (for instance, in terms of severance pay) are more likely to seek retribution in the courts. Some employers therefore sometimes use severance pay to blunt a dismissal's sting. Figure 9.9 summarizes typical severance policies in manufacturing and service industries. You can't make a termination pleasant, but at least handle it with fairness and justice.

Personal Supervisory Liability

Courts sometimes hold managers personally liable for their supervisory actions, particularly those actions covered by the U.S. Fair Labor Standards Act and the Family and Medical Leave Act.[80] The Fair Labor Standards Act defines *employer* to include "any person -

FIGURE 9.8 Questions to Ask Before Making the Dismissal Final

Is the employee covered by any type of written agreement, including a collective bargaining agreement?_____

Is a defamation claim likely?_____

Is there a possible discrimination allegation? _____

Is there any workers' compensation involvement? _____

Have reasonable rules and regulations been communicated and enforced?_____

Has the employee been given an opportunity to explain any rule violations or to correct poor performance?_____

Have all monies been paid within 24 hours after separation? _____

Has the employee been advised of his or her rights under COBRA? _____

Source: Sovereign, Kenneth L., *Personnel Law,* 4th, © 1999. Electronically reproduced by permission of Pearson Education, Inc., Upper Saddle River, New Jersey.

acting directly or indirectly in the interest of an employer in relation to any employee." This can mean the individual supervisor.

STEPS TO TAKE There are several ways to avoid creating situations in which personal liability becomes an issue.

- *Follow company policies and procedures.* An employee may initiate a claim against a supervisor who he or she alleges did not follow policies and procedures.
- Administer the discipline in a manner that does not add to the employee's *emotional hardship* (as would making them publicly collect their belongings and leave the office).
- *Do not act in anger,* since doing so undermines the appearance of objectivity.
- Finally, *utilize the HR department* for advice regarding how to handle difficult disciplinary matters.

The Termination Interview

Dismissing an employee is one of the most difficult tasks you can face at work.[81] The dismissed employee, even if warned many times in the past, may still react with disbelief or even violence. Guidelines for the **termination interview** itself are as follows:

termination interview
The interview in which an employee is informed of the fact that he or she has been dismissed.

1. ***Plan the interview carefully.*** According to experts this includes:
   - Make sure the employee keeps the appointment time.
   - Never inform an employee over the phone.
   - Allow 10 minutes as sufficient time for the interview.

FIGURE 9.9

Median Weeks of Severance Pay by Job Level

Source: Severance Pay: Current Trends and Practices, July 2007, Table 4, http://www.culpepper.com/ info/CS/default.asp.Culpepper eBulletin, July 2007. Complimentary subscriptions at: www.culpepper. com/eBulletin.

Severance Calculation Method	Median Weeks of Severance		
	Executives	**Managers**	**Professionals**
Fixed	26	6	4
Variable Amount by Employment Tenure			
1 year	4	2	2
3 years	7	5	5
5 years	10	7	7
10 years	20	12	10
15 years	26	16	15
Maximum	39	26	24

- Use a neutral site, not your own office.
- Have employee agreements, the human resource file, and a release announcement (internal and external) prepared in advance.
- Be available at a time after the interview in case questions or problems arise.
- Have phone numbers ready for medical or security emergencies.

2. *Get to the point.* As soon as the employee enters your office, give the person a moment to get comfortable and then inform him or her of your decision.

3. *Describe the situation.* Briefly, in three or four sentences, explain why the person is being let go. For instance, "Production in your area is down 4%, and we are continuing to have quality problems. We have talked about these problems several times in the past 3 months, and the solutions are not being followed through. We have to make a change."[82] Describe the situation rather than attack the employee personally by saying things like, "Your production is just not up to par." Also emphasize that the decision is final and irrevocable.

4. *Listen.* Continue the interview until the person appears to be talking freely and reasonably calmly about the reasons for his or her termination.

5. *Review the severance package.* Describe severance payments, benefits, access to office support people, and the way references will be handled. However, under no conditions should any promises or benefits beyond those already in the support package be implied.

6. *Identify the next step.* The terminated employee may be disoriented and unsure what to do next. Explain where the employee should go next, upon leaving the interview.

outplacement counseling
A systematic process by which a terminated person is trained and counseled in the techniques of self-appraisal and securing a new position.

OUTPLACEMENT COUNSELING With **outplacement counseling** the employer arranges for an outside firm to provide terminated employees with career planning and job search skills. *Outplacement firms* usually provide the actual outplacement services. Employees (generally managers) who are let go typically have office space and secretarial services they can use at local offices of such firms, in addition to the counseling services. The outplacement counseling is part of the terminated employee's support or severance package.

exit interviews
Interviews conducted by the employer immediately prior to the employee leaving the firm with the aim of better understanding what the employee thinks about the company.

EXIT INTERVIEW Many employers conduct **exit interviews** with employees who are leaving the firm for any reason. These are interviews, usually conducted by a human resource professional just prior to the employee leaving, that elicit information about the job or related matters with the aim of giving employers insights into what is right—or wrong—about their companies. Exit interview questions include: How were you recruited? Why did you join the company? Was the job presented correctly and honestly? Were your expectations met? What was the workplace environment like? What was your supervisor's management style like? What did you like most/least about the company? Were there any special problem areas? Why did you decide to leave, and how was the departure handled?[83]

The assumption, of course, is that because the employee is leaving, he or she will be candid. However, the information one gets is more likely to be questionable.[84] Researchers found that at the time of separation, 38% of those leaving blamed salary and benefits, and only 4% blamed supervision. Followed up 18 months later, 24% blamed supervision and only 12% blamed salary and benefits.

Getting to the real issues during the exit interview may thus require some heavy digging. Yet these interviews can be useful. When an Australian medical clinic laid off employees, many said, in exit interviews, "This is not a stable place to work." The firm took steps to correct that misperception for those who stayed.

Layoffs and the Plant Closing Law

Nondisciplinary separations are a fact of life, and may be initiated by either employer or employee. For the *employer,* reduced sales or profits or the desire for more productivity may require layoffs. In one recent year, U.S. employers implemented about 1,200 mass layoffs, involving a total of almost 144,000 workers.[85] *Employees* may leave to retire or to seek better jobs. The U.S. Worker Adjustment and Retraining Notification Act (WARN Act, or the plant closing law) requires employers of 100 or more employees to give 60 days' notice before closing a facility or starting a layoff of 50 or more people.

layoff
A situation in which employees are told there is no work for them but that management intends to recall them when work is again available.

A **layoff,** in which the employer sends workers home for a time for lack of work, is usually not a permanent dismissal (although it may turn out to be). Rather, it is a temporary one, which the employer expects will be short term. However, some employers use the term *layoff* as a euphemism for discharge or termination.

THE LAYOFF PROCESS A study illustrates one firm's layoff process. In this company, senior management first met to make strategic decisions about the size and timing of the layoffs. These managers also debated the relative importance of the skill sets they thought the firm needed going forward. Front-line supervisors assessed their subordinates, rating their nonunion employees either A, B, or C (union employees were covered by a union agreement making layoffs dependant on seniority). The front-line supervisors then informed each of their subordinates about his or her A, B, or C rating, and told each that those employees with C grades were designated "surplus" and most likely to be laid off.[86]

LAYOFF'S EFFECTS It's not surprising that layoffs "tend to result in deleterious psychological and physical health outcomes for employees who lose their jobs" as well as for the survivors who face uncertainty and discomfort.[87]

Furthermore, it is not just the "victims" and "survivors" who suffer. In one study, the researchers "found that the more (U.S.) managers were personally responsible for handing out WARN notices to employees, regardless of their age, gender, and marital status, the more likely they were to report physical health problems, to seek treatment for these problems, and to complain of disturbed sleep."[88]

Ironically, when some employees most need employee assistance programs—after they're laid off—they lose them. More firms are therefore extending Employee Assistance Program benefits for a month or two to former employees. For example, Florida's Sarasota County extended employee assistance program benefits for two months after laying off some employees. Most didn't use the service, but even they viewed it "like having a safety net."[89]

Global Issues in HR

Employment Contracts

Layoffs are often subject to additional constraints abroad. Businesses expanding abroad soon discover that hiring, disciplining, and discharging employees in Europe requires more stringent communication than they do in the United States. For example, the European Union (EU) has a directive (law) that requires employers to provide employees with very explicit contracts of employment, usually within 2 months of their starting work.

How employers comply with this law varies by country. In the United Kingdom, the employee must be given a written contract specifying, among other things, name of employer, grievance procedure, job title, rate of pay, disciplinary rules, pension plan, hours of work, vacation and sick-leave policies, pay periods, and date when employment began. In Germany, the contracts need not be in writing, although they customarily are, given the amount of detail they must cover, including minimum notice prior to layoff, wages, vacations, maternity/paternity rights, equal pay, invention rights, noncompetition clause, and sickness pay. The contract need not be in writing in Italy, but again, it usually is. Items covered include start date, probationary period, working hours, job description, place of work, basic salary, and a noncompetition clause. In France, the contract must be in writing, and specify information such as the identity of the parties, place of work, type of job or job descriptions, notice period, dates of payment, and work hours.

Adjusting to Downsizings and Mergers

downsizing
Refers to the process of reducing, usually dramatically, the number of people employed by the firm.

Downsizing means reducing, usually dramatically, the number of people employed by a firm. The basic idea is to cut costs and raise profitability.

To avoid unnecessary repercussions, downsizings require that employers carefully consider four matters.

1. One is *compliance with all applicable laws.*
2. Second is ensuring that the employer executes the dismissals in a manner that is *just and fair.*
3. Third is the practical consideration of *security,* for instance, with respect to retrieving keys and ensuring that those leaving do not take any prohibited items with them.
4. Fourth is to reduce the remaining *employees' uncertainty* and to address their concerns. This typically involves a postdownsizing announcement and program, including meetings where senior managers field questions from the remaining employees. Supervisors should also meet with their employees informally to encourage an open discussion of concerns.

Downsizings aren't pleasant but needn't be unfair. Information sharing (in terms of providing advanced notice regarding the layoff) and interpersonal sensitivity (in terms of the manager's demeanor during layoffs) can both help cushion the otherwise negative effects.[90]

Workforce reductions can reduce the attractiveness of the firm for prospective job applicants. However, employers who downsize but provide support to those dismissed are nearly as attractive to applicants as employers that don't downsize.[91]

Review

SUMMARY

1. Unfair treatment reduces morale, increases stress, and has negative effects on performance. Managers, and HR management, can take steps to reduce such unfairness.
2. Ethics refers to the principles of conduct governing an individual or a group, and specifically to the standards you used to decide what your conduct should be.
3. Numerous factors shape ethical behavior at work. These include individual factors, organizational factors, the boss's influence, ethics policies and codes, and the organization's culture.
4. Employees have many legal and moral rights. Laws like Title VII in the U.S. don't just list what employers can and can't do in the workplace. They also give employees (or prospective employees, and sometimes past employees) numerous rights. For example, ERISA's so-called retaliation provision gives employees who believe they were denied profit sharing or pension benefits due to discrimination the right to seek to redress the violations. On a broader level, many societies agree that people (workers included) share certain inalienable or moral rights—rights they have just because they are people living in civil societies. For example, the rights to "life,

liberty, and the pursuit of happiness" are ingrained in American culture
5. HR management can influence ethics and fair treatment at work in numerous ways. For example, having a fair and open selection process that emphasizes the company's stress on integrity and ethics, establishing special ethics training programs, measuring employees' adherence to high ethical standards during performance appraisals, and rewarding (or disciplining) ethical (or unethical) work-related behavior are some examples.
6. Firms give employees avenues through which to express opinions and concerns. For example, Toyota's hotline provides employees at a plant in the United Kingdom with an anonymous channel through which they can express concerns to top management. Firms such as FedEx engage in periodic anonymous opinion surveys.
7. Guaranteed fair treatment programs help to ensure that grievances are handled fairly and openly. Steps include management review, officer complaint, and executive appeals review.
8. A fair and just discipline process is based on three prerequisites: rules and regulations, a system of progressive penalties, and an appeals process. A number of discipline guidelines are important, including

that discipline should be in line with the way management usually responds to similar incidents, that management must adequately investigate the matter before administering discipline, and that managers should not rob a subordinate of his or her dignity.

9. The basic aim of discipline without punishment is to gain an employee's acceptance of the rules by reducing the punitive nature of the discipline itself. In particular, an employee is given a paid day off to consider his or her infraction before more punitive disciplinary steps are taken.

10. Managing dismissals is an important part of any supervisor's job. Among the reasons for dismissal are unsatisfactory performance, misconduct, lack of qualifications, changed job requirements, and insubordination. In dismissing one or more employees, however, remember that termination at will as a policy has been weakened by exceptions in many states. Furthermore, great care should be taken to avoid wrongful discharge suits.

11. Dismissing an employee is always difficult, and the termination interview should be handled properly. Specifically, plan the interview carefully (for instance, early in the week), get to the point, describe the situation, and then listen until the person has expressed his or her feelings. Then discuss the severance package and identify the next step.

12. Nondisciplinary separations such as layoffs and retirement occur all the time. The U.S. plant closing law (the Worker Adjustment and Retraining Notification Act) outlines requirements to be followed with regard to official notice before operations with 50 or more people are to be closed down.

13. Disciplinary actions are a big source of grievances. Discipline should be based on rules and adhere to a system of progressive penalties, and it should permit an appeals process.

KEY TERMS

ethics   287
organizational culture   293
opinion surveys   298
discipline   298
guaranteed fair treatment   299
dismissal   303
terminate at will   303

insubordination   303
wrongful discharge   304
termination interview   305
outplacement counseling   306
exit interviews   306
layoff   307
downsizing   308

DISCUSSION QUESTIONS AND EXERCISES

1. Describe the similarities and differences between a program such as FedEx's guaranteed fair treatment program and your college or university's student grievance process.

2. Explain how you would ensure fairness in disciplining, discussing particularly the prerequisites to disciplining, disciplining guidelines, and the discipline without punishment approach.

3. Why is it important to manage dismissals properly?

4. What techniques would you use as alternatives to traditional discipline? What do such alternatives have to do with "organizational justice"? Why do you think alternatives like these are important, given industry's current need for highly committed employees?

5. Working individually or in groups, interview managers or administrators at your employer or college in order to determine the extent to which the employer or college builds two-way communication,

and the specific types of programs that are used. Do the managers think they are effective? What do the employees (or faculty members) think of the programs if they are in use at the employer or college?

6. Working individually or in groups, review copies of the student handbook for your college and determine to what extent there is a formal process through which students can air grievances. Do you think the process should be an effective one? Based on your contacts with other students, has it been an effective grievance process?

7. Working individually or in groups, determine the rules, policies, and procedures that comprise the academic discipline process in your college. Given what you read in this chapter, do you think the process is an effective one? Would you recommend any modification of the student discipline process?

Application Exercises

For many people, Enron Corp. still ranks as one of history's classic examples of ethics run amok. During the 1990s and early 2000s, Houston, Texas-based Enron was in the business of wholesaling natural gas and electricity. Rather than actually owning the gas or electric, Enron made its money as the intermediary (wholesaler) between suppliers and customers. Without getting into all the details, the nature of Enron's business, and the fact that Enron didn't actually own the assets, meant that its accounting procedures were unusual. For example, the profit statements and balance sheets listing the firm's assets and liabilities were unusually difficult to understand.

As most people know by now, it turned out that the lack of accounting transparency enabled the company's managers to make Enron's financial performance look much better than it actually was. Outside experts began questioning Enron's financial statements in 2001. In fairly short order Enron's house of cards collapsed, and several of its top executives were convicted of things like manipulating Enron's reported assets and profitability. Many investors (including former Enron employees) lost all or most of their investments in Enron.

It's probably always easier to understand ethical breakdowns like this in retrospect, rather than to predict they are going to happen. However, in Enron's case the breakdown is perhaps more perplexing than usual. As one writer recently said,

> Enron had all the elements usually found in comprehensive ethics and compliance programs: a code of ethics, a reporting system, as well as a training video on vision and values led by [the company's top executives].[92]

Experts subsequently put forth many explanations for how a company that was apparently so ethical on its face could actually have been making so many bad ethical decisions without other managers (and the board of directors) noticing. The explanations ranged from a "deliberate concealment of information by officers" to more psychological explanations such as employees not wanting to contradict their bosses, and the "surprising role of irrationality in decision-making."[93]

But perhaps the most persuasive explanation of how an apparently ethical company could go so wrong concerns organizational culture. Basically, the reasoning here is that it's not the rules but what employees feel they should do that determines ethical behavior. For example (speaking in general, not specifically about Enron), the executive director of the U.S. Ethics Officer Association put it this way:

> [W]e're a legalistic society, and we've created a lot of laws. We assume that if you just knew what those laws meant that you would behave properly. Well, guess what? You can't write enough laws to tell us what to do at all times every day of the week in every part of the world. We've got to develop the critical thinking and critical reasoning skills of our people because most of the ethical issues that we deal with are in the ethical gray areas. Virtually every regulatory body in the last year has come out with language that has said in addition to law compliance, businesses are also going to be accountable to ethics standards and a corporate culture that embraces them.[94]

How can one tell or measure when a company has an "ethical culture"? Key attributes of a healthy ethical culture include:

- Employees feel a sense of responsibility and accountability for their actions and for the actions of others.[95]
- Employees freely raise issues and concerns without fear of retaliation.
- Managers model the behaviors they demand of others.
- Managers communicate the importance of integrity when making difficult decisions.

Questions

1. Based on what you read in this chapter, summarize in one page or less how you would explain Enron's ethical meltdown.
2. It is said that when one securities analyst tried to confront Enron's CEO about the firm's unusual accounting statements, the CEO publicly used vulgar language to describe the analyst, and that Enron employees subsequently thought doing so was humorous. If true, what does that say about Enron's ethical culture?
3. This case and this chapter both had something to say about how organizational culture influences ethical behavior. What role do you think culture played at Enron? Give five specific examples of things Enron's CEO could have done to create a healthy ethical culture.

Being in the laundry and cleaning business, the Carters have always felt strongly about not allowing employees to smoke, eat, or drink in their stores. Jennifer was therefore surprised to walk into a store and find two employees eating lunch at the front counter. There was a large pizza in its box, and the two of them were sipping colas and eating slices of pizza and submarine sandwiches off paper plates. Not only did it look messy, but there were also grease and soda spills on the counter and the store smelled from onions and pepperoni, even with the four-foot-wide exhaust fan pulling air out through the roof. In addition to being a turnoff to customers, the mess on the counter increased the possibility that a customer's order might actually become soiled in the store.

While this was a serious matter, neither Jennifer nor her father felt that what the counter people were doing was grounds for immediate dismissal, partly because the store manager had apparently condoned their actions. The problem was, they didn't know what to do. It seemed to them that the matter called for more than just a warning but less than dismissal.

Questions

1. What would you do if you were Jennifer, and why?
2. Should a disciplinary system be established at Carter Cleaning Centers?
3. If so, what should it cover, and how would you suggest it deal with a situation such as the one with the errant counter people?
4. How would you deal with the store manager?

EXPERIENTIAL EXERCISE

The Cloning Dilemma

Purpose:

The purpose of this exercise is to provide you with some experience in analyzing and handling an ethics-based situation.

Required Understanding:

Students should be thoroughly familiar with the following case, "The Cloning Dilemma," and our discussions in this chapter.

You work for a medical genetics research firm as a marketing person. You love the job. The location is great, the hours are good, and the work is challenging and flexible. You receive a much higher salary than you ever anticipated. However, you've just heard via the rumor mill that the company's elite medical team has cloned the first human, the firm's CEO. It was such a total success that you have heard that they may want to clone every employee so that they can use the clones to harvest body parts as the original people age or become ill. You are not sure you endorse the cloning of humans. You joined the firm for its moral and ethical reputation. You feel that the image presented to you was one of research and development of life-saving drugs and innovative medical procedures. The thought of cloning was never on your mind, but now it must be.

How to Set Up the Exercise/Instructions:

Divide the class into groups of four or five students. Each group should take the arbitrator's point of view and assume that they are to analyze the case and make the arbitrator's decision. Review the case again at this point, but please do not read the award and discussion.

Each group should answer the following questions:
1. What, if any, is the ethical decision to be made?
2. What would you do? Why?

ETHICS QUIZ ANSWERS

Quiz is on page 288.

1. 34% said personal e-mail on company computers is wrong.
2. 37% said using office equipment for schoolwork is wrong.
3. 49% said playing computer games at work is wrong.
4. 54% said Internet shopping at work is wrong.
5. 61% said it's unethical to blame your error on technology.
6. 87% said it's unethical to visit pornographic sites at work.
7. 33% said $25 is the amount at which a gift from a supplier or client becomes troubling, while 33% said $50, and 33% said $100.
8. 35% said a $50 gift to the boss is unacceptable.
9. 12% said a $50 gift *from* the boss is unacceptable.
10. 70% said it's unacceptable to take the $200 football tickets.
11. 70% said it's unacceptable to take the $120 theater tickets.
12. 35% said it's unacceptable to take the $100 food basket.
13. 45% said it's unacceptable to take the $25 gift certificate.
14. 40% said it's unacceptable to take the $75 raffle prize.
15. 11% reported they lie about sick days.
16. 4% reported they take credit for the work or ideas of others.

ENDNOTES

1. Bennett Tepper, "Consequences of Abusive Supervision," *Academy of Management Journal* 43, no. 2 (2000): 178–190. See also Samuel Aryee et al., "Antecedents and Outcomes of Abusive Supervision: A Test of a Trickle-Down Model," *Journal of Applied Psychology* 92, no. 1 (2007): 191–201.

2. www.walgreens.com

3. Michelle Donovan et al., "The Perceptions of Fair Interpersonal Treatment Scale: Development and Validation of a Measure of Interpersonal Treatment in the Workplace," *Journal of Applied Psychology* 83, no. 5 (1998): 683–692.

4. Gary Weaver and Linda Trevino, "The Role of Human Resources in Ethics/Compliance Management: A Fairness Perspective," *Human Resource Management Review* 11 (2001): 117.

5. Suzanne Masterson, "A Trickle-Down Model of Organizational Justice: Relating Employees' and Customers' Perceptions of and Reactions to Fairness," *Journal of Applied Psychology* 86, no. 4 (2001): 594–601.

6. Linda Trevino and Katherine Nelson, *Managing Business Ethics* (New York: John Wiley & Sons, 1999): 134.

7. Kevin Wooten, "Ethical Dilemmas in Human Resource Management: An Application of a Multidimensional Framework, A Unifying Taxonomy, and Applicable Codes," *Human Resource Management Review* 11 (2001): 161. See also "What Role Should HR Play in Corporate Ethics?" *HR Focus* 81, no. 1 (January 2004): 3; and Sean Valentine et al., "Employee Job Response As a Function of Ethical Context and Perceived Organization Support," *Journal of Business Research* 59, no. 5 (2006): 582–588.

8. Manuel Velasquez, *Business Ethics: Concepts and Cases* (Upper Saddle River, NJ: Prentice Hall, 1992): 9. See also O. C. Ferrell, John Fraedrich, and Linog Ferrell, *Business Ethics* (Boston: Houghton Mifflin, 2008).

9. For further discussion of ethics and morality, see Tom Beauchamp and Norman Bowie, *Ethical Theory and Business* (Upper Saddle River, NJ: Prentice Hall, 2001): 1–19.

10. Richard Osborne, "A Matter of Ethics," *Industry Week* 49, no. 14 (September 4, 2000): 41–42.

11. Garrett Brown, "Corporate Social Responsibility Brings Limited Progress on Workplace Safety in Global Supply Chains," *Occupational Hazards* (August 2007): 16.

12. Basically, *common law* refers to legal precedents. Judges' rulings set precedents, which then generally guide future judicial decisions.

13. Kenneth Sovereign, *Personnel Law* (Upper Saddle River, NJ: Prentice Hall, 1999): 192.

14. Ibid., 150.

15. Ibid., 236.

16. This list is from http://legaltarget.com/employee_rights.htm, accessed April 24, 2008.

17. Op. cit., 3.

18. *Miami Daily Business Review* (April 20, 2007).

19. Hugh Williamson, "Allianz Deal Set to Boost Employee Rights" *The Financial Times* (September 22, 2006): 24.

20. Sara Morris et al., "A Test of Environmental, Situational, and Personal Influences on the Ethical Intentions of

CEOs," *Business and Society* (August 1995): 119–47. See also Dennis Moberg, "Ethics Blind Spots in Organizations: How Systematic Errors in Person's Perception Undermine Moral Agency," *Organization Studies* 27, no.3 (2006): 413–428.

21. "Former CEO Joins WorldCom's Indicted," *Miami Herald* (March 3, 2004): 4C.

22. Gretchen Morgenson, "Requiem for an Honorable Profession," *New York Times* (May 5, 2002): B1.

23. "Ethics Policies Are Big with Employers, but Workers See Small Impact on the Workplace," *BNA Bulletin to Management* (June 29, 2000): 201.

24. Jennifer Schramm, "Perceptions on Ethics," *HR Magazine* (November 2004): 176.

25. From Guy Brumback, "Managing Above the Bottom Line of Ethics," *Supervisory Management* (December 1993): 12.

26. Quoted in Tom Beauchamp and Norman Bowie, *Ethical Theory and Business* (Upper Saddle River, NJ: Prentice Hall, 2001): 109.

27. James Kunen, "Enron Division (and Values) Thing," *New York Times* (January 19, 2002): A19. For another example, see Heather Tesoriero and Avery Johnson, "Suit Details How J&J Pushed Sales of Procrit," *Wall Street Journal Eastern Edition* (April 10, 2007): B1(1).

28. Dayton Fandray, "The Ethical Company," *Workforce* 79, no. 12 (December 2000): 74–77.

29. Richard Beatty et al., "HR's Role in Corporate Governance: Present and Prospective," *Human Resource Management* 42, no. 3 (Fall 2003): 268.

30. Dale Buss, "Corporate Compasses," *HR Magazine* (June 2004): 127–132.

31. This list based on Linda K. Treviño, Gary R. Weaver, and Scott J. Reynolds, "Behavioral Ethics in Organizations: A Review," *Journal of Management* 32, no. 6 (2006): 951–990.

32. R. Bergman, "Identity as Motivation: Toward a Theory of the Moral Self." In D. K. Lapsley & D. Narvaez (Eds.), *Moral Development, Self and Identity* (Mahwah, NJ: Lawrence Erlbaum, 2004): 21–46.

33. M. E. Schweitzer, L. Ordonez, and B. Douma, "Goal Setting as a Motivator of Unethical Behavior," *Academy of Management Journal* 47, no. 3 (2004): 422–432.

34. N. M. Ashkanasy, C. A. Windsor, and L. K. Treviño, "Bad Apples in Bad Barrels Revisited: Cognitive Moral Development, Just World Beliefs, Rewards, and Ethical Decision Making," *Business Ethics Quarterly* 16 (2006): 449–474.

35. J. Krohe Jr., "The Big Business of Business Ethics," *Across the Board* 34 (May 1997): 23–29; Deborah Wells and Marshall Schminke, "Ethical Development and Human Resources Training: An Integrator Framework," *Human Resource Management Review* 11 (2001): 135–158.

36. "Ethical Issues in the Management of Human Resources," *Human Resource Management Review* 11 (2001): 6. See also Joel Lefkowitz, "The Constancy of Ethics Amidst the Changing World of Work," *Human Resource Management Review* 16 (2006): 245–268.

37. William Byham, "Can You Interview for Integrity?" *Across the Board* 41, no. 2 (March/April 2004): 34–38. For a

description of how the United States Military Academy uses its student admission and socialization processes to promote character development, see Evan Offstein and Ronald Dufresne, "Building Strong Ethics and Promoting Positive Character Development: The Influence of HRM at the United States Military Academy at West Point," *Human Resource Management* 46, no. 1 (Spring 2007): 95–114.

38. Gary Weaver and Linda Trevino, "The Role of Human Resources in Ethics/Compliance Management: A Fairness Perspective," *Human Resource Management Review* 11 (2001): 123. See also Linda Andrews, "The Nexus of Ethics," *HR Magazine* (August 2005): 53–58.

39. Weaver and Trevino, op. cit.

40. Russell Cropanzano and Thomas Wright, "Procedural Justice and Organizational Staffing: A Tale of Two Paradigms," *Human Resource Management Review* 13, no. 1 (2003): 7–40.

41. "Ethical Issues in the Management of Human Resources," *Human Resource Management Review* 11 (2001): 6.

42. Gary Weaver and Linda Trevino, "The Role of Human Resources in Ethics/Compliance Management: A Fairness Perspective," *Human Resource Management Review* 11 (2001): 123.

43. Kathryn Tyler, "Do the Right Thing: Ethics Training Programs Help Employees Deal with Ethical Dilemmas," *HR Magazine* (February 2005): 99–102.

44. M. Ronald Buckley et al., "Ethical Issues in Human Resources Systems," *Human Resource Management Review* 11, nos. 1, 2 (2001): 11, 29. See also Ann Pomeroy, "The Ethics Squeeze," *HR Magazine* (March 2006): 48–55.

45. Tom Asacker, "Ethics in the Workplace," *Training and Development* (August 2004): 44.

46. M. Ronald Buckley et al., "Ethical Issues in Human Resources Systems," *Human Resource Management Review* 11, nos. 1, 2 (2001): 11, 29.

47. Gary Weaver and Linda Trevino, "The Role of Human Resources in Ethics/Compliance Management: A Fairness Perspective," *Human Resource Management Review* 11 (2001): 113–134.

48. Ibid., 125.

49. Robert Grossman, "Executive Discipline," *HR Magazine* 50, no. 8 (August 2005): 46–51. See also Jean Thilmany, "Supporting Ethical Employees," *HR Magazine* 52, no. 9 (September 2007): 105–106, 108, 110, 112.

50. M. Ronald Buckley et al., "Ethical Issues in Human Resources Systems," *Human Resource Management Review* 11, nos. 1, 2 (2001): 11, 29. See also Helge Hoel and David Beale, "Workplace Bullying, Psychological Perspectives and Industrial Relations: Towards a Contextualized and Interdisciplinary Approach," *British Journal of Industrial Relations* 44, no. 2 (June 2006): 239–262.

51. Wendy Boswell and Julie Olson-Buchanan, "Experiencing Mistreatment at Work: The Role of Grievance Filing, Nature of Mistreatment, and Employee Withdrawal," *Academy of Management Journal* 47, no. 1 (2004): 129–139. See also Helge Hoel and David Beale, "Workplace Bullying, Psychological Perspectives and Industrial Relations: Towards a Contextualized and Interdisciplinary Approach," *British Journal of Industrial Relations* 44, no. 2 (June 2006): 239–262; and Samuel Aryee et al., "Antecedents and Outcomes of Abusive Supervision: A Test of a Trickle-Down Model,"*Journal of Applied Psychology* (2007): 191–201.

52. W. Chan Kim and Rene Mauborgne, "Fair Process: Managing in the Knowledge Economy," *Harvard Business Review,* (July/August 1997): 65–75.

53. Op. cit., 114.

54. Lester Bittel, *What Every Supervisor Should Know* (New York: McGraw-Hill, 1974): 308; Paul Falcone, "Fundamentals of Progressive Discipline," *HR Magazine* (February 1997): 90–92; and Thomas Salvo, "Practical Tips for Successful Progressive Discipline," SHRM White Paper (July 2004), www.shrm.org/hrresources/ whitepapers _published/CMS_009030.asp, accessed January 5, 2008.

55. George Bohlander, "Why Arbitrators Overturn Managers in Employee Suspension and Discharge Cases," *Journal of Collective Negotiations* 23, no. 1 (1994): 76–77.

56. "Employers Turn to Corporate Ombuds to Defuse Internal Ticking Time Bombs," *BNA Bulletin to Management* (August 9, 2005): 249.

57. Dick Grote, "Discipline without Punishment," *Across the Board* 38, no. 5 (September 2001): 52–57.

58. Milton Zall, "Employee Privacy," *Journal of Property Management* 66, no. 3 (May 2001): 16.

59. Morris Attaway, "Privacy in the Workplace on the Web," *Internal Auditor* 58, no. 1 (February 2001): 30.

60. Declam Leonard and Angela France, "Workplace Monitoring: Balancing Business Interests with Employee Privacy Rights," *Society for Human Resource Management Legal Report* (May–June 2003): 3–6.

61. "After Employer Found Liable for Worker's Child Porn, Policies May Need to Be Revisited," *BNA Bulletin to Management* (March 21, 2006): 89.

62. Rita Zeidner, "Keeping E-Mail in Check," *HR Magazine* (June 2007): 70–74.

63. "Time Clocks Go High Touch, High Tech to Keep Workers From Gaming the System," *BNA Bulletin to Management* (March 25, 2004): 97.

64. Andrea Poe, "Make Foresight 20/20," *HR Magazine* (February 2000): 74–80.

65. Gundars Kaupin et al., "Recommended Employee Location Monitoring Policies," www.shrm.org, accessed January 2, 2007.

66. Eileen Zimmerman, "HR Must Know When Employee Surveillance Crosses the Line," *Workforce* (February 2002): 38–44. See also Rita Zeidner, "Keeping E-Mail in Check," *HR Magazine* (June 2007): 70–74.

67. "Workers Sharing Music, Movies at Work Violates Copyrights, Employer Finds," *BNA Bulletin to Management* (June 19, 2003): 193.

68. Cynthia Kemper, "Big Brother," *Communication World* 18, no. 1 (December 2000/January 2001): 8–12.

69. Bill Roberts, "Are You Ready for Biometrics?" *HR Magazine* (March 2003): 95–96.

70. Andrea Poe, "Make Foresight 20/20," *HR Magazine* (February 20, 2000): 74–80. See also Nancy Hatch Woodward, "Smoother Separations," *HR Magazine* (June 2007): 94–97.

71. Robert Lanza and Morton Warren, "United States: Employment at Will Prevails Despite Exceptions to the Rule," *Society for Human Resource Management Legal Report* (October–November 2005): 1–8.

72. Ibid.

73. Joseph Famularo, *Handbook of Modern Personnel Administration* (New York: McGraw Hill, 1982): 65.3–65.5. See also Carolyn Hirschman, "Off Duty, Out of Work," *HR Magazine,* www.shrm.org/hrmagazine/articles/0203/0203hirschman.asp, accessed January 10, 2008.

74. Kenneth Sovereign, *Personnel Law* (Upper Saddle River, NJ: Prentice Hall, 1999): 148.

75. Connie Wanderg et al., "Perceived Fairness of Layoffs Among Individuals Who Have Been Laid Off: A Longitudinal Study," *Personnel Psychology* 52 (1999): 59–84. See also Nancy Hatch Woodward, "Smoother Separations," *HR Magazine* (June 2007): 94–97.

76. Michael Orey, "Fear of Firing," *Business Week* (April 23, 2007): 52–54.

77. Paul Falcon, "Give Employees the (Gentle) Hook," *HR Magazine* (April 2001): 121–128.

78. Op. cit., 185.

79. "Fairness to Employees Can Stave Off Litigation," *BNA Bulletin to Management* (November 27, 1997): 377.

80. Edward Isler et al., "Personal Liability and Employee Discipline," *Society for Human Resource Management Legal Report* (September–October 2000): 1–4.

81. Based on James Coil III and Charles Rice, "Three Steps to Creating Effective Employee Releases," *Employment Relations Today* (Spring 1994): 91–94. See also Martha Frase-Blunt, "Making Exit Interviews Work," *HR Magazine* (August 2004): 9–11.

82. William J. Morin and Lyle York, *Outplacement Techniques* (New York: AMACOM, 1982): 101–131; F. Leigh Branham, "How to Evaluate Executive Outplacement Services," *Personnel Journal* 62 (April 1983): 323–326; Sylvia Milne, "The Termination Interview," *Canadian Manager* (Spring 1994): 15–16. There is debate regarding what is the "best day of the week" on which to terminate an employee. Some say Friday to give the employee a few days to "cool off"; others suggest midweek, in order to allow employees "who remain in the department or in the immediate work group some time to process the change and to talk with each other to sort it out." See Jeffrey Connor,

"Disarming Terminated Employees," *HR Magazine* (January 2000): 113–114.

83. Marlene Piturro, "Alternatives to Downsizing," *Management Review* (October 1999): 37–42; "How Safe Is Your Job?" *Money* (December 1, 2001): 130.

84. Joseph Zarandona and Michael Camuso, "A Study of Exit Interviews: Does the Last Word Count," *Personnel* 62, no. 3 (March 1981): 47–48. For another point of view, see "Firms Can Profit from Data Obtained from Exit Interviews," *Knight-Ridder/Tribune Business News* (February 13, 2001): Item 0104 4446.

85. "Workers Hit by Mass Layoffs Rose to 143,977 in February," *BNA Bulletin to Management* (April 3, 2007): 109.

86. Leon Grunberg, Sarah Moore, and Edward Greenberg, "Managers' Reactions to Implementing Layoffs: Relationship to Health Problems and Withdrawal Behaviors," *Human Resource Management* 45, no. 2 (Summer 2006): 159–178.

87. Ibid.

88. Ibid.

89. Joann Lublin, "Employers See Value in Helping Those Laid Off," *Wall Street Journal* (September 24, 2007): B3.

90. "Communication Can Reduce Problems, Litigation After Layoffs, Attorneys Say," *BNA Bulletin to Management* (April 14, 2003): 129.

91. John Krammeyer and Hui Liao, "Workforce Reduction and Jobseeker Attraction: Examining Jobseekers' Reactions to Firm Workforce-Reduction Strategies," *Human Resource Management,* 45, no. 4 (Winter 2006): 585–603.

92. David Gebler, "Is Your Culture a Risk Factor?" *Business and Society Review* 111, no. 3 (Fall 2006): 337–362.

93. John Cohan, "'I Didn't Know' and 'I Was Only Doing My Job': Has Corporate Governance Careened Out of Control? A Case Study of Enron's Information Myopia," *Journal of Business Ethics* 40, no. 3 (October 2002): 275–299.

94. David Gebler, "Is Your Culture a Risk Factor?" *Business and Society Review* 111, no. 3 (Fall 2006): 337–362.

95. Ibid.

Working with Unions and Resolving Disputes

10

When you finish studying this chapter, you should be able to:

1. *Briefly describe the history and structure of the U.S. union movement.*

2. *Discuss the nature of the major governmental labor relations laws.*

3. *Describe the process of a union drive and election.*

4. *Discuss the main steps in the collective bargaining process.*

5. *Explain why union membership dropped, and what the prospects are for the union movement.*

❶ Briefly describe the history and structure of the U.S. union movement.

Introduction

The U.S. Department of Labor's National Labor Relations Board (NLRB) recently accused Starbucks of breaking the law by trying to prevent workers in some of its New York coffee shops from unionizing. Among other things, the NLRB accused Starbucks managers there of retaliating against workers who wanted to unionize by firing two of them, threatening to terminate several others, and illegally interrogating employees about their union inclinations. A spokesperson for Starbucks said the company believes the allegations are baseless and that the firm would vigorously defend itself.[1] ■

THE LABOR MOVEMENT

Just over 15.7 million U.S. workers belong to unions—around 12.1% of all the men and women working in this country.[2] Many are still traditional blue-collar workers. But more and more white-collar workers, including doctors, psychologists, graduate teaching assistants, government office workers, and even fashion models, are forming or joining unions.[3] And about 40% of America's 20 million federal, state, and municipal public employees belong to unions.[4] In the United Kingdom, roughly 30% of employees belong to unions.

DECADES OF DECLINE However, such upbeat figures mask dramatic declines. U.S. union membership peaked at about 34% in 1955. It has consistently fallen since then due to factors such as the shift from manufacturing to service jobs, and new legislation (such as occupational safety laws). These laws provide the sorts of protections that workers could once only obtain from their unions. Indeed, hundreds of local, state, and federal laws and regulations now address the types of concerns that helped drive the early union movement.[5]

Unions Today

However, do not write off unions. In the United States, a growing number of government and white-collar employees are joining unions. In some industries (such as transportation and public utilities), it's still tough to get a job without joining a union. Union membership also ranges widely, from over 20% in Michigan and New York, down to just over 4% in North Carolina. Seven big unions recently formed their own federation, with the aim of aggressively organizing workers (more on this below). And, while union membership around the world is also declining (for example, only about 20% of workers in Germany are union members today, down dramatically from a few years ago),[6] union membership is still high in most countries—over 35% of employed workers in Canada, Mexico, Brazil, and Italy, for instance.

Furthermore, don't assume that unions are bad for employers. For example, perhaps by professionalizing the staff and/or systematizing company practices, unionization may actually improve performance. In one study, researchers found that heart attack mortality among patients in hospitals with unionized registered nurses were 5%–9% lower than in nonunion hospitals.[7] Another study found a negative relationship between union membership and employees' intent to quit.[8]

Why Do Workers Organize?

People have spent much time analyzing why workers unionize, and they've proposed many theories. Yet there is no simple answer.

It's clear that workers don't unionize just to get more pay, although the pay issue is important. In fact, union members' weekly earnings are higher than nonunion workers'. For example, recent median weekly wages for union workers in the U.S. was $781, while that for nonunion workers was $612.[9]

But pay isn't always the issue. Often, the urge to unionize seems to boil down to the workers' belief that it is only through unity that they can protect themselves from arbitrary managerial whims. For example, a butcher hired by Wal-Mart said his new supervisor told him he'd be able to start management training and possibly move up to supervisor. The butcher started work, and bought a new car for the commute. However, after the butcher hurt his back at work his supervisor never mentioned the promotion again. Faced with high car payments and feeling cheated, the butcher went to the Grocery Workers Union. It sent an organizer to speak with the employee. The store's meat cutters eventually voted to unionize. A week later Wal-Mart announced it would switch to completely prepackaged meat, and that its store no longer required butchers.[10]

RESEARCH FINDINGS A study of an Australian banking firm found that employer unfairness does play a big role: "Individuals who believe that the company rules or policies were administered unfairly or to their detriment were more likely to turn to unions as a source of assistance."[11]

In this case, unfairness alone was not enough to prompt a pro-union vote in this bank—the employees also wanted a union with clout. Employees were more likely to join where they "perceived that the union was effective in the area of wages and benefits and protection against unfair dismissals."[12]

In sum, employees turn to unions at least partly because they seek protection against the employer's whims. One labor relations lawyer put it this way, "The one major thing unions offer is making you a 'for cause' instead of an 'at will' employee, which guarantees a hearing and arbitration if you're fired."[13] Several years ago, Kaiser Permanente's San Francisco Medical Center cut back on vacation and sick leave. The pharmacists' union won back the lost vacation days. As one staff pharmacist said, "Kaiser is a pretty benevolent employer, but there's always the pressure to squeeze a little."[14]

What Do Unions Want? What Are Their Aims?

We can generalize by saying that unions have two sets of aims, one for union security and one for improved wages, hours, working conditions, and benefits for their members.

UNION SECURITY First and probably foremost, unions seek to establish security for themselves. They fight hard for the right to represent a firm's workers and to be the *exclusive* bargaining agent for all employees in the unit. (As such, they negotiate contracts for all employees, including those who are not members of the union.) Five types of union security are possible in this U.S. example:

1. *Closed shop.*[15] The company can hire only current union members. The U.S. Congress outlawed closed shops in interstate commerce in 1947, but they still exist in some states for particular industries (such as printing). They account for less than 5% of union contracts. In the United Kingdom, a closed shop employs nonunion workers, but sets a time limit within which new employees must join a union.
2. *Union shop.* The company can hire nonunion people, but they must join the union after a prescribed period of time and pay dues. (If not, they can be fired.) This category accounts for about 73% of union contracts. Unions and employers also tend to negotiate versions of the union shop, for instance, letting older workers quit the union when the contract ends.
3. *Agency shop.* Employees who do not belong to the union still must pay the union an amount equal to union dues (on the assumption that the union's efforts benefit *all* the workers).
4. *Preferential shop.* Union members get preference in hiring, but the employer can still hire nonunion members.
5. *Maintenance of membership arrangement.* Employees do not have to belong to the union. However, union members employed by the firm must maintain membership in the union for the contract period. These account for about 4% of union agreements.

Not all states give unions the right to require union membership as a condition of employment. **Right to work** "is a term used to describe state statutory or constitutional provisions banning the requirement of union membership as a condition of employment."[16] Section 14(b) of the U.S. Taft-Hartley Act (an early labor relations act that we'll discuss later in more detail) permits states to forbid the negotiation of compulsory union membership provisions, not just

closed shop
A form of union security in which the company can hire only union members. This was outlawed in 1947 for interstate commerce, but still exists in some industries (such as printing).

union shop
A form of union security in which the company can hire nonunion people but they must join the union after a prescribed period of time and pay dues. (If they do not, they can be fired.)

agency shop
A form of union security in which employees who do not belong to the union must still pay union dues on the assumption that union efforts benefit all workers.

preferential shop
Union members get preference in hiring, but the employer can still hire nonunion members.

right to work
The public policy in a number of states that prohibits union security of any kind.

for firms engaged in interstate commerce but also for those in intrastate commerce. Right-to-work laws don't outlaw unions. They do outlaw (within those states) any form of union security. This understandably inhibits union formation in those states. As of 2008, there were 23 right-to-work states.[17] In 2001, Oklahoma became the 22nd state to pass right-to-work legislation. Some believe that this—combined with a loss of manufacturing jobs—explains why Oklahoma's union membership dropped dramatically in the next 3 years.[18]

IMPROVED WAGES, HOURS, WORKING CONDITIONS, AND BENEFITS FOR MEMBERS
Once their security is assured, unions fight to better the lot of their members—to improve their wages, hours, and working conditions, for example. The typical labor agreement also gives the union a role in other HR activities, including recruiting, selecting, compensating, promoting, training, and discharging employees.

The AFL-CIO

The American Federation of Labor and Congress of Industrial Organizations (**AFL-CIO**) is a voluntary federation of about 100 national and international labor unions in the United States. It resulted from the merger of the AFL and CIO in 1955. For many people, it is synonymous with the word *union* in the United States.

However, over 7 million workers belong to unions not affiliated with the AFL-CIO. Four big unions—the Service Employees International Union (SEIU), the International Brotherhood of Teamsters, the United Food and Commercial Workers, and UNITE (formerly clothing trades workers)—left the AFL-CIO a few years ago, establishing their own Federation, the Change to Win Coalition. By 2008, Change to Win had grown to seven affiliated unions. These are: International Brotherhood of Teamsters (IBT), Laborers' International Union of North America (LIUNA), Service Employees International Union (SEIU), United Brotherhood of Carpenters and Joiners of America (UBC), United Farm Workers of America (UFW), United Food and Commercial Workers International Union (UFCW), and UNITE HERE.[19] Change to Win plans to be much more aggressive about organizing workers than they say the AFL-CIO was.[20]

UNIONS AND THE LAW

➋ Discuss the nature of the major federal labor relations laws.

Until about 1930, there were no special labor laws. Employers didn't have to engage in collective bargaining with employees and were virtually unrestrained in their behavior toward unions. The use of spies, blacklists, and the firing of agitators was widespread. "Yellow dog" contracts, whereby management could require nonunion membership as a condition for employment, were widely enforced. Most union weapons—even strikes—were illegal.

This one-sided situation lasted in the United States from the Revolution to the Great Depression (around 1930). Since then, in response to changing public attitudes, values, and economic conditions, labor law has gone through three clear changes: from "strong encouragement" of unions, to "modified encouragement coupled with regulation," to "detailed regulation of internal union affairs."[21]

Period of Strong Encouragement: The Norris-LaGuardia Act (1932) and the National Labor Relations Act (1935)

The **Norris-LaGuardia Act** set the stage for an era in which government encouraged union activity. The act guaranteed to each employee the right to bargain collectively "free from interference, restraint, or coercion." It declared yellow dog contracts unenforceable. It limited the courts' abilities to issue injunctions for activities such as peaceful picketing and payment of strike benefits.[22]

Yet this act did little to restrain employers from fighting labor organizations by whatever means they could muster. Therefore, the National Labor Relations Act (or **Wagner Act**) was passed in 1935 to add teeth to the Norris-LaGuardia Act. It did this by banning certain unfair labor practices, providing for secret-ballot elections and majority rule for determining whether a firm's employees were to unionize, and creating the **National Labor Relations Board (NLRB)** for enforcing these two provisions.

In addition to activities like overseeing union elections, the NLRB periodically issues interpretive rulings. For example, about 6 million employees fall under the "contingent" or "alternative" employee umbrella today. The NLRB therefore ruled that temporary employees could join the unions of permanent employees in the companies where their employment agencies assign them to work.[23]

UNFAIR EMPLOYER LABOR PRACTICES The Wagner Act deemed as "statutory wrongs" (but not crimes) five unfair labor practices used by employers:

1. It is unfair for employers to "interfere with, restrain, or coerce employees" in exercising their legally sanctioned right of self-organization.
2. It is an unfair practice for company representatives to dominate or interfere with either the formation or the administration of labor unions. Among other management actions found to be unfair under practices 1 and 2 are bribing employees, using company spy systems, moving a business to avoid unionization, and blacklisting union sympathizers.
3. Employers are prohibited from discriminating in any way against employees for their legal union activities.
4. Employers are forbidden to discharge or discriminate against employees simply because the latter file unfair practice charges against the company.
5. Finally, it is an unfair labor practice for employers to refuse to bargain collectively with their employees' duly chosen representatives.[24]

An unfair labor practice charge may be filed (see Figure 10.1) with the NLRB. The board then investigates the charge. Possible actions include dismissal of the complaint, request for an injunction against the employer, and an order that the employer cease and desist.

FROM 1935 TO 1947 Union membership increased quickly after passage of the Wagner Act in 1935. Other factors such as an improving economy and aggressive union leadership contributed to this as well. But by the mid-1940s, the tide had begun to turn. Largely because of a series of massive postwar strikes, public policy began to shift against what many viewed as the union excesses of the times.

Period of Modified Encouragement Coupled with Regulation: The Taft-Hartley Act (1947)

Taft-Hartley Act (Labor Management Relations Act)
A law prohibiting union unfair labor practices and enumerating the rights of employees as union members. It also enumerates the rights of employers.

The **Taft-Hartley** (or **Labor Management Relations**) **Act** reflected the public's less enthusiastic attitudes toward unions. It amended the Wagner Act with provisions aimed at limiting unions in four ways: by prohibiting unfair union labor practices, by enumerating the rights of employees as union members, by enumerating the rights of employers, and by allowing the president of the United States to temporarily bar national emergency strikes.

UNFAIR UNION LABOR PRACTICES The Taft-Hartley Act enumerated several labor practices that unions were prohibited from engaging in:

1. Unions were banned from restraining or coercing employees from exercising their guaranteed bargaining rights.
2. It is an unfair labor practice for a union to cause an employer to discriminate in any way against an employee in order to encourage or discourage his or her membership in a union.
3. It is an unfair labor practice for a union to refuse to bargain in good faith with the employer about wages, hours, and other employment conditions.

RIGHTS OF EMPLOYEES The Taft-Hartley Act also protected the rights of employees against their unions. For example, many people felt that compulsory unionism violated the basic U.S. right of freedom of association. The new *right-to-work laws* sprang up in

FIGURE 10.1

NLRB Form 501: Filing an Unfair Labor Practice

FORM NLRB 501
(2 81)

FORM EXEMPT UNDER
44 U.S.C. 3512

UNITED STATES OF AMERICA
NATIONAL LABOR RELATIONS BOARD
CHARGE AGAINST EMPLOYER

INSTRUCTIONS: File an original and 4 copies of this charge with NLRB Regional Director for the region in which the alleged unfair labor practice occurred or is occurring.

DO NOT WRITE IN THIS SPACE

CASE NO.   DATE FILE

1. EMPLOYER AGAINST WHOM CHARGE IS BROUGHT

a. NAME OF EMPLOYER   b. NUMBER OF WORKERS EMPLOYED

c. ADDRESS OF ESTABLISHMENT (street and number, city, State, and ZIP code)   d. EMPLOYER REPRESENTATIVE TO CONTACT   e. PHONE NO.

f. TYPE OF ESTABLISHMENT (factory, mine, wholesaler, etc.)   g. IDENTIFY PRINCIPAL PRODUCT OR SERVICE

h. THE ABOVE-NAMED EMPLOYER HAS ENGAGED IN AND IS ENGAGING IN UNFAIR LABOR PRACTICES WITHIN THE MEANING OF SECTION 8(a), SUBSECTIONS (1) AND _____ OF THE NATIONAL
(list subsections)
LABOR RELATIONS ACT, AND THESE UNFAIR LABOR PRACTICES ARE UNFAIR LABOR PRACTICES AFFECTING COMMERCE WITHIN THE MEANING OF THE ACT.

2. BASIS OF THE CHARGE (be specific as to facts, names, addresses, plants involved, dates, places, etc.)

BY THE ABOVE AND OTHER ACTS, THE ABOVE-NAMED EMPLOYER HAS INTERFERED WITH, RESTRAINED, AND COERCED EMPLOYEES IN THE EXERCISE OF THE RIGHTS GUARANTEED IN SECTION 7 OF THE ACT.

3. FULL NAME OF PARTY FILING CHARGE (if labor organization, give full name, including local name and number)

4a. ADDRESS (street and number, city, State, and ZIP code)   4b. TELEPHONE NO.

5. FULL NAME OF NATIONAL OR INTERNATIONAL LABOR ORGANIZATION OF WHICH IT IS AN AFFILIATE OR CONSTITUENT UNIT (to be filled in when charge is filed by a labor organization)

6. DECLARATION

I declare that I have read the above charge and that the statements therein are true to the best of my knowledge and belief.

By _____ (signature of representative or person filing charge)   (title, if any)

Address _____   (telephone number)   (date)

WILLFULLY FALSE STATEMENTS ON THIS CHARGE CAN BE PUNISHED BY FINE AND IMPRISONMENT
(U.S. CODE, TITLE 18, SECTION 1001)

19 states (mainly in the South and Southwest); as noted, these outlawed labor contracts that made union membership a condition for keeping one's job.

In general, the National Labor Relations Act does not restrain unions from unfair labor practices to the extent that it does employers. Unions may not restrain or coerce employees. However, "violent or otherwise threatening behavior or clearly coercive or intimidating union activities are necessary before the NLRB will find an unfair labor practice."[25] Examples here would include physical assaults or threats of violence, economic reprisals, and mass picketing that restrains the lawful entry or leaving of a work site. In one typical case, *Pattern Makers* v. *National Labor Relations Board,* the U.S. Supreme Court found the union guilty of an unfair labor practice when it tried to fine some members for resigning from the union and returning to work during a strike.[26]

RIGHTS OF EMPLOYERS The Taft-Hartley Act also explicitly gave employers certain rights. For example, it gave them full freedom to express their views concerning union organization. Thus, a manager can tell his or her employees that in his or her opinion unions are worthless, dangerous to the economy, and immoral. A manager can even, generally speaking, hint that unionization and subsequent high-wage demands *might* result in the permanent closing of the plant (but not in its relocation). Employers can set forth the union's record in regard to violence and corruption, if appropriate, and can play on the racial prejudices of workers by describing the union's philosophy toward integration. The only major restraint is that there can be no threat of reprisal or force or promise of benefit.[27]

The employer also cannot meet with employees on company time within 24 hours of an election or suggest to employees that they vote against the union while they are at home or in the employer's office, although he or she can do so while in their work area or where they normally gather.

national emergency strikes
Strikes that might "imperil the national health and safety."

NATIONAL EMERGENCY STRIKES The Taft-Hartley Act also allows the U.S. president to intervene in **national emergency strikes,** which are strikes (for example, on the part of steel firm employees) that might imperil national health and safety. The president may appoint a board of inquiry and, based on its report, apply for an injunction restraining the strike for 60 days. If no settlement is reached during that time, the injunction can be extended for another 20 days. During this period, employees are polled in a secret ballot to ascertain their willingness to accept the employer's last offer.

Period of Detailed Regulation of Internal Union Affairs: The Landrum-Griffin Act (1959)

Landrum-Griffin Act
A law aimed at protecting union members from possible wrongdoing on the part of their unions.

In the 1950s, senate investigations revealed unsavory practices on the part of some unions, and the result was the **Landrum-Griffin Act** (officially, the Labor Management Reporting and Disclosure Act). An overriding aim of this act was to protect union members from possible wrongdoing on the part of their unions. It was also an amendment to the Wagner Act.

The Landrum-Griffin Act contains a bill of rights for union members. Among other things, this provides for certain rights in the nomination of candidates for union office. It also affirms a member's right to sue his or her union and ensures that no member can be fined or suspended without due process (including a list of charges, and a fair hearing).

The act also laid out rules regarding union elections. For example, national and international unions must elect officers at least once every 5 years, using some type of secret-ballot mechanism.

corporate social responsibility
Refers to the extent to which companies should and do take steps to improve members of society other than the firm's owners.

The senate investigators also discovered flagrant examples of employer wrongdoing. The Landrum-Griffin Act therefore also greatly expanded the list of unlawful employer actions. For example, companies can no longer pay their own employees to entice them not to join the union. The pendulum therefore again shifted a bit back towards strengthening unions. The accompanying *Business in Action* feature helps put these shifts in perspective.

Business in Action Building Your *Social Responsibility* Knowledge

To some degree, the issue of how influential unions should be boils down to what you believe about *corporate social responsibility*. **Corporate social responsibility** refers to the extent to which companies should and do take steps to improve members of society other than the firm's owners.

Corporate social responsibility advocates say there must be a balance between what a business takes from society and what it gives back. Socially responsible behavior might include creating jobs for minorities, paying a "fair day's wage," controlling pollution, or taking employees' needs into account when contemplating closing a plant. In deciding whether to close the plant, for instance, do you just do what's best for the owners (cut costs)? Or do you try to help your employees keep their jobs? Unions, as

(continued)

we've seen, emerged at least in part to provide a way to ensure that managers didn't just consider the owners' needs.

The topic of social responsibility provokes lively debate. Many perfectly ethical people believe that a company's only social responsibility is to its stockholders. Others disagree.

MANAGERIAL CAPITALISM   The classical view is that a corporation's main purpose is to maximize profits for stockholders. This view is most notably associated with U.S. economist Milton Friedman. Basically, he said that the only social responsibility of a business is to increase its profits, so long as it stays within the rules of the game (in terms of complying with the law, for instance). He argued that all society would gain if business people made their companies as competitive as possible. (For example, how long could employees expect to keep their jobs if a company was less competitive than the one down the road?)

STAKEHOLDER THEORY   An opposing view is that business has a social responsibility to serve all the corporate stakeholders affected by its business decisions. A corporate stakeholder is anyone who is vital to a business' success. Experts in this area traditionally identify six stakeholder groups: stockholders (owners), employees, customers, suppliers, managers, and the local community. Stakeholder advocates would say top managers can't just close a plant because it's good for the owners; they must take the employees' (and community's) welfare into account (even if it means higher production costs).

So, to some extent, the whole history of labor legislation in the United States reflects (to over-simplify things) pressures from managerial capitalism advocates versus stakeholder advocates. Undoubtedly, even many managerial capitalists looked at the maltreatment some employees were suffering and willingly backed pro-union legislation. But, as we said, unions (and pro-labor laws) emerged at least in part to provide a way to ensure that managers didn't just consider the owners' needs.

THE UNION DRIVE AND ELECTION

It is through the union drive and election that a union tries to be recognized to represent employees. This process has five basic steps: initial contact, authorization cards, hearing, campaign, and election.

❸ Describe the process of a union drive and election.

Step 1: Initial Contact

During the initial contact stage, the union determines the employees' interest in organizing, and establishes an organizing committee.

The initiative for the first contact between the employees and the union may come from the employees, from a union already representing other employees of the firm, or from a union representing workers elsewhere. Sometimes, a union effort starts with a disgruntled employee contacting the local union to learn how to organize his or her place of

The Teamsters Union—already firmly in place at UPS—began an intensive organizing campaign at FedEx.

work (as at Wal-Mart). Sometimes, though, the campaign starts when a union decides it wants to expand to representing other employees in the firm or industry, or when the company looks like an easy one to organize. In any case, there is an initial contact between a union representative and a few employees.

THE UNION REP When an employer becomes a target, a union official usually assigns a representative to assess employee interest. The representative visits the firm to determine whether enough employees are interested to make a union campaign worthwhile. He or she also identifies employees who would make good leaders in the organizing campaign and calls them together to create an organizing committee. The objective is to "educate the committee about the benefits of forming a union, the law and procedures involved in forming a local union, and the issues management is likely to raise during a campaign."[28]

CONTACT PROCEDURES The union must follow certain procedures when it starts contacting employees. The law allows union organizers to solicit employees for membership as long as it doesn't endanger the performance or safety of the employees. Therefore, much of the contact takes place off the job. Organizers can also safely contact employees on company grounds during off hours (such as lunch or break time). Under some conditions, union representatives may solicit employees at their workstations, but this is rare. In practice, there will be much informal organizing at the workplace as employees debate organizing. In any case, this initial contact stage may be deceptively quiet. In some instances the first inkling management has of a union campaign is the distribution or posting of a handbill soliciting union membership.[29]

LABOR RELATIONS CONSULTANTS Labor relations consultants influence the unionization process, with both management and unions using outside advisors. The use by management of consultants (who unions often disparagingly refer to as *union busters*) has grown considerably. This so-called "union avoidance industry" includes the consultants, law firms, industry psychologists, and strike management firms that employers often turn to when the union comes to call.[30] One study found management consultants involved in 75% of the elections they surveyed.[31]

One expert says an employer's main goal shouldn't be to win representation elections, but to avoid them altogether. He says doing so means taking fast action when the first signs of union activity appear. His advice in a nutshell: Don't just ignore the union's efforts while it spreads pro-union rumors, such as "If we had a union, we wouldn't have to work so much overtime." Retain an attorney and react at once.[32]

UNION SALTING Unions are also not without creative ways to win elections, one of which is called union salting. The U.S. National Labor Relations Board defines **union salting** as "placing of union members on nonunion job sites for the purpose of organizing." Critics claim that "salts" also often interfere with business operations and harass employees.[33] A U.S. Supreme Court decision, *NLRB* v. *Town and Country Electric,* held the tactic to be legal.

union salting
A union organizing tactic by which workers who are employed by a union as undercover union organizers are hired by unwitting employers.

Improving Productivity Through HRIS: Unions Go Online

As one expert asked, "If faster and more powerful ways of communicating enable companies to compete in a quickly changing and challenging environment, shouldn't they also make unions stronger and more efficient as organizations and workplace representatives?"[34]

In fact, e-mail and the Internet have supercharged many union campaigns. Unions now can publicize their efforts online, digitally gather donations, and put membership and union authorization forms online. Of course they also mass e-mail announcements to collective bargaining unit members, and use mass e-mail to reach supporters and government officials for their corporate campaigns.

For example, the group trying to organize Starbucks workers (the Starbucks' Workers' Union) set up their own Web site (www.starbucksunion.org/). It includes notes like,

"Starbucks managers monitored internet chatrooms and eavesdropped on party conversations in a covert campaign to identify employees agitating for union representation at the coffee chain, internal emails reveal."[35]

Step 2: Authorization Cards

authorization cards
In order to petition for a union election, the union must show that at least 30% of employees may be interested in being unionized. Employees indicate this interest by signing authorization cards.

For the union to petition the NLRB for the right to hold an election, it must show that a sizable number of employees may be interested in being organized. The next step is thus for union organizers to try to get the employees to sign **authorization cards.** Among other things, these usually authorize the union to seek a representation election and state that the employee has applied to join the union. Before an election can be petitioned, 30% of the eligible employees in an appropriate bargaining unit must sign.

During this stage, both union and management typically use various forms of propaganda. The union claims it can improve working conditions, raise wages, increase benefits, and generally get the workers better deals. Management need not be silent; it can attack the union on ethical and moral grounds and cite the cost of union membership, for example. Management can also explain its record, express facts and opinions, and explain to its employees the law applicable to organizing campaigns and the meaning of the duty to bargain in good faith (if the union should win the election). However, neither side can threaten, bribe, or coerce employees. Further, an employer may not make promises of benefits to employees or make unilateral changes in terms and conditions of employment that were not planned to be implemented prior to the onset of union organizing activity. Managers also should not look through signed authorization cards if confronted with them by union representatives. Doing so could be construed as spying on those who signed, which is an unfair labor practice.

During this stage, unions can picket the company, subject to three constraints: The union must file a petition for an election within 30 days after the start of picketing, the firm cannot already be lawfully recognizing another union, and there cannot have been a valid NLRB election during the past 12 months. The union would file a petition using NLRB Form 502 (see Figure 10.2).

Step 3: The Hearing

After the authorization cards have been collected, one of three things can occur. The employer may choose not to contest union recognition, in which case no hearing is needed and a *consent election* is held immediately. The employer may choose not to contest the union's *right to an election* (and/or the scope of the bargaining unit, or which employees are eligible to vote in the election), in which case no hearing is needed and the parties can stipulate an election. Or, the employer may contest the union's right, in which case it can insist on a *hearing* to determine those issues. An employer's decision about whether to insist on a hearing is a strategic one based on the facts of each case and whether it feels it needs additional time to develop a campaign to try to persuade a majority of its employees not to elect a union to represent them.

Most companies contest the union's right to represent their employees, and thus decline to voluntarily recognize the union: They claim that a significant number of their employees do not really want the union. It is at this point that the U.S. Labor Department's NLRB gets involved. The NLRB is usually contacted by the union, which requests a hearing. Based on this, the regional director of the NLRB sends a hearing officer to investigate. (For example, did 30% or more of the employees in an appropriate bargaining unit sign the authorization cards?) The examiner sends both management and the union a notice of representation hearing that states the time and place of the hearing.

bargaining unit
The group of employees the union will be authorized to represent.

The **bargaining unit** is one decision to come out of the hearing; it is the group of employees that the union will be authorized to represent and bargain for collectively.

Finally, if the results of the hearing are favorable for the union, the NLRB directs that an election be held. It issues a Decision and Direction of Election notice to that effect and sends NLRB Form 666 ("Notice to Employees") to the employer to post, notifying employees of their rights under federal labor relations law.

FIGURE 10.2 NLRB Form 502

FORM NLRB-502
(9-07)

UNITED STATES GOVERNMENT
NATIONAL LABOR RELATIONS BOARD
PETITION

FORM EXEMPT UNDER 44 U.S.C.

DO NOT WRITE IN THIS SPACE	
Case No.	Date Filed / /

INSTRUCTIONS: Submit an original and 4 copies of this Petition to the NLRB Regional Office in the Region in which the employer concerned is located. If more space is required for any one item, attach additional sheets, numbering item accordingly.

The Petitioner alleges that the following circumstances exist and requests that the National Labor Relations Board proceed under its proper authority pursuant to Section 9 of the National Labor Relations Act.

1. PURPOSE OF THIS PETITION (if box RC, RM, or RD is checked and a charge under Section 8(b)(7) of the Act has been filed involving the Employer named herein, the statement following the description of the type of petition shall not be deemed made.) (Check One)

☐ **RC-CERTIFICATION OF REPRESENTATIVE** - A substantial number of employees wish to be represented for purposes of collective bargaining by Petitioner and Petitioner desires to be certified as representative of the employees.

☐ **RM-REPRESENTATION (EMPLOYER PETITION)** - One or more individuals or labor organizations have presented a claim to Petitioner to be recognized as the representative of employees of Petitioner.

☐ **RD-DECERTIFICATION (REMOVAL OF REPRESENTATIVE)** - A substantial number of employees assert that the certified or currently recognized bargaining representative is no longer their representative.

☐ **UD-WITHDRAWAL OF UNION SHOP AUTHORITY (REMOVAL OF OBLIGATION TO PAY DUES)** - Thirty percent (30%) or more of employees in a bargaining unit covered by an agreement between their employer and ☐a labor organization desire that such authority be rescinded.

☐ **UC-UNIT CLARIFICATION** - A labor organization is currently recognized by Employer, but Petitioner seeks clarification of placement of certain employees: (Check one) ☐ In unit not previously certified. ☐In unit previously certified in Case No. _____

☐ **AC-AMENDMENT OF CERTIFICATION** - Petitioner seeks amendment of certification issued in Case No. _____ Attach statement describing the specific amendment sought.

2. Name of Employer	Employer Representative to contact	Telephone number ( ) -
3. Address(es) of Establishment(s) involved (Street and number, city, State, ZIP code)		Telecopier Number (Fax) ( ) -

4a. Type of Establishment (factory, mine, wholesaler, etc.)	4b. Identify principal product or service

5. Unit Involved (In UC petition, describe **present** bargaining unit and attach description of proposed clarification.)	6a. Number of Employees in Unit:
Included	Present
	Proposed (by UC/AC)
Excluded	6b. Is this petition supported by 30% or more of the employees in the unit? ☐Yes ☐No *Not applicable in RM, UC, and AC

(If you have checked box RC in 1 above, check and complete EITHER item 7a or 7b, whichever is applicable)

7a. ☐ Request for recognition as bargaining representative was made on (Date) _____ and Employer declined recognition on or about (Date) _____ (If no reply received, so state).
7b. ☐ Petitioner is currently recognized as Bargaining representative and desires certification under the Act.

8. Name of Recognized or Certified Bargaining Agent (If none, so state.)	Affiliation
Address, Telephone No. and Telecopier No. (Fax) ( ) - ( ) -	Date of Recognition or Certifications / /

9. Expiration Date of Current Contract. If any (Month, Day, Year)	10. If you have checked box UD in 1 above, show here the date of execution of agreement granting union shop (Month, Day and Year) / /
11a. Is there now a strike or picketing at the Employer's establishment(s) Involved? ☐Yes ☐No	11b. If so, approximately how many employees are participating?

11c. The Employer has been picketed by or on behalf of (Insert Name) _____ , a labor organization, of (Insert Address) _____ Since (Month, Day Year) _____ / /

12. Organizations or individuals other than Petitioner (and other than those named in items 8 and 11c), which have claimed recognition as representatives ad other organizations and individuals know to have a representative interest in any employees in unit described in item 5 above. (If none, so state)

Name	Affiliation	Address	Date of Claim / /
			Telecopier No. (Fax) ( ) -

13. Full name of party filing petition (If labor organization, give full name, including local name and number)

14a. Address (street and number, city, state, and ZIP code)	14b. Telephone No. EXT ( ) -	14c. Telecopier No. (Fax) ( ) -

15. Full name of national or international labor organization of which it is an affiliate or constituent unit (to be filled in when charge is filed by a labor organization)

I declare that I have read the above petition and that the statements are true to the best of my knowledge and belief.

Name (Print)	Signature	Title (if any)
Address (street and number, city, state, and ZIP code)	Telephone No. ( ) -	Telecopier No. (Fax) ( ) -

WILLFUL FALSE STATEMENTS ON THIS PETITION CAN BE PUNISHED BY FINE AND IMPRISONMENT (U.S. CODE, TITLE 18, SECTION 1001)
PRIVACY ACT STATEMENT
Solicitation of the information on this form is authorized by the National Labor Relations Act (NLRA), 29 U.S.C. § 151 et seq. The principal use of the information is to assist the National Labor Relations Board (NLRB) in processing unfair labor practice and related proceedings or litigation. The routine uses for the information are fully set forth in the Federal Register, 71 Fed. Reg. 74942-43 (Dec. 13, 2006). The NLRB will further explain these uses upon request. Disclosure of this information to the NLRB is voluntary; however, failure to supply the information will cause the NLRB to decline to invoke its processes.

Source: http://www.nlrb.gov/nlrb/shared_files/forms/nlrbform502.pdf, accessed April 26, 2008.

Step 4: The Campaign

During the campaign that precedes the election, the union and employer appeal to employees for their votes. The union emphasizes that it will prevent unfairness, set up a grievance/seniority system, and improve unsatisfactory wages. Union strength, they'll say, will give employees a voice in determining wages and working conditions. Management emphasizes that improvements such as those the union promises don't require unionization, and that wages are equal to or better than they would be with a union contract. Management also emphasizes the financial cost of union dues; the fact that the union is an "outsider"; and that if the union wins, a strike may follow.[36] It can even attack the union on ethical and moral grounds, while insisting that employees will not be as well off and may lose freedom. But neither side can threaten, bribe, or coerce employees.

THE SUPERVISOR'S ROLE   Supervisors must know (see *HR in Practice*) what they can and can't do to legally hamper organizing activities, lest they commit unfair labor practices. Such practices could cause a new election to be held after the company won a previous election. In one case, a plant superintendent prohibited distribution of union literature in the lunchroom. Because solicitation of off-duty workers in nonwork areas is generally legal, the company subsequently allowed the union to post and to distribute union literature in nonworking areas in the plant. However, the NLRB still ruled that the initial act of prohibiting distribution of the literature was an unfair labor practice. The NLRB used the superintendent's action as one reason to invalidate an election that the company won.[37]

HR in Practice

The Supervisor's Role in the Unionizing Effort

One company helps its supervisors remember what they may and may not do with respect to unionization with the acronyms TIPS and FORE.[38]

Use TIPS to remember what *not* to do:

T—Threaten. Do not threaten or imply the company will take adverse action of any kind for supporting the union.[39] Do not threaten to terminate employees because of their union activities, and don't threaten to close the facility if the union wins the election.

I—Interrogate. Don't interrogate or ask employees their position concerning unions, or how they are going to vote in an election.

P—Promise. Don't promise employees a pay increase, special favors, better benefits, or promotions.

S—Spy. Don't spy at any union activities or attend a union meeting, even if invited.

Use FORE to remember what the supervisor *may do* to discourage unionization.

F—Facts. Do tell employees that by signing the authorization card the union may become their legal representative in matters regarding wages and hours, and do tell them that by signing a union authorization card it does not mean they must vote for the union.

O—Opinion. You may tell employees that management doesn't believe in third-party representation, and that management believes in having an open-door policy to air grievances.

R—Rules. Provide factually correct advice such as telling employees that the law permits the company to permanently replace them if there's a strike, and that the union can't make the company agree to anything it does not want to during negotiations.

E—Experience. The supervisor may share personal experiences he or she may have had with a union.[40]

RULES REGARDING LITERATURE AND SOLICITATION   To avoid problems, employers should have rules governing distribution of literature and solicitation of workers and train supervisors in how to apply them.[41] For example:

- Nonemployees can always be barred from soliciting employees during their work time—that is, when the employee is on duty and not on a break.
- Employers can usually stop employees from soliciting other employees for any purpose if one or both employees are on paid-duty time and not on a break.

■ Most employers (not including retail stores, shopping centers, and certain other employers) can bar nonemployees from the building's interiors and work areas as a right of private property owners. In certain cases, nonemployees can also be barred from exterior private property such as parking lots—if there is a business reason (such as safety) and the reason is not just to interfere with union organizers.

Such restrictions are valid only if the employer does not impose them in a discriminatory manner. For example, if company policy permits employees to collect money for a wedding shower and baby gifts or to engage in other solicitation during their working time, the employer will not be able to lawfully prohibit them from union soliciting during work time.

Finally, remember that there are many more ways to commit unfair labor practices than just keeping union organizers off your private property. For example, one employer decided to have a cookout and paid day off 2 days before a union representation election. The NLRB held that this was too much of a coincidence and represented coercive conduct; it called a second election. The union had lost the first vote but won the second.[42]

Figure 10.3 summarizes what the employer and union generally cannot do during campaigns.

STARBUCKS' EXAMPLE It's not easy for Starbucks managers at Seattle headquarters to monitor what employees are doing in its far-flung stores. The company therefore works hard to encourage employees to control themselves—by making them "partners" and by providing excellent benefits and stock option plans. As a company that provides excellent benefits

FIGURE 10.3

NLRA Union Campaign Violations

Source: Adapted from www.nlrb.gov/workplace_rights/ nlra_violations.aspx, accessed January 14, 2008.

Examples of Employer Conduct Which Violate the NLRA Are:

• Threatening employees with loss of jobs or benefits if they join or vote for a union or engage in protected concerted activity (such as 2 or more employees together asking their employer to improve working conditions and pay).

• Threatening to close the plant if employees unionize.

• Promising benefits to employees to discourage their union support.

• Transferring, laying off, terminating, assigning employees more difficult work tasks, or otherwise punishing employees because they engaged in union or protected concerted activity.

• Transferring, laying off, terminating, assigning employees more difficult work tasks, or otherwise punishing employees because they filed unfair labor practice charges or participated in an investigation by NLRB.

Examples of Labor Organization Conduct Which Violate the NLRA Are:

• Threats to employees that they will lose their jobs unless they support the union.

• Seeking the suspension, discharge, or other punishment of an employee for not being a union member even if the employee has paid or offered to pay a lawful initiation fee and periodic fees thereafter.

• Refusing to process a grievance because an employee has criticized union officials or because an employee is not a member of the union in states where union security clauses are not permitted.

• Fining employees who have validly resigned from the union for engaging in protected concerted activities following their resignation or for crossing an unlawful picket line.

• Engaging in picket line misconduct, such as threatening, assaulting, or barring non-strikers from the employer's premises.

• Striking over issues unrelated to employment terms and conditions or coercively enmeshing neutrals into a labor dispute.

and working conditions, Starbucks executives were surprised that some employees may have expressed a desire to unionize. Be that as it may, the allegations that some local managers may have tried to retaliate against employees who favored the union underscore why all employers must carefully train supervisors in how to react when the union comes to call.

Step 5: The Election

Finally, the election can be held within 30 to 60 days after the NLRB issues its Decision and Direction of Election. The election is by secret ballot. The NLRB provides the ballots (see Figure 10.4), as well as the voting booth and ballot box. It also counts the votes and certifies the results of the election. Historically, the more workers who vote, the less likely a union victory. This is probably because more workers who are not strong union supporters end up voting. Which union is important, too: For example, the Teamsters union is usually somewhat less likely than other unions to win a representation election.[43]

The union becomes the employees' representative if it wins the election, and winning means getting a majority of the votes cast, not a majority of the workers in the bargaining unit. (Remember that if an employer commits an unfair labor practice, the NLRB may reverse a "no union" election. Supervisors must therefore be careful not to commit such unfair practices.) The union typically wins just over half of such elections.

Decertification Elections: When Employees Want to Oust Their Union

Winning an election and signing an agreement do not necessarily mean that the union is in the company to stay—quite the opposite. The same law that grants employees the right to unionize also gives them a way to legally terminate the union's right to represent them. The process is *decertification*. In the U.S., there are around 450 to 500 decertification elections each year, of which unions usually win around 30%.[44] That's actually a more favorable rate for management than the rate for the original representation elections.

Decertification campaigns don't differ much from certification campaigns.[45] The union organizes membership meetings and house-to-house visits, mails literature to homes, and uses phone calls, NLRB appeals, and (sometimes) threats and harassment to win the election. Managers use meetings—including one-on-one meetings, small-group

FIGURE 10.4

Sample NLRB Ballot

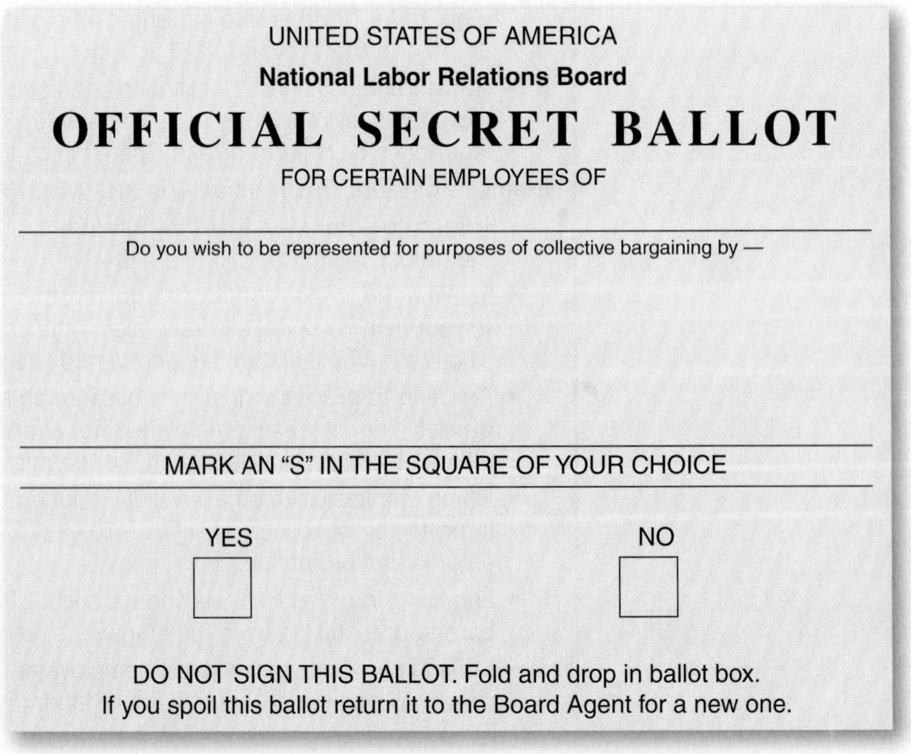

UNITED STATES OF AMERICA

National Labor Relations Board

OFFICIAL SECRET BALLOT

FOR CERTAIN EMPLOYEES OF

_____

Do you wish to be represented for purposes of collective bargaining by —

_____

MARK AN "S" IN THE SQUARE OF YOUR CHOICE

YES	NO
☐	☐

DO NOT SIGN THIS BALLOT. Fold and drop in ballot box.
If you spoil this ballot return it to the Board Agent for a new one.

meetings, and meetings with entire units—as well as legal or expert assistance, letters, improved working conditions, and subtle or not-so-subtle threats in its attempts to win a decertification vote. Employers are also increasingly using consultants.

THE COLLECTIVE BARGAINING PROCESS

④ Discuss the main steps in the collective bargaining process.

What Is Collective Bargaining?

When and if the union is recognized as a company's employees' representative, a day is set for meeting at the bargaining table. Representatives of management and the union meet to negotiate a labor contract that contains agreements on specific provisions covering wages, hours, and working conditions.

collective bargaining
The process through which representatives of management and the union meet to negotiate a labor agreement.

What exactly is **collective bargaining?** According to the National Labor Relations Act:

> For the purpose of (this act) to bargain collectively is the performance of the mutual obligation of the employer and the representative of the employees to meet at reasonable times and confer in good faith with respect to wages, hours, and terms and conditions of employment, or the negotiation of an agreement, or any question arising thereunder, and the execution of a written contract incorporating any agreement reached if requested by either party, but such obligation does not compel either party to agree to a proposal or require the making of a concession.

In plain language, this means that both management and labor are required by law to negotiate wages, hours, and terms and conditions of employment "in good faith." We'll see that court decisions have clarified the specific provisions that are negotiable.

What Is Good-Faith Bargaining?

good-faith bargaining
A term that means both parties are communicating and negotiating and that proposals are being matched with counterproposals, with both parties making every reasonable effort to arrive at agreements. It does not mean that either party is compelled to agree to a proposal.

Good-faith bargaining means that proposals are matched with counterproposals and that both parties make every reasonable effort to arrive at an agreement. It does not mean that either party is compelled to agree to a proposal. Nor does it require that either party make any specific concessions (although in practice, some may be necessary). In practice, good-faith bargaining includes things like the duty to meet and confer with the representative of the employees (or employer); the duty to supply, on request, information that is "relevant and necessary" to allow the employees' representative to bargain intelligently; and the duty to deal with whoever the employees' representative designates to carry on negotiations.[46]

WHEN IS BARGAINING NOT IN GOOD FAITH? In assessing whether the party has violated its good-faith obligations, it is the *totality of conduct* by each of the parties that is of prime importance to the NLRB and the courts.[47] As interpreted by the NLRB and the courts, examples of a violation of the requirements for good-faith bargaining may include:

1. *Surface bargaining.* This involves going through the motions of bargaining without any real intention of completing a formal agreement.
2. *Proposals and demands.* The NLRB considers the advancement of proposals as a positive factor in determining overall good faith.
3. *Withholding information.* The NLRB and courts expect management to furnish information on matters such as wages, hours, and other terms of employment that union negotiators request and legitimately require. Failing to provide such information in a timely manner and usable form may reflect bad-faith bargaining.[48]
4. *Dilatory tactics.* The law requires that the parties meet and "confer at reasonable times and intervals." It does not require management to meet at the time and place dictated just by the union. It may not be unusual for employers to try to delay the meeting so as to "disrupt a union's bargaining momentum."[49] However, inordinately delaying the meeting or refusing to meet with the other party may reflect bad-faith bargaining.
5. *Concessions.* The law does not require either party to make concessions, in other words, to give in to the other party's demand. However, being willing to compromise during negotiations is a crucial ingredient of good-faith bargaining.

6. *Unilateral changes in conditions.* This is viewed as a strong indication that the employer is not bargaining with the required intent of reaching an agreement.
7. *Bypassing the representative.* An employer violates its duty to bargain when it refuses to negotiate with the union representative.

The Negotiating Team

Both union and management send a negotiating team to the bargaining table, and both teams usually go into the bargaining sessions having done their research. Union representatives have sounded out union members on their desires and conferred with union representatives of related unions.

Similarly, management does several things to prepare for bargaining. For example, it compiles pay and benefit data, including comparisons to local pay rates and rates paid for similar jobs in the industry. Management also carefully "costs" the current labor contract and determines the increased cost—total, per employee, and per hour—of the union's demands. It also tries to identify probable union demands and to size up which are more important to the union. It uses information from grievances and feedback from supervisors to determine ahead of time what the union's demands might be and thus prepare counteroffers and arguments ahead of time.

One collective bargaining expert says, "The mistake I see most often is [HR professionals who] enter the negotiations without understanding the financial impact of things they put on the table. The thing you give up can make or break your employer. . . . For example, the union wants 3 extra days to be on holiday. That doesn't sound like a lot, except that in some states, if an employee leaves, you have to pay them for unused holiday time. Now [therefore] your employer has to carry that liability on their books at all times."[50] The accompanying *Personal Competencies* feature explains other important negotiating skills.

Personal Competencies

Building Your *Negotiating* Skills

Hammering out a satisfactory labor agreement requires negotiating skills. Experienced negotiators use *leverage, desire, time, competition, information, credibility,* and *judgment* to improve their bargaining positions. *Leverage* means using factors that help or hinder the negotiator, usually by putting the other side under pressure.[51] Things you can leverage include *necessity, desire, competition,* and *time.* For example, the union knows that an employer who needs to fill a big order fast (time) is at a disadvantage. Being able to walk away (or to look like you can) wins the best terms.

Similarly, some contract terms (such as reduced pension benefits) may be crucial. However, the employer who makes its *desires* too obvious undercuts his or her position. *Competition* is important too. There is no more convincing ploy than subtly hinting you've got an alternative (like shifting services abroad). *Time* (and particularly your deadlines) can also tilt things for or against you.

Also, as we said, "knowledge is power" when you're negotiating. Having information about the other side and about the situation puts you at an advantage. And, the other side will be trying to decide if you're bluffing, so *credibility* is important. Finally, good negotiators need *judgment:* the ability to "strike the right balance between gaining advantages

and reaching compromises, in the substance as well as in the style of [their] negotiating technique."[52]

SOME THINGS TO AVOID One expert says that negotiators typically make several big mistakes. Here's what he suggests to avoid them:[53]

- *Neglecting the other side's problems* As in all communication, negotiations usually go best when they produce a common basis of understanding—each party is "on the same page" in terms of understanding each others' point of view. Good negotiators therefore strive to understand the other person's concerns and point of view.
- *Letting price overwhelm other issues* Most of the labor agreement's elements probably come down to price, but don't neglect nonfinancial issues. Things like working conditions and disciplinary procedures may be as important as purely financial issues.
- *Neglecting BANTRA* Labor experts stress the importance of knowing your "best alternative to a negotiated agreement" (BANTRA). For example, the best alternative may be *not* getting an agreement now, but walking away and letting the other side face its constituents' pressures.

Bargaining Items

Labor law sets out *voluntary, illegal,* and *mandatory* items that are subject to collective bargaining.

Voluntary (or permissible) bargaining items are neither mandatory nor illegal; they become a part of negotiations only through the joint agreement of both management and union. Neither party can be compelled against its wishes to negotiate over voluntary items. An employee cannot hold up signing a contract because the other party refuses to bargain on a voluntary item.

Illegal bargaining items are forbidden by law. The clause agreeing to hire "union members exclusively" would be illegal in a right-to-work state, for example.

About 70 **mandatory bargaining items** exist, some of which we present in Figure 10.5. These include wages, hours, rest periods, layoffs, transfers, benefits, and severance pay. Others are added as the law evolves. For instance, drug testing evolved into a mandatory item as a result of NLRB decisions.

Bargaining Stages[54]

Bargaining typically goes through several stages.[55] First, each side presents its demands. At this stage, both parties are usually quite far apart on some issues. Indeed, labor negotiators use the term *blue-skying* to refer to demands (such as swimming pools and 17 paid holidays, including Valentine's Day) that some negotiators have been known to bring to the table. Second, there is a reduction of demands. At this stage, each side trades off some of its demands to gain others, a process called *trading points*. Third come the subcommittee studies: The parties form joint subcommittees or study groups to try to work out reasonable alternatives. Fourth, the parties reach an informal settlement, and each group goes back to its sponsor. Union representatives check informally with their superiors and the union members; management representatives check with top management. Finally, when everything is in order, the parties fine-tune, proofread, and sign a formal agreement. The *HR in Practice* feature on page 332 presents some negotiating guidelines.

voluntary (permissible) bargaining items
Items in collective bargaining for which bargaining is neither illegal nor mandatory—neither party can be compelled to negotiate over those items.

illegal bargaining items
Items in collective bargaining that are forbidden by law; for example, the clause agreeing to hire "union members exclusively" would be illegal in a right-to-work state.

mandatory bargaining items
Items in collective bargaining that a party must bargain over if they are introduced by the other party—for example, pay.

FIGURE 10.5 Bargaining Items

MANDATORY	PERMISSIBLE	ILLEGAL
Rates of pay	Indemnity bonds	Closed shop
Wages	Management rights as to union affairs	Separation of employees based on race
Hours of employment	Pension benefits of retired employees	Discriminatory treatment
Overtime pay	Scope of the bargaining unit	
Shift differentials	Including supervisors in the contract	
Holidays	Additional parties to the contract such as the international union	
Vacations		
Severance pay		
Pensions		
Insurance benefits	Use of union label	
Profit-sharing plans	Settlement of unfair labor charges	
Christmas bonuses	Prices in cafeteria	
Company housing, meals, and discounts	Continuance of past contract	
Employee security	Membership of bargaining team	
Job performance	Employment of strikebreakers	
Union security		
Management–union relationship		
Drug testing of employees		

HR in Practice

Negotiating Guidelines

1. *Set clear objectives* for every bargaining item and understand on what grounds the objectives are established.
2. *Do not hurry.*
3. When in doubt, *caucus* with your associates.
4. Be *well prepared* with firm data supporting your position.
5. Always strive to keep some *flexibility* in your position.
6. Don't just concern yourself with what the other party says and does; *find out why.*
7. Respect the importance of *face saving* for the other party.
8. Constantly be alert to the *real intentions* of the other party.
9. Be a good *listener.*
10. Build a reputation for *being fair but firm.*
11. Learn to *control your emotions;* don't panic.
12. Be sure as you make each bargaining move that you know its *relationship* to all other moves.
13. Measure each move against your *objectives.*
14. Pay close attention to the *wording* of every clause renegotiated; words and phrases are often sources of grievances.
15. Remember that collective bargaining negotiations are, by nature, part of a *compromise* process.
16. Consider the impact of present negotiations on those in *future years.*

Impasses, Mediation, and Strikes

IMPASSES Signing the agreement assumes everything is in order, and that there are no insurmountable disagreements. If there are, the parties may declare an impasse. For example, a few years ago the U.S. National Hockey League informed the NLRB that it had reached an impasse in its negotiations with the National Hockey League Players' Association.[56] The parties must get past the impasse for the contract to be agreed to and signed.

An impasse usually occurs because one party demands more than the other offers. Sometimes an impasse can be resolved through a *third party*, a disinterested person such as a mediator or arbitrator. If the impasse is not resolved in this way, a work stoppage, or *strike,* may be called by the union to pressure management.

mediation
Labor relations intervention in which a neutral third party tries to assist the principals in reaching agreement.

THIRD-PARTY INVOLVEMENT Opposing parties use three types of third-party interventions to overcome an impasse: mediation, fact-finding, and arbitration. With **mediation,** a neutral third party tries to assist the principals in reaching agreement. The mediator usually holds meetings with each party to determine where each stands regarding its position. He or she then uses this information to find common ground for further bargaining. For example,

Even professional hockey, baseball, basketball, and football players, all relatively well-paid, have gone on strike for better wages and benefits.

Southwest Airlines and its mechanics union requested federal mediation to help the parties overcome a deadlock over pay.[57] The mediator communicates assessments of the likelihood of a strike, the possible settlement packages available, and the like. The mediator does not have the authority to insist on a position or make a concession. However, he or she may—and probably will—provide leadership by making his or her position on some issue clear.

In certain situations (as in a national emergency dispute in which the president of the United States determines that a strike would be a national emergency), a fact-finder may be appointed. A **fact-finder** is a neutral party. He or she studies the issues and makes a public recommendation of what a reasonable settlement ought to be.

Arbitration is the most definitive type of third-party intervention because the arbitrator may have the power to decide and dictate settlement terms. Unlike mediation and fact-finding, arbitration can guarantee a solution to an impasse. With *binding arbitration,* both parties are committed to accepting the arbitrator's award. With *nonbinding arbitration,* they are not. Arbitration may also be voluntary or compulsory (in other words, imposed by a government agency). In the United States, voluntary binding arbitration is the most prevalent.

Arbitration may not always be as impartial as it's thought to be. Researchers studied 391 arbitrated cases in baseball over about 20 years. Arbitrator awards favored teams 61% of the time. They concluded that (at least in baseball) "self-interested behavior by arbitrators" may lead to bias against players, and particularly against players of African-American and Latin ancestry.[58]

SOURCES OF THIRD-PARTY ASSISTANCE Various public and professional agencies make arbitrators and mediators available. For example, the American Arbitration Association (AAA) represents and provides the services of thousands of arbitrators and mediators to employers and unions requesting their services. The U.S. government's Office of Arbitration Services maintains a roster of arbitrators qualified to hear and decide disputes over the interpretation or application of collective-bargaining agreements, and provides the parties involved with lists and panels of arbitrators. In the United Kingdom, the Chartered Institute of Arbitrators (www.arbitrators.org) can offer assistance. Figure 10.6 shows the form employers or unions use to request arbitrator or mediator services from the U.S. government's Federal Mediation and Conciliation Service (FMCS). Nationwide during fiscal year 2006, FMCS mediators were involved in nearly 5,500 collective bargaining disputes.[59] In addition, most states provide arbitrator and mediation services.

STRIKES A strike is a withdrawal of labor. There are four main types of strikes in the U.S. An **economic strike** results from a failure to agree on the terms of a contract—from an impasse, in other words. An **unfair labor practice strike** protests illegal conduct by

fact-finder
In labor relations, a neutral party who studies the issues in a dispute and makes a public recommendation for a reasonable settlement.

arbitration
The most definitive type of third-party intervention, in which the arbitrator often has the power to determine and dictate the settlement terms.

economic strike
A strike that results from a failure to agree on the terms of a contract that involve wages, benefits, and other conditions of employment.

unfair labor practice strike
A strike aimed at protesting illegal conduct by the employer.

An economic strike results from a failure to agree on the terms of a contract—from an impasse, in other words. The target here was Cintas Corp.

FIGURE 10.6 Form to Request Mediation Services

FMCS Form F-53
Revised 5-92

Form Approved
OMB No. 3076-0

FEDERAL SECTOR LABOR RELATIONS
NOTICE TO FEDERAL MEDIATION AND CONCILIATION SERVICE

Mail
To:

Notice Processing Unit
FEDERAL MEDIATION AND CONCILIATION SERVICE
2100 K Street, N.W.
Washington, D.C. 20427

THIS NOTICE IS IN REGARD TO: (MARK "X")

(1) ☐ AN INITIAL CONTRACT   (INCLUDED FLRA CERTIFICATION NUMBER) # _____
     ☐ A CONTRACT REOPENER   REOPENER DATE _____
     ☐ THE EXPIRATION OF AN EXISTING AGREEMENT   EXPIRATION DATE: _____

(2) ☐ *OTHER REQUESTS FOR THE ASSISTANCE OF FMCS IN BARGAINING*   *(MARK "X")*
SPECIFY TYPE OF ISSUE(S)

(3) ☐ *REQUEST FOR GRIEVANCE MEDIATION (SEE ITEM #10)*   *(MARK "X")*
ISSUE(S)

(4) NAME OF FEDERAL AGENCY   NAME OF SUBDIVISION OR COMPONENT, IF ANY

STREET ADDRESS OF AGENCY   CITY   STATE   ZIP

AGENCY OFFICIAL TO BE CONTACTED   AREA CODE & PHONE NUMBER

(5) NAME OF NATIONAL UNION OR PARENT BODY   NAME AND/OR LOCAL NUMBER

STREET ADDRESS   CITY   STATE   ZIP

UNION OFFICIAL TO BE CONTACTED   AREA CODE & PHONE NUMBER

LOCATION OF NEGOTIATIONS OR WHERE MEDIATION WILL BE HELD

(6) STREET ADDRESS   CITY   STATE   ZIP

(7) APPROX. # OF EMPLOYEES IN BARGAINING UNIT(S) >>   IN ESTABLISHMENT >>

(8) THIS NOTICE OR REQUEST IS FILED ON BEHALF OF *(MARK "X")*   ☐ UNION   ☐ AGENCY

(9) NAME AND TITLE OF OFFICIAL(S) SUBMITTING THIS NOTICE OR REQUEST   AREA CODE AND PHONE NUMBER

STREET ADDRESS   CITY   STATE   ZIP

FOR GRIEVANCE MEDIATION, THE SIGNATURES OF BOTH PARTIES ARE REQUIRED:*

(10) SIGNATURE (AGENCY)   DATE   SIGNATURE (UNION)   DATE

*Receipt of this form does not commit FMCS to offer its services. Receipt of this form will not be acknowledged in writing by FMCS. While use of this form is voluntary, its use will facilitate FMCS service to respondents. Public reporting burden for this collection of information is estimated to average 10 minutes per response, including time for reviewing the collection of information. Send comments regarding this burden estimate or any other aspect of this collection of information, including suggestions for reducing this burden, to FMCS Division of Administrative Services, Washington, D.C. 20427, and to the Office of Management and Budget, Paperwork Reduction Project, Washington, D.C. 20603.

wildcat strike
An unauthorized strike occurring during the term of a contract.

sympathy strike
A strike that takes place when one union strikes in support of another's strike.

the employer. A **wildcat strike** is an unauthorized strike occurring during the term of a contract. A **sympathy strike** occurs when one union strikes in support of the strike of another.

Strikes needn't be an inevitable result of the bargaining process. Instead, studies show that they are often avoidable, but occur as a result of mistakes made during the bargaining process. Mistakes include discrepancies between union leaders' and rank-and-file members' expectations, and misperceptions regarding each side's bargaining goals.[60]

*Picketing i*s one of the first activities occurring during a strike. The purpose of picketing is to inform the public about the existence of the labor dispute and often to encourage others to refrain from doing business with the employer against whom the employees are striking.

DEALING WITH A STRIKE Employers can make several responses when they become the object of a strike. One is to halt their operations until the strike is over. A second alternative is to contract out work during the duration of the strike in order to blunt the effects of the strike on the employer. A third alternative is for the employer to continue operations, perhaps using supervisors and other nonstriking workers to fill in for the striking workers. A fourth alternative is the hiring of replacements for the strikers. In an economic strike, such replacements can be deemed permanent and would not have to be let go to make room for strikers who decided to return to work. If the strike were an unfair labor practice strike, the strikers would be entitled to return to their jobs if the employer makes an unconditional offer for them to do so. When U.S.-based Northwest Airlines began giving permanent jobs to 1,500 substitute workers it hired to replace striking mechanics, the strike by the Aircraft Mechanics Fraternal Association basically fell apart.[61]

OTHER RESPONSES Management and labor both use other methods to try to break an impasse. The union, for example, may resort to a *corporate campaign.* This is an organized effort by the union that exerts pressure on the employer by pressuring the company's other unions, shareholders, directors, customers, creditors, and government agencies, often directly. For example, a member of the company's board of directors might wake up one day and find that the union has organized its members to **boycott**—stop doing business with—the director's own business.

Unions use corporate campaigns to good effect. Sometimes also called *advocacy* or *comprehensive campaigns,* they helped unions organize several health care firms, including Sutter Health in California, for instance.[62]

Inside games are union efforts to convince employees to impede or to disrupt production. They might do this, for example, by slowing the work pace, refusing to work overtime, holding sickouts, filing mass charges with governmental agencies, or refusing to do work without receiving detailed instructions from supervisors (even though such instruction has not previously been required).

LOCKOUTS Employers can try to break an impasse with lockouts. A **lockout** is a refusal by the employer to provide opportunities to work. The company (often literally) locks out employees and prohibits them from doing their jobs (and thus from getting paid).

The NLRB does not generally view a lockout as an unfair labor practice. For example, if your product is perishable (such as vegetables), then a lockout may legitimately serve to neutralize union power. A lockout is viewed as an unfair labor practice by the NLRB only when the employer acts for a prohibited purpose. It is not a prohibited purpose to try to bring about a settlement of negotiations on terms favorable to the employer. However, employers are usually reluctant to cease operations when employees are willing to continue working (even though there may be an impasse at the bargaining table).

INJUNCTIONS During the impasse, both employers and unions can seek injunctive relief if they believe the other side is taking actions that could irreparably harm the other party. To obtain such relief, the NLRB must show the district court that an unfair labor practice—such as interfering with the union organizing campaign—if left unremedied, will irreparably harm the other party's statutory rights. (For example, if the employer is unfairly interfering with the union's organization campaign, or if the union is retaliating against employees for trying to gain access to the NLRB, the other side might press the NLRB for 10[j] injunctive relief.) Such relief is requested after the NLRB issues an unfair labor practices complaint. The *injunctive relief* is a judicial order calling for a cessation of certain actions deemed injurious.[63]

boycott
The combined refusal by employees and other interested parties to buy or use the employer's products.

lockout
A refusal by the employer to provide opportunities to work.

The Contract Agreement

The contract agreement itself may be 20 or 30 pages long or longer. The main sections of a typical contract cover subjects such as:

1. Management rights
2. Union security and automatic payroll dues deduction
3. Grievance procedures
4. Arbitration of grievances
5. Disciplinary procedures
6. Compensation rates
7. Hours of work and overtime
8. Benefits such as vacation, holidays, insurance, and pension
9. Health and safety provisions
10. Employee security seniority provisions
11. Contract expiration date

Handling Grievances

Signing the labor agreement is not the end of the process, because questions will always arise about what various clauses really mean. The *grievance process* addresses these issues. It is the process or steps that the employer and union have agreed to follow to ascertain whether some action violated the agreement. The grievance process is not supposed to renegotiate contract points. Instead, the aim is to clarify what those points really mean, in the context of addressing grievances regarding things like time off, disciplinary action, and pay.

CONTRACT ADMINISTRATION In most U.S. unionized companies, grievance handling is often called *contract administration,* because no labor contract can ever be so complete that it covers all contingencies and answers all questions. For example, suppose the contract says you can discharge an employee only for "just cause." You subsequently discharge someone for speaking back to you in harsh terms. Was speaking back to you harshly "just cause"? The grievance procedure would handle and settle disagreements like these. It involves interpretation only, and generally would not involve renegotiating all or parts of the agreement.

SOURCES OF GRIEVANCES Employees will use just about any issue involving wages, hours, or conditions of employment as the basis of a grievance. Discipline cases and seniority problems (including promotions, transfers, and layoffs) would probably top the list. Others would include grievances growing out of job evaluations and work assignments, overtime, vacations, incentive plans, and holidays.

Sometimes the grievance process gets out of hand. For example, members of American Postal Workers Union, Local 482, filed 1,800 grievances at the Postal Service's Roanoke, Virginia, mail processing facility (the usual rate is about 800 grievances per year). The employees apparently were responding to job changes, including transfers triggered by the Postal Service's efforts to further automate its processes.[64]

THE GRIEVANCE PROCEDURE Whatever the source of the grievances, many firms today (and virtually all unionized ones) do (or should) give employees some means through which to air and settle their grievances. Grievance procedures (or processes) are invariably a part of the labor agreement. But, even in nonunion firms, such procedures can help ensure that labor–management peace prevails.

Grievance procedures are typically multistep processes. For example, step one might require the grievant to try and work out an agreement with his or her supervisor, perhaps with a union officer or colleague present. Appeals may then go to the supervisor's boss, then that person's boss, and perhaps finally to an arbitrator.

GUIDELINES FOR HANDLING GRIEVANCES It is generally best, but not always possible, to develop a work environment in which grievances don't occur in the first place. Doing so depends on being able to recognize, diagnose, and correct the causes of potential employee dissatisfaction before they become formal grievances. Typical causes include unfair appraisals, inequitable wages, or poor communications. Yet, in practice, grievances can be minimized, but not eradicated. There will probably always be a need to interpret what some clause in the agreement means. The *HR in Practice* presents important guidelines.

HR in Practice

Guidelines for How to Handle a Grievance[65]

Do

- Investigate and handle each and every case as though it may eventually result in an arbitration hearing.
- Talk with the employee about his or her grievance; give the person a good and full hearing.
- Require the union to identify specific contractual provisions allegedly violated.
- Comply with the contractual time limits of the company for handling the grievance.
- Visit the work area of the grievance.
- Determine whether there were any witnesses.
- Examine the grievant's personnel record.
- Fully examine prior grievance records.
- Treat the union representative as your equal.
- Hold your grievance discussion privately.
- Fully inform your own supervisor of grievance matters.

Don't

- Discuss the case with the union steward alone—the grievant should definitely be there.
- Make arrangements with individual employees that are inconsistent with the labor agreement.
- Hold back the remedy if the company is wrong.
- Admit to the binding effect of a past practice.
- Relinquish to the union your rights as a manager.
- Settle grievances on the basis of what is "fair." Instead, stick to the labor agreement, which should be your only standard.
- Bargain over items not covered by the contract.
- Treat as subject to arbitration claims demanding the discipline or discharge of managers.
- Give long, written grievance answers.
- Trade a grievance settlement for a grievance withdrawal (or try to make up for a bad decision in one grievance by bending over backward in another).
- Deny grievances on the premise that your "hands have been tied by management."
- Agree to informal amendments in the contract.

Dispute Resolution

Disputes—potential and real—are part of the bargaining process, and, indeed, part and parcel of managing personnel. Strikes trigger corporate campaigns and negotiations; negotiations break down and require mediators; and disciplinary actions lead to grievances, for instance. Mediators, arbitrators, grievance processes, and negotiating are all important dispute resolution mechanisms—ways to manage and resolve disputes.[66]

While union-management relations trigger many or most of the obvious employment disputes, other employment actions cause their share of disagreements. For example, an applicant believes the employer discriminated against him due to age by not hiring him; or an employee feels she would have been promoted had her boss not wanted to promote a man. Potential disputes like these are the reason why, as we saw in chapter 4, more employers are requiring applicants to sign mandatory alternative dispute resolution forms as part of their applications. For example, the employment application package for U.S.-based Circuit City requires applicants to agree to arbitrate certain legal disputes related to their application or employment with the company.

Most firms, though, don't seem to be doing a very good job of managing disputes. For example, one recent survey in the United Kingdom found that:[67]

- 79% of respondents said disputes were not handled very well in most organizations,
- 65% agreed that emotions and personal pride affected their chances of reaching a solution, and
- 47% agreed that a personal dislike of the other side led them to expensive litigation.

Given the influence of personal emotions in resolving disputes, it's apparent that employers can't rely solely on traditional dispute resolution mechanisms like grievance procedures. Instead, it's preferable that disputes don't take root or get out of hand. Employers can do at least three things to help achieve this.

ETHICS AND DISPUTES First, as we discussed in chapter 9 ("Ethics, Employee Rights, and Fair Treatment at Work"), employers need policies that encourage employees to treat each other with *fairness and respect*. For example, many grievances stem from disciplinary matters. So, prior to disciplining someone, make sure the evidence supports the charge, protect the employees' due process rights, and warn the employee of the disciplinary consequences of his or her alleged misconduct.

TRUST AND DISPUTES Second, whether dealing with disciplinary matters, grievances, or union negotiations, behave in a way that *fosters trust*. Behaviors that signal trustworthiness include:

- *Integrity*—honestly and truthfulness[68]
- *Competence*—technical and interpersonal knowledge and skills
- *Consistency*—reliability, predictability, and good judgment in handling situations
- *Loyalty*—willingness to protect and save face for a person
- *Openness*—willingness to share ideas and information freely[69]
- *Community*—willingly offer materials and resources to help the team move ahead
- *Respect*—recognize the strengths and abilities of others[70]
- *Cooperation*—behave cooperatively, and put oneself in the other person's position
- *Dependability*—partners "promise cautiously, and then keep their promises"

CONFLICT AND DISPUTE RESOLUTION Third, when disagreements do arise, some *interpersonal conflict resolution approaches* are better than others. For example, having the parties meet to confront the facts and hammer out a solution is usually better than pushing problems under a rug. Yet there are times when letting things cool down is advisable.

In practice, people usually don't rely on a single conflict-resolution style; they use several simultaneously. A study of supervisors and subordinates illustrates this.

The researchers studied how supervisors used several possible conflict-resolution styles, such as confrontation. The researchers' basic question was, "Is using some combination of these styles more effective at resolving conflicts than others?" They analyzed videotapes of 116 male police sergeants handling a standardized, scripted conflict with either a subordinate or a superior.

At least for these police sergeants, using three styles together—*problem solving* while being moderately *accommodating* and still maintaining a strong hand in *controlling* the conflict-resolution process—was an especially effective combination.

WHAT'S NEXT FOR UNIONS?

⑤ Explain why union membership dropped, and what the prospects are for the union movement.

For years, the head of Ford's United Auto Workers union fought hard for increased benefits for his union members. But recently, he's been urging his union colleagues to accept productivity-enhancing plans, like outsourcing factory jobs to lower paid workers. "Ford is in a desperate situation," he says, and "if this company goes down, I want to be able to look in the mirror and say I did everything I could."[71]

Why the Union Decline?

We saw early in this chapter that several factors contributed to the decline in union membership over the past 50 or so years. Unions traditionally appealed mostly to blue-collar workers, and the proportion of blue-collar jobs has been decreasing as service-sector and white-collar service jobs have increased. Furthermore, several economic factors, including intense international competition, have put unions under further pressure. Globalization increases competition, and competition increases pressures on employers to cut costs and boost productivity. This in turn puts unions in a squeeze. Other factors pressuring employers and unions include the deregulation of trucking, airlines, and communications; outdated equipment and factories; mismanagement; new technology; and laws that somewhat reduced the need for unions. The effect of all this has been the permanent layoff of hundreds of thousands of union members, the permanent closing of company plants, the relocation of companies to nonunion settings and mergers and acquisitions that eliminated union jobs and affected collective bargaining agreements. In the U.S., membership as a percent of people working has dropped by about two-thirds over 50 years.

How Unions Are Changing

Of course, unions are not sitting idly by and just watching their numbers dwindle.[72] The priorities of the Change to Win Coalition (whose members broke off from the AFL-CIO) illustrate what may be the new union strategies. They,

> "Make it our first priority to help millions more workers form unions so we can build a strong movement for rewarding work in America [and] unite the strength of everyone who works in the same industry so we can negotiate with today's huge global corporations for everyone's benefit."[73]

CHANGE TO WIN In practice, this means several things. Change to Win will be very aggressive about trying to organize workers, will focus on organizing women and minority workers, will focus more on organizing temporary or contingent workers, and will target specific multinational companies for international campaigns.[74]

EMPLOYEE FREE CHOICE ACT Unions are pushing the U.S. Congress to pass the Employee Free Choice Act. This would, among other things, make it more difficult for employers to inhibit workers from trying to form a union. Unions are also pushing for a new means of obtaining union recognition. Instead of secret-ballot elections, unions are pushing for a *"card check"* system. Here the union would win recognition when a majority of workers signed authorization cards saying they want the union. Several large companies, including Cingular Wireless, agreed to the card check process.[75]

CLASS ACTION LAWSUITS Unions are also using class action lawsuits to support employees in nonunionized companies, so as to pressure employers. For example, unions recently used class action lawsuits to support workers' claims under the Fair Labor Standards Act, and the Equal Pay Act.[76]

COORDINATION Unions are becoming more proactive in terms of coordinating their efforts.[77] For example, consider what UNITE (the Union of Needletrades, Industrial and Textile Employees, now part of UNITE HERE) did. They used their "Voice at Work" campaign to coordinate 800 workers at one employer's distribution center with others at the employer's New York City headquarters and with local activists and international unions throughout Europe. This forced the employer's parent company, a French conglomerate, to cease resisting the union's organizing efforts. In its "Union Cities" campaigns, AFL-CIO planners work with local labor councils and individual unions to gain the support of a target city's elected officials. In Los Angeles, this helped the service workers' union organize janitors in that city.

EXAMPLE The steps that UNITE took against Cintas Corp. illustrate some unions' new tactics. The union did not petition for an NLRB election. Instead, it proposed using the "card check" process. They also filed a $100 million class action suit against the company in support of its sales representatives. Then Cintas workers in California filed a lawsuit claiming that the company was violating a nearby municipality's "living wage" law. UNITE then joined forces with the Teamsters union, which in turn began targeting Cintas' delivery people.[78]

COOPERATIVE ARRANGEMENTS Another, somewhat more risky (for the unions) approach is to agree to enter into more cooperative pacts with employers—for instance, working with them in developing team-based employee participation programs. About half of all collective bargaining agreements encourage cooperative labor–management relationships. *Cooperative clauses* cover things like joint committees to review drug problem, health care, and safety issues.[79]

GLOBAL CAMPAIGNS Unions are also forcefully extending their reach overseas, as the *Global Issues in HR* feature illustrates.

Global Issues in HR

Unions Go Global

Any company that thinks it can avoid unions by sending manufacturing and service jobs abroad is sorely mistaken. Today, as we've seen, most businesses are "going global." Regional trade treaties like the North American Free Trade Agreement (NAFTA) are further boosting the business done by firms abroad. This fact is not lost on unions. Some are already expanding their influence abroad.

The global union campaigns reflect the belief, as the Service Employees International Union (SEIU) puts it, that "huge global service sector companies routinely cross national borders and industry lines as they search for places where they can shift operations to exploit workers with the lowest possible pay and benefits." SEIU is therefore strengthening its alliances with unions in other nations, with the goal of uniting workers in particular multinational companies and industries, around the globe.[80] For example, the head of the United States' Service Employees International Union recently worked with China's All China Federation of Trade Unions (ACFTU) to help the latter organize China's Wal-Mart stores.[81] Similarly, U.S. unions are helping Mexican unions to organize, especially in U.S.-owned factories. Thus, the United Electrical Workers is subsidizing organizers at Mexican plants of the General Electric Company.

Review

SUMMARY

1. In addition to improved wages and working conditions, unions seek security when organizing. There are five possible arrangements, including the closed shop, the union shop, the agency shop, the preferential shop, and maintenance of membership.

2. The AFL-CIO is a national federation comprising about 100 national and international unions. It can exercise only the power it is allowed to exercise by its constituent national unions.

3. During the period of strong encouragement of unions, the Norris-LaGuardia Act and the NLRA were passed; these marked a shift in labor law from repression to strong encouragement of union activity. They did this by banning certain types of unfair labor practices, by providing for secret-ballot elections, and by creating the NLRB.

4. The Taft-Hartley Act reflected the period of modified encouragement coupled with regulation. It enumerated the rights of employees with respect to their unions, enumerated the rights of employers, and allowed the U.S. president to temporarily bar national emergency strikes. Among other things, it also enumerated certain union unfair labor practices. For example, it banned unions from restraining or coercing employees from exercising their guaranteed bargaining rights. And employers were explicitly given the right to express their views concerning union organization.

5. The Landrum-Griffin Act reflected the period of detailed regulation of internal union affairs. It grew out of discoveries of wrongdoing on the part of both management and union leadership and contained a

bill of rights for union members. (For example, it affirms a member's right to sue his or her union.)

6. There are five steps in a union drive and election: the initial contact, obtaining authorization cards, holding a hearing with the NLRB, the campaign, and the election itself. Remember that the union need only win a majority of the votes cast, *not* a majority of the workers in the bargaining unit.

7. Bargaining collectively in good faith is the next step if and when the union wins the election. Good faith means that both parties communicate and negotiate, and that proposals are matched with counterproposals. Some hints on bargaining include do not hurry, be prepared, find out why, and be a good listener.

8. An impasse occurs when the parties aren't able to move further toward settlement. Third-party involvement—namely, arbitration, fact-finding, or mediation—is one alternative. Sometimes, though, a strike occurs. Responding to the strike involves such steps as shutting the facility, contracting out work, or possibly replacing the workers. Boycotts and lockouts are two other anti-impasse weapons sometimes used by labor and management.

9. Disputes are part of the bargaining process. Mediators, arbitrators, grievance processes, and negotiating are all important ways to manage and resolve disputes. Most firms, though, don't seem to be doing a very good job of managing disputes. Employers can do at least three other things to help reduce disputes. Employers need policies and practices that encourage employees to treat each other with fairness and respect, behave in a way that fosters trust, and, when disagreements do arise, some *interpersonal conflict resolution approaches* are better than others.

10. Unions are not sitting idly by watching their numbers dwindle. For example, *Change to Win* will be very aggressive about trying to organize workers. Unions are pushing Congress to pass the *Employee Free Choice Act.* This would, among other things, make it more difficult for employers to inhibit workers from trying to form a union. Unions are also using *class action lawsuits* to support employees in nonunionized companies, so as to pressure employers. And unions are becoming more proactive in terms of *coordinating their efforts.*

KEY TERMS

closed shop 317
union shop 317
agency shop 317
preferential shop 317
right to work 317
AFL-CIO 318
Norris-LaGuardia Act 318
Wagner Act 318
National Labor Relations Board (NLRB) 318
Taft-Hartley Act (Labor Management Relations Act) 319
national emergency strikes 321
Landrum-Griffin Act 321
corporate social responsibility 321
union salting 323
authorization cards 324

bargaining unit 324
collective bargaining 329
good-faith bargaining 329
voluntary (permissible) bargaining items 331
illegal bargaining items 331
mandatory bargaining items 331
mediation 332
fact-finder 333
arbitration 333
economic strike 333
unfair labor practice strike 333
wildcat strike 334
sympathy strike 334
boycott 335
lockout 335

DISCUSSION QUESTIONS AND EXERCISES

1. Why do employees join unions? What are the advantages and disadvantages of being a union member?
2. What actions might make employers lose elections?
3. Describe important tactics you would expect the union to use during the union drive and election.

4. Briefly illustrate how labor law has gone through a cycle of repression and encouragement.
5. Explain in detail each step in a union drive and election.
6. What is meant by good-faith bargaining? Using examples, explain when bargaining is not in good faith.

7. Define impasse, mediation, and strike, and explain the techniques that are used to overcome an impasse.

8. In teams of five to six students, choose an organization (such as this university, or a company in which one student works), and list the areas in which the union has had an impact.

9. Several years ago, in a dispute with management, Amtrak workers agreed not to disrupt service by walking out, at least not until a court hearing was held. Amtrak had asked the courts for a tempo-rary restraining order, and the Transport Workers Union of America was actually pleased to postpone the walkout. The workers were apparently not upset at Amtrak, but at Congress, for failing to provide enough funding to Amtrak. What if anything can an employer do when employees threaten to go on strike, not because of what the employer did, but what a third party—in this case, Congress—has done or not done? What laws might prevent the union from going on strike in this case?

Application Exercises

HR in Action
Case Incident 1   Negotiating with the Writers Guild of America

In the U.S., talks between the Writers Guild of America (WGA) and the Alliance of Motion Picture & Television Producers (producers) started off tense in 2007, and then got tenser. In their first meeting, the two sides got nothing done. As producer Dick Wolf said, "everyone in the room is concerned about this."[82]

The two sides were far apart on just about all the issues. However, the biggest issue was how to split revenue from new media, such as when television shows move on to CDs or the Internet. The producers said they wanted a profit-splitting system rather than the current residual system. Under the residual system, writers continue to receive "residuals" or income from shows they write, every time they're shown. Writers Guild executives did their homework. They argued, for instance, that the projections showed producers' revenues from advertising and subscription fees jumped by about 40% between 2002 and 2006.[83] Writers wanted part of that.

The situation grew more tense. After the first few meetings, one producers' representative said, "We can see after the dogfight whose position will win out. The open question there, of course, is whether each of us take several lumps at the table, reaches an agreement then licks their wounds later—none the worse for wear—or whether we inflict more lasting damage through work stoppages that benefit no one before we come to an agreement."[84] Even after meeting six times, it seemed that, "the parties' only apparent area of agreement is that no real bargaining has yet to occur."[85]

In October 2007, the Writers Guild asked its members for strike authorization, and the producers were claiming that the Guild was just trying to delay negotiations until the current contract expired (at the end of October). As the president of the television producers association said, "We have had six across the table sessions and there was only silence and stonewalling from the WGA leadership. . . . We have attempted to engage on major issues, but no dialogue has been forthcoming from the WGA leadership. . . . The WGA leadership apparently has no intention to bargain in good faith."[86] As evidence, the producers claimed that the WGA negotiating committee left one meeting after less than an hour at the bargaining table.

Both sides knew timing in these negotiations was very important. During the fall and spring, television series production is in full swing. So, a strike now by the writers would have a bigger impact than waiting until, say, the summer to strike. Perhaps not surprisingly, by January 2008 some movement was discernible. In a separate set of negotiations, the Directors Guild of America reached an agreement with the producers that addressed many of the issues that the writers were focusing on, such as how to divide up the new media income.[87] In February 2008, the WGA and producers finally reached agreement. The new contract was "the direct result of renewed negotiations between the two sides, which culminated Friday with a marathon session including top WGA officials and the heads of the Walt Disney Co. and News Corp."[88]

Questions

1. The producers said the WGA was not bargaining in good faith. What did they mean by that, and do you think the evidence is sufficient to support the claim?

2. The WGA did eventually strike. What tactics could the producers have used to fight back once the strike began? What tactics do you think the WGA used?

3. This was basically a conflict between professional and creative people (the WGA) and TV and movie producers. Do you think the conflict was therefore different in any way than are the conflicts between, say, the auto workers or teamsters unions against auto and trucking companies? Why?

4. What role did negotiating skills seem to play in the WGA–producers negotiations? Provide examples.

Carter Cleaning Company: The Grievance

On visiting one of Carter Cleaning Company's stores, Jennifer was surprised to be taken aside by a long-term Carter employee, who met her as she was parking her car. "Murray (the store manager) told me I was suspended for two days without pay because I came in late last Thursday," said George. "I'm really upset, but around here the store manager's word seems to be law, and it sometimes seems like the only way anyone can file a grievance is by meeting you or your father like this in the parking lot." Jennifer was very disturbed by this revelation and promised the employee she would look into it and discuss the situation with her father. In the car heading back to headquarters she began mulling over what Carter Cleaning Company's alternatives might be.

Questions

1. Do you think it is important for Carter Cleaning Company to have a formal grievance process? Why or why not?
2. Based on what you know about the Carter Cleaning Company, outline the steps in what you think would be the ideal grievance process for this company.
3. In addition to the grievance process, can you think of anything else that Carter Cleaning Company might do to make sure that grievances and gripes like this one get expressed and also get heard by top management?

EXPERIENTIAL EXERCISE

An Organizing Question on Campus[89]

Purpose:

The purpose of this exercise is to give you practice in dealing with some of the elements of a union organizing campaign.

Required Understanding:

You should be familiar with the material covered in this chapter, as well as the following incident:

"*An Organizing Question on Campus.*"

Art Tipton is a human resources director of Pierce University, a private university located in a large urban city. Ruth Ann Zimmer, a supervisor in the maintenance and housekeeping services division of the university, has just come into his office to discuss her situation. Zimmer's division of the university is responsible for maintaining and cleaning physical facilities of the university. Zimmer is one of the department supervisors who supervise employees who maintain and clean on-campus dormitories.

In the next several minutes, Zimmer proceeds to express her concerns about a union-organizing campaign that has begun among her employees. According to Zimmer, a representative of the Service Workers Union has met with a number of the employees, urging them to sign union authorization cards. She has observed several of her employees "cornering" other employees to talk to them about joining the union and urge them to sign union authorization (or representation) cards. Zimmer even observed this during the working hours as employees were going about their normal duties in the dormitories. Zimmer says a number of employees have asked her for her opinions about the union. They reported to her that several other supervisors in the

department had told their employees not to sign any union authorization cards and not to talk about the union at any time while they were on campus. Zimmer also reports that one of her fellow supervisors told his employees in a meeting that anyone who was caught talking about the union or signing a union authorization card would be disciplined and perhaps terminated.

Zimmer says that the employees are very dissatisfied with their wages and many of the conditions that they have endured from students, supervisors, and other staff people. She says that several employees told her that they had signed union cards because they believed that the only way university administration would pay attention to their concerns was if the employees had a union to represent them. Zimmer says that she made a list of employees whom she felt had joined or were interested in the union, and she could share these with Tipton if he wanted to deal with them personally. Zimmer closes with the comment that she and other department supervisors need to know what they should do in order to stomp out the threat of unionization in their department.

How to Set Up the Exercise/Instructions:

Divide the class into groups of four or five students. Assume that you are labor relations consultants retained by the college to identify the problems and issues involved and to advise Art Tipton about what to do next. Each group will spend about 45 minutes discussing the issues and outlining those issues as well as an action plan for Tipton. What should he do now?

If time permits, a spokesperson from each group should list on the board the issues involved and the group's recommendations.

ENDNOTES

1. Steven Greenhouse, "Board Accuses Starbucks of Trying to Block Union," *The New York Times* (April 3, 2007): B2.
2. "Union Members Summary," http://www.bls.gov/news.release/union2.nr0.htm, accessed April 26, 2008.
3. Ibid.
4. Joseph Adler, "The Past as Prologue? A Brief History of the Labor Movement in the United States," *International Personnel Management Association for HR* 35, no. 4 (Winter 2006): 311–329.
5. James Bennett and Jason Taylor, "Labor Unions: Victims of Their Political Success?" *Journal of Labor Research* 22, no. 2 (Spring 2001): 261–273. See also Robert Flanagan, "What Do Unions Do? A 25 Year Perspective: Has Management Strangled US Unions?" *Journal of Labor Research* 26, no. 1 (Winter 2005): 33–63.
6. John Addison et al., "The (Parlous) State of German Unions," *Journal Of Labor Research* 28, no. 1 (Winter 2007) 318.
7. Michael Ash and Jean Seago, "The Effect of Registered Nurses' Unions on Heart Attack Mortality," *Industrial and Labor Relations Review* 57, no. 3 (April 2004): 422–442.
8. Steven Abraham et al., "The Impact of Union Membership on Intent to Leave," *Employee Responsibilities and Rights* 17, no. 4 (2005): 21–23.
9. Paul Monies, "Unions Hit Hard by Job Losses, Right to Work," *The Daily Oklahoman* (via Knight Ridder/Tribune Business News) (February 1, 2005).
10. Ann Zimmerman, "Pro-Union Butchers at Wal-Mart Win a Union Battle but Lose War," *Wall Street Journal* (April 11, 2000): A14. See also Steven Greenhouse, "Report Assails Wal-Mart Over Unions," *The New York Times* (May 1, 2007): C3.
11. Donna Buttigieg et al., "An Event History Analysis of Union Joining and Leaving," *Journal of Applied Psychology* 92, no. 3 (2007): 829–839.
12. Ibid., 836. See also Lois Tetrick et al., "A Model of Union Participation: The Impact of Perceived Union Support, Union Instrumentality, and Union Loyalty," *Journal of Applied Psychology* 92, no. 3 (2007): 820–828.
13. Robert Grossman, "Unions Follow Suit," *HR Magazine* (May 2005): 49.
14. Kris Maher, "The New Union Worker," *Wall Street Journal* (September 27, 2005): B1, B11.
15. Arthur Sloane and Fred Whitney, *Labor Relations* (Upper Saddle River, NJ: Prentice Hall, 2007): 335–336.
16. Benjamin Taylor and Fred Witney, *Labor Relations Law*, (Upper Saddle River, NJ: Prentice Hall, 1992): 170–171.
17. www.dol.gov/esa/programs/whd/state/righttowork.htm, accessed January 13, 2008.
18. "Unions Hit Hard by Job Losses, Right to Work," *The Daily Oklahoman* (via Knight Ridder/Tribune Business News) (February 1, 2005). See also www.dol.gov/esa/programs/whd/state/righttowork.htm, accessed January 13, 2008.
19. UNITE (formed earlier by mergers of several unions including the ILGWU and ACTWU clothing trades workers unions) merged in 2004 with HERE (Hotel Employees

& Restaurant Employees) to form UNITE HERE. http://www.unitehere.org/about/history.php, accessed April 26, 2008. Also see, http://www.changetowin.org/about-us.html, accessed April 26, 2008.
20. Steven Greenhouse, "4th Union Quits AFL-CIO in a Dispute over Organizing," *The New York Times* (September 15, 2005): A14. See also, http://www.unitehere.org/about/history.php accessed April 26, 2008.
21. The following material is based on Arthur Sloane and Fred Witney, *Labor Relations* (Upper Saddle River, NJ: Prentice Hall, 2007): 83–132. See also http://history.eserver.org/us-labor-law.txt, accessed April 26, 2008.
22. Ibid., 106.
23. Karen Robinson, "Temp Workers Gain Union Access," *HR News, Society for Human Resource Management* 19, no. 10 (October 2000): 1.
24. See www.nlrb.gov/workplace_rights/nlra_violations.aspx, accessed January 14, 2008.
25. Michael Carrell and Christina Heavrin, *Labor Relations and Collective Bargaining* (Upper Saddle River, NJ: Pearson, 2004): 180.
26. Ibid., 179.
27. Arthur Sloane and Fred Witney, *Labor Relations* (Upper Saddle River, NJ: Prentice Hall, 2007): 102–106.
28. William Fulmer, "Step by Step Through a Union Election," *Harvard Business Review* 60 (July/August 1981): 94–102. For an example of what to expect, see Edward Young and William Levy, "Responding to a Union-Organizing Campaign: Do You and Your Supervisors Know the Legal Boundaries in a Union Campaign?" *Franchising World* 39, no. 3 (March 2007): 45–49.
29. Ibid.
30. John Logan, "New Actors in Industrial Relations—3, the Union Avoidance Industry in the United States," *British Journal of Industrial Relations* 44, no. 4 (December 2006): 651–675.
31. Arthur Sloane and Fred Witney, *Labor Relations* (Upper Saddle River, NJ: Prentice Hall, 2007): 28.
32. Jonathan Segal, "Expose the Union's Underbelly," *HR Magazine* (June 1999): 166–176.
33. "Some Say Salting Leaves Bitter Taste for Employers," *BNA Bulletin to Management* (March 4, 2004): 79; www.nlrb.gov/global/search/index.aspx?mode=s&qt=salting&col=nlrb&gb=y, accessed January 14, 2008.
34. Gary Chaison, "Information Technology: The Threat to Unions," *Journal of Labor Research* 23, no. 2 (Spring 2002): 249–260.
35. www.starbucksunion.org, accessed January 14, 2008.
36. William Fulmer, "Step by Step Through a Union Election," *Harvard Business Review* 60 (July/August 1981): 94.
37. Frederick Sullivan, "Limiting Union Organizing Activity Through Supervisors," *Personnel* 55 (July/August 1978): 55–65. Richard Peterson, Thomas Lee, and Barbara Finnegan, "Strategies and Tactics in Union Organizing Campaigns," *Industrial Relations* 31, no. 2 (Spring 1992): 370–381. See also Edward Young and William Levy,

"Responding to a Union-Organizing Campaign: Do You and Your Supervisors Know the Legal Boundaries in a Union Campaign?" *Franchising World* 39, no. 3 (March 2007): 45–49.

38. Michael Carrell and Christina Heavrin, *Labor Relations and Collective Bargaining* (Upper Saddle River, NJ: Pearson, 2004): 166.

39. Ibid., 167–168.

40. Doug Cahn, "Reebok Takes the Sweat Out of Sweatshops," *Business Ethics* 14, no. 1 (January 2000): 9; Mei Fong and Kris Maher, "U.S. Labor Chief Moves into China," *Wall Street Journal Asia* (June 22–24, 2007): 1.

41. Op. cit.

42. B&D Plastics, Inc. 302 NLRB No. 33, 1971, 137 LRRM 1039; discussed in "No Such Thing as a Free Lunch," *BNA Bulletin to Management* (May 23, 1991): 153–154.

43. Edwin Arnold et al., "Determinants of Certification Election Outcomes in the Service Sector," *Labor Studies Journal* 25, no. 3 (Fall 2000): 51.

44. Clyde Scott and Edwin Arnold, "Deauthorization and Decertification Elections: An Analysis and Comparison of Results," *Working USA* 7, no. 3 (Winter 2003): 6–20; www.nlrb.gov/nlrb/shared_files/brochures/ rpt_september2002.pdf, accessed January 14, 2008.

45. Michael Carrell and Christina Heavrin, *Labor Relations and Collective Bargaining* (Upper Saddle River, NJ: Pearson, 2004): 120–121.

46. www.nlrb.gov/nlrb/shared_files/brochures/basicguide.pdf, accessed January 14, 2008.

47. Terry Leap, *Collective Bargaining and Labor Relations* (Upper Saddle River, NJ: Prentice Hall, 1995). See also www.nlrb.gov/nlrb/shared_files/brochures/basicguide.pdf, accessed January 14, 2008.

48. Leap, op. cit., 307–309.

49. Ibid., 308.

50. Kathryn Tyler, "Good-Faith Bargaining," *HR Magazine* (January 2005): 52.

51. These are based on James C Freund *Smart Negotiating* (New York: Simon & Schuster, 1992): 42–46.

52. Ibid., 33.

53. James Sebenius, "Six Habits of Merely Effective Negotiators," *Harvard Business Review* (April 2001): 87–95.

54. Bargaining items based on Reed Richardson, *Collective Bargaining by Objectives* (Upper Saddle River, NJ: Prentice Hall, 1997): 113–115; see also Arthur Sloane and Fred Witney, *Labor Relations* (Upper Saddle River, NJ: Prentice Hall, 2007): 180–217.

55. Sloane and Witney, *Labor Relations,* 192–220.

56. "The Road to Impasse," *CBS Sports Online* (March 4, 2005), www.CDC.com/sports.

57. Monica Roman, "Southwest Air's Family Feud," *Business Week* (July 15, 2002): 48.

58. John Burger and Steven Walters, "Arbitrator Bias and Self-Interest: Lessons from the Baseball Labor Market," *Journal of Labor Research* 26, no. 2 (Spring 2005): 267–280.

59. http://fmcs.gov/assets/files/annual%20reports/ FY2006_Annual_Report.pdf, accessed January 14, 2008.

60. Jonathan Kramer and Thomas Hyclak, "Why Strikes Occur: Evidence from the Capital Markets," *Industrial Relations* 41, no. 1 (January 2002): 80–93.

61. Micheline Maynard and Jeremey Peters, "Northwest Airlines Threatens to Replace Strikers Permanently," *The New York Times* (August 26, 2005): C3.

62. Melanie Evans, "Labor Pains: As Membership Slides, Unions Have Turned to Provocative Corporate Campaigns," *Modern Health Care* 34, no. 26 (December 6, 2004): 26.

63. Arthur Sloane and Fred Witney, *Labor Relations* (Upper Saddle River, NJ: Prentice Hall, 2007): 84.

64. Duncan Adams, "Worker Grievances Consume Roanoke, VA, Mail Distribution Center," Knight-Ridder/Tribune Business News (March 27, 2001), item 1086009.

65. Walter Baer, *Grievance Handling: 101 Guides for Supervisors* (New York: American Management Association, 1970).

66. See, for example, "Top Ten Practical Tips to Achieving the Best Result through Timely Dispute Resolution," *Mondaq Business Briefing* (October 15, 2007).

67. "Ongoing Problem of Dispute Resolution," 117 *Personnel Today* (November 13, 2007).

68. Steven Robbins, *Organizational Behavior* (Upper Saddle River, NJ: Prentice Hall, 1998).

69. Ibid., 294.

70. The following is adapted from Eileen Aranda et al., *Teams: Structure, Process, Culture, and Politics* (Upper Saddle River, NJ: Prentice Hall, 1998): 116–117.

71. Jeffrey McCracken, "Desperate to Cut Costs, Ford Gets Union's Help," *Wall Street Journal* (March 2, 2007): A1, A9.

72. See, for example, Jo Blandon et al., "Have Unions Turned the Corner? New Evidence on Recent Trends in Union Recognition in UK Firms," *British Journal of Industrial Relations* 44, no. 2 (June 2006): 169–190.

73. Jennifer Schramm, "The Future of Unions," *Society for Human Resource Management, Workplace Visions* 4 (2005): 1–8.

74. Ibid.

75. "The Limits of Solidarity," *The Economist* (September 23, 2006): 34.

76. "Unions Using Class Actions to Pressure Nonunion Companies," *BNA Bulletin to Management* (August 22, 2006): 271.

77. Dean Scott, "Unions Still a Potent Force," *Kiplinger Business Forecasts* (March 26, 2003).

78. Andy Meisler "Who Will Fold First?" *Workforce Management* (January 2004): 28–38.

79. "Contracts Call for Greater Labor Management Teamwork," *BNA Bulletin to Management* (April 29, 1999): 133.

80. Jennifer Schramm, "The Future of Unions," *Society for Human Resource Management, Workplace Visions* 4 (2005): 6.

81. Mei Fong and Kris Maher, "US Labor Chief Moves into China," *Wall Street Journal Asia* (June 22–24, 2007): 1.

82. Chris Purcell, "Rhetoric Flying in WGA Talks," *Television Week* 26, no. 30 (July 23–30, 2007): 3, 35.

83. Ibid.

84. Ibid.

85. James Hibberd, "Guild Talks Break with No Progress," *Television Week* 26, no. 38 (October 8–15, 2007): 1, 30.

86. Ibid.

87. "DGA Deal Sets the Stage for Writers," *Television Week* 27 no. 3 (Jan 21, 2008): 3, 33.

88. "WGA, Studios Reach Tentative Agreement," *UPI News Track* (February 3, 2008).

89. Raymond L. Hilgert and Cyril C. Ling, *Cases and Experiential Exercises in Human Resource Management* (Upper Saddle River, NJ: Prentice Hall, 1996): 291–292.

Improving Occupational Safety, Health, and Security

11

When you finish studying this chapter, you should be able to:

1. *Discuss OSHA and how it operates.*

2. *Explain in detail three basic causes of accidents.*

3. *Explain how to prevent accidents at work.*

4. *Discuss major health problems at work and how to remedy them.*

Introduction

New York's energy utility "Con Ed" (Consolidated Edison) brings electric, gas, and steam to more than 3 million homes and businesses, and so reliability has always been a main concern. For over 180 years, its strategic mission was to "Get the lights back on fast." Con Ed's employees had a "can do" attitude. Unfortunately, that meant they sometimes ignored safety for the sake of getting outages fixed fast.

That changed recently. An explosion near New York City's Grand Central Station in July 2007 killed one person and injured several others. Some feared the explosion may have contaminated surrounding areas with asbestos. Con Ed accepted the blame, and reemphasized its new safety strategy, "Get the lights back on fast—but, first do it safely." Now it had to implement that new safety-conscious strategy throughout the firm. ■

EMPLOYEE SAFETY AND HEALTH: AN INTRODUCTION

Why Employee Safety and Health Are Important

Providing a safe work environment is important for several reasons, one of which is the staggering number of work-related accidents. For example, in one recent year, about 5,000 U.S. workers died in workplace incidents. The U.S. Department of Labor reports that over 3.8 million occupational injuries and illnesses result from accidents at work—roughly 4.4 cases per 100 full-time workers in the United States per year.[1] And these figures may underestimate (due to underreporting employers) the actual numbers by two or three times.[2]

Accidents are also expensive. For example, the health care costs of a forklift accident might be $4,500. However, the indirect costs for things like forklift damage and lost production time could raise the bill to $18,000 or more.[3] And the cost to the worker and his or her family in physical and psychological terms may be many times greater.

Dangerous workplaces aren't limited to manufacturing plants. For example, knives, hot surfaces, congestion, and slippery floors bedevil commercial kitchens. In restaurants, slips and falls account for about a third of all worker injury cases. Employers could eliminate most of these by requiring slip-resistant shoes.[4]

● Discuss OSHA and how it operates.

A Manager's Briefing on Occupational Law

Occupational Safety and Health Act of 1970

The law passed by Congress in 1970 "to assure so far as possible every working man and woman in the nation safe and healthful working conditions and to preserve our human resources."

Occupational Safety and Health Administration (OSHA)

The agency created within the Department of Labor to set safety and health standards for almost all workers in the United States.

The U.S. Congress passed the **Occupational Safety and Health Act of 1970**[5] "to assure so far as possible every working man and woman in the nation safe and healthful working conditions and to preserve our human resources." The act covers most employers. The main employers it doesn't cover are self-employed persons, farms employing only the employer's immediate family members, and certain workplaces already protected by other federal agencies or statutes. The act covers federal agencies. It usually doesn't apply to state and local governments in their role as employers.

The act created the **Occupational Safety and Health Administration (OSHA)** within the Department of Labor. OSHA's basic purpose is to administer the act and to set and enforce the safety and health standards that apply to almost all workers in the United States. Recently, OSHA had about 2,150 employees, including 1,100 inspectors working from branch offices throughout the country to ensure compliance.[6] With a limited number of inspectors, OSHA most recently has focused on fair and effective enforcement, combined with outreach, education, and compliance assistance, and various OSHA-employer cooperative programs.[7]

OSHA STANDARDS OSHA operates under the "general duty clause," that each employer:

> shall furnish to each of his [or her] employees employment and a place of employment which are free from recognized hazards that are causing or are likely to cause death or serious physical harm to his [or her] employees.

To carry out this basic mission, OSHA is responsible for promulgating legally enforceable standards. The standards are very complete and cover just about every

FIGURE 11.1

OSHA Standards Examples

Source: www.osha.gov/pls/ oshaweb/owadisp.show_document? p_id=9720&p_table=STANDARDS, accessed May 25, 2007.

> Guardrails not less than 2"× 4" or the equivalent and not less than 36" or more than 42" high, with a midrail, when required, of a 1" × 4" lumber or equivalent, and toeboards, shall be installed at all open sides on all scaffolds more than 10 feet above the ground or floor. Toeboards shall be a minimum of 4" in height. Wire mesh shall be installed in accordance with paragraph [a] [17] of this section.

conceivable hazard, in detail. Figure 11.1 shows a small part of the standard governing handrails for scaffolds.

OSHA RECORD-KEEPING PROCEDURES Under OSHA, employers with 11 or more employees must maintain a record of, and report, occupational injuries and occupational illnesses. An *occupational illness* is any abnormal condition or disorder caused by exposure to environmental factors associated with employment. This includes acute and chronic illnesses caused by inhalation, absorption, ingestion, or direct contact with toxic substances or harmful agents.

As summarized in Figure 11.2, employers must report all occupational illnesses.[8] They must also report most occupational injuries, specifically those that result in medical treatment (other than first aid), loss of consciousness, restriction of work (1 or more lost workdays), restriction of motion, or transfer to another job.[9] If an on-the-job accident results in the death of an employee or in the hospitalization of five or more employees, all employers, regardless of size, must report the accident in detail to the nearest OSHA office.

OSHA's latest record-keeping rules streamline the job of reporting occupational injuries or illnesses. The rules continue to presume that an injury or work illness that resulted from an event in or exposure to the work environment is work related. However, it allows the employer to conclude that the event was not job related (and needn't be

FIGURE 11.2

What Accidents Must Be Reported under the Occupational Safety and Health Act (OSHA)?

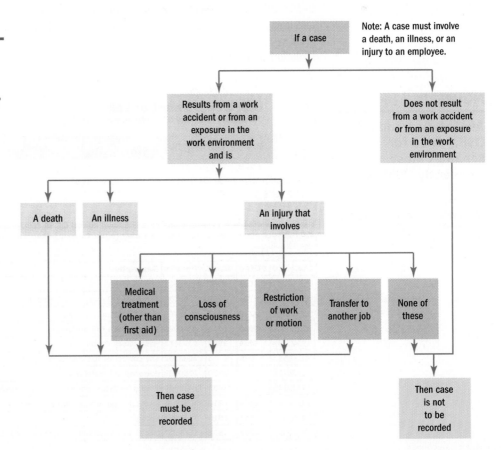

reported) if the facts so warrant—such as if a worker breaks a wrist after catching his leg on his car's bumper when parked on the company lot.

INSPECTIONS AND CITATIONS   OSHA enforces its standards through inspections and (if necessary) citations. However, OSHA may not conduct warrantless inspections without an employer's consent.

VOLUNTARY CONSULTATION   With only about 1,000 inspectors, OSHA has tried to encourage cooperative safety programs rather than rely just on inspections and citations. So, for example, OSHA provides free on-site safety and health services for small businesses. This service uses safety experts from state governments to provide safety consultations, usually at the employer's workplace. According to OSHA, this consultation program is separate from the OSHA inspection effort, and no citations are issued or penalties proposed.

The employer triggers this consultative process by requesting a voluntary consultation. When Jan Anderson, president of her own steel installation company in Colorado, realized her workers' compensation costs were higher than her payroll, she joined with similar Colorado firms for help. At the group's request, OSHA helped draft new safety systems, created educational materials, and provided inspections that were more cooperative than adversarial. As a result, says Anderson, "Our workers' compensation costs have decreased significantly, we have had no accidents, and there is an awareness that we take safety seriously."[10]

INSPECTION PRIORITIES   Such efforts notwithstanding, OSHA still makes extensive use of inspections. OSHA takes a "worst-first" approach in setting inspection priorities. Priorities include, from highest to lowest, imminent danger, catastrophes and fatal accidents, employee complaints, programmed inspections (of high-hazard industries), and follow-up inspections.[11] In one recent year, OSHA conducted just over 39,000 inspections. Of these, 9,176 were prompted by complaints or accidents, 21,576 were high-hazard targeted, and 8,415 were prompted by follow-ups and referrals.[12]

THE INSPECTION   OSHA inspectors look for violations of all types, but some potential problem areas—such as scaffolding, fall protection, and inadequate hazard communications—grab more of their attention. Figure 11.3 summarizes the 10 most frequent OSHA serious violation areas.[13]

FIGURE 11.3

Ten Safety Standards OSHA Cited for Penalties Most Frequently, 2005–2006

Source: www.osha.gov/pls/imis/ citedstandard.sic?p_esize=&p_state= FEFederal&p_sic=all, accessed May 26, 2007.

U.S. Department of Labor
Occupational Safety & Health Administration

www.osha.gov   MyOSHA   Search [ ] GO **Advanced Search** | **A-Z Index**

Standards Cited for SIC ALL; All sizes; Federal

ALL *SIC Codes*

Listed below are the standards which were cited by **Federal OSHA** for the specified SIC during the period October 2005 through September 2006. Penalties shown reflect current rather than initial amounts. For more information, see definitions.

Standard	#Cited	#Insp	$Penalty	Description
Total	111529	28183	89370521	
19260451	9774	3756	10369193	Scaffolds—General requirements.
19101200	7124	3627	1546760	Hazard Communication.
19260501	6886	6134	8346946	Duty to have fall protection.
19100134	4654	1922	1393672	Respiratory Protection.
19100147	3976	2115	3763302	The control of hazardous energy (lockout/tagout).
19100178	3183	2130	2050999	Powered industrial trucks.
19100305	3028	1863	1433020	Wiring methods, components, and equipment for general use.
19100212	2866	2310	4031408	General requirements for all machines.
19261053	2541	1910	1329484	Ladders.
19100303	2267	1692	1181507	Electrical equipment installation—General requirements.

citations
Summons informing employers and employees of the regulations and standards that have been violated in the workplace.

After the inspector submits the report to the local OSHA office, the area director determines what citations, if any, to issue. The **citations** inform the employer and employees of the regulations and standards that have been violated and of the time set for rectifying the problem.

PENALTIES OSHA can also impose penalties. In general, OSHA calculates these based on the violation's gravity, but it also usually considers factors like the size of the business, the firm's compliance history, and the employer's good faith. Penalties generally range from $5,000 up to $70,000 for willful or repeat serious violations, although they can be far higher (occasionally, in the millions). The OSHA Area Director is authorized to enter into settlement agreements that revise citations and penalties to avoid prolonged legal disputes. Therefore many cases are settled before litigation. OSHA then issues the citation and agreed-on penalties simultaneously, after the employers initiate negotiation settlements.[14]

In practice, OSHA must have a final order from the independent Occupational Safety and Health Review Commission (OSHRC) to enforce a penalty. Although that appeals process is quicker now than in the past, an employer who files a notice of contest can still drag out an appeal for years.

Inspectors and their superiors don't look just for specific hazards but also for a comprehensive safety approach. For example, factors contributing to a firm's OSHA liability include lack of a systematic safety approach; sporadic or irregular safety meetings; a lack of responsiveness to safety audit recommendations; not following up on employee safety complaints; and failure to regularly inspect the workplace, for instance, through employer walk-throughs and self-inspections.[15]

Some employers understandably view OSHA inspections with some trepidation. However, the inspection tips in Figure 11.4—such as "check the inspector's

FIGURE 11.4

OSHA Inspection Tips

Initial Contact
- Refer the inspector to your OSHA coordinator.
- Check the inspector's credentials.
- Ask the inspector why he or she is inspecting your workplace. Is it a complaint? Programmed visit? Fatality or accident follow-up? Imminent danger investigation?
- If the inspection is the result of a complaint, the inspector won't identify the complainant, but you are entitled to know whether the person is a current employee.
- Notify your OSHA counsel, who should review all requests from the inspector for documents and information. Your counsel also should review the documents and information you provide to the inspector.

Opening Conference
- Establish the focus and scope of the planned inspection: Does the inspector want to inspect the premises or simply study your records?
- Discuss the procedures for protecting trade-secret areas, conducting employee interviews, and producing documents.
- Show the inspector that you have safety programs in place. He or she may not go to the work floor if paperwork is complete and up-to-date.

Walk-Around Inspection
- Accompany the inspector and take detailed notes.
- If the inspector takes a photo or video, you should too.
- Ask the inspector for duplicates of all physical samples and copies of all test results.
- Be helpful and cooperative, but don't volunteer information.
- To the extent possible, immediately correct any violation the inspector identifies.

credentials" and "accompany the inspector and take detailed notes"—can help ensure a smooth inspection.[16]

RESPONSIBILITIES AND RIGHTS OF EMPLOYERS AND EMPLOYEES Both employers and employees have responsibilities and rights under the Occupational Safety and Health Act. For example, employers are responsible for providing "a workplace free from recognized hazards," for being familiar with mandatory OSHA standards, and for examining workplace conditions to make sure they conform with applicable standards.

Employees also have rights and responsibilities, but OSHA can't cite them for violations of their responsibilities. They are responsible, for example, for complying with all applicable OSHA standards, for following all employer safety and health rules and regulations, and for reporting hazardous conditions to the supervisor. Employees have a right to demand safety and health on the job without fear of punishment. Employers are forbidden to punish or discriminate against workers who complain to OSHA about job safety and health hazards. However, employers must make "a diligent effort to discourage, by discipline if necessary, violations of safety rules by employees."[17]

WHAT CAUSES ACCIDENTS?

❷ Explain in detail three basic causes of accidents.

Accidents occur for three main reasons: chance occurrences, unsafe working conditions, and unsafe acts by employees. Chance occurrences (such as walking past a window just as someone throws a rock through it) contribute to accidents but are more or less beyond management's control; we will therefore focus on unsafe conditions and unsafe acts.

Unsafe Working Conditions

unsafe conditions
The mechanical and physical conditions that cause accidents.

Unsafe conditions are one main cause of accidents. These include obvious factors such as:

- Faulty scaffolds
- Improperly guarded equipment
- Frayed wiring
- Unsafe storage, such as overloading
- Improper illumination, such as insufficient light
- Improper ventilation, such as insufficient air change

The basic remedy here is to eliminate or minimize the unsafe conditions. OSHA standards address potentially accident-causing mechanical and physical working conditions like these. The manager can also use a checklist of unsafe conditions, as in the *HR in Practice* feature that follows. The *Occupational Hazards* magazine Web site (http://occupationalhazards.com) is another good source for safety, health, and industrial hygiene information. *HR in Practice* summarizes typical unsafe conditions.

Although accidents can occur anywhere, there are some high-danger zones. Many industrial accidents occur around forklift trucks, wheelbarrows, and other handling and lifting areas. The most serious accidents usually occur near metal and woodworking machines and saws, or around transmission machinery such as gears, pulleys, and flywheels.

HR in Practice

Checklist of Mechanical or Physical Accident-Causing Conditions[18]

I. GENERAL HOUSEKEEPING

Adequate and wide aisles—no materials protruding into aisles

Parts and tools stored safely after use—not left in hazardous positions that could cause them to fall

Even and solid flooring—no defective floors or ramps that could cause falling or tripping accidents

Waste and trash cans—safely located and not overfilled

Material piled in safe manner—not too high or too close to sprinkler heads

All work areas clean and dry

All exit doors and aisles clean of obstructions

Aisles kept clear and properly marked; no air lines or electric cords across aisles

II. MATERIAL HANDLING EQUIPMENT AND CONVEYANCES

On all conveyances, electric or hand, check to see that the following items are all in sound working condition:

Brakes—properly adjusted

Not too much play in steering wheel

Warning device—in place and working

Wheels—securely in place; properly inflated

Fuel and oil—enough and right kind

No loose parts

Cables, hooks, or chains—not worn or otherwise defective

Suspended chains or hooks

Safety loaded

Properly stored

III. LADDERS, SCAFFOLDS, BENCHES, STAIRWAYS, ETC.

The following items of major interest to be checked:

Safety feet on straight ladders

Guardrails or handrails

Treads, not slippery

No splintered, cracked, or rickety stairs

Ladders properly stored

Extension ladder ropes in good condition

Toeboards

IV. POWER TOOLS (STATIONARY)

Point of operation guarded

Guards in proper adjustment

Gears, belts, shafting, counterweights guarded

Foot pedals guarded

Brushes provided for cleaning machines

Adequate lighting

Properly grounded

Tool or material rests properly adjusted

Adequate work space around machines

Control switch easily accessible

Safety glasses worn

Gloves worn by persons handling rough or sharp materials

No gloves or loose clothing worn by persons operating machines

V. HAND TOOLS AND MISCELLANEOUS

In good condition—not cracked, worn, or otherwise defective

Properly stored

Correct for job

Goggles, respirators, and other personal protective equipment worn where necessary

VI. SPRAY PAINTING

Explosion-proof electrical equipment

Proper storage of paints and thinners in approved metal cabinets

Fire extinguishers adequate and suitable; readily accessible

Minimum storage in work area

VII. FIRE EXTINGUISHERS

Properly serviced and tagged

Readily accessible

Adequate and suitable for operations involved

SAFETY CLIMATE Not all working condition–related causes of accidents are as obvious as faulty scaffolds. Sometimes the workplace suffers from a toxic "safety climate," in other words from a set of mostly psychological factors that set the stage for employees to act unsafely. For example, one early study focused on the fatal accidents suffered by offshore British oil workers in the North Sea.[19] Employees who are under stress, a strong pressure to quickly complete the work, and, generally, a poor safety climate—for instance, supervisors who never mention safety—were some of the not-so-obvious working conditions that set the stage for oil rig accidents.

EXAMPLE The participants in another safety climate study were 1,127 nurses working in 42 large U.S. hospitals. The researchers measured safety climate with items like "job duties on this unit often prevent nurses from acting as safely as they would like" and "the nurse manager on this unit emphasizes safety." The results revealed that "safety climate predicted medication errors, nurse back injuries, urinary tract infections, [and] patient satisfaction."[20]

OTHER WORKING CONDITION FACTORS Work schedules and fatigue also affect accident rates. Accident rates usually don't increase too noticeably during the first 5 or 6 hours of the workday, but after 6 hours, the accident rate accelerates. This is due partly to fatigue and partly to the fact that accidents occur more often during night shifts.

Accidents also occur more frequently in plants with a high seasonal layoff rate and where there is hostility among employees, garnished wages, and blighted living conditions. Temporary stress factors such as high workplace temperature, poor illumination, and a congested workplace are also related to accident rates.

Unsafe Acts

unsafe acts
Behaviors that potentially cause accidents.

In practice, it's impossible to eliminate accidents just by reducing unsafe conditions. People usually cause accidents, and no one has a surefire way to eliminate **unsafe acts** such as:

- Throwing materials
- Operating or working at unsafe speeds—either too fast or too slow
- Making safety devices inoperative by removing, adjusting, or disconnecting them
- Lifting improperly[21]

There is no one explanation for why an employee may behave in an unsafe manner. Sometimes, as noted, the working conditions may set the stage for unsafe acts. For instance, the stressed-out oil rig employees may behave in an unsafe manner even if they know better. Sometimes, employees aren't adequately trained in safe work methods; some companies don't supply employees with the right safe procedures, and employees may simply develop their own (often bad) work habits. However, it's often the employee's attitudes, personality, or skills that account for the bad behavior.

WHAT TRAITS CHARACTERIZE "ACCIDENT-PRONE" PEOPLE? Unsafe acts can undo even the best attempts to reduce unsafe conditions. The problem is that there are no easy answers to the question of what causes people to act recklessly.

It may seem intuitively obvious that some people are simply accident prone, but the research is mixed.[22] On closer inspection some apparently accident-prone people ("accident repeaters") were just unlucky, or may have been more meticulous about reporting their accidents.[23] However, there is evidence that people with specific traits may indeed be accident prone. For example, people who are impulsive, sensation seeking, extremely extroverted, and less conscientious (in terms of being less fastidious and dependable) are more likely to have accidents.[24]

Furthermore, the person who is accident prone on one job may not be so on a different job. Driving is one familiar example. Personality traits that correlate with filing vehicular insurance claims include *entitlement* ("bad drivers think there's no reason they should not speed or run lights"), *impatience* ("drivers with high claim frequency were 'always in

*People usually cause accidents, and no one has a surefire way to eliminate an **unsafe act.***

a hurry' ''), *aggressiveness* ("always the first to want to move when the red light turns green"), and *distractibility* ("easily and frequently distracted by cell phones, eating, drinking, and so on"). A study in Thailand similarly found that drivers who are naturally *competitive* and prone to *anger* are particularly risky drivers.[25]

HOW TO PREVENT ACCIDENTS

Following an accident in which four workers lost their lives, managers at the Golden Eagle refinery east of San Francisco Bay shut down the facility for four months and retrained all employees in safety methods. Then they turned to other remedies.[26] In practice, we've seen that accident causes tend to be multifaceted, so employers must take a multifaceted approach to preventing them.

Reduce Unsafe Conditions

Explain how to prevent accidents at work.

You're repairing a lamp that you think is unplugged and then learn, with a shock, that it is plugged in. Lockout/tagout aims to avoid such situations. *Lockout/tagout* is a formal procedure to disable equipment, so as to avoid unexpected releases of electrical or other energy. It involves affixing a "disabled" tag to the equipment.[27]

Reducing unsafe conditions is always an employer's first line of defense in accident prevention. Safety engineers should design jobs so as to remove or reduce physical hazards. Sometimes (as with the lamp) the solution is clear. For example, slippery floors in commercial kitchens often cause slips and falls. Employers work with safety engineers to "engineer out" potentially hazardous conditions like these, for instance, by placing non-slip mats in kitchens, or guardrails around moving machines. OSHA standards list the guidelines here.

Once this is done, management can make available *personal protective equipment (PPE)*, like safety hats and shoes. This is important. For example, the organization Prevent Blindness America estimates that more than 700,000 Americans injure their eyes at work each year, and that employers could avoid 90% of these injuries with safety eyewear.[28]

Reducing Unsafe Acts

While reducing unsafe conditions is the first line of defense, human misbehavior can short circuit even the best safety efforts. Sometimes the misbehavior, like horsing around, is intentional, but often it's not. For example, distractions—whether from cell phones or glancing back to check on a child—contribute to at least half of all car accidents. At work, not noticing moving or stationary objects or that a floor is wet often causes accidents.[29] And, ironically, "making a job safer with machine guards or PPE lowers people's risk perceptions and thus can lead to an increase in at-risk behavior."[30]

Unfortunately, just telling employees to "pay attention" is usually not enough. Instead, it requires a process. First, identify and try to eliminate potential risks, such as unguarded equipment. Next, reduce potential distractions, such as noise, heat, and stress. Then, carefully screen and train employees, as we explain next.

Use Screening to Reduce Unsafe Acts

Accidents are similar to other types of poor performance, and psychologists have had success in screening out individuals who might be accident prone for some specific job. The basic technique is to identify the human trait (such as visual skill) that might relate to accidents on the specific job. Then determine whether scores on this trait predict accidents on the job.

Again, driving is an example. Thus screening prospective delivery drivers for traits like impatience and aggressiveness might be sensible.[31]

Use Posters and Other Propaganda

Propaganda such as safety posters can also help reduce unsafe acts. In an early study, their use apparently increased safe behavior by more than 20%.[32] However, employers should combine the safety poster with other techniques, such as screening and training, to reduce unsafe conditions and acts.

Provide Safety Training

Safety training is especially important with new employees. It's essential to instruct them in safe practices and procedures, warn them of potential hazards, and work on developing their predisposition toward safety. Delta Air Lines tells supervisors to use personal anecdotes to motivate employees to wear hearing protection. For example, "a lot of the old-timers have terrible stories and terrible hearing, because whatever they did in their past jobs—whether they worked here or somewhere else—they didn't wear hearing protection."[33]

OSHA provides free on-site safety and health services for small businesses. This service uses safety experts from state governments, and provides consultations, usually at the employer's workplace. Employers can contact their nearest OSHA Area Office to speak to the compliance assistance specialist. They can also check the OSHA Training Institute training available at one of OSHA's 20 or so education centers located at U.S. colleges and universities.

Improving Productivity Through HRIS: Internet-Based Safety Improvement Solutions

Employers also use the Web to support their safety training. For example, PureSafety (www.puresafety.com) enables firms to create their own training Web sites, complete with a "message from the safety director." Once an employer installs the PureSafety Web site, it can populate the site with courses from companies that supply health and safety courses via PureSafety.com. The courses are available in various formats, including digital versions of videotape training and PowerPoint presentations. PureSafety.com also develops or modifies existing courses for employers.

Similarly, in the United Kingdom, Web sites like the U.K. Safety Network provide a listing of companies that offer a range of online health and safety training.

Use Incentives and Positive Reinforcement

Some firms award employees incentives like cash bonuses if safety goals are met. Safety incentives needn't be complicated. One organization uses a suggestion box. Employees make suggestions for improvements regarding unsafe acts or conditions. The employer follows up on all suggestions, the best of which result in gift certificates.[34] Management at San Francisco's Golden Eagle refinery instituted a safety incentive plan. Employees earn "WINGS" points for engaging in one or more of 28 safety activities, such as conducting safety meetings and taking emergency response training. Employees can earn up to $20 per month per person by accumulating points.[35]

THREE CAVEATS Some contend that safety incentive programs can, in some instances, do more harm than good. With respect to safety incentives, keep three potential drawbacks in mind.

First, such programs cannot replace comprehensive safety programs: "All other pieces/parts of a comprehensive safety program need to be in place," says one expert.[36]

Second, OSHA argued that such plans don't actually cut down on injuries or illnesses but only on injury and illness *reporting*.[37]

Third, such programs aim to produce, through reinforcement, habitual safe behavior. But safety experts caution against this. Habitual behavior occurs without thinking. When it comes to safety, employers want employees paying attention to what they're doing.[38]

One option is to emphasize nontraditional reinforcement.[39] For example, give employees recognition awards for attending safety meetings, or for demonstrating their safety proficiency.[40] The accompanying *Personal Competencies* feature shows how managers motivate employees to perform more safely.

Personal Competencies

Applying Your *Motivational* Skills

As we explained in chapter 7, goal-setting is a powerful motivation technique. People are generally highly motivated to pursue goals that they deem reasonable and acceptable. In a nutshell, that means:

1. Employees who get *specific goals* usually perform better than those who do not.
2. Put goals in *quantitative terms and include target dates* or deadlines.
3. Goals should be *challenging*, but not so difficult that they appear impossible or unrealistic

At work many employers successfully apply these concepts with *positive reinforcement programs*. For example, provide workers with safety goals, and with positive feedback on how they're doing. The feedback is usually in the form of graphical performance reports and supervisory support.

EXAMPLE   Researchers introduced one such program in a wholesale bakery.[41] The researchers set and communicated a reasonable safety goal (in terms of observed incidents performed safely). Next, employees participated in a 30-minute training session by viewing pairs of slides depicting scenes that the researchers staged in the plant. One slide showed the supervisor climbing over a conveyor; the parallel slide showed him walking around the conveyor. After viewing an unsafe act, employees had to describe "what's unsafe here?" Then, the researchers demonstrated the same incident again but performed in a safe manner, and explicitly stated the safe-conduct rule ("go around, not over or under, conveyors").

At the conclusion of training, supervisors showed employees a graph with their pretraining safety record (in terms of observed incidents performed safely) plotted. Supervisors then encouraged workers to consider increasing their performance to the new safety goal for their own protection, to decrease costs, and to help the plant get out of its last place in safety ranking. Then the researchers posted the graph and a list of safety rules.

Whenever observers walked through the plant collecting safety data, they posted on the graph the percentage of incidents they had seen the group as a whole perform safely. Workers could compare their current safety performance with both their previous performance and their assigned goal. This gave the workers positive feedback. In addition, supervisors praised workers when they performed safely. Safety in the plant subsequently improved markedly.

Emphasize Top-Management Commitment

Safety programs require a strong and obvious management commitment to safety. Here's an example:

> One of the best examples I know of in setting the highest possible priority for safety takes place at a DuPont Plant in Germany. Each morning at the DuPont Polyester and Nylon Plant the director and his assistants meet at 8:45 to review the past 24 hours. The first matter they discuss is not production, but safety. Only after they have examined reports of accidents and near misses and satisfied themselves that corrective action has been taken do they move on to look at output, quality, and cost matters.[42]

As another example of top management commitment to safety, Weyerhaeuser discharged the plant manager and safety manager at its West Virginia facility. Weyerhaeuser alleged they failed to report numerous injuries and illnesses at the plant.[43]

CON ED EXAMPLE   Safety is a problem in a large, complex utility like Con Ed, many of whose facilities go back 60 years or more.

Injecting a "safety first" mentality into all Con Ed's operations after its recent accident involved many human resource management activities. For example, Con Ed recruited and trained new people for its environmental health and safety staff. Con Ed also created thousands of pages of new policies and procedures that translate federal, state, and local environmental regulations into operating procedures its employees can actually use. Con Ed's experience shows how top management can use specific human resources strategies and practices to support its safety strategy.

The accompanying *Business in Action* feature provides another example of what "top management safety commitment" means.

Business in Action — Building Your *General Management* Knowledge

It's traditional to distinguish between two types of managers, *general managers* and *departmental or functional managers*. Plant managers, safety managers, sales managers, and human resource managers are departmental or functional managers—they focus on relatively specialized tasks and activities.

General managers are a different breed. Whether they're army "general officers," university presidents, or Vodafone's CEO, the general manager is always the person with overall responsibility for the entire organization (including all those departmental/functional managers).

When safety experts say that employee safety requires "top management" commitment, you might assume they mean the plant manager or department manager. But in fact, safety experts are very explicit: it's the company's *top manager*—usually, the CEO or president—that they mean. He or she must ensure that the whole company and chain of command commits to safety. The subordinate departmental managers then just follow the top manager's lead.

BP TEXAS CITY   An explosion several years ago at British Petroleum's (BP) Texas City, Texas, refinery shows why safety must start with the CEO (general manager). The explosion and fire killed 15 people and injured 500. It was the worst U.S. industrial accident in more than 10 years. The disaster triggered three investigations.

As one example of the investigators' conclusions, the Chemical Safety Board found that "BP's global management was aware of problems with maintenance, spending, and infrastructure well before March 2005." Apparently, faced with numerous earlier accidents, BP did make some safety improvements. However, it focused mostly on emphasizing personal employee safety behaviors and procedural compliance. The problem was that plantwide safety problems like "unsafe and antiquated equipment designs" remained.

To put the results of the three investigations into context, under its then-current top management BP seems to have been, for at least 10 years, more obviously committed to cost cutting and profits than to safety. The basic conclusion of the investigations was that cost-cutting helped compromise safety at Texas City. For several reasons, possibly including the Texas City explosion, BP's CEO stepped down soon after the investigators submitted their conclusions.

Foster a Culture of Safety

To foster the values inherent in a safety-conscious workplace culture, all managers must show by their actions that safety is important. One study measured safety culture in terms of questions like "my supervisor says a good word whenever he sees the job done according to the safety rules" and "my supervisor approaches workers during work to discuss safety issues." The workers here developed consistent perceptions concerning their supervisors' safety commitment. In turn, these workers' perceptions of the plant's safety culture apparently influenced the workers' safety behavior in the months following the survey.[44]

According to one safety expert, a facility with a safety-oriented culture exhibits:

1. *Teamwork*, in the form of management and employees both involved in safety;
2. Highly visible and interactive *communication and collaboration* on safety matters;
3. A *shared vision* of safety excellence (specifically, an overriding attitude that all accidents and injuries are preventable);
4. *Assignment* of critical safety functions to specific individuals or teams; and,
5. A *continuous effort* toward identifying and correcting workplace safety problems and hazards.[45]

Establish a Safety Policy

The company's written safety policy should emphasize that accident prevention is of the utmost importance at your firm, and that your firm will do everything practical to eliminate or reduce accidents and injuries. Figure 11.5 shows a sample policy.

FIGURE 11.5

Sample Safety Policy

Source: Employment Law Information Network, www.elinfonet.com/pickedpol/139.html, accessed January 20, 2008.

> The safety of our employees is very important. We expect all employees to be safety-conscious, follow safety rules, and to immediately alert management to any conditions in the work place that are believed to be unsafe or unhealthy. Accident prevention is important to the well being of our employees and visitors and also a factor in our costs and profits. When an accident does occur, ask yourself how it could have been prevented and take the necessary steps to prevent a similar accident in the future. Violation of safety and security rules is a serious offense warranting disciplinary action, including termination.
>
> As you go through the training program for your specific job position, additional safety procedures will be explained to you. However, every employee must be familiar with the six major causes and results of accidents in most workplaces—customers, collisions, slips and falls, cuts, lifting, and burns. The following basic safety rules have been developed to protect you and others from injury while on the job. Accidents can happen—but remember, safety is everyone's responsibility.

Set Specific Loss Control Goals

Set specific safety goals to be achieved. For example, set safety goals in terms of frequency of lost-time injuries per number of full-time employees.

Conduct Regular Safety and Health Inspections

Routinely inspect all premises for possible safety and health problems using checklists such as those in the *HR in Practice* feature on pages 352–353 and in Figure 11.6 as aids. Similarly, investigate all accidents and "near misses" and have a system in place for letting employees notify management about hazardous conditions.[46] The term *safety audit* means two things. It refers to the actual safety inspection using a checklist as in Figure 11.6. *Safety audit* also refers to the employer's review and analysis of its safety-related data, for instance, regarding accidents, workers' compensation claims, and days lost due to injuries.

Organize a Safety Committee

Employee safety committees can improve workplace safety. For example, when airborne sawdust became a problem at a pulp and paper facility, plant management appointed an employee safety committee. The committee took on the role of safety watchdog, and trained its members in hazard identification. After talking to employees who worked with the woodchips where the sawdust originated, the committee members discovered the sawdust became airborne as the workers transferred the woodchips from one belt to another. They were able to quickly correct the problem.[47]

Figure 11.7 on page 362 summarizes these and other safety steps.

Protecting Vulnerable Workers

In designing safe and healthy environments, employers need to pay special attention to vulnerable workers. These are workers who are "unprepared to deal with hazards in the workplace," either due to lack of education, ill-fitting personal protective equipment, physical limitations, or cultural reasons. Among others, they may include young workers, immigrant workers, aging workers, and women workers.[48] (While the U.S. Fair Labor Standards Act strictly limits young people's exposure to dangerous jobs, about 64 workers under age 18 died from work-related injuries in one recent year.)[49]

For example, while about half of all workers are women, vendors design most machinery and personal protective equipment (like gloves) for men. Women may thus have to use makeshift platforms or stools to reach machinery controls, or safety goggles that don't really fit. The solution is to make sure the equipment and machines women use are appropriate for their size.[50]

FIGURE 11.6 Supervisor's Safety Checklist

FORM **CD-574**
(2/03)

U.S. Department of Commerce
Office Safety Inspection Checklist for
Supervisors and Program Managers

Name:	Division:
Location:	Date:
Signature:	

This checklist is intended as a guide to assist supervisors and program managers in conducting safety and health inspections of their work areas. It includes questions relating to general office safety, ergonomics, fire prevention, and electrical safety. Questions which receive a "NO" answer require corrective action. If you have questions or need assistance with resolving any problems, please contact your safety office. More information on office safety is available through the Department of Commerce Safety Office website at **http://ohrm.doc.gov/safetyprogram/safety.htm**.

Work Environment

Yes	No	N/A	
O	O	O	Are all work areas clean, sanitary, and orderly?
O	O	O	Is there adequate lighting?
O	O	O	Is the noise level within an acceptable range?
O	O	O	Is ventilation adequate?

Walking / Working Surfaces

Yes	No	N/A	
O	O	O	Are aisles and passages free of stored material that may present trip hazards?
O	O	O	Are tile floors in places like kitchens and bathrooms free of water and slippery substances?
O	O	O	Are carpet and throw rugs free of tears or trip hazards?
O	O	O	Are hand rails provided on all fixed stairways?
O	O	O	Are treads provided with anti-slip surfaces?
O	O	O	Are step ladders provided for reaching overhead storage areas and are materials stored safely?
O	O	O	Are file drawers kept closed when not in use?
O	O	O	Are passenger and freight elevators inspected annually and are the inspection certificates available for review on-site?
O	O	O	Are pits and floor openings covered or otherwise guarded?
O	O	O	Are standard guardrails provided wherever aisle or walkway surfaces are elevated more than 48 inches above any adjacent floor or the ground?
O	O	O	Is furniture free of any unsafe defects?
O	O	O	Are heating and air conditioning vents clear of obstructions?

Ergonomics

Yes	No	N/A	
O	O	O	Are employees advised of proper lifting techniques?
O	O	O	Are workstations configured to prevent common ergonomic problems? (Chair height allows employees' feet to rest flat on the ground with thighs parallel to the floor, top of computer screen is at or slightly below eye level, keyboard is at elbow height. Additional information on proper configuration of workstations is available through the Commerce Safety website at http://ohrm.doc.gov/safetyprogram/safety.htm)
O	O	O	Are mechanical aids and equipment, such as; lifting devices, carts, or dollies provided where needed?
O	O	O	Are employees surveyed annually on their ergonomic concerns?

Emergency Information (Postings)

Yes	No	N/A	
O	O	O	Are established emergency phone numbers posted where they can be readily found in case of an emergency?
O	O	O	Are employees trained on emergency procedures?
O	O	O	Are fire evacuation procedures/diagrams posted?
O	O	O	Is emergency information posted in every area where you store hazardous waste?
O	O	O	Is established facility emergency information posted near a telephone?
O	O	O	Are the OSHA poster, and other required posters displayed conspicuously?
O	O	O	Are adequate first aid supplies available and properly maintained?
O	O	O	Are an adequate number of first aid trained personnel available to respond to injuries and illnesses until medical assistance arrives?
O	O	O	Is a copy of the facility fire prevention and emergency action plan available on site?
O	O	O	Are safety hazard warning signs/caution signs provided to warn employees of pertinent hazards?

FIGURE 11.6 Continued

FORM **CD-574**
(2/03)

Fire Prevention

Yes	No	N/A	
O	O	O	Are flammable liquids, such as gasoline, kept in approved safety cans and stored in flammable cabinets?
O	O	O	Are portable fire extinguishers distributed properly (less than 75 feet travel distance for combustibles and 50 feet for flammables)?
O	O	O	Are employees trained on the use of portable fire extinguishers?
O	O	O	Are portable fire extinguishers visually inspected monthly and serviced annually?
O	O	O	Are areas around portable fire extinguishers free of obstructions and properly labeled ?
O	O	O	Is heat-producing equipment used in a well ventilated area?
O	O	O	Are fire alarm pull stations clearly marked and unobstructed?
O	O	O	Are proper clearances maintained below sprinkler heads (i.e., 18" clear)?

Emergency Exits

Yes	No	N/A	
O	O	O	Are doors, passageways or stairways that are neither exits nor access to exits and which could be mistaken for exits, appropriately marked "NOT AN EXIT," "TO BASEMENT," "STOREROOM," etc.?
O	O	O	Are a sufficient number of exits provided?
O	O	O	Are exits kept free of obstructions or locking devices which could impede immediate escape?
O	O	O	Are exits properly marked and illuminated?
O	O	O	Are the directions to exits, when not immediately apparent, marked with visible signs?
O	O	O	Can emergency exit doors be opened from the direction of exit travel without the use of a key or other significant effort when the building is occupied?
O	O	O	Are exits arranged such that it is not possible to travel toward a fire hazard when exiting the facility?

Electrical Systems

(Please have your facility maintenance person or electrician accompany you during this part of the inspection)

Yes	No	N/A	
O	O	O	Are all cord and cable connections intact and secure?
O	O	O	Are electrical outlets free of overloads?
O	O	O	Is fixed wiring used instead of flexible/extension cords?
O	O	O	Is the area around electrical panels and breakers free of obstructions?
O	O	O	Are high-voltage electrical service rooms kept locked?
O	O	O	Are electrical cords routed such that they are free of sharp objects and clearly visible?
O	O	O	Are all electrical cords grounded?
O	O	O	Are electrical cords in good condition (free of splices, frays, etc.)?
O	O	O	Are electrical appliances approved (Underwriters Laboratory, Inc. (UL), etc)?
O	O	O	Are electric fans provided with guards of not over one-half inch, preventing finger exposures?
O	O	O	Are space heaters UL listed and equipped with shutoffs that activate if the heater tips over?
O	O	O	Are space heaters located away from combustibles and properly ventilated?
O	O	O	In your electrical rooms are all electrical raceways and enclosures securely fastened in place?
O	O	O	Are clamps or other securing means provided on flexible cords or cables at plugs, receptacles, tools, equipment, etc., and is the cord jacket securely held in place?
O	O	O	Is sufficient access and working space provided and maintained about all electrical equipment to permit ready and safe operations and maintenance? (This space is 3 feet for less than 600 volts, 4 feet for more than 600 volts)

Material Storage

Yes	No	N/A	
O	O	O	Are storage racks and shelves capable of supporting the intended load and materials stored safely?
O	O	O	Are storage racks secured from falling?
O	O	O	Are office equipment stored in a stable manner, not capable of falling?

Source: www.sefsc.noaa.gov/PDFdocs/CD-574OfficeInspectionChecklistSupervisors.pdf, accessed May 26, 2007.

Similarly, with more workers postponing retirement, older workers are doing a rising percentage of manufacturing jobs. They can do these jobs effectively. However, there are numerous physical changes associated with aging, including loss of strength, loss of muscular flexibility, reduced grip strength, and reduced blood flow. This means that employers may have to make some special provisions, for instance, providing mechanical assists and providing older workers with additional insulation if they work for long periods in the cold.[51] The fatality rate for older workers is about three times that of younger workers.[52]

SAFETY TRAINING FOR HISPANIC WORKERS With increasing numbers of Spanish-speaking workers in the United States, many employers offer special training for Hispanic workers.[53] One example was a 40-hour training course for construction workers at the Dallas/Fort Worth airport expansion project. Based on this program's apparent success, there are several useful conclusions one can draw about what a program like this should look like.

FIGURE 11.7

Steps to Take to Reduce Workplace Accidents

- Reduce unsafe conditions.
- Reduce unsafe acts.
- Use posters and other propaganda.
- Provide safety training.
- Use positive reinforcement.
- Emphasize top-management commitment.
- Emphasize safety.
- Establish a safety policy.
- Set specific loss control goals.
- Conduct safety and health inspections regularly.
- Monitor work overload and stress.

1. *Teach the program in Spanish.* OSHA requirements already demand this.
2. Recruit instructors who are from the *ethnic groups* they are training, and preferably from (in this case) construction.
3. Provide for some *multilingual cross-training* for specific phrases. For example, the course teaches non-Hispanic trainees to say "peligro" (danger) or "cuidado" (be careful).[54]
4. Address *cultural differences.* For example, the Dallas program found that some workers, such as those from Panama, usually want to be greeted first, instead of just told, "you are doing something wrong." (*Global Issues in HR,* below, provides another example.)
5. *Don't skimp on training.* Because of the multilingual aspects, the 40-hour course at Dallas/Fort Worth cost about $500 tuition per student (not counting the worker's wages).

Global Issues in HR

Crime and Punishment Abroad

Particularly when traveling in areas where medical facilities may not meet developed-country standards, sudden illnesses or accidents can be very serious. Language difficulties, cultural misunderstandings, lack of normal support, and infrastructure systems (such as poor transportation) can all make an accident or illness that may be manageable in one country a disaster in another.

Furthermore, cultural differences can cause surprises. In one hospital abroad, for instance, the doctor would not perform a heart surgery until receiving $40,000 in cash. As a result, many multinationals brief their business travelers and expatriates about what to expect and how to react when confronted with a health or safety problem abroad. Many employers also contract with international security firms. For example, International SOS has over 1,300 medical professionals staffing its regional centers and clinics.[55]

EMPLOYEE HEALTH: PROBLEMS AND REMEDIES

4 Discuss major health problems at work and how to remedy them.

Most workplace health hazards aren't obvious ones like unguarded equipment or slippery floors. Many are unseen hazards (like mold) that the company inadvertently produces as part of its production process. Other problems, like drug abuse, the employees may create for themselves. In either case, these health hazards are often as much or more dangerous to workers' health and safety than are obvious hazards like slippery floors. Typical workplace health hazards may include:

1. Alcoholism and substance abuse.
2. Chemicals and other hazardous materials.
3. Excessive noise and vibrations.

4. Temperature extremes.
5. Biohazards, including those that are normally occurring (such as mold) and man-made (such as anthrax).
6. Ergonomic hazards (such as poorly designed computer equipment that forces workers to do their jobs while contorted into unnatural positions).
7. And the many familiar safety-related hazards such as slippery floors and blocked passageways we discussed earlier.[56]

Alcoholism and Substance Abuse

Workplace substance abuse is a serious problem at work. In one recent year in the United States, of the 16.7 million illicit drug users age 16 or older, 12.4 million, or about 74%, were employed full- or part-time.[57] About 15% of the U.S. workforce (just over 19 million workers) "has either been hung over at work, been drinking shortly before showing up for work, or been drinking or impaired while on the job at least once during the previous year."[58]

Recognizing the alcoholic on the job isn't easy. Early symptoms such as tardiness are similar to those of other problems. The supervisor is not a psychiatrist, and without specialized training, identifying and dealing with the alcoholic is difficult.

TESTING For many employers, dealing with alcohol and substance abuse begins with substance abuse testing. It's increasingly unusual to find employers who don't at least test job candidates for substance abuse before formally hiring them. And many states in the U.S. are instituting mandatory random drug testing for high-hazard workers. For example, as of 2008, New Jersey requires random drug testing of electrical workers.[59]

There's some debate about whether drug tests reduce workplace accidents. The answer seems to be that pre-employment tests pick up only about half the workplace drug users, so ongoing random testing is advisable. One study, conducted in three hotels, concluded that pre-employment drug testing seemed to have little effect on workplace accidents. However, a combination of pre-employment and random ongoing testing was associated with a significant reduction in workplace accidents.[60]

DEALING WITH SUBSTANCE ABUSE Ideally, a drug-free workplace program includes five components:

1. a drug-free workplace policy,
2. supervisor training,
3. employee education,
4. employee assistance, and
5. drug testing.

The policy should state, at a minimum, "The use, possession, transfer, or sale of illegal drugs by employees is prohibited." It should also explain the employer's rationale for the policy, and the consequences for violating it (including discipline up to and including termination). Supervisors should be trained to monitor employees' performance, and to stay alert to drug-related performance problems.

TOOLS Several tools are available to screen for alcohol or drug abuse. Popular self-reporting screening instruments for alcoholism in the United States and the United Kingdom are the 4-item CAGE and the 25-item Michigan Alcoholism Screening Test (MAST). The former asks questions like these: Have you ever (1) attempted to cut back on alcohol, (2) been annoyed by comments about your drinking, (3) felt guilty about drinking, (4) had an eye-opener first thing in the morning to steady your nerves?[61] Another screening tool used in the U.K. is the Alcohol Use Disorders Identification Test, or AUDIT.

Table 11.1 shows observable behavior patterns that indicate alcohol-related problems. As you can see, alcohol-related problems range from tardiness in the earliest stages of alcohol abuse to prolonged, unpredictable absences in its later stages.[62]

A combination of pre-employment and ongoing random testing is most effective. Pre-employment drug testing discourages those on drugs from applying for or coming to work

TABLE 11.1   Observable Behavior Patterns Indicating Possible Alcohol-Related Problems

Alcoholism Stage	Some Possible Signs of Alcoholism Problems	Some Possible Alcoholism Performance Issues
Early	Arrives at work late	Reduced job efficiency
	Untrue statements	Misses deadlines
	Leaves work early	
Middle	Frequent absences, especially Mondays	Accidents
	Colleagues mentioning erratic behavior	Warnings from boss
	Mood swings	Noticeably reduced performance
	Anxiety	
	Late returning from lunch	
	Frequent multi-day absences	
Advanced	Personal neglect	Frequent falls, accidents
	Unsteady gait	Strong disciplinary actions
	Violent outbursts	Basically incompetent performance
	Blackouts and frequent forgetfulness	
	Possible drinking on job	

Sources: Gopal Patel and John Adkins, Jr., "The Employer's Role in Alcoholism Assistance," *Personnel Journal* 62, no. 7 (July 1983): 570; Mary-Anne Enoch and David Goldman, "Problem Drinking and Alcoholism: Diagnosis and Treatment," *American Family Physician* (February 1, 2002) www.aafp.org/afp/20020201/441.html, accessed July 20, 2008; and Ken Pidd, et al, "Alcohol and Work: Patterns of Use, Workplace Culture, and Safety," www.nisu.flinders.edu.au/pubs/reports/2006/injcat82.pdf, accessed July 20, 2008.

for employers who do testing. One study found that over 30% of regular drug users employed full-time said they were less likely to work for a company that conducted pre-employment screening.[63] Some applicants or employees may try to evade the test, for instance, by purchasing "clean" specimens to use. Several U.S. states have laws making drug-test fraud a crime.[64] However, a newer oral fluid drug test eliminates the "clean specimen" problem and is much less expensive to administer.[65]

The Problems of Job Stress and Burnout

Problems such as alcoholism and drug abuse sometimes stem from *job stress*. Eighty-eight percent of managers in one survey reported elevated stress levels, with most reporting feeling under more stress than they could ever remember.[66] Northwestern National Mutual Life found that one-fourth of all employees it surveyed viewed their jobs as the number one stressor in their lives.[67] Even employees with technologically advanced jobs, like computer workers, suffer high levels of stress on the job.[68]

A variety of external factors can trigger stress. These include work schedule, pace of work, job security, route to and from work, workplace noise, and the number and nature of customers or clients.[69] However, no two people react the same because personal factors also influence stress.[70] For example, those with Type A personalities—people who are **workaholics** and who feel driven to always be on time and meet deadlines—normally place themselves under greater stress than do others.

workaholic
People who feel driven to always be on time and meet deadlines and so normally place themselves under greater stress than do others.

CONSEQUENCES   Job stress has serious consequences for both the employee and the organization. The human consequences of job stress include anxiety, depression, anger, and various physical consequences, such as cardiovascular disease, headaches, accidents, and even, reportedly, early onset Alzheimer's disease.[71] Stress also has serious consequences for the employer. These include diminished performance, and increased absenteeism, turnover, grievances, and health care costs. A study of 46,000 employees concluded that health care costs of the high-stress workers were 46% higher than those of their less-stressed coworkers.[72] Yet not all stress is dysfunctional. Some people, for example, find that they are more productive as a deadline approaches.

REDUCING YOUR OWN JOB STRESS A person can do several things to alleviate stress. These include commonsense remedies like getting more sleep, eating better, finding a more suitable job, getting counseling, and planning each day's activities. In his book *Stress and the Manager,* Dr. Karl Albrecht suggests the following to reduce job stress:[73]

- Build rewarding, pleasant, cooperative relationships with as many of your colleagues and employees as you can.
- Don't bite off more than you can chew.
- Build an especially effective and supportive relationship with your boss.
- Understand the boss's problems and help him or her to understand yours.
- Negotiate with your boss for realistic deadlines on important projects. Be prepared to propose deadlines yourself, instead of having them imposed on you.
- Find time every day for detachment and relaxation.
- Get away from your office from time to time for a change of scene and a change of mind.
- Don't put off dealing with distasteful problems.
- Make a constructive "worry list." Write down the problems that concern you, and beside each write down what you're going to do about it.

burnout
The total depletion of physical and mental resources caused by excessive striving to reach an unrealistic work-related goal.

Meditation works for some. Choose a quiet place with soft light, sit comfortably, and then meditate by focusing your thoughts, for instance, by counting breaths or by visualizing a calming location such as a beach. When your mind wanders, just bring it back to focusing on your breathing, or the beach.[74]

WHAT THE EMPLOYER CAN DO The employer can also help reduce job stress. Indeed, one's relationship with his or her immediate supervisor is an important factor in one's piece of mind at work.

One British firm follows a three-tiered approach to managing workplace stress.[75] First is *primary prevention*, which focuses on ensuring that things like job designs and workflows are correct. Second involves *intervention*, including individual employee assessment, and attitude surveys to find sources of stress such as personal conflicts on the job, and supervisory intervention. Third is *rehabilitation* through employee assistance programs and counseling. Huntington Hospital in Pasadena, California, introduced an on-site concierge service to help its employees. It takes care of tasks like mailing bills and making vacation plans for them.[76] Several years ago, World Bank employees were experiencing high stress levels. Several times a week trainers from a Washington, DC-based Buddhist meditation instruction company ran meditation classes at the bank. Employees generally felt the classes were useful in reducing stress.[77]

To reduce stress, choose a quiet place with soft light, sit comfortably, and then meditate by focusing your thoughts, for instance, by counting breaths.

BURNOUT **Burnout** is a phenomenon closely associated with job stress. Experts define *burnout* as the total depletion of physical and mental resources caused by excessive striving to reach an unrealistic work-related goal. Burnout doesn't just spontaneously appear. Instead, it builds gradually, manifesting itself in symptoms such as irritability, discouragement, entrapment, and resentment.[78]

What can a burnout candidate do? In his book *How to Beat the High Cost of Success*, Dr. Herbert Freudenberger suggests:

- ■ *Break your patterns.* Survey how you spend your time. Are you doing a variety of things or the same one repeatedly? The more well rounded your life, the better protected you are against burnout.
- ■ *Get away from it all periodically.* Schedule occasional periods of introspection during which you escape your usual routine, perhaps alone, to seek a perspective on where you are and where you are going.
- ■ *Reassess your goals in terms of their intrinsic worth.* Are the goals you've set for yourself attainable? Are they really worth the sacrifices you'll have to make?
- ■ *Think about your work.* Could you do as good a job without being so intense or also by pursuing outside interests?

DEPRESSION   Stress and burnout aren't the only psychological health problems at work. For example, one *Journal of the American Medical Association* study calculated that depressed workers cost their employers $44 billion per year, either in absenteeism or in reduced performance while at work.[79] Employers apparently need to work harder to ensure that depressed employees utilize support services. One survey found that while about two-thirds of large firms offered employee assistance programs covering depression, only about 14% of employees with depression said they ever used one.[80] Training managers to recognize signs of depression—persistent sad moods, sleeping too little, reduced appetite, difficulty in concentrating, and loss of interest in activities once enjoyed, for instance—and then making assistance more readily available can help.

Asbestos Exposure at Work

There are four major sources of occupational respiratory diseases: asbestos, silica, lead, and carbon dioxide. Of these, asbestos has become a major concern, in part because of publicity surrounding numerous huge lawsuits alleging asbestos-related diseases.

OSHA standards require several actions with respect to asbestos. They require that companies monitor the air whenever an employer expects the level of asbestos to rise to one-half the allowable limit (0.1 fibers per cubic centimeters). Engineering controls—walls, special filters, and so forth—are required to maintain an asbestos level that complies with OSHA standards. Respirators can only be used if they are then still required to achieve compliance.

Computer Monitor Health Problems and How to Avoid Them

Even with advances in computer screen technology, there's still a risk of monitor-related health problems. Problems include short-term eye burning, itching, and tearing, as well as eyestrain and eye soreness. Backaches and neckaches are also widespread. These occur when employees try to compensate for monitor problems by maneuvering into awkward positions. Computer users may also suffer from carpal tunnel syndrome, caused by repetitive use of the hands and arms at uncomfortable angles.[81] OSHA has no specific standards that apply to computer workstations. It does have general standards that might apply, regarding, for instance, radiation, noise, and electrical hazards.[82]

NIOSH (the National Institute of Occupational Safety and Health) provided general recommendations regarding the use of computer screens. These include:

1. Employees should take a 3–5 minute break from working at the computer every 20–40 minutes, and use the time for other tasks, like making copies.
2. Design maximum flexibility into the workstation so it can be adapted to the individual operator. For example, use adjustable chairs with midback supports. Don't stay in one position for long.
3. Reduce glare with devices such as recessed or indirect lighting. Special "personal glare screen" eyeglasses can lower the effect of glare.[83]
4. Give workers a preplacement vision exam to ensure properly corrected vision.

5. Allow the user to position his or her wrists at the same level as the elbow.
6. Put the screen at or just below eye level, at a distance of 18 to 30 inches from the eyes.
7. Let the wrists rest lightly on a pad for support.
8. Put the feet flat on the floor, or on a footrest.[84]

Workplace Smoking

To some extent, the problem of workplace smoking is becoming moot. For example, a series of states in the U.S., have barred smoking in most workplaces.[85] Yet smoking continues to be a serious problem for employees and employers. Costs derive from higher health and fire insurance, as well as increased absenteeism and reduced productivity (which occurs when, for instance, a smoker takes a 10-minute break to smoke a cigarette down the hall).

WHAT YOU CAN AND CANNOT DO   Can employers institute smoking bans? That depends on several things, including the state in which you are located and whether or not your firm is unionized. For example, in the U.S. instituting a smoking ban in a unionized facility which formerly allowed employees to smoke may be subject to collective bargaining.[86] The United Kingdom's smoking ban was enacted in July 2007 and prohibits people from lighting up in virtually all enclosed public locations, including previously allowed indoor smoking areas. In Australia, smoking bans have been enacted on a state-by-state basis.

In general, in the U.S., you can deny a job to a smoker as long as you don't use smoking as a surrogate for some other kind of discrimination. A "no-smokers-hired" policy generally does not violate the Americans with Disabilities Act (smoking is not considered a disability), nor, in general, other federal law. About 67% of human resources professionals responding to a SHRM online survey said their companies have established smoke-free workplace policies.[87] Yet about 78% of smoker-employees in these firms said the smoke free policies did *not* motivate them to quit. Therefore also offering smoke-cessation benefits is important. The Centers for Disease Control ranks smoke cessation policies (along with aspirin therapy and childhood vaccinations) as the number 1 cost effective benefit employers can provide.[88] WEYCO Inc., a Michigan-based insurance consulting firm, first gave employees 15 months warning and offered smoking secession assistance. Then they began firing or forcing out all its workers who smoke, including those who do so in the privacy of their homes.[89]

Smoking cessation programs can more than pay for themselves. A smoking cessation program that includes therapy and selected pharmaceuticals costs about $0.45 per health plan member per month. However, it can produce annual savings of about $210 per year per smoker who quits (by reducing costs like smoking-related heart disease).[90]

Dealing with Violence at Work

A disgruntled long-term employee walked into Chrysler's Ohio Jeep assembly plant and fatally shot one worker, after reportedly being involved in an argument with a supervisor.[91]

Violence against employees is a huge problem at work and customers are more often the perpetrators than are coworkers or supervisors.[92] For example, by one early estimate, workplace violence costs employers about $4 billion a year.[93] One report called bullying the "silent epidemic" of the workplace, "where abusive behavior, threats, and intimidation often go unreported."[94] And, workplace violence isn't always aimed just at people. It also manifests itself in sabotaging the firm's property.

REDUCING WORKPLACE VIOLENCE   Most workplace violence incidents by employees are predictable and avoidable. *Risk Management Magazine* estimates that about 86% of past workplace violence incidents were anticipated by coworkers, who had brought them to management's attention prior to the incidents actually occurring. Yet management usually did little or nothing.[95] Human resource managers can take several steps to reduce the incidence of workplace violence. They include:

HEIGHTEN SECURITY MEASURES Heightened security measures are an employer's first line of defense against workplace violence, whether that violence derives from coworkers, customers, or outsiders. According to OSHA, these measures include[96] improve external lighting; use drop safes to minimize cash on hand and post signs noting that only a limited amount of cash is on hand; install silent alarms and surveillance cameras; increase the number of staff on duty; provide staff training in conflict resolution and nonviolent response; close establishments during high-risk hours late at night and early in the morning; and issue a weapons policy that states, for instance, that "dangerous or deadly weapons cannot be brought onto the facility either openly or concealed."

IMPROVE EMPLOYEE SCREENING With about 30% of workplace attacks committed by coworkers, screening out potentially explosive internal and external applicants is the employer's next line of defense.

Personal and situational factors influence workplace aggression. In general, men and individuals scoring higher on "trait anger" (the predisposition to respond to situations with hostility) are more likely to exhibit workplace aggression. In terms of the situation, interpersonal injustice and poor leadership predict aggression against supervisors.[97]

STEPS TO TAKE Employers can do much to screen out potentially violent workers before they're hired. Obtain an employment application, and solicit (and check) the applicant's employment history, education, and references.[98] Sample interview questions include "What frustrates you?" and "Who was your worst supervisor and why?"[99] Certain background circumstances, such as the following, may indicate the need for a more in-depth background investigation of the applicant:[100]

- An unexplained gap in employment
- Incomplete or false information on the résumé or application
- A negative, unfavorable, or false reference
- Prior insubordinate or violent behavior on the job
- A criminal history involving harassing or violent behavior
- A prior termination for cause with a suspicious (or no) explanation
- History of drug or alcohol abuse
- Strong indications of instability in the individual's work or personal life as indicated, for example, by frequent job changes or geographic moves
- Lost licenses or accreditations[101]

USE WORKPLACE VIOLENCE TRAINING You can also train supervisors to identify the clues that typify potentially violent employees. Common clues include:[102]

- An act of violence on or off the job
- Erratic behavior evidencing a loss of perception or awareness of actions
- Overly confrontational or antisocial behavior
- Sexually aggressive behavior
- Isolationist or loner tendencies
- Insubordinate behavior with a threat of violence
- Tendency to overreact to criticism
- Exaggerated interest in war, guns, violence, mass murders, catastrophes, and so on
- Commission of a serious breach of security
- Possession of weapons, knives, or like items in the workplace
- Violation of privacy rights of others, such as searching desks or stalking
- Chronic complaining and the raising of frequent, unreasonable grievances
- A retributory or get-even attitude

The U.S. Postal Service took steps to reduce workplace assaults. The steps include more background checks, drug testing, a 90-day probationary period for new hires, more stringent security (including a hotline that lets employees report threats), and training managers to create a healthier culture.[103] *HR in Practice* lists useful guidelines.

HR in Practice

Guidelines for Firing a High-Risk Employee

When firing a high-risk employee:

- plan all aspects of the meeting, including its time, location, the people to be present, and agenda;
- involve security enforcement personnel;
- advise the employee that he or she is no longer permitted onto the employer's property;
- conduct the meeting in a room with a door leading to the outside of the building;
- keep the termination brief and to the point;

- make sure he or she returns all company-owned property at the meeting;
- don't let the person return to his or her workstation;
- conduct the meeting early in the week and early in the morning so he or she has time to meet with employment counselors or support groups;
- offer as generous a severance package as possible; and
- protect the employee's dignity by not advertising the event.[104]

VIOLENCE TOWARD WOMEN AT WORK While men have more fatal occupational injuries than do women, the proportion of women who are victims of assault is much higher. In the U.S., the Gender-Motivated Violence Act (part of the comprehensive Violence Against Women Act passed by the U.S. Congress in 1994 and expanded in 2006) imposes significant liabilities on employers whose women employees become violence victims.[105]

Fatal workplace violence against women has several sources. Of all females murdered at work, more than three-fourths are victims of random criminal violence carried out by an assailant unknown to the victim, as might occur during a robbery. Family members, coworkers, or previous friends or acquaintances commit the remaining criminal acts. Tangible security improvements including better lighting, cash-drop boxes, and similar steps are especially pertinent in reducing such violent acts against women.

Terrorism

The employer can take several steps to protect its employees and physical assets from terrorist attack. These steps, now familiar at many workplaces, include:

- check mail carefully;
- identify ahead of time a lean "crisis organization" that can run the company on an interim basis after a terrorist threat;
- identify in advance under what conditions you will close the company down, as well as what the shutdown process will be and who can order it;
- institute a process to put the crisis management team together;
- prepare evacuation plans and make sure exits are well marked and unblocked;
- designate an employee who will communicate with families and off-site employees;
- identify an upwind, off-site location near your facility to use as a staging area for all evacuated personnel;
- designate in advance several employees who will do headcounts at the evacuation staging area; and
- establish an emergency text-messaging policy and procedure to notify affected individuals that an emergency may exist.[106]

SETTING UP A BASIC SECURITY PROGRAM In simplest terms, instituting a basic security program requires analyzing the current level of risk, and then installing mechanical, natural, and organizational security systems.[107]

Security programs often start with an analysis of the facility's *current level of risk*. The employer, preferably with the aid of security experts, should assess the company's exposure. Start with the obvious. For example, what is the neighborhood like? Is your facility close to major highways or railroad tracks (where, for instance, toxic fumes from the trains could present a problem)?

Having assessed the potential current level of risk, the employer then turns its attention to assessing and improving *three basic sources of facility security:* natural security, mechanical security, and organizational security.[108]

Natural security means taking advantage of the facility's natural or architectural features to minimize security problems. For example, do stacks of boxes in front of your windows prevent police officers from observing what's happening in your facility at night?

Mechanical security is the utilization of security systems such as locks, intrusion alarms, access control systems, and surveillance systems in a cost-effective manner that will reduce the need for continuous human surveillance.[109] Thus, for access security, biometric scanners that read thumb or palm prints or retina patterns make it easier to enforce plant security.[110]

Finally, *organizational security* means using good management to improve security. For example, it means properly training and motivating security staff and lobby attendants.[111] A SHRM survey found that about 85% of responding organizations now have a formal disaster plan.[112]

Review

SUMMARY

1. The area of safety and accident prevention is of concern to managers partly because of the staggering number of deaths and accidents occurring at work.

2. The purpose of OSHA is to ensure every working person a safe and healthful workplace. OSHA standards are complete and detailed, and are enforced through a system of workplace inspections. OSHA inspectors can issue citations and recommend penalties to their area directors.

3. There are three basic causes of accidents: chance occurrences, unsafe conditions, and unsafe acts on the part of employees. In addition, three other work-related factors—the job itself, the work schedule, and the psychological climate—also contribute to accidents.

4. Unsafe acts on the part of employees are a main cause of accidents. Such acts are to some extent the result of certain behavior tendencies on the part of employees, and these tendencies are possibly the result of certain personal characteristics.

5. Experts differ on whether there are accident-prone people who have accidents regardless of the job. Some traits do predict accidents, but the person who is accident prone in one job may not be on a different job. For example, vision is related to accident frequency for drivers and machine

operators, but might not be for other workers, such as accountants.

6. There are several approaches to preventing accidents. One is to reduce unsafe conditions. The other approach is to reduce unsafe acts—for example, through selection and placement, training, positive reinforcement, propaganda, and top-management commitment.

7. Alcoholism, drug addiction, stress, and emotional illness are four important and growing health problems among employees. Alcoholism is a particularly serious problem that can drastically lower the effectiveness of your organization. Techniques including disciplining, discharge, in-house counseling, and referrals to an outside agency are used to deal with these problems.

8. Stress and burnout are other potential health problems at work. An employee can reduce job stress by getting away from work for a while each day, delegating, and developing a worry list.

9. Violence against employees is an enormous problem at work. Steps that can reduce workplace violence include improved security arrangements, better employee screening, and violence-reduction training.

10. Basic facility security relies on natural security, mechanical security, and organizational security.

KEY TERMS

Occupational Safety and Health Act of 1970   348
Occupational Safety and Health Administration
   (OSHA)   348
citations   351

unsafe conditions   352
unsafe acts   354
workaholic   364
burnout   365

DISCUSSION QUESTIONS AND EXERCISES

1. How would you go about providing a safer work environment for your employees?
2. Discuss how you would go about minimizing the occurrence of unsafe acts on the part of your employees.
3. Discuss the basic facts about OSHA—its purpose, standards, inspection, and rights and responsibilities.
4. Explain the supervisor's role in safety.
5. Explain what causes unsafe acts.
6. Answer the question, "Is there such a thing as an accident-prone person?"
7. Describe at least five techniques for reducing accidents.
8. Explain how an employee could reduce stress at work.
9. In groups of 3 or 4 students, spend 15 minutes walking around the building in which your class is held or where you are now, listing possible natural, mechanical, and organizational security measures you'd suggest to the building's owner.

Application Exercises

HR in Action
Case Incident 1 — The Office Safety and Health Program

LearnInMotion is a dot-com firm that delivers employee training, both online and via delivery of CD/DVDs. At first glance, a dot-com is probably one of the last places you'd expect to find potential safety and health hazards—or so the owners, Jennifer and Mel, thought. There's no danger of moving machinery, no high-pressure lines, no cutting or heavy lifting, and certainly no forklift trucks. However, there are safety and health problems.

In terms of accident-causing conditions, for instance, the one thing dot-com companies have are lots of cables and wires. There are cables connecting the computers to each other and to the servers, and in many cases separate cables running from some computers to separate printers. There are 10 wireless telephones in the office, the bases of which are connected to 4.5-meter phone lines that always seem to be snaking around chairs and tables. There is, in fact, an astonishing amount of cable considering this is an office with less than 10 employees.

When the installation specialists wired the office (for electricity, high-speed cable, phone lines, burglar alarms, and computers), they estimated they used well over 8 kilometers of cables of one sort or another. Most of these are hidden in the walls or ceilings, but many of them snake their way from desk to desk, and under and over doorways. Several employees have tried to reduce the nuisance of having to trip over wires whenever they get up by putting their plastic chair pads over the wires closest to them. However, that still leaves many wires unprotected. In other cases, they brought in their own packing tape, and tried to tape down the wires in those spaces where they're particularly troublesome, such as across doorways.

The cables and wires are only one of the more obvious potential accident-causing conditions. The firm's programmer, before he left the firm, had tried to repair the main server while the unit was still electrically alive. To this day, they're not sure exactly where he stuck the screwdriver, but the result was that he was "blown across the room," as Mel puts it. He was all right, but it was still a scare. And while they haven't yet received any claims, every employee spends hours at his or her computer, so carpal tunnel syndrome is a risk, as are a variety of other problems such as eyestrain and strained backs.

One recent accident particularly scared them. The firm uses independent contractors to deliver the firm's book- and CD/DVD–based courses in London and two other cities. A delivery person was riding his bike in London when he was struck by a car. Luckily he was not hurt, but the bike's front wheel was wrecked, and the close call got Mel and Jennifer thinking about their lack of a safety program.

It's not just the physical conditions that concern the company's two owners. They also have some concerns about potential health problems such as job stress and burnout. While the business may be (relatively) safe with respect to physical conditions, it is also relatively stressful in terms of the demands it makes in hours and deadlines. It is not at all unusual for employees to get to work by 7:30 or 8:00 in the morning and to work through until 11:00 or 12:00 at night, at least 5 and sometimes 6 or 7 days per week. Just getting the company's new service operational required five of LearnInMotion's employees to work 70-hour workweeks for 3 weeks.

The bottom line is that both Jennifer and Mel feel they need to do something about implementing a health and safety plan. Now they want you, their management consultants, to help them actually do it. Here's what they want you to do for them.

Questions and Assignments

1. Based on your knowledge of health and safety matters and your actual observations of operations that are similar to ours, make a list of the potential hazardous conditions employees and others face at LearnInMotion. What should we do to reduce the potential severity of the top five hazards?
2. Would it be advisable for us to set up a procedure for screening out stress-prone or accident-prone individuals? Why or why not? If so, how should we screen them?
3. Write a short position paper on what we should do to get all our employees to behave more safely at work.
4. Based on what you know and on what other dot-coms are doing, write a short position paper on what we can do to reduce the potential problems of stress and burnout in our company.

HR in Action *Case Incident 2*	Carter Cleaning Company: Motivating Safe Behavior

Employees' safety and health are very important in the laundry and cleaning business. Each facility is a small production plant in which machines, powered by high-pressure steam and compressed air, work at high temperatures washing, cleaning, and pressing garments, often under very hot, slippery conditions. Chemical vapors are continually produced, and caustic chemicals are used in the cleaning process. High-temperature stills are almost continually "cooking down" cleaning solvents in order to remove impurities so that the solvents can be reused. If a mistake is made in this process—like injecting too much steam into the still—a boil over occurs, in which boiling chemical solvent erupts out of the still and over the floor, and on anyone who happens to be standing in its way.

As a result of these hazards and the fact that these stores continually produce chemically hazardous waste, several government agencies have strict guidelines regarding management of these plants. For example, posters must be placed in each store notifying employees of their right to be told what hazardous chemicals they are dealing with and what the proper method for handling each chemical is. Special waste-management firms must be used to pick up and properly dispose of the hazardous waste.

A chronic problem the Carters (and most other laundry owners) have is the unwillingness on the part of the cleaning–spotting workers to wear safety goggles. Not all the chemicals they use require safety goggles, but some—like the hydrofluorous acid used to remove rust stains from garments—are very dangerous. The latter is kept in special plastic containers, since it dissolves glass. The problem is safety goggles are somewhat uncomfortable, and they become smudged easily and thus reduce visibility. As a result, Jack has found it almost impossible to get these employees to wear their goggles.

Questions

1. How should the firm go about identifying hazardous conditions that should be rectified? Use data and checklists such as those in Figure 11.3 and Figure 11.6, and the *HR in Practice* feature on pages 352–353 to list at least 10 possible dry cleaning store hazardous conditions.
2. Would it be advisable for the firm to set up a procedure for screening out accident-prone individuals? How should it do so?
3. In general, how would you suggest the Carters get all employees to behave more safely at work?
4. Describe in detail how you would use motivation to get those who should be wearing goggles to do so.

EXPERIENTIAL EXERCISE

How Safe Is My University?

Purpose:

The purpose of this exercise is to give you practice in identifying unsafe conditions.

Required Understanding:

You should be familiar with material covered in this chapter, particularly that on unsafe conditions and that in Figures 11.3 and Figure 11.6.

How to Set Up the Exercise/Instructions:

Divide the class into groups of four. Assume that each group is a safety committee retained by your college or university's safety engineer to identify and report on any possible unsafe conditions in and around the school building. Each group will spend about 45 minutes in and around the building you are now in for the purpose of identifying and listing possible unsafe conditions. (Make use of the checklists in Figure 11.3, Figure 11.6, and the *HR in Practice* feature on pages 352–353.)

Return to the class in about 45 minutes. A spokesperson for each group should list on the board the unsafe conditions you think you have identified. How many were there? Do you think these also violate OSHA standards? How would you go about checking?

ENDNOTES

1. All data refer to 2006. See www.bls.gov/iif/oshwc/osh/os/ostb1757.txt, accessed January 19, 2008.
2. BLS Likely Underestimating Injury and Illness Estimates," *Occupational Hazards* (May 2006): 16.
3. David Ayers, "Mapping Support for an E. H. S. Management System," *Occupational Hazards* (June 2006): 53–54.
4. Katherine Torres, "Stepping into the Kitchen: Food Protection for Food Workers," *Occupational Hazards* (January 2007): 29–30.
5. Based on *All About OSHA*, rev. ed. (Washington, DC: U.S. Department of Labor, 1980); www.OSHA.gov, accessed January 19, 2008.
6. http://osha.gov/as/opa/oshafacts.html, accessed January 19, 2008.
7. Ibid.
8. "OSHA Hazard Communication Standard Enforcement," *BNA Bulletin to Management* (February 23, 1980): 13. See also William Kincaid, "OSHA vs. Excellence in Safety Management," *Occupational Hazards* (December 2002): 34–36.
9. "What Every Employer Needs to Know About OSHA Record Keeping," U.S. Department of Labor, Bureau of Labor Statistics (Washington, DC), report 412–3, p. 3; and http://osha.gov/recordkeeping/index.html, accessed January 19, 2008.
10. Lisa Finnegan, "Industry Partners with OSHA," *Occupational Hazards* (February 1999): 43–45.
11. http://www.osha.gov/Publications/osha2098.pdf, accessed April 27, 2008.
12. www.OSHA.gov, accessed May 28, 2005, and http://osha.gov/pls/oshaweb/owadisp.show_document?p_table = NEWS_RELEASES&p_id = 14883, accessed January 19, 2008.
13. www.osha.gov, accessed May 26, 2007.
14. http://www.osha.gov/Publications/osha2098.pdf, accessed April 27, 2008.
15. Jim Lastowka, "Ten Keys to Avoiding OSHA Liability," *Occupational Hazards* (October 1999): 163–170.
16. Robert Grossman, "Handling Inspections: Tips from Insiders," *HR Magazine* (October 1999): 41–50.
17. Arthur Sapper, "The Oft-Missed Step: Documentation of Safety Discipline," *Occupational Hazards* (January 2006): 59.
18. *Source:* Courtesy of the Insurance Services Office, Inc., from "A Safety Committee Man's Guide" (1977): 1–64.
19. For a discussion of this, see David Hofmann and Adam Stetzer, "A Cross-Level Investigation of Factors Influencing Unsafe Behaviors and Accidents," *Personnel Psychology* 49 (1996): 307–308.
20. David Hofman and Barbara Mark, "An Investigation of the Relationship between Safety Climate and Medication Errors as Well as Other Nurse and Patient Outcomes," *Personnel Psychology* 50 no. 9 (2006): 847–869.
21. List of unsafe acts from "A Safety Committee Man's Guide," *Aetna Life and Casualty Insurance Company.*
22. Duane Schultz and Sydney Schultz, *Psychology and Work Today* (Upper Saddle River, NJ: Prentice Hall, 1998): 351.
23. Robert Pater and Robert Russel, "Drop That Accident Prone Tag: Look for Causes Beyond Personal Issues," *Industrial Safety and Hygiene News* 38, no. 1 (January 2004): 50.
24. Discussed in Douglas Haaland, "Who Is the Safest Bet for the Job? Find Out Why the Guy in the Next Cubicle May Be the Next Accident Waiting to Happen," *Security Management* 49, no. 2 (February 2005): 51–57.
25. "Thai Research Points to Role of Personality in Road Accidents," *Asia and Africa Intelligence Wire* (February 23, 2005); Donald Bashline et al., "Bad Behavior: Personality Tests Can Help Underwriters Identify High-Risk Drivers," *Best's Review* 105, no. 12 (April 2005): 63–64.
26. Don Williamson and Jon Kauffman, "From Tragedy to Triumph: Safety Grows Wings at Golden Eagle," *Occupational Hazards* (February 2006): 17–25.
27. Benjamin Mangan, "Lockout/Tagout Prevents Workplace Injuries and Save Lives," *Occupational Hazards* (March 2007): 59–60.
28. James Nash, "Beware the Hidden Eye Hazards," *Occupational Hazards* (February 2005): 48–51.
29. Robert Pater and Ron Bowles, "Directing Attention to Boost Safety Performance," *Occupational Hazards* (March 2007): 46–48.
30. E. Scott Geller, "The Thinking and Seeing Components of People-Based Safety," *Occupational Hazards* (December 2006): 38–40.
31. *Asia and Africa Intelligence Wire;* Bashline et.al., op. cit.
32. S. Laner and R. J. Sell, "An Experiment on the Effect of Specially Designed Safety Posters," *Occupational Psychology* 34 (1960): 153–169; Ernest McCormick and Joseph Tiffin, *Industrial Psychology* (Upper Saddle River, NJ: Prentice Hall, 1974): 536.
33. See also Josh Cable, "Erring on the Side of Caution," *Occupational Hazards* (February 2007): 21–22.
34. J. Nigel Ellis and Susan Warner, "Using Safety Awards to Promote Fall Prevention," *Occupational Hazards* (June 1999): 59–62. See also William Atkinson, "Safety Incentive Programs: What Works?" *Occupational Hazards* (August 2004): 35–39.
35. Don Williamson and Jon Kauffman, "From Tragedy to Triumph: Safety Grows Wings at Golden Eagle," *Occupational Hazards* (February 2006): 17–25.
36. Quoted in Josh Cable, "Seven Suggestions for a Successful Safety Incentives Program," *Occupational Hazards* 67, no. 3 (March 2005): 39–43.
37. John Dominic, "Improve Safety Performance and Avoid False Reporting," *HR Magazine* 49, no. 9 (September 2004): 110–119; See also Josh Cable, "Safety Incentives Strategies," *Occupational Hazards* 67, no. 4 (April 2005): 37.
38. See Kelly Rowe, "OSHA and Small Businesses: A Winning Combination," *Occupational Hazards* (March 2007): 33–38.
39. See, for example, Deb Carl, "The Truth about Safety Incentives," *Occupational Hazards* 69, no. 9 (September 2007): 52, 54.
40. James Nash, "Rewarding the Safety Process," *Occupational Hazards* (March 2000): 29–34; Shel Siegel, "Incentives: Small Investments Equal Big Rewards," *Occupational Hazards* (August 2007): 42–44.
41. Judi Komaki, Kenneth Barwick, and Lawrence Scott, "A Behavioral Approach to Occupational Safety: Pinpointing and Reinforcing Safe Performance in a Food Manufacturing Plant," *Journal of Applied Psychology* 63

(August 1978): 434–445. See also Anat Arkin, "Incentives to Work Safely," *Personnel Management* 26, no. 9 (September 1994): 48–52; Peter Making and Valerie Sutherland, "Reducing Accidents Using a Behavioral Approach," *Leadership and Organizational Development Journal* 15, no. 5 (1994): 5–10; Sandy Smith, "Why Cash Isn't King," *Occupational Hazards* (March 2004): 37–38.

42. Willie Hammer, *Occupational Safety Management and Engineering* (Upper Saddle River NJ: Prentice Hall, 1985): 62–63. See also "DuPont's 'STOP' Helps Prevent Workplace Injuries and Incidents," *Asia Africa Intelligence Wire* (May 17, 2004).

43. James Nash, "Weyerhaeuser Fires Plant, Safety Managers for Record-Keeping Abuses," *Occupational Hazards* (November 2004): 27–28.

44. Dov Zohar, "A Group Level Model of Safety Climate: Testing the Effect of a Group Climate on Students in Manufacturing Jobs," *Journal of Applied Psychology* 85, no. 4 (2000): 587–596. See also Steven Yule, Rhona Flin, and Andy Murdy, "The Role of Management and Safety Climate in Preventing Risk-Taking at Work," *International Journal of Risk Assessment and Management* 7, no. 2 (December 20, 2006): 137.

45. Quoted from Sandy Smith, "Breakthrough Safety Management," *Occupational Hazards* (June 2004): 43. For a discussion of developing a safety climate survey, see also Sara Singer et al.,"Workforce Perceptions of Hospital Safety Culture: Development and Validation of the Patient Safety Climate in Healthcare Organizations Survey," *Health Services Research* 42, no. 5 (October 2007): 19–23.

46. "Workplace Safety: Improving Management Practices," *BNA Bulletin to Management* (February 9, 1989): 42, 47. See also Linda Johnson, "Preventing Injuries: The Big Payoff," *Personnel Journal* (April 1994): 61–64; David Webb, "The Bathtub Effect: Why Safety Programs Fail," *Management Review* (February 1994): 51–54.

47. Katherine Torres, "Making a Safety Committee Work for You," *Occupational Hazards* 68, no. 10 (Oct 2006): 51(6).

48. Sandy Smith, "Protecting Vulnerable Workers," *Occupational Hazards* (April 2004): 25–28.

49. Katherine Torres, "Challenges in Protecting a Young Workforce," *Occupational Hazards* (May 2006): 24–27.

50. Linda Tapp, "We Can Do It: Protecting Women," *Occupational Hazards* (October 2003): 26–28.

51. Cynthia Ross, "How to Protect the Aging Workforce," *Occupational Hazards* (January 2005): 38–42; and Cynthia Ross, "How to Protect the Aging Workforce," *Occupational Hazards* (February 2005): 52–54.

52. Elizabeth Rogers and William Wiatrowski, "Injuries, Illnesses, and Fatalities among Older Workers," *Monthly Labor Review* 128, no. 10 (October 2005): 24–30.

53. Hispanic worker safety is a concern. See, for example, "Hispanic Workers' Deaths Rise, Fatal Occupational Injuries Down," *BNA Bulletin to Management* (August 21, 2007): 271.

54. Quoted in Josh Cable, "Seven Suggestions for a Successful Safety Incentives Program," *Occupational Hazards* 67, no. 3 (March 2005): 39–43.

55. Ann Pomeroy, "Protecting Employees in Harms Way," *HR Magazine* (June 2007): 113–122.

56. This is based on Paul Puncochar, "The Science and Art to Identifying Workplace Hazards," *Occupational Hazards* (September 2003): 50–54.

57. Figures for 2003, see www.OSHA.gov, accessed May 28, 2005.

58. "15% of Workers Drinking, Drunk, or Hung Over while at Work, According to New University Study," *BNA Bulletin to Management* (January 24, 2006): 27.

59. "New Jersey Union Takes on Mandatory Random Drug Tests," *Record* (Hackensack, NJ, January 2, 2008).

60. Frank Lockwood et al., "Drug Testing Programs and Their Impact on Workplace Accidents: A Time Series Analysis," *Journal of Individual Employment Rights* 8, no. 4 (2000): 295–306; Sally Roberts, "Random Drug Testing Can Help Reduce Accidents for Construction Companies; Drug Abuse Blamed for Heightened Risk in the Workplace," *Business Insurance* 40 (October 23, 2006): 6.

61. http://www.dol.gov/asp/programs/drugs/workingpartners/sab/screen.asp, accessed April 27, 2008.

62. Gopal Pati and John Adkins Jr., "The Employer's Role in Alcoholism Assistance," *Personnel Journal* 62, no. 7 (July 1983): 570. See also Commerce Clearing House, "How Should Employers Respond to Indications an Employee May Have an Alcohol or Drug Problem?" *Ideas and Trends* (April 6, 1989): 53–57; "The Employer's Role in Alcoholism Assistance," *Personnel Journal* 62, no. 7 (July 1983): 568–572.

63. William Corinth, "Pre-Employment Drug Testing," *Occupational Hazards* (July 2002): 56.

64. Diane Cadrain, "Are Your Employees' Drug Tests Accurate?" *HR Magazine* (January 2003): 41–45.

65. Sally Roberts, "Random Drug Testing Can Help Reduce Accidents for Construction Companies; Drug Abuse Blamed for Heightened Risk in the Workplace," *Business Insurance* 40 (October 23, 2006): 6.

66. Marice Cavanaugh et al., "An Empirical Examination of Self-Reported Work Stress Among U.S. Managers," *Journal of Applied Psychology* 85, no. 1 (2000): 65–74.

67. www.OSHA.gov, accessed May 28, 2005.

68. Patrick Thibodeau, " Stress Causes Strains in IT Shops: Job Demands Overtax Some Workers, Data Center Pros Say," *Computerworld* 40, no. 34 (August 21, 2006): 1(2).

69. Eric Sundstrom et al., "Office Noise, Satisfaction, and Performance," *Environment and Behavior*, no. 2 (March 1994): 195–222; "Stress: How to Cope with Life's Challenges," *American Family Physician* 74, no. 8 (October 15, 2006).

70. A. S. Antoniou, F. Polychroni, A. N. Vlachakis, "Gender and Age Differences in Occupational Stress and Professional Burnout between Primary and High-School Teachers in Greece," *Journal of Managerial Psychology* 21, no. 7 (September 2006): 682–690.

71. "Failing to Tackle Stress Could Cost You Dearly," *Personnel Today* (September 12, 2006); "Research Brief: Stress May Accelerate Alzheimer's," *GP* (September 8, 2006) 2.

72. "Stress, Depression Cost Employers," *Occupational Hazards* (December 1998): 24; Patricia B. Gray, "Hidden Costs of Stress," *Money* 36, no. 12 (Dec 2007): 44.

73. Karl Albrecht, *Stress and the Manager* (Upper Saddle River, NJ: Prentice Hall, 1979): 253–255. Reprinted by permission.

See also "Stress: How to Cope with Life's Challenges," *American Family Physician* 74, no. 8 (October 15, 2006).

74. Catalina Dolar, "Meditation Gives Your Mind Permanent Working Holiday; Relaxation Can Improve Your Business Decisions and Your Overall Health," *Investors Business Daily* (March 24, 2004): 89.

75. "Going Head to Head with Stress," *Personnel Today* (April 26, 2005): 1.

76. Kathryn Tyler, "Stress Management," *HR Magazine* (September 2006): 79–82.

77. "Meditation Helps Employees Focus, Relieve Stress," *BNA Bulletin to Management* (February 20, 2007): 63.

78. Madan Mohan Tripathy, "Burnout Stress Syndrome in Managers," *Management and Labor Studies* 27, no. 2 (April 2002): 89–111. See also Jonathon R.B. Halbesleben and Cheryl Rathert, "Linking Physician Burnout and Patient Outcomes: Exploring the Dyadic Relationship between Physicians and Patients," *Health Care Management Review*, 33, no. 1 (January–March 2008): 29(11).

79. Andy Meisler, "Mind Field," *Workforce Management* (September 2003): 58.

80. "Employers Must Move From Awareness to Action in Dealing with Worker Depression," *BNA Bulletin to Management* (April 29, 2004): 137.

81. "Risk of Carpal Tunnel Syndrome Not Linked to Heavy Computer Work, Study Says," *BNA Bulletin to Management* (June 28, 2001): 203.

82. www.OSHA.gov, accessed May 28, 2005.

83. Anne Chambers, "Computervision Syndrome: Relief Is in Sight," *Occupational Hazards* (October 1999): 179–184; www.OSHA.gov/ETOOLS/computerworkstations/index.html, accessed May 28, 2005.

84. Sondra Lotz Fisher, "Are Your Employees Working Ergosmart?" *Personnel Journal* (December 1996): 91–92. See also www.cdc.gov/od/ohs/Ergonomics/compergo.htm, accessed May 26, 2007.

85. Diane Cadrain, "Smoking and Workplace Laws Ensnaring HR," *HR Magazine* 49, no. 6 (June 2004): 38–39.

86. Kenneth Sovereign, *Personnel Law* (Upper Saddle River, NJ: Prentice Hall, 1999), pp. 76–79.

87. Stephen Miller, "Employers Want to Help Employees Quit Smoking, But How?" January 2007, http://www.shrm.org/rewards/library_published/benefits/nonIC/CMS_019756.asp, accessed April 27, 2008.

88. Ibid. See also "Workplace Smoking: How Far Should You Go?" *Managing Benefits Plans* 5–6 (June 2005): 2(2).

89. Stephen Bates, "Where There Is Smoke, There Are Terminations: Smokers Fired to Save Health Costs," *HR Magazine* 50, no. 3 (March 2005): 28–29.

90. Pamela Babcock, "Helping Workers Kick the Habit," *HR Magazine* (September 2007): 120.

91. "Worker Opens Fire at Ohio Jeep Plant," *Occupational Hazards* (March 2005): 16.

92. Jerry Hoobler and Jennifer Swanberg, "The Enemy Is Not Us," *International Personnel Management Association for HR* 35, no. 3 (Fall 2006): 229–246.

93. "Violence in Workplace Soaring, New Study Says," *Baltimore Business Journal* 18, no. 34 (January 5, 2001): 24.

94. "Bullies Trigger 'Silent Epidemic' at Work, but Legal Cures Remain Hard to Come By," *BNA Bulletin to Management* (February 24, 2000): 57.

95. Paul Viollis and Doug Kane, "At-Risk Terminations: Protecting Employees, Preventing Disaster," *Risk Management Magazine* 52, no. 5 (May 2005): 28–33.

96. See "Creating a Safer Workplace: Simple Steps Bring Results," *Safety Now* (September 2002): 1–2. See also J. W. Elphonestone, "Better Safe Than Sorry: Hotels, Malls Balance Security Measures with Public Accessibility," *Commercial Property New* 19, no. 10 (May 16, 2005): 30.

97. M. Sandy Hershcovis et al., "Predicting Workplace Aggression: A Meta-Analysis," *Journal of Applied Psychology* 92, no. 1 (2007): 228–238.

98. Alfred Feliu, "Workplace Violence and the Duty of Care: The Scope of an Employer's Obligation to Protect Against the Violent Employee," *Employee Relations Law Journal* 20, no. 3 (Winter 1994/95): 395.

99. Dawn Anfuso, "Workplace Violence," *Personnel Journal* (October 1994): 66–77.

100. Alfred Feliu, "Workplace Violence and the Duty of Care: The Scope of an Employer's Obligation to Protect Against the Violent Employee," *Employee Relations Law Journal* 20, no. 3 (Winter 1994/95): 395.

101. Ibid.

102. Ibid., 401–402.

103. "Employers Battling Workplace Violence Might Consider Postal Service Plan," *BNA Bulletin to Management* (August 5, 1999): 241.

104. Paul Viollis and Doug Kane, "At-Risk Terminations: Protecting Employees, Preventing Disaster," *Risk Management* 52, no. 15 (May 2005): 28–33.

105. Kenneth Diamond, "The Gender-Motivated Violence Act: What Employers Should Know," *Employee Relations Law Journal* 25, no. 4 (Spring 2000): 29–41; "Bush Signs 'Violence Against Women Act'; Funding Badly Needed Initiatives to Prevent Domestic & Sexual Violence, Help Victims," *The America's Intelligence Wire* (January 5, 2006).

106. Lloyd Newman, "Terrorism: Is Your Company Prepared?" *Business and Economic Review* 48, no. 2 (February 2002): 7–10; Li Yuan et al., "Texting When There's Trouble," *Wall Street Journal* (April 18, 2007): B1.

107. Unless otherwise noted, the following is based on Richard Maurer, "Keeping Your Security Program Active," *Occupational Hazards* (March 2003): 49–52.

108. Ibid., 50.

109. Ibid., 50.

110. Della Roberts, "Are You Ready for Biometrics?" *HR Magazine* (March 2003): 95–99.

111. Richard Maurer, "Keeping Your Security Program Active," *Occupational Hazards* (March 2003): 52.

112. "Survey Finds Reaction to September 11 Attacks Spurred Companies to Prepare for Disasters," *BNA Bulletin to Management* (November 29, 2005): 377.

Part 5 **Special Issues in Human
Resource Management**

Managing Human Resources in Entrepreneurial Firms

12

SYNOPSIS

- The Small Business Challenge

- Using Internet and Government Tools to Support the HR Effort

- Leveraging Small Size: Familiarity, Flexibility, Fairness, Informality, and HRM

- Using Professional Employer Organizations

- Managing HR Systems, Procedures, and Paperwork

When you finish studying this chapter, you should be able to:

1. *Explain why HRM is important to small businesses, and how it's different.*

2. *Give at least four examples of how entrepreneurs can use Internet and government tools to support the HR effort.*

3. *List five ways entrepreneurs can use their small size to improve their HR processes.*

4. *Discuss how you would choose and deal with a professional employee organization.*

5. *Describe how you would create a start-up paper-based human resource system for a new small business.*

Introduction

It's not easy running a restaurant. Customers are notoriously fickle, food hygiene is always a concern, and, (perhaps most unnerving to many restaurant owners), it's exceedingly difficult to hire and keep good employees. Half of all restaurant employees are under 30 years old, and turnover of more than 100% per year is the norm.[1] So, when Joe Scripture, whose company runs 11 IHOP restaurants around Atlanta, looked at the industry's turnover statistics, he knew he and his partner needed to do something, but what?[2] ■

THE SMALL BUSINESS CHALLENGE

Why Entrepreneurship Is Important

In terms of the U.S. economy, the phrase *small business* is a misnomer. More than half the people working in the United States—about 68 million out of 118 million—work for small firms.[3] Small businesses as a group also account for most of the 600,000 or so new businesses created every year, as well as for most of business growth (small firms grow faster than big ones). And small firms account for about three-quarters of the employment growth in the U.S. economy—in other words, they create most of the new jobs in the United States.[4]

① Explain why HRM is important to small businesses, and how it's different.

Statistically speaking, therefore, most people graduating from colleges in the next few years either do or will work for small businesses—those with less than 200 or so employees. Anyone interested in human resource management thus needs to understand how managing human resources in small firms is different from doing so in huge multinationals.

How Small Business Human Resource Management Is Different

Managing human resources in small firms is different for four main reasons: *size, priorities, informality*, and the nature of the *entrepreneur*.

SIZE For one thing, it would be very unusual to find a really small business—say, under 90 or so employees—with a dedicated human resource management professional.[5] The rule of thumb is that it's not until a company reaches the 100-employee milestone that it can afford an HR specialist. That's not to say that small businesses don't have human resource tasks to attend to. Even five- to six-person retail shops must recruit, select, train, and compensate employees, for instance. It's just that in such situations, it's usually the owner and (sometimes) his or her assistant that does all the HR paperwork and tasks involved. The Society for Human Resource Management's *Human Capital Benchmarking Study* found, for instance, that even firms with under 100 employees often spend the equivalent of two-or-so people's time each year addressing human resource management issues.[6] But, that time is usually just coming out of the owner's very long workday.

PRIORITIES It's not just size but the realities of the situation that drive many entrepreneurs to expend more time and resources on non-HR issues. After studying small e-commerce firms in the United Kingdom, one researcher concluded that, as important as human resource management is, it simply wasn't a high priority for these firms: "given their shortage of resources in terms of time, money, people and expertise, a typical SME [small and medium size enterprise] manager's organizational imperatives are perceived elsewhere, in finance, production and marketing, with HR of diminished relative importance."[7]

INFORMALITY One effect of this is that human resource management activities tend to be less formalized (more informal) in smaller firms. For example, one study analyzed training practices in about 900 family and non-family small companies.[8] Training tended to be informal, with an emphasis, for instance, on methods like coworker and supervisory on-the-job training.

Such informality isn't just due to a lack of expertise and resources (although that's part of it); it's also partly a "matter of survival." Entrepreneurs must be able to quickly react to changes in competitive conditions. Given that, there's some logic in keeping things like compensation policies flexible. As one researcher says, the need for small businesses to quickly adapt to environmental realities like competitive challenges often means handling matters like raises, appraisals, and time off "on an informal, reactive basis with a short time horizon."[9]

THE ENTREPRENEUR *Entrepreneurs* are people who create businesses under risky conditions, and starting new businesses from scratch is almost always risky. Entrepreneurs therefore need to be highly dedicated and visionary. Researchers therefore believe that small firms' relative informality partly stems from entrepreneurs' unique personalities. Entrepreneurs tend (among other things) to be somewhat controlling: "Owners tend to want to impose their stamp and personal management style on internal matters, including the primary goal and orientation of the firm, it's working conditions and policies, and the style of internal and external communication and how this is communicated to the staff."[10]

IMPLICATIONS These four differences have several human resource management–related implications for small businesses.

- First, small business owners run the risk that their relatively rudimentary human resource practices will put them at a *competitive disadvantage*. We saw that big firms use practices such as Web-based recruiting, computerized testing, and intranet-based employee benefits enrollments to improve results and reduce the resources they must spend on them. A small business owner not using tools like these is accumulating unnecessary costs, and probably deriving inferior results than (larger) competitors.
- Second, there is a *lack of specialized HR expertise*.[11] In most (larger) small businesses, there are at most one or two dedicated human resource management people responsible for the full range of HR functions, from recruitment to compensation and safety and health. This makes it more likely that entrepreneurs may miss problems in specific areas, such as equal employment law, wages and hours, or occupational safety. This may produce legal or other problems.
- Third, the smaller firm is probably not adequately addressing potential *workplace litigation*. Most small business owners are well aware of the threat of employment-related litigation. However, their size and lack of HR expertise makes it unlikely that they'll address the problem. For example, most don't provide adequate (or any) employment discrimination or sexual harassment training.
- Fourth, the small business owner may not be fully complying with *compensation regulations and laws*. Compensation and benefits laws impose many restrictions on employers. These include (as examples) how to pay compensatory time for overtime hours worked, and distinguishing between employees and independent contractors. Violations have serious and expensive consequences.
- Fifth, duplication and paperwork lead to inefficiencies and *data entry errors*. For small businesses, many of which don't use human resource information systems, employee data (name, address, marital status, and so on) often appears on multiple human resource management forms. These forms include, for instance, medical enrollment forms, dental enrollment forms, tax withholding forms, and so on. Any change requires manually changing all forms. This is not only time-consuming and inefficient, but can precipitate errors.

Why HRM Is Important to Small Businesses

Entrepreneurs need to take these implications to heart. Small firms need all the advantages they can get, and for them effective human resource management is a competitive necessity. Small firms that have effective HR practices do better than those that do not.[12] For example, researchers studied 168 family-owned fast growth small and medium size enterprises (SMEs). They concluded that successful high-growth SMEs placed greater importance on training and development, performance appraisals, recruitment packages, maintaining morale, and setting competitive compensation levels than did low-performing firms: "These findings suggest that these human resource activities do in fact have a positive impact on performance [in smaller businesses]."[13]

For many small firms, effective human resource management is also a condition for getting and keeping big customers. Most suppliers (and therefore *their* suppliers) today must comply with international quality standards. This means even smaller businesses must attend to their human resource processes. Thus, to comply with ISO-9000 requirements, large customers "either directly checked for the presence of certain HR policies, or, satisfying their service demands indirectly necessitated changes in, for example, [the small vendor's] training and job design."[14]

We'll turn in this chapter to methods entrepreneurs can use to improve their human resource management practices, starting with Internet and government tools.

USING INTERNET AND GOVERNMENT TOOLS TO SUPPORT THE HR EFFORT

City Garage's managers knew they would never implement their firm's growth strategy without changing how they tested and hired employees.[15] At this fast-growing chain of repair shops, the old hiring process consisted of a paper-and-pencil application and one interview, followed by a hire/don't hire decision. The process ate up valuable management time, and was not particularly effective. City Garage's solution was to purchase the Personality Profile Analysis (PPA) online test from Thomas International USA. Now, after a quick application and background check, likely candidates take the 10-minute, 24-question PPA. City Garage staff then enter the answers into the PPA Software system, and receive test results in less than 2 minutes. These show whether the applicant is high or low in four personality characteristics.

Like City Garage, no small business owner needs to cede the advantage to big competitors when it comes to human resource management. One way to even the terrain is to use Internet-based HR resources, as City Garage has done. Another for companies operating in America, is to tap into the free resources of the U.S. government. We'll address both in this section.

Complying with Employment Laws

Complying with U.S. government (and state and local) employment law is a thorny issue for entrepreneurs. For example, "What can I ask a job candidate?" "Must I pay this person overtime?" and, "Must I report this injury?" Online and government sources can help.

❷ Give at least four examples of how entrepreneurs can use Internet and government tools to support the HR effort.

Addressing this issue starts with deciding which U.S. government employment laws apply to their size company. For example, Title VII of the Civil Rights Act of 1964 applies to employers with 15 or more employees, while the Age Discrimination in Employment Act of 1967 applies to those with 20 or more. By "employees," federal agencies mean "all employees, including part-time and temporary workers."[16] Small business owners will find the answers they need online at federal agencies' Websites like the following.

City Garage's managers knew they would never implement their firm's growth strategy without changing how they tested and hired employees.

THE DOL The U.S. Department of Labor's "*FirstStep* Employment Law Advisor" (see www.DOL.gov/elaws/firststep/) helps employers (and particularly small businesses) determine which laws apply to their business. First, the elaws wizard takes the owner through a series of questions, such as "What is the maximum number of employees your business or organization employs or will employ during the calendar year? (See Figure 12.1.)

Proceeding through the wizard, the small business owner arrives at a "results" page. This says, "Based on the information you provided in response to the questions in the Advisor, the following employment laws administered by the Department of Labor (DOL) may apply to your business or organization."[17] For a typical small firm, these laws might include the Consumer Credit Protection Act, Employee Polygraph Protection Act, Fair Labor Standards Act, Immigration and Nationality Act, Occupational Safety and Health Act, Uniformed Services Employment and Reemployment Rights Act, and Whistleblower Acts.

A linked DOL site (www.dol.gov/esa/whd/flsa/) provides information on the Fair Labor Standards Act (FLSA). It contains several specific "elaws advisors." Each one provides practical guidance on questions such as when to pay overtime. Figure 12.2 presents, from this Website, a list of elaws advisors.

THE EEOC The U.S. Equal Employment Opportunity Commission (EEOC) administers Title VII of the Civil Rights Act of 1964 (Title VII), the Age Discrimination in Employment Act of 1967 (ADEA), Title I of the Americans with Disabilities Act of 1990 (ADA), and the Equal Pay Act of 1963 (EPA). Its Web site (www.EEOC.gov/employers/) contains important information regarding EEOC matters, in particular:

- How do I determine if a business of my size is covered by the EEOC laws?
- Who may file a charge of discrimination with the EEOC?
- When can a charge of discrimination be filed?
- Can a small business resolve a charge without undergoing an investigation or facing a lawsuit?

Linked Web pages (see www.EEOC.gov/employers/smallbusinesses.html) provide small business owners with practical advice. For example, "What should I do when someone files a charge against my company?"

OSHA The DOL's Occupational Safety and Health Administration site (www.OSHA.gov/) similarly supplies guidance for small business owners. (See Figure 12.3.) OSHA's site provides, among other things, easy access to the *OSHA Small Business Handbook*. This contains practical information for small business owners, including industry specific safety and accident checklists.

FIGURE 12.1

FirstStep Employment Law Advisor

Source: www.dol.gov/elaws/firststep, accessed June 2008.

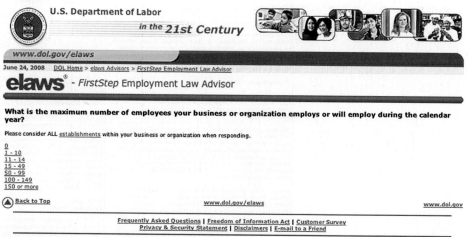

FIGURE 12.2

Sample DOL Elaws Advisors

Note: These are from http://www.dol.gov/esa/whd/flsa, accessed April 28, 2008

- The *Coverage and Employment Status Advisor* helps identify which workers are employees covered by the FLSA.
- The *Hours Worked Advisor* provides information to help determine which hours spent in work-related activities are considered FLSA "hours worked" and, therefore, must be paid.
- The *Overtime Security Advisor* helps determine which employees are exempt from the FLSA minimum wage and overtime pay requirements under the Part 541 overtime regulations.
- The *Overtime Calculator Advisor* computes the amount of overtime pay due in a sample pay period based on information from the user.
- The *Child Labor Rules Advisor* answers questions about the FLSA's youth employment provisions, including at what age young people can work and the jobs they can perform.
- The *Section 14(c) Advisor* helps users understand the special minimum wage requirements for workers with disabilities.

Employment Planning and Recruiting

Internet resources can make small business owners almost as effective as their large competitors at writing job descriptions and building applicant pools.

As we saw in chapter 4 (pages 107–108 and 138–145), the Department of Labor's O*NET (http://online.onetcenter.org) illustrates this well. Its online wizard enables business owners to quickly create accurate and professional job descriptions and job specifications.

FIGURE 12.3

OSHA Website

Source: http://www.osha.gov/dcsp/smallbusiness/index.html.

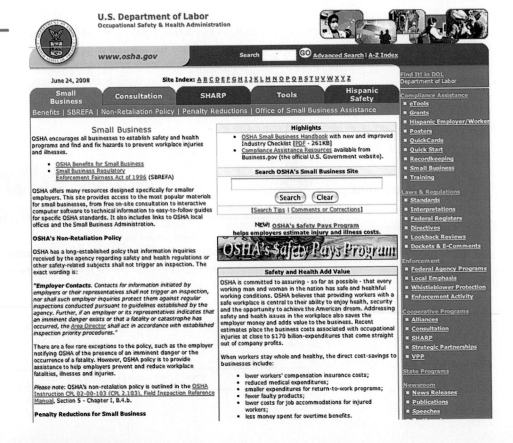

WEB-BASED RECRUITING Small business owners can and should use the online recruiting tools we discussed in chapter 4. For example, it's easy to post positions on Internet job boards on the sites of professional associations or on the sites of local newspapers.

For businesses with their own company Web sites, the dot-jobs domain can be effective. As explained earlier, it gives job seekers a simple, one-click way for finding jobs at the employers who registered at .jobs? (employers register at www.goto.jobs). For example, applicants seeking a job at Siemens can go to www.Siemens.jobs.

Employment Selection

For the small business, one or two hiring mistakes could wreak havoc. A formal testing program, like the one at City Garage, is thus advisable.

Some tests are so easy to use they are particularly good for smaller firms. One is the *Wonderlic Personnel Test*, which measures general mental ability and generally takes less than 15 minutes to administer. The tester reads the instructions, and then keeps time as the candidate works through the 50 problems in a four-page booklet. The tester scores the test by totaling the number of correct answers. Comparing the person's score with the minimum scores recommended for various occupations shows whether the person achieved the minimally acceptable score for the type of job in question.

The *Predictive Index* is another example. It measures work-related personality traits, drives, and behaviors—in particular dominance, extroversion, patience, and blame avoidance—on a two-sided sheet. A template makes scoring simple. The Predictive Index program includes 15 standard benchmark personality patterns. For example, there is the "social interest" pattern, for a person who is generally unselfish, congenial, persuasive, patient, and unassuming. This person would be good with people and a good personnel interviewer, for instance.

WONDERLIC EXAMPLE Several vendors, including both Wonderlic and Praendex (which publishes the Predictive Index) offer online applicant compilation and screening services. Wonderlic's service (which costs about $8,500 per year for a firm with, say, 35 employees) first provides job analyses for the employer's jobs. Wonderlic then provides a Web site the small businesses' applicants log into to take one or several selection tests (including the Wonderlic Personnel Test). Figure 12.4 shows a partial report for an sample applicant.

Online arrangements like these have many benefits. For example, they save the time the owners' employees might have to invest in testing candidates. For example, because it's available 24/7, prospective candidates can log in and apply anytime, wherever they are. That means a larger potential pool of applicants, and hopefully more likelihood of getting an outstanding employee.

Employment Training

While small companies can't compete with the training resources of giants like General Electric, Internet training can provide, at a relatively low cost, the sorts of professional employee training that were formerly beyond most small employers' reach.

PRIVATE VENDORS The small business owner can tap hundreds of suppliers of prepackaged training solutions. These range from self-study programs from SHRM (www.shrm.org), to specialized prepackaged training program suppliers. For example, the employer might arrange with one of these suppliers, Resource Development Ltd. of London (www.rdi.co.uk), to have its employees take stress management courses.

Skillsoft is another example (http://skillsoft.com/catalog/default.asp). Its courses include software development, business strategy and operations, professional effectiveness, and desktop computer skills. As an example, the course "interviewing effectively" is aimed at managers, team leaders, and human resource professionals. About 2 ½ hours long, it shows trainees how to use behavioral questioning to interview candidates.[18]

In the United Kingdom, the Training Journal online (www.trainingjournal.com) is one of several publications that can be used to find a vendor.

FIGURE 12.4

Wonderlic Personnel Test: Part of a Sample Report

Source: Wonderlic (www.wonderlic.com).

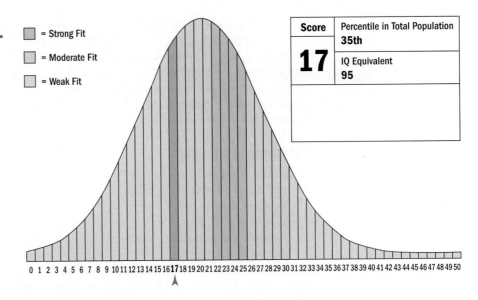

■ = Strong Fit

□ = Moderate Fit

□ = Weak Fit

Score	Percentile in Total Population
17	**35th**
	IQ Equivalent
	95

0 1 2 3 4 5 6 7 8 9 10 11 12 13 14 15 16 **17** 18 19 20 21 22 23 24 25 26 27 28 29 30 31 32 33 34 35 36 37 38 39 40 41 42 43 44 45 46 47 48 49 50

Score Interpretation

Job Fit: Test takers who score in this range do not meet the cognitive ability requirements identified for this job. The complexity present within this position may make it difficult for these individuals to meet minimum standards for job performance.

Training Potential: This test taker is likely to receive maximum benefit from training that follows a programmed or mastery approach to learning. Given enough time, this individual may have the ability to learn a limited number of lengthy, routine procedures. Allow for sufficient time with hands-on-training before requiring this individual to work independently.

THE SBA In the U.S. federal government's Small Business Administration (www. SBA.gov/training/) provides a virtual campus that offers online courses, workshops, publications, and learning tools aimed toward supporting entrepreneurs.[19] For example, the small business owner can link to "Writing Effective Job Descriptions," "Employees versus Contractors: What's the Difference?" and "The Interview Process: How to Select the Right Person." The SBA also has a growing list of online training courses (www.SBA.gov/services/training/onlinecourses/index.html). It includes online courses in areas such as writing effective job descriptions (see Figure 12.5).

NAM The National Association of Manufacturers (NAM) is the largest industrial trade organization in the United States. It represents about 14,000 member manufacturers, including 10,000 small and midsized companies.

NAM's virtual University (www.namvu.com) helps employees maintain and upgrade their work skills and continue their professional development. It offers almost 650 courses.[20] There are no long-term contracts to sign. Employers simply pay about $10–$30 per course taken by each employee. The catalog includes OSHA, quality, and technical training as well as courses in areas like business and finance, personal development, and customer service.

Employment Appraisal and Compensation

We've seen that even small employers now have easy access to computerized and online appraisal and compensation services.

For example, small employers can contract with vendors that enable them to do performance appraisals online. Thus, Employee Appraiser (www.employeeappraiser.com/index.php) presents a menu of more than a dozen evaluation dimensions, including dependability, initiative, communication, decision making, leadership, judgment, and planning and productivity.[21] Within each dimension are various performance factors, again in menu form. The eAppraisal system from Halogen Software is another example.[22]

FIGURE 12.5

Some Online Courses Offered by the Small Business Administration (SBA)

Source: www.sba.gov/smallbusinessplanner/manage/manageemployees/index.html, accessed June 2008.

Manage Employees

Managing the actions of employees is a critical component of running a business. Knowing what to do with regards to hiring, motivating, directing, reprimanding, and even firing an employee is information a business owner should know.

Writing Effective Job Descriptions

A job description describes the major areas of an employee's job or position. A good job description begins with a careful analysis of the important facts about a job, such as the individual tasks involved, the methods used to complete the tasks, the purpose and responsibilities of the job, the relationship of the job to other jobs, and the qualifications needed for the job.

Employees vs. Contractors: What's the Difference?

Whether a person is an independent contractor or an employee generally depends on the amount of control exercised by the employer over the work being done. Dictating how a job is to be done or limiting the actions of the worker may establish an employer-employee relationship.

The Interview Process: How to Select the "Right" Person

How do you select the right person for your business? There is no perfect answer, but the interview process can be a tremendous help if you use it effectively. In other words, you must have completed all of the other steps in the hiring process in order to get the most out of the interview process. Interviewing candidates for a position within your company is one of the final steps in the hiring process.

When Potential Employees Lie

When you receive a resume or job application, how can you be sure the applicant is telling the truth?

Immigration FAQs

Answers to common questions about immigration.

National Labor Relations Board FAQs

Answers to frequent questions regarding the National Labor Relations Board.

Glossary of National Labor Relations Board Terms

Learn the terms used in and about the National Labor Relations Board Teams.

Hiring Employees FAQs

Answers to commonly asked questions about hiring employees.

The U.S. Department of Labor's Employment Law Guide

Laws, regulations, and technical assistance services, provided by the U.S. Department of Labor.

Federal Government Jobs Bank

Career opportunities with the federal government.

Verify a Social Security Number

Verify employees' Social Security Numbers for accurate W-2 wage reports.

Plain English Guide to Employee Handbooks

Simple, easy guide to employee handbooks.

Planning for the Future

Know the ways to prepare for your retirement today.

Similarly, lack of easy access to salary surveys once made it difficult and time-consuming for smaller businesses to fine-tune their pay scales. Today, many career Web sites make it easy to determine local pay rates.

Employment Safety and Health

Safety is an important issue among small employers. One European study found that the majority of all the workplace accidents and serious workplace accidents occur in firms with less than 50 employees.[23]

OSHA CONSULTATION Without human resource managers or safety departments, small businesses often don't know where to turn for advice on promoting employee safety. Many even have the (inaccurate) notion that the U.S. Occupational Safety and Health Act doesn't cover small firms.[24]

OSHA provides free on-site safety and health services for small businesses. This service uses safety experts from state governments who provide consultations, usually at the employer's workplace. Employers can contact their nearest OSHA Area Office to speak to the compliance assistance specialist. According to OSHA, its safety and health consultation program is completely separate from the OSHA inspection effort, and no citations are issued or penalties imposed. (Employers can also check out the OSHA Training Institute training available in Chicago or in one of about 20 education centers located at U.S. colleges and universities.)

The employer triggers the process by requesting a voluntary consultation. There is then an opening conference with a safety expert, a walk-through, and a closing conference at which the employer and safety expert discuss the latter's observations. The consultant then sends you a detailed report explaining the findings. The employer's only obligation is to commit to correcting serious job safety and health hazards in a timely manner.

For example, when Jan Anderson, president of her own steel installation company in Colorado, realized her workers' compensation costs were higher than her payroll, she knew she had to do something. OSHA helped draft new safety systems, created educational materials, and provided inspections that were more cooperative than adversarial. As a result, says Anderson, "Our workers' compensation costs have decreased significantly, we have had no accidents, and there is an awareness that we take safety seriously."[25]

OSHA SHARP Basically, the OSHA Sharp program is a certification process through which OSHA certifies that small employers have achieved commendable levels of safety awareness. Employers request a consultation and visit, and undergo a complete hazard identification survey. The employer agrees to correct all hazards identified, and to implement and maintain a safety and health management system that, at a minimum, addresses OSHA's safety and health program management guidelines. In addition to producing a certifiably safe workplace, OSHA's on-site project manager may recommend that OSHA exempt the Sharp employer for two years from scheduled inspections.

LEVERAGING SMALL SIZE: FAMILIARITY, FLEXIBILITY, FAIRNESS, INFORMALITY, AND HRM

Small businesses need to capitalize on their strengths, so in dealing with employees they should capitalize on their smallness. Smallness should translate into personal *familiarity* with each employee's strengths, needs, and family situation. And it should translate into the luxury of being able to be relatively *flexible* and *informal* in the human resource management policies and practices the company follows. As we said earlier, smaller businesses often need to quickly adapt to environmental realities like competitive challenges. This often means that matters such as raises, appraisals, and time off tend to be conducted "on an informal, reactive basis with a short time horizon."[26] Flexibility is often key.

List five ways entrepreneurs can use their small size to improve their HR processes.

Flexibility in Benefits and Rewards

For example, the Family and Work Institute surveyed the benefits practices of about 1,000 small and large companies in the United States. They examined benefits such as flexible work, child care assistance, and health care.[27] Not surprisingly, they found that that large firms offer more *extensive* benefits packages than do smaller ones. However, many small firms seemed to overcome their bigger competitors by offering more flexibility.

A CULTURE OF FLEXIBILITY Basically, the study found that small companies, because of the relative intimacy that comes from the owners personally interacting with all employees each day, did a better job of fostering a "culture of flexibility." Most importantly, this meant "that supervisors are more supportive and understanding when work/life issues emerge."[28] For example, a furniture company in Sydney, Australia, exemplifies this. Many of the company's 17 employees have been with the firm for 10 to 20 years. An owner, attributes this in part to his firm's willingness to adapt to its workers' needs. For example, workers can share job responsibilities, and work part-time from home.

WORK-LIFE BENEFITS The point is that even without the deep pockets of larger firms, small firms can offer employees work-life benefits that large employers usually can't easily match. Here are some examples:[29]

- *Extra time off* For example, Friday afternoons off in the summer.
- *Compressed workweeks* For example, in the summer, offer compressed workweeks that let them take longer weekends.
- *Bonuses at critical times* Small business owners are more likely to know what's happening in the lives of their employees. Use this knowledge to provide special bonuses, for instance, if an employee has a new baby.
- *Flexibility* Small businesses should be able to excel at helping their employees deal with the demands of personal issues like childcare and eldercare. For example "if an employee is having a personal problem, help him or her create a work schedule that allows the person to solve problems without feeling like they're going to be in trouble."[30]
  - *Sensitivity to employees' strengths and weaknesses* The relative intimacy of the small business should enable the owner to be better attuned to his or her employees' strengths, weaknesses, and aspirations. Therefore, be attentive about what each of your employees do, ask them which jobs they feel most comfortable doing, and give them an opportunity to train for and move into the jobs they desire.
  - *Help them better themselves* For example, pay employees to take a class to help them develop their job skills.
  - *Feed them* Particularly after a difficult workweek or when some milestone (like a big sale) occurs, provide free meals every now and then, perhaps by taking your employees to lunch.
  - *Make them feel like owners* "Job enrichment" is relatively easy to achieve in small firms. For example, endeavor to give your employees input into major decisions, let them work directly with clients, get them client feedback, share company performance data with them, and give them an opportunity to share in the company's financial success.
- *Make sure they have what they need to do their jobs* Performance = Ability × Motivation. Having highly motivated employees is only half the challenge. Also ensure they have the tools they need to do their jobs—for instance, the necessary training, procedures, computers, and so on.

At Wards Furniture in Long Beach, California, workers can share job responsibilities, and work part-time from home.

■ *Constantly recognize a job well done* Capitalize on your day-to-day interactions with employees to "never miss an opportunity to give your employees the recognition they deserve."[31]

RECOGNITION Everyone likes to be recognized for a job well done. Studies show that recognition can often be as powerful as financial rewards. The relatively personal nature of small business interactions makes it both easier and more important to recognize employees. There are numerous *positive reinforcement rewards* you can use on a day-to-day basis, independent of your company's incentive plans. A short list would include:[32]

■ Challenging work assignments
■ Freedom to choose own work activity
■ Having fun built into work
■ More of preferred task
■ Role as boss's stand-in when he or she is away
■ Role in presentations to top management
■ Job rotation
■ Encouragement of learning and continuous improvement
■ Being provided with ample encouragement
■ Being allowed to set own goals
■ Compliments
■ Expression of appreciation in front of others
■ Note of thanks
■ Employee-of-the-month award
■ Special commendation
■ Bigger desk
■ Bigger office or cubicle

SIMPLE RETIREMENT BENEFITS Access to retirement benefits is more prevalent in large firms than small ones. Roughly 75% of large firms offer such benefits, while about 35% of small ones do.[33]

There are several straightforward ways that small firms can provide retirement plans for their employees. In the U.S., *Pension Protection Act of 2006* contains a provision for a new type of retirement benefit that combines traditional defined benefit and 401(k) plans.[34] Only available to employers with less than 500 employees, this provision exempts employers from the complex pension rules large employers must adhere to. With this new benefit, the employees get a retirement plan that blends a defined pension set by the plan, plus returns on the part of the investment that plan participants contributed.[35]

In the United States, probably the easiest way for small businesses to provide retirement benefits is through a *SIMPLE IRA plan*. With the *SIMPLE* (for *Savings Incentive Match Plan for Employees*) *IRA*, employers must (and employees may) make contributions to traditional employee IRAs. These plans are for employers or small businesses with 100 or fewer employees and no other type of retirement plan.

SIMPLE IRAs have many advantages—starting with simplicity. Basically, the owner need only contact an eligible financial institution and fill out several internal U.S. Internal Revenue Service forms. The IRS needs to have previously approved the financial institution. However, banks, mutual funds, and insurance companies that issue annuity contracts are generally eligible.[36] The plan has very low administrative costs. Employer contributions are tax-deductible. With a SIMPLE IRA, each employee is always 100% vested.[37]

Under these plans, the employer *must* contribute and employees *may* contribute. A typical employer contribution might match employee contributions dollar for dollar up to 3% of pay. The financial institution usually handles the IRS paperwork and reporting.

Simple, Informal Employee Selection Procedures

We saw earlier that small business managers can easily use Internet-based recruitment and selection tools to help even the recruitment/selection terrain. For example, Wonderlic's service includes a Web site that a small firm's applicants can use to take pre-screening tests. But, in general, small firms tend to rely on more informal employee selection and recruitment practices (like employee referrals and unstructured interviews) than do large firms.[38] Large firms simply have more time, resources, and specialized support to invest in formal recruiting and testing programs.

However, there are many simple, low-tech and basically costless things a small business can do to improve its selection process. We'll look at two, work-sampling tests, and streamlined interviews (see *HR in Practice*, below).

WORK-SAMPLING TESTS   What should you do if you are, say, trying to hire a marketing manager, and want a simple but more formal way to screen your job applicants?

Devising a *work-sampling test* is one simple solution. A work-sampling test means having the candidates perform actual samples of the job in question. Such tests have obvious face validity (they should clearly measure actual job duties) and are easy to devise.

The process is simple. Break down the job's main duties into component tasks. Then have the candidate complete a sample task. For example, for the marketing manager position, ask the candidate to spend an hour designing an ad, and also to spend a half hour writing out a marketing research program for a hypothetical product.

HR in Practice

A Simple, Streamlined Interviewing Process

The small business owner, pressed for time, may also use the following practical, streamlined employment interview process:[39]

Preparing for the Interview

Even a busy entrepreneur can quickly specify the kind of person who would be best for the job. One way to do so is to focus on four basic required factors—knowledge and experience, motivation, intellectual capacity, and personality. To identify the job's human requirements in this way, ask the following questions:

- *Knowledge and experience:* What must the candidate know to perform the job? What experience is absolutely necessary to perform the job?
- *Motivation:* What should the person like doing to enjoy this job? Is there anything the person should not dislike? Are there any essential goals or aspirations the person should have? Are there any unusual energy demands on the job?
- *Intellectual capacity:* Are there any specific intellectual aptitudes required (mathematical, mechanical, and so on)? How complex are the problems the person must solve? What must a person be able to demonstrate he or she can do intellectually? How should the person solve problems (cautiously, deductively, and so on)?

- *Personality factor:* What are the critical personality qualities needed for success on the job (ability to withstand boredom, decisiveness, stability, and so on)? How must the job incumbent handle stress, pressure, and criticism? What kind of interpersonal behavior is required in the job up the line, at peer level, down the line, and outside the firm with customers?

Specific Factors to Probe in the Interview

Next, ask a combination of situational questions, plus open-ended questions to probe the candidate's suitability for the job. For example:

- *Intellectual factor:* Here, ask questions that judge such things as complexity of tasks the person has performed, grades in school, test results (including scholastic aptitude tests, and so on), and how the person organizes his or her thoughts and communicates.
- *Motivation factor:* Probe such areas as the person's likes and dislikes (for each thing done, what he or she liked or disliked about it), aspirations (including the validity of each goal in terms of the person's reasoning about why he or she chose it), and energy level, perhaps by asking what he or she does on, say, a "typical Tuesday."

(continued)

■ *Personality factor:* Here, probe by looking for self-defeating behaviors (aggressiveness, compulsive fidgeting, and so on) and by exploring the person's past interpersonal relationships. Ask questions about the person's past interactions (working in a group at school, working with fraternity brothers or sorority sisters, leading the work team on the last job, and so on). Also, try to judge the person's behavior in the interview itself—is the candidate personable? Shy? Outgoing?

■ *Knowledge and experience factor:* Here, probe with situational questions such as "How would you organize such a sales effort?" or "How would you design that kind of Web site?"

Conducting the Interview

■ *Have a Plan.* Devise and use a plan to guide the interview. According to interviewing expert John Drake, significant areas to cover include the candidate's:

- College experiences
- Work experiences—summer, part-time
- Work experience—full-time (one by one)
- Goals and ambitions
- Reactions to the job you are interviewing for

- Self-assessments (by the candidate of his or her strengths and weaknesses)
- Military experiences
- Present outside activities[40]

■ *Follow Your Plan.* Perhaps start with an open-ended question for each topic, such as "Could you tell me about what you did when you were in high school?" Keep in mind that you are trying to elicit information about four main traits—intelligence, motivation, personality, and knowledge and experience. You can then accumulate the information in each of these four areas as the person answers. Follow up on particular areas that you want to pursue by asking questions like "Could you elaborate on that, please?"

Match the Candidate to the Job

You should now be able to draw conclusions about the person's intellectual capacity, knowledge and experience, motivation, and personality, and to summarize the candidate's strengths and limits. Next, compare your conclusions to the job description and the list of behavioral requirements you developed when preparing for the interview. This should provide a rational basis for matching the candidate to the job—one based on an analysis of the traits and aptitudes the job actually requires.

Flexibility in Training

Small companies also typically take a more informal approach to training and development. For example, one study of 191 small and 201 large firms in Europe found that smaller firms were much more informal in their approaches to training and development.[41] Many of the small firms didn't systematically monitor their managers' skill needs, and fewer than 50% (as opposed to 70% of large firms) had management career development programs. The smaller firms also tended to focus any management development training on learning specific firm-related competencies (such as how to sell the firm's products). They generally downplayed developing longer-term management skills.[42] They did so due to resource constraints and a reluctance to invest too much in managers who may then leave.

FOUR-STEP TRAINING PROCESS Limited resources or not, small businesses must have training procedures. Training is a hallmark of good management. Having high-potential employees doesn't guarantee they'll succeed. Instead, they must know what you want them to do and how you want them to do it. If they don't, they will improvise or do nothing productive at all. A less complex but still effective four-step training process follows.

Step 1 **Write a Job Description** A detailed job description is the heart of a training program. It should list the daily and periodic tasks of each job, along with a summary of the steps in each task.

Step 2 **Develop a Task Analysis Record Form** The individual manager or small business owner can use an abbreviated *Task Analysis Record Form* (Table 12.1) containing four columns.

- In the first column, list *specific tasks*. Here include what is to be performed in terms of each of the main tasks, and the steps involved in each task.

- In the second column, list *performance standards* (in terms of quantity, quality, accuracy, and so on).

TABLE 12.1 Sample Summary Task Analysis Record Form

Task List	Performance Standards	Trainable Skills Required	Aptitudes Required
1. Operate paper cutter			
1.1 Start motor	Start by push-button on first try	To start machine without accidentally attempting re-start while machine is running	Ability to understand written and spoken instructions
1.2 Set cutting distance	Maximum +/– tolerance of 0.007 inches	Read gauge	Able to read tolerances on numerical scale
1.3 Place paper on cutting table	Must be completely even to prevent uneven edges	Lift paper correctly	At least average manual dexterity
1.4 Push paper up to paper cutter blade		Must be even with blade	At least average manual dexterity
1.5 Grasp safety release with left hand	100% of the time, for safety	Must keep both hands on releases to prevent hand contact with cutting blade	Ability to understand written and spoken warnings

Note: This shows the first five steps in one of the tasks (operate paper cutter) for which a printing factory owner would train the person doing the cutting of the paper before placing the paper on the printing presses.

- In the third column, list *trainable skills required*—things the employee must know or do to perform the task. This column provides you with specific knowledge and skills (such as "Keep both hands on the wheel") that you want to emphasize in training.
- In the fourth column, list *aptitudes required*. These are the human aptitudes (such as mechanical comprehension) that the employee should have to be trainable for the task and for which the employee can be screened ahead of time.

Step 3 **Develop a Job Instruction Sheet** Next develop a Job Instruction Sheet for the job. As in Table 12.2, a job instruction sheet shows the steps in each task as well as key points for each.

Step 4 **Prepare Training Program for the Job** At a minimum, the job's training manual should include the job description, Task Analysis Record Form, and Job Instruction Sheet, all collected in a training manual. It might also contain a brief overview/introduction to the job, and a graphical and/or written explanation of how the job fits with other jobs in the plant or office.

With this (or any) training program, you also have to decide what training media to use. A simple but effective on-the-job training program using current

TABLE 12.2 Sample Job Instruction Sheet

	Steps in Task	Key Points to Keep in Mind
1.	Start motor	None
2.	Set cutting distance	Carefully read scale—to prevent wrong-sized cut
3.	Place paper on cutting table	Make sure paper is even—to prevent uneven cut
4.	Push paper up to cutter	Make sure paper is tight—to prevent uneven cut
5.	Grasp safety release with left hand	Do not release left hand—to prevent hand from being caught in cutter
6.	Grasp cutter release with right hand	Do not release right hand—to prevent hand from being caught in cutter
7.	Simultaneously pull cutter and safety releases	Keep both hands on corresponding releases—avoid hands being on cutting table
8.	Wait for cutter to retract	Keep both hands on releases—to avoid having hands on cutting table
9.	Retract paper	Make sure cutter is retracted; keep both hands away from releases
10.	Shut off motor	None

employees or supervisors as trainers requires only the written materials we just listed. On the other hand, the nature of the job or the number of trainees may require producing or purchasing special digital training media, PowerPoint slide presentations, or more extensive printed materials. For many generic jobs such as supervisor or bookkeeper, vendors like those we discussed in chapter 6 provide packaged multi-media training programs.

INFORMAL TRAINING METHODS   Training expert Stephen Covey says small businesses can do many things to provide job-related personal improvement without actually establishing expensive formal training programs. His suggestions include:[43]

- Offer to cover the tuition for special classes
- Identify online training opportunities
- Provide a library of tapes and DVDs for systematic, disciplined learning during commute times
- Encourage the sharing of best practices among associates
- When possible, send people to special seminars and association meetings for learning and networking
- Create a learning ethic by having everyone teach each other what they are learning

Fairness and the Family Business

Most small businesses are family businesses, in that the owner and one or more managers (and possibly employees) are family members.

Being a non-family employee here isn't always easy. They sometimes feel like outsiders. Furthermore, treating family and non-family employees inequitably can undermine perceptions of fairness, as well as morale. If so, as one writer puts it, "It's a sure bet that their lower morale and simmering resentments are having a negative effect on your operations and sapping your profits."[44] Reducing such "fairness" problems involves several steps, including:[45]

- *Set the ground rules.* One family business consultant says,

  "During the hiring process the applicant should be informed as to whether they will be essentially placeholders, or whether there will be some potential for promotion. The important thing is to make the expectations clear, including in matters such as the level of authority and decision-making they can expect to attain in the company."[46]

- *Treat people fairly.* Most employees in a family business understand that they're not going to be treated exactly the same as family members. However, they do expect to be treated fairly. In part, this means working hard to avoid "any appearance that family members are benefiting unfairly from the sacrifice of others."[47] That's why family members in many family businesses often avoid ostentatious purchases like expensive cars. (Several years ago, a book titled *The Millionaire Next Door* explained, among other things, that some small business owners were so frugal that their neighbors didn't realize they were millionaires).

- *Confront family issues.* Discord and tension among family members at work distracts and demoralizes other employees. Family members must therefore confront and work out their differences.

- *Erase privilege.* Family members "should avoid any behavior that would lead people to the conclusion that they are demanding special treatment in terms of assignments or responsibilities."[48] Family employees should come in earlier, work harder, and stay later than other employees. Endeavor to make it clear that family members earned their promotions.

The accompanying *Personal Competencies* feature shows how small business managers can use simple communication tools to improve employee-related operations.

Personal Competencies

Building Your *Communications* Skills

Seeking to shield their 11 IHOP restaurants from the industry's sky-high turnover rates, Joel Scripture and his partner hit on a solution. They dramatically reduced turnover with a new online system. It lets new employees anonymously report their opinions about the hiring process.[49] That feedback from that simple communication tool enabled them to recalibrate their firm's training and orientation methods, and reduce turnover by about a third.

Effective communications are important for any manager, but especially for those managing small businesses. With a thousand or more employees, one or two disgruntled employees may get lost in the shuffle. But in a small restaurant or retail shop with 5 or 10 employees, one or two disgruntled employees can destroy the business's quality service. Yet small business owners generally don't have the means to implement expensive communications programs. That's why simple programs, like the one at IHOP or the following ones, are important.

NEWSLETTER   In Bonita Springs, Florida, Mel's Gourmet Diner keeps employees informed with a quarterly newsletter. It distributes copies at the chain's 10 locations, but also posts it on the company Web site, and plans to translate it into Spanish. "It sounds like a cliché, but our people are the keys to our success," says the owner. "We want to make sure we give them all the information and tools they need."[50]

ONLINE   Each time employees of Tampa, Florida-based Let's Eat! go to one of the firm's computers to input a guest's order, they can quickly review the chain's menu changes, special promotions, and mandatory employee meetings.[51]

THE HUDDLE   Sea Island Shrimp House in San Antonio, Texas, keeps employees in its seven restaurants communicating with what it calls "cascading huddles." As in football parlance, the huddles are very quick meetings. At 9 A.M. top management meets in the first of the day's "huddles." The next huddle is a conference call with store managers. Then, store managers meet with hourly employees at each location before the restaurants open, to make sure the news of the day gets communicated. "It's all about alignment and good, timely communications," says the company. "Any issues on that day that needed to be communicated would happen in that huddles sequence."[52]

USING PROFESSIONAL EMPLOYER ORGANIZATIONS

The 40 employees at First Weigh Manufacturing in Sanford, Florida, don't work for a giant company, but they get employee benefits and services as if they do. That's because Tom Strasse, First Weigh's owner, signed with ADP Total Source, a *professional employer organization* that now handles all First Weigh's HR processes. "I didn't have the time or the personnel to deal with the human resources, safety, and OSHA regulations," Strasse says.[53]

At the end of the day, many small business owners, like Tom Strasse, understandably look at all the issues involved with managing personnel, and decide to outsource all or most of their human resource functions to outside vendors (generally called *professional employer organizations* (PEOs), *human resource outsourcers* (HROs), or sometimes *employee* or *staff leasing firms*).

How Do PEOs Work?

These vendors range from payroll companies to those that handle all an employer's human resource management requirements.[54] At a minimum these firms take over the employer's payroll tasks.[55] Usually, however, PEOs assume most of the employer's human resources chores.

PEOs have several characteristics. By transferring the client firm's employees to the PEO's payroll, PEOs become co-employers of record for the employer's employees. That enables the PEO to fold the client's employees into the PEO's insurance and benefits program, usually at a lower cost. The PEO usually handles employee-related activities such as recruiting, hiring (with client firms' supervisors' approvals), and payroll and taxes. Most PEOs focus on employers with under 100 employees, and charge fees of 2% to 4% of a company's payroll. HROs usually handle these functions on an "administrative services only"—they're basically your "HR office," but your employees still work for you.[56]

Why Use a PEO?

Employers turn to PEOs for several reasons:

LACK OF SPECIALIZED HR SUPPORT   Small firms with fewer than 100 or so employees typically have no dedicated HR managers, and even larger ones may have few specialists. That means the owner basically has all or most of the human resource management burden on his or her shoulders.

PAPERWORK   Many small business owners spend up to 25% of their time on personnel-related paperwork—background checks, benefits sign-ups, and so on.[57] In the U.S., the association that represents employee leasing firms estimates that the average cost of regulations, paperwork, and tax compliance for smaller firms is about $5,000 per employee per year.[58] The PEO assumes responsibility for all or most of this. Many small business owners therefore figure what they save on not managing their own human resource activities pays for the employee leasing firm's fees. For instance, when First Weigh's Strasse has a question about employee legal issues, he just calls his ADP representative.

LIABILITY   Staying in compliance with pension plan rules, and other personnel-related laws can be perilous. Legally, PEOs generally "contractually share liability with clients and have a vested interest in preventing workplace injuries and employee lawsuits."[59] The PEO should thus help ensure the small business fulfills all its personnel-related legal responsibilities. The issues that Peter McCann and his embroidery company Ideal Images faced help illustrate the liability issue. His 27-employee firm was studiously nondiscriminatory. However, a former employee still filed a charge of racial discrimination against Ideal. The investigation absorbed several tense weeks of McCann's time. Between that, and the fact that he was starting to find his chores "nearly all-consuming," he turned to Alliance Group, a PEO.[60]

BENEFITS   Insurance and benefits are often the big PEO attraction. Getting health and other insurance is a problem for smaller firms. Even group rates for life or health insurance can be quite high when only 20 or 30 employees are involved. First Weigh Manufacturing's health insurance carrier dropped the firm after its first two years, and Strasse had to scramble to find a new carrier—which he did, with premiums that were 30% higher.

That's where the leasing firm comes in. Remember that the leasing firm is the legal employer of your employees. The employees therefore are absorbed into a much larger insurable group, along with other employers' former employees. As a result, a small business owner may be able to get insurance (as well as benefits like 401(k)s) for its people that it couldn't otherwise.[61]

PERFORMANCE   Last but not least, the professionalism that the PEO brings to recruiting, screening, training, compensating, and maintaining employee safety and welfare will hopefully translate into improved employee and business results.

Caveats

Using vendors like these may sound too good to be true, and it often is: "If your PEO is poorly managed, or goes bankrupt, you could find yourself with an office full of uninsured workers."[62] Many employers view their human resource management processes as a strategic advantage, and aren't inclined to turn over strategy-sensitive tasks like screening and training to third party firms. Many employers aren't comfortable letting a third party become the legal employer of their employees. There are also more concrete risks to consider. Several years ago, for instance, the employee leasing industry tarnished itself when one or two firms manipulated the pension benefits offered to higher-paid employees.[63]

Using vendors like these can also raise its own liability concerns. In the typical employee leasing arrangement, the leasing firm and the client employer agree to share certain employee-related responsibilities, a concept known as co-employment. The question then is, who's responsible if things go wrong? For example, in the U.S. some states have not universally upheld workers' compensation as the sole remedy for injuries at work. Who's responsible if an employee here gets hurt, the PEO or the employer? One must specify whether the client company or the leasing firm is insuring the workers' compensation exposure.[64]

Several things may signal problems with the prospective PEO. One is *lax due diligence*. Because they share liability with the employer, they should question you extensively about your firm's workplace safety and human resource policies and practices.[65] Another is a *recent name change*. Search the Internet and Better Business Bureaus to see if there's been a recent name change, a possible signal of past problems. Finally, it's unlikely that the employer will gain more than a modest savings (if any) by partnering with a PEO (relative to overseeing its own HR). Therefore, be suspect of anyone *promising you substantial savings*.

Guidelines for Finding and Working with PEOs

❹ Discuss how you would choose and deal with a professional employee organization.

Employers need to choose and manage the PEO relationship carefully. Suggestions for doing so follow.

Conduct a needs analysis. Know ahead of time exactly what human resource and risk management concerns your company wants to address.

Review the services of all PEO firms you're considering. Determine which can meet all your requirements.

Determine if the PEO is accredited. There is no rating system for PEOs. However, the Employer Services Assurance Corporation of Little Rock, Arkansas (www.Esacorp.org), imposes higher financial, auditing, and operating standards on its members.[66] Also check the Web site of the National Association of Professional Employer Organizations (www.NAPEO.org) and www.PEO.com.[67]

Check the provider's bank, credit, and professional *references*. Make sure to demand specifics on things like insurance providers and creditors.

Understand how the *employee benefits are funded*. Is it fully insured or partially self-funded? Who was the third-party administrator or carrier? Confirm that participating employers will receive first-day coverage.

See if the provider contract assumes employment law *compliance liabilities in the applicable states*.

Review the service agreement carefully. Are the respective parties' responsibilities and liabilities clearly delineated?[68]

Investigate *how long the PEO has been in business*. The vendor should show a history of staying power to show that it's well-managed.

Check out the prospective PEO's staff. Do they seem to have the depth and expertise to deliver on its promises?

Ask, *how will the firm deliver its services?* In person? By phone? Via the Web?

Ask about *upfront fees* and how these are determined.

Periodically get proof that payroll taxes and insurance premiums are being paid properly and that any legal issues are handled correctly.[69]

MANAGING HR SYSTEMS, PROCEDURES, AND PAPERWORK

Introduction

Consider the paperwork required to run a five-person retail shop. Just to start with, recruiting and hiring an employee might require a help wanted advertising listing, an employment application, an interviewing checklist, various verifications—of education, and immigration status, for instance—and a telephone reference checklist. You then might need an employment agreement, confidentiality and noncompetition agreements, and an employer indemnity agreement. To process that new employee you might need an employee background verification, a new employee checklist, and forms for withholding tax and to obtain new employee data. And to keep track of the employee once on board, you'd need—just to start—a personnel data sheet, daily and weekly time records, an hourly employee's weekly time sheet, and an expense report. Then come the performance appraisal forms, a disciplinary notice, an employee orientation record, separation notice, and employment reference response.

In this final section, we'll see that the preceding list barely scratches the surface of the policies, procedures, and paperwork you'll need to run the human resource management part of your business. Perhaps with just one or two employees you could keep track of everything in your head, or just write a separate memo for each HR action, and place it in a manila folder for each worker. But with more than a few employees you'll need to create a human resource system comprised of standardized forms. As the company grows, various parts of the HR system—payroll, or appraising, for instance—will have to be computerized if the firm is to remain competitive. We'll cover manual and computerized HR systems in this final section.

Basic Components of Manual HR Systems

Very small employers (say, with 10 employees or less) will probably start with a manual human resource management system. From a practical point of view, this generally means obtaining and organizing a set of standardized personnel forms covering each important aspect of the HR—recruitment, selection, training, appraisal, compensation, safety—process, as well as some means for organizing all this information for each of your employees.

BASIC FORMS The number of forms you would conceivably need even for a small firm is quite large, as the illustrative list in Table 12.3 shows.[70] One simple way to obtain the

> 5 Describe how you would create a start-up paper-based human resource system for a new small business.

TABLE 12.3 Some Important Employment Forms

New Employee Forms	Current Employee Forms	Employee Separation Forms
Application	Employee Status Change Request	Retirement Checklist
New Employee Checklist	Employee Record	Termination Checklist
Employment Interview	Performance Evaluation	COBRA Acknowledgement
Reference Check	Warning Notice	Unemployment Claim
Telephone Reference Report	Vacation Request	Employee Exit Interview
Employee Manual Acknowledgement	Probation Notice	
Employment Agreement	Job Description	
Employment Application Disclaimer	Direct Deposit Acknowledgement	
Probationary Evaluation	Absence Report	
	Disciplinary Notice	
	Employee Secrecy Agreement	
	Grievance Form	
	Expense Report	
	401(k) Choices Acknowledgement	
	Injury Report	

Office Depot sells packages of individual personnel forms.

basic component forms of a manual HR system is to start with one of the books or CDs that provide compilations of HR forms. The forms you want can then be adapted from these sources for your particular situation. Office supply stores also sell packages of personnel forms. For example, Office Depot sells packages of individual personnel forms as well as a "Human Resource Kit" containing 10 copies of each of the following: Application, Employment Interview, Reference Check, Employee Record, Performance Evaluation, Warning Notice, Exit Interview, and Vacation Request, plus a Lawsuit-Prevention Guide.[71] Also available (and highly recommended) is a package of Employee Record Folders. Use the folders to maintain a file on each individual employee; on the outside of the pocket is printed a form for recording information such as name, start date, company benefits, and so on.

OTHER SOURCES Several direct-mail catalog companies similarly offer a variety of HR materials. For example, HRdirect (100 Enterprise Place, Dover, DE, 19901, phone: 1-800-346-1231, http://www.hrdirect.com/) offers packages of personnel forms. These include, for instance, Short- and Long-Form Employee Applications, Applicant Interviews, Employee Performance Reviews, Job Descriptions, Exit Interviews, and Absentee Calendars and Reports. There are also various legal-compliance forms, including standardized Harassment Policy and FMLA Notice forms, as well as posters (for instance, covering legally required postings for matters such as the Americans with Disabilities Act and Occupational Safety and Health Act) available.

G. Neil Company, of Sunrise, Florida (phone: 1-800-999-9111, http://www.gneil.com/), is another direct-mail personnel materials source. In addition to a complete line of personnel forms, documents, and posters, it also carries manual systems for matters like attendance history, job analyses, and for tracking vacation requests and safety records. They have a complete HR "start-up" kit containing 25 copies of each of the basic components of a manual HR system. These include Long Form Application for Employment, Attendance History, Performance Appraisal, Payroll/Status Change Notice, Absence Report, and Vacation Request & Approval, all organized in a file box.

Automating Individual HR Tasks

As the small business grows, it becomes increasingly unwieldy and uncompetitive to rely on manual HR systems. For a company with 40 or 50 employees or more, the amount of management time devoted to things like attendance history and performance appraisals can multiply into weeks. It is therefore at about this point that most small- to medium-sized firms begin computerizing individual human resource management tasks.

PACKAGED SYSTEMS Here again there are a variety of resources available. For example, at the Web site for the International Association for Human Resource Information Management (www.ihrim.org), you'll find, within the Buyers Guide tab, a categorical list of HR software vendors.[72] These firms provide software solutions for virtually all personnel tasks, ranging from benefits management to compensation, compliance, employee relations, outsourcing, payroll, and time and attendance systems.

Then, as the company grows, the owner will probably decide to transition to an integrated human resource management system; we discuss the basics in the accompanying *Business in Action* feature.

Business in Action Building Your *Human Resource Information System (HRIS)* Knowledge

information system
The interrelated people, data, technology, and organizational procedures a company uses to collect, process, store, and disseminate information.

transaction-processing systems
Provide the company's managers and accountants with detailed information about short-term, daily activities, such as accounts payables, tax liabilities, and order status.

management information systems
Help managers make better decisions by producing standardized, summarized reports on a regular basis.

executive support systems
Provide top managers with information for making decisions on matters such as 5-year plans.

human resource information systems
Interrelated components working together to collect, process, store, and disseminate information to support decision making, coordination, control, analysis, and visualization of an organization's human resource management activities.

Companies need information systems to get their work done. For example, the sales team needs some way to tell accounting to bill a customer, and to tell production to fill the order. The term **information system** refers to the interrelated people, data, technology, and organizational procedures a company uses to collect, process, store, and disseminate information. Information systems may or may not be computerized, although they often are. All the HR paperwork systems we described—for collecting information on new employees, and for keeping track of their appraisals, benefits, and training, for instance—are information systems, although they're not computerized. Of course, as the company grows, it makes sense to computerize its information systems.

LEVELS OF INFORMATION SYSTEMS Companies tend to install information systems from the bottom up, level by organizational level. **Transaction-processing systems** often come first; they provide the company's managers and accountants with detailed information about short-term, daily activities, such as accounts payables, tax liabilities, and order status.

Management information systems *(MIS)* are a level up; they basically help managers make better decisions by producing standardized, summarized reports on a regular basis. For example, an MIS may take raw data (say, on sales by location), and show the sales manager the trend of sales for the past two weeks; or show the production manager a graph of weekly inventory levels; or show the CEO a report summarizing the company's revenues, expenses, and profits for the quarter.

One more level up, **executive support systems** provide top managers with information for making decisions on matters such as 5-year plans. For example, the CEO of BMW might use his executive support system to put the sales of each of BMW's various cars last month into context, by comparing them with sales of competing brands.

As companies grow, they also often turn to integrated **human resource information**

systems (HRIS). We can define an *HRIS* as interrelated components working together to collect, process, store, and disseminate information to support decision making, coordination, control, analysis, and visualization of an organization's human resource management activities.[73] There are several reasons for installing an HRIS. The first is improved transaction processing.

IMPROVED TRANSACTION PROCESSING The day-to-day minutiae of maintaining and updating employee records takes an enormous amount of time. One study found that 71% of HR employees' time was devoted to transactional tasks like checking leave balances, maintaining address records, and monitoring employee benefits distributions.[74] HRIS packages substitute powerful computerized processing for a wide range of the firm's HR transactions.

ONLINE SELF-PROCESSING HR information systems make it possible (or easier) to make the company's employees part of the HRIS. For example, at Provident Bank, an HR compensation system called Benelogic lets the bank's employees self-enroll in all their desired benefits programs over the Internet at a secure site. It also "support[s] employees' quest for 'what if' information relating to, for example, the impact on their take-home pay of various benefits options, tax withholding changes, insurance coverage, retirement planning and more."[75] That's all work that HR employees would previously have had to do for Provident's employees.

IMPROVED REPORTING CAPABILITY Because the HRIS integrates numerous individual HR tasks (training records, appraisals, employee personal data, and so on), installing an HRIS boosts HR's reporting capabilities. In practice, the variety of reports possible is limited only by the manager's imagination. For a start, for instance, reports might be available (companywide and by department) for health care cost per employee, pay and benefits as a percent of operating expense, cost per hire, report on training, volunteer turnover rates, turnover costs, time to fill jobs, and return on human capital invested (in terms of training and education fees, for instance).

HR SYSTEM INTEGRATION Because the HRIS's software components (record keeping, payroll, appraisal, and so forth) are integrated, the employer can dramatically reengineer its HR function. Some HRIS systems route promotions, salary increases, transfers, and other e-forms through the organization to the proper managers for approval. As one person signs off, it's routed to the next. If anyone forgets to process a document, a smart agent issues reminders until the task is completed.

HRIS VENDORS Many firms today offer HRIS packages. The Web site for the International Association for Human Resource

Information Management (http://www.ihrim.org/), for instance, lists HRIS vendors.

HR AND INTRANETS Employers are increasingly creating intranet-based HR information systems. For example, an Australian energy company uses its intranet for benefits communication. Employees can access the benefits homepage and (among other things) review the company's 401(k) plan investment options, get answers to frequently asked questions about the company's medical and dental plans, and report changes in family status. Other uses for human resource intranets include, for instance: automate job postings and applicant tracking, set up training registration, provide electronic pay stubs, publish an electronic employee handbook, and let employees update their personal profiles and access their accounts, such as 401(k)s.

Review

SUMMARY

1. Managing human resources in small firms is different for four main reasons: *size, priorities, informality*, and the nature of the *entrepreneur*. These have several implications. First, small business owners run the risk that their relatively rudimentary human resource practices will put them at a *competitive disadvantage* Second, there is a *lack of specialized HR expertise*. Third, the smaller firm is probably not adequately addressing potential *workplace litigation*. Fourth, the small business owner may not be fully complying with *compensation regulations and laws*. Fifth, duplication and paperwork lead to inefficiencies and *data entry errors*.

2. The U.S. Department of Labor's "*FirstStep* Employment Law Advisor" helps employers (and particularly small businesses) determine which laws apply to their business. The DOL's site also provides information on the Fair Labor Standards Act (FLSA). It contains several "elaws advisors." The U.S. Equal Employment Opportunity Commission's (EEOC) Web site provides important information regarding EEOC matters, such as Title VII. The DOL's Occupational Safety and Health Administration site similarly presents a wealth of information for small business owners. OSHA's site provides, among other things, easy access to things like the *OSHA Handbook for Small Businesses*.

3. Internet resources can make small business owners more effective in HRM. For example, the

Department of Labor's O*NET is effective for creating job descriptions. Small businesses can use the online recruiting tools we discussed in chapter 4. Wonderlic's applicant tracking service also provides job analyses for the employer's jobs. There are many suppliers of prepackaged training solutions. These range from self-study programs from the American Management Association (www.amanet.org/) and SHRM (www.shrm.org), to specialized programs. The federal government's Small Business Administration (www.SBA.gov/training/) offers online courses. Small employers can also do performance appraisals online. OSHA provides free on-site safety and health services for small businesses.

4. Small businesses need to capitalize on their strengths, and in dealing with employees they should capitalize on their smallness. Smallness should translate into personal *familiarity* with each employee's strengths, needs, and family situation. And it should translate into the luxury of being able to be relatively *flexible* and *informal* in the human resource management policies and practices the company follows. Even without the deep pockets of larger firms, small firms can offer employees work-life benefits that large employers usually can't match.

5. Access to retirement benefits is more prevalent in large firms than small ones. Roughly 75% of

large firms offer such benefits, while about 35% of small ones do. There are several straightforward ways that small firms can provide retirement plans for their employees. For example, the *Pension Protection Act of 2006* contains a provision for a new type of retirement benefit that combines traditional defined benefit and 401(k) plans.

6. Small firms rely on more informal employee selection, recruitment, and training practices. Devising a *work sampling test* is one simple solution. Limited resources or not, small businesses must have training procedures. Training is a hallmark of good management. Having high-potential employees doesn't guarantee they'll succeed. Instead, they must know what you want them to do and how you want them to do it. We discussed a less complex but still effective job-instruction training process.

7. Most small businesses are family businesses. Inequitable treatment of family and non-family employees can undermine perceptions of fairness, as well as morale. We discussed methods for reducing problems.

8. Effective communications are important for any manager, but especially for those managing small businesses. We discussed simple programs, including newsletters and "huddles" for improving communications.

9. Many small business owners look at all the issues involved with managing personnel, and decide to outsource all or most of their human resource functions to outside vendors (generally called *professional employer organizations* or PEOs,

human resource outsourcers, or sometimes *employee* or *staff leasing firms*). At a minimum these take over the employer's payroll tasks. Usually, PEOs assume most of the employer's human resources chores. The PEO usually handles employee-related activities such as recruiting, hiring (with client firms' supervisors' approvals), and payroll and taxes.

10. Even small businesses use extensive HR-related paperwork. Very small employers start with a manual human resource management system. This generally means obtaining and organizing a set of standardized personnel forms covering each aspect of HR—recruitment, selection, training, appraisal, compensation, and safety—as well as some means for organizing all this information. Office Depot, Staples, and several direct-mail catalog companies similarly offer a variety of HR materials. As the company grows, most small- to medium-sized firms begin computerizing individual HR tasks. For example, the G. Neil Company sells off-the-shelf software packages for monitoring attendance, employee record keeping, writing job descriptions, writing employee policy handbooks, and conducting computerized employee appraisals.

11. As companies grow, they often turn to integrated human resource information systems (HRIS). We defined an HRIS as interrelated components working together to collect, process, store, and disseminate information to support decision making, coordination, control, analysis, and visualization of an organization's human resource management activities.

KEY TERMS

information system   398
transaction-processing systems   398
management information systems   398

executive support systems   398
human resource information systems   398

DISCUSSION QUESTIONS AND EXERCISES

1. How and why is HR in small businesses different than in large firms?
2. Explain why HRM is important to small businesses.
3. Explain and give at least four examples of how entrepreneurs can use Internet and government tools to support the HR effort.
4. Explain and give at least five examples of ways entrepreneurs can use small size—familiarity, flexibility, and informality—to improve their HR processes.
5. Discuss what you would do to find, retain, and deal with on an ongoing basis a professional employee organization.
6. Describe with examples how you would create a startup paper-based human resource system for a new small business.

Application Exercises

HR in Action Case Incident 1 — The New HR System

The Hotel Paris is a small, 10-room hotel, with about five full-time employees in a large city in the Midlands region of England. The hotel's owners, Marcel and Pierre, run the hotel together, and they aim, as they put it, "to use superior guest service to differentiate the Hotel Paris as an upscale boutique hotel with the finest service." The issue is how to create a set of human resource practices that will get their employees to behave in a way that guests perceive as "superior guest service."

Unfortunately, while multinational hotel chains like Ritz-Carlton have huge recruitment and training budgets and facilities, the Hotel Paris has almost nothing to spend on such activities. Just focusing on their company's training processes, for instance, the partners had reasons to be concerned. For one thing, the Hotel Paris relied almost exclusively on informal on-the-job training. After having lunch with a friend who worked for Premier Inn, Pierre had even more reason for concern. For example, in terms of number of hours training per employee per year, number of hours training for new employees, cost per trainee hour, and percent of payroll spent on training, the Hotel Paris spent about 1% of what Premier Inn did, per employee. "How can we compete with such figures?" said Pierre.

The problem, of course, was that the Hotel Paris's training wasn't just inefficient, it was nonexistent. That was the same with the Hotel Paris' human resources systems, including its incentives system (also nonexistent), appraisal system (ditto), and employee recruitment/selection systems (the same).

Questions

1. Based on what you read in this chapter and the case, what is the problem here?
2. What do you suggest Marcel and Pierre do first with respect to human resource management? Why?
3. Explain with detailed examples how Marcel and Pierre can use free online and governmental sources to accomplish at least part of what you propose in your previous answer.
4. Now, give three examples of fee-based online tools you suggest Marcel and Pierre use.
5. Do you suggest Marcel and Pierre use a PEO? Why?

HR in Action Case Incident 2 — Carter Cleaning Company: The New Pay Plan

Carter Cleaning does not have a formal wage structure nor does it have rate ranges or use compensable factors. Wage rates are based mostly on those prevailing in the surrounding community and are tempered with an attempt on the part of Jack Carter to maintain some semblance of equity between what workers with different responsibilities in the stores are paid.

Needless to say, Carter does not make any formal surveys when determining what his company should pay. He peruses the want ads almost every day and conducts informal surveys among his friends in the local chapter of the laundry and cleaners trade association. While Jack has taken a "seat-of-the-pants" approach to paying employees, his salary schedule has been guided by several basic pay policies. While many of his dry cleaner colleagues adhere to a policy of paying absolutely minimum rates, Jack has always followed a policy of paying his employees about 10% above what he feels are the prevailing rates, a policy that he believes reduces turnover while fostering employee loyalty. Of somewhat more concern to Jennifer is her father's informal policy of paying men about 20% more than women for the same job. Her father's explanation is, "They're stronger and can work harder for longer hours, and besides they all have families to support."

Questions

1. Is the company at the point where it should be setting up a formal salary structure based on a complete job evaluation? Why?
2. How exactly could Carter use free online sources like O*NET to help create the necessary salary structure?
3. Do you think paying 10% more than the prevailing rates is a sound idea, and how would Jack determine that?
4. How could Jack Carter use online government sources to determine if his policy of a male–female differential pay rate is wise and if not, why not?
5. Specifically, what would you suggest Jennifer do now with respect to her company's pay plan?

EXPERIENTIAL EXERCISE

Building an HRIS

Purpose:

The purpose of this exercise is to give you practice in creating a human resource information system (HRIS).

Required Understanding:

You should be fully acquainted with the material in this chapter.

How to Set Up the Exercise/Instructions:

Divide the class into teams of five or six students. Each team will need access to the Internet.

Assume that the owners of a small business (perhaps like the Carters, or Marcel and Pierre in Case 1) come to you with the following problem. They have a company with less than 40 employees, and have been taking care of all types of HR paperwork informally, mostly on little slips of paper, and with memos. They want you to build them a human resource management information system—how computerized it is will be up to you, but they can only afford a budget of $5,000 upfront (not counting your consulting), and then about $500 per year for maintenance. You know from your HR training that there are various sources of paper-based and online systems. Write a two-page proposal telling them exactly what your team would suggest, based on its accumulated existing knowledge, and from online research.

ENDNOTES

1. Dina Berta, "Job Trekker's Odyssey Offers HR Insights," *Nations Restaurant News* 42, no. 6 (February 11, 2008): 1, 12.
2. Dina Berta, "IHOP Franchise Employs Post-hiring Surveys to Get Off Turnover 'Treadmill,'" *Nation's Restaurant News* 41, no 39 (October 1, 2007): 6.
3. This data comes from "Small Business: A Report of the President" (1998): www.sba.gov/advo/stats. See also "Statistics of U.S. Businesses and Non-employer Status," www.sba.gov/advo/research/data.html, accessed March 9, 2006.
4. "Small Business Economic Indicators 2000," Office of Advocacy, U.S. Small Business Administration, (Washington, D.C., 2001): 5. See also "Small Business Laid Foundation for Job Gains," www.sba.gov/advo, accessed March 9, 2006.
5. Studies show that the size of the business impacts human resource activities such as executive compensation, training, staffing, and HR outsourcing. Dale Duncan and Peter Hausdorf, "Firm Size and Internet Recruiting in Canada: A Preliminary Investigation," *Journal of Small-Business Management* 42, no.3 (July 2004): 325–334.
6. *SHRM Human Capital Benchmarking Study 2007*, Society for Human Resource Management, p. 12
7. Graham Dietz et al., "HRM Inside UK E-commerce Firms," *International Small Business Journal* 24, no. 5 (October 2006): 443–470.
8. Bernice Kotey and Cathleen Folker, "Employee Training in SMEs: Effect of Size and Firm Type—Family and Nonfamily," *Journal of Small-Business Management* 45, no. 2 (April 2007): 14–39.
9. Graham Dietz et al., "HRM Inside UK E-commerce Firms," *International Small Business Journal* 24, no. 5 (October 2006): 443–470.
10. Ibid.
11. The following four points based on Kathy Williams, "Top HR Compliance Issues for Small Businesses," *Strategic Finance* (February 2005): 21–23.

12. However, one study concluded that the increased labor costs associated with high-performance work practices offset the productivity increases associated with high-performance work practices. Luc Sels et al., "Unraveling the HRM–Performance Link: Value Creating and Cost Increasing Effects of Small-Business HRM," *Journal of Management Studies* 43, no. 2 (March 2006): 319–342. For supporting evidence of HR's positive effects on small companies, see also Michael Frese et al., "Effects of Human Capital and Long-Term Human Resources Development and Utilization on Employment Growth of Small-Scale Businesses: A Causal Analysis," *Entrepreneurship Theory and Practice* 29, no. 6 (November 2005): 681–698; Andre Grip and Inge Sieben, "The Effects of Human Resource Management on Small Firms' Productivity and Employee's Wages," *Applied Economics* 37, no. 9 (May 20, 2005): 1047–1054.
13. Dawn Carlson et al., "The Impact of Human Resource Practices and Compensation Design on Performance: An Analysis of Family-owned SMEs," *Journal of Small Business Management* 44, no. 4 (October 2006): 531–543.
14. Graham Dietz et al., "HRM Inside UK E-commerce Firms," *International Small Business Journal* 24, no. 5 (October 2006): 443–470.
15. Gilbert Nicholson, "Automated Assessments," *Workforce*, December 2000, 102–107.
16. www.EEOC.gov/employers/overview.html, accessed February 10, 2008.
17. www.DOL.gov/elaws, accessed February 10, 2008.
18. Paul Harris, "Small Businesses Bask in Training's Spotlight," *T + D* 59, no. 2 (Fall 2005): 46–52.
19. Ibid.
20. Ibid.
21. www.employeeappraiser.com/index.php, accessed January 10, 2008.
22. www.halogensoftware.com/products/halogen-eappraisal, accessed January 10, 2008.

23. Jan Kok, "Precautionary Actions within Small and Medium-Sized Enterprises," *Journal of Small-Business Management* 43, no. 4 (October 2005): 498–516.

24. Sean Smith, "OSHA Resources Can Help Small Businesses with Hazards," *Westchester County Business Journal* (August 4, 2003): 4. See also www.osha.gov/as/opa/osha-faq.html, accessed May 26, 2007.

25. Lisa Finnegan, "Industry Partners with OSHA," *Occupational Hazards* (February 1999): 43–45.

26. Graham Dietz et al., "HRM Inside UK E-commerce Firms," *International Small Business Journal* 24, no. 5 (October 2006): 443–470.

27. Gina Ruiz, "Smaller Firms in Vanguard of Flex Practices," *Workforce Management* 84, no. 13 (November 21, 2005): 10.

28. Ibid.

29. These are from Ty Freyvogel, "Operation Employee Loyalty," *Training Media Review* (September–October 2007).

30. Ibid.

31. Ibid.

32. Based on Bob Nelson, *1001 Ways to Reward Employees*, (New York: Workmen Publishing, 1994): 19. See also Sunny C. L. Fong and Margaret A. Shaffer, "The Dimensionality and Determinants of Pay Satisfaction: A Cross-cultural Investigation of a Group Incentive Plan," *International Journal of Human Resource Management* 14, no. 4 (June 2003): 559(22).

33. Jeffrey Marshall and Ellen Heffes, "Benefits: Small Firm Workers Often Getting Less," *Financial Executive* 21, no. 9 (November 2005): 10.

34. www.dol.gov/ebsa/pdf/ppa2006.pdf, accessed February 18, 2008.

35. Bill Leonard, "New Retirement Plans for Small Employers," *HR Magazine* 51, no. 12 (December 2006): 30.

36. Kristen Falk, "The Easy Retirement Plan for Small Business Clients," *National Underwriter* 111, no. 45 (December 3, 2007): 12–13.

37. Ibid.

38. Adrienne Fox, "McMurray Scouts Top Talent to Produce Winning Results," *HR Magazine* 51, no. 7 (July 2006): 57.

39. This is based on John Drake, *Interviewing for Managers: A Complete Guide to Employment Interviewing* (New York, AMACOM, 1982).

40. Ibid.

41. Colin Gray and Christopher Mabey, "Management Development: Key Differences Between Small and Large Businesses in Europe," *International Small Business Journal* 23, no. 5 (October 2005): 467–485.

42. Ibid. See also Essi Saru, "Organizational Learning and HRD: How Appropriate Are They for Small Firms?" *Journal of European Industrial Training* 31, no. 1 (January 2007): 36–52.

43. From Stephen Covey, "Small Business, Big Opportunity," *Training* 43, no. 11 (November 2006): 40.

44. Philip Perry, "Welcome to the Family," *Restaurant Hospitality* 90, no. 5 (May 2006): 73, 74, 76, 78.

45. Ibid.

46. Ibid.

47. Ibid.

48. Ibid.

49. Dina Berta, "IHOP Franchise Employs Post-hiring Surveys to Get Off Turnover 'Treadmill,'" *Nation's Restaurant News* 41, no 39 (October 1, 2007): 6.

50. Kate Leahy, "The 10 Minute Manager's Guide to . . . Communicating with Employees," *Restaurants & Institutions* 116, no. 11 (June 1, 2006): 22–23.

51. Ibid.

52. Ibid.

53. Jane Applegate, "Employee Leasing Can Be a Savior for Small Firms," *Business Courier Serving Cincinnati–Northern Kentucky* (January 28, 2000): 23.

54. Robert Beck and J. Starkman, "How to Find a PEO that Will Get the Job Done," *National Underwriter* 110, no. 39 (October 16, 2006): 39, 45.

55. Layne Davlin, "Human Resource Solutions for the Franchisee," *Franchising World* 39, no. 10 (October 2007): 27–28.

56. Robert Beck and J. Starkman, "How to Find a PEO that Will Get the Job Done," *National Underwriter* 110, no. 39 (October 16, 2006): 39, 45.

57. Lyle DeWitt, "Advantages of Human Resource Outsourcing," *The CPA Journal* 75, no. 6 (June 2005): 13.

58. Harriet Tramer, "Employee Leasing Agreement Can Ease Personnel Concerns," *Cranes Cleveland Business* (July 24, 2000): 24.

59. Max Chafkin, "Fed Up with HR?" *Inc.* 28, no. 5, (May 2006): 50–52.

60. Ibid.

61. Ibid.

62. Ibid.

63. Jane Applegate, "Employee Leasing Can Be a Savior for Small Firms," *Business Courier Serving Cincinnati–Northern Kentucky* (January 28, 2000): 23.

64. Diana Reitz, "Employee Leasing Breeds Liability Questions," *National Underwriter Property and Casualty Risk and Benefits Management* 104, no. 18 (May 2000): 12.

65. Max Chafkin, "Fed Up with HR?" *Inc.* 28, no. 5 (May 2006): 50–52.

66. Robert Beck and J. Starkman, "How to Find a PEO that Will Get the Job Done," *National Underwriter* 110, no. 39 (October 16, 2006): 39, 45.

67. Lyle DeWitt, "Advantages of Human Resource Outsourcing," *The CPA Journal* 75, no. 6 (June 2005): 13, and http://www.peo.com/dnn/, accessed April 28, 2008.

68. The following items are from Layne Davlin, "Human Resource Solutions for the Franchisee," *Franchising World* 39, no. 10 (October 2007): 27.

69. Ibid.

70. For a more complete list, see, for example, Mario German, *Personnel Director* (Deerfield Beach, FL: E-Z Legal Books, 1994): vi–viii, and http://www.hoovers.com/business-forms/—pageid_16436—/global-mktg-index.xhtml?cm_ven=PAID&cm_cat=GGL&cm_pla=FRM&cm_ite=employment_contract_forms, accessed July 20, 2008.

71. Office Depot, Winter 2003 Catalog (Delray Beach, FL: Office Depot, 2003).

72. http://www.ihrim.org, accessed April 28, 2008

73. Adapted from Kenneth Laudon and Jane Laudon, *Management Information Systems: New Approaches to Organization and Technology* (Upper Saddle River, NJ: Prentice Hall, 1998): G7. See also Michael Barrett and Randolph Kahn, "The Governance of Records Management," *Directors and Boards* 26, no. 3 (Spring 2002): 45–48; Anthony Hendrickson, "Human Resource Information Systems: Backbone Technology of Contemporary Human Resources," *Journal of Labor Research* 24, no. 3 (Summer 2003): 381–395.

74. "HR Execs Trade Notes on Human Resource Information Systems," *BNA Bulletin to Management* (December 3, 1998): 1. See also Brian Walter, "But They Said Their Payroll Program Complied with the FLSA," *Public Personnel Management* 31, no. 1 (Spring 2002): 79–94.

75. "HR Execs Trade Notes on Human Resource Information Systems," *BNA Bulletin to Management* (December 3, 1998): 2. See also Ali Velshi, "Human Resources Information," *The Americas Intelligence Wire* (February 11, 2004).

Managing HR Globally

13

When you finish studying this chapter, you should be able to:

1. *List the HR challenges of international business.*

2. *Illustrate how intercountry differences affect HRM.*

3. *Explain why foreign assignments fail and what to do to minimize the problems.*

4. *List and describe the basic steps in training employees who the employer is about to transfer abroad.*

5. *Explain the main things to keep in mind when designing and implementing a global HR system.*

Introduction

Wal-Mart, notably anti-union in America, had a surprise in China. Opening stores there at a fast clip, it tried to dissuade local unions from organizing Wal-Mart's China employees. However, the All China Federation of Trade Unions (ACFTU), with strong government backing, quickly organized several stores. It now seems likely that they'll unionize many Wal-Mart China workers. ■

HR AND THE INTERNATIONALIZATION OF BUSINESS

Companies are increasingly doing business abroad. Multinationals like IBM and Sony have long done business abroad, of course. But with the growth of demand in Asia, Africa, and other parts of the world, even small firms' success depends on marketing and managing overseas.

This confronts firms like Wal-Mart with some interesting management challenges. For one thing, managers now must formulate and execute their market, product, and production plans on a worldwide basis. Ford Motor, for instance, recently implemented a new strategy called "One Ford," which basically means offering similar Ford cars internationally.

Of course, going abroad means employers like Ford must then address international human resource management issues. For example, "Should we staff our local offices in Europe with local or U.S. managers?" "How should we appraise and pay our Asia employees?" "How should we deal with the unions in our offices in Dubai?"[1]

Actually, globalization means that even employees who never leave the home office need (to some extent) to be "internationalized." As one article recently put it, "Cultural diversity isn't just for expatriates or frequent flying executives. Cube dwellers increasingly need to work, often virtually, across borders with people whose first language is not English, who don't have the same cultural touch points as U.S. employees do, and who don't approach business in the same way that Americans do."[2] We'll address such topics in this chapter.

① List the HR challenges of international business.

The Human Resource Challenges of International Business

Dealing with global human resource challenges like these isn't easy. The employer faces an array of political, social, legal, and cultural differences among countries abroad. What works in one country may not work in another: An incentive plan may work in the United Kingdom, but backfire in some Eastern Europe countries, where workers need a predictable weekly wage to buy necessities. In spite of these inter-country differences, the employer needs to create, for each country's local facility and for the company as a whole, effective human resource practices. These include methods for things like candidate selection, cultural and language orientation and training, and compensation administration.[3]

The vast distances add to the challenge. For example, how should Starbucks' chief HR officer, based in Seattle, keep track of his firm's top management performers overseas? Here's what senior international human resource managers in eight large companies said concerned them the most about managing HR internationally:[4]

- *Deployment.* Easily getting the right people skills to where we need them, regardless of geographic location.
- *Knowledge and innovation dissemination.* Spreading state-of-the-art knowledge and practices throughout the company, regardless of where they originate.
- *Identifying and developing talent on a global basis.* Identifying the firm's top talent, and developing their abilities.[5]

international human resource management
The human resource management concepts and techniques employers use to manage the human resource challenges of their international operations.

What Is International Human Resource Management?

Employers rely on **international human resource management** (IHRM) to deal with global HR challenges like these. We can define IHRM as the human resource management concepts and techniques employers use to manage the human resource challenges of their international operations. The subject matter of international human resource management generally focuses on three main topics:[6]

1. Managing human resources in global companies (*selecting, training, and compensating employees who work or are assigned abroad, for instance*);
2. Managing *expatriate employees* (those the employer posts abroad); and,
3. *Comparing human resource management practices* in a variety of different countries.

Underlying all three topics is the idea that inter-country differences in things like values and legal systems affect how employers manage human resources from country to country. Let's look at this first.

How Intercountry Differences Affect Human Resource Management

As we said, the challenges of managing human resource activities abroad don't just stem from the distances involved (though this is important). The bigger issue is dealing with the cultural, political, legal, and economic differences among countries and their people. The result is that what works in one country might fail in another.

② Illustrate how intercountry differences affect HRM.

THE ISSUE Companies operating just within the United States generally have the luxury of dealing with a relatively limited set of economic, cultural, and legal variables. Different states and municipalities do have their own laws affecting HR. However, a basic U.S. government framework helps produce a fairly predictable set of legal guidelines regarding matters such as employment discrimination, labor relations, and safety and health. Similarly, political risks within the U.S. are minimal. *Political risks* "are any governmental action or politically motivated event that could adversely affect the long-run profitability or value of the firm."[7] For example, Venezuela's president recently moved to nationalize the country's oil industries.[8]

A company operating multiple units abroad isn't blessed with such homogeneity. For example, even with the European Union's increasing standardization, minimum mandated holidays range from none in the United Kingdom to 5 weeks per year in Luxembourg. And while Italy has no formal requirements for employee representatives on boards of directors, they're required in Denmark. The point is that the need to adapt personnel policies and procedures to the differences among countries complicates human resource management in multinational companies.

CULTURAL FACTORS For one thing, countries differ widely in their cultures—in the basic values their citizens share, and in the ways these values manifest themselves in the nation's arts, social programs, and ways of doing things. In 2008 Britain's labor government asked its citizens to submit a motto that most characterized their country. The winner, in a contest sponsored by the *Times of London*, was "No mottos please, we're British."

Cultural differences mean people abroad react differently to the same or similar situations. For example, in one study of managers from Hong Kong, mainland China, and the United States, the U.S. managers tended to be most concerned with getting the job done. Chinese managers were most concerned with maintaining a harmonious environment. Hong Kong managers fell between these extremes.[9]

Several years ago, researchers surveyed the cultural values of managers in 62 countries. They concluded that the countries differed along four cultural dimensions:[10]

■ *Assertiveness*—how much people in a society are expected to be tough, confrontational, and competitive. The most assertive countries in the survey included Germany, Greece, and the United States; the least assertive were Sweden, New Zealand, and Switzerland.

- *Future orientation*—the level of importance the society attaches to future-oriented behaviors such as planning and investing in the future. The most future-oriented cultures were Switzerland and Singapore; the least future-oriented were Russia, Argentina, and Poland.
- *Performance orientation*—the importance of performance improvement and excellence in the society. The most performance-oriented cultures included Singapore, Hong Kong, New Zealand, and the United States. The least performance-oriented were Russia, Argentina, and Greece.
- *Humane orientation*—the extent to which a society encourages and rewards people for being fair, altruistic, and kind. Malaysia, Ireland, and the Philippines scored highest on humane orientation; Germany, Spain, and France scored lowest.

Cultural differences like these help shape the human resource policies and practices that work best in a particular country. For example, some argue that Americans' emphasis on individualism—on "standing on one's own feet"—helps to explain why there are fewer constraints on American human resource managers, for instance, in terms of firing employees.[11] European HR managers are much more restricted than American ones, for instance with respect to the notice they must give workers before firing them, how much severance pay the employees get, and the complexity of the legal process involved in dismissing workers. Similarly, both union membership (at about 25%–80%, depending on the European country) and union influences are much higher in Europe than in the U.S.[12]

ECONOMIC SYSTEMS Similarly, differences in *economic systems* also translate into differences in inter-country HR practices. For instance, France—though a capitalist society—imposed restrictions on employers' rights to discharge workers several years ago, and limited to 35 the number of hours an employee could legally work each week. (In 2008 they began lifting some of those limitations.)

Labor costs also vary widely. For example, hourly compensation costs in U.S. dollars for production workers range from $2.75 in Mexico to $6.43 in Taiwan, $23.82 in the United States, $27.10 in the United Kingdom, and $34.21 in Germany.[13]

There are other labor costs to consider. For example, compared to the usual 2 or 3 weeks of U.S. vacation, workers in France can expect 2 1/2 days of paid holiday per full month of service per year, and Germans get 18 working days per year after 6 months of service.

LEGAL AND INDUSTRIAL RELATIONS FACTORS Global *legal differences* can also blindside even the most sophisticated managers and companies. After spending billions of dollars expanding into Germany, Wal-Mart managers were surprised to learn that Germany's commercial laws discourage advertising that involves competitive price comparisons. They soon had to leave Germany. In 2007, the European Union decided a huge legal dispute against Microsoft, saying Microsoft made it too difficult for other firms to design compatible software products.

Wal-Mart also discovered (see the chapter opener) that China's union movement was much more powerful than were U.S. unions. And, in China, more changes are in the works. China recently passed a new employment contract law (effective January 2009). It will provide employees with some additional protections. For example, it requires that all new employees receive a written contract containing basic information on things like job description, compensation, and working hours. The law makes it somewhat easier for employers to lay off large numbers of employees. However, it also provides new benefits for laid-off employees, such as 30 days written notice.[14]

Managers of companies doing business abroad should understand what employment laws apply to them. The accompanying *Business in Action* feature provides some examples.

U.S. equal employment opportunity laws, including Title VII, the ADEA, and the ADA, impact U.S. employers doing business abroad, and foreign firms doing business in the United States or its territories.[15] For example, *foreign multinational employers* that operate in the United States or its territories (American Samoa, Guam, the Commonwealth of the Northern Mariana Islands, Puerto Rico, and the U.S. Virgin Islands) must abide by EEO laws to the same extent as U.S. employers, unless the employer is covered by a treaty or other binding international agreement that limits the full applicability of U.S. antidiscrimination laws. Similarly, *U.S. employers*—those that are incorporated or based in the United States or are controlled by U.S. companies—that employ U.S. citizens outside the United States or its territories are subject to Title VII, the ADEA, and the ADA with respect to those U.S. citizen employees. U.S. EEO laws do not apply to *non*-U.S. citizens working for U.S. (or foreign) firms *outside* the United States or its territories.

If equal employment opportunity laws conflict with the laws of the country in which the U.S. employer is operating, the laws of the local country generally take precedence. In particular, U.S. employers are not required to comply with requirements of Title VII, the ADEA, or the ADA if adherence to that law would violate the law of the country where the workplace is located. For example, an employer would have a "Foreign Laws Defense" for a mandatory retirement policy if the law in the country in which the company is located requires mandatory retirement. However, a U.S. employer may not transfer an employee to another country in order to put that person at disadvantage because of his or her race, color, sex, religion, national origin, age, or disability. For example, an employer may not transfer an older worker to a country with a mandatory retirement age for the purpose of forcing the worker's retirement.

EUROPE To see the employment effects of cultural, economic, and legal differences like these, we need look no further than Europe.

Over the past two decades, the separate countries of the former European Community (EC) unified into a common market for goods, services, capital, and even labor called the European Union (EU). Generally speaking, products and even labor can move from country to country with few impediments. The employment situation in the EU helps illustrate the legal, cultural, and industrial relations aspects of globalization.

Companies doing business in Europe (including U.S.-based companies like Ford) must adjust their human resource policies and practices to both European Union (EU) directives and to country-specific employment laws. The "directives" are basically EU laws. The directives' objectives are binding on all member countries (although each member country can implement the directives as it so chooses). For example, consider the EU directive on *confirmation of employment*. It requires employers to provide employees with written terms and conditions of their employment. However, these terms vary from country to country.[16] In England, a detailed written statement is required, including things like rate of pay, date employment began, and hours of work. Germany doesn't require a written contract. However, it's still customary to have one.

The interplay of directives and country laws means that human resource practices must vary from country to country. For example:[17]

- Most EU countries have *minimum wage systems* in place. Some set national limits. Others allow employers and unions to work out their own minimum wages.
- The EU sets the *workweek* at 48 hours, but most countries set it at 40 hours a week, and France implemented a 35-hour workweek.
- Europe has many levels of *employee representation*. In France, for instance, employers with 50 or more employees must consult with their employees' representatives on matters including working conditions, training, and profit-sharing plans and layoffs. As of 2008, most EU companies must "inform and consult" employees about employee-related actions, even if the firms don't operate outside their own countries' borders.[18]
- In many European countries, **works councils** replace the informal or union-based worker-to-management mediations typical in U.S. firms. Works councils are formal, employee-elected groups of worker representatives that meet monthly with managers to discuss topics ranging from no-smoking policies to layoffs.[19] Co-determination

works councils
Formal, employee-elected groups of worker representatives that meet monthly with managers to discuss topics ranging, for instance, from no-smoking policies to layoffs.

is the rule in Germany and several other countries. **Co-determination** means employees have the legal right to a voice in setting company policies. Workers elect their own representatives to the supervisory board of the employer, and there is a vice president for labor at the top-management level.[20] In the U.S., wages and benefits are set by the employer, or by the employer in negotiations with its labor unions. The co-determination laws, including the Works Constitution Act, largely determine the nature of HR policies in many German firms.

■ The U.S. practice of *employment at will* does not exist in Europe, where firing and laying off workers is usually time consuming and expensive.

IMPROVING INTERNATIONAL ASSIGNMENTS THROUGH SELECTION

Sending managers abroad to improve and test their global management skills is quite common. Almost 80% of *Financial Times* top 100 company CEOs recently had overseas assignments, up dramatically from 10 years ago.[21]

It's therefore disconcerting to see how often such assignments fail. In one survey, employers reported a 21% attrition rate for **expatriate** employees (those the employer posted abroad), compared with an average of 10% for their general employee populations.[22] Others stay, but are unproductive.[23] Experts attribute much of this turnover to poor expatriate entry and reentry preparations.[24]

The rate of early departures may be declining. This seems to be because more employers are taking steps to reduce typical expat problems. For example, they're selecting expats more carefully, helping spouses get jobs abroad, and providing more ongoing support to the expat and his or her family.[25]

Why International Assignments Fail

Determining why so many foreign assignments fail is a cottage industry itself. A study of 750 U.S., European, and Japanese companies provides some clues. The employers that did best in terms of sending people abroad did three things when making international assignments:[26]

■ They focus on knowledge creation and global *leadership development*;
■ They assign people overseas whose technical skills are matched or exceeded by their *cross-cultural abilities*; and
■ Their expatriate assignments include a deliberate *repatriation* process.

Let's look at some details of what makes for a successful posting abroad.

PERSONALITY Expats are increasingly younger, and single. Recent studies showed that 56% of the overseas workforce was under 40, single (43%), and female (21%). That female percentage was up from about 15% in 2004.[27]

In terms of personality, successful expatriate employees tend to be extroverted, agreeable, and emotionally stable individuals.[28] One study found three traits—extroversion, agreeableness, and emotional stability—were inversely related to the expatriate's desire to terminate the assignment; conscientiousness was positively related to the expatriate's performance. Another study found a positive relationship between sociability and cross-cultural adjustment.[29] So, not surprisingly, sociable, outgoing, conscientious people seem more likely to fit into new cultural settings.

Intentions are important too: For example, people who want expatriate careers try harder to adjust to such a life.[30] Similarly, expatriates who are more satisfied with their jobs are more likely to adapt to the foreign assignment.[31]

Studies also suggest that it's not how different culturally the host country is from the person's home country, it's the person's ability to adapt that's important. *Cultural empathy* is "a working knowledge of the cultural variables affecting management decisions."[32] Some people are so culturally at ease that they do fine transferred anywhere; others will fail anywhere.[33]

STABLE AND DYNAMIC TRAITS It seems that some of the traits required for success abroad are baked into the person's personality, while others are more easily learned.

Figure 13.1 summarizes this idea. "Stable" traits like openness and flexibility are basically part of one's personality and so are relatively fixed. Stable competencies or traits also include abilities and interests. Three researchers say that individuals who possess stable traits like those in Figure 13.1 make better expatriates, particularly for CEO-type jobs. For example, they are likely to adjust more readily to their assignments. They are also better equipped to detect and respond to cultural nuances abroad.

On the other hand, traits like knowledge and skills are "dynamic." The person acquires these through training. Dynamic traits include technical expertise and language proficiency. For example, "the ability to effectuate lean manufacturing through just-in-time procedures and flexible technologies may in fact be necessary [to succeed in the assignment abroad], but can be learned through courses or on-site training."[34] Here's how the researchers sum it up:

> [Stable traits] are the traits that expatriates not only should have but must have, and if these are lacking, the candidates should either be eliminated or should self-eliminate from consideration early in the selection process. However, if they cross this hurdle, candidates should then be evaluated for the technical expertise, functional competence, and other skills that would be necessary to perform that particular job in that particular location. With the assumption that the baseline criteria have been met, these dynamic skills can be learned.[35]

Furthermore, some stable traits (also as in Figure 13.1) may be red flags for expatriate assignments. For example,

> A *strong moral platform*, or absolute beliefs about right and wrong, may inhibit an expatriate's ability to analyze situations from multiple perspectives, and thus result in sub-par decision making.[36]

FIGURE 13.1 The Importance of Stable and Dynamic Traits in Selecting Expatriates

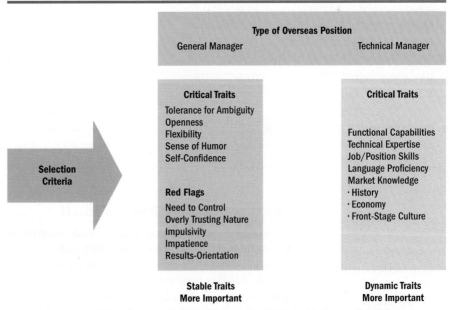

Source: Adapted from Meredith Downes, Iris I. Varner, and Luke Musinski, "Personality Traits as Predictors of Expatriate Effectiveness: A Synthesis and Reconceptualization," *Review of Business* 27, no. 3 (Spring–Summer 2007): 6(8).

Note: This figure makes the point that while stable traits are always important for expatriates, they're especially crucial for general manager-type assignments.

For foreign *general manager/CEO*-type assignments stable traits (like flexibility) are essential. This expat then needs a minimum of functional and technical competence. In addition here, "red flag" traits should signal that the person may not be CEO expatriate material.

Employers typically make foreign *technical manager*-type assignments, such as Director of Engineering, to transfer technology to the locals, so here personality-type (stable) traits are not as crucial. However, the expatriate must have the technical expertise.

FAMILY PRESSURES Family pressures loom large in expatriate failures. In one early study, U.S. managers listed these reasons for leaving early, from high to low in importance: inability of spouse to adjust, managers' inability to adjust, other family problems, managers' personal or emotional immaturity, and inability to cope with larger overseas responsibility.[37] Managers of European firms emphasized only the inability of the manager's spouse to adjust as an explanation for the expatriate's failed assignment. Other studies similarly emphasize dissatisfied spouses' effects on the international assignment.[38]

THE PROBLEM These findings underscore that it's usually not technical or even cultural incompetence, but family and personal problems that undermine international assignees. Yet employers still tend to select expatriates based on technical competence rather than interpersonal skills or domestic situations:[39]

> The selection process is fundamentally flawed. . . . Expatriate assignments rarely fail because the person cannot accommodate to the technical demands of the job. . . . They fail because of family and personal issues and lack of cultural skills that haven't been part of the process.[40] (*HR in Practice* shows how to avoid this.)

HR in Practice

Some Practical Solutions to the Expatriate Challenge

While non-work aspects of foreign assignments (like the adjustment of the spouse) can prompt assignees to leave early, that is not inevitable. Managers can take several practical steps to improve the expat's success abroad.

- First, *provide realistic previews of what to expect abroad, careful screening (of both the prospective expat and his or her spouse), improved orientation,* and *improved benefits* packages.
- Simply *shorten the length* of the assignment. One survey reports that 23% of the employers' overseas assignments lasted over 3 years, down from 32% about 10 years previously.[41]
- Use "short-term," "commuter," or "frequent-flier" assignments. These basically involve much travel but

no formal relocation.[42] Such employees are essentially international commuters.[43] This can be effective, particularly where the commutes are relatively short and inexpensive, as between Europe and the U.S.

- Use Internet-based *video technologies* and group decision-making software to enable global virtual teams to conduct business without travel or relocation.[44]
- Form *"global buddy"* programs. Here local managers assist new expatriates with advice on topics such as office politics, norms of behavior, and where to receive emergency medical assistance.[45]
- Use executive coaches to mentor and work with expatriate managers.[46]

International Staffing: Home or Local?

In general, we can classify an international company's employees as *expatriates, home country nationals, locals,* or *third-country nationals.*[47] *Expatriates* are noncitizens of the countries in which they are working. **Host country nationals** are citizens of the country in which the multinational company has its headquarters (thus, the *parent country*); these employees may also thus be expatriates when posted abroad. **Locals** (also known as *host country nationals*) work for the company abroad and are citizens of the countries where they are working. **Third-country nationals** are citizens of a country other than the parent or the host country—for example, a French executive working in the Shanghai branch of a U.S. multinational bank.[48]

WHY LOCAL? Most of the employees in a multinational company's office abroad will be "locals," for good reason. Within the United States, it's not easy bringing workers in from abroad, so using U.S. "locals" may be a necessity. Under existing rules, U.S. employers must try to recruit U.S. workers before filing foreign labor certification

host country nationals
Citizens of the country in which the multinational company has its headquarters.

locals
Employees that work for the company abroad and are citizens of the countries where they are working, also known as host country nationals.

third-country nationals
Citizens of a country other than the parent or host country.

requests with the Department of Labor. They must post open positions in the Department of Labor's job bank, and run two Sunday newspaper advertisements before filing such requests.[49]

Cost is a very big consideration in "hiring local." Some companies don't realize what it costs to send expatriates abroad. Agilent Technologies estimated that it cost about three times the expatriate's annual salary to keep the person abroad for 1 year. But when Agilent hired an outside firm to handle its expatriate program, it discovered that the costs were much higher. Agilent then dramatically reduced the number of expats it sent abroad, from about 1,000 to 300 per year.[50] Yet cost may also work in the opposite direction. For example, difficulties attracting management trainees to work in relatively low-pay U.S.-based hospitality jobs prompts some hotel chains to hire in people from abroad to fill these jobs.

Finally, politics may be a consideration. The host country's government and citizens may view the multinational as a "better citizen" if it uses local management talent.

WHY EXPATS? There are also good reasons for using expatriates—either home country or third-country nationals—for staffing subsidiaries. The main reason is that employers often can't find local candidates with the required technical qualifications. As noted earlier, companies also view a successful stint abroad as a required step in developing top managers. (For instance, the expat head of General Electric's Asia-Pacific region was transferred back to a top position as vice chairman at GE.) Control is also important. The assumption is that home country managers are already steeped in the firm's policies and culture, and thus more likely to implement headquarters' instructions and ways of doing things.

A HYBRID SOLUTION Today, the choice is not just between expatriate versus local employees; there's a hybrid solution. One survey found that about 78% of employers had some form of "localization" policy. This means a policy of transferring, for example, a U.S. employee to a foreign subsidiary (say, in France) as a "permanent transferee." The assumption here is that the employee would not be an expatriate but instead would be treated as a French local hire.[51] For practical purposes, he becomes "French." The employer in this case bought out his U.S. pension and provided temporary (not permanent) relocation assistance, and a France-based salary

OFFSHORING *Offshoring*—moving business processes such as manufacturing or call center operations abroad, and thus having local employees abroad do jobs that the firm's domestic employees previously did in-house—is growing rapidly. About 3 million jobs will move offshore between 2000 and 2015.[52] (*Outsourcing* means moving a firm's business processes to an external company. *Offshoring* therefore means outsourcing business processes abroad). Generally speaking, the need to reduce costs (by transferring jobs from high to low wage countries) is driving this trend. Reduced telecommunications costs and improved information technology are facilitating it.

Offshoring is controversial. In the 1990s, employers mostly moved manufacturing jobs overseas. Between 2000 and 2015, the U.S. Labor Department and Forrester Research estimate that about 288,000 management jobs will go offshore, 472,000 computer jobs, 184,000 architecture jobs, and almost 75,000 legal jobs and about 1.7 million office jobs. Offshoring's opponents say this job drain will mean millions of fewer white-collar jobs for American workers. Proponents say employers must offshore to remain competitive, and that the money employers thereby save boosts research and development and, eventually, creates more domestic jobs for U.S. workers.

Outsourcing jobs to lower wage countries enmeshes the employer's human resource team in the economic, political, and cultural issues we discussed earlier. The following *HR in Practice* feature illustrates how human resource managers actually deal with some of these issues.

Offshoring jobs from the U.S. to lower wage countries like India enmeshes the employer's human resource team in numerous economic, political, and cultural issues.

HR in Practice

Human Resource Management's Actual Role in Offshoring Operations

Human resource managers play a central role in offshoring decisions. IBM Business Consulting Services surveyed employers to see exactly what roles HR was actually playing in these decisions. Here's a sampling of what they found.[53]

HR's Role in Choosing the Site
It's basically impossible (or, at least, quite unwise) for employers to choose a location to which to outsource without input from the human resource team. For example, HR provides the information top management needs:[54]

- To determine *total labor costs*. These include direct wages and benefits, as well as the potential costs of exiting a market (such as government mandated costs associated with retraining and severance payments).
- To understand the *composition of local labor markets*, for example in terms of their size, education levels and the availability of language skills.
- To better understand how the firm's current *employment-related reputation* in the locale may impact any outsourcing to this locale.
- Regarding the locale's current *business environment*, for instance in terms of tax incentives, and the role of organized labor.
- Regarding how much to *integrate the local workforce* into the parent firm's corporate organization. For example, outsourced employees performing strategic

customer related tasks might best become employees. Those performing less strategic tasks might best remain independent contractors or employees of vendor firms.

HR's Role in Recruitment and selection
In IBM Business Consulting Services' discussions with employers who were offshoring, three critical recruitment/selection issues arose:

- ***Skill shortages.*** The survey team found that "Despite large candidate pools for entry-level workers, there is an ongoing "war for talent" in many of these [low wage] labor markets."[55] This often requires hiring employees from other local firms, using signing bonuses, higher wages, and improved employee retention policies (for instance, in terms of improved promotion opportunities).
- ***Hiring in bulk.*** The need to often hire hundreds or thousands of employees at once complicates the hiring process. Employers are increasingly turning to employment agencies, employee referrals, and other means, including college recruiting.
- ***Evaluation hurdle.*** "Many respondents indicated that the sheer number of potential candidates often dwarfed the firms' capacity to screen and evaluate these individuals."[56] However, the employer still must take the steps required to hire the right employees.

HR's Role in Employee retention

"Perhaps the greatest HR challenge facing globally distributed back-office and customer care centers is the retention of talented employees."[57] The often high-pressure nature of these jobs (particularly in call centers) combines with skill shortages to produce high attrition rates. To reduce high attrition, employers are taking steps such as:

- Deciding what is an acceptable *target attrition rate*, as a way to measure the employer's retention performance.
- Identifying what *"levers"* to use to reduce attrition. These levers include more training and development, improved job design and work environment, better compensation and benefits, and improved career opportunities within the centers and in the parent firm.

Values and International Staffing Policy

ethnocentric
A management philosophy that leads to the creation of home market-oriented staffing decisions.

polycentric
A management philosophy oriented toward staffing positions with local talent.

geocentric
A staffing policy that seeks the best people for key jobs throughout the organization, regardless of nationality.

Values play a role in global staffing decisions. Experts sometimes classify people's values as **ethnocentric**, **polycentric,** or **geocentric**, and these values translate into corresponding corporate behaviors and policies.[58] In a firm whose top managers tend to be *ethnocentric*, "the prevailing attitude is that home country attitudes, management style, knowledge, evaluation criteria, and managers are superior to anything the host country might have to offer."[59] In the *polycentric* corporation, "there is a conscious belief that only host country managers can ever really understand the culture and behavior of the host country market; therefore, the foreign subsidiary should be managed by local people."[60] *Geocentric* executives believe they must scour the firm's whole management staff on a global basis, on the assumption that the best manager of a specific position anywhere may be in any of the countries in which the firm operates.

STAFFING POLICIES These values translate into three broad international staffing policies. With an *ethnocentric* staffing policy, the firm tends to fill key management jobs with home (parent-country) nationals. At Royal Dutch Shell, for instance, most financial officers around the world are Dutch nationals. A *polycentric*-oriented firm would staff its foreign subsidiaries with host country nationals, and its home office with parent-country nationals. A *geocentric* staffing policy guides the firm to choose the best people for key jobs regardless of nationality. For example, U.S.-based Citigroup recently appointed as chairman a U.K. executive. Sony appointed as CEO the Englishman who'd run the firm's U.S. operations.

Ethics and Codes of Conduct

With operations in several countries, employers also need to ensure that their employees abroad are adhering to their firm's ethics codes.

Ensuring this is not easy. For example, exporting a firm's ethics rules requires more than having employees abroad use versions of its home country employee handbook. In fact, relying on such handbooks can cause problems. For instance, few countries adhere to "employment at will," like the U.S., so even handbooks with at-will disclaimers "can become binding contracts."[61] Furthermore, employees in many countries have extensive rights to consultation on working conditions under their labor laws. Here, home country-style handbooks may "breach an employer's information, consultation, and participation duty."[62]

Instead of exporting the employee handbook to foster ethical actions, one international employment lawyer recommends focusing on creating and distributing worldwide a global code of conduct. Sometimes, an American employer's main concern is establishing global standards for adhering to U.S. laws that have cross-border impacts. These employers should set policies on things like discrimination, harassment, bribery, and Sarbanes-Oxley. For other firms, like Adidas and toy maker Tomy, the main concern may be with enforcing codes of conduct for avoiding, for instance, lead-based paint or sweatshop conditions.

In any event, local cultural norms can undermine employers' attempts to institute uniform codes of conduct. Bribery, abhorrent in most counties, might be ignored in others. As another example, people in countries with a history of fascist rule still remember how their governments expected them to divulge information about their coworkers. In places like this, employees often frown on United Kingdom-type whistle-blowing rules.[63]

Selecting International Managers

In most respects, screening managers for jobs abroad is similar to screening them for domestic ones. Both types of candidates need the technical knowledge and skills to do the job, and the required intelligence and people skills.

However, foreign assignments are different. The expatriate (and his or her family) will have to cope with colleagues whose culture may be drastically different from one's own. And, there's the stress of being in a foreign land.

In spite of this, many employers don't pay much attention to expatriate screening. Researchers several years ago found that selection for a posting abroad is usually so informal they called it "the coffee machine system": Two colleagues meet at the office coffee machine, strike up a conversation about the possibility of a position abroad, and based on that and little more a selection decision is made.[64] As one recent study concluded, "[t]raditionally, most selection of expatriates appears to be done solely on the basis of successful records of job performance in the home country."[65]

TESTING Yet employers can take steps to improve the process, and testing is an obvious tool. For example, Performance Programs, Inc. (PPI) has used its Overseas Assignment Inventory (OAI) for over 30 years to help employers do a better job of selecting candidates for assignments abroad. According to PPI, "The OAI is an online assessment that measures nine attributes and six context factors crucial for successful adaptation to another culture. It is provided for both the expatriate job candidate and his or her spouse or partner. PPI establishes local norms and conducts ongoing validation studies of the OAI."[66] Figure 13.2 illustrates the OAI.

REALISTIC PREVIEWS Even in highly industrialized postings (say, to France), there will be language barriers, bouts of home-sickness and loneliness, and the need for any children to adapt to new schools and friends.

Realistic previews about the problems to expect in the new job as well as about the cultural benefits, problems, and idiosyncrasies of the country are thus another important part of the screening process. The rule should always be to "spell it all out" ahead of time, as many multinationals do for their international transferees.[67]

ADAPTABILITY SCREENING With flexibility and adaptability high on the list of what makes expats succeed, *adaptability screening* should be part of the screening process. Employers often use specially trained psychologists for this. Adaptability screening aims to assess the assignee's (and spouse's) probable success in handling the foreign transfer, and to alert them to issues (such as the impact on children) the move may involve.

Here, experience is often the best predictor of future success. Companies look for overseas candidates whose work and nonwork experience, education, and language skills already demonstrate a commitment to and facility for living and working with different cultures. Even several successful summers spent traveling overseas or participating in foreign student programs might provide some basis to believe the potential transferee can adjust when he or she arrives overseas.

Sending Women Managers Abroad

Women are underrepresented as managerial expatriates. Line managers make most of these assignments, and many of them suffer from misconceptions that inhibit them from recommending women to work abroad.[68] For example, many managers assume that women don't want to work abroad, or are reluctant to move their families abroad,

FIGURE 13.2 Overseas Assignment Inventory

Sample excerpt from the
OVERSEAS ASSIGNMENT INVENTORY

Welcome!

Enter the login information you were provided in the box on the left. This will direct you to a registration page before proceeding to your survey.

This site contains:

Overseas Assignment Inventory—A tool designed to assess cultural adaptability for employees and spouses going on international expatriate assignments.

Global Assessment Inventory—A development tool designed to assess factors related to success in multicultural interactions.

Demographics

Please complete the demographic information requested. Note, your answers will not impact the survey results. Upon completion, you will be directed to the survey.

Background Information

Employee or Spouse/Partner:	☐ Employee	☐ Spouse/Partner
Gender:	☐ Male	☐ Female
Nationality:	_____	
Age:	_____	
Number of Children:	_____	
Have Traveled Outside of Country of Citizenship:	☐ Yes	☐ No
Have Lived Outside of Country of Citizenship:	☐ Yes	☐ No

Employment

Destination Country: _____

Current Country Location: _____

[Submit]

Survey Questions *(page 1 of 6)*

Read each survey question carefully and select the bubble that corresponds to your choice. When answering the questions, keep in mind that there are no "right" or "wrong" answers. Choose the response that is reflective of what you think and do most of the time. Some of the questions appear similar; actually no two are exactly alike. Please answer each one without regard to the others.

Strongly Agree 1	Agree 2	Uncertain 3	Disagree 4	Strongly Disagree 5

1. I do not want to compromise my present standard of living. ☐1 ☐2 ☐3 ☐4 ☐5

2. The environment I am comfortable with is similar to that in my destination country. ☐1 ☐2 ☐3 ☐4 ☐5

3. Generally, my spouse/partner and I understand each other. ☐1 ☐2 ☐3 ☐4 ☐5

4. I am generally one of the first to speak and take charge in a group. ☐1 ☐2 ☐3 ☐4 ☐5

5. It is very clear to me how my work on this assignment will be evaluated. ☐1 ☐2 ☐3 ☐4 ☐5

6. I am fluent in the language spoken in my destination country. ☐1 ☐2 ☐3 ☐4 ☐5

Most surveyed women expats said that safety was no more an issue with them than it was with men.

or can't get their spouses to move because the husband is the main breadwinner. In fact, one survey found that women do want international assignments. Furthermore, they are not less inclined than male managers to move their families abroad, and their male spouses are not necessarily the families' main breadwinners.

Safety is another misperceived issue. Employers tend to assume that women posted abroad are more likely to become crime victims. However, most of the surveyed women expats said that safety was no more an issue with them than it was with men: "If it's a dangerous city, it's dangerous for whomever."[69]

STEPS There are several steps the employer can take to short-circuit misperceptions like these, and to identify more women to assign abroad. For example, *formalize a process* for identifying employees who are willing to take assignments abroad. *Train managers* to understand how employees really feel about going abroad, and what the real safety and cultural issues are. Let successful female expats *recruit prospective female* expats, and discuss with them the pros and cons of assignments abroad. Provide the expat's spouse with *employment assistance.*[70]

TRAINING AND MAINTAINING INTERNATIONAL EMPLOYEES

Careful screening is just the first step in ensuring the foreign assignee's success. The employee will then require special training. The firm will also need special international human resource policies for appraising and compensating the firm's overseas employees, and for maintaining healthy labor relations.

Training Employees on International Assignment

When it comes to providing the orientation and training required for success overseas, the practices of many multinational firms reflect more form than substance. Despite many companies' claims, there is relatively little systematic selection and training for assignments overseas.

CROSS-CULTURAL TRAINING *Cross-cultural training* seems to be the most important issue in training expatriates. Cross-cultural training "should result in the expatriate learning both content and skills that will improve interactions with host country individuals by reducing misunderstandings and inappropriate behaviors."[71] One firm in this area prescribes a four-step cultural training approach.[72]

> ④ List and describe the basic steps in training employees who the employer is about to transfer abroad.

- Level 1 training focuses on the *impact of cultural differences*, and on raising trainees' awareness of such differences and their impact on business outcomes.
- Level 2 aims at getting participants to understand how *attitudes* are formed and influence behavior. (For example, unfavorable stereotypes may subconsciously influence how a new manager responds to and treats his or her new foreign subordinates.)
- Level 3 training provides *factual knowledge* about the target country.
- Level 4 provides skill building in areas like *language* and adjustment and adaptation skills.

As Figure 13.3, illustrates, the actual cross-cultural training methods typically include things like cultural briefings and field experiences.

OTHER EXPATRIATE TRAINING Beyond cross-cultural training, employers use various other methods to train prospective expats. These include *documentary* (written materials)

FIGURE 13.3 Typical Cross-Cultural Training Methods

• Cultural Briefings	Explain the major aspects of the host country culture, including customs, traditions, and everyday behaviors.
• Area Briefings	Explain the history, geography, economy, politics, and other general information about the host country and region.
• Cases	Portray a real-life situation in business or personal life to illustrate some aspect of living or working in the host culture.
• Role Playing	Allows the trainee to act out a situation that he or she might face living or working in the host country.
• Culture Assimilator	Provides a written set of situations that the trainee might encounter living or working in the host country. Trainee selects one from a set of responses to the situation and is given feedback on if it is appropriate and why.
• Field Experiences	Provide an opportunity for the trainee to go to the host country or another unfamiliar culture to experience living and working there for a short time.

programs about the country's geography and socioeconomic and political history, *cultural assimilation* to show trainees the sorts of social and interpersonal situations they're likely to encounter, *language training*, *sensitivity training*, and actual *interactions* with people from other cultures within the trainee's own country.[73] For example, Procter & Gamble sends employees and their spouses destined for China to Beijing for 2 months of language and cultural training.[74]

TRAINING EMPLOYEES ABROAD Extending the parent company's training to its local employees abroad is increasingly important in developing markets. For Kimberly-Clark, for instance, average training per employee abroad has quickly risen from almost none to about 38 hours per year.[75] Starbucks (pronounced "Starbuck-zu" in Japan) brings new management trainees from abroad to its Seattle, Washington, headquarters. This gives them a "a taste of the west coast lifestyle and the company's informal culture," as well as the technical knowledge required to manage their local stores.[76]

Managers abroad continue to need traditional training and development. At IBM, for instance, such development includes rotating assignments that enable overseas managers to grow professionally. IBM and other firms also have management development centers around the world where executives can hone their skills. And classroom programs (such as those at the London Business School, or at INSEAD in France) provide overseas executives the sorts of educational opportunities (to acquire MBAs, for instance). Figure 13.4 illustrates some corporate programs to develop global managers.

TRENDS There are several trends in expatriate training and development.

■ First, rather than providing only predeparture cross-cultural training, more firms are providing continuing, in-country cross-cultural training during the early stages of the overseas assignment.

■ Second, employers are using returning managers as resources to cultivate the "global mindsets" of their home-office staff. For example, Bosch holds regular seminars. Here, newly arrived returnees pass on their knowledge and experience to relocating managers and their families.

■ Third, employers increasingly use software and the Internet for cross-cultural training. For example, *Bridging Cultures* is a self-training multimedia package for people who will be traveling and/or living overseas. It uses short video clips to introduce case study intercultural problems, and then guides users to selecting the strategy to best

FIGURE 13.4

Corporate Programs to Develop Global Managers

Source: Francesco, Anne Marie; Gold, Barry A., *International Organizational Behavior*, 2nd, © 2005. Electronically reproduced by permission of Pearson Education, Inc., Upper Saddle River, New Jersey.

- ABB (Asea Brown Boveri) rotates about 500 managers around the world to different countries every two to three years in order to develop a management cadre of transpatriates to support their global strategy.
- PepsiCo has an orientation program for its foreign managers, which brings them to the United States for one-year assignments in bottling division plants.
- British Telecom uses informal mentoring techniques to induct employees into the ways of their assigned country; existing expatriate workers talk to prospective assignees about the cultural factors to expect.
- Honda of America Manufacturing gives its U.S. supervisors and managers extensive preparation in Japanese language, culture, and lifestyle and then sends them to the parent company in Tokyo for up to three years.
- General Electric likes its engineers and managers to have a global perspective whether or not they are slated to go abroad. The company gives regular language and cross-cultural training for them so that they are equipped to conduct business with people around the world.

handle the situation. A sampling of cross-cultural training firms' Web sites include www.livingabroad.com, www.globaldynamics.com, www.culturalsavvy.com, and www.peoplegoingglobal.com.[77]

Team building is a big part of managing global human resources: The accompanying *Personal Competencies* feature explains how to do this.

Personal Competencies

Building Your *Global Management Team* Skills

Multinational enterprises increasingly rely on global management teams to oversee their operations. For example, Whirlpool International's business is managed by a Swede and a six-person management team from Sweden, Italy, Holland, the United States, Belgium, and Germany.[78] Globally disbursed teams like these need effective ways to foster team member trust, communication, and coordination.

Modern communications methods facilitate this. Teleconferencing, videoconferencing, and information technology devices like BlackBerry smart phones obviously make it easier to stay in touch. Group decision software enables globally disbursed team members to work on projects and reports and then hand their work-in-process on to team members in the next time zone.

Devices like these enable companies to create virtual global teams. These are teams whose members meet in person only occasionally (if at all), "with people around the world conducting meetings and exchanging information via the Internet, enabling the organization to capitalize on 24-hour productivity."[79]

Virtual teams present their own challenges. When most communications take place remotely and (often) asynchronously, the employer should make extra efforts to cultivate trust among team members. Suggestions here include:

1. Establish trust based on *performance consistency* (in other words, by doing what you are supposed to do, when you are supposed to do it), rather than based solely on social bonds;
2. Remember that *rapid responses* to virtual teammates foster trust;
3. Establish norms for *acceptable communication patterns*. For instance, each party should know how to contact each other, when to expect a response, and so on.
4. Team leaders should play important roles in reinforcing timeliness and consistency.[80]

Figure 13.5 lists other training virtual teams require.

FIGURE 13.5

Some Examples of Special Training Virtual Teams Require

Virtual teams need training on how to:
Establish trust
Lead a virtual team meeting
Resolve conflicts
Establish norms for acceptable communication patterns
Use various collaboration and communications technologies
Prepare for what to expect when working in a virtual team
Be culturally sensitive
Identify and diagnose potential virtual team problems
Deal with virtual team performance issues
Manage time conflicts with local non-virtual team supervisors

International Compensation

The whole area of international compensation presents some tricky problems. On the one hand, there is some logic in having companywide pay scales. Here, for instance, the firm pays divisional marketing directors throughout the world within the same narrow range. But this is usually not practical, given the large differences in cost of living among countries.

THE BALANCE SHEET APPROACH The most common approach to formulating expatriate pay is therefore to equalize purchasing power across countries, a technique known as the *balance sheet* approach.[81]

The basic idea is that each expatriate should enjoy the same standard of living he or she would have had at home. With the balance sheet approach, the employer focuses on four main home-country groups of expenses—*income taxes, housing, goods and services,* and *discretionary expenses* (child support, car payments, and the like). The employer estimates what each of these four expenses is in the expatriate's home country, and what each will be in the host country. The employer then pays any differences—such as additional income taxes or housing expenses.

In practice, this usually boils down to building the expatriate's total compensation around five or six separate components. For example, base salary will normally be in the same range as the manager's home-country salary. In addition, however, there might be an overseas or foreign service premium. The executive receives this as a percentage of his or her base salary, to compensate for the required cultural and physical adjustments.[82] There may also be several allowances, including a housing allowance and an education allowance for the expatriate's children. Income taxes represent another area of concern. A U.S. manager posted abroad must often pay not just U.S. taxes but also income taxes in the host country.

Table 13.1 illustrates the balance sheet approach. In this case, the manager's annual earnings are $80,000, and she faces a U.S. income tax rate of 28% and a Belgium income tax rate of 70%. You can compute the other costs using the Index of Living Costs Abroad from the U.S. Department of State's Office of Allowances, available at http://aoprals.state.gov/Web920/location.asp?menu_id=95.[83]

INTER-COUNTRY PAY DIFFERENCES Once location-specific cash premium allowances, relocation assistance, taxation, and itemized reimbursements (for things like children's schooling) are factored in, the total 3-year cost of sending the same employee abroad would vary widely by country. For example, it would range from about $432,000 for a posting

TABLE 13.1 The Balance Sheet Approach (Assumes Base Salary of $80,000)

Annual Expense	Chicago, U.S.	Brussels, Belgium (U.S.$ Equivalent)	Extra Allowance
Housing & utilities	$35,000	$67,600	$32,600
Goods & services	6,000	9,500	3,500
Taxes	22,400	56,000	33,600
Discretionary income	10,000	10,000	0
Total	$73,400	$143,100	$69,700

Source: Joseph Martocchio, *Strategic Compensation: A Human Resource Management Approach*, 2nd edition (Upper Saddle River, NJ: Prentice Hall, 2001), Table 12–15, p. 294.

to London, to $870,000 in Riyadh Saudi Arabia, and $990,000 in Tokyo.[84] Figure 13.6 summarizes typical expatriate pay premiums and benefits.

INCENTIVES While the situation is changing, performance-based incentives are still less prevalent abroad. In Europe, firms still tend to emphasize a guaranteed annual salary and companywide bonus. European compensation directors do want to see more performance-based pay. However, they first have to overcome several problems—including selling the idea of more emphasis on performance-based pay.

The employer also needs to tie the ratio of incentives to salary to local realities. In Eastern Europe workers generally spend 35% to 40% of their disposable income on basic necessities like food and utilities. They therefore require a higher proportion of more predictable base salary than do workers in many other countries.[85]

However, incentives are popular in other countries. In Japan, a worker might expect to receive as much as half (or more) of his or her total annual compensation near year end, as a sort of profit-sharing bonus. In Asia, including the People's Republic of China, incentives, even for production workers, are popular. However many employers in Asia, to preserve group harmony, make incentive pay a small part of the pay package, and team incentives are advisable.[86]

ESTABLISHING A GLOBAL PAY SYSTEM The aim of the employer's global rewards program is to make sure that the pay policies in each geographic location contribute to motivating the employee behaviors the company requires to achieve its strategic plan. The separate geographic area compensation plans should also be consistent with each other, while responsive to local conditions.[87] Designing such a global pay plan basically involves stepping back and deciding first what employee behaviors you want the pay plan to

FIGURE 13.6 Typical Expatriate Pay Premiums and Benefits

• Overseas Premium	Additional percentage of base salary (usually 10 percent) paid to compensate for inconvenience of living abroad
• Housing Allowance	Provision of comfortable housing for free or at a rate similar to what the expatriate would incur at home
• Cost of Living Allowance (COLA)	Payment of additional amount to cover extra costs to allow expatriate to live in the same manner as they did at home
• Moving Expenses	Expatriate and family transportation and goods shipment to and from assignment location
• Tuition for Dependent Education	Reimbursement for expatriate's children to receive a home country education, for example, private school in the assignment location or boarding school back home
• Home Leave	Expatriate and family transportation and time off to return home
• Tax Reimbursement Payments	Reimbursement for any additional taxes payable by expatriate as a result of living abroad

Source: Francesco, Anne Marie; Gold, Barry A., *International Organizational Behavior*, 2nd, © 2005. Electronically reproduced by permission of Pearson Education, Inc., Upper Saddle River, New Jersey.

FIGURE 13.7

Steps in Designing a Global Pay Plan[88]

- **Phase I: Formulate a global compensation framework.** This means:
  1. define your firm's global rewards philosophy (in terms how rewards will help the company achieve its strategic goals),
  2. review your current rewards programs around the world,
  3. assesses the extent to which each of these country programs are set up to help the company achieve its strategic goals, and
  4. create a preliminary compensation plan for each location.
- **Phase II: Organize jobs and appraisals.** Next, systematize job descriptions and performance expectations around the world. For example, create more consistent performance assessment practices, establish consistent job descriptions and performance expectations for similar worldwide jobs, and start planning personnel requirements and recruitment worldwide.
- **Phase III: Create detailed pay policies.** Here, devise specific pay policies for each location that make sense in terms of the firm's global compensation philosophy. Among other things, this will require surveys to assess local pay practices.
- **Phase IV: Institute a talent management framework.** Next, institute career development practices, in recognition of the fact that promotional opportunities and career progress are necessary supplements to the company's compensation programs.
- **Phase V: Reevaluate program.** Periodically reevaluate the global pay policies, given the fact that strategic needs and competitors' pay practices may change.

encourage, given the firm's strategic aims. Then, systematize job descriptions, appraisal processes, and pay policies among company facilities around the world. Figure 13.7 summarizes the steps or phases in designing a global pay plan.

Performance Appraisal of International Managers

At the Toyota factories in Toyota City, Japan, bar charts map individual workers' progress toward meeting their personal work targets. Toyota doesn't intend this public display of performance to humiliate their workers. Instead, it's to "alert [the worker's] coworkers and enlist their help in finding solutions."[89]

Several things complicate the task of appraising an expatriate's performance. Cultural differences are one. For example, an open exchange of views including criticism is often the norm in the United Kingdom, but is frowned upon in China, where "face" is a major concern.

Another complication is, who does the appraisals? Obviously, local management must have some input, but, again, cultural differences may distort the appraisals. Thus, host country bosses in Peru might evaluate an Australian expatriate manager there somewhat negatively if they find his or her use of participative decision making culturally inappropriate. On the other hand, home-office managers, not fully aware of the situation the manager faces locally, may be so out of touch that they can't provide valid appraisals.

In fact, when it comes to appraising expatriates abroad, managers don't always do what they know they should. In one study, the surveyed managers knew that having a balanced set of appraisers from both the host and home countries, and more frequent appraisals, produced the best appraisals. But, in practice, most did not do this. Instead, they conducted appraisals less frequently, and had raters from the host or the home country do the appraisals.[90]

Suggestions for improving the expatriate appraisal process include:

1. Stipulate the assignment's difficulty level, and adapt the performance criteria to the local job and situation.
2. Weigh the evaluation more toward the on-site manager's appraisal than toward the home-site manager's.
3. If the home-office manager does the actual written appraisal, have him or her use a former expatriate from the same overseas location for advice.

Safety and Fair Treatment Abroad

Safety abroad is an important issue for global employers, for several reasons. For one thing, the need to ensure safety and fair treatment doesn't stop at a country's borders. The United Kingdom has often taken the lead in occupational safety. However, other countries are quickly adopting such laws, with which anyone doing business in these countries must then comply. And, in any case, it's hard to make a legitimate case for being less safety conscious or fair with workers abroad than you are with those at home. High-profile companies including Nike, Inc. have received bad publicity for—and taken steps to improve—the working conditions, long hours, and low pay rates for factory workers in countries such as Indonesia.

The increased threat of terrorism is also affecting human resource activities at home and abroad. Domestically, for instance, new U.S. government antiterrorism regulations affect employers' ability to hire from abroad.[91] For example, the prospective employee must have an interview at his or her local British embassy abroad, and scheduling these is a relatively time-consuming process.

Employers are also facing more safety-related resistance from prospective expats. More are reluctant to accept foreign postings and take their families abroad, and those that do are demanding more compensation.[92] And for their employees and facilities abroad, employers have had to institute more comprehensive safety plans, including, for instance, evacuation plans to get employees to safety, if that becomes necessary. Even in the 1990s, the threats facing expat employees were on the rise. For example, the number of overseas kidnappings more than doubled from 830 to 1,728 during the mid-to-late 1990s.[93] Developments like these had already prompted employers to take steps to better protect their expat employees.

BUSINESS TRAVEL Keeping business travelers out of crime's way is a specialty all its own, but suggestions here include:[94]

- Provide expatriates with training about traveling, living abroad, and the place they're going to, so they're more oriented when they get there.
- Tell them not to draw attention to the fact they're British—by wearing flag emblems or T-shirts with British names, for instance.
- Have travelers arrive at airports as close to departure time as possible and wait in areas away from the main flow of traffic.
- Equip the expatriate's car and home with adequate security systems.
- Tell employees to vary their departure and arrival times and take different routes.
- Keep employees current on crime and other problems by regularly checking their home government's advisories for travel abroad.[95]
- Advise employees to remain confident at all times. Body language can attract perpetrators, and those who look like victims often become victimized.[96]

Repatriation: Problems and Solutions

One of the most unfortunate facts about sending employees abroad is that 40% to 60% of them will probably quit within 3 years of returning home. A 3-year assignment abroad for one employee with a base salary of about $100,000 may cost the employer $1 million, once extra living costs, transportation, and family benefits are included.[97] Given the investment the employer makes in training and sending these often high-potential people abroad, it obviously makes sense to do everything possible to make sure they stay with the firm.

American dual-career couples listed "the perceived impact of the international assignments upon returning to the U.S." as one of the most important issues in their willingness to relocate.[98] Yet one survey found that only about 31% of employers surveyed had formal repatriation programs for executives.[99] Formal repatriation programs are useful. For instance, one study found that about 5% of returning employees resigned if their firms had formal repatriation programs, while about 22% of those left if their firms had no such programs.[100]

STEPS IN REPATRIATION The heart and guiding principle of any repatriation program is this: Make sure that the expatriate and his or her family don't feel that the company has left them adrift. For example, one firm has a three-part repatriation program, one that actually starts before the employee leaves for the assignment abroad.[101]

First, the firm matches the expat and his or her family with a psychologist trained in repatriation issues. The psychologist meets with the family before they go abroad. The psychologist discusses the challenges they will face abroad, assesses with them how well they think they will adapt to their new culture, and stays in touch with them throughout their assignment.

Second, the program makes sure that the employee always feels that he or she is still "in the loop" with what's happening back at the home office. For example, the expat gets a mentor, and travels back to the home office periodically for meetings.

Third, once it's time for the expat employee and his or her family to return home, there's a formal repatriation service. About 6 months before the overseas assignment ends, the psychologist and an HR representative meet with the expat and the family to start preparing them for return. For example, they help plan the employee's next career move, help the person update his or her résumé, and begin putting the person in contact with supervisors back home.[102]

HOW TO IMPLEMENT A GLOBAL HR SYSTEM

⑤ Explain the main things to keep in mind when designing and implementing a global HR system.

Perhaps the most debated question in international HRM is this: "Given the cultural, legal, and political differences among countries, is it realistic for a company to institute a standardized HR system in all or most of its facilities around the world?" A study suggests that the answer is yes.

In this study, the researchers interviewed human resource managers from six global companies—Agilent, Dow, IBM, Motorola, Procter & Gamble, and Shell Oil Co.—as well as international HR consultants.[103] Here's what they found:

STEPS FOR DEVELOPING AN EFFECTIVE GLOBAL HR SYSTEM In developing *their* worldwide HR systems, best practice companies:

1. *Form global HR networks.* The firm's human resource managers around the world should feel that they're not just local HR managers, but are part of the firm's global human resource management network. Some firms formed global HR development teams to help develop the new HR systems.[104] The moral: Treat the local human resource managers as equal partners, not just implementers.
2. *Remember that it's more important to standardize ends and competencies than specific methods.* For example, IBM uses a more or less standardized recruitment and selection process worldwide. However, "details such as who conducts the interview (hiring manager vs. recruiter) differ by country."[105]

STEPS FOR MAKING THE GLOBAL HR SYSTEM MORE ACCEPTABLE Next, these companies engage in best practices to ensure that the global HR systems they develop will be *acceptable* to local managers around the world. There are two guidelines here:

1. *Remember that global systems are more accepted in truly global organizations.* These companies and their managers think of themselves as global in scope and perspective. As one Shell manager put it, "If you're truly global, then you are hiring here [the United States] people who are going to immediately go and work in the Hague, and vice versa."[106]
2. *Investigate pressures to differentiate; then determine their legitimacy.* Human resource managers seeking to standardize selection, training, appraisal, compensation, or other HR practices worldwide will always meet resistance from local managers. The latter will insist, "You can't do that here, because we are different culturally and in other ways." This study found that these "differences" are usually not persuasive. However, ascertain whether there may in fact be some reason for using a more locally appropriate system.

STEPS FOR IMPLEMENTING THE GLOBAL HR SYSTEM Finally, best practices can help ensure a more effective *implementation.* Specifically:

1. **Remember, "You can't communicate enough."** For example, "there's a need for constant contact with the decision makers in each country, as well as the people who will be implementing and using the system."[107]
2. **Dedicate adequate resources for the global HR effort.** For example, do not expect local HR offices to implement the new job analysis procedures unless the head office provides adequate resources for these additional activities.

Improving Productivity Through HRIS: Taking the HRIS Global

For global firms, it makes particular sense to expand the firm's human resource information systems to include the firm's operations abroad. For example, electrical components manufacturer Thomas & Betts once needed 83 faxes to get a head count of its 26,000 employees in 24 countries; it can now do so with the push of a button, thanks to its global HRIS system.[108] Most global HRIS do more. For example, without a database of a firm's worldwide management talent, selecting employees for assignments abroad and keeping track of each unit's compensation plans, benefits, and personnel practices and policies can be overwhelming.

When Buildnet, Inc., decided to automate and integrate its separate systems for things like applicant tracking, training, and compensation, it chose a Web-based software package called MyHRIS, from NuView, Inc. (www.nuviewinc.com). This is an Internet-based system that includes human resource and benefits administration, applicant tracking and résumé scanning, training administration, and succession planning and development.[109] With MyHRIS, managers at any of the firm's locations around the world can access and update more than 200 built-in reports such as "termination summary" or "open positions."[110] And the firm's home-office managers can access data on and monitor global human resource activities on a real-time basis.

Employers are also increasingly taking their employee self-service HR portals international. For example, Time Warner's "Employee Connection" portal lets its 80,000 worldwide employees self-manage much of their benefits, compensation planning, merit review, and personal information updating online.[111]

Review

SUMMARY

1. International business is important to almost every business today, and so firms must increasingly be managed globally. This confronts managers with many new challenges, including coordinating production, sales, and financial operations on a worldwide basis. As a result, companies today have pressing international HR needs with respect to selecting, training, paying, and repatriating global employees.
2. Intercountry differences affect a company's HR management processes. Cultural factors such as assertiveness and humane-orientation suggest differences in values, attitudes, and therefore behaviors and reactions of people from country to country. Economic and labor cost factors help determine whether HR's emphasis should be on efficiency, or some other approach. Industrial relations and specifically the relationship among the workers, the union, and the employer influence the nature of a company's specific HR policies from country to country.
3. A large percentage of expatriate assignments fail, but the batting average can be improved through

careful selection. There are various sources HR can use to staff domestic and foreign subsidiaries. Often managerial positions are filled by locals rather than by expatriates, but this is not always the case.

4. Selecting managers for expatriate assignments means screening them for traits that predict success in adapting to dramatically new environments. Such traits include both "stable" and "dynamic" traits, such as adaptability and flexibility, self-orientation, job knowledge and motivation, relational skills, extracultural openness, and family situation. Adaptability screening focusing on the family's probable success in handling the foreign assignment can be an especially important step in the selection process.
5. Training for overseas managers typically focuses on cultural differences, on how attitudes influence behavior, and on factual knowledge about the target country. The most common approach to formulating expatriate pay is to equalize purchasing power across countries, a technique known as the balance sheet approach. The employer estimates expenses for income taxes, housing, goods and services, and

discretionary costs, and pays supplements to the expatriate in such a way as to maintain the same standard of living he or she would have had at home.

6. The expatriate appraisal process can be complicated by the need to have both local and home-office supervisors provide input into the performance review. Suggestions for improving the process include stipulating difficulty level, weighing the on-site manager's appraisal more heavily, and having the home-site manager get background advice from managers familiar with the location abroad before completing the expatriate's appraisal.

7. Repatriation problems are common, but you can minimize them. They include the often well-founded fear that the expatriate is "out of sight, out of mind" and difficulties in reassimilating the expatriate's family back into the home-country culture. Suggestions for avoiding these problems include using repatriation agreements, assigning a sponsor, offering career counseling, and keeping the expatriate plugged in to home-office business.

KEY TERMS

international human resource management   406
works councils   409
co-determination   410
expatriates   410
host country nationals   412
locals   412
third-country nationals   412
ethnocentric   415
polycentric   415
geocentric   415

DISCUSSION QUESTIONS AND EXERCISES

1. What intercountry differences affect HR managers? Give several examples of how each may specifically affect an HR manager.
2. You are the HR manager of a firm that is about to send its first employees overseas to staff a new subsidiary. Your boss, the president, asks you why such assignments often fail, and what you plan to do to avoid such failures. How do you respond?
3. What special training do overseas candidates need? In what ways is such training similar to and different from traditional diversity training?
4. How does appraising an expatriate's performance differ from appraising that of a home-office manager? How would you avoid some of the unique problems of appraising the expatriate's performance?
5. Working individually or in groups, write an expatriation and repatriation plan for your professor, whom your school is sending to Bulgaria to teach HR for the next 3 years.
6. Give three specific examples of multinational corporations in your area. Check in the library or Internet or with each firm to determine in what countries these firms have operations, and explain the nature of some of their operations, and whatever you can find out about their international HR policies.
7. Choose three traits useful for selecting international assignees, and create a straightforward test to screen candidates for these traits.
8. Use a library or Internet source to determine the relative cost of living in five countries as of this year, and explain the implications of such differences for drafting a pay plan for managers being sent to each country.

Application Exercises

HR in Action Case Incident 1   "Boss, I Think We Have a Problem"

Central Steel Door Corporation has been in business for about 20 years, successfully selling a line of steel industrial-grade doors, as well as the hardware and fittings required for them. Focusing mostly in the United States and Canada, the company had gradually increased its presence from the New York City area, first into New England and then down the Atlantic Coast, then through the Midwest and West, and finally into Canada. The company's basic expansion strategy was always the same: Choose an area, open a distribution center, hire a regional sales manager, then let that regional sales manager help staff the distribution center and hire local sales reps.

Unfortunately, the company's traditional success in finding sales help has not extended to its overseas operations. With the expansion of the European Union, Mel Fisher, president of

Central Steel Door, decided to expand his company abroad, into Europe. However, the expansion has not gone smoothly at all. He tried for 3 weeks to find a sales manager by advertising in the *International Herald Tribune,* which is read by business-people in Europe and by American expatriates living and working in Europe. Although the ads placed in the *Tribune* also run for about a month in the *Tribune's* Internet Web site, Mr. Fisher so far has received only five applications. One came from a possibly viable candidate, whereas four came from candidates whom Mr. Fisher refers to as "lost souls"—people who seem to have spent most of their time traveling restlessly from country to country sipping espresso in sidewalk cafés. When asked what he had done for the last 3 years, one told Mr. Fisher he'd been on a "walkabout."

Other aspects of his international HR activities have been equally problematic. Fisher alienated two of his U.S. sales managers by sending them to Europe to temporarily run the European operations, but neglected to work out a compensation package that would cover their relatively high living expenses in Germany and Belgium. One ended up staying the

better part of the year, and Mr. Fisher was rudely surprised to be informed by the Belgian government that his sales manager owed thousands of dollars in local taxes. The managers had hired about 10 local people to staff each of the two distribution centers. However, without full-time local European sales managers, the level of sales was disappointing, so Fisher decided to fire about half the distribution center employees. That's when he got an emergency phone call from his temporary sales manager in Germany: "I've just been told that all these employees should have had written employment agreements and that in any case we can't fire anyone without at least 1 year's notice, and the local authorities here are really up in arms. Boss, I think we have a problem."

Questions

1. Based on the chapter and the case incident, compile a list of 10 international HR mistakes Mr. Fisher has made so far.
2. How would you have gone about hiring a European sales manager? Why?
3. What would you do now if you were Mr. Fisher?

HR in Action Case Incident 2 — Carter Cleaning Company: Going Abroad

With Jennifer gradually taking the reins of Carter Cleaning Company, Jack decided to take his first long vacation in years and go to Mexico for a month in January 2007. What he found surprised him: While he spent much of the time basking in the sun, he also spent considerable time in Mexico City and was surprised at the dearth of cleaning stores, particularly considering the amount of air pollution in the area. Traveling north he passed through Juarez, Mexico, and was similarly surprised at the relatively few cleaning stores he found there. On his return home, he began to think about whether it is advisable to consider expanding his chain of stores into Mexico.

Aside from the possible economic benefits, he had liked what he saw in the lifestyle in Mexico and was also attracted by the idea of possibly facing the sort of exciting challenge he faced 20 years ago when he started Carter Cleaning: "I guess entrepreneurship is in my blood," is the way he put it.

After he returned home, he had dinner with Jennifer, and began to formulate the questions he would have to ask before deciding whether or not to expand abroad.

Questions

1. Assuming they began by opening just one or two stores in Mexico, what do you see as the main HR-related challenges he and Jennifer would have to address?
2. How would you go about choosing a manager for a new Mexican store if you were Jack or Jennifer? For instance, would you hire someone locally or send someone from one of your existing stores? Why?
3. The cost of living in Mexico is substantially below that of where Carter is now located: How would you go about developing a pay plan for your new manager if you decided to send an expatriate to Mexico?
4. Present a detailed explanation of the factors you would look for in your candidate for expatriate manager to run the stores in Mexico.

EXPERIENTIAL EXERCISE

Financial Skills in Global HRM

A Taxing Problem for Expatriate Employees

Purpose:

The purpose of this exercise is to give you practice identifying and analyzing some of the factors that influence expatriates' pay.

Required Understanding:

You should be thoroughly familiar with this chapter and with the Web sites www.irs.gov, for the U.S., and similarly, www.direct.gov.uk for the United Kingdom.

How to Set Up the Exercise/Instructions:

Divide the class into teams of four or five students. Each team member should read the following: One of the trickiest aspects of calculating expatriates' pay relates to the question of the expatriate's governmental income tax liabilities. For a United Kingdom example, go to www.direct.gov.uk/en/BritonsLivingAbroad/index.htm. Your team is the expatriate-employee compensation task force for your company, and your firm is about to send several managers and engineers to Japan,

the U.S., and Saudi Arabia. What information did you find on this site that will help your team formulate expat tax and compensation policies? Based on that, what are the three most important things your firm should keep in mind in formulating a compensation policy for the employees you're about to send to Japan, the U.S., and Saudi Arabia?

ENDNOTES

1. See, for example, Helen Deresky, *International Management* (Upper Saddle River, NJ: Pearson, 2008); and Anne Marie Francesco and Barry Allen Gold, *International Organizational Behavior* (Upper Saddle River, NJ: Pearson, 2005).
2. Martha Frase, "Show All Employees a Wider World," *HR Magazine* (June 2007): 99–102.
3. Nancy Wong, "Mark Your Calendar! Important Task for International HR," *Workforce* (April 2000): 72–74.
4. Karen Roberts, Ellen Kossek, and Cynthia Ozeki, "Managing the Global Workforce: Challenges and Strategies," *Academy of Management Executive* 12, no. 4 (1998): 93–106. See also Chris Rowley and Malcolm Warner, "Introduction: Globalizing International Human Resource Management," *International Journal of Human Resource Management* 18, no. 5 (May 2007): 703(14).
5. Roberts et al., op. cit., 94.
6. Anne Marie Francesco and Barry Allen Gold, *International Organizational Behavior* (Upper Saddle River, NJ: Pearson, 2005): 145.
7. Helen Deresky, *International Management* (Upper Saddle River, NJ: Pearson, 2008): 17.
8. Ibid., 6
9. David Ralston, Priscilla Elsass, David Gustafson, Fannie Cheung, and Robert Terpstra, "Eastern Values: A Comparison of Managers in the United States, Hong Kong, and the People's Republic of China," *Journal of Applied Psychology* 71, no. 5 (1992): 664–671. See also P. Christopher Early and Elayne Mosakowski, "Cultural Intelligence," *Harvard Business Review* (October 2004): 139–146.
10. Helen Deresky, *International Management* (Upper Saddle River, NJ: Pearson, 2008): 98–99.
11. Chris Brewster, "European Perspectives on Human Resource Management," *Human Resource Management Review* 14 (2004): 365–382.
12. Ibid.
13. Annual 2006 figures, http://www.bls.gov/news.release/ichcc.toc.htm, accessed April 30, 2008.
14. Ed Frauenheim, "China's Contract Law: Something for Everyone," *Workforce Management* (August 20, 2007): 36.
15. The following is adapted from "The Equal Employment Opportunity Responsibilities of Multinational Employers," The U.S. Equal Employment Opportunity Commission: www.EEOC.gov/facts/multi-employers.html, accessed February 9, 2004.
16. Frances Taft and Cliff Powell, "The European Pensions and Benefits Environment: A Complex Ecology," *Compensation & Benefits Review* (January/February 2005): 37–50.
17. Ibid.
18. "Inform, Consult, Impose: Workers' Rights in the EU," *Economist* (June 16, 2001): 3.
19. Carolyn Hirschman, "When Operating Abroad, Companies Must Adopt European Style HR Plan," *HR News* 20, no. 3 (March 2001): 1, 6.
20. This is discussed in Eduard Gaugler, "HR Management: An International Comparison," *Personnel* (August 1998): 28. See also Carlos Castillo, "Collective Labor Rights in Latin America and Mexico," *Relations Industrielles/Industrial Relations* 55, no. 1 (Winter 2000): 59.
21. Helen Deresky, *International Management* (Upper Saddle River, NJ: Pearson, 2008): 369.
22. "Survey Says Expatriates Twice as Likely to Leave Employer as Home-based Workers," *BNA Bulletin to Management* (May 9, 2006): 147.
23. Margaret Shaffer and David Harrison, "Expatriates' Psychological Withdrawal from International Assignments: Work, Nonwork, and Family Influences," *Personnel Psychology* 51 (1998): 88. See also Jan Selmer, "Psychological Barriers to Adjustment of Western Business Expatriates in China: Newcomers vs. Long Stayers," *International Journal of Human Resource Management* 15, no. 4–5 (June–August 2004): 794–815; and Margaret A. Shaffer and David Harrison, "Forgotten Partners of International Assignments: Development and Test of a Model of Spouse Adjustment," *Journal of Applied Psychology* 86, no. 2 (April 2001): 238.
24. Helen Deresky, *International Management* (Upper Saddle River, NJ: Pearson, 2008): 348.
25. Gary Insch and John Daniels, "Causes and Consequences of Declining Early Departures from Foreign Assignments," *Business Horizons* 46, no. 6 (November–December 2002): 39–48.
26. Helen Deresky, *International Management* (Upper Saddle River, NJ: Pearson, 2008): 373.
27. "More Women, Young Workers on the Move," *Workforce Management* (August 20, 2007): 9.
28. Paula Caliguri, "The Big Five Personality Characteristics as Predictors of Expatriates' Desire to Terminate the Assignment and Supervisor-Rated Performance," *Personnel Psychology* 53, no. 1 (Spring 2000): 67–88. See also Margaret A. Shaffer, David A. Harrison, Hal Gregersen, J. Stewart Black, and Lori A. Ferzandi, "You Can Take It with You: Individual Differences and Expatriate Effectiveness," *Journal of Applied Psychology* 91, no. 1 (January 2006): 109(17).
29. Quoted in Meredith Downes, Iris I. Varner, and Luke Musinski, "Personality Traits as Predictors of Expatriate

Effectiveness: A Synthesis and Reconceptualization," *Review of Business* 27, no. 3 (Spring–Summer 2007): 16(8).

30. Jan Selmer, "Expatriation: Corporate Policy, Personal Intentions and International Adjustment," *International Journal of Human Resource Management* 9, no. 6 (December 1998): 997–1007. See also Barbara Myers and Judith K. Pringle, "Self-initiated Foreign Experience as Accelerated Development: Influences of Gender," *Journal of World Business* 40, no. 4 (November 2005): 421(11).

31. Hung-Wen Lee and Ching Hsing, "Determinants of the Adjustment of Expatriate Managers to Foreign Countries: An Empirical Study," *International Journal of Management* 23, no. 2 (2006): 302–311.

32. Helen Deresky, *International Management* (Upper Saddle River, NJ: Pearson, 2008): 90.

33. Sunkyu Jun and James Gentry, "An Exploratory Investigation of the Relative Importance of Cultural Similarity and Personal Fit in the Selection and Performance of Expatriates," *Journal of World Business* 40, no. 1 (February 2005): 1–8. See also Jan Selmer, "Cultural Novelty and Adjustment: Western Business Expatriates in China," *International Journal of Human Resource Management* 17, no. 7 (2006): 1211–1222.

34. Meredith Downes, Iris I. Varner, and Luke Musinski, "Personality Traits as Predictors of Expatriate Effectiveness: A Synthesis and Reconceptualization," *Review of Business* 27, no. 3 (Spring–Summer 2007: 16(8).

35. Ibid.

36. Ibid.

37. Discussed in Charles Hill, *International Business* (Burr Ridge, IL: Irwin, 1994): 511–515. See also Julia Richardson, "Self-directed Expatriation: Family Matters," *Personnel Review* 35, no. 4 (July 2006): 469–486.

38. Charlene Solomon, "One Assignment, Two Lives," *Personnel Journal* (May 1996): 36–47; See also Riki Takeuchi, Seokhwa Yun, and Paul E. Tesluk, "An Examination of Crossover and Spillover Effects of Spousal and Expatriate Cross-Cultural Adjustment on Expatriate Outcomes," *Journal of Applied Psychology* 87, no. 4 (August 2002): 655(12); and Julia Richardson, "Self-directed Expatriation: Family Matters," *Personnel Review* 35, no. 4 (July 2006): 469–486.

39. Barbara Anderson, "Expatriate Selection: Good Management or Good Luck?" *International Journal of Human Resource Management* 16, no. 4 (April 2005): 567–583.

40. Michael Schell, quoted in Charlene Marmer Solomon, "Success Abroad Depends on More Than Job Skills," p. 52.

41. Carla Joinson, "Cutting Down the Days," *HR Magazine* (April 2000): 90–97; "Employers Shortened Assignments of Workers Abroad," *BNA Bulletin to Management* (January 4, 2001): 7.

42. Helene Mayerhofer et al., "Flexpatriate Assignments: A Neglected Issue in Global Staffing," *International Journal of Human Resource Management* 15, no. 8 (December 2004): 1371–1389.

43. Martha Frase, "International Commuters," *HR Magazine* (March 2007): 91–96.

44. Michael Harvey et al., "Global Virtual Teams: A Human Resource Capital Architecture," *International Journal of Human Resource Management* 16, no. 9 (September 2005): 1583–1599.

45. Eric Krell, "Budding Relationships," *HR Magazine* 50, no. 6 (June 2005): 114–118.

46. Geoffrey Abbott et al., "Coaching Expatriate Managers for Success: Adding Value Beyond Training and Mentoring," *Asia-Pacific Journal of Human Resources* 44, no. 3 (December 2006): 295–317.

47. Anne Marie Francesco and Barry Allen Gold, *International Organizational Behavior* (Upper Saddle River, NJ: Pearson, 2005): 145.

48. Ibid., 106.

49. "DOL Releases Final Rule Amending Filing, Processing of Foreign Labor Certifications," *BNA Bulletin to Management* (January 11, 2005): 11.

50. Leslie Klass, "Fed Up With High Costs, Companies Winnow the Ranks of Career Expats," *Workforce Management* (October 2004): 84–88.

51. Timothy Dwyer, "Localization's Hidden Costs," *HR Magazine* (June 2004): 135–144.

52. Based on Pamela Babcock, "America's Newest Export: White Collar Jobs," *HR Magazine* (April 2004): 50–57.

53. The following is based on, "Back-office and customer care centers in emerging economies: A human capital perspective," IBM Business Consulting Services, http://www-05.ibm.com/nl/topmanagement/pdfs/back_office_and_customer_care.pdf, accessed April 29, 2008

54. Ibid., 3, 4.

55. Ibid., 5, 6.

56. Ibid., 5, 6.

57. Ibid., 10.

58. Helen Deresky, *International Management* (Upper Saddle River, NJ: Pearson, 2008): 36.

59. Arvind Phatak, *International Dimensions of Management* (Boston: PWS Kebt, 1989): 129.

60. Ibid.

61. Donald Dowling Jr., "Export Codes of Conduct, Not Employee Handbooks," *The Society for Human Resource Management Legal Report* (January/February 2007): 1–4.

62. Ibid.

63. "SOX Compliance, Corporate Codes of Conduct Can Create Challenges for US Multinationals," *BNA Bulletin to Management* (March 28, 2006): 97.

64. Hilary Harris and Chris Brewster, "The Coffee Machine System: How International Selection Really Works," *International Journal of Human Resource Management* 10, no. 3 (June 1999): 488–500.

65. Mary G. Tye and Peter Y. Chen, "Selection of Expatriates: Decision-Making Models Used by HR Professionals," *Human Resource Planning* 28, no. 4 (December 2005): 15(6).

66. www.performanceprograms.com/Surveys/Overseas.shtm, accessed January 31, 2008.

67. P. Blocklyn, "Developing the International Executive," *Personnel* (March 1989): 45. See also Paula M Caligiuri and Jean M. Phillips, "An Application of Self-Assessment Realistic Job Previews to Expatriate Assignments," *International Journal of Human Resource Management* 14, no. 7 (November 2003): 1102(15).

68. Kathryn Tyler, "Don't Fence Her In," *HR Magazine* 46, no. 3 (March 2001): 69–77.

69. Ibid.

70. Ibid.; Nancy Napier and Sully Taylor, "Experiences of Women Professionals Abroad," *International Journal of Human Resource Management* 13, no. 5 (August 2002).

71. Helen Deresky, *International Management* (Upper Saddle River, NJ: Pearson, 2008): 351–352.

72. Valerie Frazee, "Expats Are Expected to Dive Right In," *Personnel Journal* (December 1996): 31; See also Rita Bennett et al., "Cross-Cultural Training: A Critical Step in Ensuring the Success of National Assignments," *Human Resource Management* 39, no. 2–3 (Summer–Fall 2000): 239–250.

73. Helen Deresky, *International Management* (Upper Saddle River, NJ: Pearson, 2008): 353.

74. Ibid., 371.

75. Ibid., 358.

76. Ibid., 359.

77. Mark Mendenhall and Gunther Stahl, "Expatriate Training and Development: Where Do We Go from Here?" *Human Resource Management* 39, no. 2–3 (Summer–Fall 2000): 251–265. See also Geoffrey Abbott et al., "Coaching Expatriate Managers for Success: Adding Value Beyond Training and Mentoring," *Asia-Pacific Journal of Human Resources* 44, no. 3 (December 2006): 295–317.

78. Helen Deresky, *International Management* (Upper Saddle River, NJ: Pearson, 2008): 374. See also James H. Wall and Lynda Spielman, "Global Team-Building: Developing, Deploying and Connecting: Global Teams Are Quickly Becoming the Standard For Worldwide Organizations," *China Staff* 12, no. 3 (March 2006): 8(3).

79. Helen Deresky, *International Management* (Upper Saddle River, NJ: Pearson, 2008): 375–376.

80. Bradley Kirkman et al., "Five Challenges to Virtual Team Success: Lessons from Sabre, Inc.," *Academy of Management Executive* 16, no. 3 (2002): 71.

81. Charles Hill, *International Business* (Burr Ridge, IL: Irwin, 1994): 519–520; Joseph Martocchio, *Strategic Compensation* (Upper Saddle River, NJ: Pearson, 2006): 402–403.

82. Martocchio, op.cit.

83. http://aoprals.state.gov/Web920/location.asp?menu_id=95, accessed April 29, 2008.

84. Anne Marie Francesco and Barry Allen Gold, *International Organizational Behavior* (Upper Saddle River, NJ: Pearson, 2005): 164.

85. Helen Deresky, *International Management* (Upper Saddle River, NJ: Pearson, 2008): 361.

86. Gary Dessler, "Expanding into China? What Foreign Employers Entering China Should Know About Human Resource Management Today," *SAM Advanced Management Journal* 71, no. 4 (2006): 11–23. See also Joseph Gamble, "Introducing Western-style HRM Practices to China: Shop Floor Perceptions in a British Multinational," *Journal of World Business* 41, no. 4 (December 2006): 328–340; and Adrienne Fox, "China: Land of Opportunity and Challenge," *HR Magazine* (September 2007): 38–44.

87. Robin White, "A Strategic Approach to Building a Consistent Global Rewards Program," *Compensation & Benefits Review* (July/August 2005): 25.

88. Ibid., 23–40.

89. Helen Deresky, *International Management* (Upper Saddle River, NJ: Pearson, 2008): 339.

90. Hal Gregersen et al., "Expatriate Performance Appraisal in U.S. Multinational Firms," *Journal of International Business Studies* 27, no. 4 (Winter 1996): 711–739. See also Hsi-An Shih, Yun-Hwa Chiang, and In-Sook Kim, "Expatriate Performance Management from MNEs of Different National Origins," *International Journal of Manpower* 26, no. 2 (February 2005): 157–175; and Anne Francesco and Barry Gold, *International Organizational Behavior* (Upper Saddle River NJ: Pearson, 2005): 152–153.

91. "Terrorism Impacts Ability to Import, Export Workers," *BNA Bulletin to Management* (April 3, 2002): 111.

92. Ibid.

93. Frank Jossi, "Buying Protection from Terrorism," *HR Magazine* (June 2001): 155–160.

94. These are based on or quoted from Samuel Greengard, "Mission Possible: Protecting Employees Abroad," *Workforce* (August 1997): 30–32. See also Leah Carlson, "Protecting Workers in a Danger Zone," *Employee Benefit News* (September 1, 2005).

95. http://travel.state.gov/travel/cis_pa_tw/tw/tw_1764.html, accessed April 29, 2008.

96. Greengard, ibid., 32.

97. Carla Joinson, "Save Thousands Per Expatriate," *HR Magazine* (July 2002): 77.

98. Helen Deresky, *International Management* (Upper Saddle River, NJ: Pearson, 2008): 370.

99. Ibid.

100. Quoted in Leslie Klaff, "The Right Way to Bring Expats Home," *Workforce* (July 2002): 43.

101. Ibid.

102. Ibid.

103. Ann Marie Ryan et al., "Designing and Implementing Global Staffing Systems: Part 2—Best Practices," *Human Resource Management* 42, no. 1 (Spring 2003): 85–94.

104. Ibid., 89.

105. Ibid., 90.

106. Ibid., 86.

107. Ibid., 92.

108. Bill Roberts, "Going Global," *HR Magazine* (August 2000): 123–128.

109. Diane Turner, "NuView Brings Web-Based HRIS to Buildnet," *Workforce* (December 2000): 90.

110. Jim Meade, "Web-Based HRIS Meets Multiple Needs," *HR Magazine* (August 2000): 129–133.

111. Drew Robb, "Unifying Your Enterprise with a Global HR Portal," *HR Magazine* (March 2006): 119–120.

Measuring and Improving HR Management's Results

14

When you finish studying this chapter, you should be able to:

1. *Explain how and why the HR manager's job has changed, and what HR managers should focus on now.*

2. *Give examples of what human resource managers can do to move from a provider of operational services to the firm's chief "people" advisor/consultant.*

3. *Show how the consultant can establish his or her credibility as an expert, and build rapport with clients.*

4. *Discuss with examples how to conduct an HR audit.*

5. *List and explain at least five HR metrics.*

6. *Explain the process you would use to select an outsourcing vendor.*

Introduction

For many people in England and Europe, Marks & Spencer was long synonymous with retail department and food stores; its department stores were sort of the Macy's of England. Yet problems have been brewing for many years. In 2001 a confidential Marks & Spencer report noted rising costs, falling profit margins, and employee morale that had hit "rock bottom." A shake-up a few years later led to the departure of Marks & Spencer's HR head, and called for the chain's top management "to take HR seriously if it is to have any chance of regaining former glories." Now a new CEO is taking over. What changes should he make in his company's human resource management?[1] ∎

HUMAN RESOURCE MANAGEMENT'S CHANGING ROLE

A Brief Review of HR Management's Changing Role

We saw in chapter 1 that the human resource manager's job has changed over the years. As companies grew in the early 1900s, "personnel" took over hiring and firing from supervisors, ran the payroll department, and administered benefits. As technology in things like testing emerged, the personnel department began playing an expanded role in employee selection, training, and promotion.[2] The emergence of union legislation in the 1930s in the U.S. added "protecting the firm in its interaction with unions" to personnel's responsibilities. Then, when new equal employment legislation created the potential for discrimination-related lawsuits, personnel's advice and oversight grew more indispensable.[3] Figure 14.1 (repeated from chapter 1) summarizes the evolution.

Throughout these years, one thing stayed about the same: personnel/HR managers focused mostly on transactional, tactical issues. They administered benefits, screened employees, recommended appraisal forms, and oversaw labor law compliance, for instance. Today, global competition and the need to maximize employees' effectiveness are changing

❶ Explain how and why the HR manager's job has changed, and what HR managers should focus on now.

FIGURE 14.1 Issues Driving the Evolution of Human Resource Management

Decade	Major Business Issues	Common Titles for "HR"
Pre-1900s	Small businesses, and workers' guilds	No "HR" people
1900s	Growth of larger-scale enterprises due to effects of earlier industrial revolution, World War I	Labor Relations, Personnel
1920s	World-wide economic depression, Hawthorne "human relations" studies, first labor legislation	Industrial Relations, Personnel
1940s	World War II, growth of large diversified enterprises	Personnel Administration
1960s	Civil rights and compliance	Personnel
1980s	Growing impact of globalization and technology, and emergence of the knowledge/service economy, human capital	Personnel/Human Resources
2000s	Modern organizations, organization effectiveness, strategic HR planning	Human Resource Management

Source: Based on Richard Vosburgh, "The Evolution of HR: Developing HR as an Internal Consulting Organization," *Human Resource Planning* 30, no. 3 (September 2007).

that. The trend today is for the human resource unit to spend less time in operational services such as benefits administration, and more time doing two things—(1) helping top management craft and execute the firm's strategies, and (2) acting as top management's "internal consultant" for identifying and institutionalizing changes that will help the company's employees better contribute to the company's success.

Figure 14.2 shows how one expert in this area, Professor David Ulrich, sums up this idea. He says the HR manager's tasks can range (1) from day-to-day transactional tasks to strategic, future-oriented tasks and (2) from process-oriented HR tasks to people-oriented HR tasks. For example (see lower left quadrant) the HR manager's day-to-day HR processes-oriented tasks include managing compensation and benefits. The HR manager's strategic people-oriented tasks (see upper right quadrant) include talent and performance management. It's in carrying out future-oriented strategic tasks (like strategic HR planning, and performance management) that the HR manager's internal consulting skills are particularly crucial.

To sum up, the mission today of human resource management ". . . is to increase the success of the organization by improving decisions that depend on or impact people."[4] In today's jargon, HR needs to "add value." Human resource managers are therefore shifting their attention *from* providing transactional services *to* providing the advice top managers need to maximize the extent to which employees' competencies and behaviors are helping the firm execute its strategy.

New Ways to Supply Transactional Services

> ❷ Give examples of what human resource managers can do to move from a provider of operational services to the firm's chief "people" advisor/consultant.

Because of this, human resource managers need to reduce the time and effort they now put into managing transactional tasks like benefits administration. For example, by one estimate, providing transactional HR tools, processes, and services accounts for only about 25% of HR's impact on business performance.[5] The "big leap" for human resource management comes from freeing HR managers from these tasks, allowing them to focus more on applying internal consulting skills—for instance, in performance management—to boost organizational effectiveness.[6]

To make this transition to internal consultant, employers need to reinvent how they get basic HR services like benefits administration done. As we've seen in this book, employers are doing this in many ways. Technology is one. Dell uses its intranet to shift tasks like these more to *employee self-servicing*. For example, employees can log on and change

FIGURE 14.2 Human Resource Managers' Tasks Range from *Day-to-Day/Transactional* to *Strategic,* and from *Process* to *People-Oriented*

	Processes-oriented HR Tasks	People-oriented HR Tasks
Future/strategic-oriented HR tasks	Strategic HR planning HR as business partner Culture	Staffing, talent management Organizational design Performance management Training and development
Day-to-day/transactional-oriented HR tasks	Compensation Benefits HRIS Compliance	Employee relations Labor relations Safety Diversity and Equal Employment

Source: Adapted from David Ulrich and W. Brockbank, *The HR Value Proposition,* 2005, Harvard Business School Publishing.

their own benefits distributions. Dell also set up *centralized HR call centers* to answer employees' and supervisors' HR-related inquiries. *Outsourcing* one or more of these tasks to specialist outside vendors is the other option. (We'll return to outsourcing later in this chapter.)

What This Means in Practical Terms[7]

This evolution of human resource management's duties *from* supplying mostly transactional services *to* supplying more strategic and people-related consulting support has three implications for human resource managers:

1. Employers and HR units need to find *new ways to supply their traditional transactional services* (such as benefits administration), so as to free up the HR manager's time for strategic, internal consulting activities.
2. Human resource managers need to improve their business-analysis, *internal consulting skills.* And,
3. Because reducing in-house transactional services increasingly entails outsourcing some transactional services to outside vendors, human resource managers need to *improve their HR outsourcing skills.*

We've already discussed throughout this book the new methods human resource managers use to supply transactional HR services. Now, in this chapter, we'll turn to how you can build your internal consulting and outsourcing skills, starting with consulting, auditing, and measuring HR processes.

The Human Resource Manager as an Internal Consultant[8]

A human resource manager who wants to move *from* being mostly a provider of operational services *to* being the firm's chief advisor on how to leverage its human resources to add value to the company starts with three basic steps:

1. First, *know what you want to do.* This means having a plan for what transactional services to reorganize or redeploy, and how to accomplish it. That plan should make sense in terms of the company's strategic plan. We saw that *strategic human resource management* means formulating and executing human resource policies and practices that produce the employee competencies and behaviors the company needs to achieve its strategic aims. The point is to show management how you plan to make each component of the firm's HR process (recruiting, selection, and training, for instance) contribute to the firm's strategic aims ("add value"). For example, "doubling profits" may mean reducing recruitment costs by 40%, which may mean outsourcing the recruitment function.
2. Second, execute the plan to *reduce the assets and efforts* devoted to delivering transactional HR services. (We've seen that new delivery options include using more technology such as applicant tracking systems, online self-service, and call centers, and outsourcing). This will position HR to redirect its efforts to strategic and advisory activities.
3. Third, *develop the skills* required to be an effective internal consultant.

DEVELOPING HR CONSULTING SKILLS Developing internal consulting skills involves three things. *First,* master the basic human resource management functional skills, in areas like recruiting, interviewing, and equal employment compliance.

Next, acquire the *business knowledge* and strategic skills you'll need to analyze and advise how to best align employees' competencies with the firm's strategic needs.

Developing internal consulting skills involves: master the basic human resource management functional skills, and the basic business skills, and build credibility and rapport.

This means acquiring both strategic planning competencies (see chapter 3), and an adequate working knowledge of business topics like accounting, finance, marketing, sales, and operations.

Third, you'll need to build *credibility and rapport* with the firm's other managers. The following *HR in Practice* provides some guidance here.

HR in Practice

Building Credibility[9]

What makes a consultant (or anyone) credible?

Credibility starts with accomplishing what your colleagues expect of you. In this case, this means doing things like conceptualizing and driving an effective HR change management program; having a human resource management strategy that's aligned with the firm's business strategy; successfully partnering with line managers in developing business strategy; and basing human resource management recommendations on rigorous quantitative analysis.

Credibility

Beyond this, establishing credibility as an expert requires having, among other things:

- An excellent command of and understanding of the industry, organization, and competition
- Persuasive, high-quality suggestions
- A proven ability to solve business problems
- Effective interpersonal relationships and skills
- Excellent communication skills

- A reputation for creating solutions that work, and for educating clients on what is possible

Rapport

Credibility itself, though important, usually is not enough. Effective consultants must also build rapport with their clients—in this case, with the company's other managers and the firm's board of directors. Building rapport entails, for example:

- Acknowledge that the clients' situation is personal and unique and be willing to listen to their story
- Pay attention to the emotions surrounding the client's factual issues
- Focus on doing what's best for the client, rather than for yourself
- Focus on the client as an individual, not as a person fulfilling a job title
- Work to constantly find new ways to be of greater service to the client

CONDUCTING THE HUMAN RESOURCE MANAGEMENT AUDIT

Good consulting is based on good information. Most CEOs won't accept subjective, off-the-cuff explanations for the worth of projects you ask them to implement. That is why quantitative, data-based analysis is a hallmark of successful organizational consulting.

What Are HR Audits?

Within the human resource management area, such data-based analyses often start with HR managers conducting *human resource audits* of all or part of their operations. One practitioner describes an **HR audit** as "an analysis by which an organization measures where it currently stands and determines what it has to accomplish to improve its HR function."[10] Another calls it "a process of examining policies, procedures, documentation, systems, and practices with respect to an organization's HR functions."[11] The audit generally involves reviewing all or most aspects of the company's human resource function, usually using a checklist, as well as ensuring that the employer is adhering to government regulations and company policies.

HR audit
An analysis by which an organization measures where it currently stands and determines what it has to accomplish to improve its HR function.

④ Discuss with examples how to conduct an HR audit.

What Areas Should the HR Audit Cover?

HR audits vary in scope and focus. As an overview, typical broad topic areas for HR audits include:[12]

1. Roles and head count (including job descriptions, and employees by exempt/nonexempt and full/part-time status)
2. Legal issues (compliance with governmental employment-related legislation)
3. Recruitment and selection (including selection tools, background checks, and so on)
4. Compensation (policies, incentives, survey procedures, and so on)
5. Employee relations (union agreements, performance management, disciplinary procedures, employee recognition)
6. Mandated benefits (unemployment insurance, workers' compensation, and so on)
7. Group benefits (insurance, time off, flexible benefits, and so on)
8. Payroll (internal versus external payroll options, governmental compliance)
9. Documentation and record keeping (HR information systems, personnel files, citizenship and other forms, and so on)
10. Training and development (new employee orientation, workforce development, technical and safety, career planning, and so on)
11. Employee communications (employee handbook, newsletter, recognition programs)
12. Internal communications (policies and procedures, and so on)
13. Termination and transition policies and practices

Types of Audits

Beyond this, there are different types of audits, such as:[13]

1. *Compliance audits*—in particular, how well is the company complying with current governmental laws and regulations?
2. *Best practices audits*—in particular, to what extent is the employer's recruitment practices, hiring practices, performance evaluation practices, and so on comparable to those of companies identified as having exceptional practices?
3. *Strategic audits*—in particular, assessing the extent to which the employer's human resource management system is helping the company achieve its strategic goals, by fostering the required employee behaviors and organizational outcomes (such as in terms of employee turnover and length of time to fill an open position).
4. *Function specific audits*—in particular, audits here concentrate on one or more specific human resource management areas, such as compensation, or training and development.

Some Questions Prompting HR Audits

Although many employers routinely conduct human resource audits every two years or so, more often one or more questions prompt employers to conduct HR audits. These questions include:

- Are we in legal compliance? As we've seen in this book, employers need to be sure they're complying with thousands of employment laws and regulations. For example, are our employment interviewers asking any inadvisable questions? Does our application form contain the candidate's certification that all information he or she is providing is true and accurate?[14] Figure 14.3 summarizes some important legal issues to focus on.
- Are our human resource department's practices aligned with our needs and strategy? For example, are our screening and training practices producing the high levels of customer service our strategy requires?
- Are we administering our human resource management function as productively as we might be? For example, are best practice companies employing best HR practices we might benefit from?
- Did our key human resource projects or initiatives last year produce the results we intended? For example, did the company-wide training program produce improved employee performance and organizational results?

FIGURE 14.3

Sample Legal Issues to Audit

It is advisable for U.S. employers to audit how well they're complying with the various governmental laws and regulations, using checklist topics and questions like the following:

- The Fair Labor Standards Act, including minimum wage and overtime and child labor provisions. For example, *do the people we now classify as independent contractors qualify as independent contractors under the FLSA?*
- Occupational Health and Safety Act. For example, *are all machines in our plant properly guarded?*
- Consolidated Omnibus Budget Reconciliation Act (corporate). For example, *do we have new employees certify they've received notice that they can continue COBRA coverage in event of separation form the company?*
- Americans with Disabilities Act. For example, *do we postpone the medical exam until after we've made a formal job offer?*
- Age Discrimination in Employment Act. For example, *do we disregard age when making downsizing decisions?*
- Title VII of the Civil Rights Act. For example, *do we train our supervisors to avoid inadvisable age, race, gender, and national origin–related selection interview questions such as, "Are you thinking of becoming pregnant"?*
- Equal Pay Act. For example, *do we pay women who are doing the same jobs as men at the same performance levels the same as we pay the men?*
- Pregnancy Discrimination Act. For example, *do we award the same time off and other benefits for pregnancy that we do for other types of health-related absence?*
- Immigration Reform and Control Act. For example, *do we require the necessary proof of identification and eligibility to work from everyone we hire?*
- Worker Readjustment and Retraining Notification Act. For example, *do we give the necessary written notice of layoff in event of plant closings?*
- Workers' compensation laws. For example, *do we avoid asking job candidates about their workers' compensation histories?*

- Are their issues such as low morale or poor performance that might respond to improved HR practices? For example, are our incentive plans producing the behaviors we need them to produce?
- What improvements can we institute within HR to reduce costs while improving the value HR adds to our company? For example, are their human resource management activities such as benefits enrollment that we could put online and thus enable employees to self-service themselves?
- How can HR improve the company's performance management process? For example, how effective are our current processes for aligning employees' performance with company goals?
- Have we instituted policies and practices that ensure fair treatment of all employees? For example, is there a disciplinary appeals process in place?
- Are there any persistent safety and health issues we may need to address? For example, are our workers' compensation costs rising too fast?

HIGH RISK COMPLIANCE AREAS TO AUDIT   With respect to employment law compliance, most problem areas (also known as lawsuits) stem from a relative handful of sources. These are:[15]

- Hiring (including job descriptions, application forms, employment contracts, reference procedures)
- Employee evaluations (in particular performance appraisals and promotions)
- Employee discipline (evidence, rules, procedures)
- Terminations (proper warnings, adherence to complaint procedures, and so on)
- Miscalculation of exempt and nonexempt jobs
- Inadequate personnel files, including performance documentation
- Prohibited absentee policies (for instance, related to the family and medical leave)
- Inadequate or inaccurate time records (for instance, plant personnel improperly checking in early)
- Insufficient documentation (for instance, missing or incomplete I-9 forms)

When to Audit?

Most employers will conduct HR audits no more often than once every two years or so. However, several events may signal the need for an HR audit. These include:[16]

- When a business reaches various milestones such as 15 employees, 20 employees, 50 employees, and 100 employees. These are threshold employee numbers at which point various governmental regulations and laws become applicable
- When the business grows to the point where line managers can no longer make their own hiring, discipline, promotion, and other decisions without HR management's assistance
- When the employer creates or modifies an employee handbook
- When a new head of human resource management arrives
- When employee morale, turnover, attendance, or excessive discipline problems seem to signal the need to evaluate HR practices
- When the company becomes a government contractor or a subcontractor (and therefore becomes subject to new federal regulations)

The HR Audit Process

In conducting an HR audit, the basic approach is to use a checklist-type questionnaire. The team may also interview selected HR employees, and managers in other (non HR) areas, to better assess the human resource function's effectiveness.

We can summarize the basic audit process as follows:[17]

1. *Decide on the scope of the audit.* For example, will we focus on all HR functions, or just on one or two, or perhaps just on legal compliance issues?
2. *Draft an audit team.* Identify the members of the HR audit team, who the leaders are, who the team reports to, and how the team will work.

3. *Compile the checklists and other tools that are available.* For example, what do we now have in terms of internal checklists or other materials, and checklists from corporate counsel? What packaged software HR audit checklist programs are available?

4. *Know your budget.* Familiarize yourself with the audit's likely costs, and ascertain the budget before moving too far ahead.

5. *Consider the legalities.* Understand going in that what you unearth during the HR audit may be discoverable by opposing counsel in the event of a lawsuit. At a minimum, discuss the proposed audit with attorneys.

6. *Get top management support.* Top management needs to be committed to the audit and to taking the steps required to remedy any problems.

7. *Develop the audit checklist.* From various sources, including internal company checklists, packaged software programs, and reviews of other firms' best practices have the audit team create an audit questionnaire. This is usually a series of checklists. The team will use these to guide them in reviewing the areas they're about to audit. (For example, one checklist may cover what items should and should not be in the personnel file.) SHRM (www.shrm.org) is an excellent source of audit tools.[18]

8. Use the questionnaire to *collect the data* about the company and its HR practices.

9. *Benchmark the findings*, by comparing them with human resource benchmark standards (more on this below).

10. *Provide feedback* about the results to the employer's HR professionals and senior management team.

11. *Create action plans* aimed at improving areas the audit singles out.

ILLUSTRATIVE HR AUDIT CHECKLIST ITEMS In practice, many employers use off-the-shelf checklists from an HR audit software package to conduct the audit, at least for the legal compliance questions.

Beyond that, three illustrative HR audit checklist areas and checklist items would include:

Personnel Files Do our files contain information including resumes and applications; offer letters; job descriptions, performance evaluations; benefit enrollment forms; payroll change notices and/or documentation related to personnel actions; documents regarding performance issues; employee handbook acknowledgements; citizenship and immigration, medical information, and Workers' Compensation information?[19]

In practice, many employers use off-the-shelf checklists from an HR Audit software package to conduct the audit, at least for the legal compliance questions.

Wage and Hour Compliance Is our time recordkeeping process in compliance with governmental law (for instance check-in/check-out no more than 3 minutes before starting/ stopping work)? Do we conduct a random audit of timecards to ensure that practices are as they should be? [20]

Headcount How many employees are currently on staff? How many employees of these are:

■ Regular
■ Probationary
■ Temporary
■ Full Time
■ Part Time
■ Exempt
■ Non-Exempt[21]

HR METRICS AND BENCHMARKING

In conducting the HR audit, most employers will want to benchmark—compare their results to those of comparable companies. Many private human resource management consulting firms compile and offer such comparables data, as does the Society of Human Resource Management. We'll discuss in this section various types of HR metrics, benchmarks, and HR measurement systems.[22]

Types of Metrics

Employment-related metrics range from broad, overall organizational measures down to measures that focus narrowly on specific human resource management functions and activities.

Figures 14.4 and 14.5 present examples of broader measures. Figure 14.4 gives an overall sense of how efficient an employer's human resource unit is. For example, a company with about 300 employees should have (at the median) just under 1 (0.94) HR employee per company employee.

Figure 14.5 gives a quick impression of how productive the company is, in this case in terms of revenue per full-time equivalent employee (two part-timers might equal one full-time employee, for instance). *Revenue per FTE employee* provides a rough but useful first approximation for how the company is doing. If, say, the typical Dixons were generating $100,000 per employee in electronics, while Comet were generating significantly less, it would prompt questions at Comet like, "Are we overstaffed at headquarters?" "Do we have too many employees per store?" and "Can we do anything (like more training, or incentives) to boost sales per Comet employee?"

List and explain at least five HR metrics.

FIGURE 14.4 HR-to-Employee Ratios (by Organizational Size)

Organizational Size	n	25th Percentile	Median	75th Percentile
Total	751	0.73	1.12	1.88
Fewer than 100	209	1.52	2.41	3.45
100 to 249	230	0.74	1.00	1.65
250 to 499	100	0.67	0.94	1.32
500 to 999	55	0.60	0.83	1.27
1,000 to 2,499	76	0.50	0.79	1.04
2,500 to 7,499	57	0.40	0.72	1.19
7,500 or more	24	0.36	0.72	1.06

Source: SHRM Human Capital Benchmarking Study: 2007 Executive Summary.

FIGURE 14.5 Revenue per FTE (by Industry)

	n	25th Percentile	Median	75th Percentile
All industries	828	$88,497	$200,000	$539,087
Accommodations, food and drinking places	34	$43,478	$72,140	$400,000
Biotechnology	10	$90,909	$267,857	$448,430
Construction, mining, oil and gas	31	$125,000	$274,725	$555,556
Educational services	17	$73,171	$150,000	$261,216
Finance	30	$38,462	$155,956	$904,762
Government	34	$125,000	$241,270	$564,972
Health care services	71	$71,429	$140,167	$448,430
High-tech	55	$97,959	$208,421	$787,402
Manufacturing (durable goods)	95	$146,990	$264,368	$625,000
Manufacturing (nondurable goods)	44	$153,406	$287,088	$603,198
Publishing and broadcasting	22	$94,076	$166,667	$518,129
Pharmaceutical	12	$70,378	$312,927	$792,398
Retail trade	58	$111,111	$311,741	$614,704
Services (nonprofit)	70	$67,692	$128,606	$425,532
Services (profit)	161	$100,000	$200,000	$535,714
Telecommunications	16	$92,151	$112,401	$431,115
Transportation and warehousing	29	$90,909	$358,852	$600,000
Government agency (all industries)	40	$80,179	$239,048	$508,444
Nonprofit organization (all industries)	136	$68,934	$123,833	$394,560
Privately owned for-profit organization (all industries)	444	$107,787	$236,255	$655,914
Publicly owned for-profit organization (all industries)	206	$66,667	$195,890	$460,829

Note: Industries with fewer than 10 organizations were omitted from the table. They were: agriculture, forestry, fishing and hunting; insurance; real estate; and utilities.

Source: SHRM Human Capital Benchmarking Study: 2007 Executive Summary.

Figures 14.6 and 14.7 illustrate more narrowly focused human resource management metrics. Figure 14.6 shows target executive bonus percentages for different size companies. For example, for a firm with about 200 employees, the median executive bonus is about 14% of the executive's compensation. Figure 14.7 summarizes several typical HR metrics. These include absence rate, cost per hire, and health care costs per employee.[23]

Benchmarking in Action

Metrics are rarely useful by themselves. Whether it's HR metrics, financial ratios, or some other, managers generally want to "know how we're doing" in relation to something. That "something" may be historical company figures, or benchmarkable (i.e., comparable) figures from other companies.[24]

SHRM provides a customized benchmarking service; this enables employers to compare their HR-related metric results with other companies (see Figure 14.8). SHRM's service provides benchmark figures for various industries including construction and mining, educational services, finance, manufacturing, and others. The employer can request the comparable figures

FIGURE 14.6 2007 Target Bonus Percentage for Executives (Percent of Total Compensation, by Organizational Size)

	n	25th Percentile	Median	75th Percentile
All sizes	319	10%	18%	30%
Fewer than 100	78	8%	15%	25%
100 to 249	99	7%	14%	20%
250 to 499	38	15%	23%	30%
500 to 999	24	13%	20%	30%
1,000 to 2,499	33	11%	23%	30%
2,500 to 7,499	31	20%	25%	40%
7,500 or more	16	18%	28%	40%

Source: SHRM Human Capital Benchmarking Study: 2007 Executive Summary.

FIGURE 14.7 Sample Metrics from SHRM Measurements Library

HR Metrics		
Absence Rate	[(# days absent in month) ÷ (Ave. # of employees during mo.) × (# of workdays)] × 100	Measures absenteeism. Determine if your company has an absenteeism problem. Analyze why and how to address issue. Analyze further for effectiveness of attendance policy and effectiveness of management in applying policy. See white paper entitled *Absenteeism: Analyzing Work Absences.*
Cost per Hire	(Advertising + Agency Fees + Employee Referrals + Travel cost of applicants and staff + Relocation costs + Recruiter pay and benefits) ÷ Number of Hires	Costs involved with a new hire. Use *EMA/Cost per Hire Staffing Metrics Survey* as a benchmark for your organization. Can be used as a measurement to show any substantial improvements to savings in recruitment/retention costs. Determine what your recruiting function can do to increase savings/reduce costs, etc.
U.S. Health Care Costs per Employee	Total cost of health care ÷ Total Employees	Per capita cost of employee benefits. Indicates cost of health care per employee. See BLS's publications entitled *Employer Costs for Employee Compensation* and *Measuring trends in the structure and levels of employer costs for employee compensation* for additional information on this topic.
HR Expense Factor	HR expense ÷ Total operating expense	HR expenses in relation to the total operating expenses of organization. In addition, determine if expenditures exceeded, met or fell below budget. Analyze HR practices that contributed to savings, if any.
Human Capital ROI	Revenue − (Operating Expense − [Compensation cost + Benefit cost]) ÷ (Compensation cost + Benefit cost)	Return on investment ratio for employees. Did organization get a return on their investment? Analyze causes of positive/negative ROI metric. Use analysis as opportunity to optimize investment with HR practices such as recruitment, motivation, training and development. Evaluate if HR practices are having a causal relationship in positive changes to improving metric.

Source: SHRM, http://shrm.org.

CUSTOMIZED BY INDUSTRY / EMPLOYEE SIZE / REVENUE SIZE / GEORGRAPHIC
REGION / GOVERNMENT / FOR-PROFIT / NONPROFIT / PUBLIC / PRIVATE . . .
PLUS MORE

Fill the gap between expensive benchmarking services and going it alone with
SHRM's affordable, high-quality customized benchmarking reports.

- Justify additional HR staff
- Defend recruiting and HR budgets
- Make the case for better 401(k) matching
- Brief board members about return on investment
- Conduct due diligence for mergers, reorganizations and acquisitions

Whether your company size is 50 employees, 10,000 or more, we will help you
choose a customized report that compares your organization's key benchmarks
with similar organizations. In just days, you will receive your benchmarking
report, along with guidelines on how to understand and use the data,
definitions and metric calculations.

- Database of more than 3,000 organizations
- Customize based on two cuts of the data (industry, employee size or
  other cuts)
- *More than 100 benchmarks!*
    Retirement
    Employment
    HR Expenses
    Disability & Life Insurance
    Turnover
    and coming soon:
    HR Staff Salaries
- SHRM member price:
  From $245
- Receive up to 21 SPHR/PHR recertification credits

CHECK OUR WEB SITE FOR A LISTING OF ALL THE CUSTOMIZABLE
BENCHMARKS YOU CAN RECEIVE.

Source: SHRM, www.shrm.org/research/benchmarks.

not just by industry, but broken down by employee size, company revenue, industry sectors, and geographic region. (See http://shrm.org/research/benchmarks/.)

Figures 14.9 and 14.10 illustrate two of the many sets of comparable benchmark measures the SHRM Survey benchmark service would provide a specific employer who uses its service. Figure 14.9 shows HR expense data—in this case, HR expenses, HR expenses to operating expenses, and HR expenses per full-time employee for firms comparable to this client. Figure 14.10 shows important human resource management recruitment performance benchmarks, such as time required to fill open positions, and cost per hire.

Measuring the High-Performance Work System

Every company tends to adopt a human resource management system that's unique to its needs. For example, a company planning to expand to the Middle East will need to organize and staff its recruitment function in a way that supports finding good candidates in the Middle East.

FIGURE 14.9 **SHRM Customized Human Capital Benchmarking Report for [Your Organization's Name Here]**

	HR Expense Data		
	2006 HR Expenses	2006 HR Expense to Operating Expenses	2006 HR Expense per FTE
n	12	11	12
25th percentile	$320,000	5.15%	$1,358
Median	$548,215	12.86%	$2,044
75th percentile	$700,000	16.67%	$3,550
Average	$533,421	12.66%	$2,341

Source: SHRM Human Capital Benchmarking Study 2007.

high-performance work system
An integrated set of human resources policies and practices that together produce superior employee performance.

However, while each is unique in many ways, employers' human resource management systems increasingly share some common characteristics. In fact, that is basically the idea underlying the benchmarking movement—namely, *that best practice companies share common recruitment, selection, training, compensation, and other policies and practices that translate into higher employee and organizational effectiveness.* Managers often call these common sets of HR practices *high-performance work systems* (HPWS). A **high-performance work system** is a set of human resource management policies and practices that translate into organizational effectiveness.

We can trace the HPWS idea back to the 1990s. Faced with global competition, U.S. companies needed to better utilize their human resources as they strove to improve quality and productivity to compete with firms like Toyota. About this time, the U.S. Department of Labor listed several characteristics of high-performance work organizations. These were multi-skilled work teams, empowered front-line workers, extensive training, labor management cooperation, commitment to quality, and customer satisfaction.[25]

When we look at their human resource management policies and practices (recruiting, screening, and training practices, for instance), high-performance work systems are

FIGURE 14.10 **SHRM Customized Human Capital Benchmarking Report for [Your Organization's Name Here]**

	2006 Number of Positions Filled	2006 Time-to-Fill	2006 Cost-per-Hire	2006 Annual Overall Turnover Rate	2006 Annual Voluntary Turnover Rate	2006 Annual Involuntary Turnover Rate
	Employment Data					
n	16	16	14	16	14	16
25th Percentile	35	27 days	$1,000	5%	5%	1%
Median	48	55 days	$3,050	18%	18%	4%
75th Percentile	97	60 days	$7,000	20%	20%	9%
Average	65	47 days	$3,918	16%	16%	5%

Source: SHRM Human Capital Benchmarking Study 2007.

TABLE 14.1 Comparison of HR Practices in High-Performance and Low-Performance Companies

	Low-Performance Company HR System (Bottom 10%, 42 Firms)	High-Performance Company HR System (Top 10%, 43 Firms)
Sample HR Practices		
Number of qualified applicants per position (*Recruiting*)	8.24	36.55
Percentage hired based on a validated *selection* test	4.26	29.67
Percentage of jobs *filled from within*	34.90	61.46
Percent of employees in a *formal HR plan* including recruitment, *development,* and succession	4.79	46.72
Number of hours of *training* for new employees (less than 1 year)	35.02	116.87
Number of hours of *training* for experienced employees	13.40	72.00
Percentage of employees receiving a regular *performance appraisal*	41.31	95.17
Percentage of workforce whose *merit increase* or *incentive pay* is tied to performance	23.36	87.27
Percentage of workforce who received *performance feedback* from multiple sources (360)	3.90	51.67
Target percentile for total compensation (market rate = 50%)	43.03	58.67
Percentage of the workforce eligible for *incentive pay*	27.83	83.56
Percentage of difference in incentive pay between a low-performing and high-performing employee	3.62	6.21
Percentage of the workforce routinely working in a self-managed, *cross-functional,* or *project team*	10.64	42.28
Percentage of HR budget spent on *outsourced activities* (e.g., recruiting, benefits, payroll)	13.46	26.24
Number of employees per HR professional	253.88	139.51
Percentage of the eligible workforce covered by a union contract	30.00	8.98
Firm Performance		
Employee turnover	34.09	20.87
Sales per employee	$158,101	$617,576
Market value to book value	3.64	11.06

Source: Adapted from Becher et al., pp. 16–17.

measurably different from less productive ones. Table 14.1 illustrates some of the human resource policies and practices that characterize high- and low-performance work systems. This table demonstrates three things.

1. First, it shows what high-performance companies do, in terms of human resource policies and practices. For example, they hire based on validated selection tests, fill more jobs from within, organize work around self-managing teams, and extensively train employees.

2. Second, it demonstrates that high-performance work systems aim to help *workers manage themselves*. The point of such a system's recruiting, screening, training, and other human resources practices is usually to build the self-managing teams of trained, empowered, self-motivated, and flexible employees that companies today need as a competitive advantage.[26]

3. Third, it shows that we can *measure* the extent to which a particular human resource management system is (or is not) consistent with that of a high-performance work system. For instance, note the measurable differences between high-performance and low-performance companies' training policies in Table 14.1.

Strategy-Based Metrics

Benchmarking (comparing one firm's HR ratios with another's) only provides a partial picture of how the firm's human resource management system is performing.[27] It shows how the human resource management system's performance compares to the competitions'. It may *not* show how it's doing in terms of helping achieve your firm's strategic goals. For example, if our strategy calls for doubling profits by improving customer service, to what extent are our new selection and training practices helping to improve customer service?

That's an important question, and managers need *strategy-based metrics* to answer it. **Strategy-based metrics** are metrics that specifically focus on measuring the activities that contribute to achieving a company's strategic aims.[28] As an example:

strategy-based metrics
Metrics that specifically focus on measuring the activities that contribute to achieving a company's strategic aims.

- Let's say the owners of the Le Méridien hotels decide to make their hotel one of the 10 top hotels in Saudia Arabia.
- They believe doing so will translate into revenues and profits 50% higher than now.
- They decide that achieving those strategic aims requires dramatically improving customer service. They will measure customer service in terms of measures like guest returns, and guest compliments of employees.
- What can the hotel's human resource managers do to help achieve this improved customer service? They can take measurable steps, such as increase training per year per employee from 10 hours to 25, boost incentive pay (tied to guest service ratings) from zero now to 10% of total salaries, and move from no job candidates tested before hiring to 100% testing prior to hiring. The strategic metrics for Le Méridien thus include (among others) 100% employee testing, 80% guest returns, incentive pay as a percent of total salaries, and sales up 50%.[29]

A hotel's human resource managers can do many things to improve customer service, such as increase training per year per employee, and boost incentive pay.

The HR Scorecard Process

We've seen (in chapter 7, "Performance Management and Appraisal") that the *balanced scorecard process* helps the manager visualize how various metrics link to achieving the company's strategic aims. Again, the balanced scorecard is not a scorecard; it refers to a process for assigning financial and nonfinancial goals to the chain of activities required for achieving the company's strategic aims, and for continuously monitoring results.

When the focus is on the human resource management function, the manager looks more narrowly at an *HR Scorecard* process. The **HR Scorecard** refers to the process for assigning financial and nonfinancial goals *to the human resource management–related* chain of activities required for achieving the company's strategic aims, and for continuously monitoring results. The process identifies the causal links between the HR activities, and the emergent employee behaviors, and the resulting firmwide strategic outcomes and performance.[30] There are seven steps in the HR Scorecard process:[31] (Figure 14.11 summarizes the basic sequence relationships.)

HR Scorecard

Measures the HR function's effectiveness and efficiency in producing employee behaviors needed to achieve the company's strategic goals.

Step 1 Define the Business Strategy Formulate a strategy for the company, and specify the strategic goals you expect, such as "revenues and profits 50% higher than now."

Step 2 Outline a Strategy Map As we also saw in chapter 7, the strategy map is a graphical tool that shows the "big picture" of how each department's or team's performance contributes to achieving the company's overall strategic goals.

Figure 14.12 (repeated from this book's Figure 7.10) presents a strategy map for EasyJet Airline. EasyJet pursues a low-cost leader competitive strategy. The strategy map for EasyJet lays out the hierarchy of big activities required for EasyJet to succeed at reducing costs.

- At the top is achieving company-wide, strategic revenue and profitability goals.
- To boost revenues and profitability, EasyJet needs to fly fewer planes (to keep costs down), attract and keep customers, maintain low prices, and maintain on-time flights.
- In turn (further down the strategy map), fewer planes, on-time flights, and low prices require fast turnaround.
- And fast turnaround requires motivated, committed ground and flight crews.
- The human resource management team can help produce that motivation and commitment, for instance with its recruitment, selection, training, and compensation policies.

Step 3 Identify the Strategically Required Organizational Outcomes From this map, we see that to boost revenues and profitability, EasyJet needs to achieve certain organizational outcomes, namely *fly fewer planes* (to keep costs down), *attract and keep customers*, *maintain low prices*, and have *faster flight turnarounds*.

Step 4 Identify the Required Workforce Competencies and Behaviors "What competencies and behaviors must our employees show for our company to produce the strategically relevant organizational outcomes, and thereby achieve its strategic goals?" At EasyJet on-time flights, low prices, and fast turnarounds require *motivated, committed, cross-trained* ground and flight crews.

Step 5 Identify the Required HR System Policies and Activities Once the human resource manager decides what these required workforce competencies and behaviors are, he or she can decide what HR activities and policies will help produce them. For example, at EasyJet *relatively high wages, careful employee screening, and special cross-job training* should help produce faster plane turnarounds and on-time flights.

Step 6 Specify Strategic Metrics Now, the manager can set specific measurable targets—strategic metrics—for each activity. For example, "what do we mean

FIGURE 14.11

The Basic HR Scorecard Relationships

HR activities → Emergent employee behaviors → Strategically relevant organizational outcomes → Organizational performance → Achieve strategic goals

FIGURE 14.12 **Strategy Map for EasyJet Airlines**

by faster turnaround time" and "on-time flights"? EasyJet might measure turnaround time in terms of "improve turnaround time from an average of 30 minutes per plane to 26 minutes per plane this year." It might measure employee morale and customer satisfaction with periodic surveys. Table 14.2 lists some useful HR metrics (in addition to those in Figures 14.4 through 14.10, and Table 14.1).[32]

Step 7 **Report the Scorecard Measures in Digital Dashboards** EasyJet's managers may want to monitor all these metrics using digital dashboards—basically, desktop screens containing graphs and charts.[33] Doing so provides a bird's-eye view of how the human resource management function is doing. For example, a dashboard for EasyJet Airline might display daily trends for activities such as fast turnaround, attracting and keeping customers, on-time flights, and employee morale.

These "dashboards" are typically components of special performance management software systems. These systems integrate and store information from hundreds or thousands of sources (for instance, feedback from customer surveys, daily airplane turnaround statistics, employee performance measures, and on-time flights). They employ built-in analytical tools to provide managers with continuous, real-time updates regarding the employees' and company's performance.

TABLE 14.2 Some Additional HR Performance Measures

Sample measures for assessing employee attitudes, behaviors, and performance, and for assessing HR activities.

Employee attitude survey results

Employee turnover

Extent to which strategy is clearly articulated and well understood throughout the firm

Extent to which the average employee understands how his or her job contributes to the firm's success

Level of cross-cultural teamwork

Level of organizational learning

Extent to which employees are clear about their own goals

Percentage of employees making suggestions

Employee productivity

Requests for transfer to supervisor

Extent to which the employees can describe the company's core values

Employee commitment survey scores

Customer complaints/praise

Percentage of retention of high-performing key employees

Requests for transfer per employees

Percentage of employees making suggestions

Sample measures for assessing HR system activities such as testing, training, and reward policies and practices

Proportion of employees selected based on validated selection methods

Number of hours of training employees receive each year

Proportion of merit pay determined by formal performance appraisal

Percentage of workforce regularly assessed via a formal performance appraisal

Percentage of employees eligible for annual merit cash or incentive plans

Extent to which information is communicated effectively to employees

Percentage of workforce who received a performance feedback from multiple sources

Percentage of difference in incentive pay between the low-performing and high-performing employees

Percentage of the workforce routinely working in self-managed or cross-functional or project teams

Number of qualified applicants per position

Percentage of jobs filled from within

Improving Productivity Through HRIS: Tracking Applicant Metrics

The quality of a firm's new hires and of the recruitment sources that produced those new hires are useful strategic metrics.[34] Baby boomers are set to start retiring in droves, while employers also face a diminishing pool of top applicants. Furthermore we've seen that it's not rational to spend thousands of dollars recruiting and training employees unless you can measure the quality of those you're hiring, and which hiring source produces the best candidates. To do this, you need to collect and assess recruitment metrics.

The logical way to do so is with the aid of an applicant tracking system (ATS). Many vendors provide ATSs. These include specialized ATS vendors like Authoria, PeopleClick, Jobpartners, and Bond Talent, as well as outsourcers such as Accenture and IBM.

Regardless of the vendor, the measurement process involves two basic steps.

- First, the employer (and/or vendor) decides how to measure the performance of new hires. For example, with Authoria's system, hiring managers input their evaluations of each new hire at the end of the employee's first 90 days, using a 1–5 scale. Dell uses employee performance and retention metrics.[35]
- Second, the ATS enables the employer to track the recruitment sources and applicant characteristics that correlate with superior hires. (It may show, for instance, that new employees hired through "employee referrals" stay longer and work better than those from newspaper ads.) Most ATSs also enable hiring managers to keep track of all these hiring metrics on desktop dashboards.

Metrics-capable applicant tracking systems produce three big benefits. Installing an Authoria ATS enabled the global news firm Reuters to *identify the sources, candidate traits, and best practices that work best* in each place they do business.[36] This in turn enabled them to *reduce recruiting costs,* for instance, by shifting recruitment dollars from less to more effective sources. Last (but not least), the ATS should produce *better employees,* for instance, by helping the employer see which employee characteristics correlate with superior performance.

OUTSOURCING HUMAN RESOURCE MANAGEMENT ACTIVITIES

For human resource managers to devote more time to strategic matters, they must reduce the effort they put into day-to-day operational services. One way to do this is to outsource one or more specific services such as background checking and benefits administration to specialist outside vendors. We've seen that some employers outsource all or almost all their human resource functions to outside vendors like *professional employer organizations* (PEOs), *human resource outsourcers,* or sometimes *employee* or *staff leasing firms.* For example, in 2007 Starbucks outsourced many of its human resource activities to Cincinnati-based Convergys.[37] For about a year, Convergys managed Starbucks' payroll and HR administration in the U.S. and Canada, as well as Starbucks' benefits administration for Canadian employees. In 2008, facing the need to rev up Starbucks' in-store performance, the firm's top managers decided to bring HR back in-house. Now Starbucks' own human resource management team can focus on improving Starbucks employees' morale and performance.

Starbucks briefly outsourced its HR function.

Employers typically pay the outsourcing company about $400–$500 per employee per year, and sign multi-year contracts.

Outsourcing Today

A SHRM survey provides an overview of HR outsourcing today.[38]

WHO OUTSOURCES WHAT? About 58% of surveyed employers outsource at least some HR functions, 38% do not and have no plans to, and about 4% plan to outsource one or more HR functions in the next several years. Table 14.3 shows HR functions outsourced completely, partially, or not all. For example, about 49% of employers completely outsource background and criminal background checks, and 47% outsource their employee

TABLE 14.3 HR Functions That Are Outsourced Completely, Partially, or Not at All

Function	Outsource Completely	Outsource Partially	Do Not Outsource	Average Years Outsourced
Background/criminal background checks	49%	24%	27%	5
Employee assistance/counseling	47%	19%	35%	7
Flexible spending account administration	43%	24%	33%	6
Consolidated Omnibus Budget Reconciliation Act (COBRA)	38%	17%	45%	5
Health care benefits administration	24%	36%	40%	8
Temporary staffing	21%	33%	46%	7
Pension benefits administration	19%	36%	45%	8
Retirement benefits administration	17%	30%	54%	8
Employee relocation	13%	16%	71%	6
Payroll administration	13%	35%	52%	8
Retirement planning	11%	10%	80%	9
Work/life balance benefits administration	6%	5%	89%	4
Compensation and/or incentive plans administration	4%	15%	82%	7
Executive development and coaching	4%	16%	80%	6
Human Resource Information Systems (HRIS) development	4%	11%	85%	5
Recruitment/staffing of employees (nonexecutives)	4%	26%	71%	6
Recruitment/staffing of executives only	4%	24%	73%	7
Risk management	4%	8%	88%	8
Expatriate administration	2%	4%	94%	6
Employee communication plans/strategies	1%	9%	90%	5
Performance management	1%	2%	97%	6
Training and development programs	1%	20%	80%	6
Policy development and/or implementation	0%	4%	96%	5
Strategic business planning	0%	4%	96%	2

Note: Percentages are row percentages and may not total 100% due to rounding. Data based on organizations that currently outsource one or more HR functions. The percentages are not adjusted to reflect cases in which an organization may not perform a particular HR function. Average number of years outsourced includes outsourcing of HR functions both partially and completely.

Source: SHRM® Human Resource Outsourcing Survey Report, (July 2004), http://shrm.org, accessed February 2, 2006.

assistance/counseling activities. Interestingly, relatively few employers outsource core transactional HR activities such as recruitment and payroll administration.

WHY OUTSOURCE? For most employers, outsourcing seems to be more a cost-cutting tactic, rather than one to free up HR time for more strategizing. In this survey, the main reasons for outsourcing were to save money/reduce operating costs (cited by 56%), to control legal risks and improve compliance (55%), to gain access to vendor talent (47%), and to streamline human resource management operations (45%).

OUTSOURCING BENEFITS Figure 14.13 summarizes what respondents see as outsourcing's benefits. Seventy-five percent cited "HR is able to focus on core business functions," and 66% said "it allows HR to spend more time on strategy development and execution." As you can see in Figure 14.13, other reported benefits include, "improves HR metrics/measurement," and "HR had a better reputation among senior management."

OUTSOURCING PROBLEMS On the whole, about 35% of those outsourcing said they were "very satisfied" with their outsourcing vendor services and relationships, about 53% were "somewhat satisfied," and the remainder ranged from indifferent to dissatisfied. The main problem cited was lack of face-to-face contact with employees.

However, in general, HR outsourcing has not seemed to have had the effects that the employers were seeking. For example, 47% of survey participants said the outsourcing had the effect of decreasing HR job opportunities, and only 22% said it increased HR job opportunities. (Fifty-one percent said they were "not all concerned" that HR outsourcing leads to reductions in HR staff.)

To what extent did outsourcing meet organizations' overall expectations? About 21 percent (Figure 14.14) said they "strongly" agreed outsourcing met their expectations, at least to some extent and 50 percent "somewhat" agreed. Overall, the results suggest that employers must be careful to whom they outsource, and how they outsource. Let's look first at to whom employers can outsource.

To Whom Do Employers Outsource HR Functions?

There are hundreds—probably thousands—of vendors who will manage some or all of an employer's human resource management activities, for a fee. Figure 14.15 shows some top

FIGURE 14.13 Benefits of Outsourcing HR Functions for HR Professionals

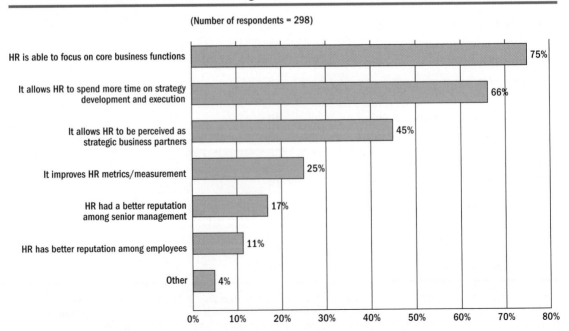

Source: SHRM® Human Resource Outsourcing Survey Report, July 2004, http://shrm.org, accessed February 2, 2006.

FIGURE 14.14

Extent to Which HR Outsourcing Has Met Organization's Expectations

Note: Percentages may not total 100% due to rounding. Based on HR professionals from organizations that currently outsource one or more HR functions. On a scale where 1 = To No Extent at All and 5 = To a Large Extent, the average level of expectation was 4.21 with a standard deviation of 0.86. A standard deviation of 1.0 or greater indicates a relative lack of consensus. Readers should proceed with caution when generalizing the results.

Source: SHRM® Human Resource Outsourcing Survey Report.

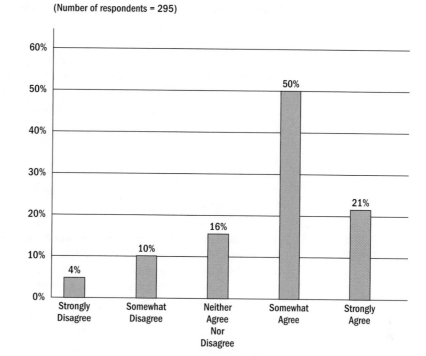

(Number of respondents = 295)

HR outsourcing providers. Most of these are very large firms, and they generally accept clients with large numbers (at least 15,000) of employees. For a directory of HR vendors see "Vendor Directory 2007," *Workforce Management* (http://bg3.mediabrains.com/client/workforcema/bg1/search.asp), as well as Web sites such as www.hr-guide.com/.

FIGURE 14.15 Some Top HR Outsourcing Vendors

Supplier	Sample Services	Sample Clients
Accenture	Talent management services; recruitment; performance and progression; learning; compensation	Best Buy, U.S. Transportation Security Administration, Unilever
IBM	Payroll, benefits; talent management (includes recruiting, learning, performance management, compensation, and succession management)	P&G, American Airlines
ADP	Payroll and benefits administration	Carmax, IKEA
Ceridian	Payroll and benefits administration; talent acquisition; regulatory compliance/administration	Comerica, FMC Corp.
Hewitt Associates	Benefits, payroll, performance management; training administration	Air Canada, Marriott
ExcellerateHRO	Compensation management; payroll, recruiting and staffing	Cardinal Health, BP Canada
Fidelity HR Services	Talent management (includes recruiting and staffing, training and development, and performance and rewards)	ABB Inc.; The Hartford
Convergys	Recruiting; compensation; HR administration; payroll, benefits	Fifth Third Bancorp., Dupont
Affiliated Computer Services, Inc	HRIS technology deployment and support; payroll, performance management, recruiting and staffing	Motorola, Delta Airlines
Northgate Arinso	Data input, time management (includes absences/presences, overtime management); payroll management	Cadbury Schweppes, Scotiabank

Sources: "Ranking the Top Enterprise HRO Providers," *HRO Today,* www.hrotoday.com/magazine.asp?artID=2074, accessed July 20, 2008; The International Association of Outsourcing Professionals, http://outsourcingprofessional.com/content/23/152/117, accessed July 20, 2008; "2008 Large Market End to End HR Outsourcing Providers," *Workforce Management,* www.workforce.com/section/09/feature/25/56/46/index.html, accessed July 20, 2008.

Some Important HR Outsourcing Competencies

The decision to outsource one or more services is a big one, and one not to be taken lightly. With less than half of the SHRM survey respondents saying that outsourcing had fully met their expectations, managers need to take care in deciding whether and what to outsource, and then in choosing and managing the vendor relationship.

THREE FACTORS The decisions on if and what to outsource depend on *employer size, financial pros and cons, and strategic issues*. In terms of *size*, many employers have little choice but to outsource. At an employer with, say, 50 employees, it's unlikely that an in-house payroll management group, background checking capabilities, or perhaps even formal employee screening capabilities will be available. Smaller firms, especially, have therefore tended to rely on vendors like employment agencies (although it wasn't called "outsourcing" in the 1990s).

The manager will also want to carefully review the *financial pros and cons* of outsourcing specific human resource management functions. For example, it's advisable to calculate the current payroll, benefits, and overhead (office space, and so on) costs of the HR function under review (such as benefits administration), so as to compare this with the prospective vendor's costs.[39] The costs of outsourcing then need to be compared to other, internal options, such as creating a central human resources call center to handle employee inquiries, or using intranet-based assets to let employees self-service routine HR tasks (as for benefits changes).

The SHRM survey (Figure 14.13) shows some of the *strategic issues* involved. For example, about 75% of respondents said outsourcing enabled them to "focus on core business functions," and 66% said it "allows HR to spend more time on strategy development and execution." The survey (see Table 14.3 above) also suggests that employers are much less likely to outsource high-impact strategic activities such as training and development, executive staffing and development, and policy development. As an example, Joseph Slawek, CEO of a small firm that manufactures flavors for foods and beverages, has two full-time and two part-time employees in his firm's HR department. With a total of 135 employees, "that costs us more than if we outsource the function," he says. However, with a unique team of scientists and others, he feels that "HR is part of our competitive advantage." An in-house human resource management team gives his firm the ability to offer the personalized career counseling and other services he feels his employees need.[40] Starbucks' decision to bring its HR back in-house probably also reflects such strategic issues. The following *HR in Practice* feature provides some guidelines on how to choose and manage the vendor relationship.

6 Explain the process you would use to select an outsourcing vendor.

HR in Practice

Outsourcing Checklist

In choosing and dealing with a vendor, suggestions include:[41]

1. Specify *which services* to outsource.
2. Agree with vendor on exactly *what HR activities will be outsourced* and what will be retained internally.
3. *Review multiple providers* and decide on one partner.
4. Clarify exactly *what services* the vendor will provide.
5. Make sure to have *metrics* to measure and hold accountable the vendor.
6. Look for *financial stability* in the prospective vendor.
7. Check the prospective vendor's *service record* with other clients.
8. Consider the *costs*, but balance short-term savings with the ability to provide long-term service.
9. Look at the prospective vendor's *technology capabilities* in terms of accommodating your growth plans.
10. Ensure the prospective vendor has an adequate *disaster recovery* plan, because it is managing crucial employee data for you.
11. Make sure the vendor will provide your in-house people with adequate *training* regarding procedures, and so on.

Managers can also apply principles of *supply chain management* when dealing with vendors, as the accompanying *Business in Action* feature explains.

Business in Action Building Your *Supply Chain* Knowledge

supply chain
Refers to all of a company's suppliers, manufacturers, distributors, and customers, and to the interactions among them.

supply chain management
All of a company's suppliers, manufacturers, distributors, and customers, and to the interactions among them.

supplier partnering
Having a limited number of suppliers, so as to build relationships that improve quality and reliability, rather than just to improve costs.

transparency
Giving supply chain partners easy access to information about details like demand, inventory levels, and status of inbound and outbound shipments, usually through a Web-based portal.

Internet-based purchasing
Internet-based purchasing automatically monitors the customer's needs online and produces the necessary products, shipping documents, and bills.

channel assembly
Having a supplier or distributor perform some of the steps required to create the company's product or service.

Companies work hard to squeeze out the wastes of unnecessary activities from everything they do. *Supply chain management* supports these aims. Indeed, world-class firms like Carrefour Group are successful largely due to how they manage their supply chains. The term **supply chain** basically refers to all of a company's suppliers, manufacturers, distributors, and customers, and to the interactions among them. **Supply chain management** "is the integration of the activities that procure materials, transform them into intermediate goods and final product, and deliver them to customers."[42] The idea is to get all the vendors, truckers, and so on "onto the same page" so they work together to cut waste and get the product or service to the customers as efficiently as possible.

SUPPLY CHAIN SOFTWARE   Companies usually build their supply chains' interconnectedness around special supply chain management software from companies like SAP and Oracle. For example, when someone places an order for a new Dell PC, Dell's software posts the order in its records. It then signals production to plan to produce the PC, and signals suppliers (like the one producing the monitor) to prepare to have one picked up. It also notifies UPS to pick up your PC from Dell (and the monitor from the supplier) on a particular day and to deliver it all to you, as ordered. And all this happens automatically.

In addition to the supply chain management software itself, four principles underlie successful supply chain management. They are *supplier partnering, transparency, Internet-based purchasing, and channel assembly.*[43]

1. **Supplier partnering** means having a limited number of suppliers, so as to build relationships that improve quality and reliability, rather than just to improve costs.
2. Supply chains also function better with *transparency*. **Transparency** basically

means giving supply chain partners easy access to information about details like demand, inventory levels, and status of inbound and outbound shipments, usually through a Web-based portal. This lets supply partners (like suppliers and truckers) accurately predict the customer's needs.

3. *Internet-based purchasing* (also called e-procurement) usually means more than just getting orders via the Web. In today's supply chains, supplier partnering and transparency usually mean that favored suppliers (like Levi's) can monitor the real-time sales of customers (like Tesco), and automatically create orders to fulfill the customer's needs. Therefore, **Internet-based purchasing** automatically monitors the customer's needs online and produces the necessary products, shipping documents, and bills.
4. Some companies also make their suppliers or distributors part of their manufacturing processes. **Channel assembly** means having a supplier or distributor perform some of the steps required to create the company's product or service. For example, Hewlett Packard (HP) doesn't send finished printers to its distributors; it sends components and modules.

Human resource managers can apply supply chain management principles such as supplier partnering, transparency, and Internet-based purchasing to dealing with vendors such as PEOs. For example, choose PEOs and other vendors based on developing a long-term relationship founded on trust, rather than just looking for the best financial deal. Create a relationship that cultivates transparency, to better enable the vendor to react quickly to your needs. And create ways to link your vendors with your own software systems, so that as many steps as possible (such as producing and paying bills) are done automatically, online.

As companies expand globally, more are outsourcing their world-wide recruitment to vendors that handle their total recruiting needs. Consultants call this recruitment process outsourcing.

The *Global Issues in HR* addresses this.

Global Issues in HR

Outsourcing the Global Recruitment Function

Here's how Robert McNabb, CEO of global recruiter Futurestep, explains the trend to recruitment process outsourcing. "Multinational companies may receive 1,000 resumes a day, and they also need to tap good passive candidates who may be entertaining four or five offers. . . . Companies with big world-class brands have discovered that the perception in the marketplace is that their recruiting process is broken."[44] So, as an example, Futurestep handles global recruiting for a large Madrid-based energy company. The employer recruits in both Europe and Latin America, and wanted a single recruiting source for all its locations.[45] (Futurestep is part of the global human resource outsourcing/executive search firm Korn/Ferry International.)

Recruitment process outsourcing (RPO) does not necessarily mean that the global vendor (such as Futurestep) does all the recruiting itself. The heart of RPO involves outsourcing the entire recruitment *process*, including deciding which sources to use and then managing them. The lead vendor may just manage the overall process. So, for example, Futurestep might be responsible for managing the employer's entire "end-to-end" recruitment activities. This would include managing all the recruiting and staffing-related people, resources, and ATS, as well as managing the external vendors such as contingent employment agencies.[46]

Review

SUMMARY

1. The human resource manager's job has changed over the years. The trend today is for the human resource unit to spend less time in operational services and more time doing two main things— (1) supporting top management's strategizing efforts, and (2) acting as the firm's "internal consultant" for identifying and institutionalizing changes that will help the company's employees better contribute to the company's success.

2. The evolution *from* supplying mostly transactional services *to* supplying more strategic and people-related consulting support has three implications for HR. Employers and HR units need to find *new ways to provide their traditional transactional services* (such as benefits administration). Human resource managers have to improve their business-analysis, *internal consulting skills.* And, human resource managers need to *improve their HR outsourcing skills.*

3. To make this transition to internal consultant, employers need to reinvent how they get basic HR services like benefits administration done. For example, Dell uses its intranet to shift tasks like these more to *employee self-servicing.*

4. Moving *from* a provider of operational services *to* the firm's chief advisor on how to better leverage its human resources entails three basic steps: First, *have an HR strategy in place.* Second, move to

reduce the assets and efforts devoted to delivering transactional HR services such as benefits administration. Third, *develop the skills* required to be an effective internal consultant.

5. Preparation for the latter starts with the basics: mastering basic human resource management functional concepts and skills in areas like recruiting, interviewing, and equal employment compliance. Next, acquire the business knowledge and strategic skills required to analyze and advise how to best align employees' competencies and development with the employer's strategic needs.

6. Studies suggest several things human resource managers can do to convince management and boards of directors that they're contributing in a strategic way to achieving the firm's strategic aims. These include conceptualizing and driving an effective change management program, and having a human resource management strategy that's integrated with the employer's business strategy.

7. Beyond this, the consultant needs to establish his or her *credibility as an expert,* and must also *build rapport* with clients—in this case, with the company's other managers and the firm's board of directors.

8. Most CEOs won't accept subjective explanations for projects they are asked to implement. Quantitative, data-based analysis is the hallmark

of successful organizational consulting. Such analyses often start with human resource managers conducting *human resource audits* of all or part of their operations. One HR practitioner describes an HR audit as "an analysis by which an organization measures where it currently stands and determines what it has to accomplish to improve its HR function."

9. HR audits vary in scope and focus. As an overview, one practitioner suggests 10 possible areas of focus for HR audits: recruitment and selection, compensation, employee relations, mandated (required) benefits, group benefits, payroll, record-keeping, training and development, employee communications, and internal communications. Beyond this, we identified four broad types of audits: *compliance audit, best practices, strategic,* and *function specific.* In conducting an HR audit, the basic approach is to use a checklist-type questionnaire.

10. In conducting the HR audit, most employers will want to compare their results to those of comparable companies. Many private human resource management consulting firms (such as Hewitt Associates) compile and offer such data, as does the Society of Human Resource Management.

11. Human resource–related metrics range from broad organizational measures to measures that focus narrowly on specific human resource management functions and activities. For example, HR-to-employee ratios give an overall feel for how efficient an employer's human resource unit is. Sales per employee provides a rough but useful first approximation for how the company is doing. More typical HR metrics include absence rate, cost per hire, and health care costs per employee. Metrics are rarely useful by themselves. SHRM provides a customized benchmarking service; this enables employers to compare their HR-related metric results with other companies.

12. Best practice companies have recruitment, selection, training, compensation, and other HR policies and practices (systems) that seem to translate into higher employee and organizational effectiveness. Managers often call these *high-performance work*

systems (HPWS). A high-performance work system is a set of employee and human resource management–related practices that translate into organizational effectiveness.

13. Benchmarking shows you how you're doing relative to the competition. It may not show you how your human resource management system is helping your company achieve its strategic goals. A strategy map outlines the causal flow of activities that contribute to achieving the company's strategy. It shows how various employee competencies, skills, and behaviors contribute to important organizational outcomes like better service, and how outcomes like better service affect organizational success.

14. Many employers use a special "scorecard" process for identifying strategic metrics. The HR Scorecard refers to a process for assigning financial and nonfinancial goals to the human resource management–related chain of activities required for achieving the company's strategic aims, and for continuously monitoring results. The process concisely highlights the causal link between the HR activities, the emergent employee behaviors, and the resulting firmwide strategic outcomes and performance.

15. For human resource managers to devote more time to strategic matters, they have to reduce the effort they put into day-to-day operational services. For more firms today, the answer is to outsource one or more services such as background checking and benefits administration to specialist outside vendors. The decisions on if and what to outsource depend on several things: employer size, financials and costs, and strategic issues. Employers are less likely to outsource high-impact strategic activities such as training and development, executive staffing and development, and policy development.

16. Human resource managers can apply many supply chain management principles such as supplier partnering, transparency, and Internet-based purchasing to dealing with vendors such as PEOs. For example, choose PEOs and other vendors based on developing a long-term relationship founded on trust, rather than just looking for the best financial deal. Create a relationship that cultivates transparency, to better enable the vendor to react quickly to your needs.

KEY TERMS

HR audit   438
high-performance work system   446
strategy-based metrics   448
HR Scorecard   449
strategy map   449
supply chain   457

supply chain management   457
supplier partnering   457
transparency   457
Internet-based purchasing   457
channel assembly   457

DISCUSSION QUESTIONS AND EXERCISES

1. Explain how and why the HR manager's job has changed, and what, in brief, HR managers want to put more of their focus on now.
2. What are the responsibilities of an internal HR consultant, exactly?
3. Give examples of what human resource managers can do to move *from* a provider of operational services *to* the firm's chief "people" advisor/consultant.
4. List what an HR manager should do to help establish his or her *credibility as an expert, and* to build *rapport* with clients.
5. Discuss with examples how to conduct an HR audit.
6. List and explain the use of at least five HR metrics.
7. Explain the process you would use to select an outsourcing vendor.

Application Exercises

HR in Action
Case Incident 1 — Marks & Spencer

As we said in the chapter introduction, Marks & Spencer was long synonymous with retail department and food stores in England and Europe. With increasing economic integration in Europe (as symbolized by the addition of more countries to the European Union, and the adoption by most EU countries outside England of the Euro currency), competition within the EU area became more intense. While Marks & Spencer's many stores continued to be crowded with shoppers, problems had been brewing for many years. In 2001 a Marks & Spencer report referred to rising costs, falling profit margins, and "rock bottom" employee morale.[47]

When Marks & Spencer's HR head left a few years later, experts told the chain's top management "to take HR seriously if it is to have any chance of regaining former glories." One consultant who had worked with Marks & Spencer said, "I have never seen the HR team get to grips with the issues that are affecting the company. HR has never been seen as a contributor for change." Concerning Marks & Spencer's new chief executive, this consultant said, "[he] is a classic example of a chief executive who has no understanding about strategic HR. You can turn a business around by cutting costs, but the likes of Marks & Spencer needs HR-driven change." Anthony Thompson, a former Marks & Spencer manager returning to the company after 8 years, found some HR-related changes that surprised him. For one thing, he saw "very few customer assistants smiling." More than 2,000 people who Marks & Spencer had hired as temporary Christmas employees failed to come to work, apparently because they were offered better jobs elsewhere.

Not surprisingly, one of the first areas the new management addressed was human resource issues, starting with pay. When the new HR manager took over, there were 429 different pay rates for the customer assistants (the retail clerks who assist customers). These rates (converted from British pounds to dollars) ranged from about $10 an hour up to $20 an hour for long-term employees. That meant newly hired customer assistants earned a bit above the minimum wage. Management changed the customer assistant pay range, so it now ranged from about $11 an hour to about $14.50. That meant long-serving customer assistants would have their pay frozen, and would receive basically no pay raises for several years. On the other hand, newly hired customer assistants could now be paid a higher rate. Long-term employees were somewhat upset that inexperienced new hires were earning close to what those with years of experience were earning. However, the new rate range would also enable M&S to hire better entry-level employees, and hopefully give all customers consistently good service.

The company implemented several other HR changes. For example, Marks & Spencer traditionally trained customer assistants through classroom-type training. To speed the process and keep more customer assistants on the floor, Marks & Spencer now trained 8,000 coaches. Their job was to go back and train customer assistants on the floor, while they were helping customers. They also streamlined the performance review process, so that identifying and (if necessary) dismissing low-performing employees was easier.

Questions

1. To what extent does management now seem to be taking a strategic HR approach to the company's problems? What do you base that on?
2. If you were an HR consultant called in by top M&S management, what would you have done if you read the confidential M&S memo, and heard the experts' comments?
3. As an HR consultant to a CEO who was not too familiar with strategic HR, what would you have done to elicit confidence in you?
4. What, as their consultant, would you do now?

| *HR in Action* | Carter Cleaning Company: The High-Performance |
| *Case Incident 2* | Work System |

On the whole, Jennifer and her father were pleased with the human resource management changes they'd implemented in the past few years. Among other things, they had new equal opportunity law compliance, selection, training, appraisal, incentive, discipline, and safety procedures. Jennifer was therefore somewhat surprised and, perhaps, disappointed when her father told her he thought they should consider outsourcing their HR activities to a professional employee organization. "We invested all this time in improving our HR practices; why outsource all this to a stranger now?" she said. "You're probably right, Jen," her father said. "But on the other hand, we may be spending way too much time and money on managing these HR tasks, and the PEO suggested they'd save us money. Really, we don't know how effective all these changes have been. I think we need to really look at the numbers."

Questions

1. Create a strategy map for a typical Carter Cleaning store.
2. List 15 HR metrics you would suggest Carter use in measuring its HR effectiveness.
3. Based on what you learned about Carter Cleaning in the previous 13 chapters and anything else you may know about the cleaning business, write a one-page outline of what you would cover in an HR audit of Carter Cleaning.
4. If the Carters asked you for a summary of why they should *not* outsource their HR activities, what would you tell them?

EXPERIENTIAL EXERCISE

Benchmarking Pay and Benefits

Purpose:

The purpose of this exercise is to give you experience in HR benchmarking.

Required Understanding:

You should be thoroughly familiar with the material in this chapter, and have access to online HR benchmarking sources.

How to Set the Exercise/Instructions:

Set up groups of three or four students for this exercise. Then read the following:

By February 2004, the strike by Southern California grocery workers against the state's major supermarket chains was almost 5 months old. Because so many workers were striking (70,000), and because of the issues involved, unions and employers across the country were closely following the negotiations. Indeed, grocery union contracts were set to expire in several cities later in 2004, and many believed the California settlement—assuming one was reached—would set a pattern.

The main issue was employee pay and benefits, including how much (if any) of the employees' health care costs the employees should pay themselves. Based on their existing contract, Southern California grocery workers had unusually good health benefits. For example, they paid nothing toward their health insurance premiums, and paid only $10 copayments for doctor visits. However, supporting these excellent health benefits cost the big Southern California grocery chains over $4.00 per hour per worker.

The big grocery chains were not proposing cutting health care insurance benefits for their existing employees. Instead, they proposed putting any new employees hired after the new contract went into effect into a separate insurance pool, and contributing $1.35 per hour for their health insurance coverage. That meant new employees' health insurance would cost each new employee perhaps $10 per week. And, if that $10 per week wasn't enough to cover the cost of health care, then the employees would have to pay more, or do without some of their benefits.

It was a difficult situation for all the parties involved. For the grocery chain employers, skyrocketing health care costs were undermining their competitiveness, and the current employees feared any step down the slippery slope that might eventually mean cutting their own health benefits. The unions didn't welcome a situation in which they'd end up representing two classes of employees, one (the existing employees) who had excellent health insurance benefits, and another (newly hired employees) whose benefits were relatively meager, and who might therefore be unhappy from the moment they took their jobs and joined the union.[48] Adding to the difficulty was the fact that several new competitors, including Wal-Mart and foreign firms like Tesco, were either in or planning to be in competition with the existing stores very soon. Each side—the retailers and the unions—decided independently that they should better understand the pay and benefits situation by seeking out benchmark figures for their industry and related industries. They want your team to use any on- or offline sources available to get them the figures they need.

ENDNOTES

1. Julia Finch, "Leaked Papers Reveal the Devastating Decline of M&S: Staff Morale Hits Rock Bottom in UK as French Take to the Streets," *The Guardian* (April 7, 2001): 26; Daniel Thomas, "Experts Warn Retailer Over Disregard of HR," *Personnel Today* (November 16, 2004): 1; "Talks Reopen in Bid to Save M&S Deal," *Grocer* (October 14, 2006): 14; Claire Warren, "This Is Not Just HR . . . ," *People Management* 13, no. 1 (January 11, 2007): 26–30.

2. "Immigrants in the Workplace," *BNA Bulletin to Management Datagraph* (March 15, 1996): 260–261. See also Tanuja Agarwala, "Human Resource Management: The Emerging Trends," *Indian Journal of Industrial Relations* (January 2002): 315–331; Shari Caudron et al., "80 People, Events and Trends that Shaped HR," *Workforce* (January 2002): 26–56.

3. "Human Capital Critical to Success," *Management Review* (November 1998): 9.

4. John Boudreau and Peter Ramstad, *Beyond HR: The New Science of Human Capital* (Boston: Harvard Business School Press, 2007): 9.

5. Dave Ulrich and W. Brockbank, *HR Value Proposition* (Boston: Harvard Business School Press, 2005), discussed in Richard Vosburgh, op. cit., 10.

6. Richard Vosburgh, "The Evolution of HR: Developing HR as an Internal Consulting Organization," *Human Resource Planning* 30, no. 3 (September 2007): 11–24.

7. Except as noted, this section based on Richard Vosburgh, "The Evolution of HR: Developing HR as an Internal Consulting Organization," *Human Resource Planning* 30, no. 3 (September 2007): 11–24.

8. Ibid.

9. Ibid.

10. Lin Greenberg-Pophal, "HR Audits: Know the Market, Land Assignments," SHRM consultants form (December 2004), accessed February 2, 2008.

11. Bill Coy, "Introduction to The Human Resources Audit," La Piana Associates, Inc., www.lapiana.org/consulting, accessed May 1, 2008.

12. Lin Greenberg-Pophal, "HR Audits: Know the Market, Land Assignments," SHRM Consultants' Forum (December 2004), accessed February 2, 2008; and Bill Coy, "Introduction to The Human Resources Audit," La Piana Associates, Inc., www.lapiana.org/consulting, accessed May 1, 2008.

13. Based on Teresa Daniel, "HR Compliance Audits: 'Just Nice' or Really Necessary?" SHRM white paper (November 2004), accessed February 2, 2008.

14. See, for example, Dana R. Scott, "Conducting a Human Resources Audit," *New Hampshire Business Review* (August 2007).

15. Teresa Daniel, "HR Compliance Audits: 'Just Nice' or Really Necessary?" SHRM white paper (November 2004), accessed February 2, 2008. See also, Dana R. Scott, "Conducting a Human Resources Audit," *New Hampshire Business Review* (August 2007).

16. From Teresa Daniel, op. cit.

17. See Teresa Daniel, op. cit.; Dana Scott, op. cit.; "Start Your HR Audit with This Checklist," *HR Focus* 84, no. 6 (June 2007): 1, 11, 13–15; and Bill Coy, "Introduction to The Human Resources Audit," La Piana Associates, Inc., www.lapiana.org/consulting, accessed May 1, 2008.

18. For additional detailed information on conducting HR audits see, for example, http://SHRM.org/HR tools/toolkits_published, accessed February 2, 2008.

19. Dana R. Scott, "Conducting a Human Resources Audit," *New Hampshire Business Review* (August 2007).

20. Ibid.

21. Bill Coy, "Introduction to The Human Resources Audit," La Piana Associates, Inc., www.lapiana.org/consulting, accessed May 1, 2008.

22. See, for example, "Using HR Performance Metrics to Optimize Operations and Profits," *PR Newswire* (February 27, 2008) and "How to 'Make Over' Your HR Metrics," *HR Focus* 84, no. 9 (September 2007): 3.

23. For additional information on HR metrics see, for example, Karen M. Kroll, "Repurposing Metrics for HR: HR Professionals Are Looking Through a People-focused Lens at the CFO's Metrics on Revenue and Income per FTE," *HR Magazine* 51, no. 7 (July 2006): 64(6) and http://shrm.org/metrics/library_published over/measurement systems TOC.asp, accessed February 2, 2008.

24. See, for example, "Benchmarking for Functional HR Metrics," *HR Focus* 83, no. 11 (November 2006): 1.

25. "With High-Performance Work Organizations, Adversaries No More," *Work & Family Newsbrief* (August 2003): 5. See also Karen Kroll, "Repurposing Metrics for HR," *HR Magazine* 51, no. 7 (July 2006), accessed from www.SHRM.org/HRmagazine/articles, February 4, 2008.

26. Robert McNabb and Keith Whitfield, "Job Evaluation and High-Performance Work Practices: Compatible or Conflictual?" *Journal of Management Studies* 38, no. 2 (March 2001): 294.

27. See Brian Becker and Mark Huselid, "Measuring HR? Benchmarking Is Not the Answer!" *HR Magazine* 8, no. 12 (December 2003), accessed from www.charmed.org, February 2, 2008.

28. Ibid.

29. Perhaps they may also want to try to quantify the extent to which HRM is helping the Ritz improve its performance. For example, the human resource manager might try to correlate (1) the new human resource performance measures (such as 100% testing), with (2) improved guest service (such as 80% of the guests returning for visits), and correlate that with (3) achieving the hotel's strategic goals (for instance, sales 50% higher).

30. The idea for the HR Scorecard derives from a broader measurement tool managers call the balanced scorecard. This does for the company as a whole what the HR Scorecard does for HR, summarizing instead the impact of various functions including HRM, sales, production, and distribution. The "balanced" in balanced scorecard refers to a balance of goals—financial and nonfinancial. Note that the *balanced scorecard* we discussed in chapter 7 reveals the links for the company as a whole. The *HR Scorecard* focuses more narrowly, just on how the human resource management system is doing.

31. Adapted in part from Becker, Huselid, and Ulrich, *The HR Scorecard: Linking People, Strategy, and Performance.*

32. Computerized HR scorecarding packages are available. See, for example,*Human Resource Department Management Report* (December 2002): 8; "Watson Wyatt Worldwide Creates the HR Scorecard Alliance," *InfoTrac*, accessed September 19, 2003.

33. For a more complete discussion, see chapter 7.

34. Connie Winkler, "Quality Check: Better Metrics Improve HR's Ability to Measure—and Manage—the Quality of Hires,*" HR Magazine* 52, no. 5 (May 2007): 93(4).

35. Ibid.

36. Ibid.

37. "Jessica Marquez, "HRO Deal Bulk of Industry," *Workforce Management* (July 23, 2007): 1, 3.

38. The following is based on a SHRM human resource outsourcing survey report (July 2004), http://SHRM.org, accessed February 2, 2006.

39. Mikio Manuel, "How to Calculate and Maximize Outsourcing ROI," www.SHRM.org/RT export/library_published, accessed February 2, 2008.

40. "HR: Outsource or In-house?" *Crain's Chicago Business* 30, no. 41 (September 8, 2007): 38.

41. The following are based on Richard Vosburgh, "The Evolution of HR: Developing HR as an Internal Consulting Organization," *Human Resource Planning* 30, no. 3 (September 2007): 11–12 and

Stephen Miller, "Collaboration Is Key to Effective Outsourcing," *HR Magazine* (2008 supp Trendbook): 58, 60–61.

42. Jay Heizer and Bernard Render, *Operations Management*, 6th ed. (Upper Saddle River, NJ: Prentice Hall, 2001): 434.

43. Kasra Ferdows et al., "Rapid-Fire Fulfillment," *Harvard Business Review* (November 2004): 104–110.

44. Fay Hansen, "Taking on the World with Recruitment Outsourcing; The Demand for Global End-to-End Recruitment Process Outsourcing, or RPO, Is Growing as Multinationals Strengthen Their Presence in a Range of Markets and Accelerate Hiring," *Workforce Management* 85, no. 20 (October 23, 2006): 34.

45. Ibid.

46. Ibid.

47. This case is based on Julia Finch, "Leaked Papers Reveal the Devastating Decline of M&S: Staff Morale Hits Rock Bottom in UK as French Take to the Streets," *The Guardian* (April 7, 2001): 26; Daniel Thomas, "Experts Warn Retailer Over Disregard of HR," *Personnel Today* (November 16, 2004): 1; "Talks Reopen in Bid to Save M&S Deal," *Grocer* (October 14, 2006): 14; Claire Warren, "This Is Not Just HR . . . ," *People Management* 13, no. 1 (January 11, 2007); 26–30.

48. Based on "Settlement Nears for Southern California Grocery Strike," *Knight-Ridder/Tribune Business News* (February 26, 2004): item 04057052.

Appendix A

COMPREHENSIVE CASES
Bandag Automotive*

Jim Bandag took over his family's auto supply business in 2005, after helping his father, who founded the business, run it for about 10 years. Based in Illinois, Bandag employs about 300 people, and distributes auto supplies (replacement mufflers, bulbs, engine parts, and so on) through two divisions, one that supplies service stations and repair shops, and a second that sells retail auto supplies through five "Bandag Automotive" auto supply stores.

Jim's father, and now Jim, have always endeavored to keep Bandag's organization chart as simple as possible. The company has a full-time controller, managers for each of the five stores, a manager that oversees the distribution division, and Jim Bandag's executive assistant. Jim (and his father, working part-time) handles marketing and sales.

Jim's executive assistant administers the firm's day-to-day human resource management tasks, but Bandag outsources most HR activities to others, including an employment agency that does its recruiting and screening, a benefits firm that administers its 401(k) plan, and a payroll service that handles its paychecks. Bandag's human resource management systems consist almost entirely of standardized HR forms purchased from an HR supplies company. These include application forms, performance appraisal forms, and an "honesty" test Bandag uses to screen the staff that works in the five stores. The company performs informal salary surveys to see what other companies in the area are paying for similar positions, and uses these results for awarding annual merit increases (which, in fact, are more accurately cost-of-living adjustments).

Jim's father took a fairly paternal approach to the business. He often walked around speaking with his employees, finding out what their problems were, and even helping them out with an occasional loan—for instance, when he discovered that one of their children was sick, or for part of a new home down payment. Jim, on the other hand, tends to be more abrupt, and does not enjoy the same warm relationship with the employees as did his father. Jim is not unfair or dictatorial. He's just very focused on improving Bandag's financial performance, and so all his decisions, including his HR-related decisions, generally come down to cutting costs. For example, his knee-jerk reaction is usually to offer fewer days off rather than more, fewer benefits rather than more, and to be less flexible when an employee needs, for instance, a few extra days off because a child is sick.

It's therefore perhaps not surprising that, while over the past few years Bandag's sales and profits have increased markedly, the firm has found itself increasingly enmeshed in HR/equal employment–type issues. Indeed, Jim now finds himself spending a day or two a week addressing HR problems. For example, Henry Jaques, an employee of one of the stores, came to Jim's executive assistant and told her he was "irate" about his recent firing and was probably going to sue. On Henry's last performance appraisal, his store manager had said Henry did the technical aspects of his job well, but that he had "serious problems interacting with his coworkers." He was continually arguing with them, and complaining to the store manager about working conditions. The store manager had told Jim that he had to fire Henry because he was making "the whole place poisonous," and that (although he felt sorry because he'd heard rumors that Henry suffered from some mental illness) he felt he had to go. Jim approved the dismissal.

Gavin was another problem. Gavin worked for Bandag for 10 years, the last 2 as manager of one of the company's five stores. Right after Jim Bandag took over, Gavin told him he had to take a Family and Medical Leave Act medical leave to have hip surgery, and Jim approved the leave. So far so good, but when Gavin returned from leave, Jim told him that his position had been eliminated. They had decided to close his store and open a new, larger store across from a shopping center about a mile away, and appointed a new manager in Gavin's absence. However, the company gave Gavin a (nonmanagerial) position in

---

*© Gary Dessler, Ph.D.

the new store as a counter salesperson, at the same salary and with the same benefits as he had before. Even so, "this job is not similar to my old one," Gavin insisted. "It doesn't have nearly as much prestige." His contention is that FMLA requires that the company bring him back in the same or equivalent position, and that this means a supervisory position, similar to what he had before he went on leave. Jim said no, and they seem to be heading toward litigation.

In another sign of the times at Bandag, the company's controller, Miriam, who had been with the company for about 6 years, went on pregnancy leave for 12 weeks in 2005 (also under the FMLA), and then received an additional 3 weeks' leave under Bandag's extended illness days program. Four weeks after she came back, she asked Jim Bandag if she could arrange to work fewer hours per week, and spend about a day per week working out of her home. He refused, and about 2 months later fired her. Jim Bandag said, "I'm sorry, it's not anything to do with your pregnancy-related requests, but we've got ample reasons to discharge you—your monthly budgets have been several days late, and we've got proof you may have forged documents." She replied, "I don't care what you say your reasons are, you're really firing me because of my pregnancy, and that's illegal."

Jim felt he was on safe ground as far as defending the company for these actions, although he didn't look forward to spending the time and money that he knew it would take to fight each. However, what he learned over lunch from a colleague undermined his confidence about another case that Jim had been sure would be a "slam dunk" for his company. Jim was explaining to his friend that one of Bandag's truck maintenance service people had applied for a job driving one of Bandag's distribution department trucks, and that Jim had turned him down because the worker was deaf. Jim (whose wife has occasionally said of him, "No one has ever accused Jim of being politically correct.") was mentioning to his friend the apparent absurdity of a deaf person asking to be a truck delivery person. His friend, who happens to work for UPS, pointed out that the U.S. Court of Appeals for the Ninth Circuit had recently decided that UPS violated the Americans with Disabilities Act by refusing to consider deaf workers for jobs driving the company's smaller vehicles.

Although Jim's father is semi-retired, the sudden uptick in the frequency of such EEO-type issues troubled him, particularly after so many years of labor peace. However, he's not sure what to do about it. Having handed over the reins of the company to his son Jim, he was loath to inject himself back into the company's operational decision making. On the other hand, he was afraid that in the short run, these issues were going to drain a great deal of Jim's time and resources, and that in the long run they might be a sign of things to come, with problems like these eventually overwhelming Bandag Auto. He comes to you, who he knows consults in human resource management, and asks you the following questions.

Questions

1. Given Bandag Auto's size, and anything else you know about it, should we reorganize the human resource management function, and if so why and how?

2. What, if anything, would you do to change and/or improve upon the current HR systems, forms, and practices that we now use?

3. Do you think that the employee that Jim fired for creating what the manager called a poisonous relationship has a legitimate claim against us, and if so why and what should we do about it?

4. Is it true that we really had to put Gavin back into an equivalent position, or was it adequate to just bring him back into a job at the same salary, bonuses, and benefits as he had before his leave?

5. Miriam, the controller, is basically claiming that the company is retaliating against her for being pregnant, and that the fact that we raised performance issues was just a smokescreen. Do you think the EEOC and/or courts would agree with her, and, in any case, what should we do now?

6. An employee who is deaf has asked us to be one of our delivery people and we turned him down. He's now threatening to sue. What should we do, and why?

7. In the previous 10 years we had only one equal employment complaint, and now in the last few years we have had four or five. What should I do about it? Why?
8. ***Change Management:*** Assuming Jim Bandag's father decides to step back in and implement the required changes, what issues might he encounter, and how exactly would you suggest he plan and execute the changes (using guidelines like those in chapter 6)?

Based generally on actual facts, but Bandag is a fictitious company. Bandag source notes: "The Problem Employee: Discipline or Accommodation?" *Monday Business Briefing* (March 8, 2005); "Employee Says Change in Duties after Leave Violates FMLA," *BNA Bulletin to Management* (January 16, 2007): 24; "Manager Fired Days after Announcing Pregnancy," *BNA Bulletin to Management* (January 2, 2007): 8; "Ninth Circuit Rules UPS Violated ADA by Barring Deaf Workers from Driving Jobs," *BNA Bulletin to Management* (October 17, 2006): 329.

Angelo's Pizza*

Angelo Camero was brought up in the Bronx, New York, and basically always wanted to be in the pizza store business. As a youngster, he would sometimes spend hours at the local pizza store, watching the owner knead the pizza dough, flatten it into a large circular crust, fling it up, and then spread on tomato sauce in larger and larger loops. After graduating from college as a marketing major, he made a beeline back to the Bronx, where he opened his first Angelo's Pizza store, emphasizing its clean, bright interior; its crisp green, red, and white sign; and his all-natural, fresh ingredients. Within 5 years, Angelo's store was a success, and he had opened three other stores and was considering franchising his concept.

Anxious as he was to expand, his 4 years in business school had taught him the difference between being an entrepreneur and being a manager. As an entrepreneur/small-business owner, he knew he had the distinct advantage of being able to personally run the whole operation himself. With just one store and a handful of employees, he could make every decision and watch the cash register, check in the new supplies, oversee the takeout, and personally supervise the service.

When he expanded to three stores, things started getting challenging. He hired managers for the two new stores (both of whom had worked for him at his first store for several years) and gave them only minimal "how to run a store" training, on the assumption that, having worked with him for several years, they already knew pretty much everything they needed to know about running a store. However, he was already experiencing human resource management problems, and he knew there was no way he could expand the number of stores he owned, or (certainly) contemplate franchising his idea, unless he had a system in place that he could clone in each new store to provide the manager (or the franchisee) with the necessary management knowledge and expertise to run their stores. Angelo had no training program in place for teaching his store managers how to run their stores. He simply (erroneously, as it turned out) assumed that by working with him they would learn how to do things on the job. Since Angelo really had no system in place, the new managers were, in a way, starting off below zero when it came to how to manage a store.

There were several issues that particularly concerned Angelo. Finding and hiring good employees was number one. He'd read the new National Small Business Poll from the National Federation of Independent Business Education Foundation. It found that 71% of small-business owners believed that finding qualified employees was "hard." Furthermore, "the search for qualified employees will grow more difficult as demographic and education factors" continue to make it more difficult to find employees. Similarly, reading the *Kiplinger Letter* one day, he noticed that just about every type of business couldn't find enough good employees to hire. Small firms were particularly in jeopardy; the *Letter* said: Giant firms can outsource many (particularly entry-level) jobs abroad, and larger companies can also afford to pay better benefits and to train their employees. Small firms rarely have the resources or the economies of scale to allow outsourcing or to install the big training programs that would enable them to take untrained new employees and turn them into skilled ones.

*© Gary Dessler, Ph.D.

While finding enough employees was his biggest problem, finding enough honest ones scared him even more. Angelo recalled from one of his business school courses that companies in the United States are losing a total of well over $400 billion annually in employee theft. As a rough approximation, that works out to about $9 per employee per day and about $12,000 a year lost for a typical company. Furthermore, it was small companies like Angelo's that were particularly in the crosshairs, because companies with fewer than 100 employees are particularly prone to employee theft. Why are small firms particularly vulnerable? Perhaps they lack experience dealing with the problem. More importantly: Small firms are more likely to have a single person doing several jobs, such as ordering supplies and paying the delivery person. This undercuts the checks and balances managers often strive for to control theft. Furthermore, the risk of stealing goes up dramatically when the business is largely based on cash. In a pizza store, many people come in and just buy one or two slices and a cola for lunch, and almost all pay with cash, not credit cards.

And, Angelo was not just worried about employees stealing cash. They can steal your whole business idea, something he learned from painful experience. He had been planning to open a store in what he thought would be a particularly good location, and was thinking of having one of his current employees manage the store. Instead, it turned out that this employee was, in a matter of speaking, stealing Angelo's brain—what Angelo knew about customers and suppliers, where to buy pizza dough, where to buy tomato sauce, how much everything should cost, how to furnish the store, where to buy ovens, store layout—everything. This employee soon quit and opened up his own pizza store, not far from where Angelo had planned to open his new store.

That he was having trouble hiring good employees, there was no doubt. The restaurant business is particularly brutal when it comes to turnover. Many restaurants turn over their employees at a rate of 200% to 300% per year—so every year, each position might have a series of two to three employees filling it. As Angelo said, "I was losing two to three employees a month." He also said, "We're a high-volume store, and while we should have [to fill all the hours in a week] about six employees per store, we were down to only three or four, so my managers and I were really under the gun."

The problem was bad at the hourly employee level: "We were churning a lot at the hourly level," said Angelo. "Applicants would come in, my managers or I would hire them and not spend much time training them, and the good ones would leave in frustration after a few weeks, while often it was the bad ones who'd stay behind." But in the last 2 years, Angelo's three company-owned stores also went through a total of three store managers—"They were just blowing through the door," as Angelo put it, in part because, without good employees, their workday was brutal. As a rule, when a small-business owner or manager can't find enough employees (or an employee doesn't show up for work), about 80% of the time the owner or manager does the job him or herself. So, these managers often ended up working 7 days a week, 10 to 12 hours a day, and many just burned out in the end. One night, working three jobs himself with customers leaving in anger, Angelo decided he'd never just hire someone because he was desperate again, but would start doing his hiring more rationally.

Angelo knew he should have a more formal screening process. As he said, "If there's been a lesson learned, it's much better to spend time up-front screening out candidates that don't fit than to hire them and have to put up with their ineffectiveness." He also knew that he could identify many of the traits that his employees needed. For example, he knew that not everyone has the temperament to be a server (he has a small pizza/Italian restaurant in the back of his main store). As Angelo said, "I've seen personalities that were off the charts in assertiveness or overly introverted, traits that obviously don't make a good fit for a waiter a waitress."

As a local business, Angelo recruits by placing help-wanted ads in two local newspapers, and he's been "shocked" at some of the responses and experiences he's had in response to his help-wanted ads. Many of the applicants left voice mail messages (Angelo or the other workers in the store were too busy to answer), and some applicants Angelo "just axed" on the assumption that people without good telephone manners wouldn't have very good manners in the store, either. He also quickly learned that he had to throw out a very wide net, even if only hiring one or two people. Many people, as noted, he just deleted because of the messages they left, and about half the people he scheduled to come in for interviews didn't show up. He'd taken courses in human resource management, so (as he said) "I should know better," but he hired people based almost exclusively on a single interview (he occasionally made a feeble attempt to check references). In total, his HR approach was obviously not working. It wasn't producing enough good recruits, and the people he did hire were often problematical.

What was he looking for? Service-oriented courteous people, for one. For example, he'd hired one employee who used profanity several times, including once in front of a customer. On that employee's third day, Angelo had to tell her, "I think Angelo's isn't the right place for you," and he fired her. As Angelo said, "I felt bad, but also knew that everything I have is on the line for this business, so I wasn't going to let anyone run this business down." Angelo wants reliable people (who'll show up on time), honest people, and people who are flexible about switching jobs and hours as required.

Angelo's Pizza business has only the most rudimentary human resource management system. Angelo bought several application forms at a local Office Depot, and rarely uses other forms of any sort. He uses his personal accountant for reviewing the company's books, and Angelo himself computes each employee's paycheck at the end of the week and writes the checks. Training is entirely on-the-job. Angelo personally trained each of his employees. For those employees who go on to be store managers, he assumes that they are training their own employees the way Angelo trained them (for better or worse, as it turns out). Angelo pays "a bit above" prevailing wage rates (judging by other help-wanted ads), but probably not enough to make a significant difference in the quality of employees that he attracts. If you asked Angelo what his reputation is as an employer, Angelo, being a candid and forthright person, would probably tell you that he is a supportive but hard-nosed employer who treats people fairly, but whose business reputation may suffer from disorganization stemming from inadequate organization and training. He approaches you to ask you several questions.

Questions

1. My strategy is to (hopefully) expand the number of stores and eventually franchise, while focusing on serving only high-quality fresh ingredients. What are three specific human resource management implications of my strategy (including specific policies and practices)?
2. Identify and briefly discuss five specific human resource management errors that I'm currently making.
3. Develop a structured interview form that we can use for hiring (1) store managers, (2) wait staff, and (3) counter people/pizza makers.
4. Based on what you know about Angelo's, and what you know from chapter 12 and from having visited pizza restaurants, write a one-page outline showing specifically how you think Angelo's should go about selecting employees.
5. *Teambuilding:* If Angelo wants to open more stores, he will have to take steps to make sure that teamwork prevails in each store—that employees in each store work together collaboratively, supportively, and in support of each store's goals. What concrete steps can Angelo take to make sure that teamwork prevails in each store?

Based generally on actual facts, but Angelo's Pizza is a fictitious company. Angelo's Pizza source notes: Dino Berta, "People Problems: Keep Hiring from Becoming a Crying Game," *Nation's Business News* 36, no. 20 (May 20, 2002): 72–74; Ellen Lyon, "Hiring, Personnel Problems Can Challenge Entrepreneurs," *Patriot-News* (October 12, 2004); Rose Robin Pedone, "Businesses' $400 Billion Theft Problem," *Long Island Business News* 27 (July 6, 1998): 1B–2B; "Survey Shows Small-Business Problems with Hiring, Internet," *Providence Business News* 16 (September 10, 2001): 1B; "Finding Good Workers Is Posing a Big Problem as Hiring Picks Up," *The Kiplinger Letter* 81 (February 13, 2004).

Google*

Fortune magazine recently named Google the best of the 100 best companies to work for, and there is little doubt why. Among the benefits it offers are free shuttles equipped with Wi-Fi to pick up and drop off employees from San Francisco Bay area locations, unlimited sick days, annual all-expense-paid ski trips, free gourmet meals, five on-site free doctors, $2000 bonuses for referring a new hire, free flu shots, a giant lap pool, on-site oil changes, on-site car washes, volleyball courts, TGIF parties, free on-site washers and dryers (with free detergent), Ping-Pong and foosball tables, and free famous people lectures. For many people, it's the gourmet meals and snacks that make Google stand out. For example, human resources director Stacey Sullivan loves the Irish oatmeal with fresh berries at the company's Plymouth Rock Cafe, near Google's "people operations" group. "I sometimes dream about it," she says. Engineer Jan Fitzpatrick loves the raw bar at Google's Tapis restaurant, down the road on the Google campus. Then, of course there are the stock options—each new employee gets about 1200 options to buy Google shares (recently worth about $480 per share). In fact, dozens of early Google employees ("Googlers") are already multimillionaires thanks to Google stock.

For their part, Googlers share certain traits. They tend to be brilliant, team oriented (teamwork is the norm, especially for big projects), and driven. *Fortune* describes them as people who "almost universally" see themselves as the most interesting people on the planet, and who are happy-go-lucky on the outside, but type A—highly intense and goal directed—on the inside. They're also super hardworking (which makes sense, since it's not unusual for engineers to be in the hallways at 3 A.M. debating some new mathematical solution to a Google search problem). They're so team oriented that when working on projects, it's not unusual for a Google team to give up its larger, more spacious offices and to crowd into a small conference room, where they can "get things done." Historically, Googlers generally graduate with great grades from the best universities, including Stanford, Harvard, and MIT. For many years, Google wouldn't even consider hiring someone with less than a 3.7 average—while also probing deeply into the why behind any B grades. Google also doesn't hire lone wolves, but wants people who work together and who have diverse interests (narrow interests or skills are a turnoff at Google). Google also wants people with growth potential. The company is expanding so fast that they need to hire people who are capable of being promoted five or six times—it's only, they say, by hiring such overqualified people that they can be sure that the employees will be able to keep up as Google and their own departments expand.

The starting salaries are highly competitive. Experienced engineers start at about $130,000 a year (plus about 1200 shares of stock options, as noted), and new MBAs can expect between $80,000 and $120,000 per year (with smaller option grants). Most recently, Google had about 10,000 staff members, up from its start a few years ago with just three employees in a rented garage.

Of course, in a company that's grown from three employees to 10,000 and from zero value to hundreds of billions of dollars in about 5 years, it may be quibbling to talk about "problems," but there's no doubt that such rapid growth confronts Google's management, and particularly its "people operations" group, with some big challenges. Let's look at these.

For one, Google, as previously noted, is a 24-hour operation, and with engineers and others frequently pulling all-nighters to complete their projects the company needs to provide a package of services and financial benefits that supports that kind of lifestyle, and that helps its employees maintain an acceptable work–life balance.

As another challenge, Google's enormous financial success is a two-edged sword. While Google usually wins the recruitment race when it comes to competing for new employees against competitors like Microsoft or Yahoo, Google does need some way to stem a rising tide of retirements. Most Googlers are still in their late twenties and early thirties, but many have become so wealthy from their Google stock options that they can afford to retire. One 27-year-old engineer received a million-dollar founder's award for her work on the program for searching desktop computers, and wouldn't think of leaving

---

*© Gary Dessler, Ph.D.

"except to start her own company." Similarly, a former engineering vice president retired (with his Google stock profits) to pursue his love of astronomy. The engineer who dreamed up Gmail recently retired (at the age of 30).

Another challenge is that the work not only involves long hours but can also be very tense. Google is a very numbers-oriented environment. For example, consider a typical weekly Google user interface design meeting. Marisa Meyer, the company's vice president of search products and user experience, runs the meeting, where her employees work out the look and feel of Google's products. Seated around a conference table are about a dozen Googlers, tapping on laptops. During the 2-hour meeting, Meyer needs to evaluate various design proposals, ranging from minor tweaks to a new product's entire layout. She's previously given each presentation an allotted amount of time, and a large digital clock on the wall ticks off the seconds. The presenters must quickly present their ideas, but also handle questions such as "what do users do if the tab is moved from the side of the page to the top?" Furthermore, it's all about the numbers—no one at Google would ever say, for instance "the tab looks better in red"—you need to prove your point. Presenters must come armed with usability experiment results, showing, for instance, that a certain percent preferred red or some other color. While the presenters are answering these questions as quickly as possible, the digital clock is ticking, and when it hits the allotted time, the presentation must end, and the next team steps up to present. It is a tough and tense environment, and Googlers must have done their homework.

Growth can also undermine the "outlaw band that's changing the world" culture that fostered the services that made Google famous. Even cofounder Sergi Brin agrees that Google risks becoming less "zany" as it grows. To paraphrase one of its top managers, the hard part of any business is keeping that original innovative, small-business feel even as the company grows.

Creating the right culture is especially challenging now that Google is truly global. For example, Google works hard to provide the same financial and service benefits in every place it does business around the world, but it can't exactly match its benefits in every country because of international laws and international taxation issues. Offering the same benefits everywhere is more important than it might initially appear. All those benefits make life easier for Google staff, and help them achieve a work–life balance. Achieving the right work–life balance is the centerpiece of Google's culture, but also becomes more challenging as the company grows. On the one hand, Google expects all of its employees to work super hard; on the other hand, it realizes that it needs to help them maintain some sort of balance. As one manager says, Google acknowledges "that we work hard but that work is not everything."

Recruitment is another challenge. While Google certainly doesn't lack applicants, attracting the right applicants is crucial if Google is to continue to grow successfully. Working at Google requires a special set of traits, and screening employees is easier if the company recruits the right people to begin with. For instance, it needs to attract people who are super-bright, love to work, have fun, can handle the stress, and who also have outside interests and flexibility.

As the company grows internationally, it also faces the considerable challenge of recruiting and building staff overseas. For example, Google now is introducing a new vertical market-based structure across Europe, to attract more business advertisers to its search engine. (By vertical market-based structure, Google means focusing on key vertical industry sectors such as travel, retail, automotive, and technology.) To build these industry groupings abroad from scratch, Google promoted its former head of its U.S. financial services group to be the vertical markets director for Europe; he moved there recently. Google is thus looking for heads for each of its vertical industry groups for all of its key European territories. Each of these vertical market heads will have to educate their market sectors (retailing, travel, and so on) so Google can attract new advertisers. Most recently, Google already had about 12 offices across Europe, and its London office had tripled in size to 100 staff in just 2 years.

However, probably the biggest challenge Google faces is gearing up its employee selection system, now that the company must hire thousands of people per year. When Google first started in business, job candidates typically suffered through a dozen or more in-person interviews, and the standards were so high that even applicants with years of great work experience often got turned down if they had just average college grades. But recently, even Google's cofounders have acknowledged to security analysts that setting such an extraordinarily high bar for hiring was holding back Google's expansion. For Google's first few years, one of the company's cofounders interviewed nearly every job candidate before he or she was hired, and even today one of them still reviews the qualifications of everyone before he or she gets a final offer.

The experience of one candidate illustrates what Google is up against. The company interviewed a 24-year-old for a corporate communications job at Google. Google first made contact with the candidate in May, and then, after two phone interviews, invited him to headquarters. There he had separate interviews with about six people and was treated to lunch in a Google cafeteria. The company also had him turn in several "homework" assignments, including a personal statement and a marketing plan. In August, Google invited the candidate back for a second round, which it said would involve another four or five interviews. In the meantime, he decided he'd rather work at a start-up, and accepted another job at a new Web-based instant messaging provider.

Google's new head of human resources, a former GE executive, says that Google is trying to strike the right balance between letting Google and the candidate get to know each other while also moving quickly. To that end, Google recently administered a survey to all of Google's current employees, in an effort to identify the traits that correlate with success at Google. In the survey, employees had to respond to questions relating to about 300 variables, including their performance on standardized tests, how old they were when they first used a computer, and how many foreign languages they speak. The Google survey team then compared the answers against the 30 or 40 job performance factors kept for each employee. They thereby identified clusters of traits that Google might better focus on during the hiring process. Google is also trying to move from the free-form interviews it has had in the past to a more structured process.

Questions

1. What do you think of the idea of Google correlating personal traits from the employee's answers on the survey to their performance, and then using that as the basis for screening job candidates? In other words, is it or is it not a good idea? Explain your answer.

2. The benefits that Google pays obviously represent an enormous expense. Based on what you know about Google and on what you read in this book, how would you defend all these benefits if you're making a presentation to the security analysts who were analyzing Google's performance?

3. If you wanted to hire the brightest people around, how would you go about recruiting and selecting them?

4. To support its growth and expansion strategy, Google wants (among other traits) people who are super-bright, who work hard (often round-the-clock), and who are flexible and maintain a decent work–life balance. List five specific HR policies or practices that you think Google has implemented or should implement to support its strategy, and explain your answer.

5. What sorts of factors do you think Google will have to take into consideration as it tries transferring its culture and reward systems and way of doing business to its operations abroad?

6. Given the sorts of values and culture Google cherishes, briefly describe four specific activities you suggest it pursue during new-employee orientation.

7. *Cross-Cultural Effectiveness:* What sorts of factors will Google have to take into consideration as it tries transferring its culture and reward systems and way of doing business to its operations abroad?

Source notes for Google: "Google Brings Vertical Structure to Europe," *New Media Age* (August 4, 2005): 2; Debbie Lovewell, "Employer Profile—Google: Searching for Talent," *Employee Benefits* (October 10, 2005): 66; "Google Looking for Gourmet Chefs," *Internet Week* (August 4, 2005); Douglas Merrill, "Google's 'Googley' Culture Kept Alive by Tech," *eWeek* (April 11, 2006); Robert Hof, "Google Gives Employees Another Option," *BusinessWeek Online* (December 13, 2005); Kevin Delaney, "Google Adjusts Hiring Process as Needs Grow," *Wall Street Journal* (October 23, 2006): B1, B8; Adam Lishinsky, "Search and Enjoy," *Fortune* (January 22, 2007): 70–82.

Muffler Magic*

Muffler Magic is a fast-growing chain of 25 automobile service centers in Nevada. Originally started 20 years ago as a muffler repair shop by Ronald Brown, the chain expanded rapidly to new locations, and as it did so Muffler Magic also expanded the services it provided, from muffler replacement to oil changes, brake jobs, and engine repair. Today, one can bring an automobile to a Muffler Magic shop for basically any type of service, from tires to mufflers to engine repair.

Auto service is a tough business. The shop owner is basically dependent upon the quality of the service people he or she hires and retains, and the most qualified mechanics find it easy to pick up and leave for a job paying a bit more at a competitor down the road. It's also a business in which productivity is very important. The single largest expense is usually the cost of labor. Auto service dealers generally don't just make up the prices that they charge customers for various repairs; instead, they charge based on standardized industry rates for jobs like changing spark plugs, or repairing a leaky radiator. For instance, if someone brings a car in for a new alternator and the standard number of hours for changing the alternator is 1 hour, but it takes the mechanic 2 hours, the service center's owner may end up making less profit on the transaction.

Quality is a persistent problem as well. For example, "rework" has recently been a problem at Muffler Magic. A customer recently brought her car to a Muffler Magic to have the car's brake pads replaced, which the store did for her. Unfortunately, when she drove off, she only got about two blocks before she discovered that she had no brake power at all. It was simply fortuitous that she was going so slowly she was able to stop her car by slowly rolling up against a parking bumper. It subsequently turned out that the mechanic who replaced the brake pads had failed to properly tighten a fitting on the hydraulic brake tubes, and the brake fluid had run out, leaving the car with no braking power. In a similar problem the month before, a (different) mechanic replaced a fan belt but forgot to refill the radiator with fluid; that customer's car overheated before he got four blocks away, and Muffler Magic had to replace the whole engine. Of course problems like these not only diminish the profitability of the company's profits but, repeated many times over, have the potential for ruining Muffler Magic's word-of-mouth reputation.

Organizationally, Muffler Magic employs about 300 people total, and Ron runs his company with eight managers, including Mr. Brown as president, a controller, a purchasing director, a marketing director, and the human resource manager. He also has three regional managers to whom the eight or nine service center managers in each area of Nevada report. Over the past 2 years, as the company has opened new service centers, companywide profits have diminished rather than gone up. In part, these diminishing profits reflect the fact that Ron Brown has found it increasingly difficult to manage his growing operation. ("Your reach is exceeding your grasp" is how Ron's wife puts it.)

The company has only the most basic HR systems in place. It uses an application form that the human resource manager modified from one that she downloaded from the Web, and it uses standard employee status change request forms, sign-on forms, I-9 forms, and so on that it purchased from a human resource management supply house. Training is entirely on-the-job. It expects the experienced technicians that it hires to come to the job fully trained; to that end, the service center managers generally ask candidates for these jobs basic behavioral questions that hopefully provide a window into these applicants' skills. However, most of the other technicians hired to do jobs like rotating tires, fixing brake pads, and replacing mufflers are untrained and inexperienced. They are to be trained by either the service center manager or by more experienced technicians, on-the-job.

Ron Brown faces several HR-type problems. One, as he says, is that he faces the "tyranny of the immediate" when it comes to hiring employees. While it's fine to say that he should be carefully screening each employee and checking references and work ethic,

---

*© Gary Dessler, Ph.D.

from a practical point of view, with 25 centers to run, the centers' managers usually just hire anyone who seems to be breathing, as long as they can answer some basic interview questions about auto repair, such as "What do you think the problem is if a 2001 Camry is overheating, and what would you do about it?"

Employee safety is also a problem. An automobile service center may not be the most dangerous type of workplace, but it is potentially dangerous. Employees are dealing with sharp tools, greasy floors, greasy tools, extremely hot temperatures (for instance, on mufflers and engines), and fast-moving engine parts including fan blades. There are some basic things that a service manager can do to ensure more safety, such as insisting that all oil spills be cleaned up immediately. However, from a practical point of view, there are a few ways to get around many of the problems—such as when the technician must check out an engine while it is running.

With Muffler Magic's profits going down instead of up, Brown's human resource manager has taken the position that the main problem is financial. As he says, "You get what you pay for" when it comes to employees, and if you compensate technicians better then your competitors then you get better technicians, ones who do their jobs better and stay longer with the company—and then profits will rise. So, the HR manager scheduled a meeting between himself, Ron Brown, and a professor of business who teaches compensation management at a local university. The HR manager has asked this professor to spend about a week looking at each of the service centers, analyzing the situation, and coming up with a compensation plan that will address Muffler Magic's quality and productivity problems. At this meeting, the professor makes three basic recommendations for changing the company's compensation policies.

Number one, she says that she has found that Muffler Magic suffers from what she calls "presenteeism"—in other words, employees drag themselves into work even when they're sick, because the company does not pay them if they are out; there are no sick days. In just a few days the professor couldn't properly quantify how much Muffler Magic is losing to presenteeism. However, from what she could see at each shop, there are typically one or two technicians working with various maladies like the cold or flu, and it seemed to her that each of these people was probably really only working about half of the time (although they were getting paid for the whole day). So, for 25 service centers per week, Muffler Magic could well be losing 125 or 130 personnel days per week of work. The professor suggests that Muffler Magic start allowing everyone to take three paid sick days per year, a reasonable suggestion. However, as Ron Brown points out, "Right now, we're only losing about half a day's pay for each employee who comes in and who works unproductively; with your suggestion, won't we lose the whole day?" The professor says she'll ponder that one.

Second, the professor also recommends putting the technicians on a skill-for-pay plan. Basically, here's what she suggests. Give each technician a letter grade (A through E) based upon that technician's particular skill level and abilities. An "A" technician is a team leader and needs to show that he or she has excellent diagnostic troubleshooting skills, and the ability to supervise and direct other technicians. At the other extreme, an "E" technician would be a new apprentice with little technical training. The other technicians fall in between those two levels, based on their individual skills and abilities.

In the professor's system, the "A" technician or team leader would assign and supervise all work done within his or her area but generally not do any mechanical repairs him or herself. The team leader does the diagnostic troubleshooting, supervises and trains the other technicians, and test drives the car before it goes back to the customer. Under this plan, every technician receives a guaranteed hourly wage within a certain range, for instance:

A tech = $25–$30 an hour

B tech = $20–$25 an hour

C tech = $15–$20 an hour

D tech = $10–$15 an hour

E tech = $8–$10 an hour

Third, to directly address the productivity issue, the professor recommends that at the end of each day, each service manager calculate each technician-team's productivity for the day and then at the end of each week. She suggests posting the running productivity total conspicuously for daily viewing. Then, the technicians as a group get weekly cash bonuses based upon their productivity. To calculate productivity, the professor recommends dividing the total labor hours billed by the total labor hours paid to technicians, or total labor hours billed, *divided by* total hours paid to technicians.

Having done some homework, the professor says that the national average for labor productivity is currently about 60%, and that only the best-run service centers achieve 85% or greater. By her rough calculations, Muffler Magic was attaining about industry average (about 60%—in other words, it was billing for only about 60 hours for each 100 hours that it actually had to pay technicians to do the jobs). (Of course, this was not entirely the technicians' fault. Technicians get time off for breaks, and for lunch, and if a particular service center simply didn't have enough business on a particular day or during a particular week, then several technicians may well sit around idly waiting for the next car to come in.) The professor recommends setting a labor efficiency goal of 80% and posting each team's daily productivity results in the workplace to provide them with additional feedback. She recommends that if at the end of a week the team is able to boost its productivity ratio from the current 60% to 80%, then that team would get an additional 10% weekly pay bonus. After that, for every 5% boost of increased productivity above 80%, technicians would receive an additional 5% weekly bonus. (So, if a technician's normal weekly pay is $400, that employee would receive an extra $40 at the end of the week when his team moves from 60% productivity to 80% productivity.)

After the meeting, Ron Brown thanked the professor for her recommendations and told her he would think about it and get back to her. After the meeting, on the drive home, Ron was pondering what to do. He had to decide whether to institute the professor's sick leave policy, and whether to implement the professor's incentive and compensation plan. Before implementing anything, however, he wanted to make sure he understood the context in which he was making his decision. For example, did Muffler Magic really have an incentive pay problem, or were the problems more broad? Furthermore, how, if at all, would the professor's incentive plan impact the quality of the work that the teams were doing? And should Muffler Magic really start paying for sick days? Ron Brown had a lot to think about.

Questions

1. Write a one-page summary outline listing three or four recommendations you would make with respect to each HR function (recruiting, selection, training, and so on) that you think Ron Brown should be addressing with his HR manager now.
2. Develop a 10-question structured interview form Ron Brown's service center managers can use to interview experienced technicians.
3. If you were Ron Brown, would you implement the professor's recommendation addressing the presenteeism problem, in other words, start paying for sick days? Why or why not?
4. If you were advising Ron Brown, would you recommend that he implement the professor's skill-based pay and incentive pay plans as is? Why? Would you implement it with modifications? If you would modify it, be specific about what you think those modifications should be, and why.
5. *Quantitative Analysis:* Create a spreadsheet showing the titles of the main measurable factors owner Ron Brown should take into consideration in analyzing whether to take the professor's pay plan advice.

Based generally on actual facts, but Muffler Magic is a fictitious company. This case is based largely on information in Drew Paras, "The Pay Factor: Technicians' Salaries Can Be the Largest Expense in a Server Shop, as Well as the Biggest Headache. Here's How One Shop Owner Tackled the Problem," *Motor Age* (November 2003): 76–79; see also Jennifer Pellet, "Health Care Crisis," *Chief Executive* (June 2004): 56–61; "Firms Press to Quantify, Control Presenteeism," *Employee Benefits* (December 1, 2002).

BP Texas City*

In March 2005, an explosion and fire at British Petroleum's (BP) Texas City, Texas, refinery killed 15 people and injured 500 people in the worst U.S. industrial accident in more than 10 years. The disaster triggered three investigations, one internal investigation by BP, one by the U.S. Chemical Safety Board, and an independent investigation chaired by former U.S. Secretary of State James Baker and an 11-member panel, organized at BP's request.

To put the results of these three investigations into context, it's useful to understand that under its current management, BP has pursued, for the past 10 or so years, a strategy emphasizing cost-cutting and profitability. The basic conclusion of the investigations was that cost-cutting helped compromise safety at the Texas City refinery. It's useful to consider each investigation's findings.

The Chemical Safety Board's (CSB) investigation, according to Carol Merritt, the board's chairwoman, showed that "BP's global management was aware of problems with maintenance, spending, and infrastructure well before March 2005." Apparently, faced with numerous earlier accidents, BP did make some safety improvements. However, it focused primarily on emphasizing personal employee safety behaviors and procedural compliance, thereby reducing safety accident rates. The problem (according to the CSB) was that "catastrophic safety risks remained." For example, according to the CSB, "unsafe and antiquated equipment designs were left in place, and unacceptable deficiencies in preventive maintenance were tolerated." Basically, the CSB found that BP's budget cuts led to a progressive deterioration of safety at the Texas City refinery. Said Ms. Merritt, "In an aging facility like Texas City, it is not responsible to cut budgets related to safety and maintenance without thoroughly examining the impact on the risk of a catastrophic accident."

Looking at specifics, the CSB said that a 2004 internal audit of 35 BP business units, including Texas City (BP's largest refinery), found significant safety gaps they all had in common, including a lack of leadership competence and "systemic underlying issues" such as a widespread tolerance of noncompliance with basic safety rules and poor monitoring of safety management systems and processes. Ironically, the CSB found that BP's accident prevention effort at Texas City had achieved a 70% reduction in worker injuries in the year before the explosion. Unfortunately, this simply meant that individual employees were having fewer accidents. The larger, more fundamental problem was that the potentially explosive situation inherent in the depreciating machinery remained.

The CSB found that the Texas City explosion followed a pattern of years of major accidents at the facility. In fact, there had apparently been an average of one employee death every 16 months at the plant for the last 30 years. The CSB found that the equipment directly involved in the most recent explosion was an obsolete design already phased out in most refineries and chemical plants, and that key pieces of its instrumentation were not working. There had also been previous instances where flammable vapors were released from the same unit in the 10 years prior to the explosion. In 2003, an external audit had referred to the Texas City refinery's infrastructure and assets as "poor" and found what it referred to as a "checkbook mentality," one in which budgets were not sufficient to manage all the risks. In particular, the CSB found that BP had implemented a 25% cut on fixed costs between 1998 and 2000 and that this adversely impacted maintenance expenditures and net expenditures, and refinery infrastructure. Going on, the CSB found that, in 2004, there were three major accidents at the refinery that killed three workers.

BP's own internal report concluded that the problems at Texas City were not of recent origin, and instead were years in the making. It said BP was taking steps to address them. Its investigation found "no evidence of anyone consciously or intentionally taking actions or making decisions that put others at risk." Said BP's report, "The underlying reasons for the behaviors and actions displayed during the incident are complex, and the team has spent much time trying to understand them—it is evident that they were many years in the

*© Gary Dessler, Ph.D.

making and will require concerted and committed actions to address." BP's report concluded that there were five underlying causes for the massive explosion:

- The working environment had eroded to one characterized by resistance to change, and a lack of trust.
- Safety, performance, and risk reduction priorities had not been set and consistently reinforced by management.
- Changes in the "complex organization" led to a lack of clear accountabilities and poor communication.
- A poor level of hazard awareness and understanding of safety resulted in workers accepting levels of risk that were considerably higher than at comparable installations.
- A lack of adequate early warning systems for problems, and no independent means of understanding the deteriorating standards at the plant.

The report from the BP-initiated but independent 11-person panel chaired by former U.S. Secretary of State James Baker contained specific conclusions and recommendations. The Baker panel looked at BP's corporate safety oversight, the corporate safety culture, and the process safety management systems at BP at the Texas City plant as well as at BP's other refineries.

Basically, the Baker panel concluded that BP had not provided effective safety process leadership and had not established safety as a core value at the five refineries it looked at (including Texas City).

Like the CSB, the Baker panel found that BP had emphasized personal safety in recent years and had in fact improved personal safety performance, but had not emphasized the overall safety process, thereby mistakenly interpreting "improving personal injury rates as an indication of acceptable process safety performance at its U.S. refineries." In fact, the Baker panel went on, by focusing on these somewhat misleading improving personal injury rates, BP created a false sense of confidence that it was properly addressing process safety risks. It also found that the safety culture at Texas City did not have the positive, trusting, open environment that a proper safety culture required. The Baker panel's other findings included:

- BP did not always ensure that adequate resources were effectively allocated to support or sustain a high level of process safety performance.
- BP's refinery personnel are "overloaded" by corporate initiatives.
- Operators and maintenance personnel work high rates of overtime.
- BP tended to have a short-term focus and its decentralized management system and entrepreneurial culture delegated substantial discretion to refinery plant managers "without clearly defining process safety expectations, responsibilities, or accountabilities."
- There was no common, unifying process safety culture among the five refineries.
- The company's corporate safety management system did not make sure there was timely compliance with internal process safety standards and programs.
- BP's executive management either did not receive refinery specific information that showed that process safety deficiencies existed at some of the plants, or did not effectively respond to any information it did receive.[1]

The Baker panel made several safety recommendations for BP, including these:

1. The company's corporate management must provide leadership on process safety.
2. The company should establish a process safety management system that identifies, reduces, and manages the process safety risks of the refineries.
3. The company should make sure its employees have an appropriate level of process safety knowledge and expertise.

[1] These findings and the following suggestions are based on "BP Safety Report Finds Company's Process Safety Culture Ineffective," *Global Refining & Fuels Report* (January 17, 2007).

4. The company should involve "relevant stakeholders" in developing a positive, trusting, and open process safety culture at each refinery.
5. BP should clearly define expectations and strengthen accountability for process safety performance.
6. BP should better coordinate its process safety support for the refining line organization.
7. BP should develop an integrated set of leading and lagging performance indicators for effectively monitoring process safety performance.
8. BP should establish and implement an effective system to audit process safety performance.
9. The company's board should monitor the implementation of the panel's recommendations and the ongoing process safety performance of the refineries.
10. BP should transform into a recognized industry leader in process safety management.

In making its recommendations, the panel singled out the company's chief executive at the time, Lord Browne, by saying, "In hindsight, the panel believes if Browne had demonstrated comparable leadership on and commitment to process safety [as he did for responding to climate change] that would have resulted in a higher level of safety at refineries."

Overall, the Baker panel found that BP's top management had not provided "effective leadership" on safety. It found that the failings went to the very top of the organization, to the company's chief executive, and to several of his top lieutenants. The Baker panel emphasized the importance of top management commitment, saying, for instance, that "it is imperative that BP leadership set the process safety tone at the top of the organization and establish appropriate expectations regarding process safety performance." It also said BP "has not provided effective leadership in making certain its management and U.S. refining workforce understand what is expected of them regarding process safety performance."

Lord Browne, the chief executive, stepped down about a year after the explosion. About the same time, some BP shareholders were calling for the company's executives and board directors to have their bonuses more closely tied to the company's safety and environmental performance in the wake of Texas City.

Questions
1. The textbook defines ethics as "the principles of conduct governing an individual or a group," and specifically as the standards one uses to decide what their conduct should be. To what extent do you believe that what happened at BP is as much a breakdown in the company's ethical systems as it is in its safety systems, and how would you defend your conclusion?
2. Are the Occupational Safety and Health Administration's standards, policies, and rules aimed at addressing problems like the ones that apparently existed at the Texas City plant? If so, how would you explain the fact that problems like these could have continued for so many years?
3. Since there were apparently at least three deaths in the year prior to the major explosion, and an average of about one employee death per 16 months for the previous 10 years, how would you account for the fact that mandatory OSHA inspections missed these glaring sources of potential catastrophic events?
4. The textbook lists numerous suggestions for "how to prevent accidents." Based on what you know about the Texas City explosion, what do you say Texas City tells you about the most important three steps an employer can take to prevent accidents?
5. Based on what you learned in this text, would you make any additional recommendations to BP over and above those recommendations made by the Baker panel and the CSB? If so, what would those recommendations be?
6. Explain specifically how strategic human resource management at BP seems to have supported the company's broader strategic aims. What does this say about the advisability of always linking human resource strategy to a company's strategic aims?

7. *Change Management:* In 2007 Lord Browne stepped down as BP's CEO, and the firm's president took charge. Based on the case, what organizational changes should BP make now and how would you suggest the new CEO go about executing them?

8. *Ethical Decision-Making:* The textbook defines ethics as "the principles of conduct governing an individual or a group," and specifically as the standards one uses to decide what their conduct should be. To what extent do you believe that what happened at BP is as much a breakdown in the company's ethical systems as it is in its safety systems, and how would you defend your conclusion? What would you have done differently, ethically? What should the new CEO do now?

9. *Managing Organizational Culture:* Based on the case, how would you characterize the organizational culture at BP companywide and at its refineries, and what exactly would you do to change that culture (assuming it needs changing)?

Source notes for BP Texas City: Sheila McNulty, "BP Knew of Safety Problems, Says Report," *The Financial Times* (October 31, 2006): 1; "CBS: Documents Show BP Was Aware of Texas City Safety Problems," *World Refining & Fuels Today* (October 30, 2006); "BP Safety Report Finds Company's Process Safety Culture Ineffective," *Global Refining & Fuels Report* (January 17, 2007); "BP Safety Record under Attack," *Europe Intelligence Wire* (January 17, 2007); Mark Hofmann, "BP Slammed for Poor Leadership on Safety, Oil Firm Agrees to Act on Review Panel's Recommendations," *Business Intelligence* (January 22, 2007): 3; "Call for Bonuses to Include Link with Safety Performance," *The Guardian* (January 18, 2007): 24.

Glossary

action learning. A training technique by which management trainees are allowed to work full time analyzing and solving problems in other departments.

adverse impact. The overall impact of employer practices that result in significantly higher percentages of members of minorities and other protected groups being rejected for employment, placement, or promotion.

affirmative action. Steps that are taken for the purpose of eliminating the present effects of past discrimination.

AFL-CIO. A voluntary federation in the United States of about 100 national and international (i.e., with branches in Canada) unions.

Age Discrimination in Employment Act of 1967. The act prohibiting age discrimination and specifically protecting individuals over 40 years old.

agency shop. A form of union security in which employees who do not belong to the union must still pay union dues on the assumption that union efforts benefit all workers.

Albemarle Paper Company* v. *Moody. Supreme Court case in which it was ruled that the validity of job tests must be documented and that employee performance standards must be job related.

alternation ranking method. An appraisal process in which the employee who is highest on a trait being measured and also the one who is lowest are identified, alternating between highest and lowest until all employees to be rated have been addressed.

Americans with Disabilities Act (ADA). The act requiring employers to make reasonable accommodations for disabled employees; it prohibits discrimination against disabled persons.

application form. The form that provides information on education, prior work record, and skills.

application service provider. An online vendor that uses its own servers and systems to manage tasks for employers, such as recruitment or training. In recruitment, they compile application information, prescreen applicants, and help the employer rank applicants and set interview appointments.

applicants tracking systems. Online systems that help employers attract, gather, screen, compile, and manage applications.

appraisal interview. The culmination of an appraisal, in which the supervisor and subordinate review the appraisal and make plans to remedy deficiencies and reinforce strengths.

arbitration. The most definitive type of third-party intervention, in which the arbitrator often has the power to determine and dictate the settlement terms.

authorization cards. In order to petition for a union election, the union must show that at least 30% of employees may be interested in being unionized. Employees indicate this interest by signing authorization cards.

balanced scorecard. Refers to a process for assigning financial and non-financial goals to the chain of activities required for achieving the company's strategic aims, and for continuously monitoring results.

bargaining unit. The group of employees the union will be authorized to represent.

behavior modeling. A training technique in which trainees are first shown good management techniques in a film, are then asked to play roles in a simulated situation, and are then given feedback and praise by their supervisor.

benefits. Indirect financial payments given to employees. They may include health and life insurance, vacation, pension, education plans, and discounts on company products, for instance.

bona fide occupational qualification (BFOQ). Requirement that an employee be of a certain religion, sex, or national origin where that is reasonably necessary to the organization's normal operation. Specified by the 1964 Civil Rights Act.

boycott. The combined refusal by employees and other interested parties to buy or use the employer's products.

burnout. The total depletion of physical and mental resources caused by excessive striving to reach an unrealistic work-related goal.

business necessity. Justification for an otherwise discriminatory employment practice, provided there is an overriding legitimate business purpose.

career. The occupational positions a person has had over many years.

career development. The lifelong series of activities that contribute to a person's career exploration, establishment, success, and fulfillment.

career management. A process for enabling the employees to better understand and develop their career skills and interests, and to use the skills and interests most effectively both within the company and, if necessary, after they leave the firm.

career planning. The deliberate process through which someone becomes aware of personal skills, interests, knowledge, motivations, and other characteristics; and establishes action plans to attain specific goals.

case study method. A development method in which the manager is presented with a written description of an organizational problem to diagnose and solve.

central tendency. The tendency to rate all employees about average.

channel assembly. Having a supplier or distributor perform some of the steps required to create the company's product or service.

citations. Summons informing employers and employees of the regulations and standards that have been violated in the workplace.

Civil Rights Act of 1964, Title VII. Law that makes it unlawful practice for an employer to discriminate against any individual with respect to hiring, compensation, terms, conditions, or privileges of employment because of race, color, religion, sex, or nation.

Civil Rights Act of 1991 (CRA 1991). This act places burden of proof back on employers and permits compensatory and punitive damages.

closed shop. A form of union security in which the company can hire only union members. This was outlawed in 1947 for interstate commerce, but still exists in some industries (such as printing).

coaching/understudy method. An experienced worker or supervisor trains the employee on the job.

co-determination. The right to a voice in setting company policies; workers generally elect representatives to the supervisory board.

collective bargaining. The process through which representatives of management and the union meet to negotiate a labor agreement.

compensable factors. Fundamental, compensable elements of a job, such as skills, effort, responsibility, and working conditions.

competitive advantage. The basis for differentiation over competitors and thus for hoping to claim certain customers.

competitive strategy. Identifies how to build and strengthen the business's long-term competitive position in the marketplace.

computer-based training. Trainees use a computer-based system to interactively increase their knowledge or skills.

content validity. A test that is *content valid* is one in which the test contains a fair sample of the tasks and skills actually needed for the job in question.

controlled experimentation. Formal methods for testing the effectiveness of a training program, preferably with before-and-after tests and a control group.

corporate-level strategy. Identifies the sorts of businesses that will comprise the company and the ways in which these businesses relate to each other.

corporate social responsibility. Refers to the extent to which companies should and do take steps to improve members of society other than the firm's owners.

criterion validity. A type of validity based on showing that scores on the test (*predictors*) are related to job performance (*criterion*).

critical incident method. Keeping a record of uncommonly good or undesirable examples of an employee's work-related behavior and reviewing it with the employee at predetermined times.

defined benefit plan. A plan that contains a formula for specifying retirement benefits.

defined contribution plan. A plan in which the employer's contribution to employees' retirement or savings funds is specified.

digital dashboard. Presents the manager with desktop graphs and charts, so he or she gets a picture of where the company has been and where it's going, in terms of each activity in the strategy map.

discipline. A procedure that corrects or punishes a subordinate for violating a rule or procedure.

dismissal. Involuntary termination of an employee's employment with the firm.

disparate impact. An unintentional disparity between the proportion of a protected group applying for a position and the proportion getting the job.

disparate treatment. An intentional disparity between the proportion of a protected group and the proportion getting the job.

downsizing. Refers to the process of reducing, usually dramatically, the number of people employed by the firm.

economic strike. A strike that results from a failure to agree on the terms of a contract that involve wages, benefits, and other conditions of employment.

Employee Assistance Program (EAP). A formal employer program for providing employees with counseling and/or treatment programs for problems such as alcoholism, gambling, or stress.

employee compensation. All forms of pay or rewards going to employees and arising from their employment.

employee orientation. A procedure for providing new employees with basic background information about the firm.

Employee Retirement Income Security Act (ERISA). Signed into law by President Ford in 1974 to require that pension rights be vested, and protected by a government agency, Pension Benefits Guarantee Corporation.

employee stock ownership plan (ESOP). A corporation contributes shares of its own stock to a trust to purchase company stock for employees. The trust distributes the stock to employees upon retirement or separation from service.

Equal Employment Opportunity Commission (EEOC). The commission, created by Title VII, empowered to investigate job discrimination complaints and sue on behalf of complainants.

Equal Pay Act of 1963. An amendment to the Fair Labor Standards Act designed to require equal pay for women doing the same work as men.

ethics. The study of standards of conduct and moral judgment; also the standards of right conduct.

ethnocentric. A management philosophy that leads to the creation of home market-oriented staffing decisions.

executive support systems. Provide top managers with information for making decisions on matters such as 5-year plans.

exit interviews. Interviews conducted by the employer immediately prior to the employee leaving the firm with the aim of better understanding what the employee thinks about the company.

expatriates. Non-citizens of the country in which they are working.

fact finder. In labor relations, a neutral party who studies the issues in a dispute and makes a public recommendation for a reasonable settlement.

Fair Labor Standards Act. Congress passed this act in 1938 to provide for minimum wages, maximum hours, overtime pay, and child labor protection. The law has been amended many times and covers most employees.

federal agency guidelines. Guidelines issued by federal agencies explaining recommended employer equal employment federal legislation procedures in detail.

flexible benefits plan. Individualized plans allowed by employers to accommodate employee preferences for benefits.

forced distribution method. An appraisal method by which the manager places predetermined percentages of subordinates in performance categories.

functional strategies. Identifies the basic courses of action that each department will pursue in order to help the business attain its competitive goals.

gainsharing plan. An incentive plan that engages employees in a common effort to achieve productivity objectives and share the gains.

gender harassment. A form of hostile environment harassment that appears to be motivated by hostility toward individuals who violate gender ideals.

geocentric. A staffing policy that seeks the best people for key jobs throughout the organization, regardless of nationality.

good-faith bargaining. A term that means both parties are communicating and negotiating and that proposals are being matched with counterproposals, with both parties making every reasonable effort to arrive at agreements. It does not mean that either party is compelled to agree to a proposal.

graphic rating scale. A scale that lists a number of traits and a range of performance for each. The employee is then rated by identifying the score that best describes his or her level of performance for each trait.

Griggs v. Duke Power Company. Supreme Court case in which the plaintiff argued that his employer's requirement that coal handlers be high-school graduates was unfairly discriminatory. In finding for the plaintiff, the Court ruled that discrimination need not be overt to be illegal, that employment practices must be related to job performance, and that the burden of proof is on the employer to show that hiring standards are job related.

guaranteed fair treatment. Employer programs aimed at ensuring that all employees are treated fairly, generally by providing formalized, well-documented, and highly publicized vehicles through which employees can appeal any eligible issues.

halo effect. A common appraisal problem in which the rating of a subordinate on one trait influences the way the person is rated on other traits.

high-performance work system. An integrated set of human resources policies and practices that together produce superior employee performance.

host-country nationals. Citizens of the country in which the multinational company has its headquarters.

HR audit. An analysis by which an organization measures where it currently stands and determines what it has to accomplish to improve its HR function.

HR Scorecard. Measures the HR function's effectiveness and efficiency in producing employee behaviors needed to achieve the company's strategic goals.

human resource information systems. Interrelated components working together to collect, process, store, and disseminate information to support decision making, coordination, control, analysis, and visualization of an organization's human resource management activities.

human resource management. The process of acquiring, training, appraising, and compensating employees, and of attending to their labor relations, health and safety, and fairness concerns.

illegal bargaining items. Items in collective bargaining that are forbidden by law; for example, the clause agreeing to hire "union members exclusively" would be illegal in a right-to-work state.

improvisation. A form of management training in which the trainees learn skills such as openness and creativity by playing games that require that they improvise answers and solutions.

incentive plan. A compensation plan that ties pay to performance.

information system. The interrelated people, data, technology, and organizational procedures a company uses to collect, process, store, and disseminate information.

in-house development centers. A company-based facility for exposing current or prospective managers to exercises to develop improved management skills.

insubordination. Willful disregard or disobedience of the boss's authority or legitimate orders.

international human resource management. The human resource management concepts and techniques employers use to manage the human resource challenges of their international operations.

Internet-based purchasing. Internet-based purchasing that automatically monitors the customer's needs online and produces the necessary products, shipping documents, and bills.

interview. A procedure designed to solicit information from a person's oral responses to oral inquiries.

job analysis. The procedure for determining the duties and skill requirements of a job and the kind of person who should be hired for it.

job description. A list of a job's duties, responsibilities, reporting relationships, working conditions, and supervisory responsibilities—one product of a job analysis.

job evaluation. A formal and systematic comparison of jobs to determine the worth of one job relative to another.

job posting. Posting notices of job openings on company bulletin boards as a recruiting method.

job rotation. A management training technique that involves moving a trainee from department to department to broaden his or her experience and identify strengths and weaknesses.

job specification. A list of a job's "human requirements," that is, the requisite education, skills, personality, and so on—a product of a job analysis.

Landrum-Griffin Act. A law aimed at protecting union members from possible wrongdoing on the part of their unions.

layoff. A situation in which employees are told there is no work for them but that management intends to recall them when work is again available.

learning organization. An organization "skilled at creating, acquiring, and transferring knowledge and at modifying its behavior to reflect new knowledge and insights."

lifelong learning. Provides employees with continuing learning experiences over their tenure with the firm, with the aim of ensuring they have the opportunity to obtain the knowledge and skills they need to do their jobs effectively.

line manager. A manager who is authorized to direct the work of subordinates and responsible for accomplishing the organization's goals.

locals. Employees that work for the company abroad and are citizens of the countries where they are working, also known as **host country nationals**.

lockout. A refusal by the employer to provide opportunities to work.

management assessment centers. A facility in which management candidates are asked to make decisions in hypothetical situations and are scored on their performance.

management by objectives (MBO). A performance management method through which the manager sets organizationally relevant goals with each employee and then periodically discusses progress toward these goals, in an organization-wide effort.

management development. Any attempt to improve current or future management performance by imparting knowledge, changing attitudes, or increasing skills.

management game. A development technique in which teams of managers compete by making computerized decisions regarding realistic but simulated situations.

management information systems. Help managers make better decisions by producing standardized, summarized reports on a regular basis.

manager. Someone who is responsible for accomplishing the organization's goals, and who does so by managing the efforts of the organization's people.

managing. To perform five basic functions: planning, organizing, staffing, leading, and controlling.

mandatory bargaining items. Items in collective bargaining that a party must bargain over if they are introduced by the other party—for example, pay.

mediation. Labor relations intervention in which a neutral third party tries to assist the principals in reaching agreement.

merit pay (merit raise). Any salary increase awarded to an employee based on his or her individual performance.

national emergency strikes. Strikes that might "imperil the national health and safety."

National Labor Relations Board (NLRB). The agency created by the Wagner Act to investigate unfair labor practice charges and to provide for secret-ballot elections and majority rule in determining whether or not a firm's employees want a union.

Norris-LaGuardia Act. This law marked the beginning of the era of strong encouragement of unions and guaranteed to each employee the right to bargain collectively "free from interference, restraint, or coercion."

Occupational Safety and Health Act. The law passed by Congress in 1970 "to assure so far as possible every working man and woman in the nation safe and healthful working conditions and to preserve our human resources."

Occupational Safety and Health Administration (OSHA). The agency created within the Department of Labor to set safety and health standards for almost all workers in the United States.

Office of Federal Contract Compliance Programs (OFCCP). The office responsible for implementing executive orders and ensuring compliance of federal contractors.

on-the-job training (OJT). Training a person to learn a job while working at it.

open shop. Type of union security in which the workers decide whether or not to join the union, and those who join must pay dues.

opinion surveys. Questionnaires that regularly ask employees their opinions about the company, management, and work life.

organization. A group consisting of people with formally assigned roles who work together to achieve the organization's goals.

organizational culture. The characteristic values, traditions, and behaviors a company's employees share.

organizational development (OD). A development method aimed at changing the attitudes, values, and beliefs of employees so that employees can improve the organization.

outplacement counseling. A systematic process by which a terminated person is trained and counseled in the techniques of self-appraisal and securing a new position.

paired comparison method. An appraisal method in which every subordinate to be rated is paired with and compared to every other subordinate on each trait.

peer appraisal. Appraisal of an employee by his or her peers.

performance analysis. Verifying that there is a performance deficiency and determining whether that deficiency should be rectified through training or through some other means (such as transferring the employee).

performance appraisal. Evaluating an employee's current and/or past performance relative to his or her performance standards.

performance management. The process through which companies ensure that employees are working toward organizational goals. It includes practices through which the manager defines the employees's goals and work, develops the employee's skills and capabilities, evaluates the person's goal-directed behavior, and then rewards him or her in a fashion consistent with the company's and the person's needs.

personnel replacement charts. Company records showing present performance and promotability of inside candidates for the firm's most important positions.

piecework. A system of incentive pay tying pay to the number of items processed by each individual worker.

polycentric. A management philosophy oriented toward staffing positions with local talent.

portability. Making it easier for employees who leave the firm prior to retirement to take their accumulated pension funds with them.

preferential shop. A type of union security in which union members get preference in hiring, but the employer can still hire nonunion members.

Pregnancy Discrimination Act (PDA). An amendment to Title VII of the Civil Rights Act that prohibits sex discrimination based on "pregnancy, childbirth, or related medical conditions."

preretirement counseling. Employer-sponsored counseling aimed at providing information to ease the passage of employees into retirement.

profit-sharing plan. A plan whereby most employees share in the company's profits.

protected class. Persons such as older workers and women protected by equal opportunity laws including Title VII.

public policy. A course of action or inaction that public authorities choose to pursue in order to address a problem.

qualifications inventories. Manual or computerized records listing employees' education, career and development interests, languages, special skills, and so on to be used in identifying inside candidates for promotion.

ranking method. The simplest method of job evaluation that involves ranking each job relative to all other jobs, usually based on a job's overall difficulty.

ratio analysis. A forecasting technique that involves analyzing and extrapolating the ratio of a dependent variable, such as sales persons required, with an independent variable, such as sales.

reliability. The characteristic that refers to the consistency of scores obtained by the same person when retested with the identical or equivalent tests.

right to work. The public policy in a number of states that prohibits union security of any kind.

salary (or compensation) survey. A survey aimed at determining prevailing pay rates. Provides specific wage rates for specific jobs.

Scanlon plan. An incentive plan developed in 1937 by Joseph Scanlon and designed to encourage cooperation, involvement, and sharing of benefits.

scatter plot. A graphical method used to help identify the relationship between two quantitative variables.

sensitivity training. A method for increasing employees' insights into their own behavior through candid discussions in groups led by special trainers.

severance pay. A one-time payment employers provide when terminating an employee.

sexual harassment. Harassment on the basis of sex that has the purpose or effect of substantially interfering with a person's work performance or creating an intimidating, hostile, or offensive work environment.

staff manager. A manager who assists and advises line managers.

stock option. The right to purchase a stated number of shares of company stock at a set price at some time in the future.

strategic human resource management. Linking HRM policies and practices with strategic goals and objectives in order to improve business performance.

supplier partnering. Having a limited number of suppliers, so as to build relationships that improve quality and reliability, rather than just to improve costs.

supply chain. Refers to all of a company's suppliers, manufacturers, distributors, and customers, and to the interactions among them.

supply chain management. The integration of the activities that procure materials, transform them into intermediate goods and final product, and deliver them to customers.

survey feedback. A method that involves surveying employees' attitudes and providing feedback to facilitate problems being solved by the managers and employees.

sympathy strike. A strike that takes place when one union strikes in support of another union's strike.

Taft-Hartley Act (Labor Management Relations Act). A law prohibiting union unfair labor practices and enumerating the rights of employees as union members. It also enumerates the rights of employers.

talent management. The end-to-end process of planning, recruiting, developing, managing, and compensating employees throughout the organization.

task analysis. A detailed study of a job to identify the skills required so that an appropriate training program may be instituted.

team building. Improving the effectiveness of teams through the use of consultants and team-building meetings.

terminate at will. The idea, based in law, that the employment relationship can be terminated at will by either the employer or the employee for any reason.

termination interview. The interview in which an employee is informed of the fact that he or she has been dismissed.

test validity. The accuracy with which a test, interview, and so on measures what it purports to measure or fulfills the function it was designed to fill.

third-country nationals. Citizens of a country other than the parent or host country.

Title VII of the 1964 Civil Rights Act. The section of the act that says an employer cannot discriminate on the basis of race, color, religion, sex, or national origin with respect to employment.

training. The process of teaching new employees the basic skills they need to perform their jobs.

transaction-processingsystems. Provide the company's managers and accountants with detailed information about short-term, daily activities, such as accounts payables, taxliabilities, and order status.

transparency. Giving supply chain partners easy access to information about details like demand, inventory levels, and status of inbound and outbound shipments, usually through a Web-based portal.

trend analysis. Study of a firm's past employment needs over a period of years to predict future needs.

unfair labor practice strike. A strike aimed at protesting illegal conduct by the employer.

union salting. A union organizing tactic by which workers who are employed by a union as undercover union organizers are hired by unwitting employers.

union shop. A form of union security in which the company can hire nonunion people but they must join the union after a prescribed period of time and pay dues. (If they do not, they can be fired.)

unsafe acts. Behaviors that potentially cause accidents.

unsafe conditions. The mechanical and physical conditions that cause accidents.

upward feedback. Having subordinates evaluate their supervisors' performance.

vested. The proportion of the employers contribution to the employee's pension plan that is guaranteed to the employee and which the employee can therefore take when he or she leaves.

vestibule/simulated training. A method in which trainees learn on the actual or on simulated equipment they would use on the job, but are actually trained off the job.

Vietnam Era Veterans' Readjustment Act of 1974. An act requiring that employers with government contracts take affirmative action to hire disabled veterans.

virtual classroom. Special collaboration software used to enable multiple remote learners, using their PCs or laptops, to participate in live audio and visual discussions, communicate via written text, and learn via content such as PowerPoint slides.

Vocational Rehabilitation Act of 1973. The act requiring certain federal contractors to take affirmative action for disabled persons.

voluntary (permissible) bargaining items. Items in collective bargaining for which bargaining is neither illegal nor mandatory—neither party can be compelled to negotiate over those items.

wage curve. Shows the relationship between the relative value of the job and the average wage paid for this job.

Wagner Act. A law that banned certain types of unfair labor practices and provided for secret-ballot elections and majority rule for determining whether or not a firm's employees want to unionize.

***Wards Cove* v. *Atonio*.** U.S. Supreme Court decision that made it difficult to prove a case of unlawful discrimination against an employer.

wildcat strike. An unauthorized strike occurring during the term of a contract.

workaholic. People who feel driven to always be on time and meet deadlines.

workers' compensation. Provides income and medical benefits to work-related accident victims or their dependents regardless of fault.

workforce planning. The process of formulating plans to fill the employer's future openings, based on (1) projecting open positions, and (2) deciding whether to fill these with inside or outside candidates.

workplace flexibility. Arming employees with the information technology tools they need to get their jobs done wherever the employees are.

works councils. Formal, employee-elected groups of worker representatives that meet monthly with managers to discuss topics ranging, for instance, from no-smoking policies to layoffs.

wrongful discharge. An employee dismissal that does not comply with the law or does not comply with the contractual arrangement stated or implied by the firm via its employment application forms, employee manuals, or other promises.

Photo Credits

Name Index

Subject Index